Contents

Change, Choice and Conflict in Social Policy

Change, Choice and Conflict in Social Policy

Phoebe Hall
Hilary Land
Roy Parker
Adrian Webb

Gower

First published 1975 by Heinemann Educational Books
Reprinted 1978

Reprinted 1986 by
Gower Publishing Company Limited,
Gower House,
Croft Road,
Aldershot,
Hampshire GU11 3HR,
England

ISBN 0-566-05301-2

Printed and bound in Great Britain by
Antony Rowe Limited, Chippenham, Wiltshire.

Acknowledgements

We have received help from a very large number of people in the course of preparing this book. The case studies, in particular, are the outcome of discussions with many of those who were connected with the events which we describe. Despite its immeasurable value it is impossible to acknowledge this assistance individually or in an adequate fashion. Politicians, civil servants, officers of associations and societies, research workers and many others gave us the benefit of their time and experience.

We are greatly indebted to the Gulbenkian Foundation for the grant without which this study could not have been undertaken. They supported us with patience and generosity over a number of years. In particular Mr Richard Mills has, on their behalf, encouraged and assisted us at all stages, as well as being an active member of our advisory group.

Indeed, we have had the privilege of being helped and constructively criticized by a most generous advisory committee. Under the chairmanship of Professor D. V. Donnison (Director of the Centre for Environmental Studies) the committee has considered our drafts, suggested ways in which the work might be improved and generally provided a means whereby we could try out our plans and our ideas. Our thanks are due to the members. They were: A. B. Cherns (Professor of Social Science, Loughborough University); J. A. G. Griffith (Professor of Public Law, London School of Economics); Margot Jefferys (Professor of Medical Sociology, Bedford College); R. Huws Jones (formerly Director, National Institute for Social Work); R. Mills (Deputy Director UK and British Commonwealth Branch, Calouste Gulbenkian Foundation); P. J. Self (Professor of Public Administration, London School of Economics); and L. J. Sharpe (Fellow, Nuffield College, Oxford).

The University of Bristol, through its Publications Committee, assisted us in the final stages with the cost of preparation. The task of typing this long book has fallen on several shoulders but we must mention in particular Trixie Hewlett, Mollie Lucas, Tina Shell and

Pamela Taylor without whose patience and care the book would not have been finished as soon as it was.

Having acknowledged our indebtedness to so many people we must make it plain that we alone are responsible for what is said or is not said and for any errors and shortcomings that the reader may detect.

Authors' Note

This book has been written by all four of us. It represents the fruits of our joint endeavours over several years. One of us has, however, taken special responsibility for writing each chapter and this is indicated in the contents. Roy Parker has acted as the 'general editor' Nevertheless, there is no chapter which is not the product of mutual deliberation and many long discussions. Were there a simple way of indicating joint and equal authorship we would have used it. As none exists we have adopted the alphabetical convention in setting our names to this book.

PART I

Introduction

In this section we introduce the book and explain the kinds of questions which led us to write it.

CHAPTER ONE

Objectives

This book is intended to help students of social administration understand why and how social policies are introduced or modified. Above all we hope that the book conveys the complexity of these questions together with a sense of the excitement to be found in trying to unravel and answer them. We also hope that it will encourage students to reflect upon the equally intriguing question of why some social issues do *not* become the subject of policy initiatives.

Although the study of social administration has always been much concerned with the development of social policies the generally available literature does not, for several reasons, adequately serve the needs of students. First, many accounts of the growth of social policy cover considerable periods of time and can devote little attention to the complicated events and processes which they encompass. The student may easily fail to appreciate these details or choose not to concern himself with them. Yet without *some* acquaintance with such detail there is the danger that superficial and often quite misleading generalizations pass as credible and satisfactory.

Secondly, even where close studies of specific developments in social policy are available they tend to be detached from the broader context and to lack the conceptual orientation necessary to use them as a means to generalization. Many are essentially historical studies of unique episodes. In these circumstances it is difficult for a student to compare one study with another and draw conclusions of a general kind.

Thirdly, there is still little material which deals directly with social policy changes in the period since the last war. More recent changes are not ignored, of course, but they are likely to be noted, criticized or evaluated rather than *explained*.

Last but not least, students of the development of social policies require a reasonable grounding in political science and its approaches to the kinds of questions with which we are concerned. Social policy choices are made through political processes and many of them are inextricably bound to the various institutions of government. Very few examples are to be found in the literature of social administration which specifically set the study of social policy-making within any political science framework. It was the desire to make good these omissions which prompted us to write this book. We were encouraged to do so by the work already published by Donnison and Chapman which aimed, in part, to meet similar needs.[1] Their studies, however, dealt with changes in policies and administrative practices at the local level. A reasonably comparable study of shifts in policies at the central or national level was, we felt, a logical and necessary next step.

Thus this book contains a major section comprising six detailed case studies of clearly identifiable changes in national social policies since the end of the last war. Although each of them conforms to a broadly similar approach and format, they vary in length, the kind of source material utilized, and the extent to which their historical antecedents are traced. This is partly because each study was the responsibility of one particular member of the team. But, in addition, each study encountered different problems. In some there was a large amount of existing and publicly available documentation; for others we had to rely upon much more limited data. In all of them, however, we discussed the changes with many of the individuals directly or indirectly involved: Ministers; MPs; civil servants; members of pressure groups and so on. It is impossible to acknowledge all these invaluable contributions, not least because many of those with whom we spoke asked that views or information should remain unattributed. The case studies can be read as accounts of the separate episodes that they examine. But their full worth can only be judged, we believe, if they are considered in conjunction with the other parts of this book.

Part II of the book was written to provide a conceptual framework for what follows and to share with the reader the kind of introduction to the political system which we ourselves have found indispensible to our studies. We are not political scientists and make no claim that our treatment of the subject is entirely satisfactory, comprehensive or especially original viewed from that standpoint. But as students and teachers of social policy this is the type of background which we have found both necessary and helpful. As far as we know it is not readily available in quite this form in any one political science text concerned with these matters.

The last part of the book is, we believe, the most ambitious section. Having completed our case studies we have, with reference to our broad conceptual framework, tried to formulate middle range proposi-

[1] Donnison, D. V. and Chapman, V., *Social Policy and Administration*, Allen & Unwin, 1965.

tions about how and in what particular circumstances certain issues attain predominance over others and become the source of new policy. We are, of course, conscious that these propositions leave much still unexplained and do not draw together all the evidence in our cases. It also needs to be stressed that the propositions are derived from the examination of substantive social policy changes. Except incidentally, we have not considered why changes do not occur and thus we cannot assume that the converse of the conditions in which issues gain priority satisfactorily explain their retardation. Quite different propositions may be required. Similarly, in our case studies we have looked at changes involving new departures, new structures or expansion. Again, somewhat different propositions may be needed in order to generalize about the withdrawal of a service or a major reduction in its scope. For these reasons the conclusions which we draw at the end of this book should not automatically be applied to all aspects of the development of social policy.

CHAPTER TWO

The Study of Changing Social Policy

I PREVAILING APPROACHES

The development of British social policy has been explained in various ways depending upon the purposes of the commentators, the level of generality and the particular aspects chosen for emphasis. Despite this diversity there appear to be certain characteristic and commonly held assumptions. They pervade much of the basic and standard literature and convey the impression of a developmental process which is substantially predetermined or, at least, carried forward through a sequence of timely responses to new situations. Social policy initiatives, it is implied, emerge because either a consensus of opinion or interest develops around a particular proposal for reform, or because it is functionally necessary in urban industrial societies reaching certain stages in their growth.

We can best illustrate the kinds of explanations that we have in mind by taking an example from one of the more widely read text books. 'By the first decade of the twentieth century the *time was ripe* for government action to secure an improvement in the national standard of physical efficiency, and *public opinion, shocked by the revelations* as to the number of army recruits rejected on grounds of physical unfitness during the fourth African War, was ready to accept it' (our italics).[1] This passage could be matched many times over by other interpretations of other developments by other authors. Such concepts as 'social pity', 'national unity', 'public enlightenment', 'the education of opinion' and 'social conscience' are used repeatedly

---

[1] Hall, M. P., *The Social Services of Modern England*, Routledge & Kegan Paul, 4th edn., 1959, p. 63. Subsequently published as *Penelope Hall's Social Services of England and Wales*, Forder, A. (ed.), 1969. This omits most of the earlier general discussion of development.

to explain changes in social policy.[2] Of course, the broad interpretive treatment of historical events relies upon simplifications like these and has to avoid the clutter of detail. Yet *some* set of assumptions, however rudimentary, is needed in order to simplify and to generalize. Although few of those who have written about the recent history of social policy have made their assumptions clear this does not mean that they do not exist. Indeed, in our view recurring themes can be recognized, especially ones related to the assumption that social policy has developed and changed along basically consensual lines.

In some ways this assumption is justifiable, for any government implementing new social policies is unlikely to proceed without what could be termed a minimum winning consensus. At the very least it must manage opposition and secure acquiescence. If, therefore, we look primarily at the formal point, such as an Act, at which change is signified it may well convey the impression of broad consensus. Furthermore, to the extent that established services or policies are studied retrospectively, the very fact of their continued existence, even when the party responsible for their introduction is superseded, suggests some kind of agreement that they *should* continue. But what of the period before the formal change? We frequently refer to winning consensus or winning support. Such phrases imply that a reform or a change is the outcome of a struggle about the resolution of differences, involving the exercise of power, the making and breaking of alliances and the settlement of terms. The outcomes may have the appearance of consensus but belie the fierce contest of interests or the protracted task of overcoming apathy which preceded them. Since many of the general accounts of the development of social policy can only locate and discuss major landmarks it is not surprising that a consensual interpretation goes largely unchallenged. Comparatively little attention is paid to defeated social policies, to what might have been rather than what is.[3] Even where there is a long and arduous campaign to establish provisions or achieve particular reforms it is those which *eventually* win through to a successful completion that most often capture the historian's attention. There are, however, other reasons why the consensual undercurrent is so strong.

One of these is connected in a complex way with the presumption

[2] If, says Bruce, summarizing his study of the development of social policies, 'the British Empire was created in a fit of absence of mind, the Welfare State has been no less the result of a fit of conscience or, rather, as the story of its progress will have shown, of a whole series of fits of conscience'. Bruce, M., *The Coming of the Welfare State*, Batsford, 1961, p. 259.

[3] Indeed, Rodgers contends that 'social policies are only interesting and worth studying if they are real policies (not mere paper plans) which are being actively pursued and which have already gone some way towards achieving their objectives'. Rodgers, B., Greve, J. and Morgan, J., *Comparative Social Administration*, Allen & Unwin, 1968, p. 12.

that social policy is benevolent in intent and in its effect.[4] The very idea of welfare, and hence of well-being, tends to suggest that once the problems arising from misunderstanding or ignorance have been resolved then dispute, conflict or opposition will melt away. Such an assumption appears to hover behind certain explanations of social policy development which attach special importance to the discovery and revelation of privation or distress. Who, after all, can be against the pursuit of well-being? Such a view is, of course, unduly simple. It ignores the fact that by increasing the welfare of one individual or group that of another may be reduced. The blanket assumption that social policy is *generally* beneficent obscures such possibilities. The point is seen most clearly perhaps in an international context. To what extent is our welfare enhanced at the cost of the reduced welfare of people in other countries? What results from an immigration policy that allows doctors and nurses easy entry but denies it to the old, the sick and the untrained from the same country? To what extent is the welfare of the Swiss or West German family partly assured by the employment of cheap immigrant labour with restricted rights to welfare? Any social policy which is effectively redistributive also implies the reduction of someone's welfare, even though this may be regarded by others as warranted. Welfare policies create both satisfactions and discontents. To the extent that they are directly concerned with regulation and control, moreover, they will rarely be seen by those who are subject to that control as contributing to *their* welfare.

There is another sense too in which social policy may have little to do with benevolence. George and Wilding, for example, contend that 'it is not a unified national effort to meet social needs or to eradicate social problems in an impartial way to the benefit of all in society. It is rather an attempt to resolve conflicting economic and other interests along social class lines'.[5] Such a view provides a valuable counterbalance to conventional perceptions of social welfare but it remains largely an assertion. There have been few attempts by marxists to examine specific social provisions in order to demonstrate just how class objectives are attained. The approach is important, how-

---

[4] Here are two examples amongst many: 'social services are benevolent in intention and ... are designed to benefit people directly or individually', in Marsh, D. C. (ed.), *An Introduction to the Study of Social Administration*, Routledge & Kegan Paul, 1965, p. 20. 'No one could hold that Welfare State social policy is harsh or negative, or springs other than from benevolent even if they are misguided intentions.' Slack, K. M., *Social Administration and the Citizen*, Joseph, 1966, p. 70. Earlier in the same book, however, she says that 'social policy is not of *necessity* positive or beneficent, nor need it spring from human sympathy'.

[5] George, V. and Wilding, P., 'Social Values, Social Class and Social Policy', *Social and Economic Administration*, vol. 6, no. 3, Sept., 1972, p. 245.

ever, because it offers an alternative standpoint from which to interpret social policy and a standpoint, moreover, which directly contests its benevolent intent or effect. It also underlines the comparative absence of explicitly ideological ways of thinking about social policy by politicians, administrators and students of the subject. This absence may itself contribute to certain assumptions about the extent of consensus, for it is an easy step from perceiving a lack of grand ideology in British politics to the belief that no ideological differences exist.[6]

A second general reason for the tacit acceptance of the assumption of consensus can be traced to certain views about the nature of the British political system. These views may be characterized as pluralist; that is, power and influence are considered to be widely distributed with no one section or elite regularly commanding a winning share. Given such an interpretation, change *can* only occur with the consent of the major interests involved. Hence the history of social policy is seen typically as a process of engineering, or awaiting, a sufficient consensus. This accords too closely with political experience to be easily dismissed but in terms of explaining what does or does not happen, whose consent has or has not to be counted, as well as how and on what terms this is obtained, it is plainly superficial. Questions like these are not wholly ignored in the social policy literature but they are frequently discussed at such a high level of generality that their contrary indications for the consensual–pluralist approach go undetected. To answer these kinds of questions it is necessary to take account of the distribution of power in society and any changes in that distribution. What, in the last analysis, does consent mean? It may be granted readily and enthusiastically or be enforced through the acquiescence of those whose ability to resist is spent. It may be bought at a high or a low price. Whose interests can be passed over because they have no power? Which interests command enough power to wrest consent from a reluctant government? Which interests are so closely affiliated with prevailing conceptions of the public good that their dominance goes unquestioned?

There is yet another reason why the undercurrent of consensus flows through much of the social policy literature, and that is because many of the general accounts of change and development are implicitly functionalist. The functionalist approach has been skilfully criticized and, in important respects, found wanting by Goldthorpe. It is unnecessary to go over such well examined ground again. We must, however, make clear the kind of approaches that are denoted by the term functionalist and the main thrust of Goldthorpe's ob-

[6] See Christoph, J. B., 'Consensus and Cleavage in British Political Ideology', *American Political Science Review*, vol. LIX, no. 3, 1965, p. 629.

jections to them. He describes the functionalist approach like this: 'some form of relatively extensive public provision against the disruptive, wasteful and debilitating tendencies within industrial, and particularly capitalist, society is taken as being in some sense a functional "prerequisite" or "imperative" for the continuing existence and development of such society'.[7] In this view, then, the explanation of the growth of social provision is *ultimately* to be given not in terms of particular group interests and pressures but rather in terms of the objective 'demands of certain social situations which are seen as virtually imposing particular courses of action'.[8] Goldthorpe sees this as a marked improvement over attributing developments in social policy to the impact of ideas, beliefs and notable public figures, for it shifts our attention to 'the description and analysis of actual social conditions and the problems which arose out of these'.[9] The difficulties and weaknesses of the approach are nevertheless formidable. Goldthorpe discusses two in particular. First, there is the problem of answering the question, what exactly we mean when we contend that a social policy is 'necessary'? Can it ever amount to more than asking: under what circumstances would a policy 'tend to be regarded as necessary?' And then, of course, we are confronted with the further quite crucial question of: by whom and to what purpose? Second, there is the difficulty which arises from the high order of generality of these forms of explanation. To argue, for example, that the combined effects of rising hospital costs, developing medical knowledge and the experience of the rigours of total war made some kind of national health service *necessary* does not help very much to explain the form which it actually took. As he points out, to answer these specific questions we have to think more 'in terms of the purposive actions of individuals and groups in pursuit of their ends'.[10]

Despite these important deficiencies in the belief that 'necessity was the mother of all policy',[11] the belief persists and continues to be conveyed to students. As a result it also plays into an easy assumption of consensus: once the implications of problems or situations are appreciated then action will eventually be generally acknowledged

---

[7] Goldthorpe, J. H., 'The Development of Social Policy in England, 1800–1914: Notes on a Sociological Approach to a Problem in Historical Explanation', *Transactions of the Fifth World Congress of Sociology*, vol. IV, 1962, pp. 50–1.

[8] *Idem.*

[9] *Ibid.*, p. 51.

[10] *Ibid.*, p. 55.

[11] The phrase is Asa Briggs'. See his 'The History of Changing Approaches to Social Welfare', in Martin, E. W. (ed.), *Comparative Development in Social Welfare*, Allen & Unwin, 1972.

as unavoidable. Consensus forms around the recognition of in-evitability. The credibility of such a view is likely to be enhanced further by broad, sweeping comparisons of the social policies of different countries. Certainly, at first sight, similar policies appear to emerge in countries at similar stages of economic and social develop-ment. An underlying and pervasive imperative may seem to be at work because the study of comparative social policy remains at its present rather superficial level.

We have argued so far that a substantial part of the literature about social policy development conveys an impression of broad consensus set in a framework of diversified power. We have also considered some of the reasons why this is so. In drawing together these obser-vations we have, inevitably, presented an unduly orderly and clear cut picture. There are many qualifications to be made, not least that a growing body of commentators is paying greater attention to the elements of conflict in the history of social policy,[12] and that there are some interpretations which unambiguously proceed from the assump-tion that conflict, arising from permanent contradictions within capi-talist society, has determined the course of social policy.[13]

The problem is not that conflict in social policy is *systematically* ignored in preference to an interpretation based upon consensus but that it is rarely made clear which kinds of assumptions authors have in mind. It is in these circumstances that the undercurrent of con-sensus takes command of the drifting ship of explanation.

Most writers on the development of social policy would deny that they pursue, say, a functionalist or pluralist approach to the task of explanation. They would probably argue that their position was more pragmatic and that they employed a variety of approaches. Indeed, such a claim could be amply supported from a study of the literature. A student as perceptive and imaginative as Titmuss moves from position to position in different parts of his work. One of his much quoted definitions implies substantial consensus: 'all col-lectively provided services are deliberately designed to meet certain socially recognized "needs", they are manifestations, first of *society's will* to survive as an organic whole and secondly of the *expressed wish of all the people* to assist the survival of some people' (our

---

[12] Kathleen Bell, for example, writes: 'my own view is that historical accounts of the development of social policy have tended to underemphasise the role of conflict in an overgeneralised picture of society inexorably expand-ing social provision to meet the demands of industrialisation. If industrialisation was the anvil, the particular shape of social policy in this country was forged on it with a good deal of heat and the striking of hammer blows'. *Disequili-brium in Welfare*, University of Newcastle, 1973, p. 4.

[13] See for example, Saville, J., 'The Welfare State: An Historical Approach', *New Reasoner*, vol. 3, Winter, 1957–8.

italics).[14] In other studies, most notably in *The Irresponsible Society*[15] and in *Income Distribution and Social Change*,[16] the issues are portrayed in the language and terms of conflict, with particular emphasis being placed upon the counter-welfare forces. In his earlier history of social policy in the Second World War, however, Titmuss adopts a mainly consensual standpoint.[17] Indeed, he regards war as an important means of achieving greater consensus whilst underplaying the extent of internal conflict which is also produced. He takes little account, for example, of the enhanced power of the trade unions and their willingness to use it in the interests of their members. To the extent that war has been accompanied by some redistribution of power the potentialities for conflict may well be increased. If one looks at certain events during the 1914–18 war, for instance, the existence of an underlying and, at times open, conflict between sections of the working class and the government is clearly apparent. The introduction of rent control in 1915 was certainly encouraged by the need to offer greater security to working class families so that men would be more willing to leave home and join the armed forces. But the necessary legislation was also rushed through as a means of reducing the working class militancy which, particularly on Clydeside, had been given further impetus by anger about rising rents.[18]

Others apart from Titmuss move from position to position in this way, but in most cases there seems to be a strong return spring carrying them back to interpretations based upon notions of consensus. This is why we have been at pains to note this orientation in the social policy literature; not because it is necessarily wrong but because, for most of the time, it goes unacknowledged. As a result some kinds of questions about how social policy is formed are more likely to be posed than others.

We can illustrate this by taking a clear statement by Donnison about the politics of British social policy. He argues that because social policies 'are so deeply embedded in society it follows that they cannot grow in a liberal democracy without the consent of the major interests – political, industrial, religious or administrative – that hold power in such a society'.[19] This is obviously true, in part at least. But if it is accepted as a *sufficient* summary of the evidence,

[14] Titmuss, R. M., *Essays on the Welfare State*, Allen & Unwin, 1958, p. 39.
[15] Titmuss, R. M., *The Irresponsible Society*, Fabian Tract 323, 1960.
[16] Titmuss, R. M., *Income Distribution and Social Change*, Allen & Unwin, 1962.
[17] Titmuss, R. M., *Problems of Social Policy*, HMSO, 1950.
[18] See for example, Moorhouse, B., Wilson, M. and Chamberlain, C., 'Rent Strikes – Direct Action and the Working Class', in *The Socialist Register*, 1972, Miliband, R. and Saville, J. (eds), Merlin, 1972.
[19] Donnison, D. V. and Chapman, V., *op. cit.*, p. 23.

as other literature as well would encourage us to do, then we fail to ask the further questions without the answers to which such a passage passes as a rounded conclusion. The further questions are ones like these: which are the 'major industrial interests' and what are the consequences of the two main sectors, the unions and the employers, frequently being in conflict? When and under what circumstances are policies introduced despite the opposition of potentially powerful groups? Is simmering discontent about a policy to be thought of as consent? In what kinds of situations can a consensus be enforced and upon which kinds of interest groups? Most writers on social policy would agree that questions like these ought to be raised and answered; yet the approach to social policy research and analysis has rarely forced them to the forefront.

Our point of departure then is that consensus, like conflict, should be treated as an interesting variable, not as a presupposition. We should not *assume* that policy arises from the building of consensus or that it represents the outcome of conflict. We must look for both and at least try to determine how each relates to the other and how their presence or absence may affect the way in which policy is or can be developed. These aspirations led us to approach our research with the aid of a series of case studies and with the intention of drawing from them certain middle or lower order generalizations about change in social policy. We were also anxious to set these cases firmly into the context of the political system and to make quite clear the framework of questions about them which guided our thinking. Part II is devoted to fulfilling these requirements, but before we do so it is necessary to examine briefly the status of the case study method in research.

II PROCEEDING BY CASE STUDIES

The use of case studies has proved an attractive way of illustrating and conveying the rich detail of various kinds of events. As a research method, however, its status remains somewhat dubious. Its application to the study of policy developments elicits two main types of criticism. These are:

(i) that the approach has not been employed in a sufficiently scientific way to advance theory, and

(ii) that the case study does not lend itself to generalization however carefully used. Hence it can never form the basis of a theory.

The implications of each of these views are clearly different. Waldo has, for instance, drawn a distinction between the optimistic and the pessimistic critics.[20] The optimistic critics are mainly disturbed by the deficiencies summarized in (i) above whilst the pessimists subscribe to the second view.[21] The former seek improvements in what they regard as potentially valuable means of developing middle-range theory whereas the latter do not regard case studies as capable of doing more than describing and illustrating.

As Waldo, one of the optimists, acknowledges, cases are often chosen in a haphazard fashion or for their dramatic impact. But if progress is to be made, he argues, then 'case studies of the "normal" should be selected, as being more representative of the real world of administration [and policy formation]. And there should be', he contends, 'a concentration of cases dealing with the same or similar phenomena, so that variables can be observed and compared.'[22] Like Waldo, others also insist that a clear research design is necessary and that the selection and use of data must arise from that framework. The fact that these requirements have not been met in all case studies arises, at least in part, from different ideas of what is useful for teaching and what for building theory. In addition, some studies of historical events which were never intended to contribute directly to the advancement of political or social theory have been treated as if this were their primary purpose.

The pessimistic critics go further and assert that there are just too many variables in the processes of policy-making to be managed by a case approach. As Waldo says, such a critic 'believes that, in investigations not amenable to controlled experimentation, science can be served only through methods that employ statistical techniques for the control and manipulation of a large universe'.[23] There is also the more extreme view that political phenomena as such are not amenable to scientific study and that we must rest content, therefore, with conclusions of an entirely speculative and impressionistic kind. Such a contention, however, hardly amounts to a substantial criticism of the case study method, since it is equally applicable to other approaches.

It should, of course, be possible to achieve the greater rigour demanded by the optimistic critics of the case study method. Indeed, there are several studies which have accomplished this difficult task. They range from Leys' early exploration of ethical issues in policy-making[24] to more recent attempts to refine and test specific hypotheses.

[20] Waldo, D., in Bock, E. A. (ed.), *Essays on the Case Method in Public Administration*, the Inter-University Case Program, 1962.

[21] This and other points have previously been made in Webb, A. L., 'Planning Enquiries and Amenity Policy', *Policy and Politics*, vol. 1, no. 1, 1972.

[22] *Op. cit.*, p. 60.

[23] *Op. cit.*, p. 62.

[24] Leys, W. A. R., *Ethics for Policy Decisions: the Art of Asking Deliberative Questions*, Prentice-Hall, 1952.

Of the latter type Paige's work on the Korean decision is one of the best known and ambitious projects.[25] Outside the sphere of foreign affairs Banfield, amongst others, has employed the case method to examine and develop hypotheses.[26] There is, we would argue, sufficient evidence to show that, given the will, case material can be used to *begin* conceptual analysis. Nevertheless, the key question remains: do case studies enable us to *test* hypotheses?

Inadequate hypotheses can certainly be challenged through case studies insofar as an episode does not accord with expectation. In reality, though, this is rarely clear cut: some aspects of a case may uphold a hypothesis whilst others appear to confound it. Data are usually so plentiful that a variety of interpretations is possible. Nevertheless, it is clear that, in principle, a case study can undermine a hypothesis if not disprove it altogether.[27] More fundamentally though, can it uphold or confirm the validity of a hypothesis?

The answer hinges mainly on the size of that category of phenomena to which cases belong. If it is large then even when the biographies of *several* closely comparable episodes are studied they will only account for a tiny proportion of the whole and will hardly justify firm conclusions. If, on the other hand, the category is small, case studies may more appropriately help us to test propositions about it. But in this case events may then be of such rare occurrence that the usefulness of the whole exercise as a generalizing endeavour is put into question.[28] For all practical purposes, therefore, we do not consider that hypotheses can be adequately upheld by the case method. In parenthesis, however, we might note that some of the hypotheses in the existing literature would seem to be remarkably difficult to confirm or refute by *any* method because of their imprecision and high level of generality.

There are many factors to be considered in the analysis of policy formation and this, of course, makes the testing of hypotheses a complicated business. One of the indictments of the case study is that although it may describe this multiplicity it offers no means of dealing with it analytically. Questions about the interdependence, overlap, weighting or relevance of variables are, it is argued, not taken into account in the case study approach. In contrast, statistical methods

[25] Paige, G. D., *The Korean Decision*, Free Press, 1968. Also his 'The United States' Decision to Resist Aggression in Korea: the Application of an Analytical Scheme', *Administrative Science Quarterly*, 3 Dec., 1958.

[26] Banfield, E. C., *Political Influence*, Free Press, 1961.

[27] How far 'the case' disproves the hypothesis will depend upon whether that hypothesis is formulated in terms of causality or probability.

[28] Of course, the idea of a universe or genre of phenomena is a convenient artifact. See Postan, M. M., *Fact and Relevance*, Oxford University Press, 1971. Note especially the essay on 'Reason in Social Study'.

are equipped to deal with such difficulties and with a large number of instances.

Those who attack the problem of explaining policy with statistical weapons have undoubtedly won ground on certain fronts. The work of people like Alt, Oliver and Stanyer, and Davies[29] traces the connection between ranges of input variables and policy outputs. However, while such studies can discover, or suggest, previously unsuspected patterns and regularities they do not show precisely how or why these occur. As Davies admits, these matters 'must be investigated using other techniques'.[30]

There are clearly many issues which neither the case study nor statistical methods can resolve satisfactorily. Objections can be raised to any method of unravelling and understanding such a complicated process as making social policy. Case studies, used systematically, have a certain heuristic merit and it is upon this ground that they can best be defended. If their weakness in providing convincing confirmation of hypotheses is accepted then at least three arguments in their favour still remain.

First, the method is as effective as other approaches in suggesting general propositions about how policy develops. Indeed, it may have the particular virtue that because such propositions emerge from the close examination of actual examples, they are likely to prompt good middle-range theorizing. This, we believe, is currently much needed in the study of social policy.

Secondly, the case study is a valuable means of conveying the immensity of the task confronting those who embark upon the journey from description to generalization in this terrain. Had more people made that journey already and were the route clearly marked then case studies might well be judged redundant; but we are still a long way from that situation.

Thirdly, at a time when the strengths and weaknesses of positivist social research are also being weighed in the balance some of the advantages of the case study may be better appreciated. It is, for instance, suited to the 'action' approach and to the exploration of the meanings actors attach to their behaviour in policy-making situations.

In our view the case method can make a contribution quite apart from its pedagogic value, but only if it is employed in a disciplined way. One of the major defects has been that an individual case study in

---

[29] For example, Alt, J. E., 'Some Social and Political Correlates of County Borough Expenditures', *British Journal of Political Science*, vol. 1, no. 1, Jan. 1971; Oliver, F. R. and Stanyer, J., 'Some Aspects of the Financial Behaviour of County Boroughs', *Public Administration*, XLVII, 1969; and Davies, B. P., Barton, A. J., MacMillan, I. S. and Williamson, V. K., *Variations in Services for the Aged*, Occasional Paper in Social Administration, Bell, 1971.

[30] *Ibid.*, p. 128.

one field could not be compared with a similar study in another field undertaken by a different researcher. Even when brought together as a compendium, isolated studies are still a poor basis for conceptual development. There are several safeguards, therefore, which seem to be necessary:

(i) There must be an acknowledged conceptual framework, however modest or rudimentary, with reference to which the cases are studied and conclusions drawn. There must be a set of questions which the cases are intended to help answer. There has to be a delimiting *context*.

(ii) There needs to be a collection of cases sharing this common framework and, as far as possible, concerned with a reasonably similar order of episodes or events. The notion of a 'collection' implies some prior system of classification.

(iii) Following from this last assumption, we must try to proceed by the comparison of cases. Generalization implies a search for regularities. The task becomes more possible to the extent that we take our first precaution: namely start with a conceptual framework. Only in this way will sufficient order be imposed upon the mass of information which case studies provide.

(iv) Finally, we must try to avoid the traps which case studies set for us. Case studies of policy-making overwhelmingly move towards a conclusion – a point of decision. Yet policy formation is clearly a flow of events and actions over time in which few of the participants will be concerned with that development alone, and some hardly conscious of it as a 'development' at all. The researcher raises it to a special position and thereby artificially removes it from the press of *other* concurrent, overlapping and competing events. Although some boundaries have to be imposed, the more the chosen case or cases are set in the context of what else was or was not happening, as well as being related to a relevant history, the less risk there will be of this oversimplification.

Thus, we believe that if there is a conceptual framework from which to depart; if there is a reasonably similar set of cases to provide the opportunity for some cautious comparison; and if we strive to look at policy-making-through-time rather than at isolated decisions the use of the case study approach is justifiable and profitable.

III THE CLASSIFICATION OF SOCIAL POLICY CHANGES

In the succeeding chapters we shall offer a conceptual framework for the case studies which follow. Here, we must pause and explain the basis upon which they were chosen. It will be recalled that we wished to focus upon changes in social policy at the national level; that is, the formal decision involved would be made by central authorities. Clearly, many such policy decisions are made at various levels in the relevant hierarchies. We wanted to make our selection, however, from those changes which were sufficiently important to have attracted some degree of 'public attention'. At the same time we were anxious that they should not be such epoch-making events that they stood exposed to the criticism that they fell outside the general run of social policy changes. We sought cases, therefore, which as issues had all been considered by the Cabinet or by cabinet committees but were not widely regarded as momentous. We further restricted our field by taking, at least as a starting point, clearly identifiable shifts of policy occurring since the end of the last war.

Even within these preliminary boundaries there remained a wide range of possible changes from which to choose. Certain other restrictions were necessary, therefore, before the task was brought within manageable proportions. Our first temptation was to concentrate upon only one area of social policy, in whichever way it might be defined. There was, for instance, the obvious course of taking a particular service (e.g. housing or education). This was rejected because we felt that it was necessary to compare what may or may not have been rather different processes at work in, say, the health or social security spheres.[31]

Other criteria had to be considered which more closely derived from the kinds of questions which we were posing and from the kind of concepts we wanted to employ. Our central concern throughout was with changes in social policy. More precisely we were preoccupied with questions of why, from a great variety of issues worthy of attention, some gain priority and form the basis for new policies. It seemed most appropriate, therefore, to devise a simple classification according to *kinds* of changes rather than kinds of policies. This we did, and from our early work identified three forms of social policy change which

---

[31] We were encouraged in this view by the work of Griffith, J. A. G., *Central Departments and Local Authorities*, Allen & Unwin, 1966.

we denoted innovation, development and reform. Let us explain more fully what each term stands for.

By *innovation* we mean the introduction of a policy which, although it may have been discussed and considered before, calls for the entry of the State into a new field of social action or for the creation of new kinds of services, rights or obligations. Logically, the converse process should also be included; namely the abolition or withdrawal of the State from previously acknowledged responsibilities.

By *development* we simply imply changes in social policy which arise from alterations in the scale or range of an existing provision. In these circumstances the State will *already* have embarked upon a particular programme but then accelerate or increase its commitment. Numbers grow, benefits rise or units of service multiply. Of course, such developments go on all the time; for some to be regarded as *clear* changes in policy they probably have to occur rapidly or on a substantial scale. Again, the converse process of contraction falls into the same category and may be thought of as negative development.

Lastly, we consider that there are yet other kinds of changes in policies which can best be called *reforms*. In these cases the change is neither an entirely new departure for the State nor a development as we have defined it. It constitutes a new way of doing something with which the State is already involved. Legislation or administrative structures are literally, re-formed. We would also include in this category instances where the objectives of an existing policy are altered radically; for instance in the matter of housing subsidies. In connection with these types of changes it is especially important to make clear that we use the term reform without any necessary connotation of progress, betterment or approval.

This rather simple trichotomy allowed us to classify many social policy changes without too much heartsearching. Its merits, for our purposes, were twofold. First, if we chose cases which fell reasonably well into each of these groups we might be better able to introduce some refinement in the propositions emerging from our studies. It might be possible, for example, to suggest that rather different conclusions hold about how innovative social policy is made from, say, how and why developments occur. In this sense we built in a basis for comparison. Secondly, it permitted us to include a mixed selection of cases in terms of the different areas of social intervention. From a pedagogic viewpoint and in order to convey the scope of social policies this was, we felt, an important advantage. We could not include every field since our resources were limited, but our cases have been drawn from the areas of social security, health, education, penal provision and environmental protection. Two cases fall into each of our three change categories and these are set out below.

CATEGORY OF CHANGE		
Innovation	*Development*	*Reform*
The introduction of Family Allowances	The growth of Health Centre provision	The improvement of measures to control air pollution
The creation of the Open University	The development of Detention Centres	The replacement of National Assistance by Supplementary Pensions and Benefits

Thus, the kinds of changes of social policy included in this study were chosen deliberately after considerable preliminary work. In contrast, we must make it plain that the final selection of examples was arbitrary. It reflects several influences; our particular backgrounds and interests, the availability of source material, and the willingness of sufficient people involved in these events to discuss them with us.[32]

The use of case studies in social research will probably remain contentious. We have explained why we believe the approach is a valuable means of understanding the complex processes behind the shifting frontiers of social policy. A last word is, however, in order. As a team working on these issues over several years we have been stimulated and have felt our understanding and grasp of social policy considerably improved by our close acquaintance with the detail and sweep of these six examples. We have felt better equipped to generalize and have shared the intellectual excitement that this enterprise brings.

However, before the case studies are presented, and the reader judges their merit for himself, it is necessary to clarify further the conceptual assumptions lying behind our approach and to offer a view of the political system within which these changes were forged. Part II is devoted to these ends.

---

[32] It is, perhaps, important to note that two other case studies were begun but abandoned because of the difficulties which became apparent.

PART II

The Political Context

In this section we offer a conceptual framework within which changes in social policies might usefully be examined, discuss key features of the political system in which they occur, and proffer a view on the fundamental issue of the nature of the distribution of power in our society and its effects upon policy-making.

CHAPTER THREE

Policy and the Political Process

The political processes which lead to changes in policies are often complicated and sometimes obscure. Our task is to find a conceptual framework which allows us to simplify and generalize. Different approaches will suit different purposes. The main questions we seek to answer are: why do certain issues gain precedence over others and why do particular kinds of change occur in social policies? To this end we have found the systems approach a useful starting point.[1] From it we have developed a simple framework which we consider helpful. However, it must be emphasized that although we begin from a systems viewpoint, this and subsequent chapters are not an attempt to produce a systems analysis of British politics. Nor shall we conduct our discussion primarily in terms of such theories. Indeed, in the final chapter of this section we turn to quite other theories which concentrate on explaining the distribution of political power. Nevertheless, a systems approach does offer certain concepts and a way of thinking which are helpful in organizing the information about social policy changes which we have assembled in the case studies.

The development and use of systems theory in the social sciences has occasioned such debate and conflict that a brief clarification of our position will avoid misunderstanding. To talk of a system implies that one is looking at a complex whole (which may in its turn be part of a larger whole) and trying to understand it in terms of the interrelation of its parts. It further implies that the whole exhibits a certain degree of organization and stability. There is little point in looking for a pattern in a kaleidoscope whilst it is turning; the scene is changing too rapidly. On the other hand the way in which a pattern is organized can be studied in more stable conditions. But the main problem is that complex social phenomena are not static even when they are relatively stable. We must reduce a myriad variables to a small number which interact with each other in a reasonably predictable

---

[1] A useful discussion of structural–functional and systems analyses of political life can be found in Morton, R D. and Lewis, V. A., *Models of Political Systems*, Macmillan, 1971.

and regular way. If all is change and there is no regularity we cannot detect a pattern and hold it in our mind for further analysis. The concept of a system can help us identify key variables and some regularities in the way they are related.

The Achilles Heel of the systems approach in the social sciences has been this very issue. It has been attacked for placing too much emphasis on the stability of systems; for a tendency to see stability as equivalent to harmony; and for a relative neglect of how social institutions can, do, and should change.[2] There is no need to enter this area of controversy; we do not make assumptions about the long-term stability of the British political system or advocate that it should be preserved in its present form.[3] We wish only to steady the kaleidoscope and point out some general features of political life that can help us understand the policy process.

The merit of starting with a systems framework is that it corrects one of the side effects of emphasizing policy-making; namely, the tendency to expect a high output of policies and to see blockages to new policies as pathological. Students of social policy commonly make this assumption because they are frequently charting unmet needs and agitating for policy change. A systems viewpoint forces us to look at the same problem in terms of the 'needs' of the system that is being called upon to produce or permit these changes. Even though the idea of a system having needs easily leads us astray, it does oblige us to look at the policy process through the eyes of the policy-maker; the person who has to work within and through the government machine. For him, the ability to block a policy may not indicate pathology but be a vital and necessary safeguard for the well-being of himself, his colleagues and the organization of which he is part. Demands made upon an organization can be a source of stress. To recognize this is not to condone undue bureaucratic delay or myopia. It is to see the picture whole and to understand some of the features of policy-making. In this chapter we will examine the policy process from the policy-maker's viewpoint by looking at two variables, demands and supports, and the ways in which they are regulated or managed.[4]

---

[2] Lockwood's article is still a valuable discussion of the problems of the systems approach. Lockwood, D., 'Some Remarks on "The Social System"', *British Journal of Sociology*, vol. VIII, no. 2, 1956.

[3] The systems approach can also be criticized for re-naming phenomena with which we are familiar, while concentrating attention on the system and not upon what it produces. However, some writers have developed an effective discussion of policy questions within a systems framework. See, for example, Vickers, G., *Value Systems and Social Processes*, Tavistock, 1968, esp. part II.

[4] The way in which we have outlined these concepts owes much to the work of David Easton and where possible we have used his terminology. However, Easton should not be held responsible for the way in which we have developed

I DEMANDS

Demands are directed towards the authorities of a political system who are being pressed, encouraged or persuaded to make certain kinds of decisions and take certain actions. Authorities may be defined as those individuals and bodies responsible for making the day-to-day decisions required of the political system. Their authority rests on the fact that most people accept their decisions as binding. In a relatively stable political system authorities are not hard to identify although they are not necessarily the most powerful individuals or institutions. In the extreme case they may be puppets in the hands of elites which themselves remain unrecognized in the formal allocation of authority. Nevertheless, the authorities with which we shall be concerned do possess considerable power and are the unequivocal target of policy demands. In the British system of government they are epitomized by the Cabinet although, as we shall see later, there are other authorities as well.

Demands present authorities with a dilemma. They must respond to a sufficient number of them if they are not to lose their support in the community, for if there is a widespread belief that authorities are unwilling or unable to respond to specific issues which are presented to them, a demand of a quite different kind may arise: that is, a call for new, more competent or responsive authorities. Yet the number and complexity of demands will almost certainly be too great for them all to be met. Demands have to be managed because other kinds of inputs which are needed to meet them are in short supply. One of the most important of these inputs is support. Governments come under pressure if large or significant groups lose faith in their policies in general or refuse to be bound by one in particular.

Not only is support in short supply but all the other key resources needed by government, such as finance, manpower, specific forms of expertise and parliamentary time are also scarce. This imposes the general need to respond selectively to demands. Even a new government with a united party behind it, served by a skilful and sympathetic civil service at full strength and able to call upon the most effective procedures for policy analysis cannot absorb all the issues that confront it and transform them into effective policy outputs. However, not even newly elected governments have everything in their favour and if they make too many mistakes, lose confidence,

and used these concepts in this chapter; for his analysis see Easton, D., *A Systems Analysis of Political Life*, Wiley, 1965; *A Framework for Political Analysis*, Prentice-Hall, 1965(a); and *The Political System*, Knopf, 1953.

purpose, enthusiasm, or key individuals, the capacity to act may fall sharply.

The political system, therefore, must clearly include a means of responding selectively to demands. The inability to deal with every issue makes this necessary. The almost infinite flow of demands that can arise must be regulated in such a way that the end result is a much smaller number of actual policy decisions. Some demands will be rejected completely whilst others will be compressed into more comprehensive issues and will almost certainly, as a result, be modified. This whole process of demand regulation will in turn influence the kinds of problems and needs which are subsequently presented to the authorities for their consideration. The nature and limits of the political process itself makes demand regulation essential, but the interaction of demands and supports influences the number, type and complexity of demands that can be, or must be, dealt with at different times. The extent to which demands have to be regulated and the kinds which are blocked or allowed through therefore vary as support varies. In other words, both the length of the queue of demands and the decisions about what should be given priority are, in part, determined by the flow of demands and by the stock as well as by the flow of *supports*. Before looking further at demand regulation, therefore, let us examine the main types of support inputs and consider how they relate to demands.

II SUPPORT

The relationship between policy-making and support is an important but complex one. Some policies clearly have a considerable impact on support whereas others have little. The content and the *timing* of many policies are fundamentally affected by considerations of support. But policies are not the only factors determining the level of support given to a government, nor are all types of support equally relevant; the relationship is not straightforward. For example, while governments quite noticeably enter periods of policy initiation which are designed to enhance their support, the same government, on other occasions, may seem quite unwilling to initiate change. Why is this? Equally, why is it that Labour governments tend to be more committed to 'programmes' and to a heavy schedule of reform? Is it entirely due to their political ideology, or does it also reflect differences in support between the parties? Why is it that governments are sometimes able to risk very unpopular actions, policies that are opposed by the majority of the electorate or by key support groups, whilst at other times they are extremely sensitive about the effects of acting on even minor issues? To answer these questions we must look at several different types of support and their impact on governmental policy.

Outputs and specific support

We are primarily interested in those outputs which we call social policies although they exhibit many of the same features and have the same significance for a political system as other kinds of output. Given the support of the populace authorities can call forth and harness the resources of a society and make allocations of values. Were the legitimacy of their acting in this way not widely recognized they would be forced overtly to coerce members of the society into accepting their decisions as binding. The use of coercion by authorities drawing their support from a small but powerful elite is too common for it to be ignored in an international study. But a study of recent British social policy can reasonably begin with the ways in which support is developed and maintained. Political coercion is only employed intermittently to enforce acceptance of particular decisions which are strongly contested. Such coercion must be viewed in Britain against a background of widespread and continuing support for authorities and for the political system, whichever political party holds office.

One source of this support is the pattern of outputs produced by authorities. Outputs, which must be defined fairly narrowly as the decisions arrived at by authorities and the actions necessary for their implementation, affect the support accorded to the authorities. A long series of acceptable outputs can lead a group to generalize its support to the authorities and the party in power *per se*. The support engendered by a single favoured output becomes less conditional if favoured outputs are frequently produced. An authority can, therefore, build up a general stock of supports by its specific actions. The political parties amass political capital by producing favoured policies. But support of this kind can be eroded just as rapidly by a series of unacceptable policies or policies which become unpopular. The danger of relying solely upon such conditional support when in office is apparent. As the authority finally responsible for all government outputs the political party in power is vulnerable. It faces numerous constraints on its policy-making compared with an opposition party and the multiple consequences of past and present outputs are difficult to control.

Easton makes several points about the hazards of depending upon specific support which are worth noting. He argues that many occasions arise where benefits have to be postponed to the medium or long-term future, while sacrifices have to be made in the present. Similarly, the diversity of interests and expectations in a community is such that even present benefits may be unsatisfactory to many. For some they are merely a partial satisfaction of their demands. The same outputs are also negatively valued by others, especially if the benefits and costs of the output are unevenly distributed. In addition, the outcome of policies are subject to time lags. Authorities reap the consequences of earlier policies but many of their present outputs will only take full effect at some future date.

Specific support based on outputs is therefore volatile and unpredictable. Authorities which depended upon it would be extremely exposed to sudden shifts in popularity. Easton's concern, of course, is with political systems in general, but the relevance of these points for party politics is clear. In economic policy, especially, time lags are inevitable and have proved a difficulty for all post-war British governments. The volatile nature of specific support is at the heart of representative government through the party system. It will already be obvious that trying to control it is therefore a major consideration in policy-making. The type of issue acted on and the way in which it is approached may vary considerably depending on whether a government has just come into office or is preparing for an election, and upon the state of its political capital; that is, upon its stock of supports. On the other hand, as we have suggested, governments cannot rely solely on their policies to give them the support they need to govern. There must be other kinds of support inputs and their impact on policy-making is more subtle.

The key question is why stability exists at all in political systems, given that few policies please everyone and specific support is difficult to predict or control. Why is it that so many people support the political system despite the fact that they are deeply divided over issues and fail to obtain a satisfactory response to all their demands? Why do people accept a political system which falls short of what they want? Why do they compromise?

One answer is that many political issues directly affect only small groups and have limited consequences for the rest of the population. The groups involved may be passionately committed to their demands and implacable in their hostility when frustrated, but against a background of lack of interest among the population as a whole they have to control very key resources if they are to be capable of creating widespread unrest. Yet sufficient issues give rise to strong emotions for politics to be an unpredictable game. Not least there are elites (representing sectional interests) that can act forcefully because of the latent power of their position. But in practice political parties, trade unions, professional bodies and other interest groups do not usually pursue their own interests to the ultimate limit. Why do moderation and compromise prevail so often?

Expediency is one answer. Although failing to obtain their

objectives, individuals and groups may be relatively content provided they obtain some influence within the political system. Groups tend to accept compromise when they feel that their power to influence events has been spent. Much apparently deep-seated conflict is precisely an attempt by organized groups to discover the limits of their power. As is apparent in industrial disputes, the limits of any one group's power may differ even in similar circumstances. Power is not a fixed commodity. Even if a group's support is constant other factors vary, not least the skill with which the various actors play the political game. The lengths to which competing groups will go in order to influence an event is usually uncertain. For this reason alone, different bodies within the political system frequently compete, jostle for advantage and engage in open conflict to test their relative strengths. But these activities are largely a prelude to, rather than a rejection of, an eventual compromise.

Various systems of representation also provide a means of managing the cleavages and conflicts that arise over the use and allocation of scarce resources. They allow diverse groups to seek influence over decisions, both formally through the electoral process and less formally through pressure group activities. The political parties not only act as channels of representation but also influence the nature of conflicts directly. Two- or three-party systems tend to soften the edge of many conflicts. Each party is itself a means of institutionalizing the balancing of interests and the pursuit of compromise. In maximizing its own support it tends to blur the conflicts engendered in smaller interest groups. It is only rarely that a large mass party can become identified with a single set of interests.

A willingness to de-politicize issues is important to the management of conflict. Issues which stimulate deep divisions present a problem for decisions about them may not be regarded as binding by one or more of the interested parties. Some issues are kept alive in party political debate largely for symbolic and morale-boosting purposes, but in many cases a self-denying ordinance is observed such that even issues which engender strong emotions will be allowed to pass (perhaps temporarily) from the centre of the political stage once a policy has been formulated. In the field of social policy the creation of the Unemployment Assistance Board in 1934 is an example where this norm was challenged but finally prevailed.[5] If most issues did not

[5] The National Assistance Board (it was replaced by the Supplementary Benefits Commission in 1966, see chapter 14) was a linear descendent of the UAB. The UAB, which was created amidst a political storm which threatened to destroy it in its infancy, in fact provided the basic organizational model for administering assistance benefits for over thirty years. This was only possible because the UAB issue was effectively de-politicized in the mid-thirties. See Millett, J. D., *The Unemployment Assistance Board*, Allen & Unwin, 1940, especially ch. 2.

cease to be politically contentious after decisions were reached they would seriously inhibit the number and complexity of new issues upon which action could be taken.

In anticipation of this norm being disastrously breached, authorities tend to withdraw some issues which threaten to remain politicized over a long period. This anticipation of stress and a possible loss of support is a spur to the mutually (albeit tacitly) approved exclusion of some kinds of issues from political consideration. A related response is not uncommon. Issues can be partially or completely removed from the political sphere by diverting them to, for example, judicial or administrative bodies. Many minor but deeply felt conflicts are left unresolved in formal political decision-making and are dealt with through delegated legislation or resolved, as it were privately, within government departments. Others, especially individually minor but recurring issues such as industrial disputes or the adjudication of disputes with a clientele (within the social services, for example), are channelled to quasi-judicial, 'independent' bodies. This cooling down by postponement is an important means of reducing political conflict, or at least containing it, and thereby easing the passage of contentious issues. Yet these responses to limited power and the management of conflict are not the only reasons for compromise. The existence of diffuse support for the regime and for the authorities is another.

Support for the regime
Of all the supports discussed by Easton, support for the regime is least affected by individual policy outputs. He sees the regime as 'sets of constraints on political interaction consisting of values, norms and a structure of authority.'[6] An absence of support for the regime would reduce or even destroy the capacity of governments to make authoritative decisions. Without the certainties and expectations about the behaviour of others that a regime allows, day-to-day political life would be riven with innumerable conflicts. An absence of even minimal agreement and support for the regime would transform each issue into 'a deep cleavage about a whole way of life'.[7] The corollary of there being support for the regime is that real limitations exist on the actors within the political system, on the way in which demands are approached and on what kinds of demands can be met. In other words, a relatively stable set of *rules of the game* can emerge in a political system. Once established and backed by precedent they can, in part, determine the sources, kinds and uses of power considered to be appropriate in political life.

Despite its over-simplification, this concept of a regime which is

---

[6] Easton, D. (1965), *op. cit.*, p. 193.
[7] *Ibid.*, p. 199.

legitimized by public support and acquiescence is of great relevance to policy-making. There are, in fact, many sets of 'rules' governing the way in which different aspects of the policy-making game are played. It is often not possible to identify them with any precision, or for that matter the groups whose support for them is crucial. But their impact on policies is no less real for that. There are, for example, rules about individual and party behaviour within Parliament which are primarily upheld by the parties themselves. There are rules about the relationship of government ministers to Parliament, the Judiciary, and to their own civil servants; and yet others which regulate the way in which civil servants themselves interact. The recent questioning of a government's 'mandate' to act in particular ways, for instance to enter the EEC or operate a new system of industrial law, illustrates the brittle quality of the rules. Nevertheless, one must not assume that there are no prescriptions or widely held expectations about how governments or other groups within the political system should behave. The fact that rules change, are stretched, ignored, or are not formally written down does not disprove their existence as a constraint on some types of actions for much of the time. For example, modern British governments have not imprisoned leading figures in the opposition party as a means of strengthening their grip on power. That they have not done so is not merely a reflection of the considerable power and autonomy of the judicial system and of the rules which guarantee that autonomy. It also reflects the fact that such an action would almost certainly be political suicide (unless the election process were abandoned) for, at the moment, governments are widely expected not to act in these ways. Although they may seem to lack teeth, there *are* rules about how the game should be played.

Many of the more specialized procedural traditions and constraints on actors in the policy-making system themselves arise from, or are justified by, the broad principles of British government The role of the House of Lords, the relationship between the Parliamentary Labour Party and the rest of the Labour movement or the power that trade unions possess vis-à-vis government have all been hotly debated issues. They illustrate the reality of the regime as a regulator of relationships in the policy-making process. They show the way in which certain principles of government, said to be supported by the electorate as a whole, are used by political actors in their struggle for power. They also confirm the often slow, but real changes which occur in the rules of the game.

Individual policies rarely influence public support for (or acquiescence with) the regime, as opposed to support for the particular government or party in power; but some policies raise questions about the rules, which then have to be clarified, defended or changed. Nevertheless, support for the regime has been a strong element of stability in modern British politics. This stability is a powerful influence not only on how policy is made, but also on what kinds of demands enter the system and what groups are most active in policy-making. It is clear, for example, that both right and left wing extremist groups would have difficulty in establishing an entirely new set of rules overnight. This is not to say that the existing regime is ideologically neutral or incapable of being used to further acts of political oppression, but the implications for groups unable to overthrow the rules are clear: they have to work within them or remain outside the policy-making process.

Working within the rules means accepting real constraints. For example, it is difficult for the Conservative Party to ignore the trade unions as an influence on policy just as it is for the Labour Party to ignore business pressures. It is not simply that these blocs have power which governments must reckon with; it is the consequences of defying the convention of consultation with such groups that demonstrates the importance of the rules. Spurning trade union or business advice has brought opprobrium to post-war British governments and increased the extent to which they have been held responsible when things went wrong. Although the practice may vary, governments are *expected* to consult with a wide range of groups,[8] and this expectation constrains their actions.

The rules of the game are important for policy-making in a number of different ways. As we have just emphasized, they begin to define limits within which political actors have to operate and policies have to be made. In doing so they may systematically favour some types of policy and retard others; we will examine this question later. Another effect of support for a regime briefly alluded to above is that it brings a degree of stability. That policy-making proceeds in an entirely different context when conflict is not managed can be seen by contrasting Northern Ireland with the rest of the United Kingdom.[9]

Fairly constant, even if imprecise, sets of rules introduce predictability and thereby facilitate much policy-making. They encourage compromise by beginning to clarify the circumstances in which groups can be said to have lost their bid to determine policy over a particular issue. There are, for example, conventions about how and how far trade unions will exert pressure on governments. 'Political' strikes are not unknown, but they are rare. Until the recent struggles over industrial relations policy the threat of overt industrial disruption

[8] This does not imply that the 'rules of the game' favour all groups equally; we are not arguing that established institutions and methods of proceeding are ideologically neutral.

[9] For a detailed introduction to the political issues and system in Northern Ireland see Rose, R., *Governing without Consensus: an Irish Perspective*, Faber, 1971.

in support of political ends has been carefully shunned. The trade unions have traditionally accepted that they have lost if a 'political' strike is the only action left to them; indeed they usually acknowledge defeat long before they reach such a situation. But let us move away from these general considerations. Does the regime help individual governments to protect themselves against rapid shifts in specific support?

Diffuse support
Support for authorities allows them to make and enact decisions. It increases their ability to enforce compromise upon other groups. Support is not just a commodity a party needs in order to win an election. It is a vital element in the handling of day-to-day problems and disputes. Much of this support comes indirectly from the widespread acceptance of the regime. Because the rules of the game are accepted, groups acting in accordance with them are thereby strengthened. 'Government by consent' does not imply consent for each individual action but for the regime. However, governments cannot sit passively by and hope that this will sustain them. They must strive to build up additional reserves of support and replenish losses.

One way of doing this is by translating specific supports into more generalized or diffuse support. As we have suggested, a long series of popular policies (producing, for example, a steady rate of economic growth combined with only limited inflation) results in more generalized support for the governing party. It is seen as a party 'fit to govern'. Indeed, a contemporary British government achieving the economic miracle of our example might happily ride out other disasters and yet be seen as the *only* party fit to govern. Given the difficulty of actually producing a long series of popular policies, however, diffuse support of this kind is not a sufficient hedge against the vagaries of party politics.

An important means of regulating political conflict and amassing diffuse support is by fostering a belief in the existence of a common or national interest. If this belief is widespread and the authorities are seen as guardians of the public good, sectional interests can legitimately be subordinated to it. This concept allows authorities to designate particular demands as not in the common interest, or to adjudicate between interests on that basis. If authorities are judged to be working for the public good they attract support and legitimacy as the body with the best vantage point from which to assess what is in the general interest. Maintaining the belief that they act in the common interest gives the authorities considerable room for manoeuvre and strengthens their ability to influence other actors in the political system. It can also bring them extra increments of diffuse support despite the fact that they act in a partisan way on many issues and may even define the public good in inconsistent ways on different occasions.

Governments enjoy advantages over other groups in any dispute about what is in the public interest. They possess much information unavailable to others. They are supremely able to set one issue against any other that is raised and to argue that the public good is not easily attained; that it lies in compromise between different issues and interests. They also have substantial access to the public through mass communication and can, therefore, use persuasion to gain support for their view of what is for the general good. Nevertheless, the concept of 'the public good' is a double-edged weapon. It is not solely the prerogative of government, for actors outside government frequently use it in seeking to exert influence over policy-makers. A group's ability to influence government is determined by the way in which its demands can be presented as well as by the number and prestige of its supporters. To present demands publicly and forcefully as a means of advancing the collective good can oblige authorities to take notice of them. Government is particularly vulnerable to such a line of argument precisely because it relates to what is seen as one of its primary functions. Yet the main point remains: governments underpin their specific support by amassing diffuse support. They do this by nurturing their image as prudent, fair and legitimate rulers. The necessity of having to do this in turn influences the way policies are made. Each aspect of support, therefore, has a bearing on policy. The types of issue acted on and the kind of action taken are in part a product of the need to increase or husband specific and diffuse support and the need to preserve the aura of legitimacy. If a government's political capital is high it gains an extra degree of freedom in its policy-making, but even then the fact that support can melt away imposes constraints.

III DEMAND REGULATION

The ways in which demands are regulated is central to a framework of ideas about policy-making. We have implied that one, admittedly crude, way of looking at policy-making is to think of a queue of demands for government action. Whether demands arise within ministries, political parties, the Cabinet or from outside the governmental system altogether they enter a queue for priority; they are subject to a process of regulation.

Two major forms of regulation occur. Control can be developed over the nature and the number of private and group wants which are presented as demands. It can also be exercised over demands that have been accorded some recognition (demands that are already being processed into possible policy initiatives) as they move through the government system. These two forms of regulation are only analytically distinct: in practice there is no discrete point at which demands enter the policy process. For convenience, however, we shall examine them separately.

Regulating the conversion of wants into demands

In all the case studies which follow, groups outside and inside the government system present new demands or requests that a policy under active consideration be modified or reconsidered. Our democratic system encourages people to express needs in the form of political demands. Its political institutions and culture ostensibly permit all citizens to convert wants into demands. The process of conversion certainly requires skills and opportunities which are not available to all. Nevertheless, if there are to be restraints on the number and content of demands, they must operate largely within the democratic ideal of not arbitrarily preventing people from expressing their viewpoints to authorities.

The conversion of wants into demands is regulated by both the structure of the political system and by the norms and values of the society. Structural regulation is effected through the existence of 'gatekeepers', and because complex political systems entail a high degree of specialization. This gives rise to distinct roles for interest groups, political parties, legislators and administrators. It also creates a hierarchy of groups through which most demands must pass. Some of these groups may specialize in presenting demands, but they all act in some ways as gatekeepers. Unusually powerful demands may result in policy changes without having passed through this maze of specialists; they may be communicated directly from the grass roots to the authorities, or they may be initiated by the authorities themselves and meet no opposition. But the majority of demands will move from one specialist group to another and at each point on their journey they are liable to be rejected or modified. A pressure group, for example, cannot simply convert every cause with which it has sympathy into a demand for government action. To do so would rapidly destroy its credibility with the authorities it wished to influence. It needs to act cautiously on those issues on which it has little information. If there is likely to be powerful opposition to a particular issue it will have to develop a correspondingly strong case, which will result in delay, or it may drop some such causes in favour of others where the chances of success are higher.

Pressure groups, like governments, also have to examine the demands they champion in terms of the consequences for their own support and their limited resources. Demands made in a way which ensures outright rejection may soon lead to the collapse of an organization which mainly exists to exercise some influence on government. Similarly the political parties, not least through their conferences and propaganda, test the support consequences of taking up different issues and indicate to the competing sectors of the party what kinds of issues cannot be promoted. The gatekeepers of the political system are not simply reducing demands to manageable proportions in a random way; they are making and transmitting judgements about what demands can appropriately be made on government via that particular channel of communication.

Important though gatekeepers undoubtedly are, there are many of them in our society. Each MP, the political parties and all pressure groups with a modicum of influence or support can bring a demand into political life. The structural regulation of demands is pervasive, therefore, but not rigorous. More powerful in many ways are the *norms* governing what kinds of demands should and should not be presented for political resolution. They constitute a set of limits on the conversion of wants which are crucial to social policy. The history of social policy is an account of attempts to modify these limits and, where possible, the values that lie beneath the political norms.

There is, in fact, a large body of agreement at any one time about the particular kinds of wants that should *not* be the concern of government. To want the replacement of a basically capitalist economy, a reduced rate of economic growth, or the abandonment of a system of exchange based on money is to want for things which stand no chance of being considered as demands. Besides such broad areas of 'agreement' there are certain other norms affecting want conversion which are more specific to each party. Different assumptions about the wants that can be translated into political action are asserted; just how much the parties differ in practice tends to be a controversial question. Both, however, operate within those 'areas of agreement' which we illustrated above.

Despite the structural and cultural limitations on the conversion of wants into demands, many demands find their way into the political system. Over the past century an increasingly large number in the field of social policy have passed through these filters. Consequently demands have to be regulated in other ways as well.

Reduction processes
Quite apart from outright rejection by an authority, most demands are modified to a significant extent. A small number are not: they move directly to an appropriate authority and become policy directives. But in order to gain sufficient support to be translated into any kind of policy action the majority of demands must undergo

change. Demands that relate to similar problems are grouped, co-ordinated and consequently become an amalgam of policy proposals. This reduction of demands not only removes some of the pressure from the political process, it also greatly increases the chance of the composite demand being accepted by the authorities. For the demands are not only reduced, they are also tailored to meet the authorities' needs and interests. Policy proposals are shorn of some of their most contentious features, compromises are made to satisfy different interests and emphases are changed to maximize the appeal and feasibility of a policy, or to minimize the loss of support it will produce. Some patently unpopular policies are often combined with sweeteners in the form of other demands that will be received favourably.

Whilst combining demands may increase grass roots or mass media support for the composite demand and reduce hostility, it also has its disadvantages. Proposals become diluted and the specialist groups involved often become disenchanted if the essential elements of their original demands are sacrificed. Demand reduction implies compromise and it often blunts the edge of radical proposals, but it is both necessary and useful to authorities. Not least because when policies finally emerge they are likely to be the result of a complicated process of fusion which enables them to be presented in a different light to different groups in order to maximize support or ease the path of implementation.

The very groups that convey demands through the political system also reduce them in the ways described. Interest groups, the political parties and the central government departments responsible for a particular area of policy are particularly important in this respect. They act as gatekeepers for issues that are progressing through the system just as they do for newly formed demands entering the system. Institutions specializing in the presentation of demands (interest groups, for example) and the authorities both take part in this reduction process.

IV THE STRENGTHS AND WEAKNESSES OF A SYSTEMS FRAMEWORK

The framework of ideas which we have distilled from Easton and other 'systems' writers has enabled us to highlight the interrelationship between demands, support and policy-making in the political system. It has also allowed us to consider two other important phenomena which we discuss at various points throughout the following chapters. The first is political stability and the second is the process of demand or issue regulation.

British political life has a strong tradition of stability; neither the continuance of parliamentary democracy nor many of the operational rules have been seriously challenged for a long time. We have suggested that conflict is quite carefully regulated and that with the expectation of stability comes a greater willingness to compromise. This facilitates much policy-making, although the rules, conventions and procedures which buttress this stability also act as a formidable set of constraints on policy-making. Not least they limit the impact of radical proposals and the divergence between party ideologies, although the *competition* for power and influence is no less real for being muted or controlled. Competition between the parties takes the form of a search for specific support through policy proposals and practice, beneath which is a continuing concern to accumulate diffuse support and to be seen as fit to govern. Party politics also operate within constraints which are embodied in the regime as well as in numerous highly specific parliamentary norms that encourage accommodation and compromise. In addition, the norms of British political life demand that governments should appear at times to transcend sectional interests and this, together with the appeal to a common or public interest, is a powerful means of regulating political conflicts.[10]

Despite the underlying stability, the outcome of conflict is uncertain in a narrower sense. The tendency for interest groups to accept compromise is lessened on particular issues where government power is known, or suspected, to be limited. It is similarly lessened over whole areas of political conflict when a government's electoral support is low and a change of government is imminent. The interaction of many groups with limited power makes compromise likely providing the support for the authorities remains high. If it does not, the outcome of the competition for power is more uncertain. The stakes are raised and the willingness to compromise is reduced. But support for the regime continues to impose limits on conflict even on these occasions. Particular policies or governments may be defeated but the system of government is rarely subject to sustained criticism or attack.

[10] The concept of a 'public' and 'general interest' has been criticized and effectively rejected by some political theorists, but this is not to deny that it is employed by the actors in the policy process and that it plays a part in the regulation of conflict in political life. See Buchanan, J. M., 'An Individualistic Theory of Political Process', in Easton, D. (ed.), *Varieties of Political Theory*, Prentice-Hall, 1966, and also Buchanan, J. M. and Tullock, G., *The Calculus of Consent: Logical Foundations of Constitutional Democracy*, University of Michigan Press, 1962.

The most important feature of the discussion of demand regulation is that it underlines the reasons *inherent in the political culture and policy process* which makes it necessary. All demands cannot be met; but not merely because the authorities are insensitive to them through their inefficiency, bureaucratic isolation or desire to ignore whole classes of problems. Authorities lack the financial, manpower, technical or informational resources to act on all demands. They also lack the political capital, for new or modified policies frequently erode support for the authorities rather than add to it. The content, cost or potential failure of a policy may all be reasons for not embarking on it. In short, demands have to compete with each other for priority; they form a queue. And the length of the queue obviously varies with changes in demands and supports. The systems framework is valuable as a means of emphasizing these central features of the policy process. It also offers one explanation of why some kinds of demands are kept out of the queue altogether. They are excluded by gatekeepers and by the norms (transmitted by these gatekeepers and contained within the political culture) about what kinds of wants should be translated into demands.

What a systems approach does not show is whether specific groups of the population suffer because their wants are continually ignored. The relative importance of ideological and technical factors in determining how many and which demands are excluded from or fail to reach the head of the queue, is unanswered. Nor does it draw attention to the possibility that governments may use their power overtly (through the suppression of a minority, for instance), or more subtly, to limit the kinds of demands that are made. This framework of concepts also obscures the fact that one political party may be more readily seen as legitimate because its composition, ideology and past record are more closely in line with the electorate's view of the nature and role of government. Many would argue that Conservative governments possess an advantage of this kind which helps them survive policy reversals and mistakes which would cripple a Labour government. The Labour Party has certainly tended to lose support rapidly during its periods in office. It shows evidence of being more dependent on, and vulnerable to, changes in specific support based on the relative attractiveness of policy proposals and their outcomes. That is, its pool of diffuse support is likely to be smaller than that of the Conservatives.

The systems approach to politics does not provide a full explanation of policy-making. The core problems tackled within it are rather different. Systems theory concentrates on the general properties of systems and on exchanges across system boundaries. It is possible to avoid some of the problems associated with a strong emphasis on system equilibrium. Easton, for example, does not assume a static political system, but explicitly recognizes that the means developed to ensure system survival may not succeed. He accepts that there can be unstable as well as stable states of equilibrium. Nevertheless, the emphasis is on how political life is sustained rather than on the kinds of outputs (policies) that arise from it.[11] The approach does not encourage one to take the viewpoint of an activist, within or outside the formal political institutions, who wishes to obtain a specific kind of policy decision. It provides a good picture of how existing holders of political power may defend their position, but does not explain the distribution of power *per se* or its consequences. Systems analysis has illuminated some aspects of power distribution, but not the impact of the overall allocation of power on policy-making.

Our discussion of demands and supports has left out any real consideration of the main participants in the political system and the nature of power relationships within it. Although some interesting data have emerged on system determinants of power distribution, the broader configurations of political power and influence must also be examined.[12] This is done in Chapter 8. However, the next four chapters identify some of the key actors and institutions involved in British policy-making at central government level and are organized around the core theme of this present chapter – the regulation or rationing of demands or issues. This process is fundamental to policy-making and to study it is to study a major determinant of policy outcomes. In addition, the image of government as merely reacting to pressures generated by outside bodies, which this chapter may have conveyed by its content and terminology, is counter balanced in the next two. Government is depicted as a powerful force at *each* stage of policy-making, from the first initiation of proposals to their final implementation.

---

[11] Some institutions which are important in the policy-making process have attracted attention from systems theorists: Fenno, R. F., *The Power of the Purse: Appropriations Politics in Congress*, Little, 1966; Buchanan, J. M. and Tullock, G., *op. cit.*, and Eulau, H., *Class and Party in the Eisenhower Years: Class Roles and Perspectives in the 1952 and 1956 Elections*, Free Press, 1962.

[12] See, for example, Riker, W. H., *The Theory of Political Coalitions*, Yale University Press, 1962.

CHAPTER FOUR

Authorities and the Policy Process

I THE NATURE OF AUTHORITIES

It seems reasonable to assume that in Britain the central authorities comprise the senior personnel working in government departments; Ministers acting individually or senior Ministers acting through the Cabinet; members of the judiciary and, arguably, Parliament in its legislative role. The kinds of decisions for which these groups can act as authorities obviously vary. Most civil servants can only make day-to-day decisions within the limits of existing policies. Members of Parliament are equally limited in that their authority is a collective one. Both groups, however, represent an important means of access to other authorities.

It would be misleading to consider authorities purely as decision-makers with respect to policy, for in dealing with issues they act in other ways as well. They add support and possibly improve the chances of a proposal being accepted by other authorities. They begin to assess the feasibility, political attractiveness and ideological appropriateness of issues. Some of them they reject on these grounds and in doing so indicate to those who present the proposals what is likely to gain government or party support. They also collect, combine and modify suggestions or demands in order to produce 'packages' which may be more readily acceptable to higher authorities. They clearly act both as advocates for some issues and as agents for the regulation and reduction of demands in general.

In communicating a demand authorities therefore make their own distinctive contribution to it. A demand conveyed by a government department to a Minister, or to the Cabinet, will already have been examined for administrative feasibility. If it appears to be utterly impracticable it will be blocked or substantially modified within the department. Senior civil servants will also consider the legislative and political implications of a demand so that they are in a position to advise their ministers. Members of Parliament who take up a demand will similarly test its political implications and potential support among their colleagues and possibly with the party leaders or the whips. As an individual, an MP can raise issues in a number of ways; for example, in the form of a parliamentary question or as isolated debating points. However, issues raised as serious policy demands usually require a more forceful presentation than this. To gain party support they would have to be examined in the light of the party's ideology, its current political needs, the stock of policies being actively favoured by its members and the likely consequences of adopting them for party support.

We cannot rigidly distinguish, therefore, between authorities and partisans; the terms are applicable to *roles*.[1] All the authorities we have mentioned may act as partisans for some issues raised by them or referred to them. Indeed, a large part of their job involves doing this with respect to those issues which they choose to support. For example, civil servants act as partisans within their own departments and with their Ministers; Ministers do so with their ministerial colleagues in Cabinet, in their party, in Parliament and with their department if they initiate their own policies. But despite their dual roles the groups we have mentioned have the distinction of being the *only* bodies who can act with authority on issues raised for central governmental resolution.

In this chapter we begin to explore the ways in which the political process at central government level impinges on policy-making. We will do so by looking at some of the principal bodies which seemingly act as authorities, asking whether they do in fact have authoritative roles, how they relate one to another and what impact they have on social policy. Two quite fundamental questions about the nature of the authorities will be raised. The first can be summarized in this way: are the authorities inert or are they creative with respect to social policy? Do they merely react to demands made upon them from external sources or do they themselves generate and champion issues? The second question is about the structure of the authorities and the ways in which they are related. Do they amount to a centralized and monolithic seat of political power? Or, alternatively, should they be regarded as a system of autonomous or semi-autonomous

---

[1] The distinction between authorities and partisans forms a central part of the thesis in Gamson, W. A., *Power and Discontent*, Dorsey, 1968. He employs the following useful definitions: 'The *authorities* are those who, for any given social system, make binding decisions in that system' (p. 21); 'potential *partisans* [are] that set of actors who for a given decision, are affected by the outcome in some "significant" way' (p. 32).

nodes of power and influence? The first of these general questions can be answered quite quickly for the time being.

Social policy and government

Policy-making can often be a process of trying to force a reluctant government to act; there are examples enough in our case studies. But to move on from this observation and characterize government and other bureaucracies as inert is unhelpful. In emphasizing the inertia of government Schaffer and Corbett, for example, run the risk of locating the initiative for policies outside government bureaucracies.[2] Although this is not their intention, it is all too easy to convey a picture of governments as reactive or obstructionist. This is a special risk in studying contemporary policy-making because the part played by authorities is difficult to determine without access to records. There are instances of governmental creativity amongst our cases (most obviously the Open University), but overall they may give an impression of slow or reluctant government responses to external pressures.

Considered from the viewpoint of policy-makers within government and, for that matter party bureaucracies, these institutions are not inert, nor are they monolithic. Party workers and civil servants would contend that their organizations often initiate changes, some of which are strongly opposed by interest groups within and outside these bureaucracies. The same people are also aware of the heterogeneous sub-systems, or groups, which comprise their organizations. These divisions can serve both to restrain and promote policy changes.

These apparently contradictory views of government, as either monolithic and resistant to change or as heterogeneous and often creative, are obviously not mutually exclusive. They depend upon one's standpoint and the type of issue or solution in which one is interested. Similarly, we do not have to define government as inert to argue that it often obstructs changes of a particular kind. It is perfectly possible for a government which is active in, say, foreign affairs to be hostile to social policy as a whole, or to a growth of public intervention in that field. This is partly a matter of rationing policy-making resources, of issue regulation, as well as a reflection of priorities and ideologies.

Modern British governments are not hostile to social policy in general, nor inert or merely reactive in their approach to social issues. However, the relationship between State responsibilities or powers and individual liberties rightly continues to be contentious. In addition, an ideological undercurrent of minimum government

---

[2] Schaffer, B. B. and Corbett, D. C., *Decisions: Case Studies in Australian Administration*, Cheshire, 1966, especially the Introduction.

has continued to influence social policy at the margin throughout the post-war period. It has surfaced more distinctly since the late sixties. This is admittedly expressed as an argument about the particular areas of social policy in which the State should be active; what the balance should be between public, market and voluntaristic provision, and about the principles on which State provision should be based. Nevertheless, these are real ideological differences and they may form the basis for resistance to social policy proposals. More specific resistance to particular proposals also arises from the ideologies or policy preferences of the political parties and from ideologies about the relationship between, for example, the economic system or the family and social policy. There are thus many reasons other than inertia or hostility why governments may keep proposals waiting in the queue.

In order to avoid casting government as inert, let us assert our belief that they should be seen as an active force in social policy; as a source of initiatives and proposals as well as a regulator of demands made upon them. We will illustrate the point in this and the following chapters. How one evaluates government initiatives depends upon one's own ideological viewpoint, but in Chapter 8 we will discuss the limits within which policy-making takes place. The rest of this and the next chapter will be devoted to our second general question; namely, do the authorities at central government level constitute a monolithic seat of power?

II THE AUTHORITIES: STRUCTURE AND INTERACTION

How are the authorities structured? What principles determine the way in which they interact? How are power and different functions distributed between them? One possible approach is to think of authorities as a hierarchy characterized by increasing degrees of power, authority or domain. However, the problems of such a view are apparent as soon as one tries to locate the apex. Is Parliament, the Cabinet or the Prime Minister the supreme authority in policy-making? These are disputed questions. The respective roles of the Premier, Cabinet and individual Ministers within the Executive is a subject of debate, as is the power and function of Parliament in relation to the Executive. We will follow a little of these debates, not in search of solutions, even less to produce a theoretical overview of British government, but to clarify some points relevant to social policy.

If a simple hierarchical model presents these problems can we replace it by something better? If we look at the process of demand or issue regulation it is possible to discern a complex system at work rather than a clear hierarchy. Government departments, the political parties, individual MPs and all the other bodies which communicate demands also participate in the process of demand regulation. Although it is not the whole picture, the governmental, parliamentary and party systems certainly seem to provide *alternative* channels for the presentation and filtering of proposals. They do not act randomly, nor do they apply just one set of criteria in regulating demands. If one accepts a 'ruling class' model of society these distinctions are, of course, unimportant. The whole State apparatus exists, from this viewpoint, to filter out demands that are unacceptable to that class. But we will operate, at least for the moment, on the opposite assumption: that several different types of issue regulation are taking place. There is certainly evidence of structural differentiation to support this view.

In practice things are not as simple as this comment suggests. Allowing one kind of issue into the policy process reduces the chances that others will flourish, since promoting and blocking issues are complementary activities. Further, the criteria used by gatekeepers in different parts of the system may be quite indistinguishable for much of the time, or on particular issues. Nevertheless, we would argue that the ability to initiate, promote and determine the format of policies is dispersed throughout the political system. It extends not only to Parliament and 'outside' groups, but also to departments within government. It is possible to argue that however weak Parliament may be, or however powerful government may appear, the ability to initiate and regulate policy demands is dispersed even within the authorities because they do not comprise a simple hierarchical or monolithic policy-making process. We are suggesting a polycentric view of policy-making. Let us explain more carefully why.

Two simple models have been suggested which might help us understand how the authorities are structured. The validity of the first, the hierarchical one, turns on the question of whether the authorities are systematically co-ordinated; that is, whether there is an omnipotent individual or institution at the apex. The second model specifies a set of parallel channels through which issues can be promoted and regulated. This presumes a polycentric structure in the sense that there would be at least two independent loci of authoritative decisions on policy issues. An obvious point at which to test these models is the interaction between government and Parliament. Are these structurally independent authorities or is one subordinate to the other? After we have considered these structural questions it will be necessary to see whether the values and interests which determine the way in which issues are handled are likely to vary from one authority to another.

Government and Parliament

What, in general terms, is the relationship between Parliament and government in policy-making? One view is that Parliament, because it is the fulcrum of the law-making process, is, or should be, dominant. This approach has been maintained by scholars from Blackstone, through Mill and Bagehot, to the present day. Set against it is an equally longstanding and quite contrary view of British government as strong, independent and dominant in many spheres of activity including the law-making function itself. 'In Britain there can scarcely be any doubt that all decisions of prime importance about major policies or new legislation are Cabinet decisions, and that those next in importance are ministerial decisions.'[3] Tivey goes on to note that a 'people's will' theory of British democracy may obscure the fact that decision-making is firmly located in the Executive. Parliament and the Electorate's representatives, the MPs, have only limited direct influence over policy. A number of writers have referred to the confusion that exists over Parliament's role, but Birch summarizes the nature of this confusion best. 'There are', he suggests, 'two languages in which the relations between Parliament and the Executive are described. One language is that of the liberal view of the constitution used by nearly all back benchers, nearly all journalists, and most academic commentators. This language emphasizes the responsibility of government to Parliament. It extols the merits of parliamentary sovereignty, of the responsibility of Ministers to Parliament ... of "the parliamentary watchdog", of the democratic advantages of a system in which there is no separation of powers between legislature and executive.'[4] The other language is used by civil servants, Ministers and leading members of the Opposition. It emphasizes 'the responsibility of Her Majesty's Government for the administration of the country, of the importance of protecting civil servants from political interference, [and] of Parliament's function as a debating chamber in which public opinion is aired'.[5] Which of these viewpoints is more appropriate to the understanding of policy-making?

Some points are indisputable. Governments have the responsibility and the power to act in those areas covered by existing legislation; that is, in the field of current administration. They do not act in

---

[3] Tivey, L., 'The System of Democracy in Britain', in Benewick, R. and Dowse, R. E., *Readings on British Politics and Government*, London University Press, 1968, p. 40.

[4] Birch, A. H., *Representative and Responsible Government*, Allen & Unwin, 1964, p. 165.

[5] *Ibid.*, p. 165.

grand isolation even here. There is a line of accountability which terminates in Parliament for many purposes, and Parliament may also be one of the many partisan bodies pressing for particular types of action; but the government has much autonomy in the day-to-day implementation and modification of policy. This is important, for the growth of government responsibility for diverse social problems means that the powers available under existing legislation are extensive. From executive decisions on the siting and design of old people's homes to major programmes of health centre construction or secondary school reorganization, governments can act without seeking specific approval from Parliament.

Government is just as clearly the locus of power when it comes to the planning of legislation. The vast majority of new legislation is developed within government; it is not generated in Parliament through Private Members' Bills. Governments dominate Parliament not only by being the source of virtually all major legislation, but also by controlling a large proportion of the day-to-day parliamentary programme. A Cabinet committee determines the flow of legislation through Parliament. The government whips and the Leader of the House advise senior Ministers and the Prime Minister on problems of timing and tactics within the House. However, this is not entirely one-sided. The Opposition also has some control over the parliamentary programme and is certainly able to cause major disruptions in a government's timetable; but this only emphasizes the basic difference in the type of power they each possess. Government, not Parliament, has the most fundamental and extensive powers in policy-making.

It would seem reasonable, therefore, to agree with Griffith when he says that 'the Government is authoritarian in decision and in action. It makes up its own mind; it puts into effect its own policy. Only if it seeks to acquire new powers by legislation must it first obtain the approval of any other body ... We speak of the sovereignty of Parliament but less confusion would be caused if we spoke of the sovereignty of the Government'.[6] His assertion not only has the merit of dispensing with confusing constitutional niceties, it also accords closely with the realities of policy-making as we perceive them. Does this leave us with government as the omnipotent policy-making authority, albeit supported by parallel systems of demand regulation? Clearly this is not the whole picture. In what ways could it be modified?

One possibility is that Parliament has some ultimate sanction, or veto, which it can exercise over the government on matters of policy.

[6] Griffith, J. A. G., 'Legislation', in Hanson, A. H. and Crick, B. (eds), *The Commons in Transition*, Fontana, 1970, pp. 15 and 18. This is a very useful discussion of the relationships between Parliament and government.

This would arise if Parliament could overthrow governments or if it could withhold new powers from government by refusing to pass legislation. In our view Parliament as a whole can hardly be said to possess such powers. Party discipline in the Commons and the nature of the responsibilities accepted by post-war governments virtually guarantee that they will not be overthrown by Parliament.[7] Of course, a government must listen to its own back benchers on occasions if it is to retain its security, but it is the party not Parliament in which the effective power to veto a policy proposal resides. Consequently, attention must be centred on Parliament's role as a base for the criticism of government and, to a certain extent, as a forum for informing and influencing the public at large.

Crick, for example, summarizes the modern role of Parliament as 'informing the electorate; influencing the Government by inquiry, debate, and scrutinizing the administration; and the indirect but powerful effect all this has on the electorate'.[8] Similarly, Beer argues for a clearer recognition of MPs and Parliament as means of explaining government policy to the electorate and of gaining the public's consent to the heavy demands government increasingly makes on it. These writers do not argue that Parliament has no role in determining policies, but they realistically emphasize other functions. Most policies are promulgated by government and are carried to legislative form with relatively few modifications being *forced* upon it within the House. However, Parliament does scrutinize the process of government. This, combined with the fact that it is the forum for legislative *activity*, puts it in a unique position without contradicting the primacy of government in policy-making. Parliament is often a powerful base from which to exert some influence on politics and it cannot be totally ignored by governments when they are formulating their programmes.

Indeed, it may be argued that to attribute policy initiatives to the government is misleading because it is largely carrying out a programme forged within Parliament and the party in response to the expression of public sentiment and demand. A government could be said to obtain a 'mandate' to act on issues selected by the interaction of party leaders, party members and the general public. This argument raises several problems.

First, it ignores the extent to which policy decisions are made outside the context of an election. Many issues arise during the life of a government; neither the priority given to them nor the solutions

---

[7] For a discussion of the consequences of the complex and technical policies administered by governments since the last war, see Beer, S., 'The British Legislature and the Problem of Mobilising Consent', in Crick, B. (ed.), *Essays on Reform*, Oxford University Press, 1967.

[8] Crick, B., 'Parliament and the Matter of Britain', in Crick (ed.), *Essays on Reform, op. cit.*, p. 208.

that are chosen need emerge from the parliamentary forum. This is most conspicuous in economic and foreign affairs where the policy environment is unstable and a long-term strategy may be difficult to fulfil; but it is also relevant to social policy. Secondly, the 'public interaction' argument raises the whole question of policy-making within parties (which will be deferred until later) and the reality of notions of representation and of public participation inherent in democracy. Thirdly, whilst the language of 'mandates' and the electorates' choice of policy proposals is widely used in political life, it can be misleading. It would be extremely difficult to disentangle the influence that parties exert over public expectations by the programmes they offer from the public influence on the content of those programmes. Moreover, if one is to use the term at all, the mandate given to a victorious party is basically a mandate to govern, based on perhaps a few major issues and qualities presented by that party to the electorate. It is clearly not a conscious and deliberate choice of a whole programme of policies. Beer argues, with good reason, that the significance of election promises is rather that they begin the process of winning acceptance for the successful party's policy programme. He accepts that a dependency effect may be operating – parties may be inducing the electorate to want what is being offered to them.[9] They may in fact be leading rather than responding to the public.

Before we proceed further let us recapitulate our argument so far. We began by asking whether Parliament and government were equal authorities, or whether one was subordinate to the other. Our initial conclusion was that Parliament is a weak authority. The authoritative decisions it makes are usually at the behest of government. The law-making function does not really give Parliament the status of an independent authority. What we are now questioning is whether, in a more general sense, *governments* are really independent. Are they not so hemmed in by their responsibility to the electorate via Parliament, the party and the electoral process, that they also lack the freedom to make policies in an autonomous way?

Governments clearly exercise leadership; on occasions in defiance of 'public opinion'. In recent years three applications have been made for membership of the European Economic Community. On each occasion the government's own party, Parliament as a whole and public opinion generally have been divided. The Cabinets of the day endorsed a policy which was not urged upon them by a powerful and united body of public opinion. For both Macmillan and Wilson this interest in Europe came at a time when few other initiatives were available in the field of economic policy. Nevertheless, their govern-

[9] Beer, S., in Crick, B., *op. cit.*, p. 96.

ments put themselves in the position of having to lead and carry public opinion with them. To take another example, the Suez débâcle was the classical instance of a policy sponsored solely by the government, but in which it was unable to gain sufficient support to continue its policy. By way of comparison, when public policy has gone ahead of public opinion on social issues it has often been expressed through the parliamentary forum, as in capital punishment and such issues as divorce or abortion.[10] The degree of leadership exercised varies greatly, but governments often initiate, rather than merely enact, policies which reflect their supporters' immediate interests and demands. Both parties believe this to be legitimate and consistent with democracy.

We have been arguing that, in the main, Parliament is not the key authority for policy decisions; government fills that role. On the other hand Parliament is clearly quite different from the galaxy of interest groups and other institutions that adopt partisan roles. A small amount of important legislation is initiated through Private Members' Bills, although even this would be impossible without a government's tacit approval. The real parliamentary influence over policy arises through the processes of debating, scrutinizing, attacking and supporting governments' actions, inactions and policy proposals. What does this tell us about the authorities?

We have not endorsed either of our earlier models wholeheartedly. Government and Parliament do seem to operate as parallel systems of issue reduction. Demands are fed into both of them from outside interests and proposals are also separately generated within each, but Parliament's authoritative role does not match that of government. They are complementary parts of the policy process and each has areas of independence, but they are not equals in policy-making. We have come near to seeing government as the omnipotent policy-maker, but have held back from adopting this hierarchical view for two reasons. The first is that Parliament is not powerless even if it is, in many ways, rather weak. We will return to its role in a later chapter. The second is that even if government is dominant we cannot simply assume that it is itself a single cohesive authority. To think of government as a straightforward hierarchy raises again the question, where is the apex? Where in government does the authority to shape and approve social policies reside?

[10] For a discussion of such issues of conscience see Richards, P., *Parliament and Conscience*, Allen & Unwin, 1970.

III THE STRUCTURE OF GOVERNMENT

The way government is organized partly determines the nature and outcome of policy. Let us begin by looking at the upper reaches of the system – at the government as opposed to the government departments. The term 'government' is used in this sense to mean the political heads of the governmental process. They comprise junior Ministers, Ministers and the Prime Minister. With few exceptions they are drawn from the ranks of Parliament. In the post-war period they have always come from a single, electorally victorious political party. It is in these hands that the power to make policy seems to be concentrated. But if this is the locus of power it is exercised in at least two distinctly different ways. Collectively, decisions are made by the government as a whole (in practice by some grouping of senior ministers) on issues of wide concern. Individually, and in departmental teams, ministers develop proposals for discussion within the Cabinet system. They also make decisions, often independent of the Cabinet, about the implementation of existing policies and programmes. This latter power is important. The average government Bill enacted by Parliament provides a mere framework within which Ministers sanction the practices that breathe life into the policy. The extensiveness of 'delegated legislation' and the responsibility for determining many questions of priority in using resources provide Ministers with substantial opportunities for making policy.

Apart from the Cabinet itself, there are two structural features of importance. Together they make it possible to handle a considerable amount of business and make decisions outside the somewhat unwieldy full Cabinet meeting. The first is the system of Cabinet committees. The functional groupings created in this way not only prepare the ground for policy-making among members of the government representing a group of related interests and departments; they also involve non-Cabinet members. Much policy formation, of routine and major importance, is thereby removed from formal meetings of the Cabinet.[11] The second is the existence of a partly informal hierarchy among ministers which extends beyond, but also into, the Cabinet.[12]

The Cabinet system and informal meetings between the Premier and his closest colleagues tend to concentrate some decision-making within a very few hands. But this is only the extreme example; power

[11] For a valuable discussion of the decision-making function of Cabinet committees see Mackintosh, J. P., *The British Cabinet*, Methuen (2nd edn), 1968, especially ch. 21 and p. 614.
[12] See Heasman, D. J., 'The Ministerial Hierarchy' and 'The Prime Minister and the Cabinet', *Parliamentary Affairs*, Summer and Autumn, 1962.

is by no means evenly distributed among ministers. As Mackintosh notes, the step from non-Cabinet to Cabinet Minister is a large one. Non-Cabinet Ministers attending a meeting of the Cabinet are at a considerable disadvantage; their opportunity to exert influence is affected by their exclusion from the circle of senior Ministers.[13] Mackintosh also accepts that the step from Cabinet Minister to Premier is a long one. In between lie the groupings of Premier and senior members of the Cabinet – of somewhat fluctuating membership depending on the subject matter – who discuss some major policies in broad outline or even in detail. These structural features influence the nature of policy-making in several ways. They reduce the time spent in Cabinet on establishing policy outlines by enabling important decisions to be raised above departmental level without involving the full Cabinet, or without involving it prematurely. In addition, they allow the Premier to reserve issues for his own consideration, or for settlement between himself and a few of his most senior colleagues.[14]

It will be clear from what has been said that the Prime Minister, who is accepted by most as at least the nominal head of his ministerial team, is certainly at the formal organizational peak of the government.[15] The Cabinet Office and the Prime Minister's private office provide a basis for controlling or reviewing those areas of policy in which he is personally most concerned. He may, therefore, exercise detailed influence on some policy issues without taking personal responsibility for a particular functional area.[16] The Premier's staff brief him and he has access to departmental information in considering an issue. The Central Policy Review Staff now assist him (and the Cabinet) in maintaining an overview of policy commitments.[17] It would seem reasonable to conclude that his power can be considerably greater than that of other ministers, or of the Cabinet as a whole.[18]

[13] Mackintosh, J. P., *op. cit.*

[14] The most famous example in recent years was the Suez intervention which was planned not by the full Cabinet but by a sub-committee of the Prime Minister and trusted colleagues.

[15] The relative power of Premier and Cabinet is still disputed, but there is wide acceptance of the view that the Prime Minister is now more than just *primus inter pares*. See Mackintosh, J. P., *op. cit.*, p. 610 and *passim* for a discussion of Prime Ministerial power.

[16] Wilson, of course, exercised considerable influence over economic policy during the 1964–70 Labour government and publicly undertook responsibility – with Shore – for economic affairs in the latter part of the period in office.

[17] *The Reorganization of Central Government*, Cmnd. 4506, 1970.

[18] Crossman, of course, argues that also being at the apex of the party and the civil service machinery puts the Prime Minister in a very powerful position indeed. See Crossman, R. H. S., introduction to Bagehot, W., *The English Constitution*, Collins, 1963, and Crossman, R. H. S., *Inside View*, Cape, 1972.

Mackintosh forcibly argues this case. He notes that much business that would have been conducted within Cabinet during the nineteenth century has gradually been relocated. The Prime Minister, in conjunction with one or more of his Ministers, is now much more of an independent decision-maker; or at least he has the opportunity to be. The Cabinet in this view exists to reconcile some important divergencies of opinion, but primarily it 'records and authorizes'.[19] Jones summarizes the argument in his critical review of this assessment of the Premier's role. 'It is often claimed that the Prime Minister has scant concern for his Cabinet whose approval of his decisions is mere formality, or which he can side-step completely. Through informal talks with individual ministers, who are more amenable alone than in Cabinet, he can infiltrate his views, influence and even reshape the Minister's proposals ... Policy will have been settled before the Cabinet stage.'[20]

The locus of policy-making has been receding before us – from Parliament to the government, to the Cabinet and now to the Premier. Given that the Prime Minister has a real concentration of power and influence at his command, within what constraints, if any, does he exercise it? The Mackintosh answer is that he is virtually impregnable and that if he is determined he has the power to enforce his view on the government. Both the restraints of Cabinet and back-bench revolt are minimized in this account. The argument is supported by some convincing examples.[21] A division of opinion in Cabinet can be resolved by compromise, or by the Prime Minister taking a strong line with the recalcitrant Ministers. The possibility of a mass resignation of senior Ministers is remote, though not impossible. But this does not mean that divergences of opinion are irrelevant, whether they occur in Cabinet or on the back benches. It is in making *anticipatory* responses to avoid or reduce conflict that Prime Ministerial or Cabinet power is modified. He may not have to, but a Prime Minister frequently will take the possibility of conflict into account in shaping policies. Jones goes further than this in arguing that the superordinate position of the Prime Minister has been exaggerated and that the traditional concept of Cabinet government has not been undermined in practice. In some respects he sees the Prime Minister's position as weak compared with that of a Cabinet minister who is acquainted with the detail and background of a policy proposal.[22] In his view the Prime Minister has to work within

[19] Mackintosh, J. P., *op. cit.*, p. 612.

[20] Jones, G. W., 'The Prime Minister's Power', *Parliamentary Affairs*, Spring 1965, pp. 170–1.

[21] Mackintosh, J. P., *op. cit.*, ch. 20 and pp. 617–22.

[22] A lack of familiarity with the detailed features of a policy is certainly one weakness that an 'overlord' Minister may encounter (see the discussion of Houghton's role in the NAB case-study, ch. 14).

limits set by his need for support from senior Ministers. Nevertheless, whatever the precise balance of power in a Cabinet, and it varies over time, a large amount of dissent can normally be tolerated by a Prime Minister who is firmly committed to a particular line of action.[23]

If the power accruing to the Prime Minister is accepted as being great, a question still remains. How far do Premiers use this power to determine policy decisions? The answer may be quite different in social policy as opposed to some other areas. It is useful to distinguish between the indirect and direct ways in which Prime Ministers can affect policy-making. Two examples will serve to illustrate the former. In the first place a particular philosophy of government, or set of priorities, may come to be identified with the Premier and this can have a general impact on policy. Certainly in the first years of the Heath administration the Prime Minister personified a distinctive style and ideology which must have had a pervasive influence even on decisions in which he was not personally involved. This is not to say that a Prime Minister can enforce a viewpoint on his colleagues for long periods if none of them feels sympathetic towards it. But as the focal point of the government he may often influence decisional premises indirectly by reinforcing general principles of government which command support in Cabinet. This kind of impact can be most easily recognized in the pre-election and immediate post-election phases of the governmental cycle when guiding philosophies are more clearly enunciated and the constraints on action are less apparent or are given less emphasis.

In the second place the Prime Minister has a key role in that he chooses his ministerial team. The choice of ministers can strongly influence policy-making within departments and the balance of advantage in the inter-departmental competition for resources. Ministers can to a certain extent choose themselves by the interests they develop, but the disposition of senior Ministers nevertheless rests with the Prime Minister. His decisions can reflect his personal priorities and prejudices as well as the need to relate seniority, standing in the party and acknowledged ability to the variations in the status of different ministerial posts. The social policy ministries are interesting in this respect. With the exception of the Home Office none of them has ranked consistently as one of the most prestigious ministerial appointments in the post-war period. Their position in the hierarchy of government posts has varied according to the priority

---

[23] Not only personality variables and party popularity, but also the actual issue involved will affect the distribution of power in the Cabinet. Successes or reversals with which a Prime Minister is associated – such as devaluation during the Wilson government – may fundamentally alter a Prime Minister's power.

given by governments to each area of social policy and the overall emphasis placed on social welfare issues in general. Even in the case of the Home Office the generally high status it has commanded has not derived from its social service functions and Home Secretaries have varied considerably in the interest they have shown in them.

Appointments to the social service ministries have tended to give Prime Ministers room for manoeuvre because, unlike the Treasury and Foreign Office, they do not automatically rate ministers of seniority. Seniority does not necessarily correlate precisely with ability of course, and a dedicated Minister working out of the limelight might be able to achieve more for his department than a senior Minister who becomes involved in government policies stretching beyond his department. Nevertheless, the possibilities are obvious enough. A second-line department to which the Prime Minister attaches little importance may suffer from being caught in a vicious circle. It may end up with a Minister who lacks the ability or political muscle to gain priority for his department's policies which consequently remain in the wings instead of gaining a place nearer the centre of the stage. This problem may have been more critical before the health, welfare and social security services were brought together in one department, but the underlying point remains: the Prime Minister partly determines the balance of power and initiative in his government when he makes ministerial appointments.

Turning to the direct impact of Prime Ministers, the main point is whether or not they become involved in specific social policy issues. In the case of the Open University Wilson's support for the idea was clearly important (see Chapter 10). He gave the policy special impetus by personally advocating it and also by giving a Minister the specific task of planning it. This latter action at least ensured that civil service resources were earmarked and that the government's commitment to the idea was publicly displayed. Similarly, the NAB case study illustrates the importance of Wilson's emphasis on poverty during the 1969 election. If for no other reason than that they attract considerable attention from the Opposition, the priorities that are personally endorsed by a Prime Minister (or future Prime Minister) can affect policy-making on those issues even long after his concern has shifted to other problems.

Nevertheless, despite these examples, Wilson's involvement in social policy issues was relatively small compared with that in economic and foreign affairs. Although he became personally involved in establishing the deflationary cuts in public expenditure during 1966, including those in the social services, this was fundamentally a matter of crisis planning rather than a detailed incursion into social policy. On balance it seems reasonable to suggest that social policy has not been a Prime Ministerial concern in recent administrations in the sense that it has not been subject to detailed intervention and long-term oversight by Prime Ministers.[24] They may have a direct impact on social policy, but the main arguments about their power are most relevant to policies on other problems: economic, foreign and industrial relations issues have figured prominently as areas in which Premiers have become involved. However, decisions in these areas of policy can, in turn, exert a powerful indirect influence on social policy. They absorb resources and politicians' energies and, as we have suggested earlier, the need to regulate issues means that giving priority to one problem can lead gatekeepers to exclude others.

We have argued that the Prime Minister's power is manifest in policy-making both directly and indirectly. Yet at the same time it has been suggested that his role is less important in social policy, despite the amount of public expenditure involved, than in some other policy areas. This apparent paradox is heightened by the last point we made: that the fate of a social policy issue partly depends upon that of other policy issues in which the Prime Minister *is* likely to be a key decision-maker (such as the correction of a balance of payments deficit). But the argument can be restated in a more tenable form. Although his *influence* may be equally great in each, the Prime Minister's *role* seems to vary from one area of policy to another. Premiers seem to be much less involved in the detail of social policy than in economic policy because the crises that develop in these respective fields are usually of a different order. Social policy issues are rarely seen to be of the same political weight or moment as those in economic or foreign affairs. Nevertheless, the Prime Minister's impact on social policy can be considerable because he, along with other factors such as the overall priorities stated or implied in party programmes and ideologies, influences the strategic decisions which determine the limits within which social policy operates. For example, in addition to the detailed priority decisions that might be discussed during public expenditure cuts, the Prime Minister is involved in strategic decisions via the continual process of public expenditure review and control. Prime Ministers seem most typically to have influenced social policy in these more indirect ways in recent years.

If we want to see where most decisions about national social policies are made we must move away from the formal pinnacle of government. We have examined a possible hierarchical model of the authorities in which the Prime Minister could be said to be at the apex. But having focused on this thesis of 'Prime Ministerial government' we must follow the logic of our argument about the Prime

[24] For an indirect confirmation of this assertion see Mackintosh, J. P., *op. cit.*, p. 625n. See also Wilson, H., *The Labour Government, 1964–70*, Wiedenfeld & Nicolson, 1971.

Minister's role in social policy and back away again. This process of retreat from a simple hierarchical model will eventually lead us to a further discussion of Parliament; but let us first look at the role of central government departments in social policy-making.

CHAPTER FIVE

Government Departments and the Development of Policy

I PLANNING AND INFLUENCE

The upper reaches of the main government departments contain many of the most influential policy-makers in British political life. Even if policies have their source outside these departments it is here that all major government policy takes shape. Interests may be consulted, negotiations conducted with the Treasury, and support may have to be gained in Cabinet committee or in the Cabinet itself, but it is in the departments that a policy acquires its ultimate form or the seal of its rejection. Government departments possess essentially similar teams of top decision-makers consisting of a few politicians and a large number of career civil servants, often augmented nowadays by a handful of temporary civil servants chosen by ministers to act as policy advisers.[1] The more political and far-reaching decisions that have to be made within departments will be taken at this level. To ask what determines whether an issue is seen as being a political or far-reaching one is to ask the central question running throughout these chapters: where and how do policy issues originate and how are they regulated?

Regulating the flow of demands is clearly an important feature of the work of government departments. Countless policy questions arise in the course of administering the social services and these are filtered through the hierarchical structure of the civil service. We will therefore discuss the different ways in which such policy questions

[1] Willson, F. M. G., 'Policy-Making and the Policy Makers', in Rose, R., *op. cit.* This is a useful and short description of policy-making in British government. It contains an outline of the 'policy-making group' (see pp. 355–61).

may reach the top of a government department. But even in a social service where contact with a clientele is a source of many pressures for change, policy-making is not a purely reactive process. Not only does the team of decision-makers at the head of a department have to deal with problems which come up to it because they cannot be adequately resolved at lower levels, but this same group of people is also the source of many policy initiatives. It is therefore both the final destination for issues filtering up for decision and the starting point for proposals and changes in policy which will filter down the departmental hierarchy. Obviously decisions are being made at all levels within the demand regulation process. The upper reaches of a government department are not all-powerful, precisely because a hierarchical system of gatekeepers filters the traffic whichever way it is flowing – up or down. Nevertheless, the top decision-makers are particularly significant and we will, therefore, pay them special attention.

The basic question of how demands are initiated and regulated will be refined into two further queries when examining the way in which policy develops at the top of a department. The first relates directly to the nature of the policy process. Is it predominantly a matter of *ad hoc* responses to current cases and pressures or, at the other extreme, does it take the form of a comprehensive reappraisal of existing and potential problems with a built-in orientation to long-term planning? The second query concerns the relative influence exercised by different members of the policy team; in particular the politicians on the one hand and the civil servants on the other. What considerations should we bear in mind when examining these questions?

Willson suggests that the nature of the workload carried by members of the policy team does not permit long-term planning. He argues that a Minister can 'only find an opportunity to discipline himself to long-term thinking when he is in opposition' and that the ideas he has when appointed 'will have to last his tenure'.[2] He makes several other pertinent points: 'it has been a popular theory that ministers have no time to think ... while civil servants have permanent tenure, familiarity with the administrative machinery, all the facilities for fact-finding and research and must, therefore, be in a favourable position for long-term reflection and the production of long-term policies ... Of course, the civil servant has all the facilities mentioned, but in truth the atmosphere could scarcely be described as being conducive to reflection. The higher one goes the less conducive it becomes, and it may be that the lower down the policy-making scale the better are the ideas being evolved.'[3]

[2] Willson, F. M. G., in Rose, R. *op. cit.*, p. 357.
[3] *Ibid.*, pp. 366–7

This offers a picture of little long-term planning: a bottleneck of day-to-day decisions at the top of departments with ministers and senior civil servants labouring under an equal pressure of immediate demands. Such a situation would obviously make it difficult to develop long-term planning within government departments and would tend to enhance the importance of the political parties in devising the outlines of much government policy. However, Willson rightly argues that there is also an important 'intermediate area of policy-making' between the more obvious interests and government.[4] This intermediate area includes the policy oriented bodies which are aligned to the political parties (such as the Bow Group or the Fabian Society) as well as research institutions (such as the Centre for Environmental Studies or the Centre for Studies in Social Policy) and smaller research groups. Both the political parties and the more powerful pressure groups are targets for some of the results of the research and policy analysis conducted by such groups. There is no firm boundary between research, pressure group activities and party politics. Altogether this 'intermediate area' of medium and long-term planning probably accounts for many of the initiatives and much of the pressure for change in social policy.[5]

This does not mean that governments do not indulge in long-term planning. Apart from what might take place in central departments (and civil servants are well placed to perceive some of the long-term needs of the social services even if they have limited opportunity to plan systematically), there are bodies which government can use for this purpose. Royal Commissions and other committees of inquiry, for example, may be established to develop policy options in specific areas. Other bodies such as advisory committees can also operate in this way if allowed to do so by the Minister concerned.[6] Although they can be used by Ministers to neutralize or delay issues, such devices as Commissions and advisory bodies are important as a means of dealing with controversial topics or of searching for agreement on the nature of a problem. They can also be used to reveiw the range of solutions available to meet a defined need and the likely consequences of adopting one solution rather than another. To varying degrees such bodies can provide the basis for, or themselves become involved in, long-term planning. But Willson's contention is that little long-term planning can be developed *inside* government

[4] *Ibid.*, p. 365.

[5] See the case studies on Health Centres, Detention Centres, Family Allowances, the Open University and National Assistance.

[6] Wheare, K. C., *Government by Committee*, Oxford University Press, 1955. For a discussion of the role of particular Commissions and of the Central Advisory Council for Education see Chapman, R. A., *The Role of Commissions in Policy-Making*, Allen & Unwin, 1973.

departments. His view leaves little room for this kind of activity or for forward-thinking civil servants to dominate Ministers.

Another view of government policy-making casts civil servants in a more dominant role. They are said to be in a position to restrict a Minister's ability to initiate policy and to communicate only that information which they wish him to have.[7] One could characterize the civil servant's role, therefore, as a formative and limiting force on Ministers' policy decisions. In so far as Ministers come into office with a programme of personal and party objectives, this may be an appropriate image. Civil servants are the major channel of communication between interest groups and government; they are not only aware of administrative constraints within the government machine but also the constraints imposed by these external groups. They give expression to the limits within which policy-making operates.

Alternatively, it may be argued that long-term planning should be and to a certain extent is the heart of the ministerial role, with the parties doing much of the preparatory thinking. This viewpoint casts the Minister as a source of inspiration and guidance about basic policy objectives. It thereby unites the question of long-term planning with that of the role of Ministers in relation to their departments. Let us look at these topics more fully by considering the origins of the social policy issues and demands that tax government departments and the ways in which they are handled.

II CENTRAL GOVERNMENT DEPARTMENTS AND SOCIAL POLICY ISSUES

Issues confronting the social service Ministers may be roughly assigned to three categories: those which arise *in the course of administering existing policies or are brought to the attention of departments by outside bodies*; those which arise from *departmental initiatives or policy reappraisals*; and those which are *raised by Ministers*. They are not mutually exclusive, but in so far as it is possible they will be examined in turn.

Issues arising from administrative and external pressures
The relationship between administration and policy-making varies according to the administrative structures and philosophies prevailing

---

[7] The most recent expression of this argument, in a modified form, is to be found in Crossman's *Inside View, op. cit.*

in a particular social service.[8] Even so a number of general points are worth noting. For example, despite the fact that some social services are actually provided by local authorities the central departments possess a formidable stock of data and experience on the operation of past and present policies. Incoming information gives forewarning of areas of practice which are, or soon will be, unsatisfactory. Even having indirect responsibility for a service ensures that a department will be the focus of pressure for reform from service personnel and their professional associations, from the users and groups representing their interests, as well as from politicians. One of the major tasks of central social service departments is to reconcile these continuous demands for changes in the services with each other and with the constraints upon expenditure. General pressure for reform will also be reinforced from time to time by incidents which highlight weaknesses or deficiences in the services.

Individual cases of grievance, hardship or apparent maladministra-. tion, for example, each elicit a civil service response. This may simply mean a defensive or explanatory letter drafted by a civil servant for a Minister to sign. In departments handling hundreds of such cases at a time the investigation of the case and even the letter may be the responsibility of a civil servant well down the hierarchy and it will have no importance for policy. However, the explanation of particularly difficult or potentially damaging cases may be read and possibly commented on at each level up to the Minister. Such cases may certainly result in discussion of the questions they raise and the advisability of modifying policy. A number of similar cases, or a request by a senior civil servant or Minister for a wider review of the problem brought to light, could begin a process of re-examination resulting in proposals for a change.

Deputations to Ministers from pressure groups or MPs also oblige a department to respond in some way. Again the initial consideration may be to defend the department, but in examining the problem the department focuses attention on issues which may not have been considered before, at least not by Ministers or by the most senior civil servants. The kind of crises produced by scandals or disasters epitomize the way in which some external pressures short-circuit the departmental hierarchy and produce results at ministerial level. For the most part, however, the initial response to an adverse criticism or comment on a department's work, or a suggestion that it does

[8] See the discussion of the different departmental approaches and philosophies in Griffith, J. A. G., *Central Departments and Local Authorities*, Allen & Unwin, 1966. The impact of different administrative structures on policy-making can be seen by comparing two social service case studies: Hindell, K., 'The Genesis of the Race Relations Bill' and Eckstein, H., 'Planning: The National Health Service', both reprinted in Rose, R., *Policy-Making in Britain*, Macmillan, 1969.

not meet needs within its areas of competence, occurs lower down the hierarchy than this. Departments collect press, television and parliamentary comments and treat them seriously in the sense that reports are prepared on important criticisms. Research bearing on a department's work is treated similarly. Whether a Minister sees reports of this kind depends on the urgency of the issue and upon his interest, but new ideas, information and criticisms can result in at least a brief examination of the adequacy of existing policy.

Not all external pressures on central government departments originate outside the government system. Some of the most influential are generated through the interaction of different levels and units of government. Countless problems of co-ordination arise and are settled at the local or field level, but some have policy repercussions. This may happen in one of several ways. The most obvious process occurs in central departments which directly provide a service themselves (for example, social security or the prison service). As there is a continuous hierarchy in these cases local issues can be pushed or pulled to higher levels if the relevant civil servant feels that it is necessary. Many problems are resolved one or two steps up the hierarchy from the point at which they first emerge and they may result in deliberate or *de facto* changes in local or regional policies. Only a small number of issues rise to the upper reaches of the hierarchy to, say, assistant secretary or even permanent secretary level, and result in national policy changes. Major breaches in prison security are instances of 'serious' problems which are examined at central as well as at local level.

The situation is rather different where local authorities provide the services. On occasion they may induce or force a department to clarify, re-examine or modify general policies. Individual local authorities may also influence central policy by accepting an innovative risk and demonstrating the merits or defects of a particular approach to a problem. Similarly, standards of good practice in current areas of administration are often developed locally and later generalized at the national level. Whether problems and developments at the field level influence the central policy-makers depends to a considerable extent on whether the government department in question has 'eyes and ears'. Some problems will nearly always move up the hierarchy quite quickly: for example, the death of a foster child or a fire in a residential home which results in fatalities. The important point is whether other less tragic problems are considered at the top of departments. Regional advisory staff and the inspectorates are the vital link between operational reality and central policy in the social services, but the strength of the link varies. The Home Office, for example, was generally considered to have good contact with the field when it was responsible for the child care services. By w contrast the old Ministry of Health was towards the other end of the continuum in its relations with the operational units of the health service, especially the local authorities. Its contact with the local authorities' welfare functions (under the National Assistance Act, 1948) was further along the continuum still.[9]

Some issues reach the top of departments by other routes. They may be promoted outside the official hierarchy by local authority and professional associations, or by more informal groupings of staff. In other instances collaboration or conflict between central government departments give rise to policy issues. Disputes about areas of responsibility can be fierce and protracted if they involve unwanted items on a department's budget or, alternatively, prestigious undertakings. A key feature of such inter-departmental issues is that a department cannot easily control how seriously the issues should be taken. A problem can rise rapidly to the top of the departmental hierarchy if the other department involved chooses to handle it at, say, under secretary or even ministerial level. The majority of inter-departmental issues are resolved, or neglected, at lower levels than this, but some of them do 'go to the top' and become important policy matters.

These demands, generated outside departments or at the operational levels within departments, are subject to a fairly strict filtering process. They are largely absorbed within the civil service hierarchy and *relatively* few reach ministerial level. Ideally the hierarchical filtering process exists to select the issues which should be conveyed to Ministers, as well as to prevent problems rising above the level at which they can be resolved effectively. The system may obviously go wrong in several ways. It may screen out too few of the minor problems of administration and, as a result, leave top policy-makers without time to plan ahead, as Willson implies. Equally it can insulate a Minister from politically sensitive or long-term policy issues which should be on his agenda. It can also exhibit both defects simultaneously. No matter how effective it is, however, in a large department with operational responsibilities (and considerable contact with a wide cross section of the public) Ministers and senior civil servants will usually be bombarded heavily with demands for decisions. This tendency is reinforced by parliamentary scrutiny of departments' work. Of course the way in which issues are dealt with must depend to a certain extent on the individuals involved. A Minister, for instance, can indicate what he wants to be in touch with by pulling some types of problems up the hierarchy for his own consideration

[9] For evidence on the departmental differences see Griffith, J. A. G., *Central Departments and Local Authorities, op. cit.*; for some of the consequences for local services see, for example, Davies, B., *Social Needs and Resources in Local Services*, Joseph, 1968.

while showing little interest in others. But before we elaborate on this aspect of a Minister's role let us look at the second category of issues that we outlined earlier.

Issues arising from departmental reappraisals of policy

Policy initiatives are developed in departments in two somewhat different ways. The first is through the traditional policy advisory role that links senior civil servants to Ministers. Civil servants systematically feed Ministers with issues arising from the administration of existing policies and try to anticipate politically sensitive problems that might arise in the near future. They also advise Ministers on possible solutions to such problems. Working groups are established to study issues that have been identified as potentially important. These may produce substantial reports without any policy change occurring and without Ministers even knowing that the problem has been studied. But if such an issue does come to life, if interesting proposals emerge that make it worth considering further, or if the opportunity of changing policy presents itself, there will be background work on which to draw.

Some ideas developed in this way may be stored within departments for long periods of time and become relevant at a later date. For example, the Family Income Supplement, introduced by the Conservative Government in 1971, was not a totally novel concept. During the period 1966–8 the Wilson Cabinet had considered the possibility of increasing family allowances or, alternatively, of introducing a means-tested system of family benefits. They chose the first course of action. Consequently, when the Conservatives came to power the civil servants were aware of the merits and shortcomings of a range of options in this field, amongst which was the means-tested alternative to family allowances.

Activities such as these – from raising issues or initiating policy study group, to giving shape to policy proposals which Ministers have launched only in outline – are well established within the civil service. The development of systematic policy analysis is a second and more recently developed source of policy initiatives. The growing emphasis upon reappraising policies and upon the improvement of social planning tend to highlight the complex inter-relationships between the social services. In the process alternative ways of doing things may be examined which challenge the appropriateness or effectiveness of existing policies. These developments are not entirely new, but their more systematic use is likely to have an increasingly important impact on policy-making. We will return to this matter later in the chapter.

The point that must be emphasized, however, is that while departments filter demands impinging upon them, they also generate issues in a number of different ways and then submit these new demands to a similar filtering process. Even demands which originate a few steps down the departmental hierarchy still have to survive a formidable regulative process. A proposal may be subject to diverse and possibly contradictory criticisms in the course of its passage. It may have to pass through the hands of superiors who are unsympathetic to its tenets, who do not see the importance of the issue to which it relates, or who are simply too preoccupied with other problems to consider it seriously. It may, equally, be given due attention but still fail to win support because it seems impracticable, politically unattractive, ill-timed or simply less useful than another proposal. The principal to deputy secretary grades of the civil service are the source and graveyard of many ideas, initiatives and issues.

This hierarchical system of gatekeepers must quite often exclude important issues and ideas as well as impractical or less important ones. Even if there were complete agreement on the criteria for deciding which was which, and even if short-term problems did not overload the system, mistakes would still be made in the selection of issues to be pushed upwards. In practice, of course, these conditions cannot be met and consequently key individuals in the civil service are important, and inevitably at times idiosyncratic, gatekeepers for ideas moving both upwards and downwards. The role of the civil service hierarchy as a communication channel is perhaps best illustrated by looking at the grade of assistant secretary. These civil servants are communicators of issues to the highest reaches of a department, but they are also the people who develop, implement and co-ordinate most of the initiatives sanctioned or promoted by these policy-makers. Any partisan (whether outside government or at a lower level in the hierarchy) who wants to influence major policies or any Minister, permanent secretary or deputy secretary wishing to develop a particular idea, needs to choose his assistant secretary with care. In practice, of course, not many advocates of policy change are in a position to do so.

One can exaggerate the importance of the assistant secretary grade. Similar comments also apply to other senior levels in the civil service. Nevertheless, the assistant secretaries are especially important and they clearly illustrate a point that has not been mentioned before. The same hierarchy that provides the basis for regulating issues and initiating policies is also a career structure. It represents rewards, satisfaction, opportunity, disappointment and unhappiness for different individuals. The ranks of the assistant secretaries are filled by the rapidly promoted and highly motivated young super-talent as well as by the disillusioned man who was promoted rather slowly and others of varying ages and dispositions who will gain no further advancement. The grade is not unique in any of these respects, but it is, we believe, a key link in the policy chain and the importance of individual variables is more easily seen at this level. As Self rightly observes, these psychological variables are something of an embarrassment to students of government[10] and we have little evidence about their impact on social policy.[11] Nevertheless, whilst we have purposely emphasized structural factors in these chapters, personality variables remain important and should not be discounted.

Issues raised by Ministers

One of a Minister's roles is to identify fairly specific objectives, problems and solutions which he feels should be incorporated or more strongly emphasized in departmental policy. But however closely a Minister defines his proposals, the idea that he has planted will first generate study and reappraisal within the department. Its administrative and economic implications will be examined, as will its congruence with, and repercussions on, existing departmental and governmental policy. Ministers are dependent on their departments to take up and develop their proposals. Many administrative or departmental considerations which a Minister may not be aware of, or not want to allow for, will be raised at this preparatory stage. Although a Minister is well placed to push a few issues very firmly, his ideas are also subject to a filtering process. They too may disappear for months or years in departmental and inter-departmental working groups or be gently relegated to a low place in the queue. The constraints discovered during this period of examination may mean a major modification of the proposal. When the cost of overcoming the limiting factors can be shown to be high or impossible to surmount in the short run the proposal may be dropped altogether.

A Minister's unique advantage in proposing change is, therefore, bounded by the now familiar process of issue regulation. This does not mean that Ministers do not initiate. Some produce a steady flow of suggestions, a proportion of which emerge as policy changes and all of which channel departmental resources into an examination of the problem highlighted. Less active Ministers may have a very limited impact; but the Minister does not influence his department solely through specific proposals. Even when he does not formulate clear ideas he can be a source of policy-thinking. The phrase 'knowing the Minister's mind' summarizes one response of alert civil

[10] Self, P., 'The State Versus Man', in Robson, W. (ed.), *Man and the Social Sciences*, Allen & Unwin, 1972, pp. 66–7.
[11] For some illuminating details, apart from those in contemporary political biography, see Boyle, E. Crossland, C. A. B. and Kogan, M. (ed.), *The Politics of Education*, Penguin, 1971; and Barnett, M. J., *The Politics of Legislation*, Weidenfeld & Nicolson, 1969.

servants. They translate general expressions of concern into specific policy reviews and attempt to anticipate some issues before they surface as problems. In this sense a Minister's indirect impact on a department can be quite substantial.

Ministers also bring particular themes into prominence and correspondingly lower the priority of others. Most Ministers become closely identified with one or more broad policy issues: for example, Sir Keith Joseph's concern with 'the cycle of deprivation'.[12] The concept of a 'cycle of deprivation' has come to the fore because it is a way of ordering some of the information accruing within the Department of Health and Social Security. But while the concept is partly a response to current problems it also influences the way these are perceived. Because of the Minister's interest, all kinds of issues may be fitted into this framework and it will encourage civil servants to notice problems which they may otherwise have ignored, and *vice versa*. Short-term priorities and long-term thinking are therefore affected; not least because research directed towards a new theme may maintain its momentum for several years. At the very least, a theme like the 'cycle of deprivation' will affect the regulation of demands and thus have an indirect impact on policy.

Ministers do not act on an entirely individual basis; they are members of a political party. Is this reflected in the way they approach policy-making? In the early phase of a party's period in office a Minister may have a substantial body of party pledges to honour. He may, therefore, represent a force for change in directions unrelated to the ongoing work of a department. He may be a potentially radical force within his ministry. This is also possible, though to a lesser degree, in the first few months of any new Minister's term of office. On the other hand not all governments come to power with a set of radical policies to implement; and even when they do a Minister's scope for pursuing a policy initiative is fraught with uncertainties. Whether he can effect desired changes in policy depends upon so many variables. The most important of these concern the quality of the party's planning; the nature of the constraints thrown up by departmental analysis; the speed with which he can establish a good working relationship with his department; the extent to which current crises dominate his work; and the impact of the party's pledges on departmental and Cabinet policy-making.

Allowing for hyperbole, Crossman's 'battering ram of change' – a Minister backed by election pledges which have to be fulfilled – summarizes one aspect of a Minister's relations with his department. The constraints within which he has to try to seek change

[12] Sir Keith Joseph was appointed Secretary of State for Health and Social Security when the Heath Administration came to power in 1970.

represent another. These constraints are clearly seen in the history of the Wilson government (1964–70). Current crises, predominantly economic, became a major preoccupation and as a result some of the social policies devised in opposition by the Labour Party lingered for too long in the civil service machine before coming to fruition or were lost altogether. Was this because individual Ministers or the whole government were diverted from longer term strategy by short-term crises? Was it because the proposals themselves were inadequate to do the job expected of them and were found wanting once examined by civil servants? Or was it because Ministers' ideas and policies were effectively neutralized by a powerful and unsympathetic civil service? These questions echo the queries which we raised at the beginning of this chapter.

Since then we have looked at several major sources of the issues which impinge on social service ministries and have considered the ways in which they are regulated and filtered. We can now examine further the two questions with which we began: namely, what is the influence of the civil service on policy; and is there any long-term policy-planning to offset the short-term horizons imposed on departments by so many of the demands made upon them? We will consider these questions in turn.

III THE CIVIL SERVANTS

Are Ministers dominated by the machine they apparently control? We have said that ideas arise, are developed and are stored within ministries. It seems quite possible, therefore, that civil servants heavily influence their Ministers. For instance, Richard Crossman sees ministerial power as a brief honeymoon, the price the civil service has to pay for its dominance. 'The civil servants take a long view. They know that the boat-loads of politicians now anchored above them are certain to be changed within five years. They also know that any ideological crusade to carry out the mandate will be blunted by failure, electoral unpopularity and sheer exhaustion. So they are prepared to concede quite a lot under the first impact of an election victory. But when this is over, they resume their quiet defence of entrenched departmental positions and policies against political change.'[13]

Similarly, evidence submitted by the Labour Party to the Fulton Committee on the Civil Service certainly suggested that information is sometimes systematically withheld from Ministers in a way that

[13] Crossman, R. H. S., *op. cit.*, p. 22.

influences their decisions and the communications which pass between them and the MPs.[14] Harold Wilson categorically dissociated himself from these charges; but in one sense they must be true. As we have seen, civil servants are gatekeepers along channels of communication. They *do* systematically withhold information from Ministers. It is their job to do so. Equally, they select the information forwarded to a Minister in a way which they believe will be conducive to rapid decisions. The point of the Labour Party evidence, of course, was that it alleged bias; a filtering of data that was, and was intended to be, detrimental to particular policy proposals or even to Labour governments in general. The dividing line is a difficult one to draw and the charge is not amenable to proof or disproof in general terms. Nevertheless, one can explore the question further. Harold Wilson argued that much depends upon the calibre of Ministers, and this is obviously true; but there are structural features affecting the relationship between Ministers and civil servants that also warrant consideration.

The assertion that radical governments meet civil service 'opposition' is one that appeals to common sense. Any government with a large programme of reforms will inevitably face problems in trying to implement them. Civil servants are aware of the many constraints that will arise and it is they who communicate most of them to Ministers. In the process they may also highlight problems which reflect their preference for the *status quo* or for incremental change, rather than elucidating the 'real' constraints. Like everyone else, civil servants have an interest in restricting changes which impose strain and tension on them and their organization. The appeal of incremental as opposed to radical change is that its effects can be more easily gauged from experience. Major changes, however, can mean promotion or greater work satisfaction as well as disruption. The problem for Ministers is that they are not in a good position to assess the motives or rationing criteria at work in the ranks of the civil service below them. All they know is that on occasions their field of action is surprisingly circumscribed and that it is the civil service which indicates these limits to them. For this reason alone Labour Ministers would have a different experience of the civil service from that of their Conservative counterparts. The fact of being dedicated to reform may well account for some Labour Party feeling that the civil service resists its measures.

An established bureaucracy is a conservative force in many respects, but whether civil servants act in a consistently biased way in policy-making is only partly an empirical question. It also depends upon the

[14] *The Civil Service; Report of the Committee*, Cmnd. 3638, 1968. For a discussion of this evidence, see Fry, G. K., *Statesmen in Disguise*, Macmillan, 1969, pp. 273–6.

ideological standpoint of the observer. What must be noted, however, is that incoming governments do not meet a body of civil servants who are utterly dedicated to continuing existing policies and totally unreceptive to the programmes of the new government. In the period before an election at least, departmental civil servants are sensitive to the policies of the Opposition as well as those of the government. The Labour government which gained power in 1964 had obtained some pre-election advice on policies from the civil service and civil servants had begun to prepare themselves for what a Labour victory would entail in terms of planning and reorganization. This is a normal feature of British government. Against this must be set the homogeneity, in terms of socio–economic background, of the small community of senior civil servants.[15] They are isolated from many of the circumstances, attitudes and life experiences of the people affected by a government's policies, although the same must be said of many Ministers and indeed of any elite with a long apprenticeship for leadership.

There are several other potential sources of friction between civil servants and Ministers which might give rise to dissatisfaction among politicians from the front and back benches. One is the amount of compromise and dilution that is generated by inter-departmental negotiations about a policy issue. The effect of proposals passing up and down the hierarchy is to introduce many modifications designed to meet particular interests or administrative constraints. When several departments become involved, which is frequent, the tension created by having to accommodate different interests is heightened. The consultations and the attempts to reach agreement, which are a central feature of the way in which the civil service works, can always result in a clear-cut proposal being emasculated. To this must be added the long-term burdens on a department which a change of policy may create. No civil servant will lightly accept a policy which threatens to become an administrative nightmare, or an unpredictably voracious consumer of public funds. Permanent secretaries and their immediate colleagues remain responsible for administering a policy after the Minister in question has moved on and often well after the government itself has been replaced. Their long-term interest in the working of the department may clash with the Minister's more immediate concern for politically rewarding results. Ministers are responsible to Parliament and their parties, but permanent secretaries are responsible to both the Treasury and Parliament for their departmental accounting over a much longer time span.

The quality of party planning can also give rise to much friction when a proposal which has been devised in opposition is introduced

[15] For a useful review of the evidence see Hill, M. J., *The Sociology of Public Administration*, Weidenfeld & Nicolson, 1972, ch. 9.

as a policy proposal. One of the merits of the party system is that it provides an alternative environment in which planning can take place. The privilege of ignoring some of the constraints accepted by civil servants is one of the strengths possessed by the political parties. A corollary is that there are also real limits to how realistic the opposition party's planning can be, even if they wish to acknowledge these constraints. It is quite clear that party planning could and often should be far more rigorous about the detailed problems raised by some kinds of proposals, although this means making more resources available to the parties. It is equally clear that some of the constraints accepted by the civil service are rejected as illegitimate or tedious impediments by party supporters. Once in power a government may be able to alter some of these, such as the rate of growth of gross national product and of public expenditure, but it is also certain that they will have to live with others that they had ignored or were not aware of during their planning in Opposition. Consequently there will always be policy issues, arising even from cautious and non-ideological party planning where, looked at from each other's viewpoint, the parties are seen as 'unrealistic' and the civil servants as 'obstructionist'.

There are thus both inherent differences of role between the parties and the civil service and a real element of civil service power underlying the complaints voiced by the Labour Party to the Fulton Committee. It is impossible to distinguish the two completely. Senior civil servants in particular do exercise a considerable influence upon the formulation and progress of issues and this influence should not be underestimated. Similarly Ministers vary in their ability to identify and appreciate key issues as well as in their willingness to initiate reappraisals of policy. The extent to which a department carries its Minister along, or is kept in action by him, does depend to a considerable extent upon who the Minister is and who the senior civil servants are. Yet, as we have tried to indicate, Ministers are not powerless. They champion some issues above others; they identify themselves with certain themes or slogans; they have enthusiasms and blind spots which affect the way their civil servants operate; they are more or less determined to make their mark in certain fields and they may project different styles of leadership or government. All these factors serve to qualify the conclusion that the real power resides with the permanent civil service. This remains a part truth which varies with the issue, the time and the personalities involved. But the fact that there are considerable structural features in the work of any department which endow civil servants with the opportunity to influence policy events is undeniable. Let us now consider how far these events are also influenced by 'rational' processes of policy analysis and planning.

IV POLICY ANALYSIS

Is policy-making a frenetic round of activities dominated by a continuous flow of demands needing to be dealt with quickly, and by the parallel need to take account of many competing interests? Alternatively, is the top of each department a haven of tranquillity protected by a fine filtering process, where an altogether more detached and impartial view of policy proposals can be taken? Do government departments set their own priorities and devise plans for the development of narrowly defined services, leaving the co-ordination of the policies which emerge to the Cabinet system? Or does the Cabinet system and the allocation of functions to departments encourage people to think across administrative boundaries at all levels of policy-making? Are policies informed by the careful examination of problems and a full review of all possible solutions? Or, in sharp contrast, are they fashioned on a confused battleground of ideas, values, individual preferences and expediency? The questions underlying these very different conceptions of policy-making are whether and to what effect a relatively thorough analysis of policy options occurs and how far policies are based on forward planning or lateral planning across administrative boundaries.

We have argued that government departments do not merely react to outside pressures. They plan their interventions with regard to numerous factors and, to a certain extent, move ahead of interest group and other pressures on some issues whilst responding slowly, if at all, on others. They certainly commit resources to many reviews of current problems or deficiencies as well as to issues on which there may be an opportunity to act in the future. Although not public, departmental working parties produce reports which often rival the output of Royal Commissions or other public enquiries in detail and careful examination. Existing data and original research as well as the work of 'lay' advisers can all be incorporated into such an analysis of a problem or the review of policy options. This process of studying issues is not wholly dominated by the immediate crises of administration.

To take one example, family poverty became a politically sensitive subject during the life of the Wilson government. That it did so owed much in the first instance to academic research and pressure group activity. No one would claim that the departmental study of the problem under Richard Crossman[16] was perfect. Nevertheless, civil service working groups did examine a range of issues, including

---

[16] He was both Secretary of State at the DHSS and chairman of the cabinet committee on social policy.

the plethora of different means tests and the possibility of co-ordinating the housing, welfare and social security benefits available to low income families. This work necessarily cut across administrative boundaries. Government departments may be criticized on many grounds, but the willingness to investigate and plan is by no means absent. They are often attacked because their priorities are not those of their critics or because they only respond to problems after sustained pressure has been mounted by outside groups and because their investigatory responses may delay action considerably. Their ability to initiate a major study of issues and solutions is not in doubt however and the research resources in the social service ministries have multiplied rapidly over the past decade. The key questions, therefore, are what kind of planning results from this variety of departmental policy analysis and what is its effect upon policy?

Because of the rapid growth of research and planning staffs in government departments it is tempting to conclude that comprehensive long-term planning is now the reality which it certainly was not before. The institution of Programme Analysis and Review (PAR), for example, ensures that some areas of a department's work are subject to reappraisal each year.[17] The attempt to develop programme budgeting also means that the policy cake is being sliced and exposed for examination in new ways. The aim of a programme budget is to collate all the available data on a specific area of policy (or policy objective) such as the care of the elderly. Because it cuts across the traditional financial boundaries between, say, hospitals and local authority residential and domiciliary care, it also cuts across administrative boundaries. This process throws the relationship between different items of service for the same need group into bolder relief. The problems that come to the fore inevitably raise questions about long- as well as short-term strategy. The impact of this kind of activity on current policy may be slight because of the filtering processes within a department and because many issues requiring immediate action occupy the time of the top decision-makers. Nevertheless, this move towards examining policy problems in ways which lengthen the time scale of analysis and cut across administrative boundaries is reinforced by changes that have been taking place outside the individual service departments. Let us look at examples of these changes.

The control of public expenditure
For over a decade now the time scale of public expenditure control has been a minimum of five years. The simple annual budget as the

[17] For an explanation of PAR and other developments discussed in this section see Keeling, D., *Management in Government*, Allen & Unwin, 1972 and Clarke, Sir Richard, *New Trends in Government*, HMSO, 1971.

sole basis of accounting is very much a thing of the past. The Plowden Report of 1961 gave rise to a system of projecting public expenditure forward over a five-year period and relating it to forecasted changes in national income and tax revenues.[18] The PESC system (the Public Expenditure Survey Committee from which the process derives its initials is the inter-departmental body which produces the collated data or survey on future expenditure) has begun to outline the strategic expenditure choices open to Ministers. As such it makes it more likely, though by no means certain, that medium term policy decisions are based on some analysis of their implications across as well as within departmental boundaries.

Not the least of the PESC system's merits is that parliamentary scrutiny of public expenditure is now also geared, especially through the House of Commons Expenditure Committee, to a longer term view of the structure and even the outcomes of public expenditure.[19] The combined effect of these changes on the way Parliament and the Treasury approach the task of controlling expenditure has certainly encouraged government departments to analyse their present and future policies somewhat differently. The concern with trends, relationships and comparative costs in and between different areas of policy has steadily increased. To this one must add the fact that the five-year cycle of PESC is by no means the longest time span over which departments now try to plan or forecast.

For example, manpower considerations cannot be dealt with on such a short time scale. Estimates of changes in the demand and supply of skilled or professional manpower has to be attempted, if at all, on a time scale that is determined by the length of training involved and the speed with which training facilities can be adjusted. Capital expenditure, especially the major public works programmes, similarly involve long periods of gestation and enforce a degree of forward thinking. The DHSS has recently introduced a system of ten-year forward planning through which it is hoped to co-ordinate policies in the health and local authority services. Once the system is fully operative and the data improve, the department will have a basis from which to plan in some detail for up to ten years ahead and on some issues over much longer time periods. None of this means that policy-makers will cease to be plagued by the needs and crises of the moment. It does mean that such decisions will not be the prime determinants of all policies. The forecasting of the resource implica-

---

[18] *The Control of Public Expenditure*, Cmnd. 1432, 1961. For a short explanation of the development and operation of the PESC system see Brittan, S., *Steering the Economy*, Secker & Warburg, 1969, ch. 4.

[19] For the Committee's enterprising attempt to study the outputs of public policies see *Relationship of Expenditure to Needs: Eighth Report from The Expenditure Committee*, H.C. 515, 1972.

tions of policies is not, however, the only way in which government policy-making has begun to change.

The Central Policy Review Staff

Two aspects of policy analysis have been referred to above. The first is the need to consider the consequences of a policy decision for related and even quite different areas of policy and the second is the concern with its long-term implications. Any analysis of policy issues which neglects these can hardly be said to provide a basis for making informed choices about priorities or about the best strategy to achieve a particular end. When, as Prime Minister, Heath created the Central Policy Review Staff (CPRS) in 1970 he set up a body that could pursue both these objectives from a wider viewpoint than that embodied in expenditure control processes, although the emphasis of the CPRS, at least for the time being, is more clearly on the first objective – seeing government policy as a whole.

It could be argued that the CPRS was created to deal with two different problems of government. The first is that although the Cabinet makes decisions corporately the departmental Ministers in the Cabinet find great difficulty in not putting their departmental interests first and the overall shape of government policy a poor second. In this sense Cabinet decisions often fall far short of the ideal – the systematic planning of the whole body of government policies. Because the Cabinet is not backed by policy advisers, as opposed to a secretariat, the CPRS is needed to brief Ministers on the wider implications of any particular policy decision. The second role for the CPRS is to keep a government from wandering from its self-appointed strategic objectives. Many governments, though not all, come to power with strategic aims (most obviously, for example, increasing the rate of economic growth while holding inflation and unemployment within politically tolerable limits). These may survive for a few months, a year or even longer; but they are continually being undermined by decisions which do not square with these aims. Governments are liable to lose their way rather quickly. It is intended that the CPRS should counteract this tendency. The CPRS discharges its functions in four principal ways.[20] First, it organizes six monthly meetings of ministers in which the government's performance is reviewed and compared with its strategic aims. These meetings are backed by a second activity, the collective briefing of the Cabinet on day-to-day issues. In other words the CPRS produces papers on

---

[20] The ways in which the CPRS operates are outlined in an unpublished paper written by one of its members, W. J. Plowden, *The Central Policy Review Staff: the First Two Years.* For a valuable comparative discussion of co-ordinative agencies, including the CPRS, see Self, P., *Administrative Theories and Politics,* Allen & Unwin, 1972, ch. 4.

issues coming before the Cabinet which are designed to bring out points of importance to it as a whole which might not otherwise be raised by the Ministers directly concerned with the issue in question. In addition to these two activities the CPRS also studies particular areas of policy rather more extensively. The point of doing this is to take trans-departmental issues and look at them from a vantage point that is outside the departments concerned but which is nevertheless in close contact with them. Ideally the CPRS has the information but not the same partisan interests and loyalties that the departments have. Finally, the project approach is mirrored in the CPRS's involvement in PAR (programme analysis and review).

The CPRS is essentially designed to further the co-ordination of policy by bridging across the functional blocks of work allocated to departments.[21] The same job also needs to be done at levels below central government, but whether the CPRS will have a role at regional or sub-regional level is not yet known. Nor, from the outside, can one easily discern its relative impact on short- and long-term planning. Nevertheless, it can be regarded as in the business of policy analysis. Its orientation is trans-departmental and even if its time scale is primarily that of the life of a government it is not overwhelmed by short-term decisions. It exists to counteract this tendency.

The implications of changes in policy analysis
Having provided these examples of the ways in which policy analysis has developed within government we must now set them against our earlier questions: what is the time scale of government policy-making and what is the role of civil servants, relative to others, in affecting decisions?

Even if the process is slow and incomplete, the time scale of policy-thinking has been lengthening. Government does now have a greater capacity to look ahead. Whether or not this capacity compares favourably with the size of the task and whether it is used appropriately are more difficult questions. The same must be said of our second major question: it is hard to assess how these developments will affect the roles of civil servants and Ministers in policy-making.

The most careful policy analysis cannot make all the options, plus their merits and defects, explicit. The policy options which are chosen for consideration are not a complete or a random set of all possibilities. Policy analysis is neither perfectly efficient nor value free. Consequently, it is important to know who makes the decisions about how a problem is to be defined, which possible solutions are to be studied, which aspects of each are going to enter the calculation of

---

[21] *The Reorganization of Central Government*, Cmnd. 4506, *op. cit.*, outlined this functional division of work.

merits and defects and how they are to be weighted. These are all political decisions in the sense of being about values: but can they all be made by politicians? Let us consider three possible ways in which the analysis of problems may be related to the taking of decisions.

First, one might begin policy-making with an 'impartial' analysis. The bargaining and decisions on political questions could come at a later stage but be based on the assembled data. In one sense this is what cost–benefit analysis offers. The problem, as we have said, is that the options to be evaluated and the methods of evaluation entail numerous value decisions which cannot easily be specified and settled in advance of the analysis, or be allowed for afterwards in many instances. The same is true of academic research and any other analysis of policy options whether or not it can be graced with the name cost–benefit. Nevertheless, much decision-making does take the results of such analyses and research as a starting point or as a source of data. The degree of critical awareness with which the results are assessed obviously varies.

Second, policy analysis can be undertaken within an established framework of ideas or policy intent. In these cases the main direction of policy may be determined by purely political forces and then the details are filled in through a more analytical process. The Seebohm Committee on the personal social services was an example of a body which worked within broad political directives in this way. Its findings were then subject to further political consideration as in the first approach mentioned above.

Both these approaches involve a sequential process in which the political and the more analytical phases of policy-making are separated into distinct stages. The third possibility is to recognize that this can never be fully attained because value decisions arise continuously. Ideally in such circumstances the 'crucial' value decisions should be made by the politician and there should be a process for detecting which these are whilst the options still remain open. In principle this is how policy-making proceeds in government; but are Ministers in a position to ensure that it works out like that in practice? Have the moves towards a more sophisticated analysis of policy issues within government affected their ability to do so? If one concentrates on the general problems involved they can be summarized in two related questions. Are there sufficient alternative sources for Ministers to enjoy a choice of information and opinions? Can the policy-making undertaken within a political party be effectively translated into government policies once that party gains power?

Our case studies provide ample evidence that during the fifties and early sixties a considerable amount of medium- and long-term thinking took place in the political parties and in the 'intermediate area' of pressure groups and research organizations. Given the lack of statisticians, economists and experienced research staff in the social service ministries at the time, the balance was tipped against the departments. The comparative freedom enjoyed by researchers and pressure groups outside government gave them the opportunity to develop a fairly wide-ranging exploration of issues in search of both long-term and more immediate strategies. The ministries were less well placed and they were often vulnerable to outside criticism because they lacked the resources to collect and use data for research as well as for administrative purposes. What we have witnessed in the past decade is a major shift in the relative positions of independent and departmental research and planning. In one sense this opens up the choices available to decision-makers. The flow of data and ideas has grown and more research is now directed specifically at policy issues of concern to Ministers and senior civil servants. A corollary is that the opportunity to influence governmental policy through research and policy analysis may have declined. Government departments are now well provided with the kinds of data and expertise needed to counteract a challenge from an outside body, should they so wish. They are also in a better position to influence the type of research being conducted outside government.

To a certain extent the growing sophistication of government forward planning also makes it more difficult to challenge existing policy from inside government. Administrative problems and the available data have always limited the room for manoeuvre, but cost–benefit studies and carefully balanced forward planning may reduce the scope for change still further. It takes more political courage for a Minister to risk major changes when faced with voluminous and apparently sophisticated scientific data which support an ongoing but unattractive set of policies, than when policies are simply based on hunches or the preferences of the preceding Minister. This does not mean that government research and planning is undesirable. It means that the nature of policy-making and the relative power of the different groups which contribute to it seem to be changing quite rapidly.[22] Paradoxically it may both expand and restrict the choices open to policy-makers. What actually happens will depend as much as anything else upon the level of understanding of planning processes which Ministers possess and upon the extent to which they can draw on them in forming their own opinions and making their own choices.

---

[22] The growing interest in social indicators, for example, illustrates the point. On the meaning, development and relevance of social indicators to policy-making, see Shonfield, A. and Shaw, S. (ed.), *Social Indicators and Social Policy*, Crane-Russak, 1972.

Similarly, with the improvement of budgeting processes incoming Ministers are likely to face a dilemma. They are the channel through which the ideas developed in the parties are fed into departments to be studied and put into effect. Ministers have to make priority decisions not only between different elements of their own programme but also between these and the policies already being developed in the department when they arrive. They now have to accomplish this task within the limits set by the five-year projections of public expenditure or persuade the Treasury and their colleagues to accept changes in these forward plans. This has always been the case in one sense. Today's decisions always affect the room for manoeuvre tomorrow; but now that plans are projected ahead in some detail and now that those involved are more aware of the inter-relationships between policies, the upheaval created by change can be correspondingly greater. The move towards more conscious and sophisticated forward planning is, therefore, a double-edged sword. It can be used to improve the quality of policy-making, but it can also impose new limits on the extent and speed with which departmental policy can be realigned around Ministers' personal or party programmes.

Political control can never be exercised over all the value choices in policy-making. Civil servants choose the options they analyse and the facts they use. Ministers cannot make all these decisions. Like everybody else civil servants employ many different criteria in making such choices; they cannot simply reflect ministerial or party values and preferences. In this sense much power does rest with them. The problem is an old one but, as Self notes, the 'effective fusion of these contributions [politicians' and civil servants'] is now more important and difficult because of the increased knowledge and experience necessary to policy-making'.[23] Does party policy-making provide Ministers with a powerful and independent viewpoint from which to appraise, and, if necessary, change the direction in which his department is moving?

The growth in departmental planning and research has not been matched by similar developments in the parties. Although they find no difficulty in producing ideas about how policy should change the parties just do not have the full-time staff to assess the administrative and financial viability of proposals. Consequently, it is difficult for them even to identify the key points at which their ideas are likely to run into problems or to identify the consequences of accepting compromise solutions on those points. There has always been an information gap between the government and an opposition party, but it shows every sign of widening. The use of academic policy

[23] Self, P., in Robson, W., *op. cit.*, p. 85. Self adds comments on the changes needed in the organization of government departments, Parliament and the political parties if the challenge is to be met. See also Self, P., *Administrative Theories and Politics, op. cit.*, ch. 5.

advisers has been one means whereby opposition parties sought a counterbalance. The greater involvement of government in research, however, has enabled the authority or knowledge of such advisers to be more easily challenged. It is doubtful whether the parties can provide their shadow Ministers with the sound policy proposals they need if they are to effect substantial changes in policy once they achieve office. The improvement in government policy analysis may reduce these possibilities even further and lead to a shift in the relative power of civil servants and Ministers to influence policy decisions.

V THE DISTRIBUTION OF POWER IN GOVERNMENT

A pluralist view of government was advanced at the outset. It has since been implied in two different senses in much of what has been said. In the first and weaker sense, administrative pluralism can be detected because government departments nurture diverse and often competitive policy proposals, objectives and aspirations. The generation of a variety of proposals and demands is not entirely offset by integrative mechanisms. Government policy is rarely a closely co-ordinated and logically consistent whole. Neither the Cabinet system nor the political parties have the power to eliminate entirely the policy consequences of this administrative diversity. The second and stronger impression that may have been gained is that in social policy government departments are the real centres of power and policy-making. This implies virtually unlimited but multiple departmental autonomy and a rubber stamping role for the Cabinet.

This stronger version of the argument underlines some important features of government even though it is exaggerated. Much policy-making arises from administrative problems and data which the responsible department alone is aware of or is in a position to interpret. A department is a repository of knowledge that gives policy-makers considerable power in their dealings with other parties and the Cabinet. Whether the power is concentrated in the hands of civil servants or channelled through Ministers, departmental autonomy is real in dealing with many issues. The nature of the commitments the parties enter into reinforces this. Many of them are vague and imprecise. Providing they operate within the broad limits of such party and government policy Ministers and their departments can enjoy large areas of autonomy. However, there *are* integrative forces within government and the question of their effectiveness must be considered. The first type of integration relates to policy as such and is expressed mainly through the Cabinet. The second hinges on the control exercised over the use of resources and it is effected chiefly through the Treasury and the Civil Service Department.

One objection to the thesis of administrative pluralism is that only enough power to make decisions on the less important issues is decentralized from the Cabinet. The definition of 'important' becomes crucial. It is certainly true, as we have argued, that the management of the economy is a Cabinet and even a prime ministerial subject. Decisions here do constrain social policy decisions. The Cabinet also allocates priorities between expensive new departures from existing policy and is one important means of co-ordinating policy and resolving conflicts in the areas of departmental overlap. The Cabinet system therefore limits departmental autonomy, especially when policies involve quite new areas of government intervention, major questions of party policy, new legislation, sensitive questions of priority or inter-departmental disputes and divergence of strategies. Nevertheless, this still leaves a degree of freedom for each department to determine the scope, timing and content of many major policy issues as well as considerable autonomy in responding to lesser problems. Within the area of social policy it has been possible for a Minister to consult the Cabinet infrequently even when he is making major decisions.[24] Does the way resources are controlled restrict this freedom?

The Treasury is in contact with all other departments and is inextricably involved in questions of policy. Almost all major policy changes have immediate or long-term financial and staffing implications. Before the Civil Service Department took over some of these responsibilities the Treasury was also concerned with the full staffing implications of a proposal; that is, changes in complements, grading, training and staffing costs. Since the advent of the Civil Service Department, policies must be referred both to it and to the Treasury before they are implemented or forwarded to Cabinet. Nonetheless, the importance of the Treasury in policy-making can hardly be over-estimated. It enters the picture directly by looking at policy proposals in terms of their cost-effectiveness, their implications for future expenditure and by examining the degree to which the financial commitments involved are open ended. Yet it is not simply concerned with the amount of financial control built into each individual policy. Its task is also to restrain public expenditure. Self expresses the situation neatly: if, he says, 'the first rule of business is market innovation, the government equivalent could be said to be market compression'.[25]

An example of how the Treasury operates in relation to spending

[24] See Crosland's comments in Boyle, E., Crosland, C. A. R. and Kogan, M. (ed.), *op. cit.*
[25] Self, P., in Robson, W., *op. cit.*, p. 74.

departments might be helpful. Successive Ministers of Pensions disclaimed responsibility for determining the rate of national assistance. They argued that an increase in scale rates could result only from a recommendation by the National Assistance Board. This was disingenuous. The NAB was not the prime mover in such decisions and neither was the Minister, although both played a part. The Treasury had the real power. The present procedure for fixing supplementary benefit scale rates illustrates this. The Supplementary Benefits Commission is asked each year for its advice on what changes should be made assuming different expenditure limits. The negotiation with the Treasury then takes place at under secretary level on the basis of this and other information. It is these negotiations which determine the overall changes in the Supplementary Benefits budget and therefore the level of the scale rates. This is a much simplified picture; the reality can be far more complex. For example, where a serious disagreement arises the chairman of the SBC would probably protest to the Treasury. The whole issue might also be discussed between the DHSS and Treasury Ministers, and at Cabinet level, if it was seen as a major problem of government priorities or electoral strategy.

Simplified as it is, two points emerge from this example. First, the SBC has relatively minor powers to fix scale rates; direct negotiations with the Treasury produce the key decisions about resources. Second, this restraint is reflected in all policy thinking in the SBC. In short, new policy proposals are examined carefully *from the Treasury viewpoint within the spending departments*. A proposal over which there can be little financial control – a blank cheque policy – will be unpopular within a department because the Treasury is unlikely to favour it. Similarly, each new expenditure proposal will be looked at in terms of its impact on existing policies and expenditures. In the final analysis an expensive new policy may only be feasible if existing costs are trimmed. The Treasury viewpoint is not merely an exogenous factor referred to at the culmination of departmental policy formulation, it is also a continuous and indirect influence throughout. Even if departmental civil servants in general were reluctant to incorporate the Treasury viewpoint into their thinking, it would still not operate as a wholly external constraint. The civil servants responsible for negotiating with the Treasury do not want to find themselves in weak and embarrassing bargaining positions. They are a voice for the Treasury in their own departments as well as the other way round. The pattern of civil service careers can also reinforce the influence of Treasury opinion. As Kogan has shown, it is far more likely that civil servants from the economic ministries will be promoted to senior posts in the social service ministries than *vice versa*. The career structure seems to reflect the dominance of economic over social objectives and values.[26]

Public social expenditure is determined by the way in which the economy is managed as well as by party ideology, but it is the Treasury which almost exclusively mediates these relationships. Willson has maintained that 'there tend to be perhaps fifty people spread over Whitehall who together can carry any case through. The art of getting one's policy proposals accepted is the art of manoeuvring for the support – active or passive – of that two and one-half score.'[27] It could be argued that the art of getting a social policy proposal through is usually, in the final analysis, that of getting Treasury approval.

Treasury control over resources is, therefore, a powerful limitation upon the autonomy of government departments. We have implied that, especially with large departments capable of planning across many services, this form of integration may be more of a constraint than the integration of policies through the Cabinet or the party. In the light of past performance, however, one is forced to conclude that Treasury control is not an adequate substitute for the co-ordination of policy. It has tended to favour least-cost policies and has not been based on extensive inter-departmental policy analysis. If child care, or services for the homeless, are taken as examples there is little evidence of an integrated set of policy decisions based upon an assessment of the most effective use of resources. Expensive residential and domiciliary services have been used in such services to meet needs which, in some cases, could be provided for more cheaply through improved cash support for families.

The control of civil service manpower has also failed to anticipate problem areas in a way which could influence policy-making. The same tendency to concentrate on subsidiary or instrumental goals has prevented the long-term administrative consequences of policies being foreseen. For example, although there are other forces involved, the pressure of work on the supplementary benefits system has been aggravated by the move towards more selective policies, by the steady flow of new policies and by the changing role of the supplementary benefits staff. They began to take 'industrial action' for the first time in 1972 and the Civil Service Department authorized a substantial increase in staff complements in an attempt to combat these grievances; but the fact that the situation arose partly reflects a failure to anticipate the consequences of change and to plan accordingly. The centralized control of manpower and financial resources is a real restraint on departmental policy-making, but it does not, as yet, constitute a long-term and wide ranging process of policy analysis. It

[26] Kogan, M., *The Government of the Social Services*, Sixteenth Charles Russell Memorial Lecture, 1969.

[27] Willson, F. M. G., *op. cit.*, p. 368.

is this need to integrate government policy-making directly, and not merely through the medium of resource control, that led to the creation of the Central Policy Review Staff. Whether or not this body becomes an important integrative force remains to be seen.

In the meantime we believe government can still be characterized as a system of semi-autonomous power bases held together to varying degrees by the Cabinet system, the Prime Minister and the Treasury. It does not comprise a set of weak administrative departments totally dominated by a single, highly centralized, policy-making body.

CHAPTER SIX

The Partisans

Many participants in the political process who act as partisans do not possess the authority to make decisions in the name of the State. Four different kinds of groups will be distinguished in the following pages: the private citizen, pressure groups, the mass media and the political parties. The questions to be asked throughout are where and how policies are initiated, brought to the attention of government, propelled forward to the point of commitment, or blocked and quietly buried. How and to what extent can these partisan groups influence government policy?

I THE PRIVATE CITIZEN

What influence does the citizen exercise over policy? The answer, quite literally, is a marginal one. At the margin, in elections at least, a small number of voters may determine the party which forms the government, but the amount of control this gives electors is severely limited. Indeed, some theorists have suggested that the opportunity to exercise influence is so small that it does not, in itself, provide a rational reason for using one's vote.[1] The rhetoric of democracy can be profoundly misleading as a representation of political reality. Given the narrow margins by which elections are won and lost, nearly half the voting electorate will have failed to exercise influence and will have little opportunity to do so for possibly a further five years.[2]

---

[1] See for example, Downs, A., *An Economic Theory of Democracy*, Harper, 1957, and for a very useful discussion of this 'economic' approach to political science Barry, B. M., *Sociologists, Economists and Democracy*, Collier Macmillan, 1970.

[2] In addition about two-thirds of all constituencies have shown a high degree of stability from one election to another and are unlikely to change hands in normal circumstances. This picture is modified somewhat by the greater volatility of the electorate in the past few years, by changes in the

Moreover, elections provide only limited opportunity to choose between the policies offered by a particular party. Elections are only
about policy choices in the broadest sense of determining the ideological stance of government and possibly one or two major issues.
The marginal or floating voters may exercise more influence to
the extent that parties direct their campaigns at them. However the
policies chosen as appealing to these voters may bear little relationship to the rest of the party programme. When the floating vote is
being wooed the hard core of party supporters may be deprived of
some of their influence. For their part the party faithful rarely, but
occasionally do, come to be seen as a floating vote. The Labour
Party experienced more difficulty in mobilizing its traditional supporters during the 1970 election than it had done for a decade. Absten-
tions by these supporters broke the pattern of the 1960s when traditional support was relatively neglected in pursuing gains among
middle-of-the-road voters. After 1970 divergent strategies once again
became a feature of a divided Labour Opposition: move left to
rekindle enthusiasm among the rank and file or keep to the centre
and look for success among less traditional supporters? That the
parties are somewhat sensitive to their supporters' opinions, or at least
to their own interpretation of what those opinions are, cannot be
denied. The extent of their sensitivity is a theme to which we will return.

What we have done so far is simply to emphasize the obvious
limitations on the electorate's influence. But the concepts of public
and party opinion are liberally evoked in policy discussions and they
are frequently used to legitimate a policy proposal or viewpoint. Does
this political language wildly over-estimate the importance of individuals' opinions? In general the answer must be yes. The politicians'
impression of public opinion is based on selective feed-back received from constituents, from the mass media and from other
sources. These concepts are employed frequently, but loosely, because
the 'rules' of a democratic system make their use necessary. Consulting electoral opinion may affect policy decisions; but its most
pervasive influence is on the milieu within which the political game is
played rather than directly on the details of policy.

On the other hand, grievances and injustices suffered by individuals can occasionally have an impact on the administration, and even
the content, of policy.[3] A small number of individuals can also be

location of population and by the re-drawing of constituency boundaries.
But the basic point remains: very many people have no *effective* impact on the
choice of government. See Hacker, A., 'Some Votes are More Equal than
Others', *New Society*, 13 Feb., 1964.

[3] Normally the status and influence of the individual in question will be irrelevant, but there are instances where these factors do seem to have a bearing
on the outcome. The famous Crichel Down affair was one. As Birch notes,

identified who, at any one time, have a distinctive if somewhat ill-defined impact on policy. The leaders of important pressure groups, trade unions, industrial corporations and professions may gain influence in their own right and on issues which are not solely related to the interests they represent. More interesting in some senses, and certainly more visible, are the people who gain prominence through the ideas they advocate. In the family allowance case study it will be shown that two of the most influential individuals were Keynes and Beveridge, men who were publicly known as brokers of formative ideas. Many other less well known individuals with access to the higher reaches of government also interpret, convey and initiate influential ideas and shifts in opinion. Nevertheless, compared with the mass of ordinary voters with whom we began, an exceedingly small number of people outside government exert direct or personal influence on policy-making.

II PRESSURE GROUPS

One of the ways in which the individual's meagre ration of influence may be augmented is through the work of pressure groups and they are a well studied aspect of the policy-making process. That is not surprising in a society where politics is regarded as a process of accommodation and of bargaining between multiple publics, each with some limited power to protect or to further their interests. The three main political parties are mass organizations which between them enjoy the support of the vast majority of the active electorate. These parties are not, in the first instance, the most convenient bodies within which to raise issues which affect, or will be supported by, only a small section of the electorate. Most interests are protected and issues articulated within smaller or more specialized groupings. These are not simply an alternative form of political organization to the parties; they are complementary. The mass parties are agglomerates in which many, frequently competing, interests are variously represented. It is normally possible to gain party support for an issue and to prevent it being diluted beyond recognition only if a more specialized grouping outside the party promotes it. Resources, experience and enthusiasm can be harnessed by such groups and used to advance the study of problems to a point where their significance for a party can be more easily assessed.

---

the complainant was a man of means, whose wife was from an aristocratic family with two close contacts in the government of the day. Birch, A. H., *op. cit.*, p. 146.

For these reasons, and also because the political culture supports it, pressure group activity has long been a widespread, and often public, feature of British politics.[4] The literature on British pressure groups takes three main forms. Some writers have approached the subject by reviewing the area of pressure group politics as a whole but distinguishing different types of groups and different kinds of influence.[5] Others have chosen to study a particular pressure group or issue in depth.[6] A third group of writers has been more concerned to discuss the role and impact of pressure groups in the context of a broader study of British politics.[7] Each of these approaches is drawn on in this section. We begin by distinguishing two basic types of pressure group, providing examples of the diversity of groups and discussing their areas of influence. The bases and limitations of their influence are then noted and, finally, the contemporary state of pressure group politics is considered.

The term pressure group is used in this book to refer to *interest* and *promotional* groups both of which are intimately involved in social policy-making. The distinction between these two kinds of pressure groups is a common one, although it is by no means the only method of classification.[8] Wooton notes, quite rightly, that it may also be misleading to the extent that the anchorage or ultimate support for a group may not be reflected in its ostensible role and objective.[9] Nevertheless it is a useful, if approximate, classification for those studying social policy.

The term interest group can be applied to any organized set of interests such as a trade union or employers' association. The protec-

[4] For a discussion of the normative support given to pressure group or lobbying activities in Britain, see Finer, S. E., *Anonymous Empire*, Pall Mall Press, 1958.

[5] Finer, S. E., *op. cit.*, Moodie, G. C. and Studdert-Kennedy, G., *Opinions, Publics and Pressure Groups*, Allen & Unwin, 1970; Potter, A., *Organised Groups in British National Politics*, Faber, 1960; Stewart, J. D., *British Pressure Groups*, Oxford University Press, 1958; and Wooton, G., *Interest Groups*, Prentice-Hall, 1970.

[6] Christophe, J., *Capital Punishment and British Politics*, Allen & Unwin, 1962; Eckstein, H., *Pressure-Group Politics: the Case of the BMA*, Allen & Unwin, 1960; Harrison, M., *Trade Unions and the Labour Party since 1945*, Allen & Unwin, 1960; Self, P. and Storing, H., *The State and the Farmer*, Allen & Unwin, 1962; and Wooton, G., *The Politics of Influence*, Routledge & Kegan Paul, 1963.

[7] Beer, S., *Modern British Politics, op. cit.*; McKenzie, R. T., *British Political Parties, op. cit.*; McKenzie, W. J. M., 'Pressure Groups in British Government', *British Journal of Sociology*, vol. 2, 1955.

[8] It has its origins in an early study by Childs – quoted in Wooton, G., *Interest Groups, op cit.*, p. 39. Other classifications of relevance to social policy include Beer's broad distinction between producer and consumer groups, which is referred to later.

[9] Wooton, G., *Ibid.*, ch. 3.

tion and furthering of members' interests are the characteristic goals of such a group. The need to enter the political arena is an incidental and, in some cases, infrequent consequence of protecting these interests. Of all interest groups, the trade unions and business organizations have perhaps the most pervasive and powerful impact on government. Through the Trades Union Congress (TUC) and the Confederation of British Industry (CBI) especially, they are now closely involved in economic management and, indirectly at least, with social policy. The trade unions, for example, had an important influence on Labour Party economic strategy in the late 1940s by withdrawing their support for physical (especially manpower) planning and forcing the government into the pattern of economic management later dubbed 'Butskellism'. Business interests played a similar part in relation to price controls.[10]

Both trade union and business interests also make direct attempts to influence social policy.[11] Yet the role of the unions is something of an enigma. They represent a large proportion of social service clients and as such can have a powerful impact in the social as well as the economic field. Unfortunately, despite their importance, their role in contemporary social policy-making is not well documented. The general issue of wage supplementation through social policy and the current problems of the poverty-wage trap in particular, illustrates the trade unions' position. They have given a clear priority to their economic and wage bargaining functions and have been critical of policies which looked like attempts to buy off discontent about living standards.[12] Where there has been an apparent clash of interests between social policy proposals and effective wage bargaining the former has been treated with suspicion; but even where this problem does not arise trade union expertise has been concentrated largely on the wages front. This choice reflects the priority accorded to earnings as a determinant of individual welfare by most trade unionists, and indeed by the whole society. It also underlines the finite power of interest groups. Given that the potential to exert influence is easily dissipated, the unions have to husband it and use it in what they see

[10] Beer, S., *Modern British Politics, op. cit.,* pp. 199–208. Other groups also influence economic policy; Beer includes an interesting example of government securing greater control over bank credit facilities. by giving the banks the inducement of higher interest rates, *Ibid.,* pp. 327–9.

[11] Beer's example of contradictory attitudes to social policy being urged on the government simultaneously by the TUC and CBI is the archetypal case (*ibid.,* pp. 363–5). but also see Harrison, M., *op. cit.,* on the trade unions' relationship with the Labour Party. See also our family allowance case study.

[12] The Family Allowance case study illustrates the complexity of these relationships between the unions and the political parties in the field of earnings supplementation.

as the most effective way. Although the unions are deeply involved in some areas of social service policy at a practical as well as an ideological level, this has not been their major preoccupation. Consequently, they have not done enough policy-thinking or research in the recent past to be really effective in those fields where wage bargaining is an incomplete response to poverty, deprivation and diswelfare. Yet if they have often and unduly neglected social policy it must also be said that research has neglected their role in policy formation.

Other interest groups are more directly involved in social policy through their role in its implementation; for example, the local authorities and the social service professions. These bodies maintain a continuing interaction with government.[13] By way of contrast, consumer groups have been slow to develop in many areas of social policy. This is partly because the interests affected by an issue may be very difficult to identify. In the case of environmental pollution, for instance, all the inhabitants of an area are presumably interested parties, but it may be impossible to define the geographical areas at risk in any instance. Furthermore, the interests affected may also be difficult to organize. The interested parties in abortion law reform and the reduction of the health hazards of smoking are unlikely to form groups with a sense of solidarity, although for quite different reasons. Stated categorically this may suggest that social policy-making is dominated by the professional groups and, more specifically, by their attempts to guard their members' interests. This is certainly a central feature of much pressure group activity. One of the outstanding studies of a social service pressure group concerns the British Medical Association (BMA) and illustrates this aspect of an interest group's role.[14] Other studies have referred to such topics as the pursuit of professionalization and improved status, working conditions and political influence on the part of social service personnel.

Nevertheless, clients' interests have not been totally unrepresented in the past for two main reasons. First, a professional association may further clients' interests while pursuing those of its members. On many issues, such as efforts to standardize professional qualifications and ethical codes or raise the quality of service, client and personnel interests may coincide, at least in part. The role of professional groups in improving the quality and range of provision is an important one and it can be vital to the development of newly established services. For example, the absence of specialist staff with their own professional association may certainly have contributed to

---

[13] On the local authority associations see Finer, S. E., *op. cit.*
[14] Eckstein, H., *op. cit.*

the chequered history of the family allowance system since its inception. Whereas, disquiet amongst medical officers and general practitioners over the organization of local health services undoubtedly contributed towards an expanded use of health centres.[15]

Secondly, consumers' interests have not been ignored completely because promotional groups as well as interest groups are active in the social policy field. The value of promotional groups is precisely that they concern themselves with issues which would be unlikely to receive effective interest group sponsorship. The essence of a promotional group's influence is the case it presents, whereas the starting point for an interest group is its ability, or claim, to represent the interests of a category of people. Promotional groups have been a prominent feature of social policy. They have taken many forms ranging from groups operating within and alongside the political parties, like the Fabian Society; national non-party groups, such as the Child Poverty Action Group which indirectly represent social service clients; and individual academic research workers producing and politicizing data on social need. Many of these groups are long-standing and multi-purpose, moving from issue to issue as problems change or even sponsoring a number of issues at the same time. Others have been short-lived, *ad hoc* combinations of people united around a highly specific issue. Even groups concerned with a single issue may exist for many years despite the fact that they make little progress. The family allowances and clean air case studies illustrate the role of single issue groups, one of which dissolved when it obtained a measure of success whilst the other continued with only small changes in direction and emphasis.

Apart from the multitude of easily recognized promotional groups, the voluntary organizations providing social services have often acted as pressure groups. They are in a sense different from either interest groups) for promotional groups as we have defined them.[16] The voluntary social services are good examples of pressure groups which maintain a low political profile; but their ability to apply pressure is real. In part their very existence can be a political pressure because they operate as an alternative to government provision and as a source of comparison for the critics of government action or inaction. They may also step directly into the field of political action if they feel a particular need is too large for them to cope with and that government should accept responsibility for it. They often fulfil the same function as research, revealing unmet and possibly unknown needs. Conversely it can be argued that as an alternative to public provision, voluntary organizations may reduce and divert the pressure

[15] See the health centre case study.
[16] They clearly illustrate that these terms are useful analytical categories, but that multiple roles are the norm for most groups.

for public action. Unfortunately, this possible effect of voluntary provision has not been fully investigated. The positive impact on social
policy is, by its nature, easier to document.

The general question we must ask of all pressure groups is why
they gain some influence on some issues. As Lindblom says it is not
at all clear why authorities pay attention to pressure group leaders.[17]
He lists three possible explanations.

(i) Pressure groups, primarily interest groups, may influence their
supporters' voting behaviour.

(i) Following Key, politics can be seen as a game played by a limited
group of participants.[18] The rules of the game demand that
all participants be allowed to participate actively. Pressure groups
are included in the game, the organization of legitimate bodies
of opinion being their distinctive function and prerequisite for
membership.

(iii) Lindblom adds his own explanation: 'Interest-group leaders
influence the proximate policy-maker through persuasion. They
try to persuade him that what they want is what he too thinks
is best – or that what he should realize is best includes what
they want.'

Lindblom rejects the first explanation, citing Key's work in support
of his argument. The basic point, that pressure groups are unable to
'deliver the vote', clearly has much force. Large interest groups
do tend to be politically heterogeneous in party terms, even if a united
front can be presented on particular issues. The Conservative government sought to neutralize opposition to the Industrial Relations
Bill (1971) on precisely these grounds. Many trade unionists, including blue collar workers, did vote for the Conservative Party in
the 1970 election. This does not mean that they specifically voted
for this particular policy, but the point remains that the trade unions
did not deliver their members' votes to the Labour Party despite their
opposition to the Conservative industrial relations policies. Smaller
interest groups and nearly all promotional groups lack the mass support necessary to influence election results directly even if they
could command their supporters' votes. What they can do is to serve
as political barometers, indicating issues that are politically sensitive
within key sectors of the electorate. Pressure groups certainly attempt
to convince the relevant authorities that this is the case.

As we have noted, the language of public opinion is greatly favoured
in politics and it is used by large interest groups, small promotional

---

[17] Lindblom, *op. cit.*, p. 63.
[18] Key, V. O., *Public Opinion and American Democracy*, Knopf, 1961.

groups and individual MPs as well as by members of a government who are defending or rejecting a policy proposal. Behind the language lies, in part, a real belief that the electorate does care about a particular issue, but it can also be seen as a kind of ritual which different groups employ in an endeavour to legitimate a course of action in other peoples' eyes by reference to 'the rules of the democratic game'. The actual or induced feelings of the electorate are less important than what the main actors in the policy process believe they feel. This is difficult to discern. No one has asked British policymakers how the concept of public opinion influences their calculations. It is not easy to discover by observation because politicians produce public opinion statements as a reflex action. The genuine belief is hard to distinguish from the customary gesture.

Nevertheless it is clear that the language is pervasive and used by all kinds of groups in jostling for political influence, sometimes with effect. Many politicians do not treat public opinion as simply an item of political mythology. People are too unpredictable for them all to be ignored by all politicians all of the time. Sample surveys of public opinion are still too infrequent, general and imprecise, and there are too many instances of unforeseen shifts in public support for the language of public opinion to be completely empty. Other policymakers (senior civil servants in particular) also reflect some of the politician's concern for public support and hence political leverage can sometimes turn on this fulcrum as well. Even pressure groups which are rarely able to 'deliver the votes' may occasionally gain nearly as much influence through the skilful use of the vocabulary of politics.

Some interest groups are more closely tied to one party than another and their members' attitudes are important to that party. Many industrial organizations and trade unions are also linked to the Conservative and Labour parties respectively because they are sources of party finance. Nevertheless, these supporters may be ignored or antagonized on occasions when the party is in power. Beer, for example, has argued that whilst the business community clearly influences Conservative administrations some sacrifice of business interests will always be accepted, if necessary, in order to attain or retain office.[19] Rather than lose their grip on political power party leaders will be tempted on occasion to give relatively low priority to the policies favoured by the party's financial supporters.

The majority of pressure groups have no financial relationship with the parties and can offer little electoral support in exchange for influence. Many of them in fact maintain some façade, or even a carefully created image of party neutrality. The Child Poverty Action

---

[19] Beer, S., *op. cit.*, pp. 359–67 and also pp. 298–301.

Group is a good example of a group which may appear to have a natural affinity to one party but which preserves the right to criticize and cultivate any party on specific policy issues. It illustrates why pressure groups seek to influence all governments rather than one party and yet how dangerous this can be. The CPAG has in turn exercised apparent influence within a Labour government in 1967–9; heavily criticized the same government during 1969–70 for neglecting poverty problems; gained support for the group's proposals from the Conservative Opposition during these latter years; and then directed critical pressure at the Conservative government for failing to enact its election promises during 1971. Some individuals within the CPAG publicly welcomed the broad principles of the 1972 tax credit proposals while they sought to influence the details of Conservative policy both directly and via the Labour Opposition.

It may be argued that this particular pressure group has sacrificed influence by having no fixed allegiance to one party; but their pattern of political activities is similar to other groups. In many circumstances it may well be a disadvantage to associate an issue with one party and thereby encourge the other main party to oppose it if there is any ideological basis for doing so. Birch is probably right in saying that the campaign for comprehensive secondary education suffered from a too rapid and partisan association with the Labour Party.[20] This may be a good tactical reason for seeking a bi-partisan approach, but many pressure groups have no choice. The chances of influencing one party's policy-making, of it gaining or retaining power and then acting on the commitment, are too low. Support has to be gained within both parties if possible. Many promotional groups adopt a bi-partisan approach simply to shorten the odds against them.

The political game may be played by a small number of participants but this number includes many pressure groups upon whom parties and governments do not obviously depend for support. Why, therefore, do they gain even a limited amount of influence? Key's answer is that they represent interests which are entitled to be heard.[21] This is a rather inadequate explanation although it conveys an important feature of pressure group activity; namely that many groups are regarded as legitimate elements in the policy-making system as a matter of tradition and established practice. Their role is institutionalized to the point where consultation rather than pressure is a more appropriate term. However, the difficult questions to answer are why and how groups attain this position; what kinds of groups do *not* enter close working relationships with government; and why even well entrenched and influential groups occasionally have to

[20] Birch, A. H., *op cit.*, pp. 220–1.
[21] Key, V. O., *op. cit.*

engage in vigorous pressure activities because their advice and wishes are ignored.

Some groups clearly obtain influence because their members play a major part in the implementation of government policy on a particular issue. A Minister of Health must take doctors' advice and comments as seriously as those of his civil servants. Both groups are intimately involved in the administration of health policies. Their co-operation is continually needed not only in executing policies, but also in spotting defects in new policies and deficiencies in existing services. In 1971 a proposal to introduce a system of prescription charges related to the market value of the drugs prescribed attracted considerable professional opposition and was subsequently withdrawn. It was a good example of an embryonic policy being criticized for its anticipated administrative and medical consequences.[22]

With the growth and increasing specialization of the social services a large number of groups of personnel have to be consulted or at least informed of policy changes before they are finalized in detail. Social service staff can be influential both by tendering professional advice and also by trade union style bargaining and coercion on matters affecting their conditions of work. Professional associations and other staff unions are frequently involved in establishing the minutiae of policies. Their interests may also be considered when the broad outlines of policy are being established, and they may initiate demands for policy change if problems about which they feel strongly arise in their area of professional competence.

Clients of a service are rarely as well organized as interest groups and a government's dependence on their co-operation is limited; but the clients' interest is represented by numerous promotional groups. On what is their influence based? One important answer is information. Governments not only need advice on the administrative consequences of their plans, they also need information on their effectiveness. Once government is seen as responsible for a wide range of social needs and policies its performance in these areas is open to criticism. It is most vulnerable to this criticism when its own information sources are inferior to those possessed by partisans. Pressure groups therefore derive much of their opportunity for influence from collecting information of a kind, or of a quality, not collected by government itself. Information is not the only tradable commodity however. Ideas, or solutions to recognized problems, are also a means of influence. Criticism of defects is not in short supply but solutions are. Specialist groups, whether they be interest, promotional or party-affiliated study groups, can have useful suggestions to make. Indivi-

[22] For references to this proposal and the opposition to it expressed by the BMA and the Pharmaceutical Society see the *Guardian*, 16 and 20 Nov., 1971.

duals may, for similar reasons, gain an opportunity for influence whether they operate from within the civil service, the party system or the intermediate area of groups and institutions concerned with policy.

The basis of pressure group power is largely agreed upon among observers of the political scene. Information, advice and ideas are the common features in nearly all instances and are the sole currency in which most *promotional* groups trade. Important *interest* groups have a stronger position in that their support is often required by government. Because of the extensive involvement of government in social and economic life they need the support of many interest groups, and not only in the sense of co-operation in administering policies. They need to legitimate their policies in the eyes of their own party supporters and, to some extent, in those of the Opposition. Interest group co-operation is widely accepted as providing a large element of legitimation. Governments not only want, but to a considerable degree are seen to have a duty, to consult affected interests; at least to consult *organized* affected interests. However radical it might be, a Labour government would be unlikely, for example, to ignore insurance interests in reforming pensions. They might have the strength and the courage to act against these interests where it seemed necessary but probably not before consulting, clarifying the areas in dispute and attempting to find a compromise. If they acted without consultation they would be attacked fiercely in Parliament, in the 'quality' press and possibly the popular press. They could also lose the support or trust of many unrelated interest groups because of their departure from 'the normal procedures'. The cost of breaking conventions can be high.

The need for information and legitimacy accounts both for the relationship of pressure groups with government departments and with the political parties. That between pressure groups and the parties is close for several reasons. The parties must be kept aware of a group's interests and demands if it is to have its cause remembered in the party programme. The parties in turn need the groups for the reasons already mentioned. Opposition parties in particular will be forming policy outlines to present at an election and yet will be deprived of most of the information and ideas flowing to government. The administrative data available to government departments are difficult to tap, but by remaining open to a wide range of groups an Opposition can keep in contact with many of the demands and suggestions impinging on government. Most pressure groups therefore want and are encouraged to maintain links with one or more parties. Most cultivate some MPs who are willing to be briefed and raise the group's demands or opinions in Parliament. Depending on the issue, pressure through Parliament can be a useful complement, or a necessary alternative to pressure through government departments.

Nevertheless, much pressure group attention, especially that of interest groups, is centred on government departments. This concentration arises precisely because of government intervention in economic and social issues. In contrast, new pressure groups and groups exploring issues in which government is not yet involved must develop influence through Parliament and the parties. Some groups never become part of the departmental policy-making machinery because they choose to remain independent of government; because their demands remain unacceptable to successive governments; or because they can be of little help.[23] But the majority of interest groups and some promotional groups whose proposals become accepted, do enter a fairly close exchange relationship with government. They are frequently consulted, sounded out or advised on issues at the earliest stages of policy formation. They may continue to play a role throughout the development of a policy and subsequently monitor its operation. Part of the price they pay is common to all situations of co-optation; they lose an element of independence and may be greatly restricted in their activities by having received confidential information about government intentions. Unless they are willing to sacrifice their position close to government their influence will have to be used discreetly. This degree of involvement with government can, therefore, be an embarrassment. It is won by creating a respectable and cautious image which would be endangered by a robustly critical campaign on an issue for which the government has little enthusiasm. One of the best examples of this problem, which was resolved by creating an independent ginger group, concerned the Howard League for Penal Reform and the campaign to abolish capital punishment.[24]

The established pressure groups largely work within private areas of policy discussion and consultation characterized by much of the caution and confidentiality of the civil servants with whom they work. They do not operate in a world charged with momentous decisions and vital state secrets; most of the interaction between them and government is at the mundane level of day-to-day administrative matters and is not about exerting influence on a broad policy front.[25]

<hr />

[23] Civil liberties and other protest groups, for example, are unlikely to be co-opted by government unless civil rights legislation is being devised.

[24] See the detention centre case study and also Christophe, J., *op. cit.*

[25] See Finer, S. E., *Anonymous Empire, op. cit.*, pp. 35–7, for evidence of the high proportion of routine matters dealt with by the FBI (now CBI) and the TUC in their contacts with government; and also see Finer, S. E., 'The Political Power of Private Capital', *Sociological Review*, vol. 3, no. 2 and vol. 4, no. 1, 1955–6.

But this somewhat uninspiring flow of communication is the basis from which influence is occasionally exercised on major issues.

The main sources of pressure group influence may, therefore, be summarized as follows:

(i) the direct manipulation of, or control over, electoral support for a particular party;

(ii) the existence of a financial relationship between political parties and a very small number of interests;

(iii) the interdependence of government and those interest groups which are directly involved in implementing government policies;

(iv) the presentation of information about unmet need or policy failures to authorities anxious to anticipate public criticism;

(v) the challenging of a government's competence by gathering information on unmet need or ineffective policies or, alternatively, the challenging of the impartiality and justice of their policies by appealing to considerations of the public good; and

(vi) the formulation of partisan analyses designed to convince an authority that partisan demands are in accord with its predispositions and interests.

A point made earlier in this chapter should now be re-emphasized. Pressure groups do not each relate to government in isolation. Their interests and objectives overlap, compete with and stand in opposition to each other. A political party is itself a confederation of groups with related interests, a forum for many diverse pressure groups whose interests cross party lines. It is a structure within which interests compete for priority and are balanced against each other. In forming alliances groups may increase their influence, though at the cost of diluting or modifying the issues which they originally brought to the alliance. In competing for influence groups may neutralize each other and they certainly give political leaders and governments the opportunity to enforce compromise or to follow their own preferred line of action. Pressure groups constrain and restrain policy-makers, but the very number of groups active on some issues may also free policy-makers to select and manipulate the interests to which they ultimately respond.

What significance then has extensive pressure group activity for policy-making? Does it modify policy in parties and government? Does it reduce the power of Parliament and the Opposition to criticize and control policy? In part it has had these results. More fundamentally it can be argued that pressure group politics has, in a complex way, transformed the nature of policy-making. Whilst pressure groups of some kind are an inherent feature of political life and have influenced social policy at all times it is possible that their impact has changed. Even discounting the fact that academic interest in this feature of political life has grown over time, it seems certain that their role in policy-making is now much greater than it was immediately before the last war. What is important is not merely that pressure groups bring demands and interests to a government's attention between elections but that, as a leading political scientist has suggested, 'taken together [they] are a far more important channel of communication than parties for the transmission of political ideas from the mass of the citizenry to their rulers'.[26] This view may be challenged in some respects, but it is widely accepted that a pluralism based on group politics has characterized the post-war period in this country. Pressure groups have certainly made for diversity within parties at times when inter-party differences have seemed small.[27]

Even so one needs to be cautious in generalizing about the role of pressure groups in social policy. They certainly do not guarantee that the power to influence decisions is widely diffused throughout society. Client-oriented groups, for example, have in most cases only nibbled at the edges of centralized political power. In this respect Beer's analysis of pressure group politics provides a useful conclusion to this discussion for he makes a distinction between 'producer' and 'consumer' interests.[28] This dichotomy is crucial to his explanation of post-war British politics and to social policy. His thesis is that both parties, and therefore successive governments, have been forced to take note of these two sets of interests. Producer interests have to be accepted as an influence on policy because a government must work with them; the 'realities of power' dictate some degree of rapport with business and trade union groups alike. It is the 'realities of winning power' in the first place that dictate concern for consumer interests, since it is largely in their role as consumers that people make their voting decisions at elections. The critical factor in his analysis is the proposition that these two sets of interests 'have a power to affect policy-making that is quite separate from their position in the system of parliamentary representation and party government.'[29] This situation has arisen, he argues, because of the collectivist

[26] McKenzie, R. T., 'Parties, Pressure Groups and the British Political Process', *Political Quarterly*, Jan.–Mar., 1958, p. 10.

[27] On the 'right' to participate in policy-making see Beer, S., *Modern British Politics, op. cit.*, p. 389. Beer's discussion of democratic one party (Conservative) government during the fifties illustrated the intra-party diversity brought about by pressure groups: Beer, S., 'Democratic One-Party Government for Britain', in Benewick, R. and Dowse, R., *Readings on British Politics and Government*, University of London Press, 1968, pp. 22–3.

[28] For further discussion of producer and consumer interests see Beer, S., *Modern British Politics, op. cit.*, ch. 22.

[29] *Ibid.*, p. 331.

nature of post-war politics. The 'Managed Economy' and the 'Welfare State' respectively guarantee the influence of at least some producer and some consumer interests.

The degree of anticipatory response to these interests implied by Beer suggests that consumer interests may be catered for even when they are difficult to organize. Indeed, he presents a picture of the parties ensnared within a process of bidding for votes, each continually competing to outbid the other. In a situation of two equally popular parties and a decline of class (or sharply ideological) politics, this represents a measure of influence for the ordinary voter. Beer accepts, as we noted earlier, that the parties shape these demands as well as responding to them. Nevertheless, power is said to be diffuse and many interests are seen as influential in shaping government policy, even if they are not directly represented by an interest or promotional group.

At least one crucial reservation must be entered at this point. It is that only *some* consumer interests gain representation in this way. A few key features of social policy are advanced by inter-party bidding. Such issues as the level of the retirement pension and the rate of house building may be a focus for party competition. But even closely related problems such as homelessness or low incomes in large families do not feature so prominently. They are not the kind of problems to which governments pay attention because of the need to bid for the support of consumer-voters. These interests require the backing of an organized pressure group working through the parties or perhaps (with a strong organization) through government departments. Social service consumer groups have not been the most powerful or rapidly growing pressure groups, and the competition for influence is keen. Beer's picture of the political parties outbidding each other for consumer support at elections suggests some measure of influence on governments, but it certainly does not guarantee success for the majority of social policy proposals. He depicts the parties as probing 'every neglected thicket in the political landscape for its quarry' and thereby ensuring representation for the consumer interest.[30] If he is right this feature of party political life would, as he argues, offset the great power of the producer interests.

His thesis is most severely tested in the field of social policy by the notion of the 'consumer as tax-payer'. The very small electoral support to be gained by introducing many kinds of social policy reform has to compete with the strong belief in consumer sovereignty and with the view of public expenditure that depicts it as a burden on the productive parts of the economy.

Beer is obviously right in seeing consumers as an important latent

[30] *Ibid.*, p. 349.

force in politics which parties may take into account despite the low level of their organization. But it is particular mass wants, such as a low level of inflation, growth in real incomes, a degree of quality control and consumer protection in the retail sector, reasonable housing costs, generous pensions, and good standards of education, to which governments try to respond. This leaves many other consumer interests with no voice, or one that is drowned by some of the contradictory consumer demands. However, a partial rebuttal of Beer's thesis does not mean that it is all discounted. Minority interests and unpopular issues may still receive support from policy-makers. Although they may not come to prominence through a party's search for the good 'consumer issue', they may reach the top of the party or governmental hierarchies by other routes. They may, for example, be pushed up the party heirarchy by their supporters and enter the governmental policy-making process when the party is in power. They may equally be brought to prominence by the mass media. Let us examine both these issues – the role of the media and the nature of the policy process within the political parties – taking the media first.

III THE MASS MEDIA

While pressure groups are the more fully researched, the mass media are the most immediately obvious source of influence on policy-making. But what is the nature of this influence? Do the media reflect a bland general public opinion shorn of any nuances, particular sectors of opinion, or one particular ideology and view of life? Do they formulate rather than reflect public opinions? Do they really influence policy at all?

Given the limited research, the honest answer to most of these questions is that we do not know. For instance, we have no data about when and in what circumstances the mass circulation newspapers have a decisive effect on policy; or whether the 'quality' press is more consistently influential. The effect of the media on elections has received some attention but this area of research has barely touched the really difficult question of whether party programmes are influenced by the existence and role of the mass media.[31] One frequently noted possibility is that the widespread use of television results in election campaigns being dominated by personalities rather than issues. But even if this is the trend, it tells us little about how policies are thereby affected.

[31] On the effects of the media on voting behaviour see, for example, Butler, D. and Stokes, D., *Political Change in Britain*, Macmillan, 1969.

The specific influence of different mass media on particular issues is a large and virtually unexplored territory. It is possible, however, to illustrate the danger of making simple assumptions about the media as channels of communication between the electorate and political elites; as organs of propaganda, or as sources of influence. The national television and radio networks, for example, carry a smaller proportion of news information than do most newspapers and they raise few local issues. Their communication with the mass public is even less two-way than that of newspapers and they do not claim to represent any particular section of the public. At the same time they are more subject to conventions of political neutrality. The fact that on occasions both parties detect political bias only emphasizes this expectation. Such factors make these media look politically somewhat impotent. Yet the size of the audience and the dramatic effects of carefully presented current affairs and documentary programmes may redress the balance. Radio, and particularly television, are ideally placed to initiate or act as a catalyst on specific issues, but they seem to be less well suited, in Britain at least, to the maintenance of steady pressure on a few topics.

Newspapers and weeklies, however, do adopt this role. One good social policy example is the attention focused on the needs of thalidomide children by the *Sunday Times* in 1972–3; but it also illustrates the problems of determining causality. Can one say that this newspaper influenced government thinking when the government of the day denied being directly influenced in this way; when the issue of compensation for thalidomide children had already dragged on for a decade; and when simultaneous exasperation was expressed in Parliament and throughout the political parties? The important point is not the precise pattern of cause and effect but the different roles played by newspapers in this kind of situation. They can provide a forum for actors in the political process, for MPs, judges, lawyers and other professionals. They can reflect the views of the ordinary or the influential citizen, act as an index of public feeling and can also pursue a consistent editorial campaign, if necessary over a considerable time. However, this does not mean that newspapers are necessarily more radical or stringent than the broadcasting media in their criticisms of public policy, or that they are more neutral representatives of the mass public. Both owners and advertisers are a constraint on the political role of the press and although they enjoy a great deal of formal freedom, the independence of newspapers from government should not be overplayed. Political neutrality is not expected and sympathetic treatment cannot easily be commanded by governments, but there are, nevertheless, important avenues of control over the press. Information can be withheld from particularly critical papers or correspondents, and the formalized or legal restriction on the publication of confidential government information can be applied with varying degrees of strictness. Although this is less critical in social policy than it is in defence or foreign affairs, governments do control and use the press in these ways as well as respond to its strictures.

In what circumstances do politicians take the media's coverage of an issue seriously and in what situations do they feel able to ignore it? These are important questions because the mass media can, on occasions, make it hard for governments to act or refrain from acting on particular issues. Yet governments and individual Ministers can also absorb large amounts of criticism by the media without difficulty on other occasions and topics. Although our case studies illustrate the roles discussed above they do not explain this paradox, nor do they determine how far the media are major or simply incidental factors in policy-making. These questions await far more detailed study than either we or any other existing research has been able to devote to them. Having said this, the mass media clearly remain, alongside the pressure groups, the political parties and Parliament, an important bridge between the centre and the periphery of the political system. They have no authority (except in rare instances such as the creation of the Open University when the BBC was closely involved in government decision-making) and their influence can easily be exaggerated, but they are ubiquitous and often powerful partisans capable of determining the extent to which issues are discussed privately or publicly. They can all give life to an issue by raising it to the level of national debate; by starting, threatening to create, or maintaining an upsurge of public concern; and by highlighting the disastrous, pathological or crisis element of a situation.

IV THE POLITICAL PARTIES

The political influence of most citizens as individuals is negligible. We have suggested that their influence in aggregate as electors may be real on some policy issues as well as in deciding which party governs. In neither case is actual influence likely to compare favourably with the political myths of democracy. The accommodation between powerful governments and the ideology of democratic control over those governments casts the political parties in a central role. They are one of the main avenues through which divergent interests can be co-ordinated and expressed. They are the primary means of political organization and in our system of government they represent the major, continuing opportunity for giving individual citizens a degree of influence in political life. How effectively do they do this and with what consequences for party policy formation? Lindblom offers one answer to this question. He points out that since the 'parties must compete to win elections, party leadership will be motivated to seek out information on citizen preferences beyond the inadequate information revealed to them by the ballot itself. In doing so they in effect give power over specific policies to citizens despite the fact that ... citizens cannot express their specific policy preferences in their vote'.[32] His contention is that the parties actively seek to discover electors' viewpoints and to represent them. This is a similar view to that held by Beer in his discussion of consumer interests.

The idea of individual electors influencing policy by their vote is assigned by Lindblom to the corpus of political myths. But in another sense he sees the public's power over policy-making as far from mythical; it is a political reality that is guaranteed by the electoral and party system. Although they seek out and represent *majority* viewpoints, Lindblom casts the political parties as the focus of influence for private citizens. He introduces an interesting argument to support the view that parties do this effectively. He notes that the two parties in the USA are often criticized for their similarity on political issues and the lack of choice they present to the electorate. However, he considers that 'the complaint confirms our argument. If the two competing parties differed greatly in the platforms they offered to voters, it would mean that at least one of the parties had failed to approximate the preference of the majority and had blundered, therefore, into a set of policies that should have been rejected well before the campaign began'.[33] We would agree with Lindblom that, as individuals, electors are only likely to gain political influence through the parties; but are even the parties likely to give them a voice in policy-making? Lindblom's is an unsatisfactory picture of the parties and of policy-making for at least four reasons.

First, it discounts the existence of even two major divergences of political opinion; although Lindblom would acknowledge the existence of multiple interests he clearly assumes that they will not prevent the emergence of consensus about major issues. As we have seen, he arrives at the position that the parties appear to provide no real choice for the electorate precisely because a single set of preferences is held by a majority of people. The key problem, as he sees it, is how to discover this set of preferences. We do not accept this belief as axiomatic. Multiple interests are the core of political life. They are overridden in favour of consensus around major issues in some circumstances. Equally, they can be the basis for divergence over major issues in other situations. The real task is to discover

[32] Lindblom, C. E., *op. cit.*, p. 55.
[33] *Ibid.*, p. 57.

what major interests are represented in political life; which of them are competing or incompatible; under what conditions differences are minimized in favour of consensus; how compromise is achieved or not, and what role the parties play in all this. We cannot simply assume that because the parties do or do not diverge on key issues they are effectively representing underlying public preferences. They may converge or disagree for other reasons.

Second, the idea that political parties seek out and respond to electoral opinion can be misleading. Opinion polls and research on public opinion may provide a relatively unbiased, if simplified, view of opinions on particular issues, but the major channels of communication with the electorate are more partial in both senses of the word. Party leaders, MPs, party workers and the mass media bridge the gap between party policies and the public. They each respond selectively to the interests, opinions and sources of opinion which are most accessible or congenial to them. In particular they each communicate with each other, within the circle of the politically active, rather than with the mass electorate. Parties do not collate and weigh comprehensive and scientifically collected data about opinions. They perceive selectively through the biases and needs of the actors involved. They are not passive recipients of voters' preferences, but groupings of the politically active populace operating within systems of bureaucratic and power relationships.

Third, parties are involved in forming opinions as well as in responding to them. Lindblom is aware of this problem and quotes Beer's comment that British parties 'have in large part framed and elicited the very demands to which they then respond'.[34] However, having raised this complicating factor he does not allow it to modify his argument to any great extent. It would seem more reasonable to assume that, at elections at least, the parties have considerable control over the issues which they emphasize. The policy questions raised by each party will presumably reflect the distribution of interests and power within the party as well as the issues which are thought to be important to the particular groups of voters the party is consciously seeking to attract. A party's ability to control the issues with which it is publicly identified is far from perfect, but it should not be dismissed as negligible, nor should the range of issues presented to the public be exaggerated.

Lastly, the electorate's influence on the political parties is further reduced by *generalized* support for the parties. We have already noted in Chapter 3 that much party support does not depend on specific policy proposals but upon variables such as family voting traditions and the question of party legitimacy. A large body of stable support allows a party to concentrate on wooing the marginal voter with specific policies or issues but compromise is required to avoid offending the former whilst focusing upon the latter. This need to compromise may be more instrumental in producing a cautious attitude to issues than in producing a drive to ascertain and satisfy voters' preferences and could, therefore, be a source of the similarities between the parties. As we have noted, the political parties (especially in a two- or three-party system) are a major source of political compromise and compromise necessarily means that many preferences will be ignored or only partially satisfied.

The parties clearly do give individual voters some control over policy-making which they would otherwise lack. But the impact of party politics on political life in general, and policy-making in particular, is an empirical question which cannot be answered in general terms. It certainly cannot be claimed that the rhetoric of democratic control of government policies by the electorate is realized through the parties. They are central to democratic representation in Britain but the major determinants of individual policies remain variable and uncertain. Nevertheless, it is possible to consider how far the parties are geared to represent grassroots opinion. A natural starting point for doing this is to be found in the contrast between the Labour and Conservative parties in their historical origins, organizations, constitutions and philosophies.

The Labour Party arose as a means of representing an existing and articulate body of interests within Parliament. From the first it was designed to be responsive to its extra-parliamentary membership and has prided itself on the commitment to democracy within the party. The Conservative Party arose as a mass movement in response to the extension of the suffrage. It developed around, and in support of, established parliamentarians and power holders. It has a tradition of strong leadership and centralized authority. The structural features of the Labour Party are intended to facilitate internal democracy, whilst those of the Conservative Party are not. Does this mean that the parties differ accordingly in the way in which they respond to grassroots opinion? It seems reasonable to assume that the rank and file members of the Conservative Party have little direct control over party policy; but can the opposite be assumed of the Labour Party?

One immediate problem is to clarify what is meant by democracy within a mass political party. If one were talking about structural features designed to permit many voices to be heard on policy issues, the answer would hardly be in doubt, as we have suggested; but this is obviously only the beginning of an answer. The real question is how these structural features are brought into play in the policy process: the essential difficulty is how to evaluate policy-making and decide whether or not it can be described as democratic. Does this adjective imply the representation of individual or organized group interests, or both? Does it mean that the mass membership should have a residual power to overthrow the party leadership if the latter's policy proposals are found wanting; that those policies should be positively approved by the membership; or that the membership should actively develop the policy proposals from which the final selection is made? In structural terms we might be talking about a number of possibilities along a continuum from a highly centralized but not omnipotent policy-making elite to a very decentralized expression of opinions and interests. Similarly we might be thinking of policy processes in which the role of the mass membership varied from that of exercising a veto in extreme circumstance to that of initiating, shaping and choosing policy proposals. Let us examine, as an example, the problem of party structure in relation to Labour, which lays the strongest claim to being democratic in this respect.

As with the whole nation, there are many competing interest blocs in the Labour Party between which trade-offs take place. Their existence is a constraint on the party leader and the ideology of democratic control legitimates their claim to influence policy. On the other hand, individual constituencies are a weaker force within the party than the label 'democracy' suggests. Much power is possessed by the major trade unions, the party leadership and other key groups within the Parliamentary Labour Party. Can individual members of the party influence policy or are they squeezed out by an oligarchy of major interest groupings? They can certainly seek representation on and submit proposals or evidence to the party's policy groups (which in turn report to the National Executive Committee), always supposing they know about these groups. Whether this constitutes an influence on policy is hard to say. The policy groups themselves represent one method of issue regulation weighing as they do the claims of competing proposals and interests.

This process is continued once a group produces an agreed policy outline. The NEC, on which all the major power blocs in the party are represented, is by no means a rubber stamp with respect to the policy groups' proposals. If a suggestion originating from an individual party member or constituency party did reach this far and was not abandoned or transformed beyond recognition along the way, it might still fail to influence party policy. It could, theoretically at least, be discarded at annual conference and might not in practice be taken seriously by members of any future Labour government. The party members do have avenues by which they can initiate or contribute to policy proposals. But the extent to which they in fact become involved, and the regulation of issues which takes place within the party, make the grassroots look far less important in the policy process than these structural features imply.

When Richard Crossman, for example, introduced *National Superannuation* (the Labour Party's policy for earnings-related pensions) to the Annual Conference in 1957 he remarked upon the fact that many people felt that ordinary members of the Labour Party could not influence policy. He hailed the pension plan as an example of how defeatist this viewpoint was, because a 'group of rank and file trade unionists, members of the Woolwich Transport and General absolutely on their own produced the first plan for pensions which bears a remarkable resemblance to our final plan'.[35] This would indeed have been an important demonstration of grassroots influence, but the pattern of policy-making is rarely as clear cut. What Crossman did not mention was that a key academic who had worked with Richard Titmuss had been in contact with this group of trade unionists and that his role presumably had something to do with the similarity between the Woolwich proposal and the Labour plan which was inspired by Titmuss.[36] Crossman's account at the time was an understandable attempt to boost the morale of the party faithful, but it seems to have been poor history.

Nevertheless, one should not judge the party simply in terms of who initiates policy. Surely annual conferences provide a negative (veto) power, or an indirect source of influence, for the mass membership which is unique to the Labour Party and justifies its claim to be democratic? Although party members have the right to vote through their local constituency representatives on policy documents presented by the NEC, and to submit motions for debate, there are two structural limitations on the influence this right confers. One, which we have already mentioned, is the power of the large trade unions expressed in their block votes. The other arises from the sheer mechanics of conference organization. The range of interests and proposals are so compressed that only a few major topics receive much attention in the general debates. The conference is beset by its own problem of issue regulation and in any situation where time is short the person who controls the agenda has considerable power. It may reasonably be argued that no one interest grouping does so exclusively in the case of Labour Party conferences. Groups within the Parliamentary Labour Party, the leader of the party, the trade unions and the constituencies have degrees of influence which fluctuate over time and by subject. Nevertheless, the centralization of power in competing elites is reflected in the way the conference

[35] Report of the Labour Party Conference, 1957, p. 119.
[36] Crossman subsequently acknowledged the more complex history of *National Superannuation*; the importance of ideas developed at the top rather than at the bottom of the party, and Richard Titmuss' role in particular, in an article on the plan's origins. *Guardian*, 5 Apr., 1963.

is managed: the importance of conference and grassroots opinion can easily be exaggerated.

Yet even if the annual conference is an elaborate façade in policy-making terms, this does not mean that it is totally irrelevant. It can still play an important indirect role in the policy process. Defeat in conference will always be damaging for the parliamentary leadership of the Labour Party as long as the party retains an internal democratic structure as its ideal. The management of conferences has an indirect influence on policy-making within both parties, but it is more important for Labour than for the Conservatives because, for the former, the possibility of a revolt in conference is far more real.

Labour leaders have certainly faced intense conflict within the party over policy issues, especially during the long periods out of office. Is this a sign of democracy at work? Does it indicate a difference between the parties? The difficulty in answering arises precisely because conflicts of this kind are far more overt in the Labour Party. Different interest groupings are more clearly and formally represented in the organization of the party so that it is easier to see when power blocs set limits on the parliamentary leadership, or are themselves overridden. As tends to happen in parties founded to seek social change, divergences of interest and opinion have traditionally been expressed more openly and trenchantly in the Labour than in the Conservative Party. This gives the impression that there is more open debate about policy in the former than in the latter, but even if this is the case one reservation must be entered. The allegiance to the idea of internal democracy has been modified to accord with some of the demands of political office. Regardless of whether or not the policy choices made in opposition derive from a form of democratic decision-making, most Labour governments have not been unduly fettered when in office by democratic control within the party.

McKenzie offers convincing arguments for this viewpoint. His thesis, leaving aside his concern with the constitutional ramifications of internal party democracy, is that the parties are essentially similar in terms of the location of power and decision-making.[37] He dismisses the different structural features as largely irrelevant. When in office, and this is the strongest part of his case, the Parliamentary Labour Party and its leaders enjoy an autonomy from the mass party which parallels the situation in the Conservative Party. McKenzie acknowledges that party leaders are not supremely powerful. His point is that while they make concessions and take account of the views of their followers, they have great authority in both parties

[37] McKenzie, R. T., *British Political Parties*, Heinemann, 1955.

and it is the parliamentary rather than the mass following which extracts concessions. He argues that the mass party is not an effective control over the party leadership. For the most part it serves the leadership loyally in both the major parties.

Questions about the extent of democratic control over social policy within the Labour Party are not easily answered at present. There is insufficient contemporary evidence to draw firm conclusions. Rose's comment on McKenzie's work, that he 'does a good job in stating where power does not lie; it does *not* rest exclusively with the one leader of the Conservative Party, nor does it rest with the mass membership of the Labour Party', cogently summarizes the state of the evidence.[38] The two main parties are complex political organizations and social policy-making is not a simple autocratic or democratic process in either of them.

Nevertheless, McKenzie's emphasis upon the importance of centralized power in both parties is helpful. If we accept it, it tells us quite a lot about the kinds of people who are making decisions on party policy. The party hierarchies reflect the stratification system of the society as a whole. To a noticeable extent in both parties MPs tend to be from a higher socio–economic background than constituency workers and are in turn inferior, in this sense, to their Cabinet (or Shadow Cabinet) colleagues.[39] The extent of control or influence on the part of the mass party is important, therefore, because the leadership is not characteristic of the party as a whole. The mass parties represent a wider range of socio–economic groupings, exhibit a wider dispersion of interests and opinions, and include more extremes of opinion than do the party elites. The compression of opinion as one moves up the party hierarchies is not surprising. As we have suggested, the political parties are as much a part of the demand regulation process as are central government departments; they channel demands but they also filter them. What are important are the criteria used in this filtering, who the key gatekeepers are, and what interests are represented in the decision-making.

However centralized policy-making becomes in the modern mass parties, it is not simply the preserve of the leader and a few of his friends. Party hierarchies are important but they are not the whole story. They are backed by central research and policy staff and by working groups which provide room for a wider range of voices in the policy process than might otherwise be the case. The Labour Party, for example, launched a set of policy proposals in the late fifties which became the basis for the platform on which the 1964 General Election was fought. The search for new policies was a

[38] Rose, R., *Policy-Making in Britain*, Macmillan. 1969, p. 154.
[39] For example, see Beer, S.. *Modern British Politics, op. cit.*, pp. 382–3; and Guttsman, W. L., *The British Political Elite*, MacGibbon and Kee, 1965.

response to electoral defeat in 1955, to the bitter 'revisionist–traditionalist' struggles within the party and to the need to provide specific examples of an electorally attractive revisionist stance. The existence of a headquarters and research staff provided a structure around which the policy planning could be co-ordinated. The groups which produced detailed proposals were drawn from the academic world, the leadership and back benches of the Parliamentary Labour Party and the trade unions. The party central staff and such groupings as the Fabian Society can be important in such planning activities: the former as a focus for and co-ordinator of planning and the latter as a source of ideas and as a continuing forum for those interested in developing policy initiatives. The general membership of the party is represented in this planning through several different channels therefore, but the party as a whole is only required to approve the policies presented to them via the annual conference and the election itself. The end result of this kind of planning is partly influenced, but not determined, by expectations of what would prove popular to the rank and file membership.

The influence of the mass membership of both parties is fundamentally an indirect one and as such it fluctuates considerably over time and from issue to issue. Party workers and the party faithful are a continuing but often subdued pressure on decision-makers within the party. The opportunity for direct involvement in policy-making and for the public expression of dissent is stronger in the Labour Party; but there is little systematic evidence of the effect of the rank and file on contemporary Labour social policy. It is a subject worthy of study. In the meantime one is left with the supposition that the active constituency members of both parties are more important in distinguishing particularly unpopular or popular proposals rather than acting as initiators of ideas. Annual conferences may highlight issues, such as pensions, which party leaders would be unwise to ignore altogether, but few policy innovations come from the floor at conferences. The precise balance of interests affecting social policy decisions in the parties is uncertain; the roles of the 'producer' groupings are as unresearched as are those of the academics, the party policy groups and the policy oriented pressure groups. Contemporary social policy formation within the parties is a difficult and comparatively neglected area of study.

V DEMAND INITIATION AND REGULATION BY PARTISANS

In this chapter we have been looking at the initiation and regulation of demands[40] which takes place outside the authorities. It is an important part of the policy process and two aspects of it need to be clarified. The first is how partisans relate to each other and to the authorities; the second concerns the criteria on which they regulate demands. These will be discussed in turn.

Crick recently wrote that his 'decade [40 plus] did not dream one could do anything but through the parties'.[41] He was not suggesting that partisan groups could not exist outside the parties, but that the latter were the brokers of political influence and the focal point for partisan activity. We have suggested that each type of partisan, including the parties, can initiate demands on government, but we have not presented the party system as the framework around which all partisan activity is structured. Both pressure groups and the mass media can and do by-pass the party system. Pressure groups are a major source of demands and they channel many of these directly to government departments or express them in a more generalized way through protest, demonstration and parliamentary pressure exerted through individual MPs. The mass media can in turn activate a demand or provide a forum for others to do so. They can be used to sustain or enliven an existing campaign or convert otherwise isolated events into wider issues[42] and in doing so they may or may not direct these demands at the parties as such. Even an attack on government may be directed quite specifically at a particular Minister or department rather than at the governing party and its record in office.

Partisan activity is not exclusively orchestrated by the political parties (any more than it is by Parliament). There are many parallel channels through which demands can be made on government. Nevertheless, the parties do remain important foci for much partisan pressure. They collect, sift and condense many partisan demands. The possibility that they might form a government attracts demands to the party in opposition. Similarly the need to win or retain power stimulates a search for policy ideas. On occasions the parties, pressure groups and the media act in complementary ways, just as they are independent and alternative routes for making policy demands in other instances.

All partisans are involved in regulating demands as well as in making them and they do this in varying ways. The nature of the problem is particularly acute for the parties because, as potential governments, they must try to cope with the task of organizing

[40] The term demand rather than issue is used here to emphasize the fact that we are discussing policy problems or proposals that are highlighted by groups outside government and presented as demands for government action.

[41] Crick, B., 'Neo-Brutal', *New Society*, 30 Nov., 1972, pp. 524–5.

[42] See the Clean Air case study.

problems in terms of their inter-relatedness, their resource implications and the priority each should receive in the party programme.[43] Nevertheless, all partisans must choose what demands to advance and how to do so. The important point to emphasize is that demand regulation involves these two different kinds of decisions. Partisans have to select the issues on which they will act and therefore reject others, but they also have to make decisions about presentation. More specifically, consciously or otherwise, they make judgements about whether a particular problem should be articulated without offering a solution, or whether it has to be tied to a specific proposal for its resolution. Equally, they define the problem in a particular way and decide whether or not to associate it with related or broader issues which might enhance its impact. The whole question of how problems become associated with certain solutions or with other problems will be discussed in Chapter 15, but such processes of combination and separation are illustrated frequently in the case studies. Demand or issue regulation is not just about rejecting some problems as unimportant or unmanageable; it is about their definition and packaging as well. All partisans, in addition to the authorities, play a part in this process.

The picture we have developed in this chapter is *one of plurality in the initiation of issues, in the channels of communication, and in the criteria employed to regulate demands.* This is not to say that all the issues which might arise in our society can be introduced into political life and gain a measure of support if presented in an appropriate way. The point we are making is not that the process of demand regulation is fair to all interests, but that it is not exclusively dominated by either government or by the party system. The administrative plurality within the authorities which we have already noted seems to be reflected in the range of institutions outside government through which many demands are launched and regulated. We must now bring the discussion together by looking at the most obvious single forum in which partisans without authority and authorities (acting both as authorities and as partisans) meet, namely Parliament. In doing so we must also mention another partisan hitherto undiscussed: that is the individual MP.

---

[43] The extent of this problem was illustrated by the Labour Party's decision in 1973 not to establish any more policy study groups because the policy-making processes were being overwhelmed by the data and recommendations emerging from the existing fifty or so groups. See for example, the *Guardian*, 20 June, 1973.

CHAPTER SEVEN

Parliament and Policy

Parliament is a forum; a market place where ideas can be expressed close to the centre of authority and where there are legal and traditional safeguards which encourage the free exchange of opinions. Is it any more than this? Earlier we noted that Griffith took the view that it is government and not Parliament which has 'sovereignty' in *making* policy. We agreed with his conclusion. Nevertheless, this still leaves several possible roles for Parliament which must be considered in looking at policy development. First, as a legislative chamber it may play an authoritative role. Second, MPs together may exercise a degree of *control* over government which has been won for Parliament over the years and which is deployed in its name. Third, Parliament may endow its individual Members with a degree of *influence* as partisans which they would not otherwise possess. Does it, however, share the authority to make policy which rests so predominantly with government?

If we return to the liberal view of the constitution we find that it embraces a philosophy which leads to a particular conception of how policy is made. From the standpoint of a distinctive and individualistic view of democratic representation Parliament, and especially the House of Commons, is cast as the final arbiter of policy issues.[1] This is a view that we have largely discounted; but let us just note what it is that we are relegating to the wings. After all, the liberal view still survives. It serves as the base line from which the more picturesque criticisms of the decline of Parliament (and many proposals for parliamentary reform) have begun.[2] In this view the Executive is responsible primarily to Parliament and thereby to the electorate.[3]

[1] For modern summaries of this current of thought and its effect on British government, see Birch, A. H., *op. cit.*, part II, and Beer, S., *Modern British Politics, op. cit.*, ch. 2.

[2] The most trenchant account of the decline in Parliament's power is Keeton, G. W., *The Passing of Parliament*, Benn, 1954.

[3] This view is widely discussed in the literature of British government, but see Butt, R., *The Power of Parliament*, Constable, 1967; and Birch A. H., *op. cit.*, part IV.

Parliament, even if it does not initiate policy, makes the final decisions. From this viewpoint Parliament is organized to control public expenditures, to formulate and control policy and to legislate.[4] These functions overlap. In principle, they confer a considerable power on Parliament to determine policy. For example, this account suggests that MPs can modify or reject government policies requiring legislation, including the levying of taxes. What we have argued is that the strength of the government and of party discipline prevent the Commons from exercising most of these nominal powers. One should not make the mistake of seeing MPs and Parliament as politically impotent. Butt, for instance, has attempted to show that back-benchers in the governing party have quite a powerful and direct impact on policy.[5] Nevertheless, such direct influence is spasmodic and difficult to disentangle from other influences, even when a major 'rebellion' is staged.

These forms of influence do not amount to an authoritative role for Parliament as a whole. There are, admittedly, narrow areas of legislative independence, for example Private Members' Bills and free votes, in which Parliament could be said to act authoritatively in its own right. Yet even these opportunities largely depend on the government's tacit or actual co-operation. Because we are concerned with policy-making we must concentrate on the influence and control Parliament exerts over the government, rather than search for the occasions when it acts in a purely authoritative capacity.

Consequently, in examining how parliamentary forces can impinge on policy we will concentrate on a few issues; namely, the roles of the Opposition, individual MPs and parliamentary committees. Together they provide a framework of ideas about how Parliament is involved in the policy process.

I PARTY INTERACTION AND THE ROLE OF THE OPPOSITION

The opposition party is one possible source of influence on government. It can try to press a government into accepting ideas which it favours. This can be done both on the floor of the House through

---

[4] This is Campion's formulation. See the *Third Report of the Select Committee on Procedure*, H. C., 189–1, 1946, p. xxiii. For a more analytical appraisal of the legislative process and Parliament's role in it – particularly delegated legislation, the growth of which has accompanied the increase in government intervention in economic and social life – see Walkland, S. A., *The Legislative Process*, Allen & Unwin, 1968.

[5] Butt, R., *The Power of Parliament, op. cit.*, chs 6–10.

individual speeches, questions to ministers, Supply Day and other debates where the topic is determined by the Opposition and through a similar range of procedures in the House of Lords. Or it can be done more privately. The Opposition can also try to influence policies which the government itself initiates. The ways of doing this are similar to those used when urging an issue on government. Much parliamentary time is consumed by opposition attempts to clarify government intentions, to expose defects or inconsistencies and thereby modify their decisions. Many of the details of legislation and the consequences of a policy are not regarded as 'party political' or are not really clear to the policy-makers themselves, or both. Oppositions can and do exercise influence on government legislation for these reasons, although the influence may be hidden in a government's amendment to its own policy. However, when a policy requiring legislation engenders party conflict the Opposition can act more directly. It can, and frequently does, pose as a mirror of public outrage and censure; but it can also set about wrecking the government's legislative timetable. These, rather than the authority to approve legislation, are the sanctions that it uses within Parliament.

Although party discipline may appear to have reduced the power of MPs to influence policy, parliamentary debate about policy is also sharpened by the interplay of party politics. Unfortunately, it is difficult to determine when governments are substantially and directly influenced by criticism from the Opposition. The problem can be illustrated quite simply. The 1959 New Towns Act, among other provisions, created a New Towns Commission to take over and manage the assets of completed New Towns (mainly housing, but also commercial and industrial property). When they launched the New Town programme in 1947 the Labour government intended, or at least suggested, that these assets should be transferred to the appropriate local authority once the towns were completed. The 1959 Conservative measure reversed this earlier 'decision'. The government was subjected to a formidable attack and the Labour Opposition used all its resources to launch and sustain it.

How does one gauge the effect of this onslaught on the government? Labour MPs feared that the Conservatives would sell a large amount of New Town property to individuals and property companies. They also believed that there would be no effective local representatives of the national commission in the individual towns. In the event promises were obtained from the Minister that neither of these things would happen. It is impossible to state categorically that the Opposition modified the government's intentions, but it is likely. In taking up this cause the Opposition had certainly presented its case far more powerfully than individual MPs could have done and it imposed a considerable loss of parliamentary time on the government. But this example also illustrates another effect of party politics in Parliament, namely that they influence opposition as well as government policies.

The conflict between parties affects the issues to which each becomes committed as well as the degree of that commitment. The Labour Opposition categorically stated that, once in office, it would reverse the Conservative decision. In fact the less dramatic procedure of commissioning a review of this aspect of New Town policy was adopted by the Wilson government.[6] Without the political excitement that developed around the 1958 Bill, however, the Labour Party might have ignored this problem altogether when it finally came to office. These indirect effects of party competition on both government and opposition policy-making are less easily measured but are, perhaps, more characteristic of parliamentary politics than the direct effects.

Government back-benchers may sometimes influence policy unobtrusively or by the threat of revolt, but opposition MPs can normally only hope to influence current policy through their party's parliamentary role as the Opposition. What then is the significance of the Opposition in policy-making? The above example suggests a number of possibilities. Its most visible purpose is to maintain a critical attitude towards the government among 'informed opinion', the mass media and the public at large. It is in this sense that Parliament is the forum in which a constant competition for electoral support takes place *between* elections. Party interaction ensures regular comparisons between the government's performance, its election pledges and alternative approaches to issues advocated by the Opposition. Opposition criticism – and criticism is institutionalized in the concept of an opposition – keeps the threat of electoral censure before the government.

This critical function can force a government to anticipate those aspects of its policies that are most vulnerable to attack. The extent to which this influences policy varies and depends in part upon the government's vulnerability on other fronts. Governments anticipate opposition criticism on most policy issues and they can tolerate a large amount of it providing they have a secure majority and their electoral support is reasonable for the phase of the electoral cycle in which they find themselves. But a government that is floundering or approaching an election tends to be more nervous about the reception a policy might receive from the Opposition. Although the most characteristic impact of opposition criticism may be on the way

[6] Cullingworth, J. B. and Karn, V. A., *The Ownership and Management of Housing in the New Towns: Report submitted to the Minister of Housing and Local Government*, HMSO, 1968.

policies are presented and defended, the existence of an alert opposition does temper policy-making.

Does the Opposition influence policy more directly? Although the majority of changes in an announced policy or a Bill are made by the responsible minister, we have argued that some of them originate in opposition criticism. Governments do not successfully anticipate all the features of their policies which will cost them popularity in the country, harsh criticism in the press, or a hard and time-consuming struggle in Parliament. The interaction of opposition and mass media criticism especially does result in policy modifications. These may emerge as amendments to a Bill in committee stage but they often take the form of an assurance from a minister on how a particular measure, power or clause will be interpreted and used. Such modification may also occur *after* the promulgation of a controversial measure, when its administrative consequences reinforce opposition criticism and force a retreat.[7]

The distinction between criticism and the initiation of a change of direction may be slight. Criticism of the effect of the 1957 Rent Act on the housing situation led, in 1963, to the establishment of the Milner-Holland inquiry into London housing.[8] This in turn became the basis for some of the Labour government's policies in the housing field. The flow of policy is continuous. A change of government does not necessarily mean a neat break in the process.

This brings us back to the point at which we began these comments about the role of the Opposition; namely that party policies arise, in some measure, from party interaction. In order to establish a distinctive image the Opposition is forced to exploit policy areas neglected by the government, or to forge a different approach to some of the issues it confronts. For example, the Labour Party's move towards a graduated pension system in the mid-fifties spurred the Conservative government into announcing its own version of this proposal before the 1959 Election.[9]

Although the overthrow of government by Parliament is scarcely an effective means of controlling policy and although parliamentary

---

[7] One of the most bitterly fought social policy issues with this kind of result was the transformation of unemployment assistance in 1934. More recently the very controversial 1957 Rent Act was amended after implementation and opposition criticism played some part in this. See Millett, J. D. *The Unemployment Assistance Board*, Allen & Unwin, 1940, ch. 2; Butt, R., *op. cit.*, pp. 215–20; and also Barnett, M. J., *The Politics of Legislation: the Rent Act of 1957*, Weidenfeld & Nicolson, 1969.

[8] *Report of the Committee on Housing in Greater London*, Cmnd. 2605, 1965.

[9] A similar example, namely the renewed interest in regional and economic planning in the early sixties, is discussed in Butt, R., *op. cit.*, pp. 300–1.

criticism rarely results in ministerial resignations,[10] Parliament can have a powerful impact on policy-making. The role of the Opposition is central to this. It acquires some direct influence over government policy by criticism and attack, but it also shapes the environment in which the government operates. This indirect influence on policy is pervasive, but difficult to predict or to control. The Opposition can have an extensive impact on policy, though not necessarily in a way that it intends or anticipates.[11]

II MEMBERS OF PARLIAMENT AND THEIR IMPACT ON POLICY

Parliament provides MPs with a unique vantage point from which to criticize and urge proposals on government, but their impact is often an indirect and limited one. Proof of this, it is widely suggested, may be found in the tendency for pressure groups (especially interest groups) to direct their attention to Whitehall rather than Westminister. Nevertheless, where well established groups are absent, or when contacts with government departments have to be supplemented or replaced by open propaganda, Parliament is an important avenue for putting pressure on the Executive. Do MPs succeed in initiating successful policy proposals or are they confined to a more reactive role by the sheer weight of government-sponsored business?

The backbench MPs on the government side have a better opportunity to influence current policy than do their counterparts on the opposition benches: but much of their impact relates to modifications sought in government-sponsored policies. Their role is similar to that of the Opposition in this respect, although they may have a greater effect by virtue of the government's dependence on their support. Butt argues that government back benchers tend to counteract the pragmatism of ministers by emphasizing the ideals and traditional goals of the party, or other canons of political virtue.[12] This is a function which is partly shared with party conferences. As Butt points out, the influence of the government's supporters comes not merely from the need to maintain morale and loyalty, but also through the way in which the British Parliament and the Executive

[10] See, for example, Birch, A. H., *op. cit.*, p. 75 and pp. 141–8; and Finer, S. E., 'The Individual Responsibility of Ministers', in Benewick, R. and Dowse, R. (eds), *op. cit.*
[11] See Morrison, H., *op. cit.*, chs 6–8.
[12] Consistent with this is his hypothesis that government backbench opinion is most influential when the Cabinet is pursuing middle-of-the-road policies. Butt, R., *op. cit.*, p. 211.

relate to each other. Ministers have strong roots in different sections of the parliamentary party and through them the government can be urged to take account of the varying shades of backbench opinion. Butt has made a detailed attempt to produce a positive picture of backbench influence. He notes a number of pertinent examples from the post-war period. Several of these, such as the 1957 Rent Act and the abolition of Resale Price Maintenance, are instances of back-benchers trying to restrain the government.[13] On the other hand different examples such as the policies towards the nationalized industries, clean air legislation and commercial television show government back benchers taking the initiative in pressing for particular types of action.[14] Fenner Brockway's persistence is introducing race relations measures as Private Members' Bills is relevant for a different reason. As a Labour MP he had little impact on the Conservative government of the day, despite the backing of an all-party group of MPs concerned with race relations. However he did induce his own party to commit themselves whilst in opposition to introduce such a measure once in power.[15] The same mechanisms are at work in the case of the thalidomide dispute, although the outcome is still uncertain at the time of writing. Some government back benchers are exerting informal pressure within their own party, matched by all-party support from MPs. The long-term impact could affect not only the decisions made by the Distillers Board of Directors, but also by the government and the Opposition on the whole question of financial support for the disabled.

Private Members' Bills on controversial, non-party issues such as abortion, homosexuality and divorce law reform became a feature of the Wilson government.[16] It has been echoed in the Heath administration by Arthur Morris' successful Chronically Sick and Disabled Persons Bill. These Bills, as we noted earlier, are an area of legislative independence for Parliament, although they need government tolerance over parliamentary time. However, their use as a lever on the MPs' own party is also a feature of parliamentary affairs worth noting. Parliament is not simply a debating chamber in which to coax, threaten or upbraid the party opposite; it is an arena in which MPs seek to influence policy-making and priorities within their *own* party, be it in power or not.

The picture of parliamentary influence on policy-making developed

[13] Butt, R., *op. cit.*, pp. 216–20; 220–26; 235–40 and 260–70 respectively. On the 1957 Rent Act also see Barnett, M. J., *op. cit.*

[14] *Ibid.*, pp. 207–11. For a discussion of the clean air legislation see the clean air case study.

[15] On the race relations legislation see Rose, E. J. B., *Colour and Citizenship*, Oxford University Press, 1969, parts I and IV.

[16] For further discussion of the developments see Richards, P. G., *Parliament and Conscience*, Allen & Unwin, 1970.

so far contains four major elements. First, we dismissed the possibility of Parliament as an authority and decided to concentrate upon its ability to control and influence government policy. The interplay of party politics was then depicted as a direct influence on some government policy, but also as an indirect force shaping policy-making within the parties. A third strand, the role of MPs in initiating policy, has just been noted. We have also argued that Parliament provides the means by which individual MPs can seek to influence policy-making within government or in their own party.[17]

The relative lack of organization among social service users and the numerous opportunities for presenting the extensive involvement of government in social welfare as incomplete or ineffective give MPs ample opportunity to advocate improved social policies. Most importantly, perhaps, some areas of social policy are not yet technically sophisticated. Because of its effect upon individual well-being a social policy issue can be taken up by a non-specialist MP more readily than, say, economic or foreign affairs. This is not to say that Parliament is the source of most social policy. At best it is one forum among others in which a government can be urged or goaded; but our studies show that it does have influence on some issues and perhaps more frequently in social policy than in other areas of policy.

III PARLIAMENTARY COMMITTEES AND POLICY

We have outlined the principal ways in which Parliament acts as a means of raising and discussing policy issues, and although this does not amount to a formal and predictable system of control over policy it clearly does influence the decisions taken in each of the political parties. So far we have not mentioned the important stream of proposals aimed at strengthening Parliament's understanding of, and its impact on, governmental activities.[18] It is a reasonable omission. Like so many other topics that could have been discussed in these chapters we have excluded it because it does not bear very directly on the period of social policy formation covered by our case studies. Nevertheless, we must mention one central theme in the debate about parliamentary reform, namely parliamentary committees.

[17] For a fuller discussion of the Backbencher see the following additional sources: Richards, P. G., *Honourable Members*, Faber, 1964; Bromhead, P. A., *Private Members' Bills in the British Parliament*, Routledge & Kegan Paul, 1956; Leonard, R. L. 'Back-bench Bills', *New Society*, 15 Jan., 1970.

[18] For a valuable summary of many of these proposals see Hansard Society, *Parliamentary Reform: 1933–60*, Cassell, 1961.

Two kinds of committee in particular could be expected to play a continuing role in the development of social policy. First, there are those exercising surveillance over public expenditure and, second, specialist committees which examine particular areas of the work of the Executive. The latter do not appear in our cases at all, principally because there has not been a specialist committee for the whole of the social service field and because the one committee which directly covers part of our field of study, the Select Committee on Education and Science, was not created until 1968 and therefore could not figure in the policy discussion which led to the creation of the Open University. Similarly, although a Select Committee on Race Relations and Immigration was created at the same time, none of our cases involve this area of social policy.

The control of public expenditure, however, is different since it impinges directly upon the whole range of public policy. The two committees concerned with the parliamentary scrutiny of public expenditure during the period of our case studies were the Public Accounts and the Estimates Committees. Their strengths and weaknesses as a method of controlling public expenditure have been discussed elsewhere,[19] but it is worth noting their role in policy-making. The Public Accounts Committee (PAC) can hardly be said to have a direct or immediate impact on policy decisions within spending departments. It is absorbed in the financial aspects of established policy, completing the process of reviewing the probity of incurred expenditures. The work of the Comptroller and Auditor General and of the PAC in examining past expenditures enforces standards of accountability that influence the way in which public moneys are used, and important policy questions, such as the extent and nature of the independence enjoyed by universities, do arise. Nevertheless, the effect on decision-making within spending departments is not crucial for our purpose.

The Estimates Committee was in a rather different position. Before it was superseded by the Expenditure Committee in 1971 it probed selected areas of government activity. It was specifically debarred from encroaching on Ministers' responsibility for substantive policies and, in this sense, it had no right to influence policy directly. Its brief was to examine the administration of policy and the financial implications of how this was conducted; but policy and implementation are not easily separated. One example can be given which relates to

[19] For example, in Hill, A. and Whichelow, A., *What's Wrong with Parliament?*, Penguin, 1964; Wheare, K. C., *Government by Committee*, Oxford University Press, 1955; Tribe, Sir Frank, 'Parliamentary Control of Public Expenditure', *Public Administration*, Winter, 1954; Hanson, A. H. and Wiseman, H. V., 'The Use of Committees in the House of Commons', *Public Law*, Autumn, 1959; and Butt, R., *op. cit.*, ch. 13.

the National Assistance Board (NAB) case study. In 1964–5 the Estimates Committee examined the administration of the Ministry of Pensions and National Insurance (MPNI). In the course of its study the sub-committee (the Estimates Committee worked through small sub-committees) expressed interest in the possibility of a merger between the NAB and the MPNI. This was advocated on the grounds of economy, but would have had the effect, *inter alia*, of reducing the marked difference between insurance and assistance benefits. It was one element in the reform and amalgamation of 1966 which is discussed in detail in the case study. Was the Estimates Committee inquiry influential in this area of policy? The most realistic answer is that it probably was not. The proposition of a merger did not receive much support from the civil service witnesses and the substantial differences in the way the two organizations operated was cited in defence of the belief that a merger would not bring substantial economies.[20] As the reports of the committee exchanges indicated, any decision to merge the two would have had to be advocated by a Minister seeking ends other than that of administrative tidiness. The changes of 1966 did in fact arise from quite a different quarter. The Estimates Committee episode was incidental to the main story in this instance.

To balance this negative example, it is worth noting the direct and indirect ways in which one of the committee's earlier investigations may have affected the development of policy within the child care services. During 1950 and 1951 the committee examined the relative merits of caring for children within institutional and non-institutional settings.[21] Having studied the evidence it came down strongly in favour of an expansion of boarding-out, as opposed to care within children's homes (mainly on grounds of cost but not exclusively so). This conclusion accorded with the view that had been gaining ground in the Home Office and its child care inspectorate. The committee's report may have directly contributed to the ascendency of this view during the succeeding years. What is indisputable is that the committee's views were used as a means of gaining support for the development of foster care in the early 1950s. The committee had an indirect impact on policy in that it stamped an important hallmark of approval on this change of direction and attitude.

These are only two instances of the kind of situation in which the committee can influence the operation of the social services. Nevertheless, perhaps the more important and certainly the more general impact of these and other parliamentary committees is

---

[20] *Fourth Report of the Estimates Committee, 1964–5*, Minutes of Evidence and Proceedings in sub-committee F; especially para. 8.

[21] *Sixth Report of the Select Committee on Estimates, 1951–2* (sub-committee D), H.C. 235, 1952.

through the information MPs acquire from them about the way in which government departments implement policy. Individual MPs are often ill-informed about the work of government departments as well as about the details of policy discussions. The Opposition party can also be out of touch with many of the realities of governing – the critical constraints within which decisions have to be made and enacted.[22] One argument for the extension of specialist committees is that it would help close this information gap between government and Parliament. An increased flow of information could assist MPs and non-governing parties in the task of devising alternative strategies and programmes to those being pursued by the government. An incidental, but worthwhile advantage would be the increased flow of information to the wider public, as can be seen from the reports of the Select Committees on the Nationalized Industries and on Agriculture, for example. Before the Estimates Committee split into functional sub-committees in 1965 there had been no regular supply of detailed information of this kind on the whole area of social policy.

Unfortunately, at least from an academic point of view, the Labour government's experimental extension of specialist committees ran quickly into problems over MPs' involvement in policy issues. The Select Committee on Agriculture, in particular, posed the question of whether the government would tolerate MPs investigating the implications for food prices of entry into the EEC.[23] The answer seems clear enough; neither of the major political parties welcomes the idea of MPs muddying the waters of contentious policy debates taking place in departments and in the Cabinet. Governments will almost certainly continue to restrict the scope of the specialist committees and preserve their own freedom to formulate policies in relative isolation. This negative conclusion is not necessarily an argument for more specialist committees, because not all MPs would see their demise as a loss. For instance, some have argued against the extension of specialist committees on the grounds that they could limit the critical functions of Parliament as a whole.[24] Leaving aside the future role of these committees, they do not at present provide a satisfactory forum for parliamentary discussion of the administration and development of social services. In time, this assertion may need to be modified in the light of the way that the Expenditure Committee (replacing the

[22] See Hill, A. and Whichelow, A., in Stankiewicz, W. J., *Crisis in British Government*, Collier-Macmillan, 1967, pp. 86–7; and Barker, A. and Rush, M., *The Member of Parliament and his Information*, Allen & Unwin, 1970.

[23] For a short but useful discussion of the Labour government's experiments with specialist committees, see Brown, R. G. S., *The Administrative Process in Britain*, Methuen, 1970, pp. 104–12.

[24] See Michael Foot's comments, *H. C. Deb.*, vol. 718, cols 208–10, quoted in Butt, R., *op. cit.*, pp. 350–1.

Estimates Committee) fits into the new and developing system of long-term planning of public expenditure.

IV THE POLICY PROCESS IN CENTRAL GOVERNMENT: A SUMMARY

In the last few chapters we have offered a broad framework of ideas about how the policy process works at central government level. Before we introduce a series of case studies against which these views can be examined, we must do two things: the first is to summarize the main points of the argument; the second, which we do in the next chapter, is to place this within the wider context of more general questions about the distribution of power in British society.

The model employed in these chapters emphasizes two basic features of policy-making; that is, the initiation and regulation of policy demands. In common with all models, however, it takes into account only a limited set of interrelated variables and consequently there is some over-simplification and distortion. Fortunately these distortions are not difficult to detect and some of them are discussed below.

To talk of *a policy process* is in many ways misleading. There are institutions geared mainly to policy-making, such as the Cabinet system, the planning groups in government departments and many of the promotional groups; but to a large extent policies are but one product of the complexity of political life. Political inter-actions are fostered by many motives other than devising, support-ing or blocking policies and political life is itself but an abstraction from the rest of social living. Furthermore, policy-making is not always as consciously perceived as we may have implied. It is not a simple or smooth progression of activities which together form a process. A second problem which arises from the need to simplify is that in isolating a few variables and institutions other important ones have been excluded. The whole system of local government has hardly been mentioned. Central government policy is pro-foundly affected by the existence of local, democratically elected (and in many ways autonomous) local authorities and also by the vast network of appointed lay bodies with planning, managerial and advisory functions. These omissions are defended, although not made less significant, by reference to the major purpose of these chapters which is to provide a framework within which the student of social policy can begin to discuss central government policy-making and our case studies in particular. The core of this framework con-tains several important elements.

The view of policy-making that has been presented is in one

sense a very centralized one. Government has been depicted as the key authority. Parliament has been characterized as a much less powerful body exercising some control and sometimes considerable influence over government, but making few authoritative decisions of its own.[25] Moreover, we have asserted that much policy-making begins in government departments and that the balance of expertise, information and power favours them on many issues. Against this we have set a distinctly non-centralized, or pluralist picture. It will have to be modified later, but it is important to draw the strands of the argument together at this point. The policy process can be regarded as pluralist in two senses. First, it exhibits diversity in a visible, structural sense; many different institutions are involved. Second, and more important, the policy process can be characterized as plural in practice. The structural diversity is reflected in the range of values, interests and viewpoints that can be detected in much policy-making. We obviously do not claim to have demonstrated the validity of all that we have said; our argument so far has proceeded mainly by assertion. Consequently, the summary of our case which follows must be regarded as a series of propositions.

1. We have suggested that the policy process is not contained within a single centrally co-ordinated system. It embraces a number of sub-systems such as Parliament, pressure groups, the political parties and other bodies like research institutions. They all act with varying degrees of autonomy. They are not wholly subordinate to nor disciplined by a single authority, nor do they form a simple hierarchy. Consequently, in structural terms, there is no monolithic apparatus for policy-making. We have further suggested that whilst there is certainly an important nucleus – government – to which these sub-systems all relate, this is itself characterized by structural differentiation. Government exhibits an administrative pluralism which strengthens the polycentric nature of the policy process.

2. These structural features are most easily discerned by looking at how demands are initiated. A wide range of institutions, including some individual citizens, can and do bring policy proposals to life. Among them is the government system itself. Government, we have argued, is not inert or merely reactive.

Once brought to life, policy demands can be carried forward by an equally varied set of actors and many proposals are developed in some detail even before they reach key decision-makers. Equally, we have noted the pressure that can be brought to bear on policy-makers by major interest groups or by groups which successfully enlist support through the mass media and within the parties. Some of

---

[25] A fuller list of authorities would include not only local government but the judiciary as well.

the forces involved can be enormously, and often unexpectedly, powerful. It is not just the entrenched pressure groups but also the reality, or fear, of public outrage (for example, at a steeply rising cost of living) which may induce governments to act quickly in ways they had not intended. By contrast we have noted the comparative weakness of the 'consumer' interest in much of social policy.

3. Whatever the origin of a policy proposal, we have argued that it must survive the processes of demand regulation if it is to become part of government policy. This is the crux of the matter. It is at this point that we move from emphasizing structural features and propose that the policy process is plural in operation as well as in form. The argument is twofold. The non-government agencies involved in policy-making are not only numerous, but differ in terms of the interests, values, ideologies and tactics which they espouse. Neither government, nor any other agency, closely controls the types of demands initiated and supported by these non-government bodies and they therefore tend to act as parallel channels of demand regulation. This plurality of institutions introduces a diversity of criteria by which demands are initially assessed and it limits the extent to which the authorities can stifle demands even before they enter the government system. Secondly, and perhaps even more important, we have maintained that the authorities include loci of power, authority and influence which are not welded into one simple hierarchical structure. There are divergences of interests, priorities and values between the authorities and even *within* government itself. The processes of demand regulation are in turn complex.

Government departments, and divisions within departments, differ in terms of their style and their methods of operation. They are also in competition over the policies they sponsor and the resources they seek. Beyond these general factors stand the politicians and civil servants. The extent of dissent within parties emphasizes the variety of views propounded by their more powerful members and by various sub-groups within them. There is no comparable evidence of differences between civil servants, but we have implied that such differences exist and are as surely an influence on policy. The political views and sympathies of civil servants vary more than the similarity of their backgrounds might suggest. Consequently, policy-making usually involves an interaction of heterogeneous views even within government departments. To this we must add, for example, the very real possibility that the growth of the social service ministries has gradually infused a distinctive philosophy into government. It is certainly arguable that they have introduced their own particular values and interests into government policy-making. If this is so they will have altered the way in which issues are regulated and policies are made.

4. None of this means that all interests or issues can be brought into play with equal chances of success, or with any chance at all. The informal and cultural aspects of demand regulation are important precisely because, almost by definition, they are systematically selective and rule out many issues. Nevertheless, we have argued that a range of interests is represented in policy-making. It is not simply the interests of, for example, the business, military or professional elites which find expression in policy-making. One of the key questions for research that our argument highlights is precisely how the structurally differentiated sub-systems of the policy process work. Do they complement each other by raising different kinds of issues, by promoting different kinds of solutions and allocating priority to proposals in different ways? Alternatively, do they reinforce each other in excluding particular types of issues and solutions? We will return to these problems in the last part of the book when we look for the regularities and common features to be found in our case studies. Our proposition at this point is that a considerable diversity of issues is initiated and is supported both outside and within government; the policy process *appears* to be plural both in its structure and in its operation.

5. These points move our discussion on to a further stage, for in presenting a model of what is happening in policy-making it is impossible not to convey some impressions about where power really lies. To tackle this question at all seriously requires more than a mere description of some of the policy actors and what they do. Some suggestions have been made en route; for example, that individual government departments – especially the economic departments and most conspicuously the Treasury – are extremely powerful within government. At the other extreme, the power of mass votes and mass opinion may occasionally be crucial. These represent different kinds of power, of course; the one is continuous and central to policy-making whilst the other operates in a more discontinuous and unpredictable way. However, such observations can only take us so far. The most detailed account of policy-making as a process may still overlook important aspects regarding the balance and operation of power. To do more we must consider, at a somewhat higher level of generality, the distribution of political power and its relevance for policy-making.

CHAPTER EIGHT

Policy and the Distribution of Power

The danger of the pluralist picture which has emerged in the preceding chapters is that the political process can easily become confused with political power. Policy-making may be a very different process from that implied by the adjective *democratic* because of concentrations of power that have not yet been discussed. Two questions underline the remaining difficulties:

(i) Are all interest groupings equally able to make themselves felt in government; is the system of representing interests just and unbiased?

(ii) Is competition for influence, the gaining of power, or the acceptance of compromise an acceptable basis for settling *every* issue? Are there not issues where a small or weak grouping of interests should be given priority?

The first question calls for a closer examination of the distribution of power as such. The second goes beyond this and casts doubt upon the fairness of any system of policy-making, however plural, which simply reflects the outcome of a competition for influence. It raises the question of whether an appeal to government's role as guardian of the public interest can resolve this problem.

The first of these two questions, however, provides the main theme of this chapter. The distribution of political power is an extremely complex and much disputed topic; to introduce it in a short space demands simplification. Perhaps the best way to do this is to produce condensed 'ideal types' of two quite opposed views of how power is distributed in Western democracies and then to explore the problems they solve and leave unresolved. For the sake of further simplicity and to avoid undue qualification, these ideal types will each be illustrated by reference to one theorist. Our versions would not necessarily be accepted by these writers as a full or balanced statement of their viewpoints. We have produced the summaries for our own purpose and they emphasize only those problems which are directly relevant to the discussion of policy-making. They identify the key variables and the approximate boundaries of the territory that we have entered.

The first position, which we shall call the pluralist–democratic case, argues that although there are defects in Western democratic political systems these are largely inescapable and residual blemishes in a basically sound and just system based upon widely dispersed power. The second case, which we shall call the class model, stresses the belief that social, economic and political power is distributed in a fundamentally unequal way in Western democratic societies.[1] Two points follow. The political system, and therefore policy-making, is not marginally but *systematically* biased and indeed repressive in effect if not in its overt form. And there are issues for which there can be no compromise satisfactory to conflicting interests.

I A PLURALIST–DEMOCRATIC MODEL

A prominent 'pluralist' has arrived at two major conclusions about Western democracies which bear on policy-making:

(i) that these political systems have developed sophisticated and, in many ways, very effective means of managing political conflict; and

(ii) that they are characterized by widely diffused political power.[2]

Dahl does not deny that conflict is a prevalent, if not ubiquitous feature of political life. His argument is that the role of the political system is to resolve this conflict and that the success with which it has been done is reflected in the absence of recent revolutionary changes in Western democracies.[3] He notes that 'even comprehensive changes are ... uncommon. The typical pattern of American politics is one of stability, moderate conflict, and incremental change'.[4] A similar conclusion can be reached in the case of Britain. Indeed, he specifically argues that although different paths have been followed,

[1] Although the terms 'class model' and 'ruling class' are rather laboured, their use avoids the kinds of confusions discussed by Poulantzas, N., 'The Problem of the Capitalist State', *New Left Review*, no. 58, 1969.

[2] Dahl, R. A., *Pluralist Democracy in the United States: Conflict and Consent*, Rand McNally, 1967; and also see Dahl, R. A., *Modern Political Analysis*, Prentice-Hall, 1963.

[3] Dahl defines change as revolutionary 'when comprehensive change in policies and relative influence is also combined with profound alterations in the operating structure of government'. *Ibid.*, p. 264.

[4] *Ibid.*, p. 429.

Britain and other European democracies are very similar to the United States in terms of the ability to regulate conflict.

The two key variables in this formulation, namely the degree of diffusion of political power and the resolution of political conflict, are said to be closely connected. They may be, but in what way? A system in which power is widely diffused may favour the resolution of conflict, but it is equally possible *a priori* that such a system would generate conflicts. The key questions for our purpose are whether patterns of conflict regulation on one hand, and the distribution of power on the other, are related to policy-making. Dahl specifies a particular relationship between the two and implies that this will have important consequences for policy-making in that there will be a considerable capacity for resolving even contentious issues and that a steady flow of policies will result from 'democratic' processes.

Let us consider first the problem of resolving conflict. Under what conditions is conflict likely to be manageable? The answer is essentially twofold: institutions devoted to conflict resolution must exist or be developed; but just as fundamental is the pattern of conflict itself. This may vary in several ways. First, conflicts may be such that a mutually advantageous solution can be negotiated by the interests involved (positive sum) or they may permit success for one party only at the expense of the other (zero sum). This is often a question of how the conflict is perceived and defined by the participants, but the difference is important. In some situations, such as the dispute over the *existing* distribution of income, wealth and political power, the conflict can hardly be other than zero sum. Conflicts of this kind, in which the stakes are high and the opportunity for compromise low, are least amenable to control.

Second, we must note that because conflicts are numerous they cannot always be treated singly and in isolation. The division of opinion on any one issue is important, but the total pattern of these divisions within the society is even more significant. If opinions divide in related ways on many disputed issues conflicts may coalesce. Conversely, if the pattern of cleavage varies from issue to issue each conflict will tend to exist in isolation from others and will be less likely to lead to a major disruption of the society. Cumulative conflict can easily lead to a group of people generalizing the conflict to the point where it threatens the stability of the society as a whole.

A fundamental assumption in the Dahl approach and one held in varying degrees by a large body of other writers, is that conflict tends to be, or can be, non-cumulative in Western democracies. How does one arrive at this kind of conclusion? Economic growth is a key factor. A 'surplus' of resources and the likelihood of further growth can transform zero sum conflicts about access to given resources into positive sum issues about future resources. In short, low income groups can be offered growth based on economic co-operation and may be persuaded to curb their militancy about the distribution of existing resources. Other groups in conflict can be similarly bought off in a high income society. Blunting the edge of conflict between income groups or social classes ensures that the myriad other grievances in society do not become cumulative. Dahl recognizes that there have been and may still be issues which encourage an accumulation of grievances but he nevertheless emphasizes that there is a basis for stability in the diversity of interests and surplus resources available in Western democracies.

This conclusion has been severely questioned by events in the recent history of the United States (which is Dahl's exemplar of pluralism). Ethnic, urban, economic and international issues (Vietnam) have been far more cumulative than his thesis suggests, even though they have not produced revolutionary changes in political and economic institutions or policies. Conscious management and the disaggregation of these conflicts has absorbed a great deal of political energy. This may seem to discredit the non-cumulative thesis and place emphasis on the skill with which cumulative discontent is handled; but one point is noteworthy. The traditional threat to political stability to which pluralists have largely reacted, namely open class conflict, has not effectively materialized even in the contemporary turbulence of American urban politics. In societies where ethnic and inter-generational conflicts have been less important, Dahl's thesis may be more applicable. However, its real value is in the questions it raises rather than in the answers it gives. It is not sufficient to assert that conflicts are or are not cumulative; nor to use the objective distribution of resources, opportunities, grievances and power as the sole evidence on which to base an answer. The real problem is to go beyond this and identify the way in which different groups within a political system perceive the distribution of these factors and how this influences their political behaviour. To argue that economic and political power is or is not concentrated in few hands and consequently that people are or are not justified in treating conflicts as cumulative, is satisfactory for some purposes; but it tells us little about policy-making.

The pluralist–democratic thesis may have a number of different implications for policy-making. The basic assertion is that inequalities in society are not so great or cumulative as to result in domination by a single elite. This leaves open the possibility of oligarchy, not least because political apathy may result in the accumulation of power in the hands of a small number of elites. In its milder forms the pluralist–democracy thesis accepts this possibility, but fundamentally insists that an oligarchy is not tantamount to a ruling class; in particular, business interests do not hold sway over all important political issues. *Competing* elites, but not a single elite, may be accepted as the dominant influence on the process of government in the weaker versions of the model.

Empirical research, conducted by adherents of the pluralist thesis, has led to an elaboration of this last point. The notion of competing elites conjures up visions of trade unions and business, for example, competing on a wide spectrum of issues (and agreeing on others). The term is most readily interpreted at a national level to mean a few ideologically differentiated groupings of an oligarchic kind. At the local level, however, it has been argued that power is not distributed in this way.[5] It is seen to be highly differentiated on a functional basis. Different issues or problems bring quite different elites into play. Power is specific to issues. Whether this is true of national politics we simply cannot determine as yet. It is a contentious issue even in terms of United States local community politics where the research has been concentrated. But the possibility is an important strand in a pluralist argument. The national oligarchic elites may often act as channels of communication for many diverse interests.

Does this pluralist–democratic conception tally with what we have said about the British political process and, if so, what are its implications for policy-making? The pluralist viewpoint is certainly favoured by many politicians as well as by students of political science and social policy. Most conspicuously, among Labour politicians, Anthony Crosland has argued both that social inequalities have been transformed and that political power is sufficiently dispersed to allow socialist aims to be pursued within a representative democratic system.[6]

The implications of the pluralist interpretation may seem to be obvious, but they are not always spelled out. When they are, the representation of diverse interests in policy-making tends to be seen as a good first step towards the attainment of a just society. Pluralism becomes identified with the elusive but highly desired virtues of democracy: indeed, the one becomes the guarantor of the other. In the words of one of its critics the pluralist thesis proposes that power 'is competitive, fragmented and diffused: everybody, directly or through organized groups, has some power and nobody has or can have too much of it. As a result, the argument goes, no government (acting on behalf of the State), can fail, in the not very long

---

   [5] This simple presentation of the pluralist viewpoint obviously neglects the wealth of detailed analysis of community politics. For a good critique of this literature see Bachrach, P. and Baratz, M. S., 'Two Faces of Power', *American Political Science Review*, vol. LVI, 1962.
   [6] Crosland, C. A. R., *The Future of Socialism*, Cape, 1956. Also his *The Conservative Enemy*, Cape, 1962.

run, to respond to the wishes and demands of competing interests – in the end everybody, including those at the end of the queue, get served'.[7]

Although we have drawn an apparently pluralist picture of British policy-making in the previous chapters, this can be challenged by practical examples. The topics of our case studies, for instance, do not include an example of a *major* public debate on social policy. The degree of client organization has been low in most areas of social policy and the trade unions, which are one channel through which client interests can be represented, are not involved in the administration of State social security schemes, for example, as they are in some European countries. Much social policy has been developed on a minimum of consultation with consumer groups and little public discussion. The pluralism of the policy *process* which we have outlined in general terms suggests that it possesses a potential for incorporating a great breadth of different interests in policy-making, but it would clearly be rash to assume that this potential is always, or frequently, realized in practice. There is ample room for argument about just how plural and democratic British policy-making is. However, the caveats noted above merely challenge the details of the theme. From a different viewpoint the entire scenario is quite simply wrong, or irrelevant. The class model of political life expresses this alternative approach.

II THE CLASS MODEL

The class view of the political system rests on affirmative answers to two questions: is there an economically dominant class in Western democracies and, if there is, does this class exercise *decisive* economic and political power? This view provides a very different interpretation of the *purpose* of the political system (it emphasizes its role in sustaining a capitalist economy); and of the political processes; and of the outcome of policy-making.

Its starting point, the structure of socio–economic classes, needs least rehearsal. Miliband reviews the available data on differentials in income, wealth, control through ownership of private enterprise and life opportunities.[8] He dismisses the thesis that managerial control has displaced ownership and thereby transformed the face of capitalism. Crosland's social–democratic approach to 'welfare capitalism' is rejected and a picture of British capitalism – reformed but

[7] Miliband, R., *The State in Capitalist Society*, Weidenfeld & Nicolson, 1969, p. 2.
[8] Miliband, R. A., *op. cit.*, ch. 2.

fundamentally unchanged – emerges. The final item in Miliband's discussion of the class system is the crucial one for policy-making. Even accepting the existence of sharp class differences it is possible, as we have noted, to argue that there are diverse and competing elites which prevent the emergence of a single ruling class. Miliband concedes that there may be this diversity and that it may express itself in real political differences, but he argues that 'specific differences among dominant classes, however genuine they may be in a variety of ways, are safely contained within a particular ideological spectrum, and do not preclude a basic political consensus in regard to the crucial issues of economic and political life. One obvious manifestation of this fact is the support which dominant classes accord to conservative parties ... different segments of these classes may support different and competing conservative parties: but they do not very much tend to support anti-conservative ones'.[9]

In short, political differences exist within dominant groups but are constrained within narrow limits. This raises the general question which must be answered if we are to make any sense of policy-making. Within what limits, if any, are the political differences found in the wider society expressed in policy-making? The answer provided by the class model is that they are almost as narrow as the distribution of power itself. The limits within which policy-making takes place are largely controlled by elites which in practice, it is argued, form a politically as well as an economically dominant *class*. In defence of this last point Miliband makes the critical distinction between the State and the government.

The State as a concept is an object of popular allegiance; as a set of institutions – the government, Parliament, the administration, the armed forces, the police, the judiciary, local government and the Monarchy – it is the locus of power. Miliband suggests, and it is fundamental to policy-making, that this 'does not mean that the government is necessarily strong, either in relation to other elements of the State system or to forces outside it ... In other words, the fact that the government does speak in the name of the State and is formally *invested* with state power, does not mean that it effectively *controls* that power'.[10] Not only may the government system be biased in favour of particular groups, but the balance of power between the State, governments and other loci of power may deny all but the formal trappings of power to the representatives of some interests or classes. In the context of recent British history, it may be specifically argued that the government system inadequately reflects the interests of the working class or of the large section of the population without

[9] Miliband, R. A., *op. cit.*, pp. 46–7.
[10] Miliband, *op. cit.*, p. 50; emphasis in the original.

property, and that even when elected into 'power' a working class party has in fact a weak grasp on real political power. To these structural limitations on the role of the Labour Party, Miliband adds the lack of political will among Labour leaders to effect radical change when in office.

This critique goes so far beyond an imputation of mere bias in the political system that the case deserves outlining in slightly more detail. The two main issues, the class backgrounds and allegiances of actors in the political process and the cultural hegemony of the dominant class, will be dealt with in turn. The first proposition to be examined is that the relationship between the economically dominant class and the State (not merely particular political parties or governments) 'is very close indeed and that the holders of state power are, for many different reasons, the agents of private economic power – that those who wield that power are also ... without unduly stretching the meaning of words, an authentic "ruling class".'[11] A major part of Miliband's case rests on the proposal that although businessmen have not 'themselves assumed a major share of government', nevertheless they 'have generally been well represented in the political executive and in other parts of the state system as well'. Moreover, it is argued that other actors in the political system are, if not businessmen, overwhelmingly members of the middle and upper classes sharing a similar range of interests.

Business interests have certainly been well represented in British governments, Parliaments and in local government.[12] Moreover, the nationalization of sectors of the economy and State intervention in the economic sphere generally have drawn the business community into closer contact with government.[13] The pursuit of administrative reform and efficiency at governmental level has also increased this interchange between government and business; an interchange which is now sought as a matter of policy. These trends support Miliband's contention that 'one of the most notable features of advanced capitalism is precisely what might be called without much exaggeration the growing colonization [by business] of the upper reaches of the administrative part' of the political system.[14] The implications for policy-making are obvious. The strong position of businessmen is only irrelevant if there are no major interests or groups whose wellbeing conflicts with their interests or if those conflicting interests are equally powerfully and directly represented in the State system. The existence of an economically subordinate class makes a clash of

[11] *Ibid.*, pp. 54–5.
[12] *Ibid.*, pp. 56–9 and Guttsman, W. L., *op. cit.*
[13] Hughes, J., *Nationalised Industries in the Mixed Economy*, Fabian Tract 328.
[14] Miliband, *op. cit.*, p. 57.

th the business community likely – though it may not be
source of such conflict. The growing interest in curbing
ntal pollution is an example which does not immediately
spectre of class conflict although it may provoke conflict
between business and other interest groups.[15] To take another
example, the growth of the social services has often been seen as
inimical to economic growth or other aspects of economic policy,
and this may be to the detriment of middle- as well as low-income
consumers.

The social background of the administrative elite is still basically
homogeneous and is fairly widely known.[16] That of the judiciary and
the financial elites is probably less well known, but not less solidly
middle or upper class.[17] This homogeneity of class background, which
is marginally but increasingly under challenge, does not itself demonstrate the overwhelming influence of an economically dominant class.
It certainly does not rule out the possibility of heterogeneous interests being represented, fostered or espoused by different individuals,
groups or institutions of the state and political systems.

The most important and powerful part of the class thesis does not
deny this possibility. It simply makes the point that dissension
generally operates within limits which are narrowly drawn. The
narrowness of these limits is partly determined by the structural
features of the system noted above, but far more fundamentally by
the processes of legitimation and the political culture within which
the political and State systems operate. Structural features alone do
not explain why there is only limited support for a more radical
critique of the socio–economic order. The most important point for
our purposes is that limited political dissension, operating within a
consensus about the legitimacy and effectiveness of capitalist institutions, has reflected mass opinion (as measured in voting behaviour)
and not merely the preferences of political and economic elites.[18] It is
the legitimacy accorded not only to the dominant class as rulers, but
to their values, norms and world view which constitutes the hegemony
– or ideological supremacy – of this class. Miliband rightly insists that

[15] Gregory, R., *The Price of Amenity*, Macmillan, 1971, esp. ch. 3; and also
Webb, A. L., 'Planning Enquiries and Amenity Policy', *Policy and Politics, op.
cit.*
[16] Hill, M. J., *The Sociology of Public Administration*, Weidenfeld & Nicolson, 1972, ch. 9.
[17] Abel-Smith, B. and Stevens, R., with Brooke, R., *Lawyers and the Courts*,
Heinemann, 1967, pp. 299–315; and Abel-Smith, B. and Stevens R., *In Search
of Justice*, Allen Lane, 1968, esp. ch. 6; Guttsman, W. L., *op. cit.*
[18] The phenomenon of working class Conservative voting fundamentally
structures the balance of political forces and the broad trends of policy-
making. For a discussion of the phenomenon see McKenzie, R. T. and Silver,
A., *Angels in Marble*, Heinemann, 1968.

hegemony cannot simply be 'something which happens, as a mere superstructural derivative of economic and social predominance. It is, in very large part, the result of a permanent and pervasive effort, conducted through a multitude of agencies, and deliberately intended to create what Talcott Parsons calls a "national supra-party consensus".'[19]

Quite apart from direct effort on the part of Conservative governments, or earlier developments in the political history of the society, the maintenance of this hegemony can be traced in the process of political socialization.[20] Political socialization is geared predominantly to the acceptance of a capitalist order through the overall bias, often unconscious, of all the major agencies of communication and socialization: the educational system, the family, the mass media, advertising, the political parties themselves and organized religion. In addition to these Miliband considers the role of 'that most powerful of all secular religions' – nationalism. It is not necessary to re-examine the evidence he advances for characterizing these institutions and ideologies as conservative. His arguments are most interesting for our purposes where issues which we have already touched upon are discussed in a very different light. Let us briefly consider two instances: the mass media and nationalism. We have already mentioned the first as a potentially important factor in the policy-making process. The second embraces one aspect of the process of legitimation mentioned at a number of points; nationalism is particularly interesting because it highlights one kind of appeal to 'the common good'.

Miliband does not deny, indeed he clearly values, the range of genuinely free expression possible through the mass media. His concern once again is with the limits of this freedom. Of newspapers he notes: 'whatever their endless differences of every kind, most newspapers in the capitalist world have one crucial characteristic in common, namely their strong, often their passionate hostility to anything further to the Left than the milder forms of social democracy, and quite commonly to these milder forms as well'.[21] Similarly, on the role of radio and television he argues that the 'assumed impartiality and objectivity is quite artificial ... [they] ... *stop at the point where political consensus itself ends*' (our italics).[22] Bias may be observed even within the areas of broad consensus and tolerated diversity. In particular the press (and the influence of television may

---

[19] Miliband, *op. cit.*, p. 181.
[20] For a discussion of the historical milestones in the development of this hegemony see Anderson, P., 'Origins of the Present Crisis', in Anderson, P. and Blackburn, R. (eds), *Towards Socialism*, Fontana, 1965.
[21] Miliband, *op. cit.*, p. 221.
[22] *Ibid.*, p. 224.

be even greater in this direction though less overt) operates for much of the time as 'a deeply committed anti-trade union force'.[23] It is not a question of continual or general opposition to trade unions as such but rather a mobilization of the concept of the public good which almost always casts trade unions as irresponsible and reckless supporters of merely sectional interests.

Whether one agrees with this analysis of mass media attitudes to the trade unions or not, the problem is inescapable: the definition of 'sectional' and 'national' or 'common' interests lies with a relatively few institutions such as governments and the mass media. What one observer may view as a clash between different sectional interests may be presented in national politics as one sectional interest pursuing its goals to the detriment of the public good. It is certainly possible for particular interests to be viewed consistently as sectional and therefore of dubious legitimacy, whilst others are not treated in this way. If to this is added a definition of the national interest which reinforces those and only those values, norms and institutions falling within the area of consensus, then the forces of political conservatism are powerful indeed. If the national interest can be kept at the forefront of political life the defences of the *status quo* are impressive.

III POLICY-MAKING: A PLURAL OR ELITIST PROCESS?

The two approaches which have been outlined are in turn drawn from broader and competing schools of thought about the distribution of political power and, although this is not always as explicit, about the kinds of policy processes and end-products that typify Western industrial societies. The class model is the polar case of a whole spectrum of elitist interpretations.[24] As a group they emphasize the

---

[23] *Ibid.*, p. 222.

[24] The term 'elite' has been avoided as far as possible in this discussion. Once one departs from the idea of a ruling class, one acknowledges the possibility that there may be a number of elites which may be in competition with each other. It can then become extremely difficult to distinguish between pluralist and non-pluralist explanations of policy-making. In accepting the notion of countervailing but oligarchic elites, many pluralists come a long way towards the non-pluralist viewpoint and we have tried to present a clear cut distinction as the foundation of our discussions. Unfortunately, a large body of literature on community politics in the US is couched in the language of elites, not ruling classes. Consequently the term 'elitist' used in the text refers to those explanations of politics which criticize the pluralist viewpoint for its underestimation of the concentration of political power. This position approaches

centralization of power in the hands of a small and, to varying degrees, cohesive sector of the society. Whether or not the *initiation* of policy demands is seen to be decentralized throughout society, the real power to *regulate* demands and to determine decisions is seen to rest with the ruling cabal of individuals and institutions. The class variant emphasizes a constellation of shared interests centring on the owner- ship and control of economic resources in a capitalist society. It also specifies important factors which help to maintain political stability in the face of inequality: for example, political socialization and opposition parties of a socialist-democratic kind (in Britain the Labour Party) which reinforce the whole edifice by seeming to offer choice while failing to act differently from the capitalist parties once 'in power'.

Pluralist models vary in terms of the degree of perfection attributed to existing democratic societies. They do not necessarily attempt to rebut all of the elitist critique. They do not insist that political power is equally distributed (indeed what that phrase might mean is hard to determine), but they do attack some of the premises and most of the conclusions of the elitist interpretation. Given inequality of access to political resources, for example, Dahl admits that there is always a danger of oligarchy. He does not deny the existence of inequalities, but argues that to condemn a 'political system for inequality is one thing; to condemn it for being dominated by a ruling elite is another'.[25] The economic determinism that sees wealth as the sole political resource is dismissed and the intellectual inheritance of Marx's and Weber's analyses of social stratification is seen as mis- leading. The pluralists advance a counter hypothesis: that any industrial society with a 'moderately free political system' tends to produce a 'dispersed and not cumulative pattern of inequalities'.[26] Consequently an absence of wealth can be overcome by the exercise of skill in mobilizing other political resources and by entering coali- tions to broaden support.

Faced by these alternatives how does one proceed? Let us first note the implications for our understanding of social policy of choosing either viewpoint as a frame of reference. The complications multiply immediately. The pluralist–democratic thesis seems to imply one obvious set of conclusions. Pluralism guarantees democracy which in turn guarantees some pay-off, including social policies, for all

that outlined in the ruling class model even though its reference to elites introduces semantic and analytical problems. For discussion of the strengths and weaknesses of the class and elitist models see Urry, J. and Wakeford, J. (eds), *Power in Britain*, Heinemann, 1973.

[25] Dahl, R. A., in D'Antonio, W. V. and Erhlich, H. J. (eds), *Power and Democracy in America*, University of Notre Dame Press, 1961, p. 80.

[26] *Ibid.*, p. 82.

interests. The high capacity for conflict resolution and political
stability presumably also means that an impressive policy output
is possible. On the other hand, even accepting the pluralist thesis,
it is possible to construct a different case. Such societies may involve
a very low capacity for policy-making because there are so many
organized, legitimate and blocking interests. A pluralist democracy
which genuinely lived up to the ideal type could well find that counter-
vailing powers too often produced a stalemate. Similarly, conflict
resolution which depends primarily on avoiding the potentially ex-
plosive zero sum definition of issues can easily mean that some issues
which *should* be treated as zero sum are not. Conflict resolution by
compromise may simply mean reaching stable 'agreed' solutions at
the expense of the weakest set of interests. This is most obviously
so when the issue is the distribution of power itself.

The class model of political life has equally uncertain implications
for social policy. Whether social policies fare well or ill presumably
depends upon the composition and attitudes of the ruling class. The
simplest assumption would be that social policy would suffer. The
ruling class would presumably be against high taxation and redistribution. Social policy would, therefore, prosper only in so far as the
ruled masses could find chinks in the armour of the ruling class.
But, the class theoretician argues, this is to accept the benevolence
assumption. In short, this view is only tenable if social policy is seen
as benevolent towards the masses, as a real gain to them. If it is seen
as a powerful buttress of class domination, as a precondition of conflict resolution by compromises which protect the *status quo*, then
all is different. If social policy is interpreted in this light it may indeed
fare well in a class society. To make the best of his position the
theorist may also claim that not all social policies arise through the
machinations of the rulers. Some, the 'real' steps forward, are forced
upon the rulers by successful, but limited, class conflict and most (if
not all) social policy starts with mass discontent which has to be
bought off, albeit at the lowest possible cost. Clearly, our two conceptions of the political system provide far from simple explanations
of social policy. They raise three different kinds of problems: that of
interpreting their implications for explaining the growth and changes
in social policy: that of evaluating social policy from different viewpoints; and that of choosing between the very different pictures of
the policy process which they offer.

It is to this last problem that we must now turn. It would be most
satisfactory if one of the approaches could be rejected on the basis
of hard evidence and policy-making could then be explored entirely
within the frame of reference provided by the other. Unfortunately,
this is not possible for two main reasons. One is that the two
approaches are contradictory precisely because they represent different

ideologies as well as two analyses of the political system and its outcomes. Much of the factual data we possess about the working of our
particular political system are common to *both* models. The majority
of the evidence can be assimilated within either. To counter the class
critique the pluralist can always accept the evidence of inequality
and redefine his position. It is worth noting Dahl's modest assertion
that 'nearly every group has enough potential influence to mitigate
harsh injustice to its members, though not necessarily enough influence
to attain a full measure of justice. The system thus tends to be self-
corrective, at least in a limited fashion. If equality and justice are
rarely attained, harsh and persistent oppression is almost always
avoided. To this extent the system attains one of the important ends
of political equality without the means'.[27] For those so inclined
ideologically, this meets the case presented by Miliband; it absorbs
his data.

But this divergence of values is matched by a sharp difference in
the type and level of explanation being offered in the two models.
The pluralists largely operate in terms of what is achieved, of the
diversity evident in politics and the lack of a visible concentration of
power in the hands of a single homogeneous class. The elitists look
mainly at what is not achieved in policy-making, at what remains
untouched because a dominant group determines what shall not be
changed. The first is predominantly a political scientist's view of who
exercises power and influence in politics; the second arises from a
more sociological concern with where power really lies, rather than
with who is visibly using it. These approaches imply quite different
interpretations of the descriptive analysis of political institutions and
processes contained in previous chapters. In an attempt to resolve the
impasse let us look for the strengths and weaknesses of each rather
than for evidence against which one might be rejected.

IV THE STRENGTHS AND WEAKNESSES OF THE TWO ANALYSES

There is much in the pluralist thesis which accords with experience
of democratic political systems. It suggests a policy-making process
that is complex, varied and capable of diverse and surprising results.
These aspects ring true for a lot of what we know about British social
policy. Nevertheless, there are topics which the thesis cannot accommodate satisfactorily. Most especially it ignores the possibility that

---

[27] Dahl, R. A., in D'Antonio and Erhlich, *op. cit.*, p. 89.

a powerful interest grouping may not have to *exert* influence to ensure that decisions favour them. As Ehrlich notes: 'the sheer fact of the possession of a power potential or resource may have been sufficient to determine the action of others ... we *do* attempt to avoid the fearful showdown, the distasteful controversy, by anticipating the reactions of those in possession of power ...'[28]

The pluralist position has been strongly criticized for its treatment of power and influence. It both concentrates attention on power that is visibly *exercised* and also tends to treat different kinds of power or influence as if they were interchangeable, or equally effective in policy-making. Some kinds of power may be difficult to activate. It is not at all clear how far and in what circumstances a reservoir of power is reduced by its use, but it may certainly be the case that different forms of political power vary in their durability once exercised.[29] Power based on an electoral mandate, for example, may be rapidly depleted if unpopular decisions are made or policies can be repre-sented as against 'the general interest'. Power that depends on the mobilization of mass support may obviously be liable to depletion if frequently employed. For this reason a working class movement may face greater problems in deciding when to exercise power than does an economic elite. To view the two as equivalent and counter-vailing forces can be profoundly misleading. The nature, context and security of their power potential is different.

Similarly, the pluralists tend to oversimplify the way in which interests are perceived and articulated. They assume that given the opportunity to do so individuals actively express their desires and preferences as they see them. It is entirely possible that people's opinions and wishes may not be formed individually and indepen-dently. An elite could avoid the overt exercise of power if *their* opinions and interests could be made widely acceptable. Dahl admits that 'political theory has barely been extended to cover this problem; in particular liberal democratic theory has often *started* with the assumption that the preferences of individuals, whether voters or consumers, should be taken as given, autonomous to the individual rather than socially determined'.[30] This assumption underlies much of the study of voting behaviour and is firmly incorporated in the expanding body of 'economic' analyses of political life. It is an ex-tremely convenient assumption to make in any discussion of democratic political systems and of policy-making. If it is discarded, however, it opens up an entirely different possibility: that the obser-

[28] Ehrlich in D'Antonio, *op. cit.*, p. 92.
[29] For a useful discussion of the complexity and difficulties of using power explanations of political decisions see March, J. D., 'The Power of Power', in Easton, D., *Varieties of Political Theory, op. cit.*
[30] Dahl, in D'Antonio and Erhlich, *op. cit.*, p. 88 (emphasis added).

vable processes of the political system are themselves an unreliable guide to how power is distributed or decisions are made.

The pluralist position, therefore, certainly has major weaknesses. Given the emphasis on the management of conflict and the absence of overt conflict it is difficult to know how some theorists would recognize cumulative discontents when confronted by them. Their minimization of the problem of conflict is important precisely because it justifies a political process which treats issues essentially as positive sum problems. It also dismisses the possibility that some major interest groupings may be unrepresented because they are denied this influence by those currently holding power. Authorities may use power actively to promote some interests at the expense of others; but they are implicitly presented by pluralists as relatively passive, unbiased adjudicators between competing interests. If, in practice, they promote particular interests it is important to consider which interests are neglected and whether a relatively narrow range of interests is consistently promoted over time. The structure and balance of political forces may in fact permit considerable political bias of this kind. If the socio–political culture under-emphasizes some interests and if authorities also deny them influence, the bias in policy-making may seem natural and unremarkable. A democratic ideology may, in these situations, veil the prolonged and almost complete suppression of even major constellations of interests.

Lindblom raises this general possibility only to dismiss it briefly. He accepts that 'interest group organization is much easier, much better financed, and hence much more effective for the educated and well-off than for the disadvantaged ...' He goes on to argue that 'the bias in policy-making is of course not limited to interest group participation. Elected and appointed proximate policy-makers are overwhelmingly from the more favoured classes ... They will therefore seek out and listen to interest group leaders with whose desires they are already sympathetic. To be sure officials do not see themselves as representing the interests of some classes against others; rather it is that they see the general interest in the light of their own group affiliations ... what is more, the prestige of middle class attitudes and political preferences is so overwhelming in some countries, the United States included, that many of the disadvantaged themselves subscribe to them, thus endorsing and perpetuating the very bias in policy-making against which they might be expected to protest.'[31]

In outline this passage is a massive indictment of the policy-making process in the western democracies. It includes as sources of bias the factors we noted above; that is, the structure of the political system, the unequal influence within this system of different group-

[31] Lindblom, C. E. (1968), *op. cit.*, pp. 67–8.

ings, the value preferences of authorities, and the entire socio-political culture. Lindblom presents a picture of bias which is so integral to the society that conscious or planned exploitation of power need not be invoked to explain the malrepresentation of different class interests in policy. Yet the passage is little more than a footnote to his general thesis and is not documented. Is bias in policy-making to be dismissed except as a temporary and peripheral problem affecting the poor, uneducated, inadequately socialized or politically disillusioned members of society?

The question is not whether a political system exhibits bias, for it can hardly fail to do so; in Schattschneider's phrase political systems represent a 'mobilization of bias'.[32] What the pluralists deny is that this bias operates systematically in one direction. Institutional pluralism is said to be matched by a plurality of values and interests in policy-making. We have argued this case for the processes by which demands are regulated in British politics. But a *degree* of plurality can be matched by substantial and consistent bias. In particular the strong position of British governments may be used to reinforce a particular definition of the public good. They do not hold the ring in a neutral way between competing interests and value systems. Nevertheless, the pluralist case has strength. To rebut it one has to show that the institutional *and* value pluralism exhibited in the initiation and regulation of demands is essentially a façade.

This of course is what elitist and most especially the class models of politics set out to do. The strength of the case is that it goes to the heart of the problem. Whatever the appearances suggest, power is not diffuse and our democracy does not give the citizen a real opportunity to choose ideologies, values and interests that will be reflected in policies. Unfortunately, the weaknesses appear to be at least as substantial as those in the pluralists' case. The class model in particular presupposes a homogeneous class culture; that is to say shared interests and the shared values which support them. Without this an elite cannot be said to be a ruling *class*, be shown to be cohesive and not a set of competing elites, or be shown to dominate other classes through the dissemination of beliefs and values sympathetic to its continuance in power. One implication seems to be that the ruling power holders efficiently perceive and pursue their own best interests. This raises problems.

For example, 'welfare capitalism' may indeed be the best guarantee of capitalism and of ruling class interests. Nevertheless, there has always been and still is considerable resistance to high public social expenditure even to offset the effects of unemployment and the discontents of low income, or black, urban populations. Although it is

---

[32] Schattschneider, E. E., *The Semi-Sovereign People*, Holt, 1960.

true that this resistance to social expenditure is often overcome, it seems possible that certain features of the capitalist ideology are impediments to its cause. The only watertight answer to this dilemma is to say that the ruling class manages to make quite precise calculations of the limits of its power to suppress discontent and of the minimum cost methods of buying off unmanageable conflict.

The alternative is to accept that social policies are not wholly manipulative and that rulers are capable of some beneficent policies, or that there are weak spots in their dominance which allow gains to be made. It is not that elite or class theories deny these latter possibilities, but they do fail to indicate where the boundary lies. If the class is not totally dominant or is not totally dedicated to furthering only its own interests and if social policy is sometimes a positive expression of values other than those of the ruling class, then the boundaries of class dominance become crucial; as do the precise mechanisms whereby that dominance can be circumvented.

The class thesis may also be criticized because it asserts that of all the conflicts in society those which underlie the class system are predominantly, or even exclusively, worthy of attention. Conflicts of interest are assumed to be cumulative along class lines even when there is little overt expression of this phenomenon. Mass indifference towards or toleration of the injustices of a class society are explained by a concept, hegemony, which is hard to test. The divergence between the priorities or social objectives held by an academic theorist and those chosen by the subordinate masses may in fact be a product of conscious choice on the part of the latter. At worst this means that the theorist is saying people *ought* to be more overtly concerned about the injustice done to them. This does not invalidate the elitist criticism of the political system; but it underlines the fact that hegemony and political socialization are extraordinarily difficult concepts to handle in a positive theory of policy-making. They should not simply be ignored, as in much pluralist argument, but the problems of applying them should not be ignored either.

The class model suffers from a lack of explanation of precisely *how* the ruling class succeeds (or fails) in its attempt to deny pressures for change which potentially threaten its position. What we really need to trace is the detailed implications of a class model for social policy. What kinds of decisions would a ruling class be likely to define as hostile and how would they, or do they, avoid such decisions being made? Is control primarily exercised, through political socialization, over the formulation of demands, or by blocking proposals once they have 'entered' the political process? What combinations of coercion; structural bias; differentially favourable rules of the game; political socialization of the mass electorate; co-optation of potential political leaders; and lack of radicalism among socialist parties do class theorists see operating in different situations and areas of policy? There are many ways by which a ruling class might retain control over policy; by administrative sabotage; by the early reversal of radical policies when in power; or by exerting economic pressures on radical governments managing capitalist economies within the wider framework of international capitalism. But there is little evidence of how ruling classes actually retain control over policy-making, short of direct coercion.

It must also be noted that the class model deflects attention from some important issues – such as divergences of interest and the mobilization of bias – which are important in *all* societies, including non-capitalist or non-elitist ones. The danger of regarding policy outcomes in capitalist societies as inadequate or largely irrelevant is that the processes by which they are arrived at will also be dismissed as irrelevant. Our concern to understand British policy-making and conflict resolution (or the engineering of consensus) is only irrelevant if class interests and conflicts are seen as the sole variables of any importance in politics. The unmodified elitist and pluralist models both 'over predict' what they observe. The elitist interpretation unduly emphasizes the power of an elite or class both in its control over political processes and the political culture. There are alternative views of the world, despite the hegemonic thesis. There is a plurality of interests, conflicts and political institutions and these do result in some changes not wholly in the interest of a ruling class. Conversely, there are ample opportunities for powerful elites or a ruling class to determine or influence the course of public policy without visibly entering the policy process, and these are under-played by the pluralists.

What evidence do our case studies provide for choosing a basic model of how power is distributed and used? In one sense the answer is none. The case studies do not allow the historical perspective from which to make such broad judgements. Indeed, if class domination of the political system rests largely upon hegemony, studying policy-making is unlikely to highlight this dominance. Hegemony is by its very nature impossible to demonstrate conclusively, especially to those who do not experience it as a constraint. However, less fundamental factors, such as the presence of bias in the policy-making process, can be sought through case studies. It is possible, for example, to note and document the relative impotence of the consumer interest in much policy-making from our studies. It is also possible, and we will do so in the last part of the book, to isolate the principal characteristics which policy proposals have to exhibit if they are to gain acceptance within government. But we cannot convincingly demonstrate whether or not the political system is dominated by a ruling class. The case studies are not themselves of the kind which could help resolve such questions. It is not just that they were directed at questions of a lower order of generality. None of them covers an issue which would fundamentally challenge the interests of a ruling class to such an extent that it would invoke overt suppression of that demand. All the demands we studied were modest – in class terms – and all interest divergences were resolved by compromise, bargaining or benign political manoeuvring such as procrastination, delay and references to other competing demands or to the 'public good'.

Yet these comments may be viewed in another light. The case studies were typical post-war policy developments. They span some major and some less prominent issues of recent social policy. They are the bread and butter of social policy. Whatever other conclusions may be drawn from this fact, it is clear that although social policy formation tends to be slow, uncertain and politically contentious, it is not currently challenging the existing distribution of power in society. British social policy is operating securely within the established economic system and power structure.

It may be objected that social policy, taken as a whole, emphasizes a normative tradition which is quite alien to that of the market economy. The proposal that social policy has modified society by restricting the range and effect of market forces and economic values can be developed along these lines. The proposition has much appeal and cannot be lightly dismissed. Universalist social policies are an essential item in the 'welfare capitalism' sought by social democrats and many policies are indeed alien to the tenets of the market place.[33] It can be argued that the distributional values of social policy have had widespread effects on the entire fabric of social life and have not been confined merely to their institutional expression – the social services.[34] For the mass of the population life may improve slowly but steadily under welfare capitalism, even if the distribution of power remains largely unchanged. We would defend this statement as a hypothesis (if somewhat more cautiously as an evaluation of substantive achievements), but we must be clear about its limits.

Even if one does not adopt the marxist critique that social welfare programmes bolster a potentially unstable economic and political system, it is possible to be critical of the role of social policy in modern Britain. It is perfectly reasonable to apply part of Miliband's

[33] 'Universalist' in this context refers to the universalist model of social policy rather than to social policy practice. This model, as opposed to the residual model, is profoundly anti-market in terms of its fundamental principles and value orientation. It has had a considerable, though by no means unchallenged impact on social welfare policies. See Pinker, R. A., *Social Theory and Social Policy*, Heinemann, 1971, pp. 106–8 for a useful discussion of this point.

[34] This is the underlying theme throughout Titmuss' writings, but he makes the argument unequivocally clear in *The Gift Relationship*, Allen & Unwin, 1970.

analysis, for example, and argue that the bias within the political system unduly restricts the range and effect of social policy. It is certainly arguable that social policy is subservient to economic considerations and to the interests of economic and political elites; that the constraints are such that only modest and economically useful proposals are adopted.

Social policy is partly a history of conflict between interests; interests which have often been concentrated in different social classes. But it is also and even more clearly a history of conflicts being resolved, of accommodation, compromise and of agreements which cut across class boundaries. The existing limits appear to encompass the vast majority of publicly expressed demands and desires and this seems to undermine the class thesis. On the other hand, this area of legitimate diversity has been established through the testing of political strength and the steady institutionalization of class conflict. Actors in the political system, as well as the general public, have learned the location of the broad boundaries of political feasibility. It is within these boundaries that social policies operate; their scope does not match the range and degree of class differences and inequalities. To say that this merely represents the pursuit over time of effective and *realistic* policies is simply to reinforce our argument. How policy proposals become defined as 'realistic' and with whose interests in mind is the limiting condition that must be explored. Some social policies certainly appear to be framed deliberately to avoid altering the prevailing distribution of privilege and power.

Our case studies cannot answer the wider questions about power because they concentrate on substantive policies. The use of political power, especially elite power, is concerned with *preventing* damaging changes in policy as well as securing advantageous ones. Whilst our cases can explore much of the policy process, therefore, they need to be interpreted within a broader conceptual framework. This must in turn be capable of explaining the paradoxical features of social policy: the powerful concern with human needs and well-being which is matched by an apparent inability to gain sufficient resources to overcome the basic hardships of low income and poorly housed communities, quite apart from reversing gross social and economic inequalities. We must also face the fact that any attempt to study policy-making in a way that seriously challenges the pluralist thesis will be extremely difficult. The power to obstruct or shape policy from afar is not the most tangible of research topics.

It is quite possible that by taking a middle path between alternatives one gets the worst of both worlds. But there does seem to be a good argument for producing a synthesis of the pluralist and class models as a basis for understanding changes in social policy. Our proposition is a simple one: that the making of day-to-day policy on social issues in Britain does operate within a distinctly pluralist *process*, but that the *limits* of policy-making are set by elites which for many purposes are indistinguishable from what Miliband calls a ruling class. The ramifications are more complex. In using the class model as an explanation of the limits of change through social policy, one is saying two things. First, with Miliband, one is accepting that in a fundamental sense policy-making is of secondary interest because the really important questions (about the distribution of economic and political power) rarely come within the ambit of social policy. Second, therefore, one is saying that social policy is largely confined to an area of activity which does not fundamentally threaten the interests of those who hold power; does not, for example, involve a substantial and effective equalization of wealth and income or challenge the maintenance of privilege through educational and occupational discrimination. However, this is less than the whole story.

Social policy is not simply limited by class interests for it can clearly serve class interests as well. It can benefit a ruling class through its contribution to economic productivity and political stability; but it can also serve the purposes of many other vested interests and social groupings, 'minor elites' below the ruling class. The disadvantage of emphasizing *only* a ruling class is that it oversimplifies the pattern and the policy consequences of power distribution. Similarly the policy-making process is not totally irrelevant simply because important questions are already resolved by the class structure. The policy process is not neutral, but nor is it wholly closed and unresponsive to groups outside the ruling classes. The preservation of economic and social privilege sets limits and influences the content of much policy, but there is also a relatively open and often unpredictable competition for influence among many other interests drawn from different classes and sectors of society.

Although we have chosen to characterize the policy process as *bounded pluralism*, one cannot assume that the class model completely explains the nature of the boundaries within which the process operates. To explore these further we must be attentive to demands that are *not* articulated; to proposals which languish interminably in the queue or are emasculated beyond recognition. In particular we must look for the decisions that are *not made*. The problems are obvious. Can one explore the failures or the limits of policy-making as opposed to its outcomes? How can one trace the complexities of political power when it is used successfully and privately to prevent things happening? How can one explore the politics of the changes that are not made, quite apart from deciding how far these reflect and demarcate the impact of class or the effect of other limiting factors?

An expanding body of research suggests that the task is not entirely hopeless. Bachrach and Baratz, for example, have explored what may be called the defensive role of power in policy-making.[35] They emphasize that without overtly exercising power an elite can both determine the way in which issues are resolved and what problems are defined as issues in the first place. In their terms, *non-decisions* and the *non-decision process* are vitally important. Their major contribution is to subject the non-decision process to empirical study. Crenson has similarly demonstrated the possibility of looking at how issues are excluded from political life.[36] We have argued throughout that policy-making is a *selective* process. The value of the conceptual and empirical work on non-decisions is that it directs attention to the consistent exclusion of particular issues, whole categories of issues or types of solutions from consideration by policy-makers.

This does not resolve all our problems. As Bachrach and Baratz argue, we still need an analysis of 'the mobilization of bias in the community; of the dominant values and the political myths, rituals and institutional practices which tend to favour the vested interests of one or more group, relative to others'.[37] It is only with the aid of this kind of analysis that we can isolate what are the *important* policy issues: the ones which challenge predominant values and the rules of the game. Without this analysis all the many issues which could feasibly arise, but which do not, would be equally worthy of study.[38] The kind of approach adopted by Miliband is still necessary, therefore, and the ideological stance of the observer must still influence the interpretation of what is happening in policy-making. What Bachrach and Baratz have done is to use part of the sociological critique of pluralist theories without assuming that a single elite or ruling-class is the source of all major limitations on policy-making. This seems to be an appropriate road for social policy research to follow for it permits a wide-ranging study of the limits on social policy in different types of society, capitalist and non-capitalist alike.

We have not attempted systematically to explore the class limits of social policy in the case studies. By studying actual social policies we have chosen to look at how policy change is achieved, not how it can be frustrated. But there is no clear distinction between the two. After the case studies we shall bring together a number of factors which were important in shaping each of the policies we studied and try to make generalizations about them. These should help us to

[35] Bachrach, P. and Baratz, M. S., *Power and Poverty: Theory and Practice*, Oxford University Press, 1970.

[36] Crenson, M. A., *The Un-politics of Air Pollution*, John Hopkins Press, 1971.

[37] Bachrach, P. and Baratz, M. S., *op. cit.*, p. 11.

[38] The methodological problems are greater than suggested here; for a discussion of this topic see Crenson, *op. cit.*, pp. 29–31.

explain why policies developed in the way they did; but they are also likely, by extension, to be useful in suggesting why many policy proposals are never accepted and why others are abandoned almost before they arise. The discussion in this chapter should serve as a reminder that in talking about policies one should not forget 'non-policies'.

Many of the factors which lead to the rejection of policy proposals may demonstrate the validity of an elitist or class model; others may reflect the exigencies of day-to-day politics; and some may be found to be universal or at least common to many different types of socio-political systems. For example, the dominance of economic values and concern with economic growth, which runs throughout the story of social policy, may be classified as a universal constraint in the developed countries. The power of economic values, the conditions defined as favourable to economic stability and growth, or the ideologies relating to public expenditure, clearly produce a policy environment which is distinctively related to our economic system. Nevertheless, economic constraints on social policy are not a purely capitalist phenomenon, nor are the limitations imposed by expenditure on armaments. National competitiveness in the military and economic fields is a varying but widespread constraint on social policies in industrial societies today. Although we have to begin at a low level of generality, the study of the limits of social policy must follow a path from the determinants of substantive policies to those of 'non-policies' and 'non-decisions'. This path must also lead to comparative international research. It is only in this way that the constraints which are peculiar to particular policy issues, political processes, political ideologies and systems of politico–economic organization can be distinguished from those which are universal, or common to a number of different types of socio–political systems.

PART III

The Case Studies

In this part we examine six cases of social policy change at the central government level.

CHAPTER NINE

The Introduction of Family Allowances: an Act of Historic Justice?

The idea of paying family allowances in recognition of the need to adjust family income to family size is a very old one. Evidence of such allowances comes to us from the time of Augustus Caesar. In this country family allowances were paid in some areas in Tudor times, and at the end of the eighteenth century William Pitt made serious proposals for a national scheme of cash allowances for children. Apart from the system of Speenhamland, which was judged a disastrous failure in Britain, little thought was given again to the idea until the turn of this century when proposals for family allowances were being seriously discussed by a variety of left wing political and feminist groups. From 1908 onwards successive governments made adjustments to the income of some groups of parents in the light of their responsibilities (for example, servicemen, the unemployed, widows and some income tax payers). However, the Family Allowances Act 1945 marked the first scheme of allowances to benefit *all* families with two or more children irrespective of the employment status of either mother or father and without proof of need or evidence of contributions.

The acceptance of such a scheme meant that the government had accepted, albeit for economic and demographic reasons, the principle that 'society should include in its economic structure some form of direct financial provision for the maintenance of children, instead of proceeding on the assumption that, save in cases of exceptional misfortune, this is a matter which concerns only individual parents and should be left to them because normally men's wages or salaries are, or ought to be and can be made to be, sufficient for the support of their families'.[1] Few supported this principle as a means of reduc-

[1] Rathbone, E., *The Case for Family Allowances*, Penguin, 1940, p. xi.

ing inequality between rich and poor, or between men, women and children; many did so as a means of achieving other objectives. The story of how such a principle was accepted by a war-time coalition government and why it was implemented in the form that it was in advance of all the other social security changes, is a useful illustration of the ways in which particular problems gain the attention of governments and how one social policy can be seen and adopted as at least a partial solution to those problems.

I THE EARLY CAMPAIGN FOR FAMILY ALLOWANCES

The variety of the sources of support for a national scheme of family allowances are an important feature of the story of how the scheme was accepted and implemented. Initially, discussions about the State sharing with parents the cost of maintaining their children took place predominantly among socialist or left wing groups who supported the principle as a worthy end in itself. Others only backed the idea as a means to other ends. During the thirties, for example, family allowances were seen by increasing numbers of people as a method of combating the falling birth rate which had given rise to widespread fear of an ever declining population. By 1942, when family allowances were debated for the first time in Parliament, the principle had acquired supporters of most shades of political opinion.

The principle and practice of state maintenance of children, 1900–20
During the decade prior to the First World War there was some discussion of proposals for the State maintenance of children. These discussions took place in the context of widespread doubts about Britain's 'national efficiency'; doubts which had arisen largely from our military incompetence during the Boer War. While such concern gained support for the provision of rate-financed school meals, proposals for *full* State maintenance had far less backing.

On 20 January, 1905, for example, the Trades Union Congress, the London Trades Council and the Social Democratic Federation (a Marxist organization) arranged a conference on the State maintenance of children. The conference was chaired by Sir John Gorst[2] and held at the Guildhall. Will Thorne, leader of the Gas Workers' Union, moved a resolution:

that this conference ... declares in favour of State maintenance

[2] Sir John Gorst was a Conservative MP until 1902 and played an important part in the reform of British State education. He was Vice-President of the Committee of the Privy Council on Education, 1895–1902.

of children as a necessary corollary of Universal Compulsory Education and as a means of partially averting that physical deterioration of the industrial population of this country which is now generally recognized as a grave national danger. As a step towards this, local authorities should provide meals for children attending 'common schools' to be paid for by the National Exchequer.[3]

While the Conference unanimously supported Treasury or rate-financed school meals only a minority was prepared to let the State share parental responsibilities more fully. Indeed, it was claimed that such 'a wide and vague expression as "State maintenance" would excite great prejudice and alarm'.[4] Ramsay Macdonald and Mrs Pankhurst, leading members of the Independent Labour Party, were among those who were opposed to the proposal on the grounds that it would seriously weaken the family as an institution. School meals, however, were acceptable because 'the common meal will be regarded as a ceremony of the greatest educational value'.[5]

The Fabians also discussed 'motherhood endowment' during this period. They were concerned about the status of mothers and children and wanted to reduce women's economic dependence on their husbands. However, they too were disturbed about the physical efficiency of the population and proposed that motherhood should be specially encouraged among the middle and upper classes in which the birth rate was declining. The eugenists also argued, on the assumption that the working classes were made up of less intelligent and less healthy stock, that if their birth rate remained higher than that of the middle and professional classes then the physical and intellectual standards of the British population must decline. In 1907 Sidney Webb, in a tract entitled (significantly) *The Decline in the Birth Rate*, wrote: 'In order that the population may be recruited from the self-controlled and foreseeing members of each class, rather than those who are feckless and improvident, we must alter the balance of remuneration in favour of the child-producing family', and therefore he concluded that 'we shall indeed have to face the problem of the

[3] *Report of the National Labour Conference on the State Maintenance of Children*, 1905, p. 15.

[4] *Ibid.*, p. 7. The proposal was certainly vague. For example, J. Hunter-Watts, a member of the SDF said: 'If the State took over the maintenance of children it would still be the workers who would really feed them, clothe them, build the good boarding schools I would like to see by the seaside, on the sandy wastes and in the great open spaces.' *Ibid.*, p. 13.

[5] Macdonald, R., *Socialism and Government*, vol. II, ILP, 1909, p. 151. Ramsay Macdonald held very strong views on the subject of motherhood endowment which he confused with the subject of 'free love'. He was therefore opposed to the idea and argued that 'the mother's and children's rights to maintenance will be honoured by the family, not by the State'. *Op. cit.*, pp. 148–50.

systematic "endowment of motherhood" and place this most indispensable of all professions upon an honourable economic basis.'[6] Other leading Fabians made similar proposals during this period and after.[7]

Meanwhile the government, in addition to allowing local authorities to provide school meals from 1906, had recognized the parental responsibilities of certain income tax payers and men in the Armed Forces. In 1909 a direct graduation in the rates of tax had been established by imposing a super tax on large incomes in addition to ordinary income tax and by taxing small earned incomes at a lower rate than the larger earned incomes. At the same time a tax allowance in respect of children of married taxpayers whose annual incomes were less than £500 was introduced.[8] At first the allowance was £10 for each child under sixteen years of age, but this and the income limit were raised during the First World War and later, in 1919, the age limit for the child was abolished provided he or she was still in full-time education. The following year, on the recommendation of the Royal Commission on Income Tax, the child allowance was increased to £30 and the income limit removed altogether on the grounds that 'in all ranges of income some regard should be had to the taxpayers' marital and family responsibilities' ... and that 'rates of tax should be so adjusted that the taxation to be borne by each class should be redistributed among the individual taxpayers in that class with due recognition of family obligations'.[9]

Only two members of the Royal Commission were concerned with redistribution *between* income groups. Their reservation stressed that 'while a bounty should be given in aid of the maintenance of children it should be given to *all* parents for *all* children and the income tax

---

[6] Webb, S., *The Decline in the Birth Rate*, Fabian Tract, no. 131, 1907.

[7] See Wells, H. G., *Independent Review*, Nov. 1906, vol. xi, p. 172. Beatrice Webb advocated a 'bairn's part' of the national income in 1918. See the *Report of the War Cabinet Committee on Women in Industry*, Cmd. 135, 1919, p. 307. Also G. B. Shaw mentions motherhood endowment briefly in a section entitled 'The Population Question' in his *The Intelligent Woman's Guide to Socialism, Capitalism, Sovietism and Fascism*, first published in 1928.

[8] Explaining this new measure, Lloyd George said: 'There is no class in the community which has a much harder struggle or a more anxious time than that composed of the men whose earnings just bring them within the clutches of the income tax collector ... When they have a family dependent upon them the obligation to keep up the appearance of respectability of all their dependants is very trying. I am strongly of the opinion that they deserve special consideration in the rearrangement of our finances.' *H. C. Deb.*, vol. 4, col. 508. William Pitt had included tax allowances in respect of children when he introduced income tax in 1796 but they were abolished in 1806 partly because of fears of over population and partly because of fraud.

[9] *Report of the Royal Commission on the Income Tax*, Cmd. 615, 1920. Section VIII.

is not the place in which to make a gift to one special minority of relatively well-to-do persons while refusing the gift to the great mass of poor parents who need it most'.[10] Although their views appeared to carry little weight they had raised a fundamental question about the relationship between tax allowances and cash allowances which remains a controversial issue. In addition, the existence of tax allowances for children was seen by others, including Beatrice Webb[11] and Seebohm Rowntree,[12] as an important precedent to be used in the argument for extending the State's recognition of parental responsibilities by the introduction of cash family allowances.

Another form of child allowance was introduced during the First World War. This was incorporated in the separation allowance paid to the wives of men in the Armed Forces. It was based on the number of dependent children in the family and was provided largely because it was found difficult to recruit men without ensuring some financial security for their families.[13] These allowances were increased during the war and by 1918 were worth four shillings for the first child, decreasing to one shilling each for fourth and subsequent children. Towards the end of the war separation allowances were extended to the families of commissioned officers.[14]

---

[10] *Ibid.* Reservation by Lilian Knowles (Professor of Economic History, University of London and member of the *Departmental Committee on the Rise of the Cost of Living to the Working Classes*, 1918) and J. Walter Clarke, para. 1. In 1920, there were 3,406,000 income tax payers of whom 1,940,000 were relieved by tax allowances. A child allowance was worth £5 8s a year to those paying tax at the standard rate of 3s and £10 16s to those (with income greater than £500) paying at the 6s rate.

[11] Beatrice Webb used this argument when stressing that it was important to adopt 'some form of State provision, entirely apart from wages, of which the present maternity benefit, free schooling, and income tax allowances constitute only the germ ... this question of public provision for maternity and childhood urgently requires investigation by a separate Committee or Commission'. *Report to the War Cabinet Committee on Women in Industry, op. cit.*, p. 307.

[12] See Rowntree, B. S., *The Human Needs of Labour*, Nelson, 1918, p. 141.

[13] During a debate on the progress of recruiting Sir Ivor Herbert said: 'In all my experiences of the last few weeks I have found hesitation as to whether to enlist or not arising from one cause, and one cause only, a doubt in the mind of the man as to whether his family was adequately provided for.' *H. C. Deb.*, vol. 64, col. 674. Debates concerning the level and method of payment of separation allowances filled many columns of *Hansard* between 1914 and 1918.

[14] Eleanor Rathbone maintained that while commissioned officers were excluded from separation allowances many able non-commissioned officers with large families were prevented from accepting commissions because to do so would have resulted in a reduction of income. This, she argued later, was a good reason for making a State scheme of family allowances universal and not restricting it to the lower income groups. See Rathbone, E., *Family Allowances*, Allen & Unwin, second edn, 1949, p. 230.

The payment of these separation allowances, which Eleanor Rathbone called 'the largest experiment in the State endowment of maternity the world has ever seen',[15] was important in two respects. First, it demonstrated that the adjustment of family income to family size had beneficial effects on the family's health and standard of living. Advocates of family allowances later used this as evidence in support of their case.[16] Second, and more crucial, the principle of paying dependants' allowances to the wives of men in the Armed Forces was carried over, albeit by a very reluctant government, into unemployment benefit.

When servicemen were demobilized in 1918 they were given a free unemployment insurance policy which entitled them to an 'out-of-work-donation' for a maximum of twenty-six weeks during the first twelve months following their demobilization. This was intended to help them return to civilian life until they found employment and, to conform with the allowances they had received in the Services, this sum included additions for dependants. The donation was similar to unemployment benefit and from November 1918 was available for periods up to a maximum of thirteen weeks to all the unemployed covered by the 1911 insurance scheme, to ex-servicemen, civilians, insured and non-insured alike. Because of continuing unemployment, the out-of-work donation was subsequently extended for further periods although the amounts paid were lower after November 1920, by which time only ex-servicemen were eligible. The scheme for civilians ended in November 1919, but some unemployed ex-servicemen continued to receive the donation until March 1921.[17]

After November 1919, therefore, all the unemployed except the ex-servicemen lost their dependants' benefits and this loss was not offset by the slight increase in the basic unemployment benefit rate made in December that year. In 1920 the unemployment insurance scheme was extended to cover all workers except those on the land, in domestic service or in the civil service. Ex-servicemen lost their dependants' allowances along with their donation the following year and in June 1921, when the number of registered unemployed stood at over two million, unemployment benefit rates were cut. However, in November that year, the government was obliged to restore small dependants' allowances in unemployment benefit as a 'temporary measure' lasting six months. They have never been withdrawn since.

[15] Rathbone, E., 'The Remuneration of Women's Services', *Economic Journal*, vol. 27, Mar. 1917, p. 55.

[16] See Rathbone, E., *Family Allowances, op. cit.*, pp. 48–51.

[17] The cost of the out-of-work donation scheme for ex-servicemen totalled over £40 million, and the scheme for civilians nearly £11 million. Ministry of Labour, *Report on National Unemployment Insurance to July 1923*, p. 56.

Table 1

CHANGE IN BENEFITS FOR THE UNEMPLOYED, 1918–22

Amounts in Shillings

	Out-of-work Donation			Unemployment Insurance Benefit						Poor Law Relief
	Nov 1918	Dec 1918	Nov 1920	Nov 1918	Dec 1919	Nov 1920	Mar 1921	July 1921	Nov 1921	Jan 1922
Men over 18	24	29	20	7	11	15	20	15	15	15
Women over 18	20	25	15	7	11	12	16	12	12	15
Wife	–	–	–	–	–	–	–	–	–	10
First child	6	6	6	–	–	–	–	–	–	6
Each additional child	3	3	3	–	–	–	–	–	1	5*

* Subsequent children received slightly less than five shillings.
SOURCE: Ministry of Labour, *Report on National Unemployment Insurance to July 1923; with a short account of the out-of-work Donation Scheme*, 1923.

While it was true that the experience of dependants' benefits demonstrated to the Ministry of Labour that 'not in a few cases they enabled respectable and industrious men and women to avoid having recourse to the Poor Law',[18] the restoration and continuation of dependants' allowances and the establishment of uniform minimum scales of Poor Law outdoor relief in January 1922 owed much to the activities of the National Unemployed Workers' Movement which organized protests nationally as well as against local Boards of Guardians.[19] In 1921 the government was clearly still fearful of social unrest. Unemployment was proving to be an intractable problem; the successful Russian Revolution was not long passed, and although the police were controlling mass demonstrations of the unemployed, using violence on occasion, they too had gone on strike in August 1918.

For the next twenty years the number of unemployed never fell below a million. As later discussion will show, the existence of a large group of men who received an income from the State which took

[18] *Ibid.*, p. 10.
[19] Some Boards of Guardians were sympathetic. In September 1921, George Lansbury and his fellow councillors in Poplar were gaoled for six weeks for over-spending on outdoor relief. A lively account of the campaign against cuts in unemployment benefit can be found in the writings of one of the leading members of the NUWM. See Hannington, W., *Unemployed Struggles, 1919–1936*, Lawrence & Wishart, 1936, chs 2 and 3.

account of their family size considerably strengthened the case for family allowances to be paid irrespective of the employment status of the parents.[20] In addition, the principle 'that relief given under the Poor Law should be sufficient for the purpose of relieving distress, but that the amount of relief so given should of necessity be calculated on a lower scale than the earnings of the independent workman'[21] still stood. This made comparisons between the circumstances of the families of the unemployed and those in work unavoidable.

The Family Endowment Society

The campaign for a national scheme of cash family allowances began in earnest with the formation of the Nineteen Seventeen Committee which became the Family Endowment Society a year later in 1918. Describing this first committee, Eleanor Rathbone wrote that they 'had been brought to the idea [of family allowances] partly by the experience of the admirable effects of war-time separation allowances [and] partly by the difficulty of otherwise reconciling the claims of equal pay for equal work with the needs of mothers and children'.[22] In the words of another founder member, Mary Stocks, the committee 'had its roots in the women's suffrage movement, but its personnel was definitely left-wing'.[23] They were all agreed that the provision of family allowances would enhance the status of women not only as mothers but as workers because 'it would strike at one of the main popular objections to "equal pay for equal work", i.e. the plea that a man requires a family wage whereas a woman requires only an individual subsistence wage'.[24] They also wished to achieve some redistribution of income in favour of families, particularly poor families. But even at this early stage they were unable to agree on the primary objectives of a scheme of family allowances.[25]

[20] For an account of the beneficial effects of dependants' benefits for the unemployed see Bowley, A. L., *et al.*, *The Third Winter of Unemployment*, King, 1922, p. 70.

[21] Ministry of Health Circular No. 240, 8 Sept., 1921, to Boards of Guardians on *Poor Law Relief to Unemployed Persons*, p. 47.

[22] Rathbone, E., *The Case for Family Allowances, op. cit.*, p. 68.

[23] The members of the committee besides Eleanor Rathbone included three members of the Executive Committee of the National Union of Women's Suffrage Societies: Kathleen Courtney, Maude Royden and Mary Stocks. The other members were H. N. Brailsford, a left wing journalist, later editor of *The New Leader* and Mr and Mrs Emile Burns, 'both good feminists, socialists and students of economics'. See Stocks, M., *Eleanor Rathbone*, Gollancz, 1949, p. 98.

[24] National Union of Societies for Equal Citizenship, *National Family Endowment*, 1920, p. 3.

[25] See *Equal Pay and the Family: a Proposal for the National Endowment of Motherhood* published by the National Union of Societies for Equal Citizenship, 1918.

"WHITHER BRITAIN?"

Jan. 27th 1934.

'For the fifth year in succession the birth rate for England and Wales was in 1933 the lowest on record.'

FAT HOPES FOR THE FUTURE

Feb. 11th 1943.

The majority were concerned only with the redistribution *between* income groups. They were convinced that equal allowances, financed out of general taxation so that the rich contributed more than the poor, should be given in all income groups because the responsibility of motherhood and the value of the child were the same whatever the status of the parents. The minority, including Eleanor Rathbone, while not opposed to the redistribution of income in favour of the poor,[26] argued that they should also be aiming at the redistribution of income in favour of those with family responsibilities *within* each income group. Eleanor Rathbone firmly believed that the only way to remove a major barrier against equal pay in professions such as teaching would be to take account of the differences in standards of living reflected in the higher costs of bringing up children in the higher income groups.[27] 'The fact remains', she wrote, 'that differences in status exist, and as long as they exist it is practically impossible, since the lives of children cannot be separated from those of their parents, to secure to all children a uniform standard of living.'[28] Acknowledging that it would appear unjust to pay higher allowances out of taxation to the middle classes, she argued that it would only be possible if the higher allowances were paid for by the income groups or occupations which benefited from them. She therefore concluded that 'it may be necessary to make the State system a flat rate one and secure the necessary gradation by supplementary allowances from an occupational pool for all the higher grade occupations'.[29]

The Family Endowment Society widened the basis of its support in the twenties because 'family allowances could be approached from so many directions with such an infinite variety of emphasis and application. It could be handled as a problem of vital statistics, housing administration, minimum wage legislation, child nutrition, national insurance, teachers' salary scales, coal mining economics, feminism, social philosophy or pure finance.'[30] As a result the society became less specifically a group of the left. It was 'committed to the principle of direct provision for the family, but to no specific scheme – concerning which there was indeed much difference of opinion among the advocates of the principle'.[31] Indeed, by the end of the twenties there were many schemes under discussion. Professor Fisher, who

[26] See for example, *Family Allowances, op. cit.*, p. 29.

[27] In 1919 the *Committee on Women in Industry* had studied the recruitment of teachers, and had recommended an occupational scheme of family allowances so that in conditions of equal pay men would still find the profession attractive. See *Report of the War Cabinet Committee on Women in Industry, op. cit.*

[28] Rathbone, E., *Family Allowances, op. cit.*, p. 233.

[29] *Ibid.*, p. 236.

[30] Stocks, M., *Eleanor Rathbone, op. cit.*, p. 102.

[31] *Ibid.*, p. 99.

followed the family allowance debate closely, said: 'It will be seen that the economic methods of establishing Family Allowances are very various. According to your political colour you can arrange the scheme to cost the Treasury £100,000,000 a year, or, by a re-allocation of wage and salary payments to cost not a penny.'[32]

The status of mothers and children

In 1925 (the year in which Eleanor Rathbone became its president) the National Union of Societies for Equal Citizenship[33] passed a resolution in favour of a State-paid scheme of flat rate family allowances. A year later the National Labour Women's Conference adopted a similar resolution. It was clear that the supporters of the scheme were concerned with the status of mothers and children just as the early members of the Family Endowment Society had been. The idea of endowment paid to a mother 'on account of her motherhood and on behalf of each of her children ... is', it was asserted, 'entirely opposed to the idea of relief of distress or poverty, because it implies a universal national provision and not a means of making up deficiencies in the incomes of particular families'.[34]

Opinion in both these movements, however, was as strongly divided as it had been among the trade union movement and the Independent Labour Party twenty years before. Only two years earlier, in 1923, the National Labour Women's Conference had rejected a resolution supporting the idea of cash family allowances. Some members believed the establishment of universal health and education services, together with improved housing provision, was more important because these services would benefit everybody, not only those with children. Linked with this idea was the belief that the economic structure of society must be changed first.[35] In addition, some were convinced that family allowances would result in lower wages, although the danger of that happening was thought to be considerably less if they

[32] Fisher, R. A., *Family Allowances in the Contemporary Situation*, an address to the Eugenic Society, 12 Apr., 1932. Professor Fisher did much work on the hereditary aspects of intelligence and later became a well-known advocate of 'the inverted birth-rate theory' (which much impressed William Beveridge).

[33] The National Union of Societies for Equal Citizenship was a suffragette organization.

[34] *Motherhood and Child Endowment*; Interim report prepared by the Advisory Committee of the Joint Research and Information Department of the Labour Party and TUC, 1922, p. 4 (Hugh Dalton was a member of this committee).

[35] As the Joint Report of 1922 referred to above stated: 'Children's pensions would require for its successful and economic administration considerable changes in the wages system as well as a very great increase in taxation and must therefore be held over for later consideration when Labour in power has been able to reorganize and stabilize Society on a better basis' (p. 4).

were financed by the State and not by employers' contributions. Others, including Dame Millicent Fawcett, never supported the idea of family allowances because, like Ramsay Macdonald, she feared they would have a detrimental effect on parental responsibility.

The majority of women's organizations, even those representing employed women, have never made family allowances one of their major preoccupations[36] although equal pay has (and still is) an issue of vital concern. Neither have women's organizations been particularly concerned with occupational schemes of family allowances. This is perhaps a little surprising for in the twenties and thirties one of the main arguments against giving women equal pay in the professions was that men have families to support whereas women do not and therefore it was only proper to pay men a higher salary.

The living wage policy

The Labour Party and the trade union movement considered family allowances again in 1926. Unlike the discussions that had taken place twenty years earlier, the wide and vague principle of State maintenance of children was superseded by more precise details and exposition. Nonetheless, varying degrees of commitment became evident but no unequivocal support for family allowances emerged.

The Independent Labour Party at its annual conference in 1926 adopted a 'Living Wage' policy. This meant the provision of a wage large enough for the needs of a man and wife supplemented by a State-paid system of allowances for all children. They had realized, as William Pitt had done, that minimum wage legislation, even if it were based on a family with three children, was not enough to meet the need of all families. 'Provision would be made for over sixteen million phantom children in the families containing less than three children, while those in excess of that number, over 1¼ million in all in families containing more than three children would still remain unprovided for.'[37] One of the ostensible purposes of the ILP policy was the redistribution of income in favour of children, particularly children of the lower income groups. As one of their members, Hugh Dalton (who was to be Chancellor of the Exchequer when family allowances were first paid in 1946) wrote in an article advocating family allowances: 'We would raid the luxuries of the rich to give a chance of life to children of the poor.'[38] For just this reason

[36] This is perhaps no longer true for the debate on the tax credit proposals has, very recently, been of much concern to many women's organizations.

[37] Rathbone, E., *Family Allowances, op. cit.*, p. 15. At that time over half the male workers over the age of twenty had no children under fourteen; 29·6 per cent had one or two; 8·8 per cent had three and 9·9 per cent more than three.

[38] Dalton, H., *New Leader*, 29 Jan., 1926. The editor of this ILP journal was then H. N. Brailsford.

the only scheme of family allowances acceptable to the Labour movement as a whole was one financed out of general taxation. Contributory or employer financed schemes, it was feared, might only help the worker with children at the expense of the childless worker. This might also weaken solidarity between workers. Even if the workers themselves made no contribution to the scheme it was argued that the cost of family allowance schemes to the employers would be used by them either as an excuse to reduce wages or at least hold back wage increases[39] or to put up prices. The latter would handicap British exports and in either case the benefit to the workers would be illusory.[40]

Therefore when, in 1926, the Royal Commission on the Coal Industry (largely at the instigation of William Beveridge, one of its members)[41] recommended the introduction of a system of children's allowances financed by the mining industry itself but with a hint that it might be accompanied by a reduction in wage rates, the Miners' Federation was only prepared to accept the proposal if financed out of general taxation.[42] In the event the issue was largely forgotten in

[39] In France there is clear evidence that employers increased family allowances in preference to making general wage increases in the twenties and thirties. There were also examples of employers using family allowances as an extra means of control over their workers. For example, some employers would not pay family allowances to workers if their older children did not go to work in their firm. See Ceccaldi, D., *Histoire des Prestations Familiales en France*, CNAF, 1954, pp. 22–3.

[40] For a full discussion of insurance-based family allowance schemes, see a report of a conference held at the London School of Economics in October 1927: *Six Aspects of Family Allowances*, Family Endowment Society, 1927. Speakers included William Beveridge, Professor Fisher, (Hon. Sec. of the Eugenics Society), H. N. Brailsford (on behalf of the ILP), Professor Mottram (University of London), Professor Murray (University of Exeter) and Mr Cohen (member of the Committee on Social Insurance of the International Labour Organization). William Beveridge had costed a contributory scheme of family allowances in 1924. He estimated that an allowance of 3s 6d for every child (except illegitimate children) could be paid for by a contribution of one shilling from each employee and employer and 9d from the State.

[41] William Beveridge was one of Eleanor Rathbone's most important and successful converts. Her book *The Disinherited Family*, published for the first time in 1924, made a considerable impression on him. Before this time he had no interest in the subject. In the epilogue to the second edition of her book he wrote: 'I read this book ... and suffered constant and total conversion. Till that time ... in concentration upon other problems of unemployment, population and so forth, I had been apt to regard her [Eleanor Rathbone] and the Family Endowment Society as slightly tiresome creatures, with a particularly loud bee in each of their bonnets.' Rathbone, E., *Family Allowances, op. cit.*, p. 270.

[42] 'If the total sum available for workers' remuneration can be kept at the present level, the allocation of a small part of this to children's allowances will raise materially the general level of comfort; if the full remuneration

the upheaval following the General Strike in 1926 although the Miners' Federation was from that time on a strong supporter of a national non-contributory scheme of family allowances.

Family allowances have never enjoyed unanimous support in the Labour movement. When, as a result of the Independent Labour Party's adoption of a 'Living Wage' policy, a joint committee of the Labour Party and Trades Union Congress examined the question in 1928 and again in 1929, two reports were issued. The majority report recommended that cash allowances financed by the State should be paid in respect of children whose parents were not subject to income tax. Those paying income tax were excluded on the grounds that their income was already adjusted to family size. There was no suggestion that children's tax allowances should be abolished. '*In our view the principle of making an allowance for each child of the income tax payer is a sound one*, in practice the middle class parent, who pays income tax receives a family allowance from the State. We do not see why the advantages should not be extended to working class people whose wages are too low to bring them within income tax limits' (our italics).[43] Any kind of contributory scheme was firmly opposed. The minority report recommended that the social services should be developed first and accorded less priority to family allowances.

At the TUC Annual Conference in 1930 the General Council recommended that the minority report be accepted. Their reasons for doing so were based on several fears: that family allowances would weaken the trade union movement by driving a wedge between the interests of single and married men and that they could interfere with wage negotiations to the detriment of wage rates. Looking at foreign experience, as the Royal Commission on the Coal Industry had also done, it was argued that the trade unions were weak in countries with family allowances and strong in countries without them. As well as these apprehensions it was also considered that the extension and development of the social services was more in keeping with collectivist principles and would not restrict benefit to families with children. Moreover, it was impractical, they concluded, to advocate cash allowances faced with the prospect of reductions in public spending.[44] The Conference adopted the minority report and family allow-

---

cannot be maintained the harmful effects of any reasonable reduction can be largely mitigated.' *Report of the Royal Commission on the Coal Industry (1925)*, vol. 1, Cmd. 2600, 1926, para. 164.

[43] *Majority Report of the Labour Party and Trades Union Congress Joint Committee on the Living Wage*, 1929, para. 4.

[44] For example, the Unemployment Insurance Fund was overspent by £44 million and Congress had at this Conference already passed a resolution which would have increased expenditure on pensions by £285 million. Their family allowance scheme was estimated to cost £70 million, based on a five shilling

ances were not discussed formally at an Annual Conference again until 1941.

The birth rate

Discussions about family allowance schemes have always involved some consideration of their impact on the size and structure of the population. In the early stages of their campaign in the twenties, supporters of family allowances were concerned lest fear of over-population militated against their proposals.[45] During this period there was a considerable body of opinion, particularly among economists, which held that the country was over-populated.[46] Partly in this belief the government was actively encouraging emigration.[47] The provision of family allowances, which could have been interpreted (at least indirectly) as encouraging people to have more children, hardly commended itself.

By the mid-thirties the Malthusian revival of the previous decade was over[48] and opinion changed with the widely publicized discovery that the country faced the prospect of a declining population. A leading article in *The Times* in September 1936 noted that: 'last year the population of our country probably reached its peak. It may increase slightly but if fertility continues to decline at the present rate that is unlikely. From now on we can only look back.'[49] Calculations based on the assumption that the fertility and mortality rates of 1933

allowance for every child. In addition it should not be forgotten that more than half the male workers over the age of twenty had no children under fourteen.

[45] Writing in 1924, Eleanor Rathbone lists fear of over-population first amongst objections to family allowances, but stressed that the opinion of experts was divided on the subject. See Rathbone, E., *Family Allowances, op. cit.*, pp. 185–98. Later in October 1927, at the conference already mentioned (see p. 168), Beveridge said that he regarded the population question as the one real difficulty in advocating family allowances.

[46] The level of unemployment, for example, was considered evidence that the country was over-populated. Beveridge (who did not believe this) and Maynard Keynes (who was more sympathetic to the view) debated this in a series of articles published during 1923 and 1924. See Beveridge, W., 'Population and Unemployment,' *Economic Journal*, vol. 23, no. 132, pp. 447–75, and Keynes, J. M., 'Reply to William Beveridge', *ibid.*, pp. 476–86. Beatrice Webb also held the view at this time that unemployment was partly due to over-population. See Cole, M. (ed.), *The Diaries, 1924–32*, Longmans, 1956, pp. 153–4.

[47] Between 1921 and 1939 there was a net emigration of 500,000 people.

[48] Maynard Keynes had moved far from classical economic theory and had put the analysis of the causes of the level of unemployment on an entirely new footing by the publication in 1936 of his *General Theory of Employment, Interest and Money*, Macmillan. He also became an advocate of family allowances. See Keynes, J. M., *How to Pay for the War*, Macmillan, 1940.

[49] 'The Dwindling Family: A Menace to the Future', *The Times*, 28 Sept., 1936.

would remain unchanged showed that the population of this country would be halved in the course of a century. On the assumption that they would continue to fall at the same rate as in the first half of the decade then, it was estimated, the population would be only one tenth of its size in a hundred years time.[50]

The international implications were clearly disturbing. Yet another leading article in *The Times* drew attention to other countries, notably Germany and Italy, which were adopting pro-natalist policies with a small measure of success.[51] 'There will be problems of defence, of transport and building, adjustment of Imperial policy confronted with the growing population of Asia and the reluctant birth-rate of the Dominions.' But, continued *The Times*, 'it may be argued that if the same thing is happening everywhere there is no need to worry. But that is not the case. Apart from the fact that Asiatic birth rates flourish and will continue to flourish, that the population of Russia may double itself to over 320,000,000 before decline begins, there is evidence of resistance [to a declining birth rate] in Germany and Italy.'[52]

The government reacted to the growing concern about population trends by establishing a Population Investigation Committee in the Autumn of 1936 and included an examination of family allowances in its terms of reference. At the Conservative Party Conference in October 1936 there was much discussion about the need for greater physical fitness, but no mention of family allowances. In his budget speech Neville Chamberlain had justified a £10 increase in the tax allowance for second and subsequent children by saying that he saw

[50] Charles, E., 'The Effect of Present Trends in Fertility and Mortality upon the Future Population of England and Wales', *London and Cambridge Economic Service Special Memorandum*, no. 40, Aug., 1935. The birth rate reached its lowest point in 1933, but it remained well below replacement level until 1941. In 1941 there were one million fewer children under fifteen than there were in 1931.

[51] In 1933, for example, Germany had passed an Act providing loans for young couples wishing to marry. The loans were interest free and a quarter of the loan was cancelled with the birth of each child. In addition to encouraging marriage and children, they were also intended to reduce male unemployment, for the loan was given to women who had been working for at least nine months of the previous two years on condition that they ceased work on marriage.

[52] 'A Case for Inquiry', *The Times*, 29 Sept., 1936. Germany's concern for her population certainly had military over-tones. In March 1937 the Fascist Grand Council stated that 'the demographic problem, being the problem of life and survival, is in reality the problem of problems, for without life there is neither youth, nor military power, nor economic expansion, no sure future of the Fatherland'. Quoted by Fisher, R. A., 'The Birthrate and Family Allowances', *Agenda*, vol. 11, no. 2, May 1943, p. 126. The Olympic Games were held in Berlin in 1936, thus drawing world-wide attention to Germany and the physical prowess of the people.

a time not too far distant 'when countries of the British Empire will be crying out for more citizens of the right breed, and when we in this country shall not be able to supply the demand. I think that if today we can give a little help to those who are carrying on the race the money will not be wasted.'[53] Family allowances did not figure in his plans. The government appeared to take little interest in the schemes of the Family Endowment Society.

There was another aspect of the population question which also caused concern. The age structure of the population was changing. By 1975 it was estimated that seven per cent of the population would be under fifteen, and thirty per cent would be over sixty, compared with twenty-five per cent and twelve per cent respectively in 1938.[54] The increasing number of old people had been noted by politicians during the twenties,[55] mainly because of the increased cost of pensions, but now, against the background of a declining population, this trend seemed more alarming. Duncan Sandys summarized the situation in this way: 'a declining population must inevitably involve a deterioration in the whole standard of life of our people. With a population whose numbers are declining, and where average age is rising, we shall be faced with the situation of a smaller and smaller proportion of active workers having to support an ever increasing proportion of old people.'[56]

There was a further feature of the birth rate problem which had concerned the eugenists in particular for many years. This was an anxiety about the steady increase of fertility down the social scale. During the twenties this fact had been used against universal family allowances because, it was claimed, they would have the 'dysgenic' effect of encouraging the idle and the feckless to have more children.[57]

---

[53] *H. C. Deb.*, vol. 300, col. 1634. The tax allowance for children as a result of this Budget was £50 for each child. Prior to April 1935 the allowance was £50 for the first and £40 for each subsequent child. The allowance was increased by a further £10 in 1936.

[54] Charles, E., *op. cit.*

[55] For example, when introducing his Budget in 1929 Winston Churchill noted that the number of old people in the country had doubled in thirty years.

[56] Duncan Sandys, *Report of the Conservative and Unionist Party Conference,* 1937. See also Glass, D. V., *The Struggle for Population,* Oxford, 1936 (David Glass was research secretary to the Population Investigation Committee); Charles, E., *The Menace of Under Population: A Biological Study of the Decline of Population Growth,* 1936; Keynes, J. M., *Galton Lecture of the Eugenic Society,* 1937, and many articles in the *Eugenic Review* between 1930 and 1940.

[57] For example, see Gray, A., *Family Endowment: A Critical Analysis,* Benn, 1927. Alexander Gray was a Professor of Political Economics. He was also opposed to family allowances on the grounds that it was 'a scheme for the nationalization of children and married women'. *Loc. cit.,* p. 78. Professor

Although there were, of course, counter arguments[58] it was not until a rapidly declining population became an acknowledged fact that the case for excluding certain groups from family allowances lost its force. By the end of the thirties sociologists and demographers could forcefully press the need to increase the birth rate among the working classes as well.[59] Thus the existence of different birth rates between classes could be used against the idea of *universal* family allowances when prevailing opinion feared over-population. When, during the thirties and forties, the concern was with the *quantity* as much as with the *quality* of population this particular objection carried little weight, although being drawn upon as a reason for not restricting a national scheme of family allowances to the working classes alone. Moreover, of course, the case for occupational family allowances and child tax allowances has always gained in strength from the existence of differential birthrates, the argument being that the more prosperous parents warranted special encouragement.[60] During the twenties and thirties interest in occupational family allowances grew but the impetus to introduce them came largely from individuals. In 1924 William Beveridge established a scheme of family allowances for the staff of the London School of Economics, of which he was the Director. Eleanor Rathbone also campaigned for their introduction whenever the opportunity arose[61] and by 1936 Leo Amery, one of the first Conservative members of the Front Bench publicly to support family allowances, was recommending occupational schemes to leading

---

William McDougall (Professor of Psychology) suggested that family endowment should be restricted to the middle and higher income groups for eugenic reasons. See McDougall, W., *National Welfare and National Decay*, Methuen, 1921, p. 195.

[58] For example, Professor Pigou (Professor of Economics) argued that 'as the birthrate of the lower group of wage earners has not apparently in the past been influenced at all by prudential considerations, it could not at all events be increased by Family Endowment since it is as large as nature permitted'. *Eugenic Review*, April 1923.

[59] 'If there is to be any significant increase in the birthrate, the major part must come from the working class. Consequently no action is likely to have a permanent influence unless it provides conditions in which the working class is able to bring up children without thereby suffering from economic and social hardship.' Glass, D. V., *op. cit.*, preface. See also Titmuss, R. M., *Poverty and Population*, Macmillan, 1938.

[60] For example, Professor Fisher wrote: 'the complete cessation of childbirth in the poorer half of the population, though it would leave a most favourable *differential* birthrate, would not take us a step nearer to arresting the process by which the eugenically valuable qualities of the nation are being destroyed'. Fisher, R. A., *op. cit.*, The Eugenic Society, 12 April, 1932.

[61] In 1930, the Family Endowment Society sent a memorandum proposing a scheme of family allowances for the Civil Service to the *Royal Commission on the Civil Service* (see appendix IV of the Minutes of Evidence). Cmd. 3909, 1931.

industrialists.[62] He introduced a scheme in a firm of which he was a director.

Poverty and malnutrition

During the thirties the inadequacies of the wage system in meeting family needs were tellingly exposed by the growing knowledge of the extent of poverty and malnutrition in the population, particularly among children. Seebohm Rowntree, in his second study of poverty in York in 1936, found that half the children in working class families were born into poverty-stricken homes and lived below the level of 'dietetic and health efficiency' during the first five years of their lives.[63] Other surveys, including those carried out in relatively prosperous areas, made similar estimates.[64] It was undeniable that low wages as well as unemployment were a major cause of poverty.[65] Although definitions of 'poverty' and adequate nutrition were (and are) debatable, the accumulation of these findings did make an impression and convinced more people of the need for family allowances, particularly when viewed against the background of a declining population at home and the pro-natalist policies of our competitors abroad.

As the thirties drew to a close and the shadow of war fell across Europe a concern about 'the State of the Nation' was clearly detectable. In 1938 Leo Amery expressed it in this way: 'when we are faced with the competition of a people who lay stress on the healthy development of their young manhood and womanhood, how can we afford a situation in which something like twenty-five per cent of the children of our country are growing up undernourished and likely to belong to the C3 rather than the A1 type when they grow up. How can we, confronted by dangers not of today and tomorrow, but of the generations which lie ahead, contemplate with equanimity the prospect of our population, already small compared with some of our competitors, steadily dwindling, above all in the younger spheres of life.'[66]

[62] By 1939 about two dozen firms, including Cadburys and Pilkingtons, had introduced family allowance schemes. Most excluded the first child.

[63] Rowntree, S. B., *Human Needs of Labour*, Longmans, 1936. See also Boyd-Orr, J., *Food, Health and Income*, Macmillan, 1936; and Department of Social Studies, Liverpool University, *Social Survey of Merseyside*, Hodder & Stoughton, 1934.

[64] Tout, H., *The Standard of Living in Bristol*, 1938. *The Times* later commented: 'these statistics are compiled for a prosperous city in a prosperous year, they disclose a disquieting amount of actual poverty'.

[65] For example, the minimum weekly earnings enforced by the Agricultural Wages Board in 1937 averaged 33s 4d. See Macmillan, H., *The Middle Way*, Macmillan, 1958 (Harold Macmillan was then in favour of a minimum income in kind provided by the State).

[66] *H. C. Deb.*, vol. 341, col. 574.

Amery was convinced of the need to introduce a scheme of family allowance even if, in the interest of economy, it was limited to third and subsequent children;[67] and now he was finding more support for that view from the Conservative benches as well as from other parties.[68] However, his suggestions concerning family allowances were 'duly ignored in Ministerial replies'[69] and he did not succeed in persuading Neville Chamberlain to have the question studied by the party research department until after the war began. Meanwhile, in spite of increasing requests in Parliament for at least an inquiry into family allowances schemes, the government did nothing, on the grounds that they 'were not aware of the widespread desire among [employers and workers] for a system of this kind'.[70]

Outside Parliament, an all-party Children's Minimum Campaign Committee had been formed in 1934 'to ensure that no child shall by reason of the poverty of its parents be deprived of at least the minimum food and other requirements for full health'.[71] All organizations working for the welfare of children were invited to affiliate. 'The Ministry of Health, the Milk Board, the Board of Education, the Statutory Committee on Unemployment Insurance and the Unemployment Assistance Board all felt the impact of its activities. Memoranda issued from it; conferences were called by it; deputations proceeded from it; researches into nutritional standards and the incidence of malnutrition were stimulated by it.'[72] The Campaign Committee used the evidence of nutritional studies not only to show the inadequacies

[67] A family allowance of five shillings for third and subsequent children in every family was estimated to cost less than £10 million per annum compared with £118 million covering every child. Leo Amery was not alone in believing the cost of a family allowance to all children would be 'overwhelming'. See Laffitte, F., *Report on the British Social Services*, PEP, June 1937, pp. 166–7.

[68] 'I got together an inter-party parliamentary committee and, well-backed by some of the younger Conservatives like Duncan Sandys and Ronald Cartland, we organized several useful debates.' Amery, L. S., *My Political Life*, vol. 3, *The Unforgiving Years, 1929–1949*, Hutchinson, 1955, p. 206. During 1938 Conservative members, Robert Boothby, Duncan Sandys and Lord Pilkington, a Labour member, David Adams, in addition to Leo Amery and Eleanor Rathbone asked for a Committee or Commission to investigate the question of family allowances (Eleanor Rathbone had been elected MP (Independent) for the combined Universities in 1929).

[69] Leo Amery professed to be perplexed by the Conservative Party's lack of response towards family allowances. 'What I would never understand was the shortsightedness of the Conservative Party in not taking up a policy so essentially sound from the point of view of a Party which professed to put family life and national strength in the forefront of its aims.' *Ibid.*, p. 206.

[70] Lennox Boyd, Minister of Labour, *H. C. Deb.*, vol. 345, col. 40.

[71] It had close connections with the Family Endowment Society. Eva Hubback, a longstanding member of the Family Endowment Society, initiated it, and another member, Marjorie Green, was the secretary.

[72] Stocks, M., *op. cit.*, p. 190.

of the wages system but also to emphasize that provisions for children in the form of school meals and milk were not sufficient in themselves to eradicate malnutrition.[73]

Nonetheless welfare provisions for school children had made progress during the 1930s although because of the frequent economic crises this progress had been rather erratic. Local authorities, moreover, had encountered difficulties in selecting children for these various benefits.[74] School meals and milk as well as education maintenance allowances increasingly came to be regarded as *complements* to a universal scheme of family allowances by its advocates rather than alternatives as had been argued, for example, at the Trades Union Congress in 1930.

Unemployment insurance and wage levels

The great depression of the thirties during which unemployment never fell below nine per cent and at one point exceeded twenty-two per cent, meant that a large section of the population was dependent on insurance and assistance benefits. It became increasingly difficult to pay insurance and assistance benefits and at the same time keep them below the level of wages. Although the system of relief under the Poor Law had changed when the Boards of Guardians were disbanded in 1929 and changes had been made in the unemployment insurance scheme, the principle of not allowing unemployment benefit to exceed a man's wages was by no means abandoned.[75] By 1938 the Unemployment Insurance Statutory Committee admitted that it could not increase dependants' benefits without pushing the level of unemployment benefit for the family man above the level of many workers' earnings. In its annual report of 1938 the Committee stated that 'the existing scale of benefits cannot be regarded as so fully meeting needs as to make it undesirable to raise them further' and continued, 'if ... the wage system made allowance for dependency, the main objection to further increase in the rates of benefit would be removed'.[76]

[73] *Ibid.*, p. 191.

[74] For example, some local authorities started to select children for free meals using an income test and not waiting for signs of malnutrition to be visible. In 1934 the Board of Education tried unsuccessfully to stop such a basis of selection being used. Others argued that school feedings was a public health measure and so should not be the responsibility of the Education Department.

[75] 'If wages were assured, whether one worked or not, the concern for and about work would be notably diminished.' *Royal Commission on Unemployment Insurance Final Report*, Cmd. 4185, 1932, para. 217. See also Beatrice Webb's supporting evidence for this rule of 'cardinal importance'. *Ibid.*, Minutes of Evidence, p. 1321.

[76] Quoted in Green, M., *Family Allowances*, Children's Minimum Council, 1938, p. 18. The median full-time weekly wages normally earned by a large sample of applicants for unemployed benefit in August 1937 was 55s 6d. At

William Beveridge, who was a member of the Committee from its inception in 1934 until 1944, was keenly aware of this problem of less eligibility and was convinced that a scheme of family allowances could help to overcome it.[77] This conclusion was obvious to others besides Beveridge. An interesting change of ground was occurring. The problem revealed by the Unemployment Insurance Statutory Committee led unquestionably to a view of family allowances as incentives to work rather than an encouragement to depend unduly on unemployment benefit. If family allowances were available to the man in work, his advantageous economic position in relation to the unemployed would be better secured.[78] Mary Stocks later wrote that 'this was a solemn thought for opponents who had formerly visualized family allowances as a threat to the wage earner's incentive ... it was her [Eleanor Rathbone's] turn to talk of economic incentive now'.[79]

The Labour movement was not, however, convinced by these arguments: rather it continued to oppose family allowances. For example, in a debate on Unemployment Assistance in July 1938, Clement Attlee described proposals for family allowances as attempts to keep down wages. This 'determined hostility of the Socialist Party generally and of the Trade Union movement in particular' which Leo Amery later described as 'a curious feature'[80] of the movement for family allowances, can perhaps be explained by two factors.

First, the Conservatives who were in favour of family allowances mostly advocated contributory or employer financed schemes and the grounds for the Labour movement's opposition to such schemes, which they had voiced in the twenties, were still valid. Indeed, the fact that Conservatives now supported such schemes heightened their suspicions. As Ellen Wilkinson (who in the twenties had been among the first women in the Labour Party to support family allowances) wrote in 1938: 'what the Amery type want is to feed the existing and potential cannon-fodder with the greatest economy and lack of waste. Pay the money for the upkeep of each child, don't give it to the individual workman who may have few or no children. In short apply the means test to wages.'[81]

50s benefit, one third of claimants were estimated to be as well off. See *Report of Unemployment Insurance Statutory Committee*, Feb. 1938. In 1936, Rowntree had estimated the 'minimum' weekly income necessary for a family of three to be 53s for an urban family and 43s for a rural family.

[77] See p. 197.

[78] See for example, *The Times*, 4 Mar., 1938. Members of Parliament, particularly Conservative Members such as Leo Amery, Duncan Sandys and Robert Boothby, started to use this as an argument for family allowances, in addition to those already mentioned.

[79] Stocks, M., *op. cit.*, p. 182.

[80] Amery, L. S., *op. cit.*, p. 206.

[81] Wilkinson, E., *Tribune*, 8 July, 1938.

The second reason for the Labour movement's hostility was that the trade unions had still to be convinced that their strength had increased sufficiently to risk reconsidering the position as declared at their Annual Conference in 1930. Achieving better wages had a much higher priority.[82] It was not until the war brought about radical changes in the strength and the economic position of the trade unions that the majority of the Labour movement felt able to accept a scheme of family allowances without fearing a serious loss of bargaining power.

The end of the first stage of the campaign for family allowances, 1920–39

By the end of the thirties the idea of a national scheme of family allowances had gained support in many quarters, although opinion was divided about the most appropriate kind of scheme. 'This support', wrote Eleanor Rathbone, 'comes from sections of opinion otherwise widely divided, from employers and trade unionists, from economists, sociologists and experts on population, from parents and would-be parents of all classes, from organizations of women and leaders of religious thought.'[83] These new converts to the cause of family allowances were different from the feminist and 'living wage' advocates of the previous decade because their primary concern was not to improve the status of women or redistribute income from rich to poor, though these aims might incidentally be attained. The main objectives were now to abolish poverty among children and halt the decline in the birth-rate. Nevertheless, family allowances had yet to become an integral part of the programme of either major political party and the trade unions remained, in the words of Eleanor Rathbone, 'suspicious and aloof'.

It was only when the war created new economic and social needs and highlighted existing problems that a universal scheme of family allowances gained sufficient additional support to be accepted and implemented. Most important of all, family allowances were seen to be relevant to the government's *economic* policy. As Maynard Keynes explained when he proposed a national scheme of family allowances in 1940: 'at first sight it is paradoxical to propose in time of war an expensive social reform which we have not thought ourselves able to afford in time of peace. But in truth the need for this reform

---

[82] As James Griffiths pointed out, the Unemployment Assistance Board's report revealed how low wages were in the country. The conclusion to be drawn was that the Minister of Labour therefore ought to raise general wage levels. *H. C. Deb.*, vol. 337, col. 2101.

[83] Rathbone, E., *The Case for Family Allowances, op. cit.*, p. xi.

is so much greater in such times that it may provide the most appropriate occasion for it.'[84]

II THE ACCEPTANCE OF FAMILY ALLOWANCES IN PRINCIPLE: 1940-43

Within eighteen months of the beginning of the war, family allowances were being discussed seriously by the Coalition government, by a large number of Members of Parliament of all parties, by the trade unions and in the press. By early 1943 the government had committed itself to introduce a national scheme of family allowances. What had brought about such a dramatic change in the importance of the issue of family allowances, which, as we have seen, the Family Endowment Society had been trying to achieve for the past twenty years?

There were several factors, all of them inter-related. First, there were important changes in the structure and distribution of power within government. Second, family allowances were seen to be relevant to the government's attempts to control inflation in a manner acceptable to the majority of people and as 'the problem of war finance centred upon the question of inflation'[85] this increased their priority enormously. Third, as the Labour movement became much more confident in its power, family allowances were no longer regarded as such a serious threat to its bargaining position. Finally, the problems of a declining population and poverty, issues to which family allowances had already been widely recognized as relevant, were highlighted by the circumstances of the war. Wishing to avoid the bitter disillusionment following the First World War and the failure of Lloyd George's reconstruction policies, many people both inside and outside government started early on in the war to pay close attention to the development of social policy.

Changes within the government, 1940
Important changes in the government occurred in May 1940 when Neville Chamberlain resigned and Winston Churchill became Prime Minister. Attlee, Bevin, Morrison, Cripps, Dalton and Greenwood became members of Churchill's coalition government, thus bringing into positions of real power several Labour leaders. This was important not so much because these men were necessarily keen advocates of family allowances (Attlee and Bevin certainly were not), but because

[84] Keynes, J. M., *How to Pay for the War, op. cit.*, p. 32.
[85] Harrod, R. F., *The Life of John Maynard Keynes*, Macmillan, 1951, p. 490.

with such men in power the trade unions could be more confident that their interests would be looked after. In particular, Ernest Bevin became Minister of Labour and National Service and he successfully withstood government demands to interfere in wage negotiations.[86]

The membership of the War Cabinet was important. Apart from being smaller than the usual peace time Cabinets its composition until September 1943 was very unusual. When Kingsley Wood became Chancellor of the Exchequer in May 1940, replacing John Simon, the Chancellor ceased to be a member of the Cabinet for the first time. He returned as a member in October 1940 along with Ernest Bevin but was excluded again between February 1942 and September 1943. Chester explains this omission from the Cabinet in terms of the weak position of the Treasury at the time.[87]

When the government changed in May 1940 its economic advisers changed too. In particular, Keynes became their chief adviser. The Economic Section was part of the War Cabinet Secretariat and worked to the Lord President of the Council who, until 1943, was John Anderson. He was a member of the Cabinet and a man 'trusted and respected by leaders of the Parties in the Coalition and by the Prime Minister ... he had not been involved in the bitter Party controversies of the inter-war period'.[88] These changes had the effect of substantially reducing the Treasury's opposition to Keynes' more radical economic policies and at least guaranteed them a hearing in the Cabinet.[89] In other words, the war brought Keynes into a position directly influencing the country's financial policies. Describing the pressures making for changes in Treasury views during the war, Professor Sayers later wrote: 'it also happened that among the Chancellor's war-time advisers there were powerful advocates of the view that more attention should be given, in financial policy to "social needs". This strand of thought was expressed mainly by Mr Keynes and Mr Henderson.'[90]

---

[86] Bevin had stated very clearly at the beginning of the war that trade union co-operation depended on the government treating them as equals and 'equality not merely in the economic sense but in the conception and the attitude of mind of those in power'. Bevin, E., *Transport and General Workers Union Record*, Oct. 1939.

[87] 'When Mr Churchill's Government took office in May 1940, the political atmosphere was definitely antagonistic to the Treasury ... and the Permanent Secretary of the Treasury (Sir Horace Wilson) had unfortunately become associated in the public mind with Mr Neville Chamberlain's appeasement policy. So for the first time the Chancellor of the Exchequer ceased to be a member of the Cabinet.' Chester, D. N. (ed.), *Lessons of the British War Economy*, Cambridge University Press, 1959, p. 6 (Chester was Secretary to the 'Beveridge Committee' in 1942).

[88] Chester, D. N., *op. cit.*, p. 10.

[89] *Ibid.*, p. 18.

[90] Sayers, R. S., *Financial Policy, 1939–1945*, HMSO, 1956, p. 96 (Hubert Henderson was also a supporter of family allowances).

The government's economic policy

One of the most important features of the background against which a policy of family allowances became accepted was the fact of a national coalition government kept together by the overriding necessity to win the war. On the one hand conditions of war justified government policies which would never have been acceptable in peace time, but on the other hand the need to avoid political and industrial controversy placed considerable restraints on their actions. The role of the government's economic policy and the limitations placed upon that role during the war are important examples of this.

At the beginning of the war prices and wages had risen rapidly,[91] focusing the government's attention on the need to avoid inflation. In a war economy the goods available for civilian consumption must be limited and if inflation is to be avoided some means of withdrawing excess purchasing power must be introduced. It inevitably draws attention to the distribution of the remaining purchasing power. This background is important in understanding why a national scheme of family allowances would seem attractive: it might be effective in reducing demands for higher wages and avoiding across the board increases whilst at the same time appearing to spread the costs of the war in a more equitable manner.

At the beginning of the war Keynes published a plan which 'endeavoured to snatch from the exigency of war positive social improvement',[92] but that would at the same time curb inflation. He proposed to 'link further changes in money rates of wages, pensions and other allowances to changes in the cost of a limited range of rationed articles of consumption, an iron ration as it has been called, which the authorities will endeavour to protect one way or another, from rising prices'. In addition he wanted further protection for 'those whose standard of life offers no sufficient margin'[93] by introducing a sharply progressive income tax scheme with an exempt minimum and a system of family allowances. Some aspects of this plan were found in Kingsley Wood's first budget. This included several strong anti-flationary measures. Direct taxation was increased substantially. The married man's allowance was reduced from £170 to £140 and the child's allowance from £60 to £50. The earned income allowance was reduced from one sixth to one tenth subject to a minimum of £200. The standard rate of income tax was increased from 8s 6d to

---

[91] See *Ministry of Labour Gazette*, Feb. 1946, p. 32.

[92] Keynes, J. M., *How to Pay for the War, op. cit.*, p. 10. This book was based on Keynes' articles in *The Times* during November 1939. The other major elements of the plan were a deferred savings scheme (which emerged later, somewhat altered, as the Post-War Credit Scheme) and a general capital levy to be made after the war.

[93] *Ibid.*, p. 11.

10s; purchase tax and excess profit tax (at 100 per cent) were continued; prices were controlled; food prices subsidized and rationing extended by the introduction of the 'points system' for food and clothing. Income tax allowances and tax rates did not change again until after the end of the war. But as a result of this large increase in direct taxation, together with the general increase in the level of earnings, many more men were brought into the groups paying income tax. As a consequence, during the war, many more married men with families benefited from children's income tax allowances. In 1941–2 four million tax payers received tax allowances in respect of five and a half million children.[94] In particular 'for the first time typical married men belonging to the working classes were paying income tax and . . . were benefiting from the children's income tax allowance'.[95] Before the war a married man earning an average wage did not pay income tax even if he had no children.[96] As Table 2 shows, in 1942 men with average earnings were affected by income tax allowances for children, although those with low earnings gained nothing from them.[97]

Table 2

VALUE OF INCOME TAX CHILD ALLOWANCES, 1941–2

Order of child in family	Earned weekly income*				
	Under £3 10s	£3 10s	£5 10s	£6 10s	£7 10s
First	–	3s	5s 8d	6s 3d	9s 7d
Second	–	–	5s 8d	6s 3d	9s 7d

* Average adult male employee's weekly earnings were £5 11s 10d in 1942.

[94] In 1941–2 there were 5·6 million families including 10·1 million children. See *The White Paper on Family Allowances: Memorandum by the Chancellor of the Exchequer*, Cmd. 6534, 1942.

[95] Booker, H. S., 'Income tax and Family Allowances in Britain', *Population Studies*, vol. III, no. 3, Dec. 1949, p. 243. This article contains a detailed discussion of the tax changes that occurred during and immediately after the war.

[96] In October 1938 average adult male weekly earnings were £3 9s (£175 a year). A married man did not pay income tax until he was earning £225, and if he had one child he did not pay tax until he earned £300.

[97] A study of taxation published in 1942 showed that the tax structure had become noticeably more progressive from the middle income groups upwards but was still regressive among the low income groups. See Findlay Shirras, G. and Rostas, L., *The Burden of British Taxation*, National Institute of Economic and Social Research, 1942.

Thus, in 1941 'the budget had in fact ceased to serve its peace time purpose of providing finance for all government activities and had become solely an engine for preserving, in the face of colossal defence expenditure at home and abroad, reasonable stability in the value of money and *adequate incentives consistent with a distribution of the burden that people would accept as broadly just*' (our italics).[98] At the same time the impact of war on civilian life was increasing the importance of the social services. New problems arose from the dislocations in family life brought about by evacuation and the bombing.[99] It became important also to maintain civilian morale. The Treasury attitude towards the development of social policy changed, therefore, in the face of pressure not only from the Chancellor's wartime advisers but also from those departments which had to deal with these new problems.

Initially, growth in war expenditure hindered development of social policy[100] but 'as soon as the 1941 budget had established Keynes' prime object of financial stability, he formulated for 1942 suggestions for a budget which should be fit to be described as a *Social Policy Budget*, and should primarily aim at adjusting various social anomalies which have been developed out of the war situation and also out of the previous budget itself'.[101] A scheme of family allowances was among the developments proposed at this time. 'In urging such a plan [family allowances] Mr Henderson especially used the arguments that were of equal force in peace-time, though the pressure of war-time taxation on the family man was the occasion of its urgency.'[102]

Wages Policy

The Treasury however had also wanted to include government control of wages in their anti-inflationary policies because they believed that without it inflation would be impossible to control.[103] The trade unions, however, had told the Chancellor of the Exchequer (Sir John Simon) at the outbreak of war that they were totally opposed to any such policy and they expressed this view just as strongly in 1941.[104]

---

[98] Sayers, R. S., *op. cit.,* p. 69.

[99] See Titmuss, R. M., *Problems of Social Policy*, HMSO, 1950.

[100] For example, the improvement in old age pensions which was being discussed in 1939 was not implemented in the early part of the war.

[101] Sayers, R. S., *op. cit.,* p. 97.

[102] *Idem.*

[103] Early in 1940 among the chief advocates of direct wage control were Lord Stamp, then economic adviser to the Cabinet, and William Beveridge.

[104] 'We have stood for no interference with the wage system. We repeat that, but it does not mean that our General Council is not prepared to look at any practical scheme that is put before us to try and solve this very anxious

Ernest Bevin was a firm advocate of their views inside the government. The arguments he used are a good example of the constraints facing a coalition government in a situation in which the country's resources, in particular its manpower, must be utilized to the full. First, he stressed the need to preserve 'adequate incentives'. This was crucial, and 'he recognized that the responsibility he had been given of supplying and distributing manpower to meet essential requirements was dependent upon their being an appropriate rate of wage for the different jobs to be done. Workers could not be expected to change their employment if the transference would involve for them a serious loss of money. Conversely, if the competing offer of high wages by employers in the munitions industries were allowed to continue, there would be a restless movement of workers in pursuit of higher earnings.'[105] Thus some regulation of wages might be necessary but it must be voluntary, because the government had to maintain industrial peace. Bevin was also 'anxious that in whatever measures he decided to take he should have the support of the associations of employers and trade unions. To override their objections would merely precipitate industrial strife.'[106] In any case, Bevin concluded, the government would be the first to ignore a wage freeze if industrial peace was threatened.[107]

Second, Bevin argued that wage rates could be stabilized if prices were held steady because, in the early months of the war, most pay claims had been justified in terms of the higher cost of living. Subsequently, therefore, a constant eye was kept on the cost of living index and by concentrating subsidies on those items weighing heavily in the basket of goods used for the index, and by avoiding any addi-

---

difficulty. One thing we are certain of: that the solution will not be found in trying to interfere with the system which has been established and which on the Government's own testimony has worked so admirably' (Sir Walter Citrine's speech at the TUC Annual Conference 1941). *TUC Annual Report, 1941.* See also TUC statement: *The Trade Unions and Wage Policy in War-Time, 1941.*

[105] Parker, H. M. D., *Manpower*, HMSO, 1957, p. 425.

[106] *Ibid.*, p. 425.

[107] Bevin was right, for in the summer of 1941 the miners wanted more money because of the rise in the cost of living: 'the major issue of industrial peace must come first. A sufficient rise in the price of coal, allowing increased wages was conceded, but the War Cabinet insisted that the "cost of living" justification should be soft pedalled and forgotten as soon as possible; and it decided also that early steps must be taken to educate the trade union movement in the compulsions of war economy.' Sayers, R. S., *op. cit.*, p. 60. Allan Bullock reports a similar concession made to the railwaymen at the end of 1941. See Bullock, A., *The Life and Times of Ernest Bevin, vol. 2, Ministry of Labour, 1940–45*, Heinemann, 1967, p. 89.

tional purchase tax on these items, rises in the index were kept to a minimum.[108]

However, the most telling argument for a coalition government was the necessity to avoid political controversy. Increased taxation and stabilized prices, held down with the help of subsidies financed out of general taxation, were acceptable methods of combating inflation because the cost was born by the community in general. Wage control on the other hand was a method of fighting inflation at the expense of one section of the nation and thus was not one the trade unions could accept as broadly just without comparable sacrifices from the employers. 'If wage control was imposed by the State, Bevin made it perfectly clear that Labour would demand the socialization of industry.'[109] A wartime coalition government could not afford to stir up a political controversy of that order. Indeed, 'the Minister's defence convinced his colleagues and brought to an end once and for all discussions within the Government about the advisability of a direct control over wages'.[110]

The government therefore had to rely on voluntary wage restraints together with price stabilization, increased taxation and the encouragement of savings to combat inflation. Post-war credits were introduced in January 1942 and although no scheme of compulsory savings was ever introduced, voluntary savings grew rapidly.[111] Throughout the spring and summer of 1942 the government continued to be criticized in the press and in the House of Commons for not pursuing a tougher wage policy. By October 1942, however, its retreat from wage control ceased to be seriously challenged in Parliament where the main topic of controversy now centred on the military conduct of the war.

Changes in attitude in the Labour movement

One of the major reasons for the Labour movement's antagonism towards a scheme of family allowances during the twenties and thirties was the fear that such a scheme would undermine its bargaining position. By 1941 the position of the Labour movement was substantially stronger; perhaps stronger than it had ever been. In addition

---

[108] During the war 2½ million workers had their wage rates directly tied to the cost of living. (The cost of living index was a very old one, including candles and excluding electricity for example; therefore it did not really measure the cost of living). See Sayers, R. S., *op. cit.*, pp. 65, 75 and 127.

[109] Bullock, A., *op. cit.*, p. 91.

[110] Parker, H. M. D., *op. cit.*, p. 431.

[111] 'If voluntary saving is found to be inadequate then we shall be faced with other and more stringent means. It is no use shutting our eyes to it.' (Walter Citrine at the TUC Annual Conference in 1941.) Once Kingsley Wood had promised that up to £375 'lent to the nation' would not be included in any means test assessment for unemployment benefit, the flow of small savings rose from its pre-war level of £57 million a year to £733 million in 1943.

to Bevin's successful stand against direct wage control, unemployment was falling.[112] In the light of these changes the Labour movement was at last prepared to consider family allowances again. The National Executive of the Labour Party reported to their Annual Conference in 1941 that it was 'opportune' to examine the proposal for family allowances because 'there have been substantial developments in the social services: the principle of children's allowances has been widely applied in schemes of social assistance, much scientific inquiry has been made into the incidence of poverty on the family; the Trade Union movement has grown in strength and stature; and now there are the widespread economic and social changes due to the war'.[113] Great emphasis was placed on the last two arguments. The report continued: 'if doubts remain as to the wisdom of a permanent system of children's allowances, there is an especially strong case for paying such allowances under the present war-time conditions. In terms of purchasing power, wage rates generally have declined, and although some earnings have increased because of longer working hours and over-time, the real wage incomes of many of the poorest families have been reduced. It is more difficult than ever for the low paid worker with a large family to make both ends meet. We do not think that the payment of allowances during the war would materially handicap the unions in their present fight to maintain and improve standards.'[114]

At the Annual Conference of the Trades Union Congress a motion in favour of a State-paid scheme of family allowances was proposed for similar reasons, with stress on the 'circumstances of war'. In 1941, however, not all sections in the Labour movement were equally convinced by the new arguments. Some unions remained opposed[115] and the question of family allowances was referred back to a joint committee of the Labour Party and the Trades Union Congress for further discussion.

Changing attitudes towards the problems of poverty and the development of the social services

The coming of the Second World War heightened the problems of a declining population and poverty in several ways. In the first place, like previous wars it increased concern for the next generation upon whom not only the country's future defences would rest, but upon whom the continuation of the existence of the society for which they

[112] Unemployment still stood at one million at the end of 1940 but it was falling and by 1943 it had dropped to 100,000.

[113] *Report of the Labour Party Annual Conference*, 1941, p. 190.

[114] *Ibid.*, p. 192.

[115] The principal opponents were the Transport and General Workers Union, the Associated Society of Locomotive Engineers and Firemen and the National Union of General and Municipal Workers.

were fighting depended. The likelihood of heavy war casualties among civilians as well as among men and women in the Armed Services, together with fears that the war situation itself would in any case lead to a reduction in the number of births[116] magnified the dangers of a birth rate below replacement level. 'A state of population growth which seems likely to lead to a rapidly diminishing population and possibly to extinction in some of the leading civilized communities of the modern world'[117] acquired a new significance.[118]

Evacuation policy revealed to a wider section of the public than had hitherto been aware of it 'that the submerged tenth described by Charles Booth still exists in our towns like a hidden sore, poor, dirty, and crude in its habits, an intolerable and degrading burden to decent people forced by poverty to neighbour with it'.[119] Many of the complaints about the evacuees who came from large overcrowded cities concerned their behaviour, standards of hygiene or ill manners. Those who complained seemed mainly concerned with improving standards of mother-care by means of better education rather than with increasing family incomes. Despite these emphases this mass exodus from the cities at least brought home to many more people the fact that in spite of the development of the social services in the past thirty years, much still remained to be done.[120]

In addition to these changes new war-time arrangements for service pay and allowances were introduced which 'threw into sharper prominence the fact that in industrial society money rewards take no account of family responsibilities'.[121] As a member of the National

---

[116] 'The war is likely to affect the figures. It is estimated that the war of 1914–18 resulted in about half a million fewer babies being born than would have otherwise seen the light.' Rathbone, E., *The Case for Family Allowances, op. cit.*, p. 50.

[117] Charles, E., *op. cit.*, pp. 192–3.

[118] Both in her writing and in parliamentary debates of this period, Eleanor Rathbone also clearly felt it appropriate to use nationalist and sometimes even racialist arguments in support of her campaign for family allowances. 'As time went on and *in response to growing public concern with a falling birth rate*, she [Eleanor Rathbone] gave it increasing prominence, and indeed it added a new zest to her labours during the final stages of the family allowance campaign.' Stocks, M., *op. cit.*, p. 316 (our italics).

[119] Bondfield, M., Preface to Women's Group on Public Welfare, *Our Towns a Close Up: A Study Made During 1939–1942*, Oxford University Press, 1944, p. xiii.

[120] *Ibid.*, p. xvii.

[121] Titmuss, R. M., 'War and Social Policy', in his *Essays on the Welfare State*, Allen & Unwin, 2nd ed., 1963, p. 82. In his essay, which discusses the effects of modern warfare, he writes: 'perhaps the dominating one has been the increasing concern of the State in time of war with the biological characteristics of the people. The growing scale and intensity of war has stimulated a growing concern about the *quantity and quality* of the population'. (our italics), p. 78.

Executive of the Labour Party pointed out at the Party Conference in 1941, we had reached a 'stage where the only people who do not enjoy family allowances are the poorly paid civilian workers'.[122] Indeed, by the beginning of 1942 the cost of allowances paid in respect of children was considerable. As well as the dependants' benefit in unemployment insurance and assistance, workmen's compensation, widows' and orphans' pensions and income tax, the war had brought about the need for additional allowances. The children of servicemen and unaccompanied evacuated children attracted allowances. After income tax allowances the latter two schemes were the most costly (see Table 3).

Table 3

COST OF CHILD DEPENDENCY BENEFITS, 1941–2

Scheme	£ millions
Unemployment Insurance	0·5
Unemployment Assistance	0·5
Contributory widows' and orphans' pensions	3·0
Payments by Ministry of Pensions	0·6
Billeting payments in respect of unaccompanied evacuated children	8·6
Service allowances	20·0
Income tax allowances	80·0
Total	113·2

SOURCES: Benefits except service allowances, *White Paper on Family Allowances, op. cit.*, p. 8. Service allowances, *Report of Labour Party Conference, 1942*, Appendix.

The very nature and intensity of the war, requiring the total effort of civilians as well as those in the Armed Forces, underlined the need to pay attention to the society for which they were fighting. It was not sufficient to ensure the maintenance of society. To sustain both civilian and service morale there had to be the prospect of a new and better social order. At the end of 1940 the government, aware of this and of the need to consider the problems that would face the country when the war was over, gave Arthur Greenwood, a member of the War Cabinet (and since June 1940 Chairman of the Economic Policy Committee), the task of planning a reconstruction policy. At the time there was considerable pressure from the Trades Union

[122] Mrs Ayrton Gould, *Report of the Labour Party Annual Conference, 1942*, p. 133.

Congress for a review of social insurance provision. This pressure had increased when the Royal Commission on Workman's Compensation, set up in 1939, intimated that it could not continue in wartime conditions. So in June 1941 Arthur Greenwood established an Inter-Departmental Committee on Social Insurance and Allied Services. William Beveridge, at Bevin's suggestion,[123] was appointed its chairman. Writing of this later, Janet Beveridge said, 'the Government hoped that the new Committee would, under William's chairmanship, placate the TUC, who viewed the relinquishment of the duties of the Royal Commission with concern and dismay'.[124] The appointment of this committee also involved the question of morale and was regarded by many as 'more useful in the battle against Hitler's conception of a new order, than a whole catalogue of high sounding war aims'.[125]

Aware of the propaganda value of the establishment of this committee, at home as well as abroad, Arthur Greenwood gave its appointment considerable publicity.[126] The public welcomed such news because, together with the disappearance of the threat of invasion in 1941, it seemed to bring the end of the war much nearer.[127] As later discussion will show, throughout 1942 the press waited eagerly for the publication of Beverldge's report and gave it enormous publicity when it came. This put the government in a difficult position because the report contained widesweeping and controversial changes over which ministers held divergent views, thus posing a threat to the coalition. Churchill, in particular, was determined not to commit the government to the committee's recommendations and he at least had underestimated the speed with which Beveridge would complete his report. Attempts to delay its publication and give it minimal publicity[128] only served to increase public interest. Nevertheless, in spite of the government's ambivalence towards the published report and its proposals, the appointment of the Beveridge Committee was

[123] This was mainly because Bevin no longer wanted Beveridge to work in his Ministry where he did not get on well with the senior civil servants. Arthur Greenwood was hardly likely to have been unaware of Beveridge's considerable interest in social security. See Bullock, A., *op. cit.*, p. 225.

[124] Beveridge, J., *Beveridge and His Plan*, Hodder & Stoughton, 1954, p. 42.

[125] Editorial, *Spectator*, 13 June, 1941, p. 625.

[126] For example, on 8 June, 1941, two days *before* the appointment of the Beveridge Committee, *Reynolds News* carried a headline 'Greenwood's Security Plan Move'.

[127] A headline in the *News Chronicle* on 11 June, 1941 read: 'Social Security for All after the War is being Planned: a vast scheme to ensure no-one shall want.' The propaganda value did not go unnoticed either. From documents captured from the Germans it was clear that they took the Beveridge Committee very seriously. See Beveridge, J., *op. cit.*, ch. 14.

[128] See page 205.

important in encouraging the public to think in terms of major changes in social security provisions.

Against this background of interwoven events, solutions to the problem of poverty were widely regarded as a precondition for the new and better post-war Britain. If allowed to continue, poverty and malnutrition, particularly among children, would jeopardize the building of this new society. 'These are the children that are to build the new Britain you and I talk about; how can they build a new Britain if in the early stages of their life, their bodies, minds and souls are warped by poverty?'[129] asked James Griffiths, introducing a motion in favour of a national scheme of family allowances at the Labour Party Conference in 1942.

During this time the dislocations of family life arising out of the war-time situation were putting additional strain on the existing social services. Government departments found themselves facing many new problems as well as those of poverty and malnutrition. As we have seen above, during a war involving the total population these problems cannot be ignored, not least in order to maintain civilian morale. Their solutions could only be found if the extension of the social services ceased to be regarded as a luxury to be postponed until the war was over. Thus the Treasury was subjected to increasing pressures from other government departments to give social policy high priority.[130]

Growing support in Parliament

Keynes' plan for economic policy, including a scheme to pay cash family allowances, which was contained in his book *How to Pay for the War* was widely talked about outside as well as inside government and in 1940 he discussed his economic plans with 250 Members of Parliament from all parties.[131] Although initially these were not well received in many quarters, including the Treasury,[132] they at least defined the nature and magnitude of the economic problems to be overcome, and prepared people for the necessity of drastic action. However, as we have already seen, in time opinion did change in his favour. Moreover his proposals added a further, crucial weapon to the campaigners for family allowances who lost no time in using it. For

[129] *Report of the Labour Party Annual Conference*, 1942, p. 133.

[130] See Sayers, R. S., *op. cit.*, pp. 96–8.

[131] He also discussed it on the radio: he addressed a TUC group and the Fabian Society. He also interviewed many eminent financiers, including the Governor of the Bank of England, who commented favourably. See Harrod, R., *op. cit.*, p. 440.

[132] See Sayers, R. S., *op. cit.*, p. 33. The Labour Party were also far from enthusiastic initially, although they only had vague proposals to put in its place. See *The Keynes Plan – its Danger to the Workers*, Labour Research Dept, 1940.

example, Beveridge, commenting on the Prime Minister's recent warning of the danger of inflation and the necessity to cut down on consumption, said in a letter to *The Times* on 12 January, 1940: 'if we are to restrict consumption we must not do so at the expense of vital needs. Above all we must not do so at the cost of children. The needs of every family in the country vary with the size of family: the greatest single cause of poverty in this country is young children. The relatively high standard of health shown by children in the last war was in part a result of the system of separation allowances for men in the Forces; these take account of family needs. The extension of this principle to all classes of the community is a war-time measure whose necessity can hardly be questioned by anyone who accepts the Prime Minister's thesis.'

In the changed economic and social circumstances of the war the campaign for family allowances was making considerably headway in Parliament. The all-party members' group in favour of family allowances formed at the end of the thirties had gained the support of 152 MPs by 1941. Among them were many more Labour Party members, including James Griffiths. During 1941 the Parliamentary Labour Party itself announced that it was in favour of a State scheme of family allowances, although the Conservative 1922 Committee did so first.

Questions concerning family allowances were frequently put to the Chancellor of the Exchequer in the early part of 1941 and on 16 June, 1941 a deputation of MPs headed by Leo Amery took a memorandum to the Chancellor of the Exchequer asking him to investigate a scheme of family allowances. Their reasons for advocating national allowances were as follows:

(i) to prevent an increase in malnutrition due to poverty aggravated by high prices;
(ii) to prevent the spread of discontent between:
    (a) the richer and poorer classes; and
    (b) those who get allowances – evacuees, the servicemen and the unemployed – and those who do not;
(iii) to prevent a fall in the birth rate;
(iv) to fulfil (i)–(iii) without inflation, and
(v) to prevent an overlap between unemployment benefit and wages because family allowances are paid to one and not to the other.

Reporting on the deputation's meeting with the Chancellor who 'was fortified by representatives from the Ministry of Health, Food and Pensions, though not of Education', the *Spectator* said that 'Sir Kingsley Wood's reply was disappointing. He produced all the stock arguments and then announced that he would personally conduct an investigation into the practicality of the scheme.'[133] The all-party group then tried to obtain a debate on the subject and signed the following Motion:

> That this House would welcome the introduction of a National State-paid scheme of allowances for dependent children, payable to their mothers or acting guardians, as a means of safeguarding the health and well-being of the rising generation; this House urges His Majesty's Government to give immediate consideration to the formulation of such a scheme.

However, the debate did not occur until 1942, by which time the government had considered and replied to the above memorandum and it was becoming clear that the Labour movement was viewing the idea with greater sympathy.

1942: 'Three ifs bar way to family allowances'[134]

This year brought the strands of support for family allowances closer together than ever before. Inside the government there was increasing pressure on the Treasury to consider such a measure; the activities of a substantial proportion of Members of Parliament were making serious consideration of such a scheme hard to avoid; the Labour movement was beginning to view family allowances with more favour; Beveridge and his committee were considering them and the press were alive to the issues and were giving the development of the idea wide coverage.

In May 1942 the government published its own exploratory white paper on family allowances[135] in reply to the all-party MPs memorandum received in 1941. The arguments for family allowances were seen to be as follows: that they would reduce the risk of malnutrition in large families; would avoid the necessity of inflationary wage increases sufficient to meet the needs of parents of large families; parenthood might be encouraged, thus counteracting the decline in the birthrate and, finally, parents who were not liable to tax would receive a similar benefit to those getting income tax relief in respect of their children. The contrary arguments were that such a scheme would prejudice wage negotiations and require money better spent in the development of other social services, especially those such as health, housing and education which could only be provided for

---

[133] *Spectator*, 20 June, 1941, p. 647. The reasons given by the Chancellor of the Exchequer for wanting more time before debating family allowances were not only that time was needed to consider various schemes but that: 'I have to take into account the views of other people.' See *H. C. Deb.*, vol. 380, col. 1992. 'Other people' in particular meant the trade unions.

[134] From a report of Kingsley Wood's speech in the House of Commons, *Daily Herald*, 24 June, 1942.

[135] *White Paper on Family Allowances, op. cit.*

collectively. No attempt was made to assess the respective merits of the arguments.

The Chancellor was clearly in favour of a flat rate and universal scheme, for the savings to be made by restricting it to those covered by the existing unemployment and health insurance schemes, for example, were negligible.[136] Discussion in the white paper was mainly confined to methods of financing such a system and the possibility of making savings by abolishing income tax allowances and the other allowances for children under the existing insurance and assistance schemes. The Chancellor 'wisely refrained, "for a variety of reasons," to add to the planned reduction of £7 million by any savings on the separation allowances for the children of servicemen'.[137] This, as later discussion will show, was important.[138]

Although the White Paper did not commit the government to a particular scheme, it was seen by *The Times*, for instance, as clearing the way 'for a universal scheme of direct allowances ... What it involves is the transfer of a fraction of the resources of those who have no dependent children to those who have responsibilities. Equity and national interest combine to justify this transfer. This is an issue where *progress towards building the healthier society of the future need not await the end of hostilities*' (our italics).[139] Indeed, shortly after the publication of the Chancellor's memorandum the way was further cleared when family allowances were debated fully in the House of Commons for the first time. The Motion, signed this time by 211 Members, differed only slightly in form from that of the previous year. The debate ranged over all the by now familiar arguments for and against family allowances.

The majority of Members were in favour of a national scheme and most talked in terms of it being financed by the Exchequer. James Griffiths said that the Labour Party were only prepared to accept a non-contributory scheme which included every child.[140] Among the supporters of family allowances were those who were only prepared to support State intervention in cases of need. Family allowances were a method of meeting one of the current defects of the economic system but they looked forward to the time when higher levels of earnings would make them unnecessary. Those on the extreme Left

---

[136] In the light of recent discussions about the Family Income Supplement, it is interesting that the Chancellor felt that the object of family allowances was not to correct a wage system that paid little regard to family responsibilities, because that would imply an allowance equal to the deficiency of the wage and that would lead back to Speenhamland.

[137] 'Family Allowances', *The Times*, 4 June, 1942.

[138] See p. 210.

[139] Leader in *The Times*, 11 May, 1942.

[140] *H. C. Deb.*, vol. 380, col. 1873.

held the same view as those on the extreme Right: family allowances were undesirable, though for very different reasons. The former argued that a reduction in inequality and hence the abolition of poverty was impossible in a capitalist economy, so family allowances were basically only a compromise leading to the pauperism of the poor. They therefore advocated far more social services and a guaranteed minimum provided by the State in kind. The champions of *laissez-faire* on the far Right regarded family allowances as the thin end of the wedge of State intervention in the family which would destroy initiative, the incentive to work and generally demoralize the country. Apart from Edith Summerskill and Eleanor Rathbone, few voiced the feminist arguments concerning the need to improve the status of women and children. Eleanor Rathbone had far more support for her nationalistic arguments in favour of family allowances. An underlying theme throughout the debate was the need to increase the population.

At the end of the debate the Chancellor of the Exchequer, Sir Kingsley Wood, explained the government's position on family allowances. 'If the Motion is adopted by the House, the Government, as it requests them to do, will give it full consideration. This subject must however be considered by the Government in the light of the considerations I have mentioned – the report of the Beveridge Committee, the further conclusions of organized labour and the financial position. In conclusion I will say that it should be possible for all these matters to be adequately considered in the Autumn. I think we shall have the reports I have mentioned by then and they will be given our immediate attention. Conclusions will be reached as rapidly as possible.'[141] He clearly expected Beveridge to have considered family allowances in his report, for he had already said 'family allowances are not strictly within the terms of the enquiry, but it is obviously a matter which is very closely associated with it, and which must, I think be considered in conjunction with any report from the Committee'.[142] Although only three weeks previously the Labour Party Conference had voted in favour of a national scheme of family allowances, the Chancellor was less sure about the reactions of the trade unions. He considered this 'a matter of special importance [for] family allowances have long been the subject of discussion in trade union circles which have been particularly apprehensive about their effect on wage negotiations'.[143] The Motion however was duly accepted by the House of Commons and so the government was committed to a policy of family allowances provided the Beveridge Committee reported in its favour (a foregone conclusion); the Trades

[141] *H. C. Deb.*, vol. 380, col. 1941.
[142] *Ibid.*, col. 1941.
[143] *Ibid.*, col. 1940.

Union Congress accepted such a policy; and the economic situation allowed it.

The press greeted this decision as enthusiastically as they had greeted the news earlier in May and June that the Co-operative conference, the Labour Party conference and the National Labour Women's conference had passed resolutions in favour of family allowances. 'The Nation Needs Children'; 'Children's Allowances Win by a Million Votes'; 'Of Course we want Family Allowances' ran headlines in the *Daily Herald*.[144]

By the autumn of 1942 the Trades Union Congress had passed, but not unanimously, a resolution in favour of a universal State-paid scheme of family allowances at their annual conference. Beveridge had made such a scheme the first underlying assumption of his plan for social security. The economic situation of the country still warranted the inclusion of such a scheme in the Chancellor's financial policy. Quite apart from the growing pressure to consider reconstruction policies[145] the fight against inflation was not over.[146] Thus, 'with opinion in the House well disposed towards family allowances, organized labour acquiescent if not enthusiastic, and such a scheme firmly embedded in the popular Beveridge scheme of social security, the new year of 1943 ushered in hopes of Government action'.[147]

Summary, 1940–3

In three years family allowances had gained the attention and the interest of the government that twenty years of campaigning by the Family Endowment Society had failed to achieve. Support for a scheme of family allowances had become widespread since its introduction was seen to be relevant to a number of problems facing a war-time coalition government. First, the threat of a declining population and continuing poverty, particularly among children, had acquired greater significance to a country fighting for its survival. As these were problems to which a scheme of family allowances had already been recognized as offering a partial solution, they were accorded greater priority. Second, the need to consider and develop social policies not only to deal with social problems thrown up by the war-time situa-

---

[144] *Daily Herald*, 26 and 28 May and 22 June, 1942.

[145] '*From 1942 onwards* these considerations of post-war reconstruction became rapidly more prominent, until in 1944 and 1945 the Chancellor's eye could never be off them for one moment' (our italics). Sayers, R. S., *op. cit.*, p. 98.

[146] Looking back in his budget speech of 1942, Sir Kingsley Wood said: 'During the last year we have definitely held our own against the onset of inflation. The enemy is still at our gates. Our vigilance must not be relaxed for a moment, but we can at least claim that as yet he has not established a bridgehead across our financial defences.' Quoted by Sayers, *ibid.*, p. 96.

[147] Stocks, M., *op. cit.*, p. 309.

tion but as a means of reconstructing a better and more equitable society could not be ignored if civilian morale was to be maintained, and the bitter disillusionment following the First World War was to be avoided. The immediate introduction of a scheme of family allowances was important to these aims. 'We insist on planning for the post-war future. But we must plan not only in terms of bricks and mortar. We must build the inhabitants of the new world as steadily as we build its cities ... there should be no waiting for the end of the war.'[118] Third, family allowances had also become a means offered to the government by Keynes, one of their chief economic advisers, of curbing inflationary wage demands but at the same time protecting families with children. A social policy which becomes relevant to a government's economic policies gains enormously in priority. Finally, with unemployment substantially diminished and their representatives firmly established in positions of power, the Labour movement no longer regarded family allowances as likely to undermine its bargaining position over wages.

The changed economic and political circumstances brought about by the war had strengthened the various strands of support for family allowances and interwoven them with important new strands. In the next section we shall explain why the family allowance scheme took the form that it did and why, when the policy had gained so much support as a necessary war-time measure, it was not introduced until the war was almost over.

III FROM PRINCIPLE TO PRACTICE

'If family allowances were introduced they would, by reason of their wide scope, naturally be regarded as the basic social service payment for children and other schemes involving payments in respect of children of certain classes would have to be adjusted in the light of new circumstances.'[149] So wrote the Chancellor of the Exchequer in his exploratory White Paper on family allowances in May 1942. How wide was the scope of the scheme proposed in the Beveridge Report and later by the government? What was its relationship to the dependency allowances already in existence? What pressures were there to restrict the cost of the scheme? The answers to these questions are important not only in understanding the scheme of family allowances finally introduced in 1946 and its later chequered development, but also because they may help to explain why family

---

[148] *Daily Herald*, 11 June, 1941.
[149] *White Paper on Family Allowances, op. cit.*, p. 6.

allowances were not introduced earlier during the war, although many expected them to be.[150]

Beveridge's scheme of family allowances

A general scheme of cash children's allowances was the first of three assumptions underlying the Beveridge committee's plan of social insurance; the other two assumptions being that full employment would be maintained and a comprehensive health service introduced. He based his proposals for these allowances on the argument first, that 'it is unreasonable to seek to guarantee an income sufficient for subsistence, while earnings are interrupted by unemployment or disability without ensuring sufficient income during earning'. Second, 'it is dangerous', he pointed out, 'to allow benefit during unemployment or disability to equal or exceed earnings during work', and finally, 'children's allowances can help to restore the birth rate both by making it possible for parents to bring them into the world without damaging the chances of those already born, and as a signal of the national interest in children, setting the tone of public opinion'.[151] He therefore proposed, in addition to benefits in kind, a State-financed allowance graduated by age and worth on average eight shillings for each child after the first. Keynes' ideas were an important influence on the financial design of these proposals, for he was one of Beveridge's chief advisers. 'The finance on which its practical success depended was planned with the co-operation of the best actuarial minds available. It was scrutinized and approved by the unquestioned authority of William's close but highly critical friend in such matters, Maynard Keynes. Other Treasury officials, including Professor Robbins lent for war service there, played their part.'[152] The total cost of implementing Beveridge's proposals was a crucial factor. Beveridge himself wrote of 'a deal' with Keynes which was confirmed in August 1942. 'The gist of the deal was that Keynes promised to support my Report if I would keep the additional burden on the Treasury down to £100 million a year for the first five years; after that, he said the Treasury should have no difficulty in meeting these charges. I found myself able to satisfy Keynes' condition for support, provided that I spread the introduction of adequate contributory pensions over a substantial period of transition ... The total additional cost to the Exchequer and to rates in the first year of the scheme was reduced to £86 million, all of which resulted from the grant of children's allowances.'[153]

[150] 'Preparation had commenced in 1943 and Ministers were sometimes envisaging the commencement of allowances *during* the war.' Sayers, R. S., *op. cit.*, p. 98.
[151] *Social Insurance and Allied Services*. A Report by William Beveridge, Cmd. 6404, 1942, p. 154.
[152] Beveridge, J., *op. cit.*, p. 6.
[153] Beveridge, W., *Power and Influence*, Hodder & Stoughton, 1953, p. 309.

In his exploratory memorandum on family allowances, the Chancellor of the Exchequer had estimated that a scheme including all dependent children would cost £132 million annually, assuming the allowance was worth five shillings for each eligible child. This was more than Beveridge was 'allowed' to spend, although he already considered that five shillings a week was too low to cover the subsistence needs of a child.[154] Basing his estimates on subsistence needs (as estimated by Rowntree in 1938) and allowing for a 25 per cent increase in post-war prices over 1938 prices, Beveridge had arrived at an allowance graduated by age, worth on average nine shillings for each child included in the scheme. However, in view of the substantial increase in the provision of school meals and milk that had occurred during the war he arrived at a cash allowance worth on average eight shillings, the value of provision in kind being equivalent to an additional shilling on the allowance.[155] This was clearly going to cost well over £100 million, for the only savings he envisaged making in dependency benefits already in existence, was £11 million on unemployment insurance and assistance, widows' and orphans' pensions and workmen's compensation. Like the Chancellor of the Exchequer, he did not even consider making savings on the servicemen's separation allowances.

He could have reduced the cost of the scheme to the Treasury in three ways. First, he could have put the scheme on a contributory basis as he proposed to do for unemployment and sickness benefits. Beveridge had always been in favour of such a method and in 1924 had worked out a scheme of family allowances based on equal contributions from employees and employers and a smaller contribution from the State. The Conservative Party also favoured a contributory arrangement and had presented such a scheme to Kingsley Wood, who had turned it down.[156] In 1942 the Chancellor of the Exchequer had estimated that a five shilling allowance for all dependent children could be financed by a contribution of 2s 8d per week in respect of every employed person. As *The Times* commented: 'distributed between employer and employee, possibly helped by a State contribution, these figures, taken by themselves, may not seem formidable. But they have to be weighed together with the existing burden of social

[154] *Beveridge Report, op. cit.,* p. 88. Indeed five shillings was the sum being considered in 1920.

[155] In July 1940, 130,000 children were receiving school meals each school day (free and paid). By February 1945 1,650,000 children were receiving school meals (14 per cent of them free, the rest paying 4d to 5d a meal). In July 1940, 50 per cent of school children received milk at school compared with 73 per cent in February 1945. Titmuss, R. M., *Problems of Social Policy,* HMSO, 1950, p. 510.

[156] See Amery, L. S., *op. cit.,* p. 207.

insurance contributions as a method of financing the social services.'[157] Beveridge accepted much the same reasons for not making family allowances contributory. The major consideration must have been, however, that the Labour movement would only accept a State-financed scheme. Beveridge knew this for he had frequent consultations with the TUC while he was writing his report. Moreover, the government had stated in June 1942 that its acceptance of a scheme of family allowances was conditional upon the trade unions' approval. He therefore had to find another way of cutting the cost.

There was a second possibility. He could have proposed abolishing income tax allowances in respect of children which, in 1941, were costing the Exchequer £80 million; more than enough for his purpose. It was an option which Keynes, the Chancellor of the Exchequer and others had already contemplated. At the outbreak of war Keynes had considered financing a national scheme of family allowances along just these lines. His reasons were not only economic. He wrote: 'the system of children's allowances under the existing income tax appear highly anomalous when it is examined in detail. For a man with an earned income of £250 gets £7 per annum for the first child and nothing for any subsequent, then it gradually rises with income to a maximum of £8 13s for every child. For the non-income tax payers there are no general children's allowances though allowances are paid in a number of special cases. In lieu of the whole of the present system of children's allowances, I propose a flat payment of five shillings per week per child or £13 per annum, for income tax payers and for the insured population.'[158]

The Chancellor of the Exchequer in his white paper on family allowances also considered the relationship between income tax allowances in respect of children and cash family allowances. He had examined a scheme for linking income tax relief to family allowances under which family allowances would be renounced by those parents benefiting from tax relief. He rejected this on two grounds. First, because such a scheme would have the 'unexpected consequence' that changes in income tax would lead to changes in family allowances[159] and, second, because there was a difference, or so he argued, in principle between tax remission and directly paid allowances. 'Tax relief given in respect of children represents a recognition of the fact that the possession of children *reduces the capacity to pay*.'

[157] Leader in *The Times*, 11 May, 1942.
[158] Keynes, J. M., *op. cit.*, p. 86.
[159] 'The fact that parents would qualify for new or increased cash payments when and because their tax liability was reduced would mean that the link between family allowances and income tax would increase the cost of reducing income tax, particularly on the lower ranges of income, and so might postpone the time at which some relief from the present severity of income tax will be possible.' *White Paper on Family Allowances, op. cit.*, p. 5.

On the other hand 'the family allowance is assumed to be intended *to reduce financial hardship arising from the maintenance of children'* (our italics).[160] There was, therefore, as *The Times* said: 'a strong case for letting them run concurrently and allowing income tax payers to enjoy both'.[161]

We have already seen that there was no pressure from the leading members of the Family Endowment Society to abolish tax allowances in respect of children. On the contrary they wanted a national scheme of flat rate family allowances supplemented either by occupational schemes of family allowances or bigger income tax allowances extended to include surtax payers. Beveridge himself was also opposed to the abolition of these tax allowances. 'The idea sometimes mooted that the granting of children's allowances on a subsistence scale, as proposed in my Report, should lead to an abandonment of income tax rebates is wrong and reactionary' he wrote at the time.[162] He wished to see generous occupational family allowances developed in addition to increased tax rebates.[163]

At its annual conference in 1941 the Labour Party considered, but did not pass, a resolution in favour of a State-paid scheme of family allowances. This resolution included a clause relating to the abolition of income tax allowances in respect of children. A year later a similar resolution was passed but without the clause relating to income tax allowances.[164] Increased earnings together with the sharp increases in direct taxation already mentioned had brought the benefits of children's allowances to the average wage earner for the first time. Moreover, children's tax allowances were worth about six shillings a week in respect of each child of the average wage earner with three children, rising to a maximum of nearly ten shillings for those with higher earnings. An eight shilling cash allowance would have seemed an ungenerous substitute and could hardly be considered just compensa-

---

[160] *Idem.*

[161] 'A National Responsibility', *The Times*, 4 June, 1942.

[162] Beveridge, W., *The Pillars of Security*, Allen & Unwin, 1943, p. 159.

[163] In his Galton lecture to the Eugenics Society in February 1943 (while his report was being debated in the House of Commons), Beveridge proposed extending occupational schemes and increasing income tax rebates in respect of children because 'from the eugenic point of view flat subsistence allowances ... did not go far enough'. *The Times*, 17 Feb., 1943.

[164] At the Annual Conference of the Labour Party in 1941 a report including the costs of various dependency benefits was discussed. In this report the estimated annual costs of income tax allowances in respect of children in 1940–1 was given as £10 million. By the time of their conference in 1942 the true costs of these tax allowances for 1941–2 had been given wide circulation by the publication of the Chancellor of the Exchequer's White Paper on Family Allowances a month before. Perhaps this brought home to many trade unionists the extent to which tax allowances now benefited their members (the true cost was £80 million).

tion for taxing the family man more heavily. Perhaps even this would not have prevented Beveridge at least putting forward the suggestion for substituting family allowances for tax allowances; after all, 'the administrative simplification of getting rid of income tax rebates and other special allowances now made in respect of children must also be taken into account as a far from negligible factor'.[165] But there was a further objection to abolishing income tax allowances for children and this was almost certainly the crucial one. This was the view that direct taxation had reached its limits, thus making it politically impossible to tax the family man more heavily, which would have been the effect of removing the allowances. It will be remembered that the government had 'imposed a rapidly growing burden of taxation during the first years of war and then during the later years had to review the detailed structure so as to minimize the harmful repercussions this heavy burden was *believed* to be having upon the war effort'[166] (our italics). Concern for preserving (quite apart from improving) 'the war effort' had already prevented the government from imposing strict control over wages and had obliged it to increase the remuneration of men in the Armed Forces even though this was an area over which it had direct control. The whole question of optimum levels of direct taxation fell into the same set of considerations and largely accounts for Beveridge's disinclination to solve the problem of keeping down the cost of family allowances by a withdrawal of income tax allowances in respect of children.[167]

Throughout the campaign for family allowances there had never been any suggestion, except from the Conservative Party in the late thirties on the grounds of economy, that the first child in a family should not receive a family allowance. None of the dependency benefits paid by the State in 1942 excluded the first child. On the contrary, the allowance for the first child in the family was often worth more than the allowances for subsequent children and was never worth less. The exclusion of first children, however, nearly halved the cost of the scheme, thus saving seven times as much as the limitation of the scheme to parents earning, say, less than £420 (the income limit for the existing health and unemployment insurance scheme). If Beveridge

---

[165] Leader, *The Times*, 11 May, 1942.

[166] Sayers, R. S., *op. cit.*, p. 5.

[167] For example, Winston Churchill wrote to the Chancellor of the Exchequer on 19 Feb., 1941: 'I have been much disturbed by what you told me yesterday of your intentions. I cannot believe that an income tax of that rate would be compatible with national thrift or enterprise. Taken with the super tax it amounts to almost complete confiscation of the higher rates of income ... If you suppose you can collect at these high rates without waste or great diminution of effort, without striking a deadly blow at good housekeeping and good management in every form, you are greatly mistaken.' Quoted by Sayers, R. S., *ibid.*, Appendix IV, p. 557.

wanted his scheme to be accepted by the government he had no alternative but to limit its scope by excluding from it the first child in every family. This was his third and chosen solution. However, he justified this course of action not in terms of the need for economy, but because 'to give full subsistence allowances for all the children of a man or woman at work may be described as wasteful ... It would be an unnecessary and undesirable inroad on the responsibilities of parents.'[168] In the circumstances, it is hard to accept this as much more than a convenient rationalization.

The relationship between family allowances and the existing dependency benefits

How did the family allowances proposed by Beveridge in his report compare with those already being paid with respect to the children of servicemen, war pensioners, civilian widows, the unemployed and various other categories?

Table 4

SEPARATION ALLOWANCES FOR CHILDREN PAID TO THE WIVES OF MEN IN THE ARMED FORCES, 1939–45

Order of Child in Family	Pre-war	Nov. 1939	Nov. 1940	Mar. 1942	Sept. 1942	May 1944
First	5s	5s	7s 6d	8s 6d	9s 6d	12s 6d
Second	3s	4s	5s 6d	6s 6d	8s 6d	12s 6d
Third	2s	3s	4s	5s	7s 6d	12s 6d
Fourth and subsequent	1s	3s	4s	5s	7s 6d	12s 6d

The system of separation allowances introduced in the First World War was developed further during the Second. The wives of all men and officers in the Armed Forces received a marriage allowance together with an allowance for each dependent child. The value of the marriage allowance increased with rank but the compulsory contribution or 'allotment' to the allowance made by each man varied

[168] *Beveridge Report, op. cit.*, p. 15. He had less scruples about making inroads into the sense of responsibility of university teachers. In the scheme Beveridge introduced for the teaching staff at the London School of Economics in 1925, £30 a year was paid on behalf of each child under thirteen years of age and £60 for each older child until age twenty-three years if still in full-time education.

with his rate of pay. Children's allowances, to which no compulsory contribution was made, varied with rank. Those received by the wives of officers were higher for the first two children than those received by the families of the lower ranks. Captains and subalterns (and their equivalent ranks in the Navy and Air Force) received higher child allowances than officers in higher ranks.[169] By the end of 1944, 55 per cent of men in the Services were married and it was estimated that there were approximately two and a half million husbands in the Armed Forces living away from their families.[170] Separation allowances, therefore, were of vital importance to a considerable number of families. It is also important to remember that these allowances were not subject to income tax.

The level of unemployment dropped considerably during the war. In 1940 there were still as many as one million unemployed but by the summer of 1943 the number had fallen to 100,000 and a year later to the lowest level of 75,000.[171] Assistance payments for children were increased in the early years of the war when prices were rising rapidly and payments for the unemployed were increased (by one shilling for each dependent child) towards the end of the war in 1944. The latter increase was mainly justified in terms of easing the problem of resettlement.[172]

Parents were expected to contribute to the cost of keeping their evacuated children according to their means. Nevertheless, the State contribution was substantial and in 1941, for example, the average cost to the State of keeping an evacuated child was 8s 6d a week. Between September 1941 and the end of the war 118,300 unaccompanied children were placed under the Government Evacuation Scheme.[173]

Although Beveridge's proposal of eight shillings for each child after the first compared unfavourably with the allowances introduced

[169] For example, between September 1942 and May 1944 a major's wife received each week 52s 6d for herself and two children compared with a subaltern's wife and two children who received 59s 6d. A serving man's wife received 38s for herself and two children.

[170] Ferguson, S. and Fitzgerald, K., *Studies in the Social Services*, HMSO, 1954, p. 3.

[171] Sayers, R. S., *op. cit.*, Appendix III, p. 524. In June, out of 15 million men of working age 4·3 million were in the Armed Forces (see table 10 p. 350).

[172] Writing of the autumn of 1944, Alan Bullock says: 'Bevin remarked that most of the trouble after 1918 had come not from those who had stayed at home but from the ex-soldiers disillusioned on their return to industry. With that in mind he laid as much stress upon the measures proposed for resettlement as on the arrangements for demobilization ... The White Paper on Full Employment might be regarded as part of the policy, together with a bill which Bevin had introduced to provide increased unemployment benefit during the transition from war to peace.' Bullock, A., *op. cit.*, p. 334.

[173] Titmuss, R. M., *op. cit.*, Appendix 11, p. 564.

Table 5

UNEMPLOYMENT INSURANCE, WIDOWS, ORPHANS AND WORKMEN'S
COMPENSATION, 1942: ALLOWANCES FOR CHILDREN

Order of Child in Family	Unemployment Insurance	Contributory Widow's Pension	Contributory Orphan's Pension	Workman's Compensation (1940 Act)	Public assistance and unemployment assistance
First	4s	5s	7s 6d	4s	average per child 6s*
Second	4s	3s	7s 6d	4s	
Third and subsequent	3s	3s	7s 6d	3s	

*Varied by age from 4s 9d for under fives to 7s 9d for fourteen year olds.
SOURCE: *Beveridge Report, op. cit.*, p. 230.

specifically to meet situations arising from the war, they were better than existing allowances under the public assistance and national insurance schemes. Moreover, he proposed to pay the allowance for *all* children including the first of families in receipt of other social security benefits. Under his scheme, therefore, the financial position of the families of the sick, unemployed and widowed would be improved.

Acceptance of the policy
The Beveridge Report received enormous publicity. On the day of publication it usurped the war news on the front page of many newspapers. The BBC broadcast a summary of the report in twenty-two languages throughout Europe,[174] Beveridge prepared a summary for distribution to men in the Armed Forces and the daily newspapers gave their readers comprehensive but simple 'thumbnail sketches of life of the family in Beveridge's Britain'.[175] Although Beveridge had played down the population aspects in his report,[176] family allowances

[174] Several Members of Parliament, including Bevan and Shinwell, were very angry because the Beveridge Report was circulated to the BBC and the press before it was given to Members of Parliament.
[175] *Daily Herald*, 2 Dec., 1942. In 1964, it was estimated, that the family allowance would have increased to 36 shillings a week per child.
[176] He explained later that he did not elaborate on the population question in his Report because it was outside his terms of reference. This was not because he thought it any less important. See Beveridge, W., *The Pillars of Security, op. cit.*, p. 152.

were presented primarily in the context of concern about a falling birth-rate.[177]

The government tried to reduce the enormous interest the public was showing in the Beveridge proposals by clamping down on all official publicity. Churchill in particular was anxious to do this and on his insistence the summary of the report circulated to the Armed Forces was withdrawn. He was opposed to committing the government to a 'cloud of pledges and promises which arise out of the hopeful and genial side of man's nature and are not brought into relation with the hard facts of life'.[178] The war was not yet won, the economic position at the end of the war was unknown and both Labour and Conservative Ministers were well aware that taken as a whole Beveridge's plan was controversial. They were anxious not to weaken the coalition. (See the cartoon opposite page 205.)

However, demands were continuously voiced in the press that the government should commit itself to implementing the report's proposals. 'Action upon the Beveridge Report is an essential war measure; essential because it would invaluably stimulate our people, essential because it would strikingly exemplify our war aims, essential because freedom from want is a vital prop of the peace structure which must be erected in advance.'[179]

The government broke its weeks of silence when it faced Parliament for a debate on the Beveridge Report in February 1943. By then it had received a report from the committee it had set up to examine Beveridge's proposals in detail and the Cabinet, the day before the debate, accepted this report which had recommended that most of his proposals, including all three 'Assumptions' be accepted. Churchill had made it clear to the Cabinet, however, that 'it is desirable that should the measures be produced it should be an integral conception', and, he went on to emphasize, 'we cannot initiate the legislation now or commit ourselves to the expenditure involved'.[180] The government mishandled the debate in the House of Commons and John Anderson's[181] statement accepting most of the report only in principle 'because in the nature of things there could be no final commitment'[182] seemed so unenthusiastic that a sizeable group of younger Conservative Members led by Quintin Hogg as well as many Labour Members led

[177] For example, a leader in the *Daily Herald* said: 'State to Share Family Keep ... Britain must have more children. Children's allowances ... will help indirectly to produce them.' (2 Dec., 1942.)

[178] Churchill, W. S., *The History of the Second World War*, vol. IV, Cassell, 1951, p. 86.

[179] *Daily Herald*, 18 Dec., 1942, quoted from a leader.

[180] Churchill, W. S., *op. cit.*, p. 862.

[181] John Anderson became Chancellor of the Exchequer in September 1943 when Kingsley Wood died.

[182] *H. C. Deb.*, vol. 186, col. 1678.

by Aneurin Bevan, threatened to vote against the government by rejecting Anderson's statement as inadequate. After three days of debate and much pressure on the Parliamentary Labour Party by Labour Ministers, the government won.[183] Outside Parliament, the result of this debate, contrary to Churchill's intentions, was to increase the pressure on the government for a clearer statement of its plans for reconstruction including social insurance.

The proposal to introduce a national scheme of family allowances, however, had ceased to be controversial. Indeed, the government had already appeared to have made up its mind about such a scheme in the previous year. It was, therefore, rather more forthcoming about family allowances than it was on Beveridge's plan as a whole and on 16 February, 1943, the first day of the debate, Anderson announced the government's acceptance of the principle of family allowances. 'Apart from the Beveridge Report, the Government have had under consideration for some considerable time this important and somewhat difficult problem. Before the publication of the report they had come to one clear and definite conclusion; that whatever might be decided about cash allowances, by far the best and the most effective measure, within the limits of its possibilities, is the fullest development of the various child welfare services which bring the benefits directly to the children ... It is the intention of the Government to see that the provision of welfare services is developed to the fullest possible extent and their intention is that there shall be in addition a cash allowance of five shillings per week, starting with the second child.'[184]

The government's reasons for reducing the allowance to five shillings were first that it would be supplemented by services in kind to a greater extent than envisaged by Beveridge and, second, it was important that it 'should not be at a rate which would in practice prove an obstacle to the fullest development of the welfare services ... [and] we see no difficulty whatever in providing services equivalent in money value to 2s 6d per head ... as against the one shilling assumed by Sir William Beveridge'.[185] Anderson denied, however, that the reduction was made to save money, because 'the Government are fully alive to all the implications of the population trend which is brought out so clearly in the Beveridge Report'.[186]

Members from all parties tried to get the government to say when family allowances would be introduced because 'everybody now has become more or less a convert to the payment of family allowances',[187]

---

[183] For a fuller discussion of the debate on the Beveridge Report see, for example, Bullock, A., *op. cit.*, pp. 225–34 and Beveridge, J., *op. cit.*
[184] *H. C. Deb.*, vol. 386, cols. 1666–7.
[185] *Ibid.*, col. 1667.
[186] *Ibid.*, col. 1667.
[187] *Ibid.*, col. 1787.

and they were to be granted 'from an angle entirely different from that which is involved in catering for social security as embodied in the Beveridge plan. Children's allowances would have come in any case.'[188] Although Kingsley Wood said 'immediate steps' would be taken, he also echoed Churchill's caution by saying that 'it was not in the interests of the country or of the scheme itself to treat any of these matters in isolation'. He regarded 'family allowances as one of the main matters appertaining to the [Beveridge] scheme'.[189] The government was not prepared to commit itself to a timetable even for the introduction of family allowances.

In March 1943, to stem the continuing criticism of his government's attitude towards post-war planning, Churchill made a broadcast explaining their cautious approach. He emphasized that the 'supreme task' facing Britain was that of winning the war. He therefore proposed a four-year plan of social and economic reforms to be implemented only when the war was over, although preparations for some of the necessary preliminary legislation would commence at once. Stressing the need to halt the decline in the birthrate so that the country could 'keep its high place in the leadership of the world and ... survive as a Great Power', planning for 'the care of the young and the establishment of sound hygienic conditions of motherhood was vigorously proceeding'. He warned his listeners meanwhile 'of a danger of it appearing to the world that we here in Britain are diverting our attention to peace, which is still remote and to the fruits of victory, which have still to be won'.[190]

The broadcast received much comment in the press.[191] Although the government's attitude to post-war planning had been clarified and presented in a more positive manner than in the House of Commons the month before there was much regret that 'no foretaste of the forthcoming reforms can be offered even while the war lasts', because, as a leader in *The Times* explained, 'the realization now of some instalments of the future social plan – family allowances are perhaps the most conspicuous case in point – will not be to divert men's minds from their supreme effort of winning the war'.[192]

Family allowances, 'a cause neglected by the powerful organized interests, economic or political', had clearly only ceased to be neglected

[188] *Ibid.*, col. 1775.

[189] *Ibid.*, cols. 1834–5.

[190] 'After the War: the Prime Minister's Broadcast', *The Times*, 22 Mar., 1943.

[191] Copies of the text of his broadcast were distributed by *The Times* and it was published in full in the June 1943 issue of *Current Affairs*, the bulletin of the Army Bureau of Current Affairs, which was used by officers for leading discussion groups with their troops. This issue was devoted to social security and, in addition to a summary of the Beveridge Report, was designed to help the officers 'in driving home what the Prime Minister said'.

[192] 'The Four Year Plan', *The Times*, 22 Mar., 1943.

in conditions of war when 'they passed above the strife of party controversy'.[193] Support inside the government and in the Labour movement for such a scheme had been won on the grounds that it was at least an appropriate war-time measure. After the publication of the Beveridge Report, the government presented family allowances, in public at least, as part of its plans for reforming social security, and as such belonging to post-war reforms. Although Hubert Henderson was a strong critic of the plan as a whole,[194] he nonetheless opened pre-budget discussions in 1943 with a request to consider a scheme for family allowances and preparations to implement the scheme did in fact start that year. In the event the payment of the first family allowances did not begin until after the war was over. Why was there a delay? Ironically, did the scheme's association with Beveridge's plan reduce the priority family allowances had acquired since the outbreak of war or were there other pressures for delay?[195]

Pressures for delay

The family allowance scheme proposed by Beveridge would have cost £86 million annually. By reducing the size of the allowance to five shillings the government cut the cost of introducing them to less than £60 million in the first full year. We have seen that financial considerations had restricted Beveridge's proposals and in spite of Anderson's assurances to the House of Commons that the government plan to reduce the amount of the family allowance was not made 'to save money', the wish to economize was a determining factor. Financial considerations had already played their part in limiting the scope of these allowances. They also affected the timing of their introduction.

'We must consider the financial priorities ... in relation to other claims and we must put Defence first. The maintenance of the level of labour is supremely important ... and then we will take into account

---

[193] Sayers, R. S., *op. cit.*, p. 97.

[194] 'It is fairly open to question whether a scheme founded on its [the Beveridge Report] principles would not introduce more anomalies, more complications, and more illogicalities than it would remove. It would certainly cost immensely more, and it would do nothing that could not be much more easily done otherwise, to diminish want.' Henderson, H., 'The Principles of the Beveridge Plan' a memorandum written in August 1942, when Beveridge was discussing his proposals with the Treasury. See Clay, H. (ed.), *The Inter-War Years and other Papers*, Clarendon Press, 1955.

[195] John Walley argues that the inclusion of a family allowance scheme in Beveridge's plan for reforming social security gave those opposed to family allowances an opportunity to delay them, on the grounds that the plan must be taken as a whole and should not be implemented during the war. One of these opponents was the Secretary of the new Assistance Board, Sir George Reid, who had also been a member of the Beveridge Committee. He had 'a thoroughly old-fashioned dislike of the whole idea of children's allowances'. See Walley, J., *Social Security: Another British Failure*, Knight, 1972, p. 71.

this social security scheme, together with other claims upon the nation's purse.'[196] So explained Herbert Morrison to the House of Commons at the end of the long and angry debate on the Beveridge Report. He was referring to the whole security plan, not just family allowances, but they, like the whole plan had to compete with other claims on the nation's resources. Where was the Exchequer to find the money to implement a scheme of family allowances?

In 1942 Keynes and Henderson proposed to the Chancellor that a scheme of family allowances should be financed by new or additional luxury taxation. Suggestions of this kind however 'met strong opposition from the Inland Revenue Department on the grounds that "the purpose of the income tax is not the redistribution of income". In the face of this opposition the Chancellor fought shy of the more far-reaching and more detailed proposals of this kind.'[197]

An alternative might have been to increase direct taxation. However, as we have seen already there were limits to the amount of money the government felt it could raise in this way. Churchill certainly still held that view which he repeated in his broadcast on the Beveridge Report in March 1943.[198] In the latter half of the war, Keynes also subscribed to the general view that direct taxation had reached its limit.[199]

There was perhaps a further difficulty in initiating expenditure of this kind during the war. The Americans, through the introduction of lend-lease in 1941, were supplying Britain with large amounts of dollars and by June 1942 Keynes could write of the dollar shortage being over.[200] However, 'the Americans saw to it that no more dollars were forthcoming than were necessitated by genuinely austere standards. The enforcement of these standards inevitably became a major concern of the Treasury which had to take the lead in the more fundamental negotiations on lend-lease; negotiations which continued throughout the whole remaining length of the war. Moreover condi-

[196] *H. C. Deb.*, vol. 386, col. 2048.

[197] Sayer, R. S., *op. cit.*, pp. 97–8.

[198] In this speech he said: 'Direct taxation on all classes stands at unprecedented and sterilizing levels. Besides this there is indirect taxation raised to a remarkable height.' *The Times*, 22 Mar., 1943.

[199] For example, in a paper to the Chancellor of the Exchequer Keynes wrote in 1944: 'The fact that direct taxation has now passed the point which can be justified on merits, is effecting change in the psychology of the taxpayers, which if it is not soon reversed, may become permanent. Everyone nowadays is concerned in re-arranging his affairs so as to attract as little taxation as possible and this as a general universally excused phenomenon is something new in this country.' Quoted by Sayers, R. S., *op. cit.*, p. 142.

[200] In June 1942 Keynes wrote: 'We are in no serious risk of running short of dollars ... it is now quite out of date to regard our dollar problem as the essence of our financial difficulties. That is a hangover from the pre-lend-lease and early lend-lease days.' *Ibid.*, p. 357.

tions were attached to lend-lease.'[201] An indication of the Americans' views towards the introduction of such a scheme as family allowances is suggested (but *only* suggested) by the revision they made to the fifth clause of the Atlantic Charter in August 1941. This clause, which was proposed and drafted by Bevin and accepted by the War Cabinet, read: 'they [Britain and America] support the fullest collaboration in the economic field with the object of improving labour standards, abolishing unemployment and want, securing economic advancement and social security for all people'.[202] The revised version omitted the reference to the abolition of unemployment and want. This, perhaps, is one of the considerations the government had in mind when deciding not to implement a scheme of family allowances until the war was over.

Another reason for delaying the implementation of family allowances may have arisen from the 'difficulties' Kingsley Wood mentioned, 'not in connection with the principle, but in connection with the very many adjustments that will have to be made when, as the Government have agreed, these children's allowances are of a universal character. All sorts of questions arise in connection with income tax allowances and matters of that sort. This is ... a very formidable subject.'[203] It is clear from what has already been said that income tax allowances were extremely unlikely to be replaced by family allowances. Moreover, discussion about extending occupational family allowance schemes and income tax allowances was growing throughout 1943. Certainly the five shilling allowance did not compare well with the existing dependency benefits under the insurance and assistance schemes but in any case these would have had to be reviewed under Beveridge's proposals even if the level of benefit was whittled down too. It seems likely that the dependency benefits that most concerned the government while the war was still on were those being paid to servicemen's families. They were also the allowances which the government took most carefully into account when considering the impact that family allowances might have on other schemes, in large

[201] Sayers, R. S., *op. cit.*, p. 18.

[202] Quoted in Bullock, A., *op. cit.*, p. 69. Describing her surprise at Churchill's attitude towards the 'Beveridge Report', Janet Beveridge later wrote: 'It was said to us that the Prime Minister had at first been moved to accept the Report, but that strongly hostile influences from a quarter he did not feel able to resist had been brought to bear, to which he had yielded.' Beveridge, Janet, *op. cit.*, p. 172. Did these 'hostile influences' originate from high places in America or from members of his own party? The latter seems unlikely to have carried so much weight because a substantial number of Conservatives favoured the proposals contained in the Report. Beveridge himself said that he believed Churchill's attitude stemmed 'either from his inner consciousness or from bad advice'. See Beveridge, W., *Power and Influence*, Hodder & Stoughton, 1953, pp. 331–2.

[203] *H. C. Deb.*, vol. 386, col. 1833.

part because they were the subject of much controversy.[204] The government could not gain direct control over the earnings of men and women in industry but throughout the war it was in a position direc¹ly to determine the incomes of an ever increasing number of men in the Armed Forces. This did not mean, however, that it was prepared to resist pressure to increase servicemen's pay and allowances. There were several reasons for this.

At the beginning of the war prices rose sharply and although average wage rates did too, real incomes increased comparatively slowly. Those on fixed incomes or low wages were most affected by rising prices and, as we have seen, during 1940 and 1941 unfavourable comparisons were made between the condition of the family of the poorly paid civilian worker and the family of the serviceman whose income took account of the number of children he had to support. However, from 1942 onwards comparisons between a civilian worker's earnings and servicemen's pay became less favourable to the serviceman. The government consistently refused throughout the war to make comparisons between civilian and servicemen's pay because, in its view, 'no valid comparison can be made between such wages and emoluments of soldiers'.[205] Nevertheless, it must have been aware that it would be extremely difficult to transfer men from industry into the Services if the discrepancy became too large; and the morale of the troops themselves would suffer.

The United States had entered the war at the end of 1941 and by 1942 American soldiers began to be stationed in this country. Men in the Armed Forces therefore could compare their pay with that of their opposite numbers in the American forces as well as with that of civilian workers.[206] There was widespread concern with the fact that the 'war for social justice is being fought for us by men who are themselves the victims of a colossal injustice'.[207] Thus, for a variety of reasons the level of servicemen's pay and allowances was the subject of discussion in the House of Commons and in the press throughout 1942. In February separation allowances were increased but by such a small amount (see Table 4), that it failed to stem the clamour for further reconsideration. A survey of manpower resources and demands which was completed in October 1941 had shown that by June 1942 two million additional men and women would be needed

---

[204] 'Wages policy continued to be a subject of controversy *particularly* Service pay and allowances, until almost the end of the war' (our italics). Bullock, A., *op. cit.*, p. 84.

[205] Secretary of State for War, *H. C. Deb.*, vol. 397, col. 1722.

[206] 'From time to time he encounters the excellent soldiers who receive up to 8s a day. Everybody does the same, he reasons, so why should one get more than another?' Leading article 'Ten Bob Tommy has these Grouses', *Daily Herald*, 28 May, 1942.

[207] Leader *Daily Herald*, 28 May, 1942.

in the Armed Forces and the war industries. It was clear that the existing conscription scheme would only provide 60 per cent of the men required for the services and civil defence. Three hundred thousand more had to be found and to do this a greater degree of compulsion would be necessary to direct men into the Armed Forces and women (referred to as 'dilutees') into industry to replace them. It was essential that this should be done with the minimum of discontent.

Throughout the summer of 1942 the press kept up their complaints about the level of servicemen's pay while they reported with enthusiasm growing support for family allowances, and Members of Parliament badgered the government in Parliament. 'Of all the Home Front issues, none requires the attention of Parliament more urgently,' declared a leader in the *Daily Herald* on 2 June. On 13 July the Prime Minister asked the Chancellor of the Exchequer 'what is the difference between the yearly pay of a British soldier anywhere and an American soldier quartered in this country?'[208] He was clearly interested in establishing a greater degree of parity for he also wanted to know how much it would cost to increase British pay to half the American level, suggesting that at the same time the United States reduced theirs, keeping the surplus in the United States. British servicemen's pay and allowances were increased again a few weeks later in September.

The next and last changes made to Service pay and allowances did not occur until May 1944. The end of the war was in sight but the Allies had not yet landed in France and victory still had to be won. Another manpower survey in the autumn of 1943 showed once again that there was a gap between the demand and supply. This time, however, it had to be closed by drafting men from industry into the services in the knowledge that they could not be replaced. Moreover, having decided to take the risk that the European war would be over by the end of 1944, men were not only drafted from the 'less essential' industries but from the munitions and aircraft industries as well. Earnings in these industries were well above the average.[209] By this time too, more American troops were stationed in this country.

Throughout the early part of 1944 the government was asked by Parliament to produce comparisons of servicemen's incomes with those of civilians and, in the light of these comparisons, to review and increase them. At the beginning of March there was a five-hour

---

[208] Churchill, W. S., *op. cit.*, vol. IV, appendix C, p. 780.

[209] For example, during 1944 the average earnings of adult males in government factories were at least 20s a week higher than the average (122s) for all employees. See *Ministry of Labour Gazette*, Feb. 1946, p. 32.

George Whitelaw's **CONFERENCE CARTOON**

CRUMBS!

May 27th 1942.

FIRST pay-day under the Family Allowances Act took place yesterday. For more than 30 years Eleanor Rathbone advocated financial aid for parenthood. Before she died last January, aged 73, she saw her major proposals accepted and about to become law.

But if she were alive today it is likely that her voice would be heard in protest against one aspect of the new Act. That is the decision to reduce relief payments for tuberculosis and public assistance from families receiving family allowances. A selection of letters below shows what readers think of this new Means Test.

FAMILY ALLOWANCES

VICKY.

Aug. 7th 1946.

parliamentary debate on the subject during which the government refused to promise further increases on the grounds first, that there was 'a fundamental difference between civilian and Army earnings'[210] and, second, because large increases in allowances would be inflationary.[211] The government majority fell to 23. Though undefeated it did agree to give the issue further consideration. Meanwhile demands for increased pay for servicemen were given wide coverage in the press. For example, the day after the debate a leader in the *Evening Standard* emphasized that 'feeling was strong that Army pay is inadequate and without doubt there is large support for that view in the country and in the Forces. The startling contrasts with the rates paid to American and Dominion troops, the sudden fall in income which most families must feel when the wage earner is called up ... tend to produce a sentiment of discontent.'[212]

It was at this time that the Prime Minister wrote to the Chancellor of the Exchequer saying that although he was not prepared to make changes in basic pay he did feel increased allowances were justified. 'The war has been going on a long time and this, together with the arrival of a large number of better paid American Service personnel, does justify some concessions to our own forces ... I think that special consideration should be given to married personnel and in this category, especially to the lowest paid classes.'[213] At the end of April 1944 further increases in separation allowances were granted. They were the largest that were made during the war and represented a substantial improvement,[214] particularly in children's allowances, which became 12s 6d tax free for each child. They occurred at a time when every effort was needed finally to win the war but also at a time when plans for demobilization were in preparation. It is hard to believe that the increases would have been quite as large if the Minister of Pensions had not been able to say that 'in dealing with allowances, it is well known that they are only of a temporary nature. If, as the Prime Minister forecast ... we are getting nearer the end of the war

---

[210] James Grigg, Secretary of State for War, *H. C. Deb.*, vol. 397, col. 1722.

[211] The government had estimated that it would cost £900 million to bring the level of British soldiers' pay up to that of the Dominions and the United States. However, during March 1944 groups of leading economists from both Oxford and Cambridge wrote to *The Times* arguing that increases in servicemen's pay would not increase inflation very much, and that their inflationary impact could be nullified completely by increasing the standard rate of income tax by one shilling and indirect tax by 10 per cent. See *The Times*, 8 and 14 Mar., 1944.

[212] *Evening Standard*, 3 Mar., 1944.

[213] Churchill, W. S., *op. cit.*, vol. V, appendix C, p. 610.

[214] A recruit in the Army at the outbreak of war received 14s basic pay and 26s for his wife and two children: 5s of this was subject to tax. After May 1944 and until the end of the war a recruit received 21s basic pay together with 56s 6d for his wife and two children; none of this was taxable.

we shall get to the end of the allowances for wives and children when men are demobilized.'[215]

The pressure to increase servicemen's allowances, particularly those in respect of their children were, therefore, considerable throughout the war. It is not surprising then that discussions concerning the cost of a national scheme of family allowances did not include the suggestion that savings might be made by withdrawing the servicemen's allowances until the details of the Family Allowance Bill were published in March 1945. Even the White Paper on Social Insurance published in September 1944 did not specifically state that separation allowances would be replaced with family allowances.[216] It had been widely assumed in 1942 that the Chancellor of the Exchequer's 'wise refusal' to consider savings on the separation allowances should family allowances be introduced 'would mean in effect a welcome addition to the incomes of married men in the Forces'.[217] If family allowances had been introduced during the war, servicemen's families would have had to have been included and unless the value of the allowance was substantially greater than the five shillings the government were prepared to pay, family allowances would not have been considered adequate to *replace* servicemen's separation allowances. This might not have mattered if, in 1943, the government (particularly Churchill) had been confident that further increases in servicemen's pay would be unnecessary. Such an assumption, however, was unrealistic. There had been a year of continual grumblings about the level of this pay; the government had been forced to give two increases in 1942; it lacked complete control over civilian earnings and, in addition, the duration of the war remained uncertain. Therefore, if it was going to have to spend additional money on children during the war, why not reserve it for servicemen's children where need was generally recognized to be very great and certainly greater than among civilian families?[218]

---

[215] *H. C. Deb.*, vol. 402, col. 666.

[216] 'There will be no duplication with allowances payable under other schemes.' *White Paper on Social Insurance*, part I, Cmd. 6550, 1944, p. 16.

[217] 'Family Allowances: From the Principle to the Methods', *The Times*, 4 June, 1942.

[218] For example, 'it seemed to be the general impression that the family income of many working class householders is now large enough to obviate the necessity of expectant mothers to go out to work. All agree however that there is one outstanding exception, that of the serving man's wife ...' Quoted from a Ministry of Labour report made in August 1943 in Titmuss, R. M., *Problems of Social Policy, op. cit.*, p. 420. This is not to say that there was no poverty among civilian workers. In a statement Seebohm Rowntree made for a deputation on Family Allowance to the Chancellor of the Exchequer in January 1943, he pointed out that all but four Trade Boards fixed weekly wages below 72s 7d (his estimate of the poverty line at 1943 prices).

The introduction of family allowances was, therefore, delayed because in a situation in which taxation was thought by many, inside as well as outside the government, to have reached its limits, greater priority was given to servicemen's families. The level of expenditure on separation allowances and the cost of a State scheme of family allowances were certainly of a similar order towards the end of the war. The cost of servicemen's children's allowances in 1944 was considerable. The *increase* from 9s 6d to 12s 6d introduced at the beginning of May 1944 was estimated to cost £18 million in 1944. The total cost of these allowances from May 1944 to May 1945 must have been in the region of £80 million. Family allowances in their first year cost £57 million.

Had family allowances replaced separation allowances, civilian earnings and servicemen's pay would have been more directly and easily comparable. In those circumstances it would certainly have been more difficult to avoid increasing the servicemen's basic rates across the board. This would have cost the government considerably more than adjustment to the complicated system of allowances which, in any case, ensured that at least the income of wives of serving men did not *appear* to be too far below those of civilian workers. The government had behaved with regard to servicemen's pay exactly as the trade unions predicted employers would behave if they financed schemes of family allowances for their workers: basic wage levels would be depressed.[219]

Increased children's allowances for servicemen were in part an alternative to increases in their basic pay during the war[220] just as in the early years of the war a national scheme of family allowances was an attractive alternative to general wage increases in a period of inflation. Ostensibly, prices rose less rapidly after 1941 because the government tinkered with the cost of living index[221] and pressure for increasing servicemen's allowances derived not from rising prices,

[219] This had happened in France where family allowances were (and still are) financed by special Funds to which employers contribute in proportion to their wage bills. 'This consequence is generally recognized; and the extension of the system of children's allowances has in effect been accepted as *an alternative to larger wage increases* in periods of rising prices. Thus the French system is virtually one under which workers without dependent children contribute heavily to the assistance of family men' (our italics). *Report of the Royal Commission on the Population*, Cmd. 7695, 1949, p. 167, para. 447. Also see Sellier, François, *Dynamique des Besoins Socaux*, Les Editions Ouvrières, pp. 191–5.

[220] This was a point not unnoticed by some MPs. Talking of separation allowances, a Captain Cobb said, 'to pretend that that is an act of generosity on the part of the Government is quite wrong. It is nothing of the sort. It is merely an excuse to enable the Government to underpay the bachelor soldier.' *H. C. Deb.*, vol. 410, col. 2691.

[221] See page 184.

but from rising civilian earnings in certain industries and the presence of higher paid American and Dominion troops. These were factors over which the government had little control. It was not until March 1945, when the war was nearly over, that the government felt able even to *suggest* withholding family allowances from servicemen and, as the following discussion will show, that possibility caused as much debate as the rest of their family allowance proposals put together. In the event family allowances were not withheld from servicemen, for once the war was over men who had served in the Armed Forces either lost their separation allowances on demobilization or in 1946 when the government withdrew them and introduced a new pay structure[222] a month before the family allowance scheme came into operation. Thus, in practice servicemen's children's allowances were replaced by the national scheme of family allowances. In other words for them a tax free allowance of 12s 6d for every dependent child was replaced by a taxable allowance of five shillings for every dependent child excluding the first.

The white paper on social insurance, September 1944
The government proposals for a reformed system of social security which were published in September 1944 reduced the previously suggested scope of family allowances.[223] First, the allowance was not to be graduated by age. One of the major reasons for this was probably the government's desire to keep the scheme as administratively simple as possible. Commenting on Beveridge's proposals in 1942, the Government Actuary had written: 'the administration of children's allowances is likely to be more expensive than might be expected. The changes in the size of family, variation in rate of allowances with age of child and the intermittent payment of allowances for the first child where the parent is unemployed, disabled, etc., will necessitate very frequent administrative action.'[224] Eleanor Rathbone too was aware of the need for simplicity and she opposed a variable allowance on the grounds that it would be 'administratively troublesome'.[225] Second, the allowance was to cease when the child reached the age of sixteen irrespective of whether he or she continued in full-time education. Administrative considerations were probably one of the reasons for this as well, together with the fact that it

---

[222] See *Post-War Code of Pay, Allowances and Service Pensions and Gratuities for Members of the Forces Below Officer Rank*, Cmd. 7615, 1945.

[223] *White Paper on Social Insurance*, part I, Cmd. 6550, 1944.

[224] *Beveridge Report, op. cit.* Memorandum by the Government Actuary, p. 202, para. 72.

[225] See Evidence to the *Royal Commission on the Population* given by Eva Hubback and Eleanor Rathbone on behalf of the Family Endowment Society, 1944.

would reduce the cost of the scheme slightly. Altogether the cost of administering the proposed cash allowances was estimated to be £2 million a year, a little under four per cent of the total annual cost. The government was still only prepared to pay a five shilling allowance although aware that this would not meet the subsistence needs of a child. It justified this on the grounds that the State must not take away parents' responsibilities, although it was in the national interest for the State to help parents discharge their parental duties. This was an extension of Beveridge's rationalization for excluding first children. The family allowance scheme, therefore, was now presented as 'a *general contribution* to the needs of families with children'[226] (our italics). The government did, however, intend to extend the provision of free school milk and meals to all children and this, it argued, would compensate for the reduction in the cash value of the family allowance.[227] Pressure for this change must have come in part from the Board of Education whom Beveridge reports as having tried to urge him to give allowances wholly or mainly in kind. The cost of cash family allowances was estimated to be £57 million. School meals and milk when available to at least 74 per cent of school children were estimated to cost £60 million of which £20 million would be administrative costs.

A more detailed justification for abandoning subsistence level allowances was given in the debate on the White Paper which took place in the House of Commons early in November 1944. There was much mention of 'parental responsibility' by the leading government speaker, Sir William Jowitt (Minister of National Insurance) and by R. A. Butler (Minister of Education) who said that 'the system of family allowances is intended to help the general economy of the family and is not intended to be based on any standard of subsistence ... [because] the family should continue to have responsibilities of its own'.[228] However, he did add that the first child was to be excluded for 'a more mundane reason, and that is that the addition of the first child at a cost of five shillings would cost some £73 million. That would make a total of £130 million for cash allowances.'[229] Much importance was attached by government spokesmen to the rapid development of school meals and milk. Butler said that school milk would definitely be free to all children by the time family allowances were introduced and that there would be a substantial increase in school meal provisions.[230] Building work on school dining rooms would be sanctioned

[226] *White Paper on Social Insurance*, part I, *op. cit.*, p. 14.
[227] See pp. 215-6.
[228] *H. C. Deb.*, vol. 404, col. 1111.
[229] *Ibid.*, col. 1112. In 1944 14,000 of 28,000 schools provided meals. All but 1,000 schools served milk.
[230] *Ibid.*, col. 1125.

more readily and it was to rank with urgent housing needs as a priority for scarce building resources.

Conservative Members were glad that the government was not committing itself to provide subsistence level benefits. The level of taxation necessary to maintain such a heavy commitment would, they felt, be a serious disincentive. 'I do not believe we can transfer from war to peace production effectively unless taxation is materially reduced ... Are we building up a scheme under which people can just lie back and be comfortable, sapping the energy and enterprise which have built up the country and pulled it through the war?' asked Sir Spencer Summers, for example. Nonetheless, he supported family allowances 'because of the part they play in overcoming the disparity between those on benefit and those at work'.[231]

Labour and Liberal Members (now including Beveridge) criticized the government for abandoning subsistence standards. They were concerned primarily to prevent poverty. 'The principle', said Beveridge, 'should be that we should regard it as a primary aim of social policy to ensure every child against want, against going hungry, cold, ill-clad and ill-housed, not because the parents are spending their money badly but because the family income is not sufficient to provide the bare necessities of healthy life.'[232] He and other Liberal and Labour Members were not convinced that school meals and milk would compensate for the small cash allowance. Children under school age and school children during the school holidays would not benefit from them and serious doubts were expressed about the ability of the government to expand these facilities as rapidly as Butler envisaged. There was some discussion too about linking the level of benefits to the cost of living or at least guaranteeing to maintain their purchasing power, but the government was not prepared to consider that proposal. The scheme it was proposing, explained the Minister of National Insurance, 'is not and does not pretend to be a scheme of social security.... Economic justice, political justice, justice everywhere, full employment, organization of the health services, maintenance of a stable price level, a satisfactory housing policy – these things and many others are all necessary ingredients in a policy of social security, our task is a humbler one.'[233]

However, certain important areas of agreement were demonstrated in this debate. First, it was clear that the government was prepared to introduce changes in the social insurance and assistance schemes by stages instead of as a single package, and it was prepared to acknowledge that in any case family allowances were not an integral part of

[231] *Ibid.*, col. 1000.
[232] *Ibid.*, col. 1125.
[233] *Ibid.*, col. 984.

the social insurance scheme.[234] This was a reversal of the policy instigated by Churchill two years earlier. The end of the war seemed nearer and reconstruction policies had gained in priority both inside and outside the government. Secondly, there was no opposition to the government's intention to give them priority. Greenwood, who, when responsible for reconstruction planning had appointed the Beveridge Committee, welcomed this change. 'I am not prepared to wait until the whole plan is ready in legislative form, nor are my friends. I was glad to hear the Minister say that early in the next session a bill for Family Allowances will be brought forward.'[235] Reasons for wanting to give family allowances priority varied. It was generally felt that as family allowances had been agreed in principle for many months there should be no further delays. Eleanor Rathbone stressed that 'from the population point of view we've not a year to lose ... from about 1960 onwards the population will be beginning to decrease so much that in each generation, that is, about twenty-eight years, we shall lose from a fourth to a fifth of our population. That is a positively terrifying prospect.'[236] Mrs Gazalet Keir (Labour), while not believing family allowances would do much to alter the birth rate, hoped 'the government will see their way to implement them at the earliest possible movement, *as it has nothing to do with the insurance scheme*' (our italics).[237]

Finally, it was clear that family allowances were not going to replace income tax allowances for children.[238] Indeed, there was considerable support, particularly among Conservative Members, for making family allowances tax free because 'otherwise they would be of little benefit to the middle income group'.[239] Family allowances were, therefore, regarded as a universal benefit, not one exclusively for the poor.

Thus family allowances still had widespread support in Parliament during the discussion of the social security proposals. However, their relationship to the rest of the social insurance and assistance schemes was unclear and the coalition government was not yet committed to any of the details for their reform which were contained in the White Paper on Social Insurance. In addition, the future of provisions for

---

[234] 'The cost of these family allowances will be met wholly from the proceeds of taxation; they are thus outside the bounds of the scheme of social insurance properly so called.' *White Paper on Social Insurance*, part I, *op. cit.*, p. 6.

[235] *H. C. Deb.*, col. 999, vol. 404.

[236] *Ibid.*, col. 1169.

[237] *Ibid.*, col. 1052.

[238] 'It will be found desirable to continue the system of income tax relief for children notwithstanding the introduction of a system of family allowances.' Anderson, *Ibid.*, col. 1201.

[239] Tory Reform Committee, *Tomorrow's Children*. This was a booklet published the day of the debate on the White Paper on Social Insurance by a group of Conservatives formed to secure the acceptance of the main features of the Beveridge Report.

school children, which were regarded as complementary to cash family allowances, depended upon promises the government was in no position to guarantee.

The Family Allowances Act 1945

The Family Allowances Bill was published in March 1945 and debated in Parliament during the following weeks. The scheme contained in the Bill was the same as that outlined in previous government statements, namely a five shilling allowance payable on behalf of every child after the first and financed out of taxation. The allowance was to be taxable and power to exclude families in receipt of children's allowances under existing schemes were contained in the Bill. This time it was clear that servicemen's families would be excluded from the schemes for 'regulations may provide that there shall be no duplication with service or other children's allowances'.[240]

The provision to withhold family allowances from servicemen provoked immediate criticism in the press.[241] Churchill wrote at once to the Chancellor of the Exchequer expressing his concern because 'considering the object in view is to encourage the birth and extra nourishment of children, I cannot see why this additional benefit should be denied to those classes [servicemen and women]. In fact I should think that the prejudice which such a decision would arouse would greatly detract from the popularity of the scheme, for which nevertheless an immense annual sum is to be paid.'[242] Members of all parties criticized the government for even considering such a proposal and when the Bill was debated in Parliament this, together with the question of which parent should receive the allowance, attracted the most discussion.

Members refused to accept the government's reasoning that servicemen's pay and allowances, which in any case they would be reviewing, were not comparable with civilians' earnings and that the exclusion of the former from the scheme was merely following the principle of no duplication with other allowances for children.[243] 'The nation, and particularly the Armed Forces of the Crown, regard this child's allowance as something of a pledge, which is to be spread uniformly over the whole community' the Chancellor was told.[244] At the Committee stage in the House of Commons the clauses giving the government

[240] H. C. *Deb.*, vol. 408, col. 2259.

[241] See for example, the leader in *The Times*, 9 Mar., 1945.

[242] Churchill, W. S., *op. cit.*, vol. IV, appendix C, p. 627.

[243] The other families whose benefits would be adjusted if they received family allowances included those receiving orphans' pensions, and children's allowances under workman's compensation and public assistance. This was also a controversial clause but Labour members did not succeed in removing it from the Bill.

[244] H. C. *Deb.*, vol. 410, col. 2721.

power to make regulations excluding servicemen were negatived. In the House of Lords, after an assurance from Lord Woolton that servicemen were to get family allowances *in addition* to what they were already getting, the Second Reading lasted only twenty minutes and the Bill passed through the Committee stage and Third Reading without debate. When the Bill returned to the House of Commons for the Third Reading on 11 June, Churchill specifically stated that agreement had been reached about servicemen's pay: 'if there is no agreement there will be no Bill'.[245] The Act therefore contained no clause excluding servicemen's families from the scheme.

Eleanor Rathbone spoke mainly about the clause which stated that the family allowance would be received by the father and not the mother. Concerned with improving the status of mothers since the beginning of the campaign for family allowances, she was prepared not to vote for the Bill if the allowance was paid to the father because this would be 'practically throwing an insult in the faces of those to whom the country owes most, the actual or potential mothers'.[246] During the Second Reading all but one of the nineteen speeches on this aspect of the Bill were in favour of paying the allowance to the mother. Comparisons were made with servicemen's allowances which were paid directly to the mother. After a free vote on the clause at the Committee stage, it was agreed that the mother should receive the allowance. Eleanor Rathbone had less support for her proposal that the allowance should be regarded as belonging to the child, although this was an idea with which Churchill was sympathetic.[247]

There was very little debate about the objectives of a State-paid scheme of family allowances although there was some discussion about its limitations. Labour Members regretted the exclusion of the first child and wished the allowance were larger. Liberal Members wanted the value of the allowance tied to the cost of living 'for if this was not done, the whole thing may prove to be a hollow sham',[248] and Beveridge repeated his warning that 'unless as the family increases you make certain that the whole cost of the child is covered by your allowance, you cannot make sure that the children will in every case be free from want'.[249] Conservative Members placed more emphasis on the development of services in kind rather than cash for 'there is less chance of diversion from the children to other and less worthy

[245] *H. C. Deb.*, vol. 415, col. 1071.

[246] *H. C. Deb.*, vol. 408, col. 2283.

[247] In a memorandum to the Chancellor of the Exchequer, he wrote: 'surely these sums should be free from income tax and should be considered the property of the children? Would not this save a great many complications?' Churchill, W. S., *op cit.*, vol. IV, appendix C, p. 627.

[248] *H. C. Deb.*, vol. 408, col. 2340.

[249] *Ibid.*, col. 2309.

purposes',[250] and some regretted family allowances were to be taxable because 'the allowance should be of benefit to everybody ... they must be of value to the middle income ranges'.[251] Again comparisons were made with the non-taxable servicemen's allowances.

Members of all parties admitted, in the words of the Minister of National Insurance, that 'the baby is a very little one. We feel it will have to be a good deal fattened and cosseted before it reaches its proper stature.'[252] It was not at all clear how and when the scheme would receive extra nourishment. Indeed, there was no guarantee that it would even get regular attention for, unlike the National Insurance Act passed the following year, there was no requirement that the Government Actuary or any other member of the administration should regularly review the scheme. Although there was no agreement that its main objective was to encourage parenthood, Labour Members believed that family allowances were one of the many measures needed to abolish poverty; those who were optimistic about the future growth of the scheme seemed tc base their confidence in the belief that 'the trend in the birth rate will force a change'.[253] After all the government had appointed a Royal Commission on Population in 1944[254] and it seemed certain at the time that they would consider and recommend more generous allowances for children.

Outside Parliament the introduction of family allowances was associated with the need to increase the birth rate. *The Times,* for example, described the scheme as 'something more than a measure to mitigate want caused by size of family. It is ... the first very limited step taken by the State with the deliberate intention of encouraging parenthood.'[255] In a broadcast on the evening before the Bill gained Royal Assent, Churchill talked of 'the perils of a falling population' and he gave family allowances as an example of the National Government's 'stress on all that surrounds the life of the home and of bringing into the world in satisfactory conditions the largest number of children ...'[256] During the campaign leading up to the General Election in 1945 the party manifestos presented the development of family

---

[250] *Ibid.,* col. 2261 (Minister of National Insurance).

[251] *Ibid.,* col. 2313.

[252] *H. C. Deb.,* vol. 411, col. 1418.

[253] *H. C. Deb.,* vol. 408, col. 2277 (Eleanor Rathbone).

[254] The Royal Commission on the Population was appointed on 3 Mar., 1944, 'to examine the facts relating to the present population trends in Great Britain; to investigate the causes of these trends and to consider their probable consequence; to consider what measures, if any, should be taken in the national interest to influence the future trend of population and to make recommendations'.

[255] *The Times,* 9 Mar., 1945.

[256] Report of Churchill's speech, *Evening Standard,* 14 June, 1945.

benefits and services in a similar context.[257] It is not surprising, therefore, that a public opinion survey conducted towards the end of the war showed that family allowances were generally associated first, with the government's wish to encourage the birth of more children and second, with the need to help poor families, particularly those with several children.[258] The exclusion of the first child was taken to imply that it was a measure designed for large rather than small families.

The views of the Family Endowment Society, the TUC, women's organizations and other pressure groups on the scheme of family allowances finally introduced can be found in the evidence these groups gave to the Royal Commission on the Population and to the Royal Commission on Equal Pay. There was general concern that the value of the allowance was too small but, as in Parliament, it was believed that an increase would be necessary if the scheme was to have any impact on the birth rate.

Family allowances, described by the Chancellor of the Exchequer only three years before as 'the basic social service payment for children',[259] had been reduced in scope to do no more than 'ease the financial burden which at the present time oppresses parents with large families'.[260] In the circumstances (and with the advantage of hindsight), it is difficult to believe that the Act was 'an Act of historic justice to the family'.[261] First, it had been passed in isolation from all the other social security reforms. Second, the small cash allowance was to be supplemented at some unknown future date with free school meals and with milk for all children and these were measures over which the Minister of National Insurance had no control.[262] Indeed, their priority would have to be established and maintained in the face of other demands on the education budget, not the social security budget. Finally, nobody had given detailed consideration to the scheme's future development. It was merely assumed that concern

---

[257] A healthy family life must be fully ensured and parenthood must not be penalized if the population of Britain is to be prevented from dwindling.' *Let us Face the Future*, Labour Party Manifesto, 1945. '. . . on the proper feeding and the healthy upbringing of a substantially increased number of children depends the life of Britain and her enduring glory.' *Conservatism in a Nutshell*, Conservative Party Manifesto, 1945.

[258] Mass Observation, *Britain and Her Birth Rate*, Curwin Press, 1945.

[259] See page 196.

[260] The Minister of National Insurance introducing the Second Reading of the Family Allowances Bill, *H. C. Deb.*, vol. 408, col. 2259.

[261] *The Times*, 6 Aug., 1946 (the first day on which family allowances were paid).

[262] The Minister of Education announced on 28 Mar., 1946 that school milk would be free of charge to all school children when payment of family allowances commenced, and that school meals would be free to all from the beginning of April 1947. School meals were never made free to all children.

about population trends would continue to strengthen the case for bigger allowances. It had been forgotten that family allowances were supported for very different reasons and that most support had been won on the grounds that such a scheme was a means to a variety of other ends: curbing inflation, maintaining the incentive to work and reducing poverty among children. The *principle* that 'children should receive a little share of the national income given to them not in respect of their father's service in industry but in respect of their own value to the community as its future citizens and workers' was far from established.[263]

Once family allowances had been introduced they attracted very little attention. The Report of the Royal Commission on Equal Pay, published two months after the scheme came into operation, might have been the occasion of further discussion.[264] The commission recommended that equal pay be introduced in the teaching profession and non-industrial government employment, recognizing that this would almost certainly lead to a demand for occupational family allowances. However, the Report was never debated in Parliament, in spite of frequent requests from Labour Members throughout the winter and spring of 1947. The Labour government was facing severe economic difficulties in the transition from war to peace. As Hugh Dalton, the Chancellor of the Exchequer, explained when refusing to implement the commission's proposals, they were 'not in the national interest' because the introduction of equal pay would mean higher production costs with no guarantee that productivity would be increased. Moreover he said that 'if the pay of unmarried women were raised to equality with that of married men, a married man with a family would be left in a relatively worse economic position than any other section of the community'.[265] It would be difficult therefore, in his view, to resist demands for occupational family allowances, thus involving the government in even more expenditure.

Two years later the Report of the Royal Commission on the Population was published.[266] It contained proposals for substantial increases in State family allowances, the extension of occupational family allowances and an increase in the value of income tax reliefs. This report, like the one on Equal Pay, was never debated in Parliament.

[263] Eleanor Rathbone speaking in the first parliamentary debate on family allowances. *H. C. Deb.*, vol. 380, col. 1866.

[264] *Report of the Royal Commission on Equal Pay*, Cmd. 6937, 1946. The commission had been established by Herbert Morrison in October 1944, 'to consider the social, economic and financial implications of the claims for equal pay for equal work'.

[265] *H. C. Deb.*, vol. 440, col. 1070. Dalton was aware of the needs of the family man to some extent, for in his 1947 budget he increased the child tax allowance from £60 to £70.

[266] *Report of the Royal Commission on the Population*, Cmd. 7695, 1949.

The government was still grappling with economic problems and by 1948 concern about the birth rate had declined somewhat, for the population trends had appeared to alter during the five years that the Commission was sitting.[267] Moreover, the advent of nuclear weapons in 1945 had reduced the military advantage of sheer numbers.

Perhaps the publication of these two reports could have been used to bring family allowances to the attention of the government, Parliament and the press once again, but there was no one sufficiently interested to do so. Eleanor Rathbone had died in January 1946 and with her the Family Endowment Society died. She had provided much of the finance for it and in many ways the society had become a platform for her and her ideas.

In the following two decades issues once closely associated with family allowances became separated from them. An increasing proportion of married women[268] joined the labour market and acquired an economic status of their own, albeit an inferior one to men. In addition their earnings now supplemented the family income at a time when there were still dependent children in the family. Women had therefore found and used other methods of acquiring an economic status and supplementing their family's income. Family allowances became less relevant as a means to these ends and by the end of the sixties were no longer associated with the issue of equal pay. In recent months a renewed interest in using family allowances paid to the mother as a means of recognizing her status has materialized, associated with the debate on the tax credit proposals.[269]

The problems of poverty and a declining birth rate, concern for which had underpinned the final stages of the campaign for family allowances and which, in the eyes of the public, were the main reasons for their introduction, ceased to be issues in the fifties and early sixties. Unemployment was far lower than Beveridge and many economists had dared to hope, and with rising average real wages, poverty was no longer associated with the families of wage earners.[270] Income tax allowances for children were regularly increased so that the tax payer's income continued to be adjusted to his family size. The maintenance of a gap between a family man's earnings and the benefit he received while unemployed did not require the operation of the 'wage stop' on a large scale and was, therefore, a problem of

---

[267] In 1941 the birth rate had fallen to 13·9 per 1000 population, the lowest ever recorded. A year later it was the highest since 1931, at 15·6 per 1000 population and by 1947 it had increased to 20·6 per 1000 population.

[268] There were over a million more married women in employment at the end of the fifties than at the beginning of that decade.

[269] See *Select Committee on Tax Credit, 1972–73*, H. C., 341, vol. 1.

[270] In his Report Beveridge had assumed an unemployment rate of 8 per cent, but by the end of the war he had lowered this to 4 per cent.

much smaller dimensions than in the twenties and thirties.[271] It was widely believed, particularly by those concerned with social security, that the birth rate trends in the fifties suggested a stable population rather than a declining one.[272]

Inside government, therefore, those involved in the administration of social security became preoccupied with other more major sectors of that system, notably pensions. Apart from the difficulties posed by the wage stop, there was no way in which the decline in the real value of family allowances could pose problems for those who administered the social security system. In contrast, the question of inadequate insurance pensions did make a big impact on the work of the National Assistance Board.

Finally, there was no pressure group specifically interested in family allowances. The TUC was very concerned that the government should improve the inadequate insurance benefits but it had nothing to say about family allowances throughout the fifties. Women's organizations were more preoccupied with campaigning for equal pay and nursery and welfare provisions for children. There was no equivalent of the Family Endowment Society until the formation of the Child Poverty Action Group in 1965.

This separation of once closely associated issues had important implications for the subsequent development of family allowances. The debate on the aims of the scheme and the principle of the State sharing the financial cost of children were allowed to lapse and family allowances were increased only twice in the first twenty years of their operation and then only partially to offset the effect of removing food subsidies.[273] By the early sixties there was even talk in Conservative circles of paying them only to third and subsequent children. It seemed that Enoch Powell was right when he said 'yet we have these payments still in 1964, their origin forgotten, their value eroded. Nobody says much about them nowadays ... Still there they are.'[274] When family allowances did become an issue again in the mid-sixties the context of the debate was considerably narrower.

More recently the discussion has broadened once again after family

[271] The 'wage stop' refers to the procedure whereby a man's benefit is reduced to what are considered to be his 'normal' earnings. It applied to National Assistance and Supplementary Benefits.

[272] In fact the birth rate continued to rise from 1942 until 1964, but there was a considerable time lag before this trend was recognized. For a more detailed discussion on the Government Actuary's perception of demographic trends see Land, H., 'Women, Work and Social Security', *Social and Economic Administration*, July 1971.

[273] In 1952 the allowance was increased to eight shillings for every eligible child and in 1956 the allowance for third and subsequent children was increased to ten shillings. They were not increased again until 1967.

[274] *Spectator*, 12 June, 1964.

allowances were threatened with extinction in a reorganization of the income tax system.[275] A more vocal women's movement and, more important, the government's need to curb wage demands in a period of the most rapid inflation since the war, have brought issues long ago associated with family allowances alongside them again. As a result, family allowances look as if they may at last become 'the basic social service payment for children'.[276]

IV CONCLUSION

This case study describes the long and chequered path which the campaign for family allowances had to travel before gaining the serious attention of the government. We have tried to explain why a coalition government accepted the idea of a State-financed scheme of family allowances in principle during war-time and then delayed implementing the idea until the war was over. In studying the introduction of this new policy, there are some general conclusions to be drawn.

1. The objectives of a scheme of family allowances did not remain the same either before or after the policy was implemented. As the objectives changed, so did the character and extent of support for the policy.

2. The policy was not even considered by a government until the problems with which it was associated were believed to be the proper concern of government. Family allowances were supported in the early days as a means of reducing inequalities between rich and poor, and between men and women. To socialists and feminists these were worthy ends in themselves but were not regarded as legitimate ends for government social policy until the Second World War. Broader support from Liberals and Conservatives was forthcoming only when family allowances became linked with other problems: a declining birth rate, poverty and malnutrition among children, the maintenance of work incentives and the need to curb inflation. These problems were established concerns of government and thus, by association, the legitimacy of family allowances was enhanced.

3. It was hard to establish the legitimacy of this policy which, it was believed, would interfere with prevailing patterns of family responsibility thus reducing the dependency of wives on husbands and children on parents.

[275] See the Green Paper, *Proposals for a Tax-Credit System*, Cmnd, 5116, 1972.

[276] The subsequent development of child benefits which started to replace family allowances and child tax allowances in April 1977 is described in H. Land, 'The Child Benefit Fiasco' in Jones, K. (ed.), *Year Book of Social Policy*, Routledge and Kegan Paul, 1977, pp. 116–32.

4. It was also difficult to establish a policy which modified market forces in ways which were believed to be detrimental to the workings of that market. Thus, sections of the Labour movement opposed family allowances on the grounds that they would restrict trade union freedom in wage bargaining and Conservatives opposed them on the grounds that they would weaken work incentives. Only when both had been convinced that this would not be the case – the former because their bargaining position had improved for other reasons and the latter because it could be shown that family allowances were needed to *preserve* incentives – did family allowances gain widespread support. Until that time policies which had less impact on wage levels were preferred, namely social services in kind for children.

5. Family allowances gained priority when they became relevant to government economic policy. They were accepted by the government at the beginning of the war because, it was argued, they were a weapon against inflation. It is no coincidence that family allowances were given a new lease of life in the recently recommended tax credit scheme by a Conservative government facing similar economic problems.

6. The introduction of temporary or selective measures strengthened the case for moving to a universal scheme of family allowances by demonstrating that the policy was feasible and had beneficial rather than detrimental effects. Once apparently successful they weakened the case of those who opposed the policy in principle. Thus the introduction of separation allowances for the wives of servicemen during the First World War was important, first because it demonstrated that adjusting family income to family size improved the health of the children and, second, because it was difficult to maintain a distinction between the unemployed ex-serviceman and the unemployed civilian. As a result unemployment benefit had to include allowances for dependants.

7. The association of the policy with trends, such as demographic changes, which were unpredictable to governments and pressure groups alike led to erratic development of the policy because support for it waxed and waned in an unforeseen manner. This was mainly because the other objectives of the policy had not been made explicit and had not won unequivocal support. The development of family allowances after 1945 may have been hindered by associating them, in the public's eyes at least, with the need to increase the birth rate and with little else.

8. Circumstances changed so that the policy which was once thought to make the achievement of certain objectives easier was believed to make it more difficult. Universal family allowances were regarded as a potentially valuable means of reducing the total wage bill to tolerable limits but separation allowances were increasingly needed,

and used, to keep the total expenditure on pay for men in the Armed Forces to a minimum. If universal family allowances had been introduced at that time it would have been difficult to use them as an alternative to general increases in servicemen's pay. The relationship between servicemen's pay and allowances strengthened the case for universal family allowances at the end of the First World War and at the beginning of the Second, but weakened it between 1941 and 1945, thus delaying their introduction.

9. Some of the objectives to which the policy became attached were subsequently achieved by other policies. In these circumstances support for the policy was weakened. Family allowances became less relevant to the government's economic policy after 1941 because wage increases were kept in check without them. Similarly, after 1945 more married women acquired a degree of economic independence by taking paid employment, so that the importance of family allowances as a means of giving women an economic status of their own declined. Income tax allowances were regularly increased thus updating the adjustment of the tax payer's income to family size. Taxable cash allowances therefore became less relevant as a means to that end. It is difficult to understand why arguments for a particular policy get forgotten. For example, why was it forgotten that income tax allowances for children were often discussed in relation to cash family allowances and that, whereas their existence was used as an argument for introducing cash allowances, the majority, including the TUC, wanted cash allowances *in addition*, not as an alternative to tax allowances? The relationship between tax allowances and family allowances was 'discovered' in the late fifties as if for the first time.

10. As the policy was first discussed and debated outside government it had to be taken up by people within government. In the case of family allowances this was not achieved until Keynes, when he was appointed an economic adviser, brought the idea in with him. He had been convinced of the case for introducing family allowances on economic grounds, as well as for reasons of equity, before his appointment. His entry into the heart of government at a time when the Treasury was weak enabled him to put new ideas to the policy-makers quickly and with force.

11. Once introduced, family allowances were not monitored either outside or inside government. There were no pressures, therefore, for their value to be maintained, far less increased. They were easily forgotten because the ministry responsible for their administration had no duty to review them regularly and, after Eleanor Rathbone died, there was no pressure group outside government with a specific interest in them until 1965. Thus, opportunities for evaluating family allowances provided, for example, by the publication of the reports of the

Royal Commissions on Equal Pay and on the Population were not used.

12. In operation, family allowances made little impact upon the administration of related policies. They were isolated from the development and administration of other social security benefits and therefore their declining value was overlooked, particularly during a period of low unemployment. When unemployment increased and earnings-related benefits were introduced in the early sixties, the inadequacy of family allowances became more visible and therefore attracted more attention.

CHAPTER TEN

Creating the Open University

The Open University is a unique institution within our system of higher education. It now provides degree and post-degree courses for students from a wide variety of backgrounds, age-groups and levels of educational attainment. Its uniqueness derives in part from the nature of its students, but more particularly from its methods of teaching. A high proportion of the material is taught by correspondence but this is supplemented, as most of us are aware, by the use of 'lectures' on radio and television and by tutorials at local centres and summer schools.

After only two complete years in operation the Open University was already a sizeable organization; its budget for 1972 was estimated to be £8,403,000 and the total number of students taking courses that year was 32,356; there were 349 full-time, centrally based staff[1] and 279 regional tutorial and administrative employees; at that time twenty-two undergraduate courses were being offered but by 1975 there were to be at least seventy-five.[2]

The creation of the Open University followed a distinctive pattern of development, its success being dependent largely on the personal influence of a few individuals in positions of authority who took the most important decisions without the help of much expert advice. Very little public debate on the concepts and issues involved took place until the later stages, when information about the precise nature of the scheme became more widely known but, by this time, the basic framework had already been agreed.

The decision to create a *University of the Air* originated within the Labour Party, in Opposition, in 1963, and when the party was returned to power in 1964 the task of developing the new institution was entrusted to Miss Jennie Lee, then Parliamentary Under Secretary

---

[1] Includes full-time teaching staff in faculties and the Institute of Educational Technology, plus staff tutors and senior counsellors.

[2] Figures provided by the Open University (unpublished).

for the Arts. Responsibility for the policy remained within the Department of Education and Science until September 1967 when a Planning Committee was established. The university finally received its Charter in July 1969 and began its courses in January 1971.

There are five fairly distinct stages in the development of the Open University which are used in this study to demarcate its main sections. The first period is the background before autumn 1963; the second, on planning within the Labour Party, extends until March 1965; the third examines from then until 1966, when a white paper was published; the fourth, to September 1967, covers a period when the policy seemed dormant and the last continues to the beginning of 1969 when the Open University becomes a reality.

I THE BACKGROUND TO THE POLICY: BEFORE AUTUMN 1963

On 8 September, 1963 at a rally in Glasgow, Harold Wilson announced that his party was working on plans for a *University of the Air* and nationally organized correspondence courses. These would be intended for a wide variety of potential students; for instance, technicians and technologists who left school at sixteen or seventeen and later felt they could qualify as graduates, others who would like to acquire new skills and qualifications and those who had no facilities for taking GCE at 'O' or 'A' level. 'What we envisage,' he said 'is the creation of a new educational trust, representative of the Universities and other educational organizations, associations of teachers, the broadcasting authorities, publishers, public and private bodies, producers capable of producing television and other educational material. This trust would be given State financial help and all the government assistance required. Broadcasting time could be found either by the allocation of the fourth television channel, together with the appropriate radio facilities or by pre-empting time from the existing three channels and the fourth when allocated.'[3] Educational programmes would be made available for supplementary study at educational institutes such as technical colleges.

What were the origins of this scheme? How and why did the *University of the Air* secure a place within the Labour Party programme for education? The answer to these questions lies in the coincidence of two trends: growing pressures on the educational system and the development of broadcasting. This resulted in a

---

[3] Extract from the press release of the speech.

number of similar but independent proposals for using broadcasting to extend educational facilities, one of which was adopted by the Labour government when it was returned to power in 1964.

Pressures to improve higher and further education

During the late 1950s and early 1960s interest in education, and especially post-school education, was increasing as the need for a rapid expansion of facilities became apparent.[4] The pressures on higher and further education came from three main sources: from the increasing demand for places in higher education; from the need to improve industrial and technological training, and from a recognition of the wastage of talent arising from unequal educational opportunities.[5]

The increasing demand for places in higher education arose primarily from two factors, the 'bulge' and the 'trend'. The former refers to the inflated number of children born towards the end of the Second World War, and especially after it had ended. As a result there was a massive increase in the number of eighteen year olds in the early 1960s, from 642,000 in 1955 to 963,000 in 1965.[6] This in itself would have raised the demand for higher education. In addition, however, there was the 'trend', which refers to the increase in the proportion of persons of a given age who obtain good school leaving qualifications and may therefore wish to seek higher education.[7]

The second source of pressure was derived from the need to improve industrial training facilities and to adjust occupational training more closely to future demands for skills.[8] The Zuckerman Report[9] of 1959 estimated that by 1970 the number of qualified scientists and engineers trained each year would have to be doubled. What Harold Wilson was later to call the 'white-heat' of the scientific

---

[4] See Peters, A. J., *British Further Education*, Pergamon, 1967, pp. 228–91, for a short discussion of the growing interest shown in higher and further education during this period.

[5] Definitions of 'higher' and 'further' education vary. The definition used here is based on that provided in *The Impact of Robbins* by Layard, R. *et al.*, Penguin, 1969, pp. 146–7. 'Higher' education refers to advanced courses provided at universities and former colleges of advanced technology. 'Further' education comprises all other full-time post-school education leading to advanced qualifications provided at institutions maintained by LEAs or receiving direct grants from central government, except colleges of education.

[6] *The Report of the Committee on Higher Education* (*Robbins*), 1963, Cmnd. 2154, p. 56.

[7] For statistics on the 'trend' see the Robbins Report *ibid.*, Appendix 1, part IV, Tables 10, 12, 14 and 33, pp. 112–51.

[8] See Wellens, J., *The Training Revolution*, Evans, 1963, p. 10 for a discussion of the need for manpower planning.

[9] *The Report on Scientific and Engineering Manpower in Great Britain*, Cmnd. 902, 1959.

revolution[10] was creating a need for the expansion of technological education.[11]

Inadequate and unequal educational opportunities in general was a third preoccupation of the late 1950s and early 1960s. The Crowther Committee, which reported in 1959, expressed concern over this problem. It was argued that 'the available resources of men [and presumably also of women] of high ability are not fully used by the present system' and, the report continued, 'there is hardly one amongst the advanced English-speaking countries who would profess itself content with so small a trickle as one in eighteen continuing in full-time education into the later teens'.[12] Not only was the proportion small but the social background of children was an important factor in determining their educational careers; the lower the social class, the greater the degree of educational wastage.[13] The Robbins Report illustrated this point with reference to higher education. It stated that 'the proportion of young people who enter full-time higher education is 45 per cent for those whose fathers are in the "higher professional" group compared with only four per cent for those whose fathers are in skilled manual occupation ... The link is even more marked for girls than for boys'.[14] Moreover, they argued that 'the relative chances of reaching higher education for middle-class and working-class children have changed little in recent years'.[15]

The pressures on the post-school sectors of the education system led to a reappraisal of the possibilities for its extension. It was partly as a response to these pressures that the Robbins Committee was established in 1961 to review full-time higher education and advise the government on long-term planning. Its report, published in 1963, concluded that a large-scale expansion was necessary. The committee devoted most of its attention to formulating the long-term aims of higher education and discussing how these could be achieved. In this part of the report the use of broadcasting and correspondence

[10] 'Labour and the Scientific Revolution', in the *Report of the 62nd Annual Conference*, Labour Party, 1963.

[11] For discussions of the problems faced in the provision of industrial and especially technological education see: Robinson, E., *The New Polytechnics*, Penguin Education Special, 1968. Wellens, J., *op. cit.*, *passim*. Peters, A. J., *op. cit.*, pp. 87–90 and 124–7.

[12] The Central Advisory Council for Education (England), *15–18: A Report*, p. 316. This committee has two links with the Open University. Lord Crowther, its Chairman, later became the first Chancellor of the new university and Sir Peter Venables, a member, became Chairman of the Open University planning committee.

[13] *Robbins Report, op. cit.*, p. 51.

[14] *Idem.* See also Jackson, B. and Marsden, D., *Education and the Working Class*, Routledge, 1962. Jackson later became a founder member of the National Extension College, a forerunner of the Open University.

[15] *Robbins Report, op. cit.*, Appendix I, part 2, p. 52.

was totally ignored. It was recognized, however, that besides a long-term plan, measures to overcome the short-term crisis would be necessary. The committee made two recommendations. Evening teaching for first degrees should be introduced and, secondly, some universities should establish correspondence courses. It was in conjunction with these emergency measures that television was thought to be important. The committee stressed, however, that although correspondence courses and teaching by television might afford some temporary easing of pressure, the effect could only be marginal.[16]

The Robbins Report was not the only forum for discussion of emergency measures. Three articles published in the *Spectator* in the summer of 1963 outlined a number of proposals. The first aired the possibility of extending and improving correspondence courses;[17] the second suggested that a private university, which charged fees, should be established;[18] and the third argued that more part-time universities at which students paid their own fees was the answer.[19] The proposals for using television to extend post-school education must be seen as part of a general search for new ideas about how facilities might be expanded to meet the increasing demands on this sector.

The development of broadcasting

It is unnecessary to provide a detailed account of technical progress in radio and television. What follows is a brief summary of the developments in broadcasting which have made its use as an effective educational medium feasible. Three factors are especially important: they are an increase in the amount of broadcasting time available; an improvement in the coverage and quality of the services; and a growth in the number of radio and television sets in use.

Ever since the British Broadcasting Company received its licence to broadcast in 1923,[20] competition for the use of air space (broadcasting time) has been fierce. From the very beginning educational programmes were produced but the provision of programmes linked to examinations would have required considerably more transmission time than could be spared for only one of the BBC's many functions.

The first television service was established in 1936 but it was suspended during the Second World War. In June 1946 it was restarted in London and stations in the Midlands and the North began transmitting in 1949 and 1951 respectively. The Independent Television

[16] *Robbins Report, op. cit.*, pp. 262–3.
[17] Cotgrove, S., 'The Forgotten Tenth', *Spectator*, 17 May, 1963.
[18] Margeson, J., 'Emergency University', *Spectator*, 24 May, 1963.
[19] Phillips Griffiths, A., 'Part-timers', *Spectator*, 28 June, 1963.
[20] It became the British Broadcasting Corporation in 1927.

Authority was formed in 1954[21] on the authorization of the Post-master General for a ten-year trial period and in 1964 permission was granted for its continuance.[22] The BBC began a second service in 1964 when BBC 2 came into operation. This was an important addition. Together the two channels provided the corporation with almost a hundred hours of transmission time a week.[23] Since it was explicitly stated that the new channel would cater for minority interests, it was then possible to consider seriously the provision of systematic educational programmes.

The extent to which the broadcasting services covered the whole country and the technical quality of the programmes received were factors which had to be taken into account when planning the provision of systematic teaching through radio and television. In the case of radio broadcasting, national coverage and good quality reception has been achieved only gradually. In 1950 one long and twelve medium wavelengths were allocated to the BBC but these were inadequate for national coverage. During the fifties the quality of reception grew poorer as the number of European broadcasting stations increased. Experiments with transmissions on very high frequencies (VHF) enabled the BBC to reduce interference and therefore it was decided to use VHF to supplement the long and medium wavebands. By 1960 there were twenty VHF stations in operation. The use of three wavebands resulted in coverage for over 97 per cent of the population of the United Kingdom.[24] The introduction of a number of satellite transmission stations extended the coverage to ninety-nine per cent and it is now virtually complete.

Total coverage is also the aim for television. By 1961 BBC 1 could be received by 98·8 per cent of the population of the United Kingdom. The percentage rose to ninety-nine per cent in 1963 and to 99·5 per cent by the end of 1966.[25] BBC 2 was available to sixty per cent of the population by this time but, with the introduction of ultra high frequencies (UHF) interference was reduced and coverage extended to more than eighty per cent of the public by 1970.[26] By 1967 programmes produced by the Independent Television Authority could be received by ninety-eight per cent of the population.

An effective nationwide educational television service depends not only on the extent of broadcasting coverage but also on the number and distribution of radio and television sets. By 1963 it was thought

[21] The Television Act, 1954, Sect. I (3).
[22] The Television Act, 1964.
[23] *BBC Handbook*, 1967, p. 25.
[24] *BBC Handbook*, 1960, *passim*.
[25] *BBC Handbook*, 1967, p. 105.
[26] *BBC Handbook*, 1970, p. 119.

that almost every household had a radio set[27] but there is, unfortunately, no data on the exact number of radio and television sets in use. The only indication we have is the number of broadcast receiving licences in existence which is presumably considerably fewer than the actual number of sets. From 1951 to 1969 the number of licences held in the UK increased from some twelve million to almost eighteen million.[28]

In this case study the part played by technological advances was important. By the early 1960s radio and television had achieved the sophistication necessary for use as a teaching medium. The existence of a well developed broadcasting system provided an enabling factor, a necessary condition for proposals suggesting the expansion of educational facilities through this medium. Taken alone, however, technical progress does not explain the exact timing of the University of the Air. The possibility of utilizing radio for educational purposes had existed since the 1920s, and suggestions for educational television were made from the early 1950s onwards.

The use of broadcasting for higher and adult education: an early experiment

The harnessing of broadcasting facilities for educational purposes is no new idea. Even in the earliest days of the wireless, education was considered of great importance. From 1923, the year in which the British Broadcasting Company received its licence, a regular series of educational talks was included in the evening programme, but there was no syllabus. In September 1924 an attempt was made to reorganize the programmes in consultation with the Adult Education Committee of the Board of Education and the British Institute of Adult Education. Regular talks were arranged and 20,000 copies of a printed syllabus were circulated. In 1927 a separate Adult Education Section at the BBC was formed.

Later the same year a Committee of Enquiry was established jointly by the BBC and the British Institute of Adult Education under the Chairmanship of Sir Henry Hadow.[29] Its report, published in 1928,[30] made several important recommendations, including the allocation of a long wave station for educational purposes with a director of high standing in the academic world and a staff of specialists who would experiment in the use of the new medium. Failing a special service, definite hours were to be set aside for formal education. It

[27] *BBC Handbook*, 1963.

[28] *BBC Handbook*, 1970, p. 219.

[29] Sir Henry Hadow was also chairman of one of the most famous reports on education ever produced, *The Report on the Education of the Adolescent*, 1926.

[30] *New Ventures in Broadcasting: a Study in Adult Education*, BBC and BIAE. 1928.

was suggested that a Central Council for Adult Education should be formed to plan the programmes and distribute educational publications. The country was to be divided into large regions and fourteen area councils were to be created. Discussion groups related to the radio programmes would be established within each area.[31]

Most of the Hadow Report proposals, except that of a long wave station for education, were implemented. For the next eighteen years a great deal of time and energy was devoted to the group listening scheme and at first it seemed remarkably successful. By the year 1930–1 there were over 1,000 listening groups in existence. There was, initially, considerable excitement over the possibilities of extending the scheme, but gradually interest began to wane. The local organization was weak; only four of the fourteen area councils were ever established and the scheme was gradually cut down from 1934 onwards until by 1938 the number of groups fell to below 600. The BBC made it clear that it would not continue to give financial assistance to local listening groups after 1940, and in 1946 the scheme was abandoned.

The reasons put forward for the failure of the scheme are interesting for they point to problems which have been important in discussions on the Open University. The first concerns the lack of central organization, which Asa Briggs[32] sees as the main weakness of the group listening scheme. Its success depended upon the BBC reaching agreement with a number of rival bodies. Some of those associated with adult education saw the scheme as superficial, whilst others thought it lacked imagination and enthusiasm. Opposition to broadcasting adult education during peak hours was aroused, especially amongst organizations representing listeners.[33] Within the BBC there was uncertainty over the relationship between 'Talks' and organized 'Adult Education'. Briggs argues that it has always been difficult to maintain momentum in adult education and that consequently its history has been one of peaks and troughs. Particularly in the provinces successes in schools broadcasting had the effect of attracting BBC professional effort away from adult education, which suffered in consequence. The second reason offered to explain the failure of the group listening scheme at the local level was the problem of 'group leaders'. Mary Stocks believed that the quality of the group leaders lay at the root of the schemes' troubles.[34] She considered that

[31] It is interesting to note that the committee received a proposal from a Dr Fournier d'Albe for a 'Wireless University'.

[32] Briggs, A., *The History of Broadcasting in the United Kingdom*, vol. II, Oxford University Press, 1965, pp. 218–26.

[33] For example, The Wireless League and the Radio Association.

[34] Stocks, M., *The Workers' Educational Association – the First 50 Years*, Allen & Unwin, 1953.

groups were only successful where a well-qualified group leader was present and in these circumstances the need for a wireless lecturer was not great. A third reason was suggested by Peers[35] who argued in 1958 that lack of technical sophistication created difficulties for the scheme. The project came before the days of VHF transmission; air space was very limited and hence competition for time was intense. 'Recent technical advances in VHF broadcasting and the possibility of multiple channels for television transmissions suggest', he wrote, 'that the time is ripe for a reconsideration of the place of broadcasting in adult education and for an examination of the question whether in the future, adult education must continue to compete for a place within the programmes of a monopoly devoted mainly to popular entertainment. In this connection much might be learned from developments in the USA.'[36]

Proposals during the fifties and early sixties
The group listening scheme outlined above did not attempt to provide systematic courses leading to examinations and hence qualifications. Indeed the Adult Education section of the BBC followed the traditional approach of the Workers' Educational Association,[37] one of the foremost providers of adult education in Britain. Emphasis was placed on general enrichment rather than on rigorous vocational training. From the late 1950s, however, suggestions that more examination orientated programmes should be developed began to appear.

In 1960 Professor Sir George Catlin suggested a 'University of the Air'.[38] He maintained that Ellen Wilkinson, Minister of Education in the 1945 Labour government, had envisaged the use of established wavelengths to transmit the lectures of eminent academics such as Huxley and Hogben, to a wide audience. During the early fifties Catlin had arranged informal discussions with the BBC but had met with the response that systematic educational broadcasts of this nature would be impracticable. His proposal for a Television University was not, therefore, based on transmissions by the BBC. 'What is required,' he said, 'is an autonomous system of educational broadcasting under a Corporation on which both the Ministry of Education and the Universities and the Arts Council will be represented.' The Corporation would use the new third channel.[39]

[35] Peers R., *Adult Education*, Routledge & Kegan Paul, 1958, pp. 234–5.

[36] Peers, R., *op. cit.*, p. 235.

[37] The WEA is a non-sectarian, non-party political federation of educational and workers' organizations founded in 1903 to widen educational opportunities for working men and their children.

[38] Catlin, Sir G., 'A University of the Air', *Contemporary Review*, 1960. In 1960 he was professor of political science at McGill University. He was a member of the National Broadcasting Development Committee at the time.

[39] Discussed on p. 242.

In March 1961 Woodrow Wyatt introduced a Private Member's Bill in the Commons which was designed to facilitate the expansion of adult education programmes. It would have obliged the Postmaster General to allow any television service, whether commercial or the BBC, which wished to provide adult education outside the permitted hours at its own expense.[40] Woodrow Wyatt was concerned about the inadequacy of higher education, particularly in science. He argued that it was necessary to give added powers to both channels immediately without waiting for the Report of the Committee on Broadcasting which was at that time considering future policy on this and other subjects. The Postmaster General, Reginald Bevins, argued that it was necessary to wait until the committee reported. Commenting on the failure of his Bill, Mr Wyatt said that 'everybody agreed in principle but nobody did anything in practice'.[41]

R. C. G. Williams, Chairman of the Electronics and Communications Section of the Institution of Electrical Engineers, argued in January 1962 that a 'Televarsity' should be established.[42] He maintained, like Sir George Catlin, that a university employing television could be used to improve facilities for higher education, especially in the field of technology. Williams developed his proposal in a number of speeches and articles during 1962 and 1963.[43] His arguments are very similar to those later advanced by Harold Wilson. In a speech in October 1963 Williams said: 'A Television University is a fundamentally different concept from education programmes as we now know them which, valuable as they are, lack an academic link between student and teacher. A link could be developed through associated correspondence courses, textbooks and visits to the university. This would not only provide an opportunity for further education for many young people who are tied to the house by domestic responsibilities but at the same time help to break down the barriers between the minority who have had the privilege of a higher education and the vast majority who have never seen a university.'[44] Suggestions such as these were known to the Labour Party Research Department at the time when its own University of the Air proposals were being

[40] The Postmaster General had the power to limit the number of hours of broadcasting a week.

[41] Private correspondence.

[42] Since the early fifties he had emphasized the importance of educational television, e.g. Williams, R. C. G., Speech to the Institution of Electrical Engineers (IEE), 1952; and Chairman's address to the IEE, 1956.

[43] Williams, R. C. G., 'A Television University', *Screen Education*, no. 13, Mar./Apr. 1962; and 'The Next Twenty-five Years of Television', a lecture to the IEE, 31 May, 1962.

[44] Williams, R. C. G., in the Chairman's Address to the Electronics Division of the IEE, 23 Oct., 1963.

formulated but there is no evidence that the idea sprang directly from any of them.

From 1960 a committee chaired by Lord Pilkington had been considering the future of the broadcasting services.[45] When the Committee's report was published in June 1962 the positions of individuals and groups on the subject of educational television became much clearer. One of the most important aspects of the committee's work was to consider the implications of the proposed change in the definition of British television from 405 to 605 lines and the use of ultra high frequency bands. With this modification it was thought that four television services with nearly complete coverage could be provided. BBC 1 and the Independent Television Authority already commanded two channels, and the committee was in favour of the third being reserved for a second BBC service. This left one channel unallocated. Several groups giving evidence suggested that the fourth channel should be devoted entirely to education but the committee finally rejected this solution for three reasons. First, if one service specialized in educational programmes then the other channels would tend to be devoted to 'other' broadcasting. Gradually, the general educative function of all but the specialized channel would cease to exist. To make their second point they quoted the Ministry of Education's evidence: 'Education in the wide sense is part of living and not a separate activity to be confined to some ages or some times of day . . . A service which was labelled "educational" would tempt very few of those for whom broadcasting should have most to offer.'[46] Third, it was maintained that educational programmes would benefit from the association of producers with the producers of other programmes and *vice versa*. These two groups, therefore, should be kept in close proximity with each other.[47]

Those who were attracted by the idea of a University of the Air or something similar can have derived little comfort from the committee's conclusions. More important, however, was the fact that most of the bodies whose co-operation would be essential to the success of any future television college or university also rejected a specialized educational television service. They included the Ministry of Education; the BBC; the Association of Education Committees; the National Union of Teachers; the Workers' Educational Association; and the Universities' Council for Adult Education.[48]

---

[45] The Post Office, *Report of the Committee on Broadcasting, 1960*, Cmnd. 1753, 1962.
[46] *The Report of the Committee on Broadcasting, op. cit.*, p. 276.
[47] *Ibid.*, pp. 273–84.
[48] The UCAE comprises representatives of the extra-mural departments of those universities providing external adult education. It was founded in 1945 to formulate common policies on extra-mural education.

In its evidence the BBC stated that to the best of its knowledge there did not exist amongst education authorities and organizations any demand for an educational service outside the context of general services. The view held by all the bodies mentioned above was that the main task of the national television services should be to awaken the imaginations of the many rather than provide specialized programmes for the few.

Only a minority of those giving evidence took the opposite view. Foremost amongst them was the ITA, which advocated a separate television channel devoted solely to educational programmes. It argued that three general services were adequate to meet public demand and rather than add a fourth it would be better to provide a specialized service. This should be locally organized and directed by educational bodies. The authority gave four reasons for its proposal. Three general services already existed, a fourth specifically educational service would benefit the nation more than another general one. Secondly, the ITA contended that 'the urgencies of Britain's position in the world' demanded an extension of educational facilities. Thirdly, the increasing leisure many people enjoyed could, in part, be used constructively through this service. Lastly, they argued that the discontinuous nature of instruction in programmes of general interest was felt to be unsatisfactory and the content was not the responsibility of educationalists.

This proposal does not appear to have been an influential contribution to ideas concerning education and television because the motives behind it came into question. The authority was accused of using the issue of educational television to further its own ends.[49] When it became known that four television services would be available once the transfer to 625 line transmission and UHF took place, the ITA had changed its evidence to the Pilkington Committee, and included the suggestion for a specifically educational service. Of the four available channels one was allocated to the BBC (a non-commercial body) and one to the ITA (commercial). It was argued that the ITA's intention was to achieve the establishment of a non-party, non-profit making third channel devoted to education in order that the fourth channel could then be allocated to a commercial group.[50]

Despite their insistence that educational programmes should not be provided as a separate service, the Pilkington Committee were aware of the potential value of television to adult education. 'There is', they commented, 'clearly much room for experiment. It has been

[49] See for example, 'The Phoney Fourth Service', *New Statesman*, 12 Dec., 1961.
[50] *Ibid.*, and also comment by Marcus Lipton MP, *H. C. Deb.*, vol. 651, col. 885.

proposed to us that the BBC and ITA should, for example, consider experiments in broadcasting courses of adult education of a vocational nature, or provide refresher courses at times convenient for house-wives ... The two broadcasting authorities should, we suggest, consult with professional bodies to see how far the idea would be practicable.'[51]

The government accepted the Pilkington Committee's conclusions concerning educational television. A White Paper, published in July 1962, argued that it would be a mistake to separate educational from other programmes by providing a specialized channel.[52] The government was, however, anxious to begin providing more educational programmes for adults. Between 1961 and 1963 the BBC had been negotiating with the Universities' Council for Adult Education on the development of adult education programmes. Following the White Paper attempts were made by the extra-mural departments to provide courses related to the increased number of television programmes but by the end of 1963 they had met with little success; only a few departments were in active negotiation with the broadcasting authorities. One of the main problems concerned the times of transmitting the programmes, a difficulty later encountered by those planning the Open University.

The whole debate on the future of the BBC and the ITA[53] which took place during the early sixties served to crystallize ideas and publicize the views of individuals and groups on many issues including that of educational television. Although the Pilkington Committee was rarely referred to when the University of the Air was being discussed either within the Labour Party or the ministry, it provided information concerning the likely reactions to the proposal from those interested in the subject. It also showed clearly that in the opinion of most groups within the fields of broadcasting and higher education, the national television services should continue to provide programmes of general cultural enrichment rather than systematic courses leading to examinations.

By far the most important pioneering work on the uses of educational television and correspondence teaching in further education resulted from the efforts of a few Cambridge academics during the early sixties. Michael Young and Brian Jackson, Chairman and Director respectively of the Advisory Centre for Education (ACE),[54] were

---

[51] The *Report of the Committee on Broadcasting, op. cit.*, p. 284.

[52] *Memorandum on the Report of the Committee on Broadcasting, 1960*, Cmnd. 1770, 1962, p. 5.

[53] The activities of both the BBC and the ITA were to be reviewed in 1964.

[54] The Advisory Centre for Education was established in 1959 to disseminate information and provide a forum for discussion on educational problems.

the leading figures amongst a small group who were becoming increasingly concerned at the restricted entry requirements of the universities, the inadequacy of educational opportunities in general for large sections of the community, and the impending problems created by 'the bulge'. In the autumn of 1962 Michael Young published an article entitled 'Is your child in the Unlucky Generation?'[55] In it he discussed the increased demand for university entrance likely in the mid-sixties and the possible means of expanding education facilities. One of these was the formation of an 'Open University'. After consideration of the ways in which ACE might publicize its views the group came to the conclusion that before political action would be taken on new ideas of this nature it would be necessary to demonstrate that educational television and correspondence teaching could be effective. Therefore, rather than attempt direct influence on the Labour Party, with which Michael Young had retained close connections for many years,[56] it was decided to devise means of testing out their ideas. Three projects were prepared: a study of correspondence education; a week of televised lectures by eminent Cambridge academics to home students – the 'Dawn University', and the launching of a pilot body known as the 'National Extension College' (NEC) to begin combining correspondence and television with residential schooling.[57]

The following year the Advisory Centre began its projects. The study of correspondence education in Britain found that the number of students wishing to take commercially run correspondence courses at that time could be as high as 500,000. Here was a group of students unreached by State education and unprotected by universal standards. The study found that the courses provided were largely of low quality. The second project – the Dawn University – was successfully completed in October 1963. It consisted of six televised lectures transmitted by Anglia Television at 7.15 a.m. from 21 October for one week. The results were encouraging. The experiment received considerable publicity and a survey of viewers revealed a demand for a larger project and for written work to support the programmes. The third and most important project – The National Extension College – began in the winter of 1962-3. It was originally hoped that the college would not only demonstrate the effectiveness of combining correspondence, television and higher education and provide premises

[55] Young, M., 'Is Your Child in the Unlucky Generation?', *Where*, no. 10, Autumn, 1962.

[56] Dr Young was Secretary of the Labour Party Research Department from 1945–1951. During the 1964 general election he was recalled as research director.

[57] Young, M. and Jackson, B., *The Story of the National Extension College*, unpublished, 1970.

in the vacations for the benefit of home students[58] but also, eventually, 'act as the nucleus of an "open university" and work closely with London's External Registrar'.[59] The NEC is now closely involved with the Open University in providing gateway courses for intending students but certain differences of opinion between those who planned the Open University and those running the NEC effectively prevented the college from playing a more central role in planning the policy.

Michael Young and his colleagues formed their ideas concerning correspondence, television and an open university before Harold Wilson and the Labour Party became interested in them. However, despite close links with the party's research department they believed that unless the practicability of their plans could be demonstrated, an open university would not be politically acceptable. Their assumptions were incorrect. Within a few months of Michael Young's first published suggestion for an open university Harold Wilson welcomed and developed a similar notion, the impetus for which, he claims, came from elsewhere. Wilson maintains that the original inspiration for his 'University of the Air' resulted from contacts he made whilst travelling abroad and from the evidence of foreign experiments. In a speech to the First Congregation of the Open University he gave his account. 'It was in fact', he recalled, 'my own observations on what was being done in two very different countries – the Soviet Union and the United States – that led me to think what could be done on an even more hopeful scale in the fruitful soil of British communications and the British system of education.'[60] However, although there was no direct communication, Mr Wilson was clearly aware of the work being carried out in Cambridge. On the announcement of the 'University of the Air', Young contacted him, bringing the Advisory Centre's work to his attention. Wilson replied that he was being kept informed about the 'Dawn University' and added that the experiments, particularly the NEC, were very much on the lines of what was wanted.[61]

Foreign influences
The most important source of ideas on educational television and correspondence teaching appears to have been that of foreign experience and experiments in these fields. The USSR was of special interest because it was providing correspondence courses on a large

[58] Young, M., 'Announcing the National Extension College', *Where*, Autumn, 1963.

[59] Young, M., 'Is Your Child in the Unlucky Generation?' *op. cit.*

[60] Speech by Harold Wilson to the First Congregation of the Open University at the Royal Society, London, 23 July, 1969.

[61] Private correspondence.

scale at this time. So was the USA where television for educational purposes was starting to develop.

By the beginning of 1963 there were eighty educational television stations in the United States, most of them concentrating on schools broadcasting, but university level programmes were slowly being introduced. At this time the number of such stations forecast for 1970 was 200. From the early fifties the Western Reserve University, Iowa State University, and the University of Houston had used television for teaching but the first systematic broadcasting of a complete college curriculum took place in Chicago in the late 1950s. Although it was concerned with teaching at pre-university level, its organization and results were of great interest to those in Britain considering a Televarsity. Mr Wilson made a regular lecture tour of the United States each winter at the invitation of Senator Benton, owner of the *Encyclopaedia Britannica*, and it was during his visit of 1962–3 that the American projects were brought to his notice. Senator Benton was interested in the use of both correspondence and television for educational purposes and it was primarily through Wilson's discussions with Benton that he claims he formulated the idea of the University of the Air. Britain was well placed to consider a national scheme of educational television and correspondence, being relatively small and compact and having a nationwide television service. Wilson had to curtail his visit to America that year on hearing that Hugh Gaitskell, the leader of the Labour Party, was gravely ill, but further information on educational television in the United States and on Russian correspondence schemes[62] was subsequently sent to him by the Senator.[63]

While the Americans were exploiting the possibilities of educational television the Russians were making considerable use of correspondence teaching for higher education. In 1960–1, for the first time, the majority of all their entrants to higher education were in correspondence colleges and 40 per cent of all graduations from higher education resulted from students taking correspondence courses.[64] By the end of 1962 interest in the application of both educational television and correspondence techniques by the USA and USSR was beginning to develop in this country. Peter Laslett, who visited America during 1962 on behalf of the Advisory Centre for Education, returned very enthusiastic about his findings. He concluded an article on American television teaching by saying: 'This is the one new thing that we can

[62] Benton visited Moscow in summer 1962.

[63] A memorandum on University-level television in the United States was prepared for Benton by the *Encyclopaedia Britannica*, in October 1963.

[64] *Robbins Report, op. cit.*, p. 39. For further evidence see Appendix V, pp. 197–202.

still call upon to expand and to adapt British education to the needs of the late twentieth century.'[65]

In April 1963 an Anglo-American conference on education by correspondence and television was held by the Oxford University Department of Education.[66] During Easter that year Wilson wrote his first speech on the subject of the University of the Air in which he drew heavily upon the information gathered for him by Senator Benton and on a report produced by Television International Enterprises Ltd, outlining the various educational uses of television throughout the world. The effective influences upon the leader of the Opposition at this time were not those of individuals and groups at home but ones from abroad where evidence, although somewhat tenuous, was already available.

Summary: the period before autumn 1963
The prospect of an unusually heavy demand for higher and further education in the mid-sixties resulted in a wide range of proposals for extending the existing facilities. Amongst these there was a small number which capitalized upon technological advances in broadcasting. These ideas were, however, mostly made by individuals who had little success in persuading others of their practicality. The discussions within the Pilkington Committee on the uses of the existing television services for educational purposes indicated clearly that the majority of interested bodies were against using a separate channel purely for televised courses, and were in favour of retaining general educative programmes on the existing networks. The Advisory Centre for Education could be forgiven for thinking that before educational television would be accepted by any political party a demonstration of its effectiveness would be essential.

In this case the often prolonged process of persuading authorities to accept a fairly radical innovation was fore-shortened because the idea was taken up independently by the leader of the Labour Party. In the event it was unnecessary to provide a practical demonstration that educational television would be effective. The crucial evidence which enabled the incorporation of the policy in a party's programme was drawn from experiments abroad. The projects carried out by the Advisory Centre for Education were of more value to the planners of the Open University at a later stage when it was necessary to justify the proposals more carefully.

---

[65] Laslett, P., 'Teaching by Television', *Where*, no. 11, Winter, 1963, pp. 4–5.
[66] For a report of the conference see *Universities Quarterly*, vol. 18, Dec. 1963, p. 180.

II THE DEVELOPMENT OF THE POLICY WITHIN THE LABOUR PARTY: AUTUMN 1963 TO MARCH 1965

'Really radical change', a recent commentator has maintained, 'probably comes most easily from political levels and from a Minister looking at problems with a fresh eye, from the election manifesto of a new government.'[67] The creation of a University of the Air was certainly one policy which emerged during a party's pre-election preparatory period. By the beginning of 1963 the Labour Party had been in opposition for eleven years and, with the knowledge that a general election had to be called by October 1964, great efforts were being devoted to its electoral programme. The research department was instructed to concentrate on producing new ideas with the accent on invention rather than cost. The priorities would be decided later.

Within the party a University of the Air was first publicly suggested by the Taylor Committee,[68] a study group established in March 1962 by Hugh Gaitskell, then leader of the party. The committee, under the chairmanship of Lord Taylor, were asked to consider proposals for the party's contribution to the debate on higher education. Their report, published in March 1963, pointed out the necessity for a rapid and continuing expansion of higher education on an unprecedented scale. They argued that the use of radio and television for adult education should be greatly extended and it was proposed that 'as an experiment the BBC sound radio and television and the ITA should be required to co-operate in organizing a "University of the Air" for serious planned adult education. Alternatively, the fourth television channel might be used exclusively for higher education'.[69] Their proposal for a University of the Air was of no direct policy significance. It was included because the committee were aware of Wilson's interest in the subject but they made no attempt to develop the suggestion or to place it in an educational context.

As we have already noted, Mr Wilson was concurrently and independently pursuing the possibility of introducing adult education through television and correspondence. Before the committee reported he had collected information about correspondence courses in the USSR and about educational television in the United States. By Easter 1963 he had prepared his plans and written his introductory

[67] Brown, R. G. S., *The Administrative Process in Great Britain*, Methuen, 1970, p. 162.
[68] *The Years of Crisis*, Report of the Labour Party's Study Group on Higher Education, 1963.
[69] *Ibid.*, p. 34.

speech on the subject but at this stage no members of the research department were closely involved. Because, as will become more clearly apparent, Wilson's personal commitment to the University of the Air was essential to the success of the scheme, it is important to understand his reasons for suggesting and supporting it.

It has often been stated that the main reason why Wilson proposed the University of the Air was to provide electoral capital.[70] The idea was undoubtedly used in this way for both the 1964 and 1966 elections. Although Wilson's interest in a university based on television was aroused before he knew that he would succeed Gaitskell as leader of the party, he utilized the suggestion subsequently to derive maximum political benefit. He had prepared a speech on the subject by spring 1963, yet he did not use it until September at a rally to mark the launching of the Labour Party's pre-election campaign in Scotland. It is important to see the germination of this idea within the context of the time it was proposed. The party was anxious to establish an image for itself as the progressive party, able to respond to the needs of the modern world. The second time the new university was mentioned was a few weeks later at the Labour Party Conference. Here it formed part of the policy statement delivered by Wilson to the delegates in which he emphasized the need for Britain to adapt to a rapidly changing environment. It was a rousing address calculated to unite and inspire the party for its election task ahead. The reason for his speech entitled 'Labour and the Scientific Revolution' was, he said, because 'the strength, the solvency, the influence of Britain, which some still think depends upon nostalgic illusions or upon nuclear posturings – these things are going to depend in the remainder of this century to a unique extent upon the speed with which we can come to terms with the world of change'.[71] Despite its theme of change however, Wilson's speech contained very few concrete proposals. He suggested that a Labour government should establish several new ministries[72] and a State-sponsored chemical engineering consortium, but none of these was outlined in the same detail as the University of the Air. The idea added some substance to a speech lacking in other well-developed proposals.

A University of the Air projected the image the party was trying to create. Four main reasons for the proposal were given by Wilson both to the Conference and in his election speech. The first of these was the need to take full advantage of technological progress. 'We must

---

[70] See for example: 'An Exaggerated Idea', *The Times*, 29 Jan., 1969; Chataway, C., *H. C. Deb.*, vol. 715, col. 808, and Kelly, T., correspondence to *The Times*, 7 May, 1966.

[71] 'Labour and the Scientific Revolution', *op. cit.*, p. 136.

[72] Ministries for Higher Education, for Science, for Disarmament, and for Overseas Development.

organize British industry', he said, 'so that it applies the results of scientific research more purposively to our national production effort'.[73] Secondly, it was essential to utilize the untapped talent which existed as a result of an inadequate education system. He argued that 'we simply cannot as a nation afford to cut off three-quarters or more of our children from virtually any chance of higher education. The Russians do not, the Germans do not, the Americans do not and the Japanese do not and we cannot afford to either'.[74] The third reason given was the egalitarian one. Not only would the scheme recommend itself to those interested in economic and technological issues therefore, but also to the radical socialist element of the party. Wilson maintained that the University was designed to provide an opportunity for those who had not been able to take advantage of higher education. He saw it making 'an immeasurable contribution to the cultural life of our country, to the enrichment of our standard of living'.[75] The fourth, and very general reason for his proposal was the need to maintain British prestige abroad. He concluded his speech by asserting that 'we must use all the resources of democratic planning, all the latent and underdeveloped energies and skills of our people to ensure Britain's standing in the world'.[76] The University of the Air, however insubstantial the scheme might be, fitted perfectly with Wilson's theme of change since it illustrated his arguments on all the above points. It is important to add that he was very careful to stress that the new university was not to replace any existing policies for higher education. He stated very firmly that this was 'not a substitute for our plans for higher education, for our plans for new universities and for our plans for extending technological education'.[77]

At this stage the proposal bore the marks of a policy suggested primarily for electoral purposes and it is perhaps not surprising that on balance there was an adverse reaction in the press. The *Economist* was the only periodical to welcome Wilson's suggestion, saying, 'it is one of the best things he has done, and provides a real hope that he is not going to be inhibited in his approach to higher education by Labour's formidable, and orthodox tail of supporting academics'.[78] The *Spectator* thought it unlikely that any of Wilson's proposals to the Conference would reach completion. 'Panaceas are ... understandable, even permissible at party conferences', it stated, 'but that should not lead us to take them for more than they are or to mistake

[73] 'Labour and the Scientific Revolution', *op. cit.*, p. 135.
[74] *Ibid.*, p. 136.
[75] *Ibid.*, p. 137.
[76] *Ibid.*, p. 140.
[77] *Ibid.*, p. 137.
[78] *Economist*, 14 Sept., 1963.

the war-cry before the charge for the operational orders which will actually be executed'.[79] An editorial in *The Times* referred to the idea as a 'heady prospect' but maintained that Wilson defeated his object by 'the sheer magnitude of his dream'. It was argued that the existing television facilities could not support even a limited range of studies let alone a whole university course. 'Where', the editorial asked, 'are we to get the money? Where are we to get the manpower?' Rather than adopt Wilson's plans, which smacked of 'socialist idealism', a careful study should be made of how the existing facilities could be improved.[80]

There was little published reaction to the idea on the part of educational and broadcasting groups; partly, one suspects, because none of them had been consulted on the initial formulation of the plan and were therefore without the necessary information for comment.[81] Even Wilson referred to the University of the Air soon after his Glasgow speech as an 'inchoate idea'. He did, however, receive a large number of encouraging letters from interested individuals.

From the autumn of 1963 to March 1965 plans for the university progressed very little. Wilson promised that if reaction to his suggestion were favourable he would arrange for a working party to be established but, despite his assurances that the immediate response was encouraging,[82] no such group was formed. There were several reasons for this. The University of the Air had never been official Labour Party policy. It was not put to the vote at conference nor officially recognized by the National Executive Committee. Therefore, in the busy months before the election in October 1964, it is unlikely to have had very high priority. A large number of working parties were already in existence. In any case it was rather late to establish another one. At this time (late 1963 and early 1964) it was not known when the election would take place and a working party would probably have lasted from nine months to a year.

The only work produced was a paper written by members of the Labour Party research department in May 1964. It presented the plans as far as they had progressed and concluded by posing a number of questions which remained to be settled. The purpose of the University of the Air was clear: to provide a variety of courses mainly leading to recognized qualifications or examinations. But this was all. The size of the audience, its exact composition, the organization, the allocation of time on radio and television all remained 'questions for further discussion'. In fact no decisions had been taken since autumn 1963.

[79] *Spectator*, 11 Oct., 1963.
[80] *The Times Educational Supplement*, 13 Sept., 1963.
[81] The WEA, in a discussion paper *Viewing and Learning*, Apr., 1964, referred to the proposal as 'a bold and imaginative idea'.
[82] In his speech to the First Congregation of the Open University, July, 1969.

It must be added that despite the emphasis given to the new university in Wilson's early election speeches, no mention of it was made in the party manifesto for the 1964 election.

Labour assumed office in October 1964 and for the first few months there was no indication that the idea was still alive. Even officials of the Department of Education and Science were uncertain as to whether the government would pursue it. In February 1965, however, Wilson made his intentions to encourage the policy quite clear. Miss Jennie Lee was transferred from the Ministry of Public Building and Works to the Department of Education and Science where she was given special responsibility as Secretary of State for the Arts and for supervising the development of the new university. The practice of giving responsibility for a particular policy to a junior Minister was one which Wilson reserved for his particularly cherished projects.[83] The university's chance of survival was further improved by the choice of Miss Lee as its patron. She is an unorthodox and powerful woman and was known to be a close personal friend of the Prime Minister.

Summary: the policy within the Labour Party

Several important features emerged during this stage of the university's development which later resulted in widespread criticism from interest groups. One of these was the policy's political origins. Although once in office Wilson made it clear that he intended to pursue the policy, attacks on the university as an electoral gimmick continued. Many ideas arise during a pre-election period and can be subject to similar criticism but few have been so closely linked to one prominent political figure. The University of the Air was, therefore, open to the additional charge of arising from personal whim rather than from more 'rational' processes of evaluation.

The second aspect which fell prey to ready criticism also arose from the use of the idea for electoral purposes. Since the policy had been justified on several different grounds it could be attacked for its inadequacies with respect to each in turn. Wilson had claimed that there were technological, economic, egalitarian and political gains to be made from creating the university. Depending on the special interests of the critic, particular parts of the whole could be, and were, isolated for scrutiny.

The other main feature of the University of the Air scheme was its isolation. This exposed it to attack. It was kept entirely separate from the Labour Party's main policies for higher education and, in addition, it was planned by a small number of people (a tactic which was maintained, as we shall see, until the Planning Committee

---

[83] Wilson, H., *The Labour Government, 1964–1970*, Weidenfeld & Nicolson, 1971, p. 10.

stage). When announcing the university to the party conference Wilson introduced the idea as a 'supplement' to his plans for higher education rather than as an integral part of them. Within the Labour Party only a few members of the research department assisted in drawing up the initial blueprint. Miss Lee was not involved until she assumed special responsibility and no interested groups from the fields of higher and adult education or broadcasting were asked for advice. It was believed, even at this early stage, that if the university was to be a success, it would require very careful management. The containment of the policy at this and later periods aroused additional opposition. The more private the policy the fewer allies there are likely to be.

III THE DEVELOPMENT OF THE POLICY WITHIN THE DEPARTMENT OF EDUCATION AND SCIENCE: MARCH 1965 TO EARLY 1966

This period covers the preliminary planning of the university within the Department of Education and Science (DES) to the time at which a white paper outlining the government's views on the policy was published in February 1966. As soon as Miss Lee entered the department she made it clear that she did not intend to deviate from the Prime Minister's original plan in any way but to build upon it. This attitude resulted in certain difficulties. Most of the senior civil servants involved in the higher education section of the department were opposed to the Prime Minister's plan, arguing that it was an unnecessary frill and that resources should not be diverted to this end when they could be better spent in other ways. Added to the general hostility was a more specific reason for antagonism in some quarters.

For several months before Miss Lee entered the department a joint working party of the DES and the BBC had been meeting regularly to devise an experimental service of educational television. It was to be a pilot project designed to test the case for allocating the fourth television channel entirely to an educational service. Within the BBC's own education sections there was a general movement away from the view that programmes should be provided for 'enrichment' to an examination orientated approach based on a curriculum. By early 1965 a scheme had been worked out, costed, approved by the Secretary of State and was ready to be considered by the Cabinet.[84] The scrapping of this project in favour of the

---

[84] Recently, the BBC has tried to resurrect the plan but it has been rejected.

University of the Air, at this stage no more than an outline, came as a disappointment to certain officials at the DES and to members of the BBC.

The isolation of the proposed University from the mainstream of higher education policy during its early development was noted when we discussed the previous period. The 'hiving off' of the policy became even more noticeable when Miss Lee took over. The Secretary of State for Education and Science, Mr Crosland, was giving first priority to his policies for higher education at this time. In two speeches made early in 1965 he outlined his plans to expand the colleges of education and technical colleges,[85] but no mention was made of the embryonic university. Throughout 1965 planning for higher education continued entirely divorced from that of the Open University. The results of both planning processes were published as separate white papers, one on the University of the Air[86] and one on the polytechnics.[87] Neither report mentioned the existence of the other.

In the summer of 1965 an advisory committee on the University of the Air was established. It had two unusual features. The first was that Miss Lee herself was chairman. Most committees of this kind are chaired by someone chosen from outside the ministry or department involved and the Minister to whom the committee is reporting then has the power to accept or reject the committee's conclusions. The advisory committee was, therefore, to some extent restricted in its deliberations. The second unusual feature was its terms of reference. They were peculiarly specific. The committee was 'to consider the educational functions and content of a University of the Air, as outlined in a speech made by Mr Harold Wilson in Glasgow on 8 September 1963'. It was clear that a policy decision had already been taken to the effect that the proposed institution was to be nothing less than a degree awarding university.

The committee was composed of members serving in an individual capacity rather than as representatives of specific groups or interests.[88]

---

[85] See Robinson, E., *The New Polytechnics, op. cit.,* p. 35.

[86] *A University of the Air,* Cmnd. 2922, 1966.

[87] *Polytechnics: a Plan for Polytechnics and Other Colleges,* Cmnd. 3006, 1966.

[88] The members were as follows: Miss J. Lee (chairman), Joint Parliamentary Under Secretary of State, DES; Professor K. J. Alexander, Professor of Economics, University of Strathclyde; Lord Annan, Provost, King's College, Cambridge; *Dr E. W. Briault, Deputy Education Officer, ILEA; *Dr Brynmor Jones, Vice-Chancellor, University of Hull; Mr D. G. Holroyd, Director, University of Leeds Television Centre; Mr P. Laslett, Fellow of Trinity College, Cambridge; *Mr N. I. MacKenzie, Lecturer in Sociology, University of Sussex; Mr A. D. C. Peterson, Director, Department of Education, University of Oxford; Dr O. G. Pickard, Principal, Ealing Technical College; Professor F. Llewellyn-Jones, Principal, University College of Swansea; *Mr J. Scupham,

One prominent group expressed annoyance that the members were asked not to divulge the proceedings of the committee, thus keeping their colleagues in ignorance of the policy's development. The committee's membership was drawn from a limited range of backgrounds: there were thirteen members, including Miss Lee, of whom nine came from universities. Only one was from a technical college and there was no member from the local authorities generally. In view of his research on educational television and correspondence courses one might have expected that Michael Young would have been included but it is understood that he was unable to agree to the committee's restricted terms of reference.

The committee was asked to complete its work with speed, a request which it realized was based on the government's wish to produce a white paper on the subject before the general election of March 1966. Although the subsequent white paper maintained that 'broad agreement' had been reached within the committee, there were some differences of opinion amongst the members. First, although the subject was strictly outside its terms of reference, there was disagreement about the educational level at which the new institution should operate. Should it be a college offering diplomas rather than a degree-giving body? The argument put forward by supporters of a college was that the experience of the National Extension College (NEC) had shown that the current need for further education centred around the diploma level rather than the degree. The decision to recommend a university was upheld by the committee which also agreed that the NEC could not form the basis of the new institution because its emphasis was primarily on pre-degree level work.

A second point of some disagreement in the committee was the part to be played by radio and television. It was maintained by certain members that for practical reasons the university would have to rely largely upon correspondence teaching, with broadcasting as the supporting medium rather than vice versa. Broadcasting was vital because it was universally available but it could only play a subsidiary role because of the lack of air space (broadcasting time) and the cost of producing programmes, especially those for television. In the event it was decided that the university's programmes should be divided equally between radio and television but that the part played by broadcasting in general would need careful examination. From a purely tactical point of view undue emphasis on radio and television laid the proposed institution open to the charge of failing to provide enough individual contact between staff and students. The status of

retired, formerly Controller of Educational Broadcasting, BBC, and *Professor H. Wiltshire, Profesor of Adult Education, University of Nottingham.

 * Refers to those members also on the planning committee established later in 1967.

the broadcasting element was an important issue. The term 'University of the Air'[89] indicates the extent to which this feature had predominated before the committee was established. Miss Lee, rather reluctantly, accepted the advice of the members to reduce the emphasis on broadcasting. Although in October 1965 she stated in the Commons that she felt the 'University of the Air' was an appropriate title,[90] by May 1966 she had changed her mind and began to use the term 'Open University' when answering questions in the House. There is no clear and definite point at which the title generally used actually changed.

The white paper based on the committee's report, which was never published, was brief and somewhat indecisive. The announcement of the government's intention was carefully worded so that there was no definite commitment. 'The Government *believe that* ... an open university providing degree courses as rigorous and demanding as those in existing universities can be established' (our italics).[91] There was no mention of whether or when it would be started. The paper outlined the purposes of the university, which were threefold; to contribute to educational, cultural and professional standards generally; to provide degrees, and to help students in many parts of the world. Miss Lee's determination that the institution should be no less than a university was stated in unequivocal terms. 'From the outset it must be made clear that there can be no question of offering to students a make-shift project inferior in quality to other universities. That would defeat its whole purpose ...'[92]

Then followed comments on the type of degree course to be offered, the media which would be used and the organizational framework. It was maintained that although the university should offer primarily courses leading to degrees, courses of a professional, technical, refresher and conversion kind should also be included. The presentation of courses would involve a combination of television, radio, correspondence, tutorials and practicals, short residential courses as well as study at communal viewing centres. Despite the advisory committee's discussion of the limitations of the role of television, the white paper emphasized its special contribution. Television would 'build up the corporate feeling of a University' and give the project 'its unique impact and coverage'.[93] Programmes should be screened at peak viewing time on a national network, a

---

[89] See *Adult Education*, vol. 6, no. 4, Nov. 1968, for a short discussion of this change of emphasis by a member of the planning committee, Professor R. Shaw. Also Gregory, D., 'The Open Promise', *Education*, 9 May, 1969.

[90] *H. C. Deb.*, vol. 924, col. 330.

[91] *A University of the Air, op. cit.*, p. 3.

[92] *Idem.*

[93] *Ibid.*, p. 6.

requirement which later resulted in difficult negotiations with the BBC. Finally, the organizational framework of the university was to resemble, as closely as possible, that of other universities. The 'educational trust' suggested by Mr Wilson in his 1963 speeches was abandoned although, in essence, the scheme had altered little.

Reactions to the proposed university while the advisory committee was sitting and following the publication of the white paper were on the whole unfavourable. In October 1965 the National Extension College held a one-day conference on the 'University of the Air', which was attended by about seventy people with an interest in the education of adults by television.[94] Two of the main speakers Mr E. Hutchinson, Secretary of the National Institute for Adult Education, and Mr L. E. Ball, External Registrar of London University, were not convinced of the need for a University of the Air. The former maintained that information collected by the NIAE led them to the conclusion that there were not many people missing the opportunity of taking degrees. The latter argued that there was little demand for places on correspondence courses to qualify technologists and engineers. Brian Jackson, Director of the National Extension College, wished to see the government delay its plans on the grounds that more research was needed into the educational needs of British society and that the international knowledge in this field should be tapped. In all, the conference gave some indication of the powerful opposition, at this stage, of those with interests in adult education.

Just before the white paper was published, the *Sunday Times* published an article which claimed that the announcement on the university was being postponed because of a Cabinet split on the scheme. The article stated: 'Although some Ministers, including Mr Wilson himself, are apparently keen that a "University of the Air" should be established quickly, some of his senior Ministers believe that other election promises carry more priority ... Mr Anthony Crosland, the Education Minister, is understood to be one of those who feel that if the Treasury has any money to spare for this department, it should go towards plans for raising the school leaving age to 16 in 1970 ... Mr Anthony Wedgwood-Benn, the Postmaster General, takes the line that the "University of the Air" scheme cannot be settled apart from the plans for the future of broadcasting and the fourth channel, now under study by the Cabinet.'[95]

Following the white paper a *Times* leader voiced disquiet about the costs involved. 'The big question is whether all the money the "University of the Air" will cost will be worthwhile. There may well

[94] Bailey, P., 'Cambridge Conference on the University of the Air', *Visual Education*, Dec. 1965.
[95] Chapman, C., 'Cabinet Split on Plan for University of the Air', *Sunday Times*, 23 Jan., 1966.

be a relatively high audience to begin with. How fast and how far will it run down? ... The BBC's valiant efforts at direct adult education many years ago had to be abandoned for lack of support ... No one wants to throw cold water on good intentions. But a minimum of four years would be a long time to hold students to something as tenuous as a television course. The cost per degree could be fantastic.'[96]

An article in the *Observer*[97] the following day reported that in reply to enquiries sent out by Miss Lee, the Independent Television Authority and the BBC had both denied that they would have much suitable air time for the university's programmes. The BBC announced that it would be opposed to any arrangement which restricted BBC 2's future development. The article mentioned the opposition shown by some educationalists to the idea as well as the division within the Cabinet and added, 'many of its advocates are sorry that so much committee work and good intentions have yielded no more than a white paper that raises more awkward questions than it answers and commits the Government to virtually nothing'.

Further criticisms of the white paper were expressed at the annual conference of the Association for Adult Education. One fear was that, for economic reasons, the WEA and the university extra-mural tutors would find themselves 'hoisted on this degree-awarding bandwagon'.[98] At the Library Association conference the government's plans were attacked for omitting a discussion of the increased demand for books and libraries which would ensue.[99]

The Conservative Party made no formal policy statements concerning the new university at this point but two debates in the Commons indicated the general stance taken by Conservative members. The first one took place in April 1965 and attracted little interest. Although the debate was lengthy, attendance in the House was small. Only three Conservative Members spoke, arguing for locally organized, closed-circuit[100] systems for educational television.[101] They considered that the University of the Air was too ambitious, too costly

[96] The Leader, *The Times*, 26 Feb., 1966.

[97] Ardagh, J., 'TV Degrees Still Far From Reality', *Observer*, 27 Feb., 1966.

[98] 'TV University under Fire', *The Teacher*, 29 Apr., 1966.

[99] Reported in the *Local Government Chronicle*, 11 May, 1966.

[100] There are two types of network which could be used for educational television; a closed-circuit or an open-circuit system. The former consists of a co-axial cable linking the transmission studio with the receiver and only points connected by the cable can receive signals. The cable is expensive but it can carry several channels at once (up to about six). The latter system which links transmitter and receiver by radio waves is more flexible but the number of channels is limited and costly.

[101] Christopher Chataway, MP, produced a pamphlet in 1964 entitled *Educational Television*, proposing a local closed-circuit system.

and could only cover a minute part of normal university work.[102] The proposal received a second airing in a debate on broadcasting policy in general, initiated by the Opposition. Many of the speakers made lengthy comments on the university, most of those from the Opposition being unfavourable. It was referred to as 'a completely bogus institution' and an 'unlovely centralised colossus', the main bones of contention being its cost, its organization, the lack of research and its political origins. The Postmaster General was asked by several speakers to reveal the cost of the project but he declined to comment. As in the previous debate, the Opposition speeches concentrated on the merits of local closed-circuit television rather than a nationally organized scheme based on very little research. Finally, the government's motives were called in question. One Opposition member stated that 'the most truthful reason for it came to me from a Socialist who said "Well, Harold insists on having it!"' That may be a good reason in the Socialist Party, but it is not a good guide to educational advance'.

Summary: policy within the Department of Education and Science, March 1965 to early 1966

This period saw the basic framework for the university laid down but several fundamental questions, such as the organization and provision of the broadcasting element and the cost, remained unresolved. The most obvious feature of the policy's development at this stage was its isolation, a feature which was evident from 1963 until the planning committee began its work. It was isolated in two respects. Firstly, it remained entirely separate from educational policy-making in general: the idea was developed by Miss Lee and a small number of civil servants without the help of those involved in the further and adult education sectors of the department. Secondly, the extent and nature of expert opinion brought to bear at this stage was carefully controlled: opinions were canvassed from a few individuals only. Moreover, before any advice from interested individuals was sought, it had been decided that the new institution would be nothing less than a degree-awarding body. The isolation of the policy was in part a deliberate tactic designed to protect an idea towards which hostility was anticipated. Early debates on educational television had demonstrated considerable differences of opinion and Miss Lee was aware of opposition from some civil servants when she entered the department.

It was mentioned earlier that Mr Wilson justified his suggestion on several grounds, the most important being those of increasing educational opportunities, of benefiting the economy by utilizing

---

[102] *H. C. Deb.*, vol. 709, col. 2007.

wasted talent especially in order to provide more scientists and technologists and of capitalizing upon technological advances in radio and television. This broadly based case resulted in opposition on each of these grounds from groups with widely differing interests and opinions. Both the National Extension College and the secretary of the NIAE maintained that inequality of opportunity would not be significantly reduced because it was diplomas rather than degrees which most educationally disadvantaged people would wish to pursue. Several groups and individuals took the view that the project was so impracticable and broadcasting so limited an educational medium that the university could not produce a sizeable increase in the number of scientists and technologists. Certain Conservative MPs interested in educational television and several commercial bodies contended that to transmit systematic educational programmes on a national network was to misuse technological advances in broadcasting. The development of local closed-circuit systems would be much more effective.

During this period the policy still carried the handicap of having been used for electoral purposes. The idea was given extravagant coverage in the Labour Party's manifesto produced for the general election of March 1966. 'It will mean', the manifesto announced, 'genuine equality of opportunity to millions of people for the first time.'[103] The white paper on the new university was timed to appear one month before the election date. This meant that the advisory committee worked under considerable pressure. In addition, the policy could be attacked as 'party political' and therefore impracticable and frivolous.

IV THE DEVELOPMENT OF THE POLICY WITHIN THE DEPARTMENT OF EDUCATION AND SCIENCE: FEBRUARY 1966 TO SEPTEMBER 1967

Between February 1966 and September 1967 the precise details of the scheme's development are difficult to trace.[104] Despite a large number of parliamentary questions on the subject in the Commons, Miss Lee remained non-committal. It is known, however, that discussions were taking place between the Department and the Treasury, the BBC and the Post Office. At the same time the costs of alternative types of

[103] The Labour Party Manifesto, *Time for Decision*, March 1966.
[104] The DES were unable to provide information on their negotiations with interested bodies during this period.

organization were being examined. Replying to a question in the Commons in July 1966 Miss Lee announced that a preliminary survey including a review of costs and television channels had been completed.[105] By March 1967 a firm estimate of both capital and running costs was available,[106] yet it was not until September 1967 that a planning committee was appointed to formulate detailed proposals.

Why was the decision to proceed with detailed planning of the scheme so protracted? There seem to be three main reasons. The first concerns the overall state of the nation's economy. In July 1966 the sterling crisis resulted in the bank rate being raised to seven per cent, tax increases, credit restraints and a prices and incomes standstill. Building projects for further education had been deferred for six months in July 1965 but were unaffected by the freeze of the following year. There was some speculation that the new university might be one of the projects axed instead. Indeed a member of the DES has commented that this appeared to be a very precarious period for the project. Although the idea survived, the need for economic restrictions delayed decisions on the project and aggravated the second problem, that of costs.

The question of costs had been of great importance from the very beginning of the scheme. Since the educational value of the university could not be convincingly demonstrated it was essential that its overall costs should be kept as low as possible. Much of the opposition to the plan centred around the argument that this was a project of unproven worth.[107] Miss Lee and her advisers predicted that the largest single cost element in the running of the university was likely to be payments for broadcasting and hence considerable time was devoted to discussions on alternative means of providing programmes. The most important of these was that the fourth television channel might be used for the university.[108] The Postmaster General reported in the Commons that the capital cost of developing this channel would be between £30 and £40 million spread over eight to ten years and 'many millions of pounds per year' to run it.[109] Although the fourth channel alternative was rejected on grounds of cost, the idea was not abandoned altogether. The white paper on *Broadcasting* of December 1966 made an important statement to the effect that no allocation of frequencies to a fourth television service would be authorized for at least three years because of 'the possibility that the network would be required for a specialised service of educational television

[105] *H. C. Deb.*, vol. 732, cols 1875–7.

[106] *H. C. Deb.*, vol. 742, col. 127.

[107] For example, the opinion of officials at the National Extension College and the WEA. See also *The Times*, 26 Feb., 1966; the *Observer*, 27 Feb., 1966; and the *Sunday Telegraph*, 3 July, 1967.

[108] See p. 242.

[109] Wedgwood-Benn, A., *H. C. Deb.*, vol. 725, col. 1574.

forming part of the structure of the Open University'.[110] Those working on plans for the university were greatly encouraged by the white paper's comment that 'the decision to reserve the fourth network would enable the requirements of the Open University to be appraised in the light of practical experience'. It was interpreted as a commitment by the government to continue developing the policy. Negotiations between Lord Goodman (on behalf of the Department) and the BBC resulted in the decision that air space could be provided on BBC 2 at reasonable cost.

The financial problems were accentuated by the unknown quantities involved. No estimate had been made of the likely number of students, of their characteristics and their distribution. It was argued by officials at the DES that until a more detailed plan was devised a survey would be valueless, as an informed choice by those interested in becoming students could not be made. Yet, without such information, a precise estimate of costs for the Treasury was impossible. The fact that no precise figures were published left those opposing the policy somewhat at a loss. One speaker in the debate on broadcasting[111] speculated that the cost of the Open University degree might be as much as that of training a Ph.D student but he had no data on which to base his assertions. It is interesting to note that at no stage prior to this had Mr Wilson or Miss Lee raised the question of cost per student.

Another problem was that of reaching agreement with the BBC over the amount of air time which would be made available for the university's programmes. Co-operation with the BBC was essential to the success of the university once it was decided that the fourth channel could not, at the outset, be used. It must be remembered that the BBC is an independent body and as such was in a position to bargain with the department over the timing of the proposed programmes and the levels of payment involved. The advisory committee made formal approaches to the Director General of the BBC and the discussions continued throughout 1966. By March 1966 the BBC had agreed in principle to act as agent for the Open University but several important points remained to be settled. This part of the planning process was extremely delicate. Discussions were protracted by a number of problems, the first of which was the times of transmission for the university's programmes. The advisory committee, and later representatives of the department, were insistent that the university's programmes should be provided at peak viewing time in order to reach a large proportion of the population, but the controllers of broadcasting at the BBC were reluctant to surrender their peak times for educational programmes. From a com-

[110] *Broadcasting*, Cmnd. 3169, 1966, p. 6.
[111] *H. C. Deb.*, vol. 725, col. 1514.

mercial point of view it is valuable to provide programmes of great popular appeal at these times and it was especially important for the BBC to attract new viewers to BBC 2. Moreover, the university was competing for programme time on BBC 2 with the further education programmes provided by the BBC itself. A third difficulty was that of reaching agreement on the precise functions of the corporation's production teams and the academic staff of the University with regard to programme content and presentation. Peak viewing time was finally obtained for radio and television but since the television programmes were on BBC 2 – a channel with less than nationwide coverage – they would not be received by a large number of those whom the university was originally designed to help. Radio transmissions were on VHF, another medium with a limited range.

Agreement upon the exact times at which the university's programmes should be transmitted required protracted negotiations. In March 1966 a letter was sent by Sir Hugh Greene, Director General of the BBC, to Lord Goodman offering certain specific times. Evenings between seven and eight o'clock on BBC 2 would be devoted to educational programmes but as the BBC's own further education programmes filled the period from 7.30 to 8.00 p.m. the Open University was offered 7.00 to 7.30 p.m. This was agreed. However, in August 1967 Sir Hugh wrote to Miss Lee saying that the corporation had decided to fill the 7.30 to 8.00 p.m. peak time with news in colour and that the time available for educational programmes was therefore being moved forward to the hour between 6.30 and 7.30. This decision left a complex task for the planning committee which had to re-negotiate the time available.

In addition to the difficulties faced in the negotiations outlined above there were problems at a higher level. It has been suggested[112] that agreement with the BBC was delayed by the 'dual control system' operating on broadcasting policy decisions. For historical reasons[113] the Postmaster General has the power to prescribe hours of broadcasting and to veto any particular broadcast or class of broadcasts. Since the Second World War the importance of broadcasting decisions has become greater and they have often been referred to the Cabinet. However, the Postmaster General has not usually been a member of the Cabinet and therefore questions of broadcasting policy have frequently been made the responsibility of a Cabinet Minister.[114]

---

[112] Wedell, E. G., *Broadcasting and Public Policy*, Joseph, 1968, p. 56.
[113] Wedell, *op. cit.*, p. 56.
[114] The responsibility has usually been assigned to one of the members of the Cabinet without departmental responsibilities. The members to assume responsibility for broadcasting in addition to their Cabinet role were Lord Home in 1962, Herbert Bowden in October 1964 and Richard Crossman in August 1966.

Wedell explains the effect of this two-tier arrangement. 'Even where only one Minister is involved, the permanent officials whose task it is to ensure the continuity of administrative practice often finds the rate of ministerial turnover frustrating ... Where two Ministers are concerned who, moreover, are not in the same department, the delays and frustrations are compounded. In the absence of clear proposals, decisions are shelved or overlaid by more urgent matters. In this way decisions on the proposal to establish a "University of the Air" and on the development of local sound broadcasting were deferred from one year to another.'[115]

The period from February 1966 to September 1967 was a crucial one for the reasons given above. By September 1967, however, although no finance had been allocated to the project, the establishment of a planning committee composed of many distinguished members was a clear indication that the government intended to proceed with its proposals. How had the scheme survived despite the difficulties it encountered?

The driving force undoubtedly came from Miss Lee, whose contribution to the survival of the scheme was immense. Although she was not closely involved with the plan until the Prime Minister gave her special responsibility for it in 1965, her personal commitment to its success was obvious. In explaining her enthusiasm for the project she points to her socialist background, coupled with a great respect for university education. Others, including Mr Wilson, have mentioned the part played by Miss Lee's husband, Aneurin Bevan, in the formulation of the National Health Service, and her own wish to make a similar lasting contribution. Her first task was to establish a productive working environment despite an initially hostile department. This she did by detaching herself and her advisers and by maintaining direct contact with the Prime Minister. Her skill and singlemindedness were important especially during her chairmanship of the advisory committee. During 1966 and part of 1967 several of those closely connected with the university's development have maintained that her contribution was to keep the project alive while many others were sacrificed for economic reasons. In public statements she always showed unwavering support for the project. For instance, in May 1966, a particularly uncertain period for the scheme, she spoke to the Association of Broadcasting Staffs at Brighton: 'We would be entirely out of tune with the times if we thought men and women working either full-time or part-time for their living would thank you for being palmed off with a kind of paddy-the-next-best-thing.'

Despite her commitment, however, Miss Lee's attitude towards

[115] Wedell, E. G., *op. cit.*, p. 60.

the university may have constrained its development. She refused to compromise on her vision of the new institution, adhering to the view that it should have the highest academic status; providing degrees, being staffed by university teachers and being termed a university. The conception led to criticism even from some of those who most ardently wished to see the State provide educational television. It must be added that her rigidity was undoubtedly in part a function of her belief that compromise in a situation of considerable hostility might have destroyed the scheme completely.

Although Miss Lee's contribution was vital, without the existence of certain extremely favourable factors the scheme could not have survived. Some of these should be mentioned. By far the most important was the personal interest and commitment of the Prime Minister, Mr Wilson. His support for the project during the economic difficulties of 1966 demonstrated that he had more than an electoral interest in the idea (at this stage he had a firm working majority in the Commons for another five years). In his speech to the first Congregation of the Open University in July 1969 he referred to the university as 'a cherished project of mine for many years'.[116] He saw his most important contribution as initiator of the project and claimed, in a masterpiece of understatement, to have done 'only two things since 1964. The first was to put the whole project in the hands of the Minister of State, Miss Jennie Lee, and the second was to give her at all times, no matter what difficulties she faced, and finance was only one of them, all the backing a Prime Minister can give'. According to Mr Wilson the university was continually high on the Treasury's list of non-essential projects and available for cutting but realizing the powerful backing this project in particular enjoyed, they did not press hard for its withdrawal.

A second important factor in explaining the whole project's survival was the existence in the DES of a few fairly senior civil servants who were both well-versed in the field of higher education and eager to pursue the planning of the new university. Miss Lee was heavily dependent upon their briefing especially when she first arrived at the Department. This small group, the most senior of whom was an Assistant Secretary, followed the project through from 1965 to the conferring of the Charter and provided a focal point for negotiation, discussion and criticism. Miss Lee also had the legal assistance of Lord Goodman, who was especially valuable in the negotiations with the BBC.

The strategy of detachment continued and was the third factor making for its survival. By refusing to publicize details of the plans

---

[116] Speech by the Prime Minister to the First Congregation of the Open University at the Royal Society, London, 23 July, 1969.

and by restricting the numbers involved in the planning, any effective opposition was delayed until it was too late to destroy the policy. The adoption of this tactic had mixed results; it may have kept the idea alive but, as was mentioned earlier, it also led to the build up of considerable ill-feeling on the part of interested groups. The completely separate development of the Open University from the rest of higher education and particularly the polytechnics has already been discussed. During the advisory committee stage a suggestion was made that the Council for National Academic Awards[117] should confer the degrees for the Open University but this was rejected by Miss Lee as bestowing the university with a second rate status.[118]

Those concerned specifically with adult education felt excluded from the discussions but criticism from this quarter was anticipated by the department. The new university was an untested idea which would cost several million pounds a year. In contrast, adult education has remained a neglected area within the education system as a whole, having to work within very tight financial limits. It was foreseen that even with careful public relations the new university would be received somewhat coolly. To avoid delays the Universities' Council for Adult Education, the Workers' Educational Association[119] and the co-ordinating body for the field of adult education as a whole, the National Institute for Adult Education, were left in the dark about a project towards which they felt they could contribute.[120] Although none of the organizations recorded official views during this period, the secretaries of both the UCAE and the WEA wrote to *The Times* expressing disquiet. Thomas Kelly, secretary of the UCAE, wrote that his organization was 'unanimous in desiring an extension of adult education through television and radio', and that the extra-mural departments would 'collaborate wholeheartedly in the "University of the Air", should it be established' but he expressed the personal opinion that the proposal as it stood was premature because enough research into student demand had not been carried out. He suggested as an alternative that an Adult Education Broadcasting Council should be established to ascertain the needs of students and the most effective broadcasting services.[121] In another letter to *The Times* Mr Harry Nutt, general secretary of the WEA, argued that his organization had a fine reputation but that its activities were restricted by

---

[117] The Council for National Academic Awards confers degrees for the polytechnics and colleges of education outside the university system.

[118] Robinson, E., *op. cit.*, p. 235.

[119] See footnote 37.

[120] Derived from interviews with Mr E. Hutchinson, secretary of the NIAE, Mr B. Groombridge, former deputy secretary of the NIAE; the UCAE files and the WEA files.

[121] Correspondence in *The Times*, 7 Mar., 1966.

lack of funds. Some of the finance allocated to the Open University should be diverted to the more traditional means of providing adult education.[122]

The local education authorities were another group whose suspicion was increased by ignorance at this stage. The body which showed most interest was the Association of Municipal Corporations whose secretary wrote to the DES following the publication of the white paper on the university, expressing their desire to be included in the subsequent planning.[123] The department replied that they could give the association no indication as to when consultations would take place. The AMC together with the County Councils' Association and the Association of Education Committees became increasingly anxious that the scheme might involve their member councils in additional expenditure.[124] Opposition from one other quarter should be mentioned. Officials at the National Extension College, the small group which had shown such interest during the policy's early stages, became somewhat isolated from the university's development after one of their members had disagreed with the basic conclusions of the advisory committee. Thereafter, the NEC remained critical of the direction the plans seemed to be taking.[125] The hostility built up towards the policy during this period had little effect on the direction or timing of its development but was important because it made the planning committee's task of securing co-operation extremely delicate.

The final factor which helped to improve the university's survival chances was of a more general kind. This was the growing interest in educational television. From 1964 onwards an increasing amount of research took place in this field. One notable experiment was undertaken at Nottingham University by Harold Wiltshire, Professor of Adult Education.[126] In January 1963 the idea of building television into a teaching system was outlined in *The Times Educational Supplement*. Although the response was mixed, a warm reception came from Mr N. Collins, Deputy Chairman of ATV, and a grant was provided by the Leverhulme Trust whereby ATV agreed to produce thirteen twenty-minute programmes on economics. These were transmitted between 27 September and 21 December 1964. Those who enrolled paid a fee, in return for which they were given a handbook

---

[122] Correspondence in *The Times*, 27 Sept., 1967.

[123] *Municipal Review*, Mar. 1966, p. 142.

[124] From an interview with Sir William Alexander, general secretary of the AEC.

[125] From interviews with Dr M. Young and Mr B. Jackson, chairman and director of the NEC respectively.

[126] Professor Wiltshire was later a prominent member of the Open University planning committee.

and assigned a tutor. The conclusions of the research were published jointly by the NIAE and the University of Nottingham.[127] It was found that a television course could recruit and hold many good students who would not be attracted otherwise. Also, it was found possible to teach effectively through television provided it was coupled with active learning and brought students into contact with tutors. The cost need be no greater than class teaching and, on a larger scale, it could be less. It was not necessary to show programmes on adult education at peak times. Wiltshire and Bayliss argued that 'tele-teaching' should be recognized as a normal method of adult and further education and that a regular service of 'telecourses' should be established under the control of a body of educators; for instance, a National Centre for Broadcasting Education could be formed. The results of this research were adopted by the UCAE which proposed such a centre instead of the Open University.

Experiments with closed-circuit television had been taking place in Glasgow since 1964. In a pamphlet called *A Strathclyde View* it was maintained that 'the arguments in favour of the establishment of a "University of the Air" seem overwhelming'.[128] The pamphlet suggested that preparatory and degree courses should be provided nationally, but that one hundred per cent coverage by broadcast television was probably unrealistic on the grounds of expense and was in any case undesirable, being 'an inefficient exploitation of the few broadcast channels likely to be available for education television'.

It maintained that some sixty to seventy per cent coverage could be achieved very economically by low-power transmitters at the centres of conurbations. The remainder of the population could be covered more economically by conventional film projection at home or in local halls. Further experiments were carried out at Queen's University, Belfast, Kingston-upon-Hull and by the National Extension College.

Summary: the second phase within the DES
This was a period of considerable uncertainty for the scheme. However, by September 1967, although no finance had been approved by the Treasury, the government's intention to pursue the university was made clear by the appointment of a planning committee. The outstanding feature of this period was the way in which a project of unproven merit, of unknown cost and with many enemies, survived a period of great economic uncertainty. Without doubt the most important single factor was the personal backing of the Prime

[127] Wiltshire, H. and Bayliss, F., *Teaching Through Television*, National Institute of Adult Education and Nottingham University, 1965.
[128] *University of the Air – A Strathclyde View*, University of Strathclyde, June 1965, p. 1.

Minister, but the policy's chances of success were enhanced by Miss Lee's skilful management.

V THE PLANNING COMMITTEE STAGE: SEPTEMBER 1967 TO JANUARY 1969

By the autumn of 1967 the most important decisions concerning the Open University had already been taken but there were many more detailed aspects still to be settled. It was at this stage that the process of asking advice and gaining support was begun. Having kept the policy development carefully contained within the DES it was now important to win the co-operation of interested groups in the education, broadcasting and local authority spheres.

In September 1967 a planning committee was appointed by the Secretary of State for Education and Science. This was a major step forward in that, following a long silence, it provided unequivocal evidence that the government intended to pursue its plans for the university. Once it was clear to the opponents of the scheme that the policy would almost certainly succeed it was advantageous for them to join the committee or assist it in its work since the room for manoeuvre was now limited to influencing the detailed plans. A few individuals who had made public their opposition to the plans were asked to join the committee and two have since said that their views were modified as a result of being included. The group was remarkable in that it comprised a large number of respected and powerful individuals from the university, adult education, broadcasting and local authority fields. Six of the nineteen members were, or had been, vice-chancellors, and the chairman was Sir Peter Venables, the vice-chancellor of the University of Aston, Birmingham. Sir Peter had for many years been interested in widening educational opportunities[129] and was an experienced and well respected educationalist, especially in the field of technical training.[130] The membership of the committee was important because besides providing an efficient team it also endowed with academic respectability a project which hitherto had been closely associated with the political arena.

The formation of such an impressive committee must be attributed largely to Miss Lee (now Lady Lee)[131] who made great efforts to con-

---

[129] He was a member of the Crowther Committee and was especially interested in those aspects of the committee's work which dealt with widening opportunities for technical education. See Central Advisory Council for Education (England), *15–18*, 1959–60.

[130] See Venables, P. F. R., *Technical Education*, Bell 1956.

[131] She was made Baroness Lee of Asheridge in 1970.

vince several of the more reluctant members to join. Nevertheless, she ensured that the group, like the earlier advisory committee, discussed the details rather than the essentials of the plan. The committee's terms of reference were again fairly specific. It was asked 'to work out a comprehensive plan for an Open University as outlined in the white paper of February 1966 *A University of the Air* and to prepare a draft Charter and Statutes'. By asking the committee to build on the white paper the original ideas were safeguarded. The group was limited by two further considerations. The date for the university to begin was fixed beforehand at January 1971. A general election had to be called before May 1971 and by setting the starting date of the university near to the election Miss Lee believed that a Conservative government, should it be returned, would have little opportunity to abandon it. This decision indicates the extent to which the project was still a party political issue. It meant that from the beginning the committee had to work with considerable speed. The second factor was that when it began its work no funds had formally been allocated to the university. Negotiations between the DES and the Treasury were continuing; the first estimates were submitted in February 1968. A sum of £400,000 was estimated[132] and agreed as the total cost for the first year (1968-9), but since the expenditure during that period was expected to be exceptional the committee had little idea of how much the Treasury would be willing to sanction in the future. The committee's report stated that 'present uncertainties make it impossible for us accurately to forecast at this stage either the recurrent expenditure or the income of the Open University. There are altogether too many unknowns ...'[133]

The group worked hard to improve the respectability of the university. First, it consulted a wide range of interested groups who had not previously been given a chance to express their views. Second, to reduce the political associations of the university the committee itself rather than the department appointed the principal officers. The Vice-Chancellor was Dr Walter Perry, formerly Vice-Principal of Edinburgh University. He was a well known figure in the education world but was publicly uncommitted to any particular stance politically or within adult education. The choice of Lord Crowther as Chancellor gave the university a figurehead who had been associated with the expansion of educational opportunity for many years. Third, for the first time in the policy's development, research on the possible demand for Open University places was commissioned. The National Institute for Adult Education was asked to conduct a survey from the results

[132] *Civil Estimates 1968-9, Class VII*, Education and Science, 1968.
[133] *The Open University*, Report of the Planning Committee to the Secretary of State for Education and Science, Jan. 1969, p. 28.

of which the committee concluded that the possible student number could be between 34,000 and 150,000.[134]

The planning committee's report, published in January 1969, was not a detailed document, but it clarified certain aspects of the project especially those concerning its aims and organization. It was maintained that the university should be independent and autonomous and focus upon adult students. Degrees, at honours and general level, would be conferred by the accumulation of a certain number of 'credits' and no formal academic qualifications would be required for enrolment. The committee decided that the administrative structure should consist of four parts: the central administrative office, the academic departments, the administrative staff concerned with educational technologies and the administrative staff linking the central office with local regions. Initial broadcasts would be on BBC 2 between 5.30 and 7.30 p.m. and would be supplemented by correspondence tuition. To begin with the University would be financed by a grant-in-aid from the DES.

The committee's task of reducing opposition was not easy. One difficulty involved negotiating with the Further Education Advisory Committee of the BBC over the allocation of the 6.30 to 7.30 p.m. time on BBC 2. A compromise enabling the two groups to divide the peak time between 7.00 and 7.30 was finally agreed. The most intractable groups, however, were the local authority associations who wished to see the plans postponed for economic reasons. In January 1968 the government announced that local authorities were going to be asked to restrain their expenditure for 1969–70 to a level only three per cent above that of 1968–9.[135] The Association of Municipal Corporations was the most vociferous in its opposition although the County Councils' Association took a similar view. In January 1968 the education committee of the AMC resolved that 'in view of the current financial situation implementation of the project should be deferred until such time as economic circumstances are more favourable'. Meetings with the Planning Committee did little to allay the association's fears since the committee made it clear that it was the department's responsibility to make financial decisions of this nature. In September 1968 Sir William Alexander, general secretary of the Association of Education Committees and a member of the planning committee, voiced his doubts publicly. He asked why, in view of the grave economic pressures on higher education, the government insisted on proceeding with the university.[136] In December the AMC expressed concern that the LEAs might be expected to accept certain commitments, including

---

[134] *Ibid.*, p. 3. Based on the numbers reporting that they intended to register as students.

[135] *Public Expenditure in 1968–9 and 1969–70*, Cmnd. 3515, 1968.

[136] 'Dispute on the Open University', *The Times*, 19 Dec., 1968.

financial support for students on courses, the provision of resources for premises, staff and funds for books. The association informed the department of its view, saying: 'We consider it to be inevitable that all the financial liabilities arising from the project must be regarded as being entirely the responsibility of central government.'[137] The reply[138] they received was extremely vague, giving the local authorities none of the assurances they sought. This meant that by the time the planning committee reported the authorities were still bitterly opposed to the plans as they stood. In fact it was another year and a half before more specific arrangements satisfying the local authority associations were made.

Although most of the views expressed by educationalists at this stage were private, there are indications that some still had reservations, especially those interested in adult education. At the Joint Conference of the Association of Teachers in Adult Education and the Association of Adult Education, at which Miss Lee spoke, the disadvantageous financial position of this sector of education was stressed. The secretary of the NIAE made a highly critical speech which was well received by the delegates. The WEA, the NIAE, and the UCAE all expressed disappointment at not being consulted more fully by the planning committee[139] and, in particular, at the lack of consideration given by the committee to educationally disadvantaged groups. Members of the National Extension College took a similar view. In an article in *The Times*, its director wrote: 'I fear that we are in considerable danger of creating yet another university institution for the middle-class, and especially for that middle-class housewife seeking a liberal arts course ... The Open University has many splendid uses ... but if it is centrally to reconnect adult education with a major working-class audience ... then it must go and get them.'[140]

Two organizations which showed general support for the policy at this juncture were the National Union of Teachers and the Association of University Teachers. The former realized for the first time the value of the University for training teachers and became very interested in the proposal. Negotiations with Open University representatives continued after the committee reported on the size of the quota for teachers and the number of credits[141] needed by those already possess-

---

[137] Report of the Education Committee, *Municipal Review Supplement*, Feb. 1969, p. 17.

[138] Reproduced in the Education Committee Report, *Municipal Review Supplement*, Mar. 1969, p. 61.

[139] From WEA and UCAE files (especially the UCAE memorandum of March, 1969) and from an interview with the secretary of the NIAE.

[140] Jackson, B., *The Times*, 25 Nov., 1969.

[141] A degree was to be achieved by an accumulation of credits for individual subjects. Six credits were needed for an ordinary degree and eight for an honours degree.

ing a first degree or a diploma of education. The AUT supported the committee in general but was concerned about the proposed credits system and the contracts of service for the teachers involved. After the planning committee report was published the association indicated its support by including the university amongst its schedule of institutions recognized as universities and a local branch of the AUT was inaugurated.[142]

The most important reason for the speed at which the planning committee was forced to work can be found in the belief held by Miss Lee and her colleagues that the Conservative Party, once in power, would abandon the scheme. This fear was based on conjecture since no official policy statement was made by the party until after the planning report was published. On 27 January 1969, however, Sir Edward Boyle, chief Opposition spokesman on education, made a statement setting out the party's views: 'The Opposition cannot hold out any prospect at this time that funds of the order of an annual rate of £3·7 million, as mentioned in the Report can be counted on for the future.'[143] It seems in retrospect, therefore, that the quest for a speedy conclusion may have been justified.

Summary: the planning committee stage

The planning committee was handed an extremely difficult public relations exercise to perform in a relatively short period. It undertook this task with considerable skill, for although opposition to the University remained in some quarters, the support of a large number of influential educationalists was won. The largest unsolved problem concerned the financial implications for local authorities – a problem which took many months to overcome.

The government was clearly anxious to accept the report's recommendations and transfer the final stage of the development work to the new officers of the Open University. On the same day that the report was published the Secretary of State for Education, Mr Edward Short, made a statement in the Commons. He said: 'The Government fully accept the outline plans for development set out in the Report. It will now be for the University authority, as an autonomous and completely independent institution, to carry the project forward, and in this it can count on the support of the Government.'[144] On 22 July 1969 the Open University officially received its Charter. Although much still needed to be done, the policy to establish a university based on television and correspondence had reached fruition.

[142] Information gained from correspondence with AUT officials.
[143] Conservative Central Office press release, Statement by Sir Edward Boyle, 27 Jan., 1969.
[144] *H. C. Deb.*, vol. 776, col. 941.

VI CONCLUSION

The planning process which led to the formation of the Open University tells us little about education policy-making in general. No single case-study can do that. Nevertheless it highlights a number of features worth exploring in future studies of policy change.

1. The effective pressures for change in this case came from the highest ranks of the Opposition party machine, which meant that the often slow process of persuading one of the major parties to adopt a new idea was unnecessary. The influence of pressure groups in the initial stages was, therefore, slight; the essence of the idea having been derived, Wilson claimed, from foreign experience.

2. Technological developments played an important part. They do not explain the exact timing of the policy but were prerequisites to its introduction. Without broadcasting facilities of high quality and wide coverage the whole idea would have been untenable.

3. Similarly, population change was a key background variable. The increased numbers in those age groups requiring higher and further education in the early sixties created pressures which encouraged the search for new ways of expanding facilities.

4. Above all, this study demonstrates the important part powerful individuals can play in promoting their favoured proposals despite opposition from ministries, the Treasury, civil servants and well-established interest groups. Without the continued support of the Prime Minister it is extremely unlikely that proposals for an Open University would have been implemented. He was able to entrust the planning of the project to an influential and committed junior Minister who could operate secure in the knowledge that the Premier's support would be forthcoming if the project met difficulties. The original idea was further safeguarded by carefully controlling the role of experts. The advisory committee was chaired by Miss Lee herself and later the planning committee was given very restricted terms of reference, thus limiting their room for manoeuvre.

5. The rationale which Wilson gave for introducing the policy highlights both the advantages and disadvantages of using a broad based defence to justify change. It may increase support by attracting groups with widely differing views but it may also expose a policy to greater criticism. Wilson claimed that there were good technological, economic, egalitarian and political reasons for an Open University. In this case the tactic appeared to increase support only slightly and probably attracted unnecessarily diverse criticism.

6. The proposal for a University of the Air was first publicly floated during a party's pre-electoral campaign and was clearly used subsequently for political ends. As a new and superficially attractive

he Case Studies

s, etc.' could be made available.[4] Despite this requirement, how-
he development of health centres was extremely slow: between
and 1963 only eighteen were built throughout England and
. The numbers began to increase during the mid-sixties, 121
opened between 1964 and the end of 1969 (see Table 6). This
examines the reasons for the early failure of the scheme and the
rs contributing to a re-emergence of interest in the idea twenty
s after its enactment.

Table 6

LTH CENTRES OPENED BEFORE 31 DEC., 1969 IN ENGLAND AND WALES*

	England	Wales	England and Wales
1949–51	1	–	1
1952–4	4	–	4
1955–7	3	–	3
1958–60	5	–	5
1961–3	5	–	5
1964–6	11	2	13
1967–9	97	11	108
Total	126	13	139

* Compiled from figures provided by the Department of Health and Social Security. The table includes only those centres newly built since 1949 and not those adapted from voluntary clinics, dispensaries etc. The only centres closed during these years were such adaptations or temporary ones later replaced by permanent buildings.

I THE BACKGROUND TO THE HEALTH CENTRE CONCEPT BEFORE 1948

Since this study is concerned primarily with the developments in health centre policy following the National Health Service Act, 1946, we shall not examine in detail the various suggestions made before then.[5] Nevertheless, the background to the health centre scheme cannot be ignored for it contains features which adversely affected the subsequent progress of the proposals.

[4] The National Health Service Act, 1946, Section 21.
[5] The suggestions made early this century for reorganizing the health services, including proposals for health centres, would make a fascinating study. One question which requires examination is why the suggestions for medical centres propounded from 1914 onwards by prominent administrators we shelved during the 1920s.

idea its chances of acceptance were probably enhanced by its being suggested during a pre-electoral period when the accent was on projecting the right party image. The importance of pre-electoral periods in the selection and planning of policy proposals requires further investigation. What kinds of suggestions are put forward and how does their use as a rallying cry affect their subsequent progress? Much of the criticism directed towards the Open University resulted from its promotion during the 1964 and 1966 electoral campaigns.

7. Although when the Treasury was first approached it was clearly somewhat reluctant to meet the costs of the Open University, the financial commitment involved did not present a major hurdle. This was probably because the level of expenditure could be quite easily controlled and limited in the future if necessary. The initial outlay on buildings and equipment was not very great and the scale of the University's operations could be adjusted thereafter.

8. The introduction of an Open University was an extremely contentious proposal and hence the effective management of opposition was crucial. In this instance a tactic of 'containment' was used, the project being deliberately insulated from debates about the education service as a whole. If the proposal had been seen as part of education policy generally, it would have been placed in the queue of proposals competing for DES attention and its merits would have been debated alongside those of other policies being considered at the time, such as the expansion of polytechnics. Its chances of success would probably have been slim. There was no hard research to support it, the only evidence being that of foreign experiments. Its cost could not be estimated accurately since elements such as the size of the student population and the nature of the regional organization were not decided until after it had become fairly clear that the project would be accepted by the government. Throughout the development of this policy, its survival was heavily dependent upon its separation.

9. The study also illustrates the disadvantages of containment or cocooning. By excluding those whose co-operation will subsequently be needed for the implementation of the project, opposition can be aroused which is later difficult to convert into necessary support. In this case a committee of inquiry, often the machinery adopted by departments to effect a public relations exercise, was not used. Instead, an *ad hoc* and prestigious planning committee was formed to win the co-operation of interested groups in education, broadcasting and local administration. This indicates that even at this late stage, however, the policy was being protected; the submission of evidence to a committee of inquiry could have resulted in undue publicity for its critics. The planning committee received no such formal evidence although it met many of those interested in or involved

in implementing the university. The reduction of opposition, however, was only partially successful using this method. The committee could not allay the fears of the local authority associations whose member councils stood to lose financially from the introduction of the scheme. Where opposition had arisen through ignorance or lack of early consultation the group had more success. The key feature of this committee was its membership. By persuading an eminent group of individuals to join it, Miss Lee demonstrated that the project had some powerful support outside the DES and that it was unlikely that the university would be scrapped altogether. Under such circumstances the tactics of the opposition tended to be modified. Previous critics either became supporters or they attempted to influence the *details* of the scheme rather than to destroy it completely.

CHAPTER ELEVE

The Development o
Centres

The number of health centres in England and W rapidly during the late sixties.[1] By the end of Decem were 307 in operation, from which 1,625 family doctors ing.[2] This represented a doubling in two years both o of centres and of the general practitioners involved. It w the Department of Health and Social Security was eager even further expansion. A circular sent to authorities in designated centres as 'top priority' for capital expendi sequently, Lord Aberdare, Minister of State at the DHSS, a that the department expected there to be more than 500 c the end of 1974 from which 3,000 family doctors would be pr

The health centre was planned as an integral part of th National Health Service reform enacted in 1946. Political bar produced a tripartite structure of health administration – the h the local authority services and the executive council services – required co-ordination. It was argued at the time that health ce established on a nationwide basis could provide a valuable ventu which personnel from the three parts of the service could w together to provide community medical care. A duty was, therefo placed upon every local health authority to 'provide, equip and mai tain' centres at which 'general medical services, general dental service pharmaceutical services, local health authority services, specialis

[1] This study covers the growth of health centres in England and Wales.
[2] Figures provided by the Department of Health and Social Security and the Welsh Office.
[3] This statement was made on 21 February, 1973 at a conference in Cambridge on local authority health services. The Minister was anxious to encourage local authorities to continue planning health centres despite the fact that the latter's responsibility for health services lapsed in April 1974 with National Health Service reorganization.

idea its chances of acceptance were probably enhanced by its being suggested during a pre-electoral period when the accent was on projecting the right party image. The importance of pre-electoral periods in the selection and planning of policy proposals requires further investigation. What kinds of suggestions are put forward and how does their use as a rallying cry affect their subsequent progress? Much of the criticism directed towards the Open University resulted from its promotion during the 1964 and 1966 electoral campaigns.

7. Although when the Treasury was first approached it was clearly somewhat reluctant to meet the costs of the Open University, the financial commitment involved did not present a major hurdle. This was probably because the level of expenditure could be quite easily controlled and limited in the future if necessary. The initial outlay on buildings and equipment was not very great and the scale of the University's operations could be adjusted thereafter.

8. The introduction of an Open University was an extremely contentious proposal and hence the effective management of opposition was crucial. In this instance a tactic of 'containment' was used, the project being deliberately insulated from debates about the education service as a whole. If the proposal had been seen as part of education policy generally, it would have been placed in the queue of proposals competing for DES attention and its merits would have been debated alongside those of other policies being considered at the time, such as the expansion of polytechnics. Its chances of success would probably have been slim. There was no hard research to support it, the only evidence being that of foreign experiments. Its cost could not be estimated accurately since elements such as the size of the student population and the nature of the regional organization were not decided until after it had become fairly clear that the project would be accepted by the government. Throughout the development of this policy, its survival was heavily dependent upon its separation.

9. The study also illustrates the disadvantages of containment or cocooning. By excluding those whose co-operation will subsequently be needed for the implementation of the project, opposition can be aroused which is later difficult to convert into necessary support. In this case a committee of inquiry, often the machinery adopted by departments to effect a public relations exercise, was not used. Instead, an *ad hoc* and prestigious planning committee was formed to win the co-operation of interested groups in education, broadcasting and local administration. This indicates that even at this late stage, however, the policy was being protected; the submission of evidence to a committee of inquiry could have resulted in undue publicity for its critics. The planning committee received no such formal evidence although it met many of those interested in or involved

in implementing the university. The reduction of opposition, however, was only partially successful using this method. The committee could not allay the fears of the local authority associations whose member councils stood to lose financially from the introduction of the scheme. Where opposition had arisen through ignorance or lack of early consultation the group had more success. The key feature of this committee was its membership. By persuading an eminent group of individuals to join it, Miss Lee demonstrated that the project had some powerful support outside the DES and that it was unlikely that the university would be scrapped altogether. Under such circumstances the tactics of the opposition tended to be modified. Previous critics either became supporters or they attempted to influence the *details* of the scheme rather than to destroy it completely.

CHAPTER ELEVEN

The Development of Health Centres

The number of health centres in England and Wales expanded rapidly during the late sixties.[1] By the end of December 1971 there were 307 in operation, from which 1,625 family doctors were practising.[2] This represented a doubling in two years both of the number of centres and of the general practitioners involved. It was clear that the Department of Health and Social Security was eager to promote even further expansion. A circular sent to authorities in April 1971 designated centres as 'top priority' for capital expenditure. Subsequently, Lord Aberdare, Minister of State at the DHSS, announced that the department expected there to be more than 500 centres by the end of 1974 from which 3,000 family doctors would be practising.[3]

The health centre was planned as an integral part of the larger National Health Service reform enacted in 1946. Political bargaining produced a tripartite structure of health administration – the hospital, the local authority services and the executive council services – which required co-ordination. It was argued at the time that health centres established on a nationwide basis could provide a valuable venue at which personnel from the three parts of the service could work together to provide community medical care. A duty was, therefore, placed upon every local health authority to 'provide, equip and maintain' centres at which 'general medical services, general dental services, pharmaceutical services, local health authority services, specialist

[1] This study covers the growth of health centres in England and Wales.
[2] Figures provided by the Department of Health and Social Security and the Welsh Office.
[3] This statement was made on 21 February, 1973 at a conference in Cambridge on local authority health services. The Minister was anxious to encourage local authorities to continue planning health centres despite the fact that the latter's responsibility for health services lapsed in April 1974 with National Health Service reorganization.

services, etc.' could be made available.[4] Despite this requirement, however, the development of health centres was extremely slow: between 1949 and 1963 only eighteen were built throughout England and Wales. The numbers began to increase during the mid-sixties, 121 being opened between 1964 and the end of 1969 (see Table 6). This study examines the reasons for the early failure of the scheme and the factors contributing to a re-emergence of interest in the idea twenty years after its enactment.

Table 6

HEALTH CENTRES OPENED BEFORE 31 DEC., 1969 IN ENGLAND AND WALES*

	England	Wales	England and Wales
1949–51	1	–	1
1952–4	4	–	4
1955–7	3	–	3
1958–60	5	–	5
1961–3	5	–	5
1964–6	11	2	13
1967–9	97	11	108
Total	126	13	139

* Compiled from figures provided by the Department of Health and Social Security. The table includes only those centres newly built since 1949 and not those adapted from voluntary clinics, dispensaries etc. The only centres closed during these years were such adaptations or temporary ones later replaced by permanent buildings.

I THE BACKGROUND TO THE HEALTH CENTRE CONCEPT BEFORE 1948

Since this study is concerned primarily with the developments in health centre policy following the National Health Service Act, 1946, we shall not examine in detail the various suggestions made before then.[5] Nevertheless, the background to the health centre scheme cannot be ignored for it contains features which adversely affected the subsequent progress of the proposals.

[4] The National Health Service Act, 1946, Section 21.

[5] The suggestions made early this century for reorganizing the health services, including proposals for health centres, would make a fascinating study. One question which requires examination is why the suggestions for medical centres propounded from 1914 onwards by prominent administrators were shelved during the 1920s.

First, in 1946 a specific duty to provide centres was placed upon local authorities at a time when the concept of a health centre was still unclear. There were differences of opinion as to the optimum size of centres, the functions they should perform and who should control them. A brief description of several suggestions will illustrate the diversity of ideas. The first fairly detailed proposal for a nation-wide provision of health centres[6] was put forward in 1920 in the Interim Report of the Dawson Committee on the Medical and Allied Services.[7] The committee argued that two types of centre should be established; 'primary' centres staffed by general practitioners should deal with frontline medical care while 'secondary' centres, staffed by specialists, would treat the more complicated cases. The country would be divided into administrative areas for health purposes and the centres controlled by the proposed authorities for each area.

During the twenties the 'health centre' idea was adopted by a number of left-wing organizations which put forward a variety of proposals. A memorandum published by the Labour Party in 1921[8] advocated that centres should be established in the public hospitals of large towns to provide accommodation for all medical activities. Two years later the Trades Union Congress suggested a similar scheme. In towns with a population of 6,000 or more all medical facilities should be provided from the hospitals in the area. Where the population was below 6,000 'treatment centres', with well-equipped surgeries and a few beds, were recommended. Doctors would work in groups focusing upon the hospitals or centres. In 1930 the Socialist Medical Association (SMA) produced a plan for much larger centres.[9] Each was to have a staff of about twenty-four doctors together with health visitors, district nurses and midwives, serving a population of 60,000. In rural areas a system of clinics administered by the counties and county boroughs was proposed. This suggestion was adopted officially by the Labour Party in 1934 but the party's plans remained ill-defined. In 1943 a leaflet developing Labour's future policy for the health services argued for 'some kind of health centre supported by the community',[10] but no precise scheme was put forward. During the

---

[6] In September 1918 Sir A. Newsholme, Chief Medical Officer to the Local Government Board, suggested in his last report *The Needs of the Future*, Supplement to the 47th Annual Report of the LGB, 1917–8, Cd. 9169, that the services of doctors could be used more economically if provided through centres, but the proposal was not developed further.

[7] *Interim Report of the Committee on the Future of the Medical and Allied Services* (Dawson Report), Cmd. 693, 1920, pp. 9–14.

[8] Prepared by the Party's Advisory Committee on Public Health.

[9] The Socialist Medical Association was established in 1930. From the outset it was committed to the implementation of a nationalized health service, including health centres. It became affiliated to the Labour Party in 1933.

[10] *A National Service for Health*, Labour Party pamphlet, 1943.

early forties a number of pamphlets advocating health centres were issued by the Socialist Medical Association but they were mostly propagandist and contained little hard information. Similarly the Communist Party published several leaflets on the health services. They all suggested that health centres should consist of ten or more doctors, aided by nurses and auxiliaries and should provide 'nearly every kind of service that the patient needs'.[11] No mention was made of whether specialist facilities should be included or who should control the centres.

Organizations representing various groups within the medical profession began to make their views on health centres clearer during the war years. Whereas the left-wing proposals had differed primarily on the size of a centre and the functions it should perform, the plans put forward by medical groups displayed differences of opinion as to who should own and administer the centres. The Medical Practitioners' Union (MPU)[12] published its ideas in 1939 and again in 1943.[13] Its plans were similar in some respects to those put forward by the SMA but while the latter proposed that large authorities under the general control of the Minister of Health should run all the medical services in each area, the MPU wished to see the medical profession controlling health centres. Not unexpectedly, the Society of Medical Officers of Health agreed with the SMA that centres should be provided, administered and maintained by the local authorities.[14] They were joined in this view by the Liberal Party.[15]

The British Medical Association (BMA), representing a large proportion of general practitioners,[16] published two reports during the 1930s advocating the integration of the local health services into single administrative units[17] but neither document tackled the organization of general practice. In 1942, however, when the Interim Report of its Medical Planning Commission[18] was published it became clear that the BMA was then in favour of a network of centres. The commission, which was established by the BMA in conjunction with the

[11] Communist Party, *Good Health for All*, May, 1944.

[12] The MPU was formed in 1913. Although often thought of as a left-wing organization (it is affiliated to the TUC), its policies have not maintained any consistent ideological position. Its membership is about 5,000.

[13] MPU, *Design for Family Doctoring*, 1966–7, pp. 90–2.

[14] Society of Medical Officers of Health, *A National Health Service*, Nov. 1942.

[15] Liberal Party, *Health for the People*, 1942.

[16] The BMA represented 63 per cent of GPs in 1940; 77 per cent in 1950; 80 per cent in 1955. (Source: *British Medical Journal*, Supplement, 1950, i, 7 Jan., 1950, p. 4 and *BMJ*, Supplement, 1956, ii, 7 Apr., 1956, p. 46).

[17] BMA, *Proposals for a General Medical Service for the Nation*, 1930. Also BMA, *A General Medical Service for the Nation*, 1938.

[18] 'The Medical Planning Commission Draft Interim Report', *British Medical Journal*, 20 June, 1942, pp. 744–50.

Royal Colleges[19] and other professional organizations, suggested that health centres would reduce the isolation of GPs. The report recommended that although doctors might wish to form their own centres during the early stages, in the long-run they should be provided and administered by a statutory health authority (set at regional level). Although the commission's 73 members represented a fairly broad cross-section of medical opinion, their views on the control of centres were not unanimous. Another report produced in 1942 by a group of younger doctors maintained that the buildings should be provided by central rather than local authorities.[20]

It would be erroneous to suppose that the views put forward by groups within medical and political circles constituted a coherent debate. The ideas outlined above were produced in apparent isolation, with no reference to one another. Indeed, the term 'health centre' disguised a very wide variety of views on the local organization of medical services. The only common ground was a wish to see certain medical services brought together under one roof for the purpose of prevention and cure of disease and that such groups of medical personnel and facilities should be linked to the hospital service.

The white paper of 1944 on the future organization of the health services[21] recognized the ill-defined nature of the health centre concept by announcing the government's intention to provide a number of centres on an experimental basis with a view to more widespread development if the trials were successful. The types established initially would be varied but basically the design was to include individual consulting rooms, simple laboratories, nursing and secretarial staffs, telephone services and other accessories. In some cases recovery and rest rooms, dark rooms, facilities for minor surgery and auxiliary aids would be added as well. No mention was made of specialist services or of attaching health centres to hospitals. In contrast to the approach of the white paper, the National Health Service Act of 1946 made no references to the need for experimentation. Instead it placed a specific duty on every local health authority to provide and maintain centres and in February 1947 the Ministry of Health sent a circular to each health authority requesting that plans should be submitted.[22]

A second feature which later affected the policy's implementation was that conflict over the local control of centres was unresolved by the process of bargaining and negotiation leading to the National Health Service Act. This omission was crucial because the subsequent

[19] The Royal Colleges represented physicians, surgeons and obstetricians and gynæcologists.
[20] 'The Medical Planning Research Interim General Report', *Lancet*, 21 Nov., 1942, pp. 614, 616–7.
[21] *A National Health Service*, Cmd. 6502, 1944.
[22] Ministry of Health Circular, 22/47.

development of centres depended upon close working relationships between GPs and local authority health departments. We have already noted that proposals for health centres made before the publication of the white paper in 1944 had differed over the issue of control. The National Health Service Act placed the provision of centres and their maintenance on the shoulders of the counties and the county boroughs, although there was considerable evidence to show that many GPs would be unwilling to work in local authority-owned premises. When the Conference of Panel Practitioners met in 1942, a motion approving the principle of health centres was qualified by a statement that the establishment of centres should not be compulsory and that in any event they should be built on the initiative of GPs.[23] In answer to a BMA questionnaire circulated to determine doctors' reactions to the white paper, only 23 per cent of GPs were in favour of being under contract to local authorities; 63 per cent were against.[24] Eckstein maintains that the fundamental reason for this distrust of local government was 'class contempt'. 'The operative upper-class stereotype of the councillor is pronouncedly petit bourgeois . . . The doctors were less afraid of central control because civil servants of the administrative class and MPs are (. . . at least in popular mythology), a rather different species from their local counterparts.'[25] In addition, memories of the long battle fought by the BMA against the maltreatment of MOsH by local councils lingered on. The image of 'bureaucracy', salaried payment and the parlous state of local authority services completed the case made by GPs against local control.[26]

From 1945 the bitter and protracted negotiations over the nature of health centres which took place between the BMA and Aneurin Bevan, Minister of Health from 1945, did nothing to relieve the suspicions of general practitioners regarding health centre practice in the early stages of its development. The Medical Planning Commission's Report of 1942 indicated BMA support for some form of health centre scheme but the publication of both the Beveridge Report in 1942 and the white paper on the health services in 1944 produced adverse reactions from the Association.[27] It was argued that health centre practice would be unacceptable to the medical profession if a salaried service were introduced, if the centres were lay-controlled and finally if private practice from within centres were forbidden. We have already noted that the results of the BMA questionnaire of 1944

[23] *British Medical Journal*, Supplement, 5 Dec., 1942, p. 70.

[24] Eckstein, H., *The English Health Service*, Harvard University Press, 1958, p. 148. Selected questions from BMA questionnaire (unpublished).

[25] Eckstein, H., *Ibid.*, p. 150.

[26] Eckstein, H., 'The Politics of the BMA', *Political Quarterly*, vol. xxvi, no. 4 (1955), pp. 345–59.

[27] 'The BMA and the Beveridge Report', *British Medical Journal*, 13 Feb., 1943; also *British Medical Journal*, 13 May, 1944, p. 645.

indicated that the rank and file medical opinion on lay control was consistent with the published policy of the BMA. Answers to questions concerning the desirability of health centres *per se* and to the intractable problem of a salaried service, however, suggest that the opinion of the majority of BMA members differed from the official stance on these issues; sixty-eight per cent were in favour of the principle of health centres and twenty-four per cent were against. Surprisingly, sixty-two per cent of the replies favoured a totally or partially salaried service and only twenty-nine per cent opposed the idea.[28] Nevertheless, the BMA continued its opposition to a salaried service within health centres. Eckstein maintains that the Association managed to persuade the Minister of Health in the coalition government, Henry Willink, to modify the white paper proposals on health centres.[29] He argues that Willink agreed to drop the idea of a salaried service and to substitute a scheme whereby local authorities let health centres to GPs who would be paid on a capitation basis and who would be free to practise privately if they wished.

However, following the 1945 election, a Labour government was returned to power and the new Minister of Health, Aneurin Bevan, refused to accept the modifications agreed by his predecessor. Partly as a result of the Minister's uncompromising attitude, there were further clashes with the BMA both before and after the National Health Service Act was passed.[30] Under the Act the counties and county boroughs were to provide and administer health centres but the remuneration of GPs was largely left open. Statements made by Bevan indicated that he was in favour of a small salary, plus a capitation fee for each patient on the doctor's list. The BMA reacted adversely to this compromise on remuneration with the result that before the Act came into effect on 5 July 1948, Bevan agreed to introduce an Amending Act abandoning the universal basic salary in favour of capitation payments for most doctors. Despite the favourable views expressed concerning the principles of health centre practice and a salaried service on the part of GPs in 1944, a postal inquiry by the BMA in 1951 found that only thirty-eight per cent of GP principals approved of health centres in general.[31] A survey conducted by Hadfield in the same year found that forty-seven per cent were opposed to the health centre scheme.[32] It appears, therefore, that the

[28] Eckstein, H., *The English Health Service, op. cit.*
[29] Eckstein, H., *ibid.*, pp. 155–6. Eckstein points out that there is little evidence to indicate the exact course followed by the negotiations.
[30] For fuller accounts of the negotiations see: Lindsey, A., *Socialised Medicine in England and Wales*, Chapel Hill, 1962, pp. 41–72, *passim*. Also BMA, *Health Services Financing*, 1970, pp. 33–50.
[31] *British Medical Journal*, Supplement, 26 Sept., 1953, p. 125.
[32] Hadfield, J., 'A Field Survey of General Practice, 1951–52', *British Medical Journal*, 26 Sept., 1953, p. 702.

official discussions which were held before the enactment of the health centre proposals did little to reduce hostility towards the scheme.

Health centres were introduced in 1946 as part of a 'package' of policies relating to health care. Aneurin Bevan made it quite clear in his speech during the second reading of the National Health Service Bill that the government attached 'very great importance indeed' to the health centre concept.[33] For, within the health service as a whole, it was seen to provide the much needed link between the general practitioner and the local health authority services – a point which was made forcibly by Bevan. Despite the professed importance of centres, however, two aspects of their history presaged a difficult future for the scheme. The term 'health centre' had no precise meaning and yet a duty was placed upon local authorities to provide them. Although the duty was soon to be lifted, health departments were left to experiment in isolation, with little help from the ministry. Secondly, the process of negotiation and enactment, which can sometimes effect a change in attitudes towards social issues and their solutions, failed to create a favourable climate of opinion amongst GPs – a group whose co-operation was to be vital in the planning and implementation of the policy. In 1944 general practitioners had demonstrated their reluctance to being under contract to local authorities and this reluctance had, if anything, increased by the time of the BMA's postal inquiry in 1951.

II THE EARLY DEVELOPMENTS: 1948–51

This period provided great opportunities for launching a health centre scheme. The National Health Service as a whole began to operate in 1948 and, if centres were to become an integral part of the system, it was essential to begin planning them in concert with the decisions affecting other parts of the service.

The National Health Service Act was due to come into operation on 5 July 1948, but in December 1947 local health authorities received a circular cancelling the requirement to submit proposals for health centres under Section 21 of the Act.[34] A further circular in January 1948 emphasized the importance of centres as 'a key feature in the general reconstitution of the country's health service' but stated that the Minister of Health did 'not expect local health authorities nor-mally to submit any proposals to him yet for the immediate provision of health centres'.[35] On the appointed day, twenty-seven dispensaries

[33] *H. C. Deb.*, vol. 422, col. 58.
[34] Ministry of Health, Circular 176/47.
[35] Ministry of Health, Circular 3/48.

and clinics were taken over from voluntary organizations and medical aid societies to be used as health centres by local authorities but the Ministry of Health's Annual Report for 1949 announced that newly built centres would be given priority only in 'those areas where there is an immediate need for accommodation for doctors and dentists and for clinics'.[36]

Why was the decision to postpone the scheme taken? Two reasons were given in the circular of January 1948. They were 'the sheer practical impossibility of a new building programme and the need for intensive research and thought about design'.[37] The first of these reasons was undoubtedly important. The unfavourable economic situation and acute shortages of material and labour in the immediate post-war period resulted in fierce competition for building resources. In September and October 1947 capital investment for the following years was reviewed and cuts were made in the estimates proposed by departments.[38] Devaluation took place in September 1949 and further capital expenditure cuts were announced that October. Even before the full extent of the economic crisis became known, Aneurin Bevan, whose Ministry encompassed both the health services and housing until 1951, was aware of the need to determine building priorities. During the committee stage of the National Health Service Bill he stated 'the first priority must be in the provision of houses and hospitals because the quicker we can provide enough decent houses, the less we shall need health centres . . . The provision of hospital facilities must come second because there is a very lamentable situation in some parts of the country at present.'[39] In June 1947 he was questioned in the House on the powers of local authorities to acquire sites for centres and replied that 'it is no use at the moment acquiring them [sites] too far ahead of time for lack of building materials and labour owing to the prior claims of housing'.[40] When questioned about the circular of January 1948 he went further, stating that 'no immediate substantial increase of building work under the Act has ever been promised or regarded as feasible'.[41] It was quite clear that in the battle for scarce building resources health centres were not to be accorded very high priority.

The second reason given for rescinding the obligation upon local authorities to prepare plans for health centres – that of the need for research before launching a widespread project – also appears (in

[36] Ministry of Health, *Annual Report for the Year Ended 31 Mar., 1949*, p. 254.
[37] Ministry of Health, Circular 3/48.
[38] *Economic Survey for 1948*, Cmd. 7344, 1948, para. 172, p. 38.
[39] *H. C. Deb.*, Standing Committee C, Session 1945-6, May–July, col. 1515.
[40] *H. C. Deb.*, vol. 439, col. 662.
[41] *H. C. Deb.*, vol. 447, col. 53.

retrospect) to have been valid. Apart from the Peckham experiment of the thirties[42], which was far too ambitious and costly to have been implemented on a national scale, there had been no attempt to evaluate different types of centre. During the committee stage of the National Health Service Bill, Bevan made clear the nature of the trial period he envisaged for centres. 'It is obvious', he stated, 'that we shall have to have some experimentation. Nevertheless, there is no experimenting with the initial idea; there is only experiment as to how it is to be carried out, for instance, with regard to building.'[43] The 1948 circular indicated that the Ministry of Health would refuse to countenance the widespread conversion of existing buildings to create centres, on the grounds that there was a lack of suitable accommodation in the right places and, more important, that this strategy might 'prejudice the attractiveness of the whole health centre conception. Health centre development is essentially something which, if it is to be done at all, must be done well'. At the same time the ministry announced that the newly established Central Health Services Council was being asked to form a committee to collate all existing information relevant to the future of the centre scheme and to suggest 'the best kinds and purposes of health centres at which development should aim'.[44] The conclusion reached by this committee, which reported in 1950, was that there ought to be a short-run and a long-run strategy. The former should include the establishment of centres with general but not necessarily specialist facilities in areas where the medical services required immediate expansion. The latter involved developing a nationwide programme of centres and the reservation of sites by local authorities for its eventual implementation.[45] It must be added that the initial experimental nature of the health centre scheme was a condition laid down by the BMA when negotiating the terms under which the profession would be willing to enter the service.[46]

A further reason for the postponement of the policy is offered by Eckstein.[47] He maintains that the above reasons are inadequate and that the only alternative explanation is that the government had a change of heart over the desirability of establishing centres. He argues that following the circular of January 1948 the Minister made no further attempts to encourage local efforts. Ryan[48] disagrees with this view on the grounds that the circumstantial evidence cited by Eckstein

[42] For information on this experimental centre see Pearse, I. H. and Crocker, L. H., *The Peckham Experiment*, Allen & Unwin, 1943.

[43] *H. C. Deb.*, Standing Committee C, *op. cit.*, col. 1513.

[44] Ministry of Health, Circular 3/48.

[45] Central Health Services Council, *Health Centre Committee Report*, 1950.

[46] See Ryan, M., 'Health Centre Policy in England and Wales', *British Journal of Sociology*, Mar. 1968, p. 35.

[47] Eckstein, H., *The English Health Service, op. cit.*, pp. 248–52.

[48] Ryan, M., *ibid.*, p. 35.

does not necessarily lead to such a conclusion. Certainly there is evidence to suggest that, within the limits imposed by the economic circumstances of the time, Bevan made attempts to encourage some projects. The 1948 circular itself made it clear that 'particularly urgent new projects and attractive practicable conversions would be considered by the Ministry'.[49] In addition, attempts were made by the ministry to arrange discussions between the appropriate local health authority and the Executive Council in all cases where an estate of 2,500 or more houses (which might be expected to contain about 10,000 people) were being constructed.[50] Not all local authorities were discouraged from proceeding with plans; by the end of 1951, there were seventy projects which were known to the ministry. Eckstein maintains that sixty-five of these applications for loan sanction were rejected, but this is incorrect. It is true that only five schemes were approved, but many of the projects had not progressed beyond the preliminary stages and loan sanction was never requested.[51] A further two schemes were sanctioned but subsequently met with insuperable problems at a local level.[52] It is impossible to resolve this debate conclusively but there appears to be sufficient evidence to show that the Labour government was, at this stage, anxious to avoid abandoning the scheme altogether.

Nevertheless, it is clear that the government failed to take advantage of a situation which, in some respects, favoured the widespread development of centres. The disruptions caused by a wartime situation were beginning to subside but the health services were still in a state of flux. Many demobilized GPs were searching for new practices at this time and evidence from the BMA questionnaire of 1944 had indicated that a high proportion of doctors in the Services, who were accustomed to working for a salary within a bureaucratic framework, were willing to consider health centre practice. Indeed, eighty-three per cent of these doctors were in favour of health centres *per se* and seventy-four per cent stated that they would be willing to work on a salaried basis. However, even doctors in this group were reluctant to work under contract to local authorities; only thirty-five per cent replied that they would be willing to accept an appointment under these conditions.[53] Following Bevan's assurances concerning a salaried service the BMA was prepared to be conciliatory in its attitude towards centres. In July 1948 the

[49] This point was reiterated by the ministry in a letter to local health authorities on 13 Apr., 1948.
[50] Ministry of Health, *Annual Report for the Year Ended 31 Mar., 1949,* p. 254.
[51] It is not known exactly how many projects were formally submitted for loan sanction.
[52] Ministry of Health, *Annual Report for the Period Ended 31 Dec., 1951,* p. 71.
[53] Eckstein, H., *op. cit.,* p. 148.

Council of the Association produced an Interim Report on Health Centres in which it concluded that 'The Council ... is satisfied that the most satisfactory form of practice at present and in the immediate future is partnership practice from a common surgery. It believes that the logical future development will be the provision of specially designed health centres from which both general practitioners and the present local authority services can be provided.'[54]

Many local health authorities appeared eager in the early years to begin their programme. This was demonstrated by the seventy projects known to the Ministry. The *Local Government Chronicle* recorded comprehensive health centre planning by some of the larger authorities including London, Birmingham, Manchester and Bristol.[55] The ministry's rejection of proposals created despondency and some ill-feeling amongst authorities. Birmingham Council was aggrieved when its scheme for a health centre estimated to cost £38,000 was not approved, whilst the London County Council's project at Woodberry Down was sanctioned at a cost of £187,275.[56]

The Trades Union Congress expressed its dissatisfaction with the 'continued postponement of the health centre programme' at its annual conference in 1949. It passed a resolution pressing the government 'to sanction and arrange for the building of at least a hundred health centres forthwith and to announce its determination to complete in ten years the full programme of health centres needed for the whole population'.[57] The Minister of Health replied in correspondence to the TUC that the economic situation made this impossible but, undeterred, the Medical Practitioners' Union moved a resolution at the next TUC annual conference that 'the Minister of Health . . . proceed with the erection of a number of small economical health centres with diagnostic facilities for general practitioners in selected areas',[58] in order that experience might be gained for subsequent expansion of the scheme.

The National Health Service as a whole began operating in a climate of considerable economic stringency following the war, when shortages of capital, labour and materials resulted in fierce competition for the right to build. In retrospect the fact that a nationwide network of centres remained a statement of intent during this early period seems unsurprising. Although a duty had been placed upon authorities to provide centres, the whole scheme was experimental and, as such, was unlikely to be accorded high priority when pressure to build houses, schools and hospitals was so great.

---

[54] BMA, *Council Interim Report on Health Centres*, July 1948, p. 12.
[55] *Local Government Chronicle*, no. 4054, 26 Aug., 1944, p. 513; no. 4180, 25 Jan., 1947, p. 86; and no. 4291, 26 Mar., 1949, p. 293.
[56] *Local Government Chronicle*, no. 4291, *ibid.*
[57] TUC, *Annual Report 1949*, General Council Report, pp. 498–500.
[58] TUC, *Annual Report 1950*, Resolutions List, p. 585.

The results of this slow start were unfortunate since there is some evidence to show that many of those involved in planning centres at a local level – both GPs and health authorities – were interested in the potential afforded by this new machinery. In the subsequent years, however, initial enthusiasm waned as the difficulties for both central and local government became apparent.

III THE 'FAILURE' OF THE POLICY: 1951-63

By 1963 only eighteen health centres had been purpose built in England and Wales, four by county councils, eleven by county boroughs[59] and three by London boroughs. Most of these were located in urban areas but only one, Peterlee, was built in a New Town.[60] They were developed in roughly equal numbers by Labour- and Conservative-controlled councils. Since the execution of the health centre policy relied on the decisions of both central and local groups, factors affecting these two sectors will be discussed in turn.

Centralized policy

Government policy throughout this period remained remarkably uniform; the health centre programme was to be restricted to the creation of a small number of units only. In 1951 a Conservative government was returned to power. The following year the new Minister of Health, Mr Macleod, announced in the Commons that any general expansion of health centres would be impracticable due to the shortage of building resources.[61] Throughout the fifties the limitations on capital expenditure coupled with the need to retain the experimental nature of the scheme were offered as explanations of the policy adopted. The annual report of the Ministry of Health for 1954 gave the standard reasons. 'The amount of money available for capital work in the health service is still severely limited and the few new health centres which are being provided are of very different types and are regarded as being experimental. For some time ahead the Minister believes that the building of a health centre is likely to be justified only where a largely new population needs to be provided with health services . . . The Minister remains willing to consider proposals for economically built health centres in

[59] Including one municipal borough and one urban district with delegated health authority powers.
[60] For a useful article on the numbers and characteristics of health centres built up to mid-1969 see Curwen, M. and Brookes, B., 'Health Centres: Facts and Figures', *Lancet*, ii, 1969, p. 945.
[61] *H. C. Deb.*, vol. 502, col. 212.

these circumstances.'[62] Subsequent statements indicated that the policy remained unchanged.[63] In its preamble to the Health and Welfare Plans of 1963, the ministry announced that 'the circumstances which now justify [health centre] provision do not arise frequently; there must be a local need for new premises, coinciding with a keen desire on the part of both local health authority and general practitioner to develop this particular form of co-operation'.[64]

The reasons for limiting the health centre programme consistently for twelve years are varied but undoubtedly the most important factor, especially during the early years, was the limitation on capital expenditure. The rate of capital formation within the health services as a whole suffered in comparison with building in other sectors of the social services. Between 1949 and 1959 local authority capital expenditure on housing fluctuated between £228m and £399m; expenditure on education and child care rose steadily from £38m to £123m while expenditure on local authority health services remained at £3m, rising only to £4m in 1959.[65] It was not until the sixties that capital expenditure on local health services began to rise (from £5m in 1960 to £14m in 1967).[66] It is clear that health centres fell within a group of services not accorded high priority at this time.

Although the overall economic situation gradually improved during the early fifties, considerable anxiety was expressed concerning the costs of the National Health Service in general. Partly as a result of under estimation of future expenditure before the service was introduced, a ceiling beyond which expenditure was forbidden to rise was imposed in 1950. It was raised in 1951 and the total Health Service budget was kept within these limits until 1954–5. This general cost constraint, which in part arose from the increased defence expenditure associated with the Korean war, had important repercussions on the health centre scheme. In 1953 the Guillebaud committee was established to examine the costs of the National Health Service.[67] Its report, published in 1956, noted that the great majority of those giving evidence to the committee had taken the line that centres must for some time remain in the experimental phase and that group practices provided 'some at least, of the benefits of a

[62] Ministry of Health, *Annual Report for the Year Ended 31 Dec., 1954*, p. 105.

[63] *H. C. Deb.*, vol. 541, cols. 1641–2. *H. C. Deb.*, vol. 601, col. 418. *H. C. Deb.*, vol. 626, cols. 964–5.

[64] Ministry of Health, *Health and Welfare: the Development of Community Care*, Cmnd. 1973, 1963, p. 11.

[65] Central Statistical Office, *National Income and Expenditure*, 1960, p. 38.

[66] CSO, *National Income and Expenditure*, 1968, p. 57.

[67] *The Report of the Committee of Enquiry into the Cost of the National Health Service* (Guillebaud), Cmd. 9663, 1956.

health centre at a much lower cost'.[68] The following year an announcement was made in the Commons on behalf of the Minister to the effect that he accepted the committee's recommendation that health centres should remain experimental.[69]

Apart from the financial reasons for a 'go slow' on centres, the ministry was also constantly aware of the BMA's views on the subject. In 1948 the Association stressed the need to proceed with caution and adopt an experimental approach.[70] This remained its opinion throughout the fifties.[71] In September 1959, when the Medical Practitioners' Union representative on the General Medical Services Committee of the BMA pressed the committee to clarify its views on health centre planning the chairman stated that its current policy was that health centres should be provided on an experimental basis only.[72] The Association's strategy was twofold: to ensure that general practitioners practising from centres obtained favourable terms of service and to protect those doctors working in close proximity to health centres. During 1950–1 the Association was engaged in lengthy negotiations with the London County Council over the form of the contract between the authority and the Executive Council and other aspects of the arrangements at the Woodberry Down health centre. In 1959 the BMA complained to the Minister that inadequate consultation was taking place with GPs before the plans were finalized.

It is important to see the implementation of the health centre proposals within the context of the Ministry of Health's approach towards local authority planning generally. Griffith discusses the department's traditionally *laissez-faire* attitude towards the local authorities at some length.[73] With regard to health centres, it was certainly clear that it adopted a non-interventionist role; the extent of its influence on the development of the scheme being the approval or otherwise of the plans submitted for loan sanction and the rather haphazard dissemination of information by the department's medical officers. Its approach was summarized by Sir George Godber, the Deputy Chief Medical Officer to the Ministry of Health. 'It would not be right', he argued, 'to formulate a plan for the development of general practice centrally and then impose it ... The function of planning is to provide outside aids to the extent that they may be desired, and to make sure that the other parts of the health service

[68] *Guillebaud Report, ibid*, p. 207.

[69] *H. C. Deb.*, vol. 564, col. 4.

[70] BMA, *Interim Report on Health Centres, op. cit.*

[71] The Local Medical Committee for the County of London took a different viewpoint. This is discussed on p. 295.

[72] *British Medical Journal*, Supplement, ii, 26 Sept., 1959, p. 101.

[73] Griffith, J. A. G., *Central Departments and Local Authorities*, Allen & Unwin, 1966, pp. 488–500.

292 The Case Studies

are planned for their proper supporting role; in fact, to give general practice the best possible conditions for evolution.'[74] In July 1960 a spokesman for the Ministry of Health made it quite clear that the ministry's role was essentially passive. In answer to a parliamentary question, he replied: 'In recent years loan sanction has been given in all cases where there has been local agreement to a health centre project but the initiative in these matters must come from the locality concerned.'[75]

Local decisions

The local planning of health centres depended upon the co-operation of two groups; health authorities and GPs. We will consider each in turn. As has already been noted, it was impossible for the health authority to proceed with plans at a local level unless ministerial sanction for each project was obtained. There is some evidence to suggest that in the early years of the scheme local health authorities had a considerable interest in planning centres; by the end of 1951, as we have said, seventy projects were known to the Ministry. However, continual discouragement to the submission of plans for loan sanction contributed to a decline in enthusiasm at the local level. The Ministry's *laissez-faire* attitude induced some local authorities, including the LCC, to complain of the lack of encouragement given by the department during the fifties.[76]

The task of planning and establishing centres at a local level was not easy. Their provision was a costly undertaking for any authority. The estimated cost of a health centre receiving sanction in 1954 was £36,000 in comparison with an average estimated cost of £10,000 for a maternity and child welfare clinic during the same year.[77] By 1958 the average estimated cost of health centres receiving sanction was £24,500 while for clinics it was £13,500. Despite a decline in the capital cost of centres during the fifties they still represented a sizeable investment for the local authority.

Current costs too placed a burden on the authority since, in addition to paying for their own staff working in the centre, many had to subsidise the rents of the general practitioners. The ministry's guidance on this aspect of the planning process was very general: 'the charge to be made to general practitioners should be a reasonable computation of what it would cost the doctors to provide facilities for practice from

[74] Godber, Sir G., 'Health Services, Past, Present and Future', *Lancet*, ii, 1958, pp. 2–6. Sir George became Chief Medical Officer in 1960.
[75] *H. C. Deb.*, vol. 626, cols 964–5.
[76] See London County Council, *Development of Health and Welfare Services, 1962–1972*, p. 5.
[77] Ministry of Health, *Annual Report for the Year Ended 31 Dec., 1958*, p. 198.

their own surgeries in the neighbourhood of the centre'.[78] In many cases general practitioners had refused to join any scheme unless a low rent, usually a non-economic rent, was charged. Health centres were used as branch surgeries by many doctors who argued that rent had to be paid for a main surgery elsewhere and that therefore they could not afford high centre rents in addition. Although local authority subsidies to general practitioners working at centres were not very great in terms of the total health authority budget, the principle involved was important. Any widespread expansion of centres based on this financial arrangement would have been costly for the authorities.

Apart from the expense involved, the practical difficulties of planning and establishing centres were considerable. Three of these were basic. First, the acquisition of suitable sites was not easy, especially in densely populated areas. In October 1951, the Ministry of Health informed the County Medical Officer of Kent that the acquisition of land for health centre building could only be sanctioned for the immediate erection of centres.[79] During the early years of the scheme some authorities attempted to retain sites for future centres but were eventually forced to relinquish them.[80] The LCC complained that its health centre policy had been retarded by the Minister's refusal to allow it to reserve sites.[81] Second, the local medical officer had to mastermind an extremely complex planning process necessitating the co-operation of several groups hitherto unused to working together. There was the Executive Council[82] which entered into the health centre contract with the local authority on behalf of the doctors involved; the Local Medical Committee[83] which represented all the GPs in the area; the doctors themselves as well as members of other local authority departments such as planners, architects, surveyors and treasurers. Lastly, the most intractable difficulty faced by authorities was that of persuading general practitioners to enter health centre practice. The *Lancet* carried a number of articles during the early fifties discussing the family doctors' reluctance to co-operate in the scheme. This problem was especially important since without the full co-operation of general practitioners

[78] Ministry of Health, NHS Act 1946, *Local Health Authorities' functions and financial arrangements in relation to health centres* (Sect. 21), p. 3.

[79] *County Councils' Association Gazette,* vol. XLIV, no. 10, Oct., 1951, p. 183.

[80] *Medical Officer,* vol. 119, 1 Mar., 1968. In separate articles the Medical Officers of Oxford and Bristol commented upon this problem.

[81] LCC, *Development of Health and Welfare Services, op. cit.*

[82] Under the National Health Service structure obtaining to April 1974, the Executive Councils administered medical, dental, ophthalmic and pharmaceutical services in areas corresponding to the major local authority boundaries.

[83] Under the National Health Service Act 1946 the Minister of Health may designate any committee a Local Medical Committee if it is recognized to represent local practitioners. Many of the committees are, in practice, run by local divisions of the BMA.

in the area, the Minister would not sanction local plans. The Medical Officer for Staffordshire expressed his regret at being unable to continue planning for lack of sufficient support.[84] A small number of authorities such as Oxford, Bristol and Hampshire attempted to win the confidence of their general practitioners by starting attachment or liaison schemes,[85] but before 1960 less than twenty were actually operating. By 1964 they numbered 414.[86] In negotiating contracts for the early centres great difficulty was experienced in reaching agreement over rents. As already mentioned, the outcome in many cases was an undertaking on the part of the local authority to subsidise the general practitioners but the debate could take months, sometimes years (as in the case of Woodberry Down) to settle. Moreover, objections to this rent subsidy were sometimes raised by other general practitioners in the area concerned.

The health authorities clearly found it difficult to negotiate with GPs. It is interesting therefore to examine the views of the latter a little more closely since these help to explain why so few centres were built. It is fairly easy to understand some of the reservations held by general practitioners concerning health centres. Many were undoubtedly influenced by the antagonistic views of the British Medical Association. Their reluctance was reinforced by the experimental nature of the scheme. Clearly, if a scheme is labelled experimental this implies risks for the participants. Furthermore, it is important to remember that the growth of partnerships and group practices is largely a post-war phenomenon. Most general practitioners were unused to working in close contact with their medical colleagues let alone with the local health authority officials, towards whom many were hostile, and with para-medical staff whose potential value they did not appreciate. In 1956 an inquiry into Health Visiting declared that GPs were quite clearly insufficiently aware of the functions of health visitors.[87] Two years previously a committee of the Central Health Services Council examining general practice compared health centres with group practices and concluded: 'Many of the advantages

---

[84] 'Obstructions to Health Centre Development', *Medical Officer*, vol. 96, 21 Dec., 1956, p. 383. Information in the *Annual Report of the CMO for Staffordshire.*

[85] Precise details vary from area to area but usually in an *attachment* scheme the health visitor (district nurse or midwife) is responsible for all the patients on the lists of specified GPs. In a *liaison* scheme the HV is responsible both for a geographical district and for the patients on the list of a specified GP. Where patients live outside the district but within the local authority boundary the health visitor is responsible for liaison with the GP.

[86] Anderson, J. A. D. and Draper, P. A., 'The Attachment of Local Authority Staff to General Practice', *Medical Officer*, vol. 117, 3 Mar., 1967, p. 113.

[87] Ministry of Health Working Party, *An Enquiry into Health Visiting* (Jameson Report), 1956, pp. 113–15 and 122–3.

both to doctors and to patients which have in the past been urged in favour of health centres, may, it is hoped, be more easily secured through the evolution of group practices consisting of doctors who have chosen to work together in communal premises which they own themselves.'[88] The committee pointed out several of the objections voiced by doctors. GPs doubted whether patients would follow them if the location of their practice was moved. They feared becoming too dependent on centres and felt that relationships with colleagues might become strained. In addition, they suggested that once accustomed to a centre their patients would be unwilling to follow them if they wished to withdraw.

Experiments and alternatives

Two further factors affected the decisions taken by the ministry, the local authorities and the general practitioners. These were, first, the results of experimental schemes conducted during the fifties and, second, the existence of alternative solutions to the problems it was originally hoped health centres would alleviate. Each must be examined if we are to understand the sluggish development of health centres up to 1963.

Despite the emphasis placed on the experimental nature of the health centre scheme throughout the fifties few efforts were made to evaluate and compare those which were established. The first systematic attempt was made in 1956 by the Local Medical Committee for the County of London. Its report on four health centres and one group practice was based on a comparison of the siting, building, accommodation, ancillary help, extent of partnership, use as branch surgeries, local authority services and costs, both capital and current. It concluded that group practices 'gave a more flexible approach and much less costly results', but regretted that the local health authority was excluded from the picture under these arrangements. 'We think this is a most unfortunate result and we hold that there is an urgent need for the erection in London of other health centres of modest proportions.'[89] Reaction to the early centres was not always so favourable. For example, following the opening of Bristol's first centre, one councillor questioned whether in the light of experience at the *William Budd*, health centres were really necessary. Diagnostic clinics would be so much cheaper to run.[90] In 1960 a small survey of health centres and group practices was under-

[88] Central Health Services Council, *Report of the Committee on General Practice within the NHS* (Cohen Report), 1954, p. 21.

[89] Local Medical Committee for the County of London, *Report on Health Centres*, 1956, p. 11.

[90] 'Are Health Centres Necessary?', *Local Government Chronicle*, no. 4542, 16 Jan., 1954, p. 73.

taken by two medical officers at the Ministry of Health.[91] The authors maintained that group practices should be encouraged since 'this type of organization can provide a full range of extra-hospital care',[92] but that in financial terms there need be little difference between the two types of organization and that 'a modest programme of health centres construction should be maintained'. Centres had the advantage of providing the conditions for experimental developments and of offering single handed practitioners help in the form of ancillary aid and contact with colleagues.[93] The most comprehensive study of the centres built before 1960 was made by the Medical Practitioners' Union. A questionnaire was sent to all the Section 21 centres operating in 1959 and to diagnostic centres, group practices and teaching units. The study concluded that 'health centres have failed to fulfil the role envisaged for them in the Planning Commission report, the White Paper or the Act itself. The answer lies in a large number of factors – financial, technical, administrative and psychological . . . Both the Ministry of Health and the profession need to develop a new and positive approach.'[94]

The attitude of the Ministry of Health towards pursuing an experimental policy appears to have hardened by the early sixties. Its annual report for 1961 stated that 'in practice those health centres established under Section 21 of the Act have been designed primarily to associate general medical practice with the maternity and child welfare service and the school health service. Viewed as an experiment in this limited field, they have shown that they do not always completely solve the problems of integration'.[95] Between 1949 and 1963 only fifteen per cent of doctors practising in health centres used the centre as their main surgery.[96] Added to this, in many cases the design militated against close working relationships. In eight of the centres built before 1961 all the firms of GPs had separate suites and in only four were they shared with the local authority staff.[97] The failure to integrate the personnel of health centres was an obvious defect of the early centres. Another was the size of the capital costs involved. We have already noted that the cost of centres in compari-

[91] Lees, W. and Carr, T. E. A., *Survey of Health Centres and Group Practices–1960,* Ministry of Health, 1961, unpublished.

[92] *Ibid.,* p. 29.

[93] *Ibid.*

[94] Medical Practitioners' Union, *Health Centre Report,* 1960, compiled and written by J. Sluglett.

[95] Ministry of Health, *Annual Report for the Year Ended 31 Dec., 1961,* p. 88.

[96] Brookes, B. and Curwen, M., *Lancet, op. cit.*

[97] Medical Practitioners' Union Handbook, *Design for Family Doctoring,* 1967, p. 77.

son with that of local authority clinics was high, but the centres built in the early fifties were especially expensive.

Table 7

TOTAL CAPITAL COST OF CENTRES OPENED, 1952–6*

Centre	Year Opened	Total Capital Cost (£)
Woodberry Down (Hackney)	1952	198,000
William Budd (Bristol)	1952	21,340
Harold Hill (Havering)	1954	45,000
Cheltenham (Gloucestershire)	1955	26,500
Aveley (Essex)	1955	41,441
Alderman Jack Cohen (Sunderland)	1956	71,000

* Medical Practitioners' Union Handbook, *Design for Family Doctoring*, 1967, p. 77. The table includes new buildings only.

Another reason given for regarding the early 'experimental' centres as unsatisfactory was that the size and design of many resulted in forbidding, unfriendly buildings similar to small hospitals and contrasting unfavourably with the image of the cosy, comfortable premises of the traditional family doctor.

Not only was the success of the early experimental schemes unproven but during the fifties *alternative* means of facilitating close working relationships both between general practitioners themselves and between GPs and local authority staff were developed, the most important of these being the expansion of group practices. In 1950 the Central Health Services Council report on health centres saw the encouragement of group practices as an interim measure 'to obtain immediately some of the advantages which health centres are intended to provide and to ensure as far as possible that no new obstacles to their satisfactory introduction are created'.[98] A Group Practice Loan Scheme was announced in 1953 and began operating two years later when interest-free loans became available from the ministry for partnerships of three doctors or more. Financial assistance was provided in order to reduce the burden of raising capital to build group practice premises. From December 1955 to May 1967, when the scheme ended, 756 applications for loans were approved and the total financial assistance amounted to some £4¾ million. Thus general practitioners had means by which they could work together in the same

[98] Central Health Services Council, *Report for the Period Ended 31 Dec., 1950*.

premises, without taking the risks many of them believed to be inherent in entering local authority-owned centres.

Several official committees preferred the group practice to the health centre, seeing the former as the predominant type of general practice organization in the future. We have already noted that these views were expressed in the Cohen[99] and the Guillebaud[100] reports. In 1963 a further document prepared for the Central Health Services Council concluded 'that there remained much to explore in developing the advantages of group practices and their premises'. It seemed to them 'improbable that health centres would develop the full potential originally envisaged by, for example, Lord Dawson of Penn ...'[101] While general practitioners could avoid the health centre by establishing group practices, local authorities could bypass the scheme if they wished by continuing to build clinics for their own staff, while trying at the same time to forge closer links with the GPs through attachments.[102] Another possibility was to use general powers under housing legislation[103] to provide local authority-built housing incorporating surgeries in areas where an extension of medical facilities was necessary. Although a few authorities used these powers to provide both local authority and general practice accommodation, most schemes involved the latter only.

Summary
The development of health centres constitutes an evolutionary policy; that is, one which is formed by the aggregation of a series of day-to-day decisions. The extent and nature of the scheme depended on both central and local government but while loan sanction was very difficult to obtain, clearly the former played the major role. The most important reason given by the ministry for limiting the scheme was the need to restrict capital expenditure but the question then arises as to why centres were not given higher priority. This is partially answered by the fact that capital expenditure on the health services in general rose more slowly than that in other parts of the social services; the entire health service suffered from an excessive cost consciousness in its early years. In addition health centres were expensive units

[99] *Report of the Committee on General Practice within the NHS, op. cit.*

[100] *Report of the Committee of Enquiry into the Cost of the NHS, op. cit.*

[101] Central Health Services Council, report by a sub-committee of the Standing Medical Advisory Committee, *The Field of Work of the Family Doctor* (Gillie), 1963, p. 32.

[102] See p. 301.

[103] Housing Act 1957, Section 93, empowered a local authority with the consent of the Minister of Housing and Local Government to provide and maintain in connection with housing accommodation ... buildings or land which in the opinion of the Minister will serve a beneficial purpose in connection with the requirements of the persons for whom the housing accommodation is provided.

to build in comparison with the average local authority clinic. The further problem of relationships between general practitioners and local authorities was recognized by the ministry when it stated quite specifically that plans would only be passed if there was a willingness on the part of *both* groups to establish a centre.

At the local level, the knowledge that loan sanction was difficult to obtain discouraged many authorities from beginning to plan, and those which attempted to do so faced great problems since the planning process involved securing the co-operation of groups unused to working together. Achieving such co-operation was often a difficult task and fell primarily upon the medical officers of health. The local authority thus needed to be committed to the development of health centres and their MOH required to have the confidence of general practitioners, plus considerable negotiating skill. To add to the obstacles involved the early experimental centres provided no encouragement to those wishing to begin a health centre programme.

Until the early sixties therefore a number of pieces had to be fitted together in a complicated jigsaw if a health centre was to be established. Most authorities preferred to adopt 'alternatives' which were cheaper, easier to implement and solved, at least in part, the problems health centres were intended to overcome.

IV EXPANSION OF THE HEALTH CENTRE SCHEME: 1963–70

As late as 1963, eighteen years after the National Health Service Act made provision for a nationwide network of centres, there was still no firm central government commitment to the health centre scheme and it was a further two years before such support was forthcoming. In February 1966 the Minister of Health stated in the Commons that he was 'anxious to encourage the development of health centre practice'.[104] The first sign of renewed interest, however, came not from the Minister but from local authorities in 1963 with the publication of their Health and Welfare Plans.[105] In total the local authorities proposed to increase the number of centres from seventeen to fifty-five by 1972. Three years later, in the plans for the 1966–7 period, they indicated their intention to provide nearly three hundred centres by March 1976.[106]

[104] *H. C. Deb.*, vol. 724, col. 158.
[105] Ministry of Health, *Health and Welfare: the Development of Community Care*, Cmnd. 1973, 1963.
[106] Ministry of Health, *Health and Welfare, Revision to 1975–6*, Cmnd. 3022, 1964.

The re-emergence of interest in health centres came largely from three sources: the difficulties faced by local authorities; problems within general practice; and an increasing willingness on the part of the government to reconsider the possibility of a widespread development of centres. In many respects the problems faced by general practitioners and local authorities were inter-linked. Deficiencies resulting from the tripartite structure of the National Health Service affected both groups. The Porritt Committee Report, published in 1962, maintained that the separation of social medicine, family doctoring and hospital practice into three distinct administrative compartments prevented them from operating as a team.[107] One of their recommendations to improve the situation was to extend the number of group practices with attachment schemes and to continue experimenting with different types of health centre. As the main reason for introducing health centres in 1946 was to provide a link between the three parts of the Service, it is scarcely surprising that the idea should be resurrected when co-ordination was felt to be becoming increasingly difficult.

The most important single factor behind the decision of some local authorities to reconsider the potential of the health centre was the policy of community care adopted by the Ministry of Health in the late fifties. The costs of institutional care in general were rising rapidly. Within the Health Service the increasing expenditure on hospital in-patient treatment was causing considerable concern. At the same time evidence on the detrimental effects of prolonged institutionalization was accumulating.[108] In 1962 the ministry published a Hospital Plan in which it was stated that the total number of hospital beds was to be reduced in favour of a policy of care within the community 'for all those who do not require the special types of diagnosis and treatment which only a hospital can provide'.[109] It was clear that if such a policy was to be pursued the existing community health and welfare services would require strengthening and to this end local authorities were asked by the Minister to submit their plans for the following ten years. It was in reply to this request that proposals for fifty-two centres by 1972 were made. The extension of community care offered opportunities to those medical officers who had been interested in the concept for many years but who had been frustrated by the difficulties of obtaining loan sanction for their proposals.[110] It must be remembered, how-

[107] *A Review of the Medical Services in Great Britain*, Report of a committee established jointly by the BMA and Royal Colleges, Social Assay, 1962.

[108] See for example, Barton, R. W., *Institutional Neurosis*, Wright, 1959, and Goffman, E., *Asylums*, Doubleday, 1961.

[109] Ministry of Health, *A Hospital Plan for England and Wales*, Cmnd. 1604, 1962, p. 9.

[110] For example, the medical officers of Bristol, Oxford, Hampshire and the West Riding of Yorkshire.

ever, that the ten-year plans submitted by the authorities were not binding. The preamble to the plans stressed that they were not definitive but rather '... a basis for continuing consultation'.[111]

Despite incentives to reconsider centres, local authorities still faced many of the problems which had arisen when planning centres in the fifties. The capital cost of such projects remained high; much higher than that of building further clinics. Moreover, medical officers realized that it would still be necessary in many cases to subsidise the general practitioners working from centres, that this would impose a financial burden on the health authority and that it would provoke complaints on grounds of inequity from other GPs in the vicinity. It was still necessary to bring together a large number of local groups in the planning process and the major difficulty continued to be that of persuading GPs that it would be in their interests both professionally and sometimes economically to co-operate with the health authority. However, the barriers to smooth working relationships between the GPs and the staff of the MOH were very slowly being broken down.

By the early sixties there was evidence that some groups were willing to co-operate with local health authority staff. At the end of 1964, some seven hundred local authority nurses, midwives and health visitors were reported to be working in general practice attachment schemes in England and Wales.[112] A small survey carried out in 1963 found that fifty-four per cent of GPs would accept district nurses and midwives attached to their practices but only twenty-five per cent were in favour of including health visitors as well. Another study, conducted in 1964, found sixty-eight per cent in the first category and forty-seven per cent willing to accept health visitors.[113] Although there was some evidence of changing attitudes on the part of GPs, criticisms of their isolationist approach remained. In 1966 the Queen's Institute of District Nursing commented that most GPs remained ignorant of the qualifications and functions of a district nurse.[114]

A number of factors contributed to the increasing willingness of some GPs to consider health centre practice rather than the major alternative – group practice. Financial reasons were the most import ant. First, there was the problem of current expenses. The system of reimbursement for practice expenses obtaining until 1966 was such

[111] *Health and Welfare Plans*, 1963, *op. cit.*, p. 48.
[112] Anderson, J. A. D. and Draper, P. A., *Medical Officer, op. cit.*, p. 113. The figure of seven hundred represented 3·4 per cent of these groups of local authority staff.
[113] Both surveys are published in *Reports from General Practice II*, 'Present State and Future Needs', Royal College of General Practitioners, 1965, p. 42.
[114] Queen's Institute of District Nursing, *Feeling the Pulse*, 1966.

that there was little incentive for practitioners to improve their facilities. The Ninth Review Body on Doctors' and Dentists' Remuneration pointed out the disadvantages of the 'pool' system, as it was known. 'Though the pool [fund] is credited with the estimated total practice expenses of the profession, the distribution of the total to individual doctors is determined primarily by the size of lists. While the size of list no doubt has a considerable influence on the amount of practice expenses incurred, no attempt has hitherto been made to relate what the individual doctor received to his actual expenses.'[115] This meant that GPs suffered personal financial loss if they provided facilities which were more expensive than those provided by other GPs with similar sized lists. The single-handed doctor was at a particular disadvantage since there was no scope for sharing facilities and costs. In a health centre on the other hand the provision of equipment and staffing was the responsibility of the local authority and the rent paid by the doctors for the use of these facilities was, in many cases, subsidised.

Second, for many GPs the position regarding capital expenditure was unsatisfactory. The provision of group practice premises required heavy capital expenditure and such costs were beyond the resources of many, especially the newly qualified. For those who could raise the necessary capital, practice premises were not a particularly attractive investment. They do not appreciate in value at the same rate as most other property since premises of such a specialized nature are not in great demand. The interest-free loan scheme was of limited use; in total only 756 of the 1,310 applications were approved,[116] a ceiling was placed on the amount which each doctor could borrow and loans were not available for partnerships of two. In 1967 this scheme was superseded by the General Practice Finance Corporation but it also imposes limitations on the size of the loan and the number of principals who can benefit (three to six). Thus, despite considerable growth in the number of group practices the financial barriers to their establishment remained insuperable for many GPs. Health centres, on the other hand, offered the prospect of improved facilities without heavy capital expenditure.

For some GPs practical problems were (and often still are) the most important reason for accepting health centre practice. Slum clearance in urban areas often presented some established practices with the need to find alternative premises. In such areas the acquisition of sites was often difficult and in consequence general practitioners found it necessary to approach the local authority with a view to entry into a health centre. Another problem was that of finding

[115] *Review Body on Doctors' and Dentists' Remuneration, Fifth Report,* Cmnd. 2585, 1965.
[116] Statistics provided by the Department of Health and Social Security.

replacements for general practitioners who left practices in less attractive parts of the country. A Ministry of Health Working Party on General Practice commented in 1964[117] on the great difficulty encountered in filling vacancies in underdoctored areas. The permanent loss of a member of a group practice places a greater burden of expenditure on the remaining doctors, whereas within a centre the responsibility for finding replacements and for paying the proportion of expenses of the missing partner becomes that of the Executive Council.

The discussion so far has concentrated on the local aspects of health centre development. Yet it must be remembered that local enthusiasm is wasted without the approval of the Minister of Health through the loan sanctioning process. In the Autumn of 1964 a Labour government was returned to power and from the beginning of its term of office it faced severe problems within the health and welfare field. First, it inherited a policy of community care which was in need of translation from theory to action. It was clear that the new government was in favour of pursuing the policy. The Labour Party Manifesto produced for the 1964 election promised to give 'new impetus' to the community care services.[118] The Minister of Health asked local authorities to make revisions to their ten-year plans for health and welfare. Second, the incoming government was almost immediately faced with the 'Doctors Crisis' as it later became known. Following what was considered by the BMA to be an unsatisfactory pay award by the Review Body on Doctors' and Dentists' Remuneration in 1963, a further claim was submitted by the Association in 1964. The Review Body's decision, made public in January 1965, created great discontent amongst the officials of the BMA and also amongst rank and file members. A request from the association to its members asking for undated resignations resulted in 18,000 being submitted within three weeks from a total of 22,000 GPs. Faced with this clear demonstration of dissatisfaction, the Minister of Health agreed to negotiate with the BMA and discussions focusing upon the 'Doctors' Charter' drawn up by the Association began. Amongst the issues raised were the nature of the premises required by GPs, the extent of diagnostic aids and the ancillary help needed. Thus the combined effect of the government's wish to improve local authority health and welfare services plus pressure from the BMA backed by its members resulted in a general reappraisal of the possibilities afforded by health centre practice. Since the thirties the Labour Party and the 1945 Labour government had, in theory, supported the health centre concept; in the mid-sixties the scheme could be seen as not only desirable

[117] Ministry of Health, *Working Party on General Practice*, July 1964.
[118] *Let's Go with Labour for a New Britain*, Labour Party, 1963.

but also uniquely fitted to provide at least a partial solution to the growing problems faced by health authorities and general practitioners.

The extent to which health centre building had risen in priority became clearer when in July 1965 a tough economic package was announced. It required the postponement for six months of many capital projects involving public expenditure. A similar request for cuts in expenditure on local authority building had been made in 1956[119] and this had resulted in the deferment of several health centre projects but by 1965 centres were listed as 'urgently needed' and thus exempted from the requirement to postpone building.[120]

While negotiations over the Doctor's Charter were taking place the overall system of remuneration for GPs was being considered by their Review Body and one of the results of these deliberations was a change in the financial framework within which health centres operated. As far as the development of health centres was concerned the most important aspect of the revised arrangements which were introduced in 1967 to replace the 'pool' system[121] was the provision whereby reimbursement for the practice expenses of GPs was paid directly to the doctor by the Executive Council. In most cases reimbursement was made for the total amount of rent and rates, together with a proportion of expenditure on auxiliary staff. It is a matter for debate whether these changes have increased the incentives for general practitioners to consider health centres since the direct payments apply to all GPs regardless of how the practice is organized. Within a centre doctors still have to pay for a proportion of the expenditure on auxiliary staff, plus their share of the heating, lighting and services. The revisions regarding reimbursement were, however, much more important for the local authorities, for GPs could now be charged an economic rent since they could recover a large proportion from the Executive Council. Thus the subsidisation of GPs working in centres could be avoided. This certainly removed one possible disincentive for a local authority to provide health centres.

In the above discussion it has been argued that problems within the local health and welfare services plus those facing general practice created a more favourable environment within which to consider the health centre idea than had existed throughout the fifties. The Ministry of Health, which had consistently refused to encourage centres while local enthusiasm seemed lacking, reacted positively to the interest shown by health authorities. Commenting in 1966 on the Health and Welfare Plans Revision for 1966–76, in which nearly three hundred

[119] The implications for local health authorities were explained in the Ministry of Health Circular 3/56.
[120] Ministry of Health Circular, 20/65.
[121] See p. 302.

centres were proposed by March 1976, the ministry stated that it represented 'a remarkable and welcome rate of development'.[122] The same year, the Chief Medical Officer to the Ministry of Health publicly put his stamp of approval on the expansion of the scheme. 'The interest in health centres which had lain dormant for many years has been recently reawakened for they offer, *as no other project could offer* [our italics], a means of providing groups of doctors with suitable premises adequately staffed, with ancillary help and with the opportunity to work in the closest co-operation with the professional staffs of the local health authorities.'[123]

Thenceforth the ministry began to give more general encouragement to health centre building. In April 1967 a circular was sent to health authorities because it was thought that they might 'welcome further guidance on this subject'.[124] It gave general information on the new financial arrangements and planning procedures but omitted any detailed advice. Later that year the ministry initiated a conference, to be held annually, for the GPs practising at centres in order to disseminate information on the subject.[125] The following year a subcommittee of the Standing Medical Advisory Committee to the Ministry of Health was established to examine the organization of general practice in detail; a brief which included the consideration of health centres. An interim report of a Design Guide on Health Centres was produced[126] in 1967 and has now been published in its final form.[127] In addition to such guidelines the central department has begun the systematic evaluation of health centres. Since 1968 it has examined the centres opened each year and produced a report in order to assess different types of design.

Increasing encouragement from the ministry has been part of a general 'snowballing effect'. Whereas the early experimental centres adversely affected attitudes towards the scheme's expansion the new wave of centres built from 1964 onwards attracted much interest in local authority and general practice circles. A few projects such as the Hythe Health Centre in Hampshire[128] and the St George Centre in Bristol[129] became showpieces, inundated with requests for visits

[122] *Health and Welfare: the Development of Community Care, Revision to 1975–6, op. cit.*, p. 6.

[123] *Annual Report of the Chief Medical Officer to the Ministry of Health*, 1966, p. 206.

[124] Ministry of Health, Circular 7/67.

[125] Reported in *British Medical Journal*, iv, 30 Dec., 1967, p. 800.

[126] Ministry of Health, Circular 7/67.

[127] Department of Health and Social Security, *Health Centres: A Design Guide*, 1970.

[128] 'Hythe Health Centre', *British Medical Journal*, ii, 3 July, 1965, p. 42. 'Integration in Hampshire', *Medical World*, vol. 104, no. 3, Mar. 1966, p. 10.

[129] 'Oldest and Newest – Bristol', *British Medical Journal*, i, 25 June, 1965, p. 1662. 'Big City Centre', *Medical World, ibid.*, p. 7.

and publicized widely in the medical press. In 1965 alone the *British Medical Journal* carried fifteen articles about health centres. As more were planned and built the medical officer's rather complex task of bringing together the groups involved became easier and more familiar. For example, the necessity of including the GPs and the Executive Council in the planning procedure from the very beginning in order to avoid friction at a latter stage was recognized. It had been a prerequisite often overlooked in the development of earlier schemes.

Scant reference has been made to the views of professional and other organizations. This is because, apart from the BMA, they have played only a very minor role. The BMA, which had appeared hostile to the idea of centres during the fifties and had counselled that a policy of experimentation should be adopted, continued to suggest that GPs should be wary of working from centres. As late as 1967 the Association was still suggesting that an experimental approach was necessary and warned GPs not to begin practising from centres until the terms of tenancy agreements were clarified. Doctors were asked to submit their contracts to the legal advisers of the BMA for official scrutiny. In May the chairman of the General Medical Services Committee of the BMA explained that their policy was to encourage doctors, as far as possible, to buy their own premises, but he acknowledged that the demand for centres from the profession was almost insatiable. He concluded: 'I do not see my role to be a King Canute, holding back the waves. But we have a responsibility to those doctors and we will do everything possible in the GMSC to save them from themselves and see that, whatever agreements they reach, they do so with their eyes open.'[130] It appears that despite very strong opposition from their association many general practitioners were willing to take the risk and try health centre practice. The traditional advocates of a nationwide programme of centres, the TUC,[131] the Medical Practitioners' Union[132] (which was one of the major influences on the TUC's health centre policy) and the Socialist Medical Association[133] continued to present their views but there is no evidence that this made any impact on government decisions.

It is important not to overemphasize the results of the changes discussed above. The increased rate of growth of centres was to begin with, very slow; in England and Wales only eight were built in 1966, fourteen in 1967 and thirty-nine in 1968. By the end of 1969, however, 149 were in operation and it appears that the return to power of a Conservative government did not affect the priority given to centres.

[130] *British Medical Journal*, ii, Supplement, 13 May, 1967, p. 90.
[131] TUC, *Congress Report*, 1964, pp. 504–7. TUC, *Congress Report*, 1965, p. 439.
[132] Stated at the MPU, *National Health Centre Conference*, 6–7 May, 1967.
[133] SMA, *The Case for Health Centres*, 1964.

Sir Keith Joseph, the incoming Secretary of State at the Department of Health and Social Security, made a statement to this effect in July 1970 when he forecast that by the end of 1972 there could be as many as three hundred centres in operation, serving four million patients and accommodating 1,600 general practitioners working from main surgeries. In the event this number of centres was reached by the end of 1971.

The nature and extent of health centre development depended upon both central and local decision makers but the relative importance of the actors in the process changed. Whereas the pattern of health centre building during the fifties was largely determined by the ministry, through the regulation of loan sanction, the renewal of interest came initially from some local health departments. Their reconsideration of the health centre concept arose largely from a request by the ministry to strengthen local services in accordance with the policy of community care. At first only a few authorities responded by proposing centres but the interest spread quickly. The general significance of the Health and Welfare Plans should not be overlooked. For the first time the combined intentions of local authorities were published, providing important declarations of local policy. Simultaneously economic and practical problems within general practice – ones which group practice did not adequately solve – were resulting in a greater willingness on the part of some GPs to consider centres. For the medical officer of health these new units could provide a focal point for community medicine and for the GP the problems of acquiring a site, financing and equipping his own surgery, filling vacant medical posts in the practice and providing ancillary help were removed. The health centre could provide, for both groups, solutions to some of their problems and because it was still a vague concept it was possible to apply it to a wide variety of situations.

As the first amongst the new wave of centres were completed, a 'snowballing' effect began to operate. Once health authorities had expressed an interest in planning centres the ministry began to encourage the programme. Moreover, the new centres, unlike their earlier counterparts, were interpreted as successful experiments, thus creating a stimulus to other ventures. By the late sixties the provision of a centre was no longer a pioneering effort involving undue risks for the participants. Here was a general idea which had lain dormant for many years but one which bore re-examination as the functions, finances and practical problems of health department work and general practice changed.

V CONCLUSION

The growth of health centres provides us with an example of an evolutionary policy; a policy which emerged as a result of decisions made by a variety of groups, both central and local, administrative and professional. Many of our social policies are of this type, being the aggregation of numerous small decisions taken sometimes over many years. Several aspects of the health centre study could be tested against other evolutionary policies.

1. The association of the concept with other issues had both positive and negative effects on its progress. In the mid-forties the bracketing of health centres with a *group* of policies accentuated the importance of the former. It is unlikely that a health centre scheme would have been publicly accorded such approval by the Minister of Health if it had not been seen as a part of the National Health Service plan. The tripartite structure of health administration which resulted from several years of difficult negotiation required linking mechanisms; health centres, although untried, were a convenient solution to the problem. However, as only one comparatively small part of a larger scheme they had to compete for priority with other health programmes, and were affected by measures directed at the health service as a whole. Hence, during the fifties, health centres competed for resources with capital building such as clinics and hospitals and suffered the consequences of attempts to limit health expenditure generally. Their subsequent association with a different policy, 'community care', which had become an important catch-phrase by the mid-sixties, enhanced their priority; the recognition of health centres as a solution to some of the problems raised by this approach helps to explain renewed interest in the concept.

2. When the term 'health centre' was first coined it was applied by a variety of groups to significantly different schemes. Despite these differences, the widespread use of the same label created the spurious impression of general agreement over the introduction of a health centre policy. Thus the vagueness of the concept was of some advantage when enacting the policy but the problems of such ambiguity became only too apparent when attempting to plan the early centres.

3. The study demonstrates that the enactment of a policy may prove to be an article of faith rather than a statement of intent. Although the establishment of health centres on a nationwide basis was provided for under the National Health Service Act, for economic and practical reasons implementation on this scale was clearly impossible in the short run. Even before the Act was passed it was apparent that there would be shortages of capital and building materials for some time to come. Similarly, it was clear that general

practitioners and local authority officials were on the whole reluctant to work together.

4. The labelling of a scheme as 'experimental' can affect its progress in several respects. Apart from being particularly vulnerable in times of economic stringency it is perhaps generally easier for policy-makers to delay such programmes since it can reasonably be argued that they are in the process of evaluation. Moreover, interpretation of the success or failure of experiments can seriously affect the future of a whole programme. The early health centres were seen as failures and thus their example discouraged subsequent trials, but the second period of experimentation provided an impetus to expansion since many of the models established in the mid-sixties were interpreted as successful. A further implication of calling a scheme experimental is that it suggests that there are risks for the participants. Many local health authorities and general practitioners were unwilling to take the risks health centre practice in the early years implied. Conversely, the rewards for those who take the risks and succeed are considerable. Health centres such as the Hythe centre in Hampshire and the St George centre in Bristol were extremely valuable advertisements for their respective authorities.

5. The balance of central and local decision-making was an interesting feature of this study. Whilst, for economic and practical reasons, the Ministry of Health was unwilling to sanction many projects, there was little that the few enthusiastic medical officers and general practitioners could do. Thus, the pattern of health centre building was determined primarily by the ministry during the fifties, but the resurrection of the concept was a direct result of decisions taken by individual health authorities spurred on by the need to find ways of strengthening their community service. The ministry, when faced with spontaneous demonstrations of local support, was willing to begin encouraging the scheme itself.

6. The introduction of health centres in the early years of the scheme was undoubtedly seriously affected by the existence of 'alternative' policies. Most general practitioners preferred to try group practice rather than risk co-operating with the local authority; most medical officers were content to continue building clinics. Health centres assumed a new importance only when these alternatives were to some extent discredited, when group practice became impractical and too costly for many family doctors and clinics were seen as inadequate bases for community health teams.

7. This study demonstrated the power of the general practitioner to determine the delivery of his own service. The importance of independent groups of professionals in affecting the outcome of some social policies was clearly underestimated by civil servants in this case. Here was a scheme which depended for its success upon the support

of the general practitioner yet no attempt was made either to gauge the likely reactions of this group or to sell them the idea. It illustrates the reluctance of civil servants to interfere in any positive way with the autonomy of this section of the medical profession. Once antipathy towards health centres was demonstrated by general practitioners, government officials were content to await a change of mind rather than attempt to enforce it.

8. In sharp contrast to the power of the general practitioner was the weakness of *organized* pressure groups; the latter played a relatively unimportant part in affecting the pattern or rate of health centre growth. Those groups which had proposed health centre schemes from the thirties, notably the Socialist Medical Association, the Medical Practitioners' Union and the Trades Union Congress continued to press for their implementation throughout the fifties but with little success. There is no evidence to show that the representations of these groups contributed in any way to the renewal of interest in the concept. The British Medical Association was consistently opposed to the widespread introduction of centres, but its official policy was ignored by a few of its members – both medical officers and general practitioners – in the fifties and subsequently by larger numbers. The BMA's views may have contributed to some family doctors feeling uncertain in the early stages but these apprehensions were later overridden by the practical and economic difficulties facing many of those in general practice. The major reason for the failure of organized groups to influence the crucial decisions is probably that in a situation where local initiative is felt by the department in charge to be prerequisite to widespread implementation, centralized pressure groups are unlikely to play a large part.

CHAPTER TWELVE

Detention Centres: the Experiment Which Could Not Fail

Detention centres provide a short period of residential training for young offenders. Descriptions of their regime from their beginning have typically contained adjectives such as sharp, strict, rigorous and, more recently, brisk and firm. The establishment of detention centres and their subsequent expansion have been controversial. Their initial development was slow but by the early sixties detention centres had ceased to be an experimental method of dealing with certain types of offender and had become the standard short-term custodial treatment for young offenders. Originally, in 1948, detention centres were expected, and intended, to be primarily deterrent and punitive institutions. Over the years the regimes in detention centres have been modified with increasing emphasis placed on education. However, attempts to reconcile a punitive and deterrent system with one that professes to be both educational and reformative are inherently contradictory. Therefore changes in detention centre provision have not been based on progress towards a consistent set of objectives but have emerged from, and thus illustrate, the conflict between very different views about the goals of penal policies and the most appropriate methods of pursuing them.

The Criminal Justice Act of 1948 made provision for the establishment of detention centres as an attempt to deal with the young offender 'to whom it seems necessary to give a short but sharp reminder that he is getting into ways that will inevitably lead him to disaster'.[1] The 'short sharp shock', as the detention centre regime subsequently became known, was intended to provide a more effective alternative

[1] The Home Secretary introducing the Second Reading of the Criminal Justice Bill, *H. C. Deb.*, vol. 444, col. 2138. A 'young offender' is an offender aged between fourteen and twenty-one years of age, a 'juvenile offender' is an offender under seventeen years of age.

both to short terms of imprisonment and to corporal punishment. Under the same Act imprisonment was to be restricted to those over sixteen coming before the lower courts and to those over fourteen dealt with by the higher courts. Further restrictions were envisaged, for the government was given powers to make an Order in Council prohibiting magistrates' courts from sending anyone under twenty-one to prison. Judicial corporal punishment was abolished.

There was widespread support for the broad aim of keeping young offenders out of prison and, as a means to this end, the introduction of detention centres was regarded favourably by most individuals and organizations concerned with penal policy, including the more liberal members of the judiciary and of Parliament. However, this new form of custodial treatment was a replacement for corporal punishment which was an entirely punitive method of dealing with offenders. With widespread concern about rising crime rates among young people at this time,[2] there was far from sufficient support for removing all elements of punishment and retribution from penal policies concerning young offenders. Government spokesmen therefore presented detention centres as a tough alternative to corporal punishment and it is clear from the debates surrounding the 1948 Criminal Justice Act that detention centres, although the regime was only vaguely defined, were intended to be tough, punitive institutions. In the sense that the introduction of detention centres represented a departure from the policy followed for decades of treating young offenders in institutions where the main emphasis was on education and reform, this new form of custodial treatment could be regarded as a retrograde step.

The introduction of detention centres with the kind of regime implied by the Act was, therefore, subject to two major but conflicting criticisms. On the one hand there were fears that this short-term custodial treatment would not be sufficiently deterrent. Therefore attempts were made to retain corporal punishment. On the other hand there were fears that the regime would not be beneficial and moves were made, also unsuccessfully, to modify the clauses relating to detention centres in order to place a greater emphasis on education and training.

Thus, from its inception the 'short, sharp, shock' has been regarded by some as not sharp enough to be a deterrent and by others as too short and sharp to be in any way beneficial and, worse, to be damaging. Detention centres, therefore, have always been controversial and

[2] For example, the *Report of Commissioner of Police for the Metropolis* stated: 'The year of 1946 has been a difficult year for the Metropolitan police. Crime is far above the pre-war level ... A disturbing feature is the number of crimes attributable to youths in the age group 14 to 20.' Quoted in Parliament, *ibid.*, col. 2138.

as soon as the first centres were opened their aims, regimes and their results were the subject of much interest, investigation and debate. As a result some of the punitive and deterrent aspects of a detention centre sentence have been removed and replaced with more opportunities for education and training. Nevertheless, if the development of detention centres is to be understood, it must be remembered that their objectives have remained inconsistent, for they have continually reflected both the view that toughness deters and that education reforms.

The main purpose of this case study is to describe the pressures that built up at the end of the 1950s and which led to the population of detention centres being increased fivefold between 1959 and 1964 in marked contrast to a very slow initial development. We shall also discuss and explain the processes by which these pressures resulted in an increase in the number of detention centre places. How far did provision increase because, as an experiment, the centres had been judged 'successful' and therefore worthy of expansion? If so, given their contradictory objectives, who defined success and who had to be convinced of it? Who were the groups and individuals who were influential in developing detention centre policy?

The Home Secretary was, and still is, responsible to Parliament for the prevention of crime and the treatment of offenders in general, but during the period of this case study[3] many of the powers necessary to do this rested in the hands of the Prison Commissioners. They were responsible for the superintendence, control and inspection of all institutions to which the Prison Acts applied. The chairman of the Prison Commission was a senior civil servant, usually with long Home Office experience, directly responsible to the Home Secretary through the Permanent Under Secretary of State. In practice he was the head of a minor department assisted by four Commissioners and several Assistant Commissioners, and had a good deal of autonomy. Indeed, Lionel Fox, the chairman during the greater part of the period covered by this case study, wrote that 'the work of the Prison Commissioners is self-contained and they are primarily responsible for

---

[3] The Prison Commission was dissolved in March 1963 and its staff and functions transferred to the Home Office where they are now managed by a Prison Board. The Prison Board has no functions directly given to it as the Prison Commission had, and membership of the Prison Board is subject to the postings and crosspostings which normally take place in civil service departments. Therefore the Prison Commission enjoyed a far greater degree of autonomy and its membership was more permanent, thus providing a large degree of continuity in policy. One of its most famous members, Alexander Paterson, who brought many new ideas and attitudes to the commission, was a member for nearly twenty years. For a fuller account of the work of the Prison Commission see Fox, L., *The English Prison and Borstal System*, Routledge & Kegan Paul, 1952, ch. 5.

both the formulation and application of policy'.[4] The commission dealt directly with the Treasury in matters of finance, establishment and supply and its funds were subject to a separate parliamentary vote. The greatest restrictions on the commission's work were often financial[5] and to win the additional resources necessary for the implementation of new policies it needed powerful allies. In this way the interests and priorities of the Home Secretary and his senior civil servants in the Home Office had an important impact on the development of penal policy.

The judiciary also plays an important role, for it implements important aspects of penal policy and the Executive has far less control over it than, say, over the civil servants in the Department of Health and Social Security who administer social security policies. In addition the Magistrates' Association, particularly its Council, which is often more forward looking than the general membership, is a powerful pressure group which expects to be and is consulted by the government on penal matters. Both the Home Office and the Prison Commissioners suffer the consequences if offenders are sentenced inappropriately.

There are other pressure groups trying to influence penal policy both from within and outside the Home Office. The Prison Officers' Association is an example of the former and the Howard League for Penal Reform an important example of the latter.[6] Although the membership of the league is small, it has influence because its members are found in the legal profession, among leading magistrates, in Parliament and on the Home Office Advisory Council for the Treatment of Offenders. It is regarded by the Home Office and by the Prison Commissioners as an important source of informed opinion and until the Home Office developed its own research unit in the late 1950s they were often the sole collectors and purveyors of general information about penal matters. Lionel Fox once described them as 'HM's Opposition to the Prison Commission'.[7]

What impact did these various groups have on the way in which detention centre policy developed? How important were trends in the crime rates among young people? Criminal statistics always make news, often reaching the headlines, and a government which appears unable to maintain law and order quickly begins to lose credibility.

---

[4] Fox, L., *op. cit.*, p. 78.

[5] On his retirement as chairman of the Prison Commission, Lionel Fox said that his years in office 'have been spent not so much in overcoming the forces of reaction as in dragging open the public purse'. Quoted by Alice Bacon, H.C., *Standing Committee B of Criminal Justice Bill*, 2 Feb., 1961, vol. 1, col. 435.

[6] For a full account of the history of the Howard League for Penal Reform see Rose, G., *The Struggle for Penal Reform*, Stevens, 1961.

[7] Quoted in Rose, G., *op. cit.*, p. 275.

Another factor, therefore, to be accounted for in the development of any penal policy is public reaction to an increase in crime rates as conveyed in the newspapers, by the radio and television.

Before we consider questions such as these, however, the origins of detention centres must be briefly described, for these help to identify some of the important strands in the story of their later development.

I THE BACKGROUND TO THE INTRODUCTION OF DETENTION CENTRES

The treatment of young offenders since the middle of the last century has been based on the principle of keeping them out of prison and exposing them to more educational and remedial measures. Concern centred around the fear that imprisonment, for however short a period, was not only a damaging experience for young people but was also not a very efficient deterrent. These fears were summarized by a committee reporting in 1927 on the treatment of young offenders. 'What matters so profoundly', it pointed out, 'is the communication of a wrong outlook on life, cynical, depraved, selfish or all three. That is the real contamination which changes character definitely for the worse and this perverted attitude towards life and fellow human beings is likely to be absorbed by the impressionable lad or girl from the daily sights of the ordinary prison ... There is also the risk of weakening the deterrent effect of imprisonment. The young offender, once imprisoned, is apt to lose the dread which he once felt. Familiarity has dispelled the terror of the unknown and he is now an initiate.'[8] The need to find a better deterrent was not too pressing in 1927, because crime rates among young people were falling. This may partly explain why the committee rejected a proposal to establish special places of short-term detention on the grounds that they would be 'undesirable', particularly for offenders of school age, as it would interrupt their education without giving sufficient time for rehabilitative training.

It had been possible to send a young person under seventeen to 'a place of detention' rather than to prison since 1908. Section 106 of the Children Act, 1908, abolished imprisonment for children under fourteen and only allowed a sentence of imprisonment on young persons between the ages of fourteen and sixteen if it had specifically been stated that they were 'too unruly and depraved' to be sent to 'a place of detention'. Other young offenders who were found guilty

[8] *Report of the Departmental Committee on the Treatment of Young Offenders* (Malony), Cmd. 2831, 1927, pp. 81–2.

of an offence punishable in the case of an adult by imprisonment, or liable to imprisonment in default of payment of a fine, could be sent to 'a place of detention' which would be 'in lieu of' imprisonment. The 1927 departmental committee recommended that committal to 'a place of detention' as well as to prison should be abandoned as far as possible.

Section 54 of the Children and Young Persons Act, 1933, transferred the duty to provide 'places of detention', henceforth known as 'remand homes', from the police to county and county borough councils, where normally they became the responsibility of the education department. In 1948 they were transferred to the new local children's departments. In 1933 no young person was sent to detention but numbers rose from 1935 onwards as recorded crime among young people increased. Many sentencers began to express their frustration with the lack of an alternative to short-term imprisonment, particularly for those offenders who were not thought to need long-term institutional training but were unsuitable for probation.[9] In 1937 Basil Henriques, chairman of the Young Prisoners Committee of the Royal Society for the Assistance of Discharged Prisoners, speaking at the Magistrates' Association annual conference, recommended that special institutions should be set up for boys on remand, awaiting transfer to borstal or serving sentences. He was disturbed that offenders under twenty-one were being sent to prison as a sentence in itself or to await removal to borstal. That year 1,355 offenders between the ages of sixteen and twenty-one years had been sent to prison on conviction, over a third of them being first offenders. A further 2,694 were sent to prison on remand or awaiting trial and were not sent to prison subsequently.[10] The Magistrates' Association suggested establishing young offenders' centres, 'run on the lines of a borstal, in which young people between seventeen and twenty-three would spend from three to twelve months followed by a year's supervision by a probation officer'.[11]

A more punitive approach was considered by the Departmental Committee on Corporal Punishment in 1938. They heard 'a good deal of evidence' which suggested that juvenile courts lacked the opportunity to deal in a satisfactory way with minor offences 'due in the main to nothing more than a misguided sense of adventure'.[12] Views had been expressed that this type of offender needed 'some form of

[9] The probation service had grown since the beginning of the century and was put on a national basis by the Criminal Justice Act of 1925.
[10] See *The Magistrates' Association, 16th Annual Report and Statement of Accounts*, 1936–7, pp. 16–17.
[11] Quoted by the Home Secretary introducing the Second Reading of the Criminal Justice Bill, 1938, *H. C. Deb.*, vol. 342, col. 272.
[12] *Report of the Departmental Committee on Corporal Punishment*, Cmd. 5684, 1938, p. 45.

short and sharp punishment which will pull him up and give him the lesson which he needs'.[13] Witnesses differed about the form this punitive detention should take and about its duration. There were proposals for depriving the young offender of his liberty on Saturdays as well as for special places of detention, not associated with remand homes, where 'discipline would be strict and the inmates would be required to do a great deal of work'.[14] The committee felt that it was beyond its terms of reference to examine these proposals in detail but it did suggest that if judicial corporal punishment were abolished, as it recommended, juvenile courts would need additional powers to deal with those needing 'some form of punishment which will operate effectively as a deterrent'.[15]

The committee's recommendations on the abolition of corporal punishment were included in the Criminal Justice Bill of 1938, the progress of which was halted by the declaration of war. One of the main objects of this Bill as the Home Secretary, Sir Samuel Hoare, explained in introducing its second reading, was 'to effect an immediate reduction in the numbers of young people received into prison and to provide for the ultimate abolition of imprisonment as a method of treatment of young offenders convicted of such offences as are dealt with by courts of summary jurisdiction'.[16] However, the alternatives to short-term imprisonment and corporal punishment which were proposed in this Bill did not include the provision of special places of punitive detention. Instead, compulsory attendance centres (where the young offender would spend a maximum of three hours a day during Saturdays or evenings over a period of up to six months) and Howard Houses for those needing a short period of residential care, were proposed. The main purpose of these two provisions was to restrict the young offenders' liberty without interrupting their normal working life. The Home Secretary argued that restriction of liberty was sufficient punishment. Therefore Howard Houses, which were hostels in which offenders would be required to live for a period of six months followed by six months' supervision, were not intended to be primarily punitive institutions. As the Under Secretary of State to the Home Department explained to the House of Commons during the debate on the Bill, 'considerable freedom would be given to the housemasters in their arrangements for the life of the institutions ... it is not at all to be a prison ... It is to be a place where the boys can live under good conditions and good influences and where discipline can be learned.'[17]

[13] *Ibid.*, p. 46.
[14] *Ibid.*, p. 48.
[15] *Ibid.*, p. 49.
[16] *H. C. Deb.*, vol. 342, col. 273.
[17] *Ibid.*, col. 726.

Much of the debate during the Bill's passage through the House of Commons centred on the more controversial proposals to abolish capital punishment and judicial corporal punishment. However, the clauses giving the government powers to establish Howard Houses and attendance centres were passed together with that abolishing corporal punishment, although the clause prohibiting magistrates from sending sixteen-year-olds to prison was defeated. But the Bill did not reach the House of Lords and so, failing to complete all its stages before emergency legislation for the oncoming war intervened, it was set aside and never reached the Statute Book.

At the end of the war, when the Home Secretary asked the standing Advisory Council on the Treatment of Offenders, which had been appointed in 1944, to review the provisions of the 1938 Bill, the treatment of young offenders was a much more urgent problem. There had been a big increase in recorded crimes among the young. The number of young offenders aged between seventeen and twenty-one found guilty of indictable offences had increased by nearly 50 per cent between 1939 and 1945.[18] As a result greater use was made during these years of corporal punishment, punitive detention in remand homes and short terms of imprisonment.[19] This was criticized from several quarters.

In 1944 a Committee of Inquiry had to be established to investigate a complaint that a young girl detained in a remand home in London had been allowed to associate with older girls of 'bad moral character'.[20] Two years later the Curtis Committee on the care of children deprived of a normal home life recommended that remand homes 'should be merely places of transit. A child committed to custody for purposes of punitive detention ... should not in our opinion be admitted to the ordinary remand homes.'[21] Because of the pressure on accommodation due to the increase in juvenile delinquency, magistrates found it difficult to find places in remand homes for all those they thought required a period of punitive deten-

[18] In 1939 13,655 offenders aged between sixteen and twenty-one were found guilty of indictable offences. The numbers rose to 19,707 in 1941, fluctuated in subsequent years and by 1945 reached 21,133.

[19] In 1941 the number of sentences of corporal punishment reached a peak of 567 compared with 65 in 1938. These numbers fell sharply thereafter and in 1947 were 58. But in 1947 1,636 young offenders were sent to prison for three months or less. In 1939 134 children and 45 young persons (fourteen to sixteen years old) were committed to detention in a remand home. During the war numbers rose even higher: from 309 and 123 respectively in 1940 to 377 and 152 in 1947.

[20] *Report of Committee of Inquiry on London County Council Remand Homes*, Cmd. 6594, 1944–5.

[21] *Report of the Care of Children Committee* (Curtis), Cmd. 6922, 1946, p. 170.

tion.[22] In any case many were not happy about doing so because, as John Watson, chairman of the south east London juvenile court, wrote: 'The first essential to a short, sharp punishment is that it shall be to some extent unpleasant and a remand home is not – or should not be unpleasant.'[23] Those whose behaviour was too 'refractory and violent', or simply those for whom there was no room in a remand home, could be remanded in prison. However, short terms of imprisonment were felt to be unsatisfactory for the same reasons advanced by the Malony Committee in 1927. Instances of school-children sent to prison aroused much criticism in the press.[24]

In April 1945 the Council of the Magistrates' Association sent a resolution to the Home Office expressing 'concern at the absence of any alternative to prison as a place of detention in custody for persons of both sexes between the ages of sixteen and twenty-three ... during their period of remand, also for young prisoners who are too unruly to be held in remand homes or young prisoners committed to Borstal after absconding from Home Office schools; it records its opinion that special institutions should be established for all such persons, and it regards this provision as a matter of such prime importance that it should be included in any contemplated legislation'.[25] Pending such a change, it asked the Home Office to get certain approved schools to agree to accept young persons whom the courts wished to sentence to punitive detention. A year later it sent a memorandum to the Home Office for its consideration when drafting the new Criminal Justice Bill. It asked 'that the provision of Howard Houses be included in any new Bill, the Council being in favour of the residential custody which would be provided by Howard Houses as laid down in the 1938 Bill'.[26] It also recommended the abolition of powers to pass a sentence of corporal punishment. When the provisions of the Criminal Justice Bill were published the council was concerned that detention centres would become little more than short-term prisons for the young, but decided not to oppose the measure formally.

However, from some of the discussion that took place in the journals

---

[22] In 1940 the Home Office had to send a circular in April and another in July requesting managers of approved schools to release more boys under licence earlier in order to relieve some of the pressure on remand homes, as well as to meet the additional demands due to the evacuation of approved schools in dangerous areas.

[23] Watson, J., *The Child and the Magistrate*, Cape, 1942. Revised Edn., 1950, p. 203.

[24] A case of a boy sent to an Oxford prison aroused much comment and later was used in Parliament as an example of the dangers inherent in the existing system. See *H. L. Deb.*, vol. 155, col. 403.

[25] Magistrates' Association, *25th Annual Report and Statement of Accounts*, 1944–5, p. 15.

[26] *Ibid.*, p. 14.

and newspapers at this time it is clear that there was considerable interest in a form of detention that would provide a shorter, sharper punishment than Howard Houses. Echoing some of the witnesses to the 1938 Committee on Corporal Punishment, John Watson had written in 1942 that 'what is needed is a small local establishment in which the discipline is strict, the food plain, where things are done "at the double" and with a maximum of healthy hard work and a minimum of amusement: the kind of place the offender would not want to visit twice and against which he would warn his companions'.[27] The experience of military detention had clearly made some impact on those who were thinking about penal policy and searching for a more acceptable form of short-term custodial treatment for young offenders than that provided by prisons or remand homes. Certainly experience of the use of detention in the Armed Forces during the war had encouraged thinking about the lines of subjecting young offenders to a punitive regime for a short period. For example, during the passage of the new Criminal Justice Bill (introduced to Parliament in 1947) through the House of Lords, the Lord Chancellor, having commented on military detention and how successful this had been with even the most 'unsuitable material', hoped that he had 'said enough to show that the Bill, so far from being the result of superficial sentiment or wishful thinking, is the result of hard practical experience that has not only been established in the field of penal treatment but *in the actual experience of the three Fighting Services during the war*' (our italics).[28]

With a background of higher crime rates among young people and a judiciary determined to have some form of short-term custodial treatment for young offenders at its disposal which it considered tough enough to be a deterrent, it is not surprising that the proposals for the treatment of young offenders in 1948 were of a harsher nature than those contained in the 1938 Bill. Moreover, in February 1947 at Standon Farm Approved School[29] a master was murdered and the publicity this received served to confirm the belief that the courts and approved schools were now having to deal with very difficult boys. Certainly if the government still wished to abolish judicial corporal punishment it had to be seen to be putting something severe in its place. Detention centres with a regime incorporating some

[27] Watson, J., *op. cit.*, p. 203.
[28] *H. L. Deb.*, vol. 155, col. 468. See also Choppen, V., 'The Origins of the Philosophy of Detention Centres', *British Journal of Criminology*, vol. 10, no. 2, 1970, p. 162, where she refers to a lecture entitled 'Lessons from the Army for Penal Reformers' given in June 1946 by Lt Col J. C. Penton, RAMC, at which he spoke of military detention camps as being a useful method of dealing with delinquents whether army or civilian.
[29] See *Standon Farm Approved School, Report of Committee of Inquiry*, Cmd. 7150, 1947.

features of military detention camps were more likely to be an accept-able alternative to corporal punishment than Howard Houses, which were not in any case mentioned in the new Bill. This is surprising since Chuter Ede, the Home Secretary in 1948, had spoken in their favour during the second reading of the 1938 Criminal Justice Bill, and, as we have seen, the Council of the Magistrates' Association had proposed they be included in the Bill.

Some of those who were familiar with Chuter Ede's views prior to and during the passage of the 1948 Criminal Justice Bill, suggest that he may have been influenced by the views of his senior civil servants, in particular Sir Frank Newsam, with whom Chuter Ede worked closely.[30] This could explain, for example, why Chuter Ede supported the death penalty while in office but reverted to being an abolitionist once he had left. An alternative explanation is that Chuter Ede and his senior officials were reflecting the views of the people who actually had to deal with offenders. In 1947 the police and the prison service were understaffed and needed recruits. Given the rising crime rates among the young at the time, any measure which appeared to be dealing with them leniently may well have been thought to endanger the morale of the prison service and the police.

The 1948 Act abolished corporal punishment and raised the pro-hibition against imprisonment to seventeen-year-olds for the magistrates' courts, and to fifteen-year-olds for the higher courts. Instead, those over fourteen and under seventeen could now be sent to a detention centre for three months by a magistrates' court and for up to six months by a higher court. Where a detention centre existed a court could no longer sentence this group of offenders to one month's detention in a remand home as a punishment. Those over seventeen and under twenty-one could be sent by magistrates' courts to a detention centre or to prison for six months, and higher courts could send anyone over fifteen to prison for any length of time. An offender could not be sent to a detention centre if he had previously been to prison or in Borstal or, since the age of seventeen, had been committed to a detention centre. The courts were also only to use this form of punishment when they had 'considered every other method (except imprisonment) by which the court might deal with him and is of the opinion that none of these methods is appropriate'. Also, the offence had to be one for which a term of imprisonment could have been imposed.[31] Finally, detention centres were to be added to the list of institutions administered by the Prison Com-mission.

[30] Christophe, J., *Capital Punishment and British Politics*, Allen & Unwin, 1962, pp. 39–40.
[31] These include wilful damage, offences of drunkenness and disorderly behaviour and all forms and degrees of larceny.

These formal provisions tell us little about the kind of institution a detention centre was intended to be; about the characteristics of offenders thought likely to respond best to its regime or indeed what that regime would be. The debates in both Houses of Parliament revealed much muddled thinking about detention centres and naturally most attention was paid to the controversial issues of abolishing capital punishment[32] and judicial corporal punishment. Nevertheless it is instructive to see what was said about the aims and underlying philosophy of the as yet non-existent detention centres.

Concern about rising crime rates among the young was frequently voiced and there seems little doubt that the need to find an effective deterrent for young offenders was uppermost in many Members' minds. Introducing the Second Reading, the Home Secretary, Chuter Ede, said: 'Undoubtedly the most difficult and distressing problem which confronts us is the problem not merely of the juvenile but of the adolescent criminal, and in any consideration we give to this matter we must have those persons very clearly in mind because we must prevent them becoming habitual criminals.'[33] Some Members were quick to point out that this was a good reason for retaining corporal punishment. The need to counteract this line of argument was no doubt one of the reasons which led the government spokesmen to stress that the courts must be provided with tough alternatives to corporal punishment which could be used when necessary. The Home Secretary was at pains to point out that the Bill was not 'concerned primarily to provide milder penalties; it is rather concerned to permit the widest possible variety of types of treatment. It is concerned to provide that this treatment shall be decided upon in the most intelligent manner so that we may reform the prisoner according to the circumstances of his case.'[34] In a similar vein, Kenneth Younger, Parliamentary Under Secretary of State to the Home Office, when summing up for the government, explained that detention centres were 'for the young offender for whom a fine or probation would be inadequate, but who does not require the prolonged period of training which is given by an approved school or a borstal institution. There is a type of offender to whom it seems necessary to give a short but sharp reminder that he is getting into ways that will inevitably land him in disaster.'[35] The regime in a detention centre would, therefore, consist of 'brisk discipline and hard work'.

Most Members seemed satisfied with variations of the slogan 'short

---

[32] The government had omitted any provision to abolish capital punishment in the Bill. However a clause to do so was introduced by Sydney Silverman during the Second Reading. For a full account of this aspect of the 1947 Criminal Justice Bill see Christophe, J., *op. cit.*, ch. 2.

[33] *H. C. Deb.*, vol. 444, col. 2128.

[34] *Ibid.*, col. 2345.

[35] *Ibid.*, col. 2138.

and sharp punishment' and few asked what this would actually mean in practice. As George Benson pointed out after the Second Reading debate had lasted over nine hours: 'No one has yet enquired as to what corrective training is to be given ... The value of this Bill will not rest in names – whether these places are called detention centres or remand centres – but what type of institution is to be set up by the Home Office and what happens therein.'[36] A little more of the Home Office's views and intentions regarding detention centres was revealed in the House of Commons Standing Committee and in the House of Lords in response to enquiries by Members who were closely associated with sentencing and the treatment of young offenders.[37] These enquiries were concerned with the extent to which short sentences could be really deterrent and whether or not the staffing and siting of the buildings would be good enough to avoid the characteristics of prisons.

It was clear from the government's response to amendments concerning the regime and the after-care that the primary aim of the detention centre was deterrent. In rejecting an amendment to the clause concerning the establishment of detention centres which would have added 'where he will receive education and reformative training', the Home Secretary said that 'education and reformative training will I hope go on simultaneously; but I do not want these places turned into a kind of junior or specialized approved schools. They are entirely different in their purpose and I think we should impose a quite impossible task on the people who have to conduct them if we inserted these words.'[38] The punitive aspect of detention centres was stressed again when Sir George Manningham Buller's[39] amendment, which would have required a period in a detention centre to be followed by an equal period under supervision, was also rejected by the Home Secretary. In his view voluntary after-care was sufficient and would avoid the problem of finding a suitable sanction for those

[36] *Ibid.*, col. 2286. George Benson was an active member of the Howard League for Penal Reform. Later on in the 1950s he became chairman of the executive committee of the league and at this time was also a member of the Advisory Council for the Treatment of Offenders.

[37] Notably Viscount Simon and Viscount Templewood, both of whom had been Home Secretaries, the former from June 1935 to May 1937, the latter (then Sir Samuel Hoare), from May 1937 to September 1939. As we have already seen, Samuel Hoare spoke strongly in favour of less punitive ways of dealing with young offenders during the debates on the 1938 Criminal Justice Bill. He maintained his interest in penal policy and was Vice-President of the Magistrates' Association from 1947 to 1952.

[38] *H. C., Standing Committee A of the Criminal Justice Bill*, 1948, vol. 1, col. 971.

[39] Sir George Manningham Buller was later the Solicitor General (November 1951 to October 1954) and then became Attorney General (October 1954 to 1962).

needing compulsory supervision. The threat of return to a detention centre was an unacceptable sanction, he argued, because he 'could not contemplate using these detention centres as places to which young people should return time after time. Clearly if they have not profited by the short, sharp lesson then some other means will have to be found because a series of short, sharp lessons is apt to lose its effect.'[40] In the House of Lords, Lord Chorley for the government stated that 'the primary object of this type of sentence is not by any means reformatory because it is obviously not possible to take in hand the serious reformation of this type of young man on the basis of a period of three months detention'.[41]

There was very little information about who would staff detention centres. Introducing the Second Reading in the House of Lords, the Lord Chancellor stressed that 'the success of any such scheme depends primarily not upon the bricks and mortar, but upon the staff and the regime. We must do everything we can to see that we provide, in addition to the building, a highly qualified and highly trained staff.'[42] In the House of Commons, Kenneth Younger had said that he had 'no doubt that one of the limiting factors, unfortunately, will be the provision of suitable staff'.[43] However, Viscountess Davidson's suggestion that the Bill should make provisions for the recruitment and training of men and women 'of higher character and ability' gathered little support.

The location of detention centres was the subject of rather more discussion. It did not go unnoticed that the Bill would give powers to the Prison Commissioners to set up detention centres in buildings that might have been a former prison. This made some Members of both Houses wonder how detention centres in fact would be, as Lord Chorley described them, 'divorced from the sordid and unpleasant atmosphere of the ordinary prison'.[44] However, Kenneth Younger assured them that the government did not intend to use out-of-date prison buildings.

The practical details of the regime were still to be decided. So Viscount Templewood received no answer to his question 'What methods of training are to be used for the variable times of detention?'[45] The government was so vague indeed that some of their lordships said they did not believe such centres would ever exist, especially in the face of building difficulties and staff shortages. This was the view of Lord Schuster, who moved an amendment to delete

[40] *H. C., Standing Committee A, op. cit.*, col. 976.
[41] *H. L. Deb.*, vol. 156, col. 780.
[42] *H. L. Deb.*, vol. 155, col. 393.
[43] *H. C. Deb.*, vol. 444, col. 2349.
[44] *H. L. Deb.*, vol. 156, col. 780.
[45] *Ibid.*, col. 298.

the power to provide detention centres from the Bill altogether in order, he said, to give the Lord Chancellor an opportunity to say what detention centres were.[46] Lord Goddard[47] suggested that the government should remove the centres from the Bill until they had a policy and Viscount Simon commented that it was very odd to have a phrase in an Act of Parliament 'which in itself means nothing at all ... I know what a prison is, and I know what a Borstal is, but nobody reading this can ever know what a detention centre is. For all I know it might be a shopping centre.'[48] However, as the Lord Chancellor had admitted 'there is not much chance of building them at the present time [and] it will be some time before remand centres and detention centres can be built, but it is just as well now to take the power to build them so that when the opportunity does arise we shall be able to do so'.[49] In the Commons, the Home Secretary had merely said that 'these centres are experimental. I hope we shall be able to start them without inducing the people in charge of the experiment to give undue consideration to any one point.'[50]

But if so much was to be left to those who actually ran the centres by what criteria were the staff to be selected? What sort of offenders were these centres going to receive? If it was important that particularly for young offenders 'their treatment must be decided on by reference to their character, their social background and circumstances and not merely by reference to the crimes for which they are convicted',[51] how were the courts to decide who was suitable for detention centres? It was at least clear that there would be different detention centres, some for those aged between fourteen and seventeen and others for those aged between seventeen and twenty-one, but much still remained to be decided.

In the circumstances the proposal to establish detention centres was hard to oppose. Those who would have preferred to retain corporal punishment seemed apparently satisfied with the notion of 'a short and sharp punishment' with emphasis on 'discipline' and 'hard work'. Those, including the Council of the Magistrates' Association, who feared the establishment of an institution little better than prison could only wait and see because the government had described the regime and purpose of detention centres in such vague terms. Moreover, it is very difficult to oppose an 'experiment'. To call a measure experimental may be an effective tactic for getting it through Parliament but, as in this case, it leaves a large number of unanswered

---

[46] *Ibid.*, col. 404.
[47] Lord Goddard was Lord Chief Justice from 1946 to 1958.
[48] *H. L. Deb.*, vol. 156, col. 784.
[49] *H. L. Deb.*, vol. 155, col. 550.
[50] *H. C., Standing Committee A, op. cit.*, col. 971.
[51] *H. C. Deb.*, vol. 444, col. 2139.

questions for those who have to implement the policy.

The operation of the Act with respect to young offenders and detention centres depended to a considerable extent on the way in which the Prison Commission, together with the Home Office, interpreted these measures. The Prison Commission's ability to acquire the resources for building and staffing these institutions was crucial and this depended to a large extent on the Home Secretary's bargaining position both in the Cabinet and with the Treasury, as well as the nature and extent of his interest in penal reform. This is why, as we shall see, the appointment of R. A. Butler as Home Secretary in 1957 marked a turning point in the story of detention centres.

The way in which the courts wanted to use these new detention centres was also important and this, in turn, partly depended on concern about the incidence of crime among young people as expressed by the mass media as well as by the politicians. It is, furthermore, necessary to note first that in spite of the Act's intention to restrict imprisonment for young offenders it was still possible, in certain circumstances, to send to prison persons over fourteen and under seventeen on remand, awaiting trial or awaiting removal to approved school. Those aged between seventeen and twenty-one on remand or awaiting a place in a Borstal allocation centre also went to prison until the proposed remand centres came into existence over ten years later. In other words young people could still find themselves in prison even before they had been found guilty and this would only cease when remand centres were widely available. Second, a detention centre order was a replacement for punitive detention in a remand home.[52] This meant that if detention centre places were insufficient to satisfy the courts' demands for places of short-term custody they would continue to use prisons and remand homes inappropriately. In addition to the unfavourable publicity this practice attracted, the Home Office had to face the criticisms of the staff of prisons and remand homes, the latter with whom they were more directly concerned after the Children Act, 1948.[53]

[52] Section 18 of the Criminal Justice Act, 1948, included an amendment to the 1933 Children and Young Persons Act which said that 'a court shall not make an order that an offender who is not less than fourteen years of age be committed to custody in a remand home under Section 54 of the Children and Young Persons Act, 1933, if it has been notified by the Secretary of State that a detention centre is available for the reception from that court of persons of his class or description'.

[53] As already stated, in 1933 local authority education departments were usually responsible for providing remand homes but after the 1948 Children Act remand homes were staffed and provided by the new children's departments. Thus, after 1948, the Children's Department of the Home Office was closely concerned with the use of remand homes for the detention of young offenders under seventeen.

II THE EARLY DETENTION CENTRES: 1952 TO 1957

The first detention centre was not opened until 1952, four years after the passing of the Criminal Justice Act. Why was there a delay of four years and why was the first detention centre for junior boys between the ages of fourteen and seventeen? The availability of existing and new resources which could be called upon by the Prison Commissioners provides some important answers.

The late forties and early fifties were still times of austerity. Money and materials were in short supply and new houses had priority over new prisons. Lionel Fox subsequently wrote: 'The Commissioners originally took the view that specially provided buildings would be required for detention centres, but when it became clear that such buildings could not be provided, they decided at least to experiment with adapted buildings if any suitable could be found.'[54] In their Annual Report for 1950 the Prison Commissioners announced that negotiations were in progress for two sites in south east England. Such negotiations were always protracted 'due to long, local sieges against the arrival of detention centres', as a junior minister to the Home Office later wrote.[55]

The Conservative Party was elected to office in October 1951 with the slogan 'Set the People Free'. It was committed to a reduction of 'socialist controls' and, amongst other things, had promised a reduction in the number of civil servants. This forced a standstill in recruitment to the Prison Service. It was, therefore, impossible for the Prison Commissioners to obtain special staff for the new centres. Instead wardens and officers came as volunteers from elsewhere within the prison system. Likewise, the Prison Commissioners could not gain additional resources in the form of new buildings. The Conservative government had inherited a record balance of payments deficit,[56] as well as a commitment to defence expenditure connected with the Korean War.[57] It wished, nevertheless, to reduce taxation. So the economic and political climate did not, on the whole, favour more generous expenditure on the social services.[58] In addition, build-

[54] Fox, L., *op. cit.*, p. 342.

[55] Deedes, W. F., 'Crossroads for the Young Offenders', *Daily Telegraph*, 23 Sept., 1960.

[56] There was a balance of payments deficit of £700 million in 1951. By then UK reserves had risen to £800 million but sterling liabilities were still at £3,000 million.

[57] Defence spending rose from 7 per cent of Gross National Product in 1950 to 10·5 per cent in 1952.

[58] Expenditure on the social services fell from 18 per cent of Gross Domestic Product in 1952 to 16 per cent in 1955.

ing materials were still in short supply in the early fifties. Harold Macmillan, a powerful Minister of Housing in the new government, was committed to building 300,000 houses a year[59] and by 1953 this target had been passed in spite of the continuing shortage of materials. The Home Secretary, David Maxwell-Fyfe, did not command as powerful a position in the Cabinet and anyway was not especially interested in penal policy.

Clearly, therefore, the economic situation at the end of 1951 was far from favourable to the development of new forms of custodial treatment requiring additional capital and current expenditure. However, on the other side of the coin, detention centres had been labelled 'experimental' which at least enabled a modest start to be made without any commitment to further development on a major scale in the near future; crime rates among fourteen to seventeen-year-olds were continuing to rise (see Table 8); the courts were determined to use some form of punitive detention, and the child care staff of remand homes did not like their homes being used as places of punishment.

As we have already seen, the courts could continue to use remand homes as places of punitive detention until detention centres were available to them. In 1950 altogether 589 children and 277 young persons were sent to remand homes as a punishment. But magistrates as well as remand home staff were dissatisfied with this procedure, especially as they knew that the Prison Commissioners had the powers to make alternative provisions.[60] At the Annual General Meeting of the Magistrates' Association in 1950 a resolution was adopted deploring the 'delay in establishing remand and detention centres and urging the Home Secretary to take necessary steps without further delay'.[61] He replied that he was aware of the desirability of remand centres but could not hold out any prospects of provision at an early date, but 'with regard to detention centres it is hoped to establish one or two such centres in existing premises suitably adapted for these purposes'.[62]

The Home Secretary was subject to pressure from his Children's

---

[59] In 1951, 195,000 houses were completed. In the first year of Conservative government in 1952 house completions increased to 240,000 and by 1954 completions totalled 347,000 in spite of the shortage of building materials.

[60] 'A short, sharp punishment is what many delinquents need, but it is doubtful whether a month is long enough, and it is quite certain that the remand home is the wrong place for it. It is quite impossible to segregate those receiving punishment from those who are there for observation or awaiting removal to an approved school.' Henriques, B., *The Indiscretions of a Magistrate*, Harrap, 1950, p. 160.

[61] The Magistrates' Association, *Annual Report and Statement of Accounts*, 1950–1, p. 14.

[62] Magistrates' Association, *ibid.*, p. 4.

Table 8

INCIDENCE OF INDICTABLE OFFENCES; OFFENCES OF VIOLENCE AND ROBBERY, AND ASSAULT WITH INTENT TO ROB AMONG DIFFERENT AGE GROUPS

Year	Males found guilty of indictable offences*		Males found guilty of offences of violence against the person†			Robbery and assault with intent to rob: all ages	
	Under 17	17 and under 21	Under 17	17 and under 21	All ages	Crimes known to police	Persons found guilty‡
1938	26,400	10,100	110	147	1355	287	127
1949	37,300	10,800	210	379	2973	990	466
1950	39,100	10,900	311	447	3523	1,021	550
1951	43,800	12,400	345	474	3619	880	424
1952	41,300	12,400	314	563	3751	1,002	456
1953	35,300	10,700	376	579	3961	580	554
1954	31,800	10,100	426	745	4257	812	465
1955	32,600	11,300	439	921	4604	823	415
1956	35,800	13,400	596	1,120	5648	965	496
1957	41,800	17,500	751	1,595	6727	1,194	636
1958	47,700	21,300	1,012	2,051	7528	1,692	882
1959	48,900	22,400	1,201	2,323	8736	1,900	1,031

* See Home Office, Statistics Relating to Crime and Criminal Proceedings for the Year 1960, Cmnd. 1437, 1961.
† See Report of the Advisory Council on the Treatment of Offenders on Corporal Punishment, Cmnd. 1213, 1960, Appendix C, p. 32.
‡ Ibid., Appendix D, p. 33.

Department as well. It was being pressed to economize by reducing the average length of stay of children and young persons committed on remand and, where possible, by the closing of some remand homes.[63] In 1951 six-monthly figures instead of annual figures of the numbers and length of stay in remand homes were introduced 'to give a better picture of the use made of remand homes'.[64] In a situation in which remand home places for children and young persons under observation or awaiting a place in an approved school were becoming increasingly scarce, the staff were even less happy about using their precious places for punitive detention. The Children's Department was, therefore, keen to see detention centres established. The Prison Commissioners were less enthusiastic, not only because of their lack of resources but also because they did not wish to become responsible for offenders as young as fourteen, an age group with which they were so far unfamiliar.

In their annual report for 1951, the Prison Commissioners noted that they were planning to open a junior detention centre, a 'pilot' scheme, at Kidlington near Oxford. The premises to be converted were built as a workhouse in 1939 and during the war had been used as an agricultural camp. Campsfield House at Kidlington was opened in August 1952 and operated under the rules contained in the Prison Act, 1952. The centre had accommodation for an average of forty-four boys. The twelve staff and two instructors were volunteers from within the Prison Service.

The first junior detention centre

It is clear that the Prison Commissioners relied heavily on the advice of the Home Office Children's Department. They thanked it 'for co-operation and advice in preparation of the Statutory Rules and arrangements for setting up the first centre'.[65] Under Section 43 of the Prison Act, 1952, the Commissioners had, in any case, to work in consultation with the Children's Department because in all other respects the junior age groups were the latter's responsibility. Indeed, the Children's Department Inspectors had the same powers of inspection as the Commissioners with respect to junior detention centres.[66]

---

[63] *Sixth Report with Evidence taken before Sub-Committee D of the Select Committee on Estimates, Session 1951–2* (235), 'Child Care', p. 12.

[64] *Ibid.*, p. 104. In 1949 12,995 children and young persons were committed on remand for an average length of stay of 37 days. By the first half of 1951 the average length of stay was 28 days.

[65] *Report of the Prison Commissioners for 1952*, Cmd. 8948, 1953, p. 92.

[66] Under the Children and Young Persons Act, 1969, this rather anomalous position will be resolved when 'community homes' take the place of junior detention centres. Throughout the period under discussion in this chapter,

The Commissioners' annual report in 1952 discussed the operation of this first detention centre but conveyed little of how they had 'devised a regime appropriate to the declared principles of this new form of treatment'.[67] This, they stressed, had presented them with 'novel problems' because they had not been concerned with the junior age group before. Repeating many of the catch-phrases used during the debates in 1947 and 1948 they said that the essence was 'a short, sharp shock' and that 'from the start a boy is told that he must do as he is told and that he lives in a community where second best is not accepted'.[68] The boys were required to change into shirts with collars and ties for each meal and these changes, together with those necessary for PT, meant changing ten times a day: such was the emphasis on cleanliness, tidiness and routine. However, although the regime was strict and primarily deterrent in intention, every effort was made to 'develop formative influences and to encourage self-discipline'.[69] To avoid 'any prison flavour' in the centre the officers did not wear uniform. The warden, a former Borstal housemaster, was quoted as saying that 'although emphasis is and always will be on the punitive aspects, two vital elements were introduced which would elevate punishment into positive intensive training. The reformative and educative influences were introduced to play a prominent part in the life of the course.'[70] It is not clear what these 'reformative and educative' influences were. The boys' formal education was provided by a schoolmaster seconded from the Oxford County Education Authority. After-care was thought essential and every effort would be made to persuade the boys to accept it.

Looking to future development of detention centres after 1952, the Prison Commissioners reported that 'economic conditions for some time precluded any development of this scheme and even now the provision of no more than three centres has been authorized. The same conditions have equally precluded the erection of special buildings for centres.'[71] In any event it would be some years, it was argued, before the work of such centres could be fully assessed. To help with this task Dr Max Grünhut of Oxford University was commissioned in 1952 to study and follow up the first hundred receptions to Campsfield House. In this sense, at least, the provision of detention centres was taken seriously as an experiment, although it is a pity that so few lessons were learnt from past experience of punitive

---

however, the Children's Department Inspectorate was responsible for junior detention centres and the Prison Commissioners (later Department) were responsible for inspecting senior detention centres.

[67] *Report of the Prison Commissioners for 1952, op. cit.,* p. 92.
[68] *Ibid.,* p. 93.
[69] *Idem.*
[70] *Idem.*
[71] *Report of the Prison Commissioners for 1952, op. cit.,* p. 91.

detention, a study of which was published in the same year by the Cambridge department of Criminal Science.[72] Indeed, the problems facing those concerned with detention centres were to some extent predicted in this report which attempted to evaluate the effects of punitive detention in remand homes. For this reason its results warrant brief summary.

The findings relate first to the characteristics of offenders likely to respond to punitive detention and the characteristics of those for whom it appeared unsuitable. In general, detention in remand homes had not been very successful; nearly half of those aged between fourteen and sixteen had been reconvicted within three years. Of these, the majority (eighty per cent) had been reconvicted within a year of leaving the remand homes. Offenders with low intelligence or low educational achievement, with a history of truancy or those who had been previously convicted had a considerably higher rate of failure. So too did those offenders whose home backgrounds were unsatisfactory.

It was also clear from the Cambridge study that courts were using detention in remand homes differently. In Birmingham it was found that 'the main consideration in committing to detention has been given to guidance and to afford such training as is practicable within the limited time',[73] whereas in Liverpool and Manchester, for example, 'a need is felt for an establishment to which the tough type of young offender could be sent for some months and where the regime would be very rigorous'.[74] It is worth noting that the older boys from the Birmingham remand home where the warden saw 'little to be gained by emphasizing the punitive aspects'[75] achieved a considerably higher success rate (seventy-one per cent) although their characteristics were similar to the boys in the total sample. Finally, the report concluded, on the basis of the remand homes wardens' views, that after-care was an essential part of this form of treatment for young offenders.[76]

The first senior detention centre

The first detention centre for boys aged between seventeen and

---

[72] *Detention in Remand Homes: A Report of the Cambridge Department of Criminal Science on the Use of Section 54 of the Children and Young Persons Act 1933*, Macmillan, 1952. This was a study of 2,000 offenders who, between 1945 and 1948, had been committed to punitive detention and to remand homes in four urban areas.

[73] *Ibid.*, p. 62.

[74] *Ibid.*, p. 64.

[75] *Ibid.*, p. 63.

[76] Some magistrates, for example Basil Henriques, ensured after-care by giving a probation order at the same time as committing the offender to a month's punitive detention. This was a practice later used by some magistrates with respect to detention centres. See Henriques, B., *op. cit.*, p. 60.

twenty-one was opened at Cranbrook in Kent in April 1954. Although while this centre was in preparation the prison population had been falling[77] and the number of young offenders sent to prison had dropped by half between 1948 and 1952,[78] there was still concern that 328 young offenders had been sent to prison in 1952 for a first offence and that 600 had gone there for a sentence of less than three months. The Commissioners wrote: 'It may be that the opening of a detention centre for boys over seventeen years of age will help to reduce the number of these deplorable short sentences of imprisonment on young people.'[79] A major reason for opening a senior detention centre for boys was, therefore, to keep young offenders *out of prison*; for junior detention centres the reason was to keep them *out of remand homes*.

The Commissioners' initial doubts seemed to be focused on whether there would be sufficient demand for places in such a centre.[80] They need not have worried. A waiting list became necessary very soon because 'the Centre rapidly filled up and was running to near maximum capacity within a few weeks'.[81] The *Justice of the Peace and Local Government Review* reported that 'magistrates and others interested in the treatment of young offenders have been hoping for the establishment of detention centres in various parts of the country so that all courts may eventually have this method open to them'.[82] The object of the regime was stated to be the same as that of the junior centre: 'to provide short, sharp punishment'. This meant, a Home Office memorandum to the courts in 1954 pointed out, that 'there will be brisk activity under strict discipline and supervision beginning with early morning PT followed by domestic duties and work. In the evening there will be classes for further education, PT, gymnastic instruction and other activities. Particular attention will be given to the inculcation of personal standards of cleanliness, obedience and good manners.'[83] The warden interpreted this guidance very strictly in his first year, for he believed that a short sentence could only be effective if the men at the centre were made to 'concentrate on even the most minute detail and no man must even be allowed to think

[77] The average population in prisons, borstals and detention centres in 1952 was 22,568; in 1954, 21,337 and in 1955, 20,156. *Report of the Prison Commissioners for the Year 1953*, Cmd. 9199, 1954, p. 19.

[78] In 1948, 2,488 males under 21 were sentenced to prison, compared with 1,255 in 1952. *Ibid.*, p. 19.

[79] *Ibid.*, p. 21.

[80] See *Report of the Prison Commissioners for the Year 1954*, Cmd. 9547, 1955, p. 86.

[81] *Ibid.*, p. 86.

[82] *Justice of the Peace and Local Government Review*, vol. 114, 13 Dec., 1952, p. 797.

[83] Quoted in *Justice of the Peace and Local Government Review*, vol. 118, 24 June, 1954, p. 399.

"this will do"; only their best will do and nothing else should be accepted. Particular attention is paid to their general appearance and dress, their deportment, their table manners in the dining room; they must conform and respond to an order without question, in fact they must always be on their toes and not give way to the slovenly habits that are all too well known to them.'[84]

Another junior detention centre, Foston Hall, a converted country house in Derbyshire, was opened in 1956 and a year later a second detention centre for senior boys was ready at Werrington, Staffordshire.

Sentencing policy

There were two major areas of uncertainty confronting the courts in operating Section 18 (detention centres) of the 1948 Criminal Justice Act. How were offenders suitable for detention centres to be selected and how was supervision for the boys to be provided after leaving? Statements by the Home Secretary during the debate on the 1948 Act had implied that detention centres were not suitable for all offenders but, at the same time, he looked forward to the time when short prison sentences for young offenders would be abolished because there were sufficient detention centres available. The first consideration calls for a much more specific sentencing policy than the second. Certainly Dr Grünhut's findings based on the first hundred boys sentenced to detention centres showed very clearly that a poor response to the regime (i.e. further convictions) was associated with certain characteristics and not others. In the light of previous studies of punitive detention his findings were not entirely unexpected, although detention centres were clearly dealing with more serious cases than the remand homes. For example, over one in five of the boys committed to remand homes for punitive detention were first offenders compared with less than one in ten sent to Campsfield House. Similarly less than three per cent of the twelve to sixteen-year-olds detained in remand homes had three previous convictions compared with fourteen per cent of the detention centre boys.

Home background was a significant factor in determining the boys' response to the regime. One in three had a bad home background[85] and half of those with definite symptoms of social maladjustment, apart from their delinquency, were reconvicted within six months. The boys most likely to be reconvicted had had previous institutional experience, usually in approved school. Over half of this group had

---

[84] *Report of the Prison Commissioners for the Year 1954, op. cit.*, p. 88.
[85] It is interesting to note that there was insufficient information to assess the home background of 11 per cent of the boys. Grünhut, M., 'Juvenile Delinquents under Punitive Detention', *British Journal of Delinquency*, vol. 5, no. 3, Jan. 1955, p. 196.

been reconvicted within six months compared with just over a quarter for the whole group. Dr Grünhut concluded that 'failure after repeated treatment of different kinds is a stronger indication of unsuccessful treatment in the Detention Centre than the gravity of a boy's criminal activities'.[86] In contrast only four of the forty-four who were either concurrently on probation or had been probationers were reconvicted within six months, not least because 'where probation continued, it fulfilled the function of personal after-care, undertaken by an officer whom the boy knew before'.[87] Grünhut's second conclusion, therefore, was that 'constructive after-care must begin immediately after the boy's release from detention and continue for a considerable time'.[88]

With these reservations, together with a warning that early findings did not allow final judgements to be made, he felt able to state that 'a moderate criminal experience in the past does not rule out a fair prospect of success after a period of detention'.[89] This statement encouraged the Prison Commissioners and particularly magistrates, many of whom ignored Dr Grünhut's reservations and his warning that 'even with an intensified after-care effort, the possibilities of punitive detention should not be overestimated'.[90]

It is perhaps not surprising that some courts were sending boys who clearly needed more than 'a short, sharp shock'. As Dr Grünhut said: 'The magistrates are confronted with a dilemma – they are obviously and understandably reluctant to commit first offenders without serious social maladjustment to what is, to all intents and purposes, a severe punishment and they are not infrequently inclined when probation and Approved Schools have failed to overcome lasting social maladjustment to try this new and apparently more intense form of punishment.'[91] Even so he found considerable variations between courts: for example, London courts were more likely to send serious cases to detention centres whereas the courts in the Black Country were reluctant to send ex-approved school boys.

How much assistance were the courts given once such information was available? The Home Office memorandum sent to the courts when Blantyre House, the first senior detention centre, opened in 1954, stated that 'justices may like to know that boys with previous

[86] *Ibid.*, p. 201.
[87] *Ibid.*, p. 208.
[88] *Idem.*
[89] *Idem.*
[90] *Ibid.*, p. 209.
[91] *Ibid.*, p. 144. The Howard League for Penal Reform made a similar observation and commented that 'as long as Detention Centres are meant to be deliberately unpleasant – deterrent – the courts will go on sending the most unpleasant boys, for the notion that the punishment should fit the crime dies hard'. *Howard Journal*, vol. 9, no. 3, 1956–7, p. 197.

institutional training were unlikely to benefit from the regime and that it was important that the boys should be physically fit'. A few months later when pressed in the House of Commons to give further guidance, the Home Secretary, Major G. Lloyd George, made it clear that he felt 'it would not be proper to advise courts how to deal with a convicted person ... all [that] magistrates have to consider [is] whether it is better to send a man to a detention centre or a prison'.[92] Later, in 1956 when Foston Hall, the second junior detention centre, was opened the Home Office dispatched another circular drawing the same point to magistrates' attention and adding that 'those who show serious symptoms of mental disturbance or who are dull mentally or unfit physically' were unsuitable and that detention should not be used as a substitute for long-term training. The circular made it clear that 'the application of appropriate selection standards would make only a small proportion of young offenders appear eligible for punitive detention'.[93]

It was also necessary to ask magistrates *not* to give six-month sentences, for only higher courts had that power, and also to point out that it was 'desirable' that they should ascertain that there was a vacancy before making a detention centre order. The courts were also informed that wardens were prepared to give them a report on a boy upon the completion of his detention if requested.

Providing the courts with information and guidance was no guarantee that they would act accordingly; nor did evaluation of the regime seem to have much impact on sentencing policy. Although the proportion of first offenders sent to Campsfield House within the first two years increased from eight per cent to twenty-seven per cent, the proportion fell thereafter, and the proportion of those with three or more previous convictions remained constant. In the first two years the senior detention centre was sent a high proportion of boys with a bad home background: thirty-six per cent as compared with eighteen per cent of junior detention centre boys.

There was much wider agreement among the courts that after-care was an essential part of a detention centre order. From the beginning many magistrates were concerned that there was no statutory after-care and some attempted to solve this problem by making a probation order as well as a detention centre order if the boy was found guilty on two charges. However, although a detention centre order running concurrently with a probation order was not within the spirit of the 1948 Act,[94] initially there was not thought to be a valid legal

[92] *H. C. Deb.*, vol. 546, col. 2501.

[93] Home Office Circular, no. 371, 1956.

[94] A detention centre order was only supposed to be given after the courts had considered all other forms of treatment except imprisonment, and had rejected them as being unsuitable for that particular offender. It was therefore

objection and magistrates used this device for ensuring after-care. In 1956, for example, of the 358 boys released from the senior centres, over a third (154) were subject to compulsory after-care for this reason. However, only 85 of the remaining 204 boys opted for voluntary supervision.

The operation of the early detention centres
The wardens and their officers faced several problems in running these early centres. Some resulted from the sentencing policies of the courts. Offenders who were physically or mentally handicapped caused considerable difficulties for they could not participate fully in a regime based on a large amount of strenuous activity whether it took the form of parading, marching at the double, physical training or general labouring. It was difficult to know what to do with them and sometimes they spent most of their sentence in the sickbay. Moreover, while the obviously handicapped boy could be excused from various activities without the other boys thinking it strange or unfair, the boy with a weak heart, for example, appeared to the others to be getting off lightly. In addition, with a regime involving close and continued supervision, coping with exceptions made considerable demands on the staff.

The wardens also found difficulty in dealing adequately with boys sent to them for longer than three months because 'the centres are geared to an intensive ten weeks course of discipline and training, and boys with other lengths of sentence are inevitably out of gear'.[95] Until detention centres were established which allowed fully for a six-month training programme, boys serving longer sentences merely repeated the ten-week cycle.

The nature of the regime and the brevity of the sentence meant that the staff had few sanctions at their disposal. Therefore, 'it was thought desirable to provide for the earning of some remission both to encourage the boys to behave well and to provide an effective disciplinary sanction in view of the small privileges which can be provided and the comparative mildness of the available punishment'.[96] Boys could earn two weeks remission for good behaviour but those who failed to do so spent the full twelve weeks at the detention centre. They too did not fit into the neat ten-week cycle.

The staff would have been faced with similar problems had after-care been made compulsory on leaving the centre. The usual sanction against breaking the conditions of after-care is a return to the institu-

---

also illogical to act on the basis that a probation order was suitable *at the same time* as a detention order.

[95] *Report of the Prison Commissioners for the Year 1953, op. cit.*, p. 95.
[96] *Report of the Prison Commissioners for the Year 1955*, Cmnd. 10, 1956, p. 111 (the boys could earn two weeks remission for good behaviour).

tion from which the offender has been released but as Chuter Ede had said during the debates on the Criminal Justice Bill, 'a series of short, sharp lessons is apt to lose its effect'.[97] Certainly the staff of the early centres would have faced practical difficulties in having offenders back for a short period after leaving.

Another problem arose from the keeness of magistrates to send offenders to detention centres. From the early days the senior detention centres were always full. As Dr Grünhut suggested later, the staff of the detention centres and the Prison Commissioners 'probably feared that a statutory combination of a form of probation [with a detention centre order] might induce magistrates to make more frequent use of a form of treatment intended only for a small selection of young offenders'.[98] Therefore, although the wardens of the two early centres had initially expressed concern about the lack of after-care they apparently changed their views. After a year's experience the warden of the senior centre said that he was no longer so sure about the need for compulsory supervision and thought that 'if the system is left as it is it will find its own level'.[99] He was encouraged by the fact that of all the boys discharged from his centre up until the end of 1955 almost seventy per cent had not appeared again in court by the end of that year (in fact *half* of those leaving during 1955 were reconvicted within three years).

There were also fears that with such a mixed bag of delinquents being sent by the courts,[100] those with criminal experience would contaminate the rest. However, the strict regime and the constant turnover hindered the development of relationships between the boys, and the warden of the senior centre felt able to say that he was 'confident this intermixing does not have a detrimental effect; there is very little time for friendships to mature and each man is so dependent upon his own effort that he cannot afford to be influenced'.[101] In those circumstances one wonders whether a relationship of much value could develop between the officers and their charges. Nevertheless, the warden believed that the development of the right relationship between the staff and the boys depended on the officers showing 'firmness with kindness, an element of humour with hard work and complete fairness and impartiality'.[102]

Other difficulties arose from the nature of the detention centre sentence. New boys could arrive daily while others were leaving daily.

[97] See p. 324.
[98] Grünhut, M., 'After Effects of Punitive Detention', *British Journal of Criminology*, vol. 10, Jan. 1960, p. 189.
[99] *Report of the Prison Commissioners for the Year 1954, op. cit.*, p. 90.
[100] The first senior centre received 232 boys in the first nine months, including delinquent soldiers, conscientious objectors and 'Edwardians'.
[101] *Report of the Prison Commissioners for the Year 1954, op. cit.*, p. 86.
[102] *Ibid.*, p. 87.

A constantly changing population not only made it difficult to devise a programme which could be entered at any point in the ten-week cycle but also made it difficult to treat the boys individually. In 1955 an attempt to alleviate this problem was made by allotting a small group of boys to each officer and 'in order to cover the personal work which is badly needed, especially for boys in the senior centre, the Commissioners are loaning a housemaster to Blantyre House for an experimental period of six months'.[103] However, the following year it was reported that this housemaster had relieved the warden from the pressure of 'administrative work'.

Great emphasis was placed on the part played by physical training in the regime. Physical training, the warden of Blantyre House explained, 'is mainly responsible for the fresh and healthy outlook on life that is achieved ... A greater sense of cleanliness is apparent and the doctrine of "if one feels good, one will be good" comes to the fore.'[104] However, the major role of physical training highlights the contradictions in the basic objectives of the detention centre. If the experience was meant to be sufficiently unpleasant so that the offender would not want to return then once the boys started *enjoying* the physical exercise this objective was defeated. On the other hand it was regarded as an achievement if the boys did come to enjoy it: this was reckoned as one of the positive aspects of their stay. 'Experience shows that while detention is irksome and the scale of effort demanded very high, a corporate spirit exists among the inmates, interest in personal progress and pride in achievement is observed in most of them.'[105]

Finally, it should be remembered that a regime which is 'strict and rigorous, the highest possible standards being required at the quickest possible tempo',[106] is not only tough for the offenders but sets a fast pace for the disciplinary staff. Moreover, as the Howard League for Penal Reform said in 1956 'a deliberately deterrent regime is not easily imposed on young men of, perhaps, nineteen and twenty who are physically fit – stronger perhaps than some older members of staff. There may be a tendency to reinforce it by the dangerous way of trying to humiliate the offender. Another reason is that it may be difficult to obtain or keep really suitable staff, for it is hard to feel pride in doing something that is mainly deterrent and therefore mainly

---

[103] *Report of the Prison Commissioners for the Year 1955, op. cit.*, p. 111.

[104] *Report of the Prison Commissioners for the Year 1956*, Cmd. 322, 1957, p. 111.

[105] *Report of the Prison Commissioners for the Year 1955, op. cit.*, p. 90. One physical training instructor we met who had worked in a detention centre was outraged at being told by a visiting committee that what he was doing was barbaric. He was proud that the boys came to *enjoy* his PT sessions.

[106] Description of detention centre regime contained in *Prison and Borstals England and Wales*, HMSO, 1957, p. 59.

negative.'[107] It is quite clear from talking to some of those who worked in the early centres that the later 'mellowing' of the regime was due partly to the needs of the staff being taken more into account.

General criticisms of the regime

The detention centres attracted much attention besides that of Dr Grünhut and, during their early years, they received more visitors than offenders. In 1958 a small sub-committee of the Magistrates' Association was established to visit and report on Campsfield House 'in view of difference of opinion about the value of a period of detention in the detention centre'.[108] Three members of this committee were clearly unhappy at some aspects of the system. Whilst recognizing that the 'regime must be strict and primarily deterrent in intention', they felt that the supervision was too strict.[109] They were also concerned that many of the boys had 'already received an impression from the courts committing them that they will undergo severe punishment; consequently they arrive embittered and hard and the staff have a difficult task in overcoming this initial resentment'.[110]

The work consisted of domestic, kitchen and laundry work together with labouring and gardening, some of it unnecessarily tedious. For example, there was only one small iron in the laundry. The committee noted that boys were being sent to the centre who were medically unfit for its rigours. It was recommended that such boys should be screened out by having a medical report available to the courts. Ex-approved school boys should also be excluded. They agreed with the warden that 'the simple delinquent coming from a family of offenders and brought up in an atmosphere of crime cannot benefit from committal', but they were not convinced that the warden was right in saying that 'even the offender who puts up a façade of toughness as compensation for his unhappiness and insecurity will benefit from the training and his moral fibre strengthened'.[111] They therefore recommended that the Home Office should issue a circular to the courts giving details of the methods of treatment used in a detention centre and the type of offender suitable for this treatment.

The Magistrates' Association made this report public in the autumn of 1954 and it received considerable coverage. ' "Shock" Detention Centre for Boys Criticized: Unsuitable Types Sent', ran a headline

[107] *Howard Journal*, vol. 9, no. 3, 1956–7, p. 197.

[108] The Magistrates' Association, *39th Annual Report and Statement of Accounts*, 1953–54, p. 8.

[109] 'The boys are never left for one moment unsupervised and this seems to be implicit in the form of training. We consider this unfortunate and needs relaxing.' *Ibid.*, p. 46.

[110] Former staff of the early detention centres have confirmed that some boys arrived clearly expecting harsh treatment.

[111] *Ibid.*, p. 52.

in the *Daily Telegraph*, for example.[112] The association was criticized by the Home Office for making the report public and for drawing attention to the difference in views about the value of detention centres. Consequently, two years later when another sub-committee reported on the second junior detention centre at Foston Hall (opened in January 1956) and opinions were still somewhat divided, the association decided not to publish its report and used the experimental nature of detention centres as a reason for not coming to any firm judgement.

However, it is clear that the members of this sub-committee were not favourably impressed with junior detention centres. They reported that they were opposed in principle to detention centres for the junior age groups 'though for the older group (seventeen to twenty-one years) it is considered that such centres may be of use in *a limited number of cases* and may keep some young men from going to prison'.[113] In other words in 1956 detention centres were still regarded as an experimental type of custodial treatment only suitable for certain offenders, and it was felt that their value had still to be proved.

The Howard League for Penal Reform had also been concerned about the development of detention centres since they were first proposed, and although recognizing that such centres would prevent some young offenders from being sent to prison it saw no reason to suppose that hard work and discipline would deter. It preferred short-term schools and compulsory attendance centres.[114] By 1956 it was very concerned that the regime in detention centres was still primarily deterrent, and as a result receiving some very difficult boys. But these were the boys, it pointed out, least likely to benefit from the experience for 'if character traits are strongly anti-social and delinquency really deep-rooted, deterrence does not work and punishment cannot teach'.[115] It therefore recommended that as detention centres were stated to be experimental and the Criminal Justice Act had not specified how they should work in detail, the Prison Commissioners should try 'a regime more on the lines of a short-term Borstal or Approved School with more emphasis on training and an extra staff member so that there is greater opportunity to enter into the boys' personal problems'.[116]

Questions about detention centres were not often asked in Parliament, but when they were, they too centred mainly on the selection of offenders and the nature of the regime. The need to ensure that

[112] *Daily Telegraph*, 25 Sept., 1954.
[113] Magistrates' Association, *32nd Annual Report and Statement of Accounts*, 1956–57, p. 16.
[114] See *Howard Journal*, vol. 7, no. 3, 1947–8.
[115] *Howard Journal*, vol. 9, no. 3, 1956–7, p. 197.
[116] *Ibid.*, p. 198.

only boys who were physically fit were sent to detention centres was emphasized by Members but, as we have already seen, requests to give courts firmer guidance were refused. In December 1955 concern was expressed about conscientious objectors being sent to a detention centre because there were allegations that the warden had used 'terms of opprobrium' to them. The Home Secretary said he had accepted the staff's denial that this had happened.

The Prison Commissioners were clearly conscious of the need to counter adverse criticism. They felt obliged to emphasize the positive aspects of detention centres in their annual reports, and reviewing developments in penal policy from 1946 to 1955 they said: 'The regime of these centres has been the subject of some controversy, the feeling being expressed that a merely deterrent regime must be retrograde and harmful. The Commissioners for their part, while mindful of the expressed purpose of these centres, have sought to make the regime as formative as is practicable in so short a time as three months. In particular they have made sure that neither in the buildings they have acquired nor in the staff, nor in the regime shall there be any flavour of prison. So far the evidence suggests to them that a regime of strict discipline and high tempo does have the effect desired on the majority of boys who come to the centres, with no signs of the harm that may be done by harshness and repression.'[117] In all their reports in the early years of detention centres the Commissioners continued to stress the experimental nature of the provision. They drew attention to the junior centre warden's report that during 1954 there had been a 'noticeable mellowing in the atmosphere of the centre'.[118] By 1955 they were also sure that the senior detention centre did not set standards which were too high: 'The general reaction has been quite extraordinary, the weak and spineless have striven hard to make their mark and the stronger character soon gives way to the challenge and conforms enthusiastically.'[119]

At this time, therefore, they were aware of certain difficulties in running detention centres, conscious of informed and responsible criticism as well as being uncertain of their ability to expand the programme. The prospects of there being any marked expansion looked slight. 'When trends both of prison population and national economic conditions are so unpredictable', the Commissioners wrote, 'it would be unprofitable to speculate as to whether and when it may became both necessary and practical to augment the present programme.'[120] Nevertheless, placed alongside the priority being given to certain other features of penal provision, especially remand centres,

---

[117] *Report of the Prison Commissioners for the Year 1955, op. cit.,* p. 26.
[118] *Report of the Prison Commissioners for the Year 1954, op. cit.,* p. 87.
[119] *Report of the Prison Commissioners for the Year 1955, op. cit.,* p. 88.
[120] *Report of the Prison Commissioners for the Year 1956, op. cit.,* p. 134.

Table 9

EXPERIENCE OF PRISON BY YOUNG OFFENDERS, 1959–62

	Sent to prison for first offence	Sent to prison for less than three months	Total offenders under twenty-one sent to prison under sentence	Number under twenty-one committed to prison before conviction or remanded for trial who did not subsequently return to prison	
				Found guilty	Not guilty
1952	328	606	1,255	2,565	119
1953	328	600	1,149	2,593	101
1954	324	580	1,067	2,256	58
1955	267	604	1,068	2,499	104
1956	304	690	1,404	2,907	81
1957	321	738	1,543	4,061	285
1958	308	905	1,782	4,094	164
1959	661	1,356	2,498	4,184	203
1960	356	1,225	3,099	3,233	146
1961	360	1,170	3,029	3,284	284
1962	313	810	2,691	4,369	201

SOURCES: *Reports of the Prison Commissioners* for the years 1952–62 and *Report of the Work of the Prison Department, 1968* (statistical tables).

detention centres seemed to have scored well. They were relatively cheap to establish and the short sentence involved meant that they provided many more places for offenders each year than the same number of places in prison or borstal.

Detention centres and remand centres
One of the avowed aims of establishing detention centres, in particular senior detention centres, was to keep young people out of prison. Their introduction was, therefore, evaluated not only in terms of the impact of the regime on offenders sent to them but also in terms of whether or not fewer young people were experiencing imprisonment. As table 9 shows, the number of young offenders being sent to prison had not been substantially reduced by the opening of the first senior detention centre, at Goudhurst in 1954. On the contrary, whereas the number of young offenders being sent to prison had fallen in the two years *prior* to the opening of Goudhurst, by 1956 numbers were increasing again. The Prison Commissioners explained in their annual report for that year how the increase could be explained broadly in terms of increases in crimes of violence, breaking and entering, larceny, Highway Act offences and non-indictable assaults. However, in July 1955, the Home Secretary, Lloyd George, had requested the Advisory Council on the Treatment of Offenders to examine alternatives to short-term imprisonment for both young and adult offenders. Earlier that year the Howard League for Penal Reform had asked him to consider ways of avoiding short spells in prison. First, because short sentences were not only useless for the purposes of training but also likely to do more harm than good as deterrents. Second because, with fewer short-term prisoners, hard pressed prison staff would have more time to deal with the others.

A sub-committee of the Advisory Council duly reported early in 1957.[121] It proposed that attendance centres, as envisaged in the 1948 Criminal Justice Act, should be established for the seventeen to twenty-one-year-olds (only junior centres existed at the time); that courts should consider imposing heavy fines as an alternative to prison and that section 17 of the Act should be extended to adult first offenders.[122] It recommended that remand centres should be set up

---

[121] Report of the Advisory Council on the Treatment of Offenders, *Alternatives to Short Terms of Imprisonment*, 1957. The sub-committee which studied the subject included George Benson, MP, Margery Fry, B. J. Hartwell, Dr Radzinowicz and Sir Henry Studby. George Benson and Margery Fry were both members of the executive committee of the Howard League for Penal Reform at the time.

[122] Section 17 provided that imprisonment shall not be imposed on a person under twenty-one years of age unless the court is of opinion that no other method of dealing with him is appropriate; and that for the purpose of determining whether any other method is appropriate the court shall obtain and

as soon as possible, for none existed in 1957, and courts should be encouraged to make greater use of remands for enquiry, on bail in the majority of cases. An indication of the lack of widespread concern about young offenders in 1957 is the fact that the report made *no* mention either of detention centres or corporal punishment.

At this time the Home Office was under increasing pressure from other quarters to establish the remand centres promised in the 1948 Criminal Justice Act. At their annual meeting in 1956 the Magistrates' Association had passed the following resolution: 'Since much of the value of the alternatives to prison is lost if they have to spend a period in prison while such alternatives are considered or awaited, this Magistrates' Association urges the Government to set up remand centres as provided for in the Criminal Justice Act.'[123] Then, early in 1957, Charles Royle, vice-chairman of the Magistrates' Association succeeded in getting an Adjournment Debate in the House of Commons on remand centres. He argued that the lack of remand centres led to the inappropriate sentencing of offenders to prison *and* detention centres. He deplored the fact that nearly two and a half thousand young people had been remanded in prison in 1955 and estimated that since 1948, 20,000 young people had served a few weeks or days in prison awaiting trial. If remand centres were provided there would be no need to send the majority of these young people to prison. He regretted that economic conditions had prevented this. Therefore, he would rather see remand centres built instead of detention centres particularly as the need for detention centres would not be as great if this was done. 'I believe', he said, 'that some magistrates are so concerned about the situation and are so determined that under no circumstances will they send young people to prison even on remand that they have been tempted to and actually do send them to detention centres in sheer desperation.'[124]

In reply the Joint Under Secretary of State for the Home Department, Mr J. E. Simon, said that remand centres were not a substitute for detention centres: the former were for detention and observation *before* trial or sentence, the latter a method of treatment *after* trial and conviction. He agreed that there was a real need for such facilities and it was particularly disturbing that during 1954, for example, 314 boys and eight girls under seventeen had been remanded in prison.

---

consider information about the circumstances and shall take into account any information before it which is relevant of the person's character and his physical and mental condition. The court also had to state the reason for its opinion that no other method was appropriate. The First Offender Act was passed in 1958, and brought into effect. It extended this provision to adult first offenders.

[123] Quoted by Charles Royle during the Adjournment Debate, *H. C. Deb.*, vol. 555, col. 760.

[124] *Ibid.*, col. 763.

The atmosphere of a local prison was undesirable and their presence contributed towards overcrowding. However, the provision of remand centres was a matter of priorities and the most urgent needs were new prisons and borstals. He did not think remand centres were of greater importance than detention centres. He gave two reasons.

First, it was hoped that one day detention centres would be sufficiently numerous so that it would be possible to put an end to sentences of imprisonment for all persons under twenty-one by magistrates' courts. Second, detention centres were much cheaper to establish than remand centres. Unlike detention centres, remand centres had to be purpose-built and, if used to best advantage, needed to be combined with observation and classification centres. The Prison Commissioners had estimated that seven such centres were needed and these would cost over £7 million. In contrast, four detention centres complete with staff housing had been built for less than £300,000. 'From the point of view of the Treasury, which has to consider every demand on the national economy – security, the social services such as education, housing, hospitals and a rising consumption not only for the wage earner but for the retirement pensioner and others in a similar position – the sum (for remand centres) is obviously a very large one.'[125] However, Simon did agree that the need was a real one and that young offenders were 'urgent claimants on our sympathy'.

Summary: the first five years of detention centres, 1952 to 1957

The first five years of the development of detention centres had been slow, cautious and controversial. Throughout the period the Prison Commissioners were in a weak position to gain more resources. Neither Home Secretaries were strong ministers and the economic situation did not favour an increase in public expenditure. After 1951 crime rates, especially among the young, appeared to be falling[126] and were not seemingly the cause of public concern and, apart from attempts to abolish capital punishment in 1956, penal policy was not the subject of widespread comment in the press. The experimental nature of detention centres was continually emphasized by the Prison Commissioners in order to justify this slow development as well as to counter criticism both from those wanting a more rapid increase in their number and those who were concerned about the punitive aspects of the regime.

The courts were faced with the problem of deciding which offenders might benefit from a detention centre sentence: the offender for whom all other forms of treatment had failed or the first offender in need of a 'short, sharp shock'. Their varied views about the character-

[125] *Ibid.*, col. 760.
[126] See Table 8, p. 329.

istics of offenders suitable for detention centres posed problems for those running them but as long as the staff were not overwhelmed by numbers and while the experimental nature of the regime allowed modifications, these problems were not insurmountable.

Thus by 1957 there were only four detention centres and little to suggest that in the next five years this form of provision would undergo a rapid and substantial growth. Our next section traces this marked development and endeavours to explain why it happened.

III THE PERIOD OF GROWTH: 1957 TO 1961

'While the centres will not cease to develop or to seek means of improving their work, the experimental stage of this new form of treatment is coming to an end. Application for a fifth centre is being sought in the North East, but there are other areas in the country where courts have expressed the need for detention centres.'[127] So wrote the Prison Commissioners of developments during 1957. This year was an important one for it marked the beginning of pressure for change and development which were to culminate in the Criminal Justice Act of 1961.

In January 1957, R. A. Butler[128] was appointed Home Secretary when Anthony Eden resigned and Harold Macmillan became Prime Minister. Here was a Home Secretary apparently committed to penal reform *and* with sufficient power to gain the additional resources to implement change. He was a senior member of the Cabinet and was well acquainted with penal affairs for, as Leader of the House, he had helped the government to defeat the Bill to abolish capital punishment. Moreover, he had been Chancellor of the Exchequer from October 1951 to December 1955 and so knew the Treasury well. In any case the argument that the economic situation and the priorities of the building programme did not permit expenditure for improving the prison system became weaker, for 1958 and 1959 were years of economic expansion compared with the preceding years of restriction.

During 1957 Butler made several important new appointments among his senior civil servants. A. W. Peterson, who had previously been an Assistant Secretary at the Home Office, became his personal assistant in his capacity as Lord Privy Seal and was later that year appointed a Prison Commissioner upon the retirement of R. C. Bradley (Bradley had been the Commissioner responsible for develop-

---

[127] *Report of the Prison Commissioners for the year 1957*, Cmnd, 496, 1958, p. 91.
[128] For an interesting description of Butler's role during the debates on capital punishment, see Christophe, J., *op. cit.*, ch. 6.

ing early detention centre policy). This was an important appointment, for Peterson was made deputy chairman of the commission and later became its chairman when Lionel Fox retired in September 1960. At the Home Office Frank Newsam, who had been its permanent head, retired in June 1957 and Butler replaced him with Charles Cunningham from the Scottish Home Department. Thus not only was there a new Home Secretary in 1957 but changes as well in the ranks of senior civil servants concerned with penal policy.

Shortly after becoming Home Secretary Butler was given the opportunity of making a declaration of intent with respect to penal policy. The Opposition allowed him to open the debate in the Supply Committee on Supplementary Estimates in which the government was seeking approval for an additional £107,000 for the salaries and expenses of the officers of the Prison Commission, prisons, borstals and detention centres. Anthony Greenwood explained that a debate on the prison service had been requested because it had always been 'the Cinderella' of the social services and he hoped that Mr Butler was going to be a 'reforming Home Secretary'. The Opposition had, therefore, wanted to give him the chance of 'enunciating certain principles'.

Mr Butler did so. His first priority, he explained, was to expand the Home Office's research programme, for in the past twelve years they had spent only £12,000 on research and he believed 'accurate knowledge is an indispensable tool of administration'.[129] Next he was going to look at sentencing policy because he considered that the increase in the numbers in prison (3,000 between 1938 and 1955) was partly due to increases in the length of sentences. This, he admitted, involved considerations which were the concern of the judiciary and not of the Executive, 'although the Executive certainly has a distinct concern with the effects'. Being bolder than previous post-war Home Secretaries, he continued, 'there are ways in which the Executive, within its proper limits, may well seek to collaborate with the judiciary in this all important question of sentencing policy'.[130] In order to assess an offender's need for treatment remand centres were of great importance and must be established. Finally, he wanted to see changes in the treatment of offenders with less emphasis on punishment. 'I believe', he declared, 'that we might one day come to think of our prisons not as places of punishment – though that must be since deprivation of liberty must always be a punishment; not only as places where offenders are trained to be better men and better citizens, which is what they seek, however imperfectly, to be now; but also as places where an offender could work out his own or her own personal redemption by paying his or her debt not only to society

[129] *H. C. Deb.*, vol. 566, col. 1142.
[130] *Ibid.*, col. 1146.

whose order he has disturbed but to the fellow members of that society whom he has wronged.'[131] At this time it was too early to detect the change from downward to upward trends in both crime rates and in the prison population. However, as we have already seen, the courts were complaining of major difficulties arising from the lack of remand centres and the subject had been discussed by Parliament. A month after his appointment Butler announced that the first remand centre would be built.

In the Queen's Speech in November 1957, for the first time for some years, there was a reference to the government's policy with respect to penal reform: 'They will continue to pay particular attention to penal reform and the treatment of offenders and they will develop improvements in the prison system in the light of an imaginative programme of research.'[132] A vague commitment and one that aroused little comment in Parliament at the time. However, in the following months, against a background of rising crime, especially crimes of violence,[133] politicians, the courts and apparently the 'public' demanded effective deterrents. The debate about corporal punishment was renewed and magistrates asked for more detention centres. The number of young offenders sent to borstal and prison increased, as Table 10 shows, reversing the trend of the few previous years. This, together with a disturbing number of young people, especially those under seventeen, being remanded to prison, strengthened demands for remand centres as envisaged in the 1948 Act and added urgency to the provision of alternatives to short terms of imprisonment.

The government had, therefore, soon to develop some very specific proposals. In May 1958, Butler asked the Advisory Council on the Treatment of Offenders to review the treatment of young adult offenders because 'the system has been subjected to severe strains as a result of the great increase in crime in this age-group'.[134] What were these 'severe strains', who felt them and how did the Home Secretary and the Prison Commissioners respond?

The prison service felt the pressure most for several reasons. First, the borstal population increased from 2,800 at the beginning of 1956 to over 4,400 at the end of 1958. During 1958 four prisons were converted into borstals and two redundant service camps were adapted for this purpose. Offenders sentenced to borstal training had frequently to wait for as long as three months in prison before being transferred to a borstal reception centre. Second, young prisoners serving sentences of three months or more, although eligible for transfer to a young

---

[131] *Ibid.*, col. 1154.

[132] *H. C. Deb.*, vol. 577, col. 7.

[133] See Table 8, p. 329.

[134] Advisory Council on the Treatment of Offenders, *Penal Practice in a Changing Society*, Cmnd. 645, 1959, p. 10.

Table 10

CHANGES IN THE CUSTODIAL TREATMENT OF MALE YOUNG OFFENDERS, 1952–65

	Detention Centres		Prison: total receptions	Borstals: receptions	Total receptions	Total receptions per 100,000 in 16–21 age group
	Total receptions	Average population				
1952	75	40	1,255	2,124	3,454	257
1953	210	44	1,149	1,812	3,171	230
1954	247	108	1,067	1,523	3,069	221
1955	586	124	1,132	1,478	3,196	225
1956	818	'165	1,320	1,899	4,037	279
1957	1,093	234	1,574	2,367	5,034	337
1958	1,302	271	1,782	3,047	6,131	420
1959	1,356	274	2,498	3,062	6,916	462
1960	1,295	275	3,099	3,476	7,870	507
1961	2,311	462	3,029	3,588	8,928	555
1962	3,595	754	2,691	3,746	10,032	613
1963	4,743	1,032	2,412	3,548	10,703	573
1964	5,780	1,295	2,593	3,715	12,088	615
1965	6,740	1,522	2,957	3,923	13,620	686

SOURCE: *Report of the Prison Commissioners for the Year 1960*, Cmnd. 1647, table C. 10, and the *Report on the Work of the Prison Department, 1968* (Statistical Tables), Cmnd. 4266, table C. 10.

prisoners' centre, were increasingly having to serve their whole sentence in local prisons. This placed a considerable burden on local prisons: more than an increase in adult offenders would have done, because the policy was to give each young offender a single cell and not to allow the doubling or trebling up which occurred among adult prisoners.[135] Third, the courts were sentencing more first offenders to prison and giving more short sentences.[136] Last, detention centres as well were reported to be not only full but sometimes overfull by the end of 1957.[137] Wardens could not refuse boys sent to their centre and had, therefore, to accommodate them in the sick bay or even in the isolation cells.

The courts were also experiencing difficulties. Although at last a remand centre had been promised, it did not yet exist. As Charles Royle had said in the House of Commons, some magistrates were sending young offenders to detention centres rather than remanding them or sentencing them to prison. However, when the demand for detention centre places grew as the number of young offenders coming before the courts increased they could not always do this. Moreover, once they had been notified that a detention centre was available to them they no longer had the power to use remand homes for punitive detention. Magistrates were, therefore, often faced with a situation in which there was no detention centre vacancy. What were they to do with an offender whom they wanted to send there? A detention centre order took effect immediately so that it was illegal to remand a boy to await a vacancy, once they had made the order. Some magistrates adopted the practice of remanding boys under section 14 (sub-section 3) of the Magistrates' Court Act, 1952, under which a court may adjourn the hearing and remand a defendant for the purpose of determining the most suitable method of dealing with him. Strictly speaking to use this section of the Act in order to remand a boy with the intention of making a detention centre order at the next hearing if there was a vacancy, was against the spirit of the Magistrates' Court Act. Other magistrates, finding no vacancy at a detention centre, took tougher measures. For example, a case was reported of an eighteen-year-old whom both the probation officer and the magistrates thought should be sent to a detention centre but because there was no vacancy for over three weeks he was committed in custody to Quarter Sessions with a view to borstal training.[138]

Perhaps this procedure would have attracted less attention if

[135] By the end of 1958, 6,000 men were sleeping three in a single cell. *Ibid.*, p. 13.

[136] See Table 9, p. 343

[137] *Report of the Prison Commissioners for 1957, op. cit.*, 1958, p. 8.

[138] *Justice of the Peace and Local Government Review*, vol. 122, 12 July, 1958, p. 442.

magistrates had been able to remand in custody to a remand centre. But because there were, as yet, no remand centres and not always a vacancy in a remand home, boys were remanded in prison. Instances of these, particularly where they involved boys and girls under seventeen, received considerable publicity during 1958 and 1959. In August 1959 there was a case of a fifteen-year-old London boy who was repeatedly remanded in custody for three weeks at a time (the maximum remand period a court may impose at one hearing) so that he spent a total of three months in prison.[139] As a result of this case magistrates were strongly advised against the practice of remanding in custody in the absence of a vacancy in a detention centre. This increased the courts' determination to get more detention centres.

The Prison Commissioners were certainly made increasingly aware of the magistrates' dissatisfaction with the lack of detention centres.[140] The judiciary were putting further pressure on the Prison Commissioners at this time by making it harder for them to retain one of the few means they had for curbing the demand for detention centre places. Without statutory after-care some magistrates were very reluctant to send boys to detention centres. Thus to concede to demands for statutory after-care would, as Dr Grünhut had noted,[141] further increase the pressure on detention centre places.

In 1958 the issue of ensuring after-care came to a head when the Lord Chief Justice ruled[142] that a probation order on a boy named Evans at the same time as a detention centre order was contrary to the spirit and intention of the Criminal Justice Act, 1948. Moreover, it was held that the two orders were inconsistent because probation could not start until after the boy had left the detention centre and the courts could not know in advance whether he would need probation at that point. This decision effectively halted this means of securing after-care and those concerned with young offenders regarded 'the position [as] so serious that it would be helpful if the Home Office as a matter of urgency put forward a short Bill declaring the past practice to be lawful and legalizing the practice in the future'.[143] Later, in the House of Lords during the debate on the Criminal

---

[139] *Justice of the Peace and Local Government Review*, vol. 123, 29 Aug., 1959, p. 439.

[140] For example, on 17 Sept., 1958 the *Surrey Comet* reported that Surrey magistrates had decided to ask the Home Secretary to receive a deputation about the provision of additional detention centres, quoted in the *Justice of the Peace and Local Government Review*, vol. 122, 18 Oct., 1958, p. 677. See also *Report of the Prison Commissioners for the Year 1958*, Cmnd, 825, 1959, p. 89.

[141] See p. 338.

[142] In *R. v. Evans* (1958) 3 All ER 673.

[143] *Justice of the Peace and Local Government Review*, vol. 123, 28 Mar., 1959, p. 201.

Justice Bill in 1961 Lord Parker was to explain that ever since the case of Evans he had hoped provision for statutory after-care following commitment to a detention centre would be introduced. In other words this was almost certainly a decision taken by the judiciary with a view to forcing the government into making statutory provision for after-care.

During 1958 Grünhut's sequel study of the effects of the detention centres' regime on the senior age group became available to the Home Office and the Prison Commissioners were encouraged by his findings. At that time only thirty-four per cent of the boys who had left Blantyre House between 1954 and 1957 had been reconvicted. With so much demand for increased detention centre provision they took comfort from Dr Grünhut's conclusion that 'there is a fair chance that a boy can be led back to a law abiding life even under unfavourable circumstances. This observation justifies the proposition that detention in a detention centre has a legitimate place in a differentiated system of penal and corrective methods for juvenile and adolescent offenders.'[144] Less attention seems to have been paid to his view that those suitable for punitive detention were a small proportion of offenders.

In all these circumstances the Prison Commissioners felt justified in making proposals to establish sufficient detention centres so that they could ultimately replace short terms of imprisonment. In addition they wanted all short and medium term sentences of imprisonment for young offenders to be abolished and the principle of indeterminacy applied to all medium term sentences for young offenders. It was these proposals that the Home Secretary asked the Advisory Council on the Treatment of Offenders to consider in May 1958.

Meanwhile concern about rising crime rates, especially among the young, was becoming the subject of lively public debate. In March 1958, for example, the *Sunday Times* ran a series of articles on crime, to which the magistrate John Watson, Viscount Samuel and R. A. Butler all contributed. The cause of increased criminal activity among the young was attributed to several factors but one of the underlying themes in all three articles was that a reduction in a sense of personal and family responsibility was responsible for the increasing numbers of young offenders. 'Against the great material advantages of the welfare state', wrote John Watson, 'must be weighed a dangerous tendency to undermine the responsibility of parents for their children – and thus to lessen their determination to control them.'[145] Viscount Samuel likewise spoke of 'unhappy and undisciplined

---

[144] *Ibid.*, p. 98 (see also Grünhut, M., 'After Effects of Punitive Detention', *op. cit.*, p. 192).
[145] *Sunday Times*, 9 Mar., 1958.

children' being the product of loosening family relationships. There was a need, therefore, to 'instil discipline and improve restraint'.[146] Many of the letters in response to these articles echoed these sentiments and it was clear that penal policy was expected to treat young offenders in a way that would make up for the lack of discipline in the home. The Home Secretary in the final article promised to 'develop and improve the facilities available to the courts'.[147] Pressure was mounting for the government to take tough measures, including the reintroduction of corporal punishment, to curb the rising crime rate. This took a variety of forms and came from mixed sources.

At the Conservative Party Conference in October 1958, for instance, detention centres came under attack for not being tough enough to deter the rising number of young thugs. The restoration of corporal punishment was offered as a more effective alternative, but a less specific resolution was actually passed: 'That this Conference, recognizing that the disturbing increase in criminal offences has shown the failure of existing methods of punishment and reform, calls for an immediate review of the causes of crime and the application of more effective measures to reduce it.' Butler spoke during the debate on the motion and gave an undertaking 'to deal resolutely, so far as I can, with juvenile crime, whatever methods may be felt best and however strong those methods may have to be'.[148] However, this did not mean that he was prepared to reintroduce corporal punishment and it was clear that he was offering more detention centres as an alternative to this. 'I do not believe the whole thing can be settled by flogging or birching. *I have in mind in particular the new detention centres which we are setting up.*' He continued: 'I wish to have time to fashion my proposals thoroughly with the aid of my colleagues, the Magistrates' Association and other bodies such as the Advisory Council on the Treatment of Offenders who also advise me.' Meanwhile, he said, with reference to offenders of all ages, 'what we have to do is to classify these prisoners, to have a building programme for the prisons and that I am arranging in conjunction with my friend the Chancellor.'[149]

But although detention centres might in part placate the more vociferous advocates of corporal punishment the Prison Commissioners were at the same time being attacked from other quarters for allowing the regime in these centres, particularly the junior centres, to be too punitive. At the Annual Conference of Children's Officers in September 1958, for example, the President deplored the fact that

[146] *Sunday Times*, 2 Mar., 1958.

[147] *Sunday Times*, 16 Mar., 1958.

[148] *Report of the 78th Conference of the National Union of Conservative and Unionist Associations*, 1958, p. 95.

[149] *Ibid.*, p. 102.

the Prison Commissioners rather than local authorities were responsible for junior detention centres. He was very worried that the centres were subject, in nearly every aspect, to prison law. This included regulations concerning photographing and finger printing for the criminal records office. 'At Kidlington one of the first things we saw was a special room in which these youngsters have their photographs and their finger prints taken and sent to Scotland Yard. Even the laundry baskets were labelled "HMP Kidlington".'[150] This, together with the fifteen-foot barbed wire fence surrounding the centre, the sight of a physical training lesson with a teacher in front and a 'discipline' officer standing on either side led him, and the party with him to conclude 'that it was the finest inoculation against any fear of prison that we could imagine but we could see very little that was really constructive'. These views were widely reported in the press but, of course, many did not share his views. For example, the *Justice of the Peace and Local Government Review*, reporting the speech under the heading 'Detention Centres have again come under fire', disagreed with his observations and could find nothing objectionable in the fact that the Prison Commissioners were responsible for detention centres. 'The fact must be faced that being sent to a detention centre is meant to be a punishment and sometimes punishment leads to amendment.'[151]

Penal policy became the subject of serious discussion in Parliament during the next session, 1958–9. In the Queen's Speech, changes in the penal system were promised and, unlike the previous year, were set in the context of the increasing crime rate: 'My Government views with gravity the increase in crime. In the light of the most up to date knowledge and research they will seek to improve the penal system and to make methods of dealing with offenders more effective.'[152] This time the subject aroused greater discussion[153] in Parliament, and with both wings amongst the critics of detention centres represented, the debate following the Queen's speech highlighted the inherent contradictions in detention centre policy.

Mr Butler spoke confidently of the value of detention centres but did not put as much emphasis on their tough, punitive nature as he had at the Conservative Party Conference. He talked of detention centres as one of a *variety* of ways of dealing with young offenders. 'The first rule in dealing with young offenders', he said, 'is to preserve

[150] Presidential address, *Annual Report and Statement of Accounts of the Association of Children's Officers*, 1958, p. 6.

[151] *The Justice of the Peace and Local Government Review*, vol. 122, 27 Sept., 1958, p. 6.

[152] *H. C. Deb.*, vol. 594, col. 6.

[153] The debate on crime and the penal system filled over a hundred columns of Hansard, compared with less than two columns the year before.

elasticity of judgement and diversity of treatment suited to the individual young person.'[154] However, if variety of treatment is stressed – and this after all is what the 1948 Criminal Justice Act was supposed to have provided – then the question of selection of offenders cannot be avoided. As Gordon-Walker said, referring to the Home Secretary's speech at the Conservative Party Conference, 'I hope that the Right Honourable Gentleman will not over-emphasize the usefulness of these centres as a way of placating his supporters ... I believe that we want more detention centres but they are only useful for a limited number of boys and the more we develop diversity of treatment the more need there is for the better sorting out of prisoners.'[155] Other Members, too, were also less certain of the value of detention centres and drew attention to the contradiction between the notion of a 'short, sharp shock' and 'positive' training. James MacColl felt that this should be resolved by making sentences shorter: 'A detention centre ought to be unpleasant and should be primarily based on getting people on to their toes and teaching them that orders are orders: and it should be done quickly.'[156] Anthony Greenwood was more sceptical: 'We shall need a great deal more evidence on this matter before we are certain that the detention centres are being as useful as it was hoped when they were established.'[157] He reminded the House that in the past ten years only two per cent of the young offenders found guilty by the higher courts had been to a detention centre. What evidence was there for contending that detention centres are effective in deterring young offenders from further crime? In reply David Renton, Under Secretary of State to the Home Office, quoted Dr Grünhut's conclusion that a period in a detention centre 'has a legitimate place in a differentiated system of penal and corrective methods for juvenile delinquents and adolescent offenders' but without adding Dr Grünhut's reservations.[158]

The contradictions in detention centre policy mentioned above were also illustrated in the Prison Commissioners Report for 1958. Wardens were reported to be concerned about the boys being selected by the courts as suitable for a detention centre sentence. There had been an increase in the number of physically unsuitable boys and forty per cent of the boys sent to Werrington senior centre had had at least three previous convictions. One boy had spent five years in two approved schools and had had four probation orders. 'It is unfortunate when places in centres are scarce that they should be taken up by boys

[154] *Ibid.*, col. 510.

[155] *Ibid.*, col. 484.

[156] *Ibid.*, col. 550. James MacColl was Chairman of the Panel of London Juvenile Courts between 1946 and 1964.

[157] *Ibid.*, col. 562.

[158] See p. 335.

with such unhopeful prospects.'[159] The Prison Commissioners reported that as in previous years there was emphasis in the centres on discipline and physical training, especially circuit training. ' "Stickability" and the mastering of tedium are obstacles for any adolescent but more so for many detention centre boys.'[160] On the other hand 'the wardens have increasingly sought to use the period at the centres to help the boys in personal difficulties so as to improve their prospects after release'[161] and, with this in mind, it was noted that a woman social worker had been appointed to Campsfield House.

Penal practice in a changing society

The white paper *Penal Practice in a Changing Society* was published in February 1959 and was the first formal government response to the mounting concern over the increase in crime. The treatment of young offenders was considered at some length because 'in the last few years there has been a startling increase in convictions of young men aged, roughly, from 16 to 21'.[162] In addition to a rising crime *rate* among this age group, there were, in any case, more of them in the population. This was something over which, of course, no control was possible and combined with the rising rate of crime it foreshadowed even greater pressures on the penal system in the near future.

In contrast, the white paper did not discuss the treatment of juvenile offenders (those under seventeen) because, it was said, the government wanted to await the report of the Ingleby Committee which had been appointed in October 1956 and was still taking evidence.[163] At this time, however, there was far less anxiety about juvenile crime for trends among this lower age group were not increasing dramatically. It had been possible to close approved schools throughout the fifties and, although the first detention centre opened was a junior one, in 1958 the Prison Commissioners reported that it was 'seldom used to capacity'. The main emphasis in the subsequent development of detention centres was to be on increasing the number of senior centres. Only two more junior centres were opened compared with a

[159] *Report of the Prison Commissioners for the Year 1958, op. cit.*, p. 9.
[160] *Ibid.*, p. 90.
[161] *Idem.*
[162] *Penal Practice in a Changing Society: Aspects of Future Development,* Cmnd. 645, 1959, p. 1. In 1938 the total number of persons in the age group seventeen and under twenty-one found guilty of offences of violence against the person was ten per cent of the total number of persons found guilty of these offences; in 1958 the figure was twenty-six per cent.
[163] Its terms of reference required the committee to examine 'the working of the law' relating to the proceedings, powers and constitution of juvenile courts, remand homes, approved schools and the prevention of cruelty to children.

further eleven senior centres and, under the Children and Young Persons Act, 1969, junior detention centres were to cease to exist as they become part of the local authority system of community homes. (In fact between 1969 and 1973 the number of juveniles sent to detention centres increased by 67 per cent.)

We shall, therefore, follow the development of senior centres for it was concern with the young offender aged seventeen to twenty-one and not the juveniles which dominated the debates during the late fifties and early sixties and resulted in the rapid expansion of detention centre places. The treatment of offenders under seventeen was caught up in the wider debate about the care of children and young persons and, from the mid-fifties, the story of junior detention centres becomes part of a rather different series of developments.

The 'counter-attack' on crime involved the development of methods for dealing with offenders sentenced to some form of detention, as well as having an efficient police force and ensuring that the sanctions for the enforcement of criminal law were adequate. The government's recommendations were, therefore, much concerned with the custodial treatment of young offenders aged between seventeen and twenty-one and were broadly the same as those made by the Prison Commissioners a year earlier.

More detention centres were to be built and were to become the *standard* short-term custodial treatment. Offenders needing longer custodial treatment in borstals would be given a single indeterminate sentence with a maximum of two years, within which they could be released (under supervision) at any time after a minimum of six months depending on their response to training. Serious offenders would be given a determinate sentence of upwards of three years in prison with the possibility of a third remission. The operation of these proposals depended on the existence of sufficient remand and observation centres and this the government planned to provide.

Once more Dr Grünhut's evaluation of detention centres was used to justify their expansion. His results were said to be 'encouraging, in terms both of reappearances in court and of character improvement',[164] and again it was claimed that 'it has been possible to adapt the original conception of the "short, sharp shock" to include a limited, but positive, form of training'.[165] Therefore, to reduce the numbers of young persons sent to prison 'where conditions make it impossible to organize a form of training for young offenders which is both corrective and exacting [and] ... in view of the encouraging results of the detention centres and the manifest desire of many courts to be able to use this form of treatment, it is proposed to accelerate the provision of more centres so that as soon as possible all sentences of

[164] *Ibid.*, p. 9.
[165] *Idem.*

six months or less may be of detention and not of imprisonment'.[166]

The government was already prepared for an expansion in the detention centre programme, and provision for additional centres proposed in the white paper was included in the Civil Estimates for Prisons 1959–60, published at about the same time. These estimates included the cost for building the two additional centres for which sites had already been found[167] and the first instalment for the building of six additional centres. The Home Secretary had, therefore, been moderately successful in his quest for additional resources for this part of the Prison Service.

Three months later the Advisory Council on the Treatment of Offenders published its report.[168] It endorsed the Prison Commissioners' proposals which were substantially contained in the white paper. The objects of these proposals as it interpreted them were, first, to keep young offenders out of prison for the reasons usually given; and 'to ensure the protection of society by providing that such offenders can be given the amount and type of training best suited to their needs and from which they are likely to derive the most benefit'.[169]

Detention centres should change, the Advisory Council recommended, from an experimental form of custodial treatment for which only a small proportion of young offenders would be eligible to the standard short-term custodial sentence. As soon as detention centres were available to every court it would be possible to prohibit magistrates from sending any offender under twenty-one to prison. The council did not feel that these proposals were a departure from the principles of 1948 because 'the system has already shown some flexibility in expanding the original conception of a regime based primarily on deterrence to include elements of positive personal training. We believe that in this wider context it will be well able to maintain the same brisk and exacting regime which will be ... both more rigorous and constructive than is possible for short sentences in local prisons.'[170] At the same time the council recognized that its recommendations implied that 'youths of widely differing

---

[166] *Ibid.*, p. 10.

[167] *Report of the Prison Commissioners for the Year 1958, op. cit.*, p. 89. Sites were extremely difficult to find and keep, for invariably there were local planning objections. For example, Mr Butler reported that in 1959 the Prison Commissioners submitted to six local planning authorities proposals for the provision of five centres. Each aroused local objections and there was a public enquiry in two cases. See *H. C. Deb.*, vol. 612, col. 1127.

[168] *The Treatment of Young Offenders: A Report of the Advisory Council on the Treatment of Offenders*, 1959. Seventy per cent of young offenders sent to prison in 1957 received sentences of six months or less.

[169] *Ibid.*, p. 7.

[170] *Treatment of Young Offenders, op. cit.*, p. 10.

characteristics, abilities and states of health'[171] will be sentenced to detention centres. Nevertheless, it appeared confident that the regimes in each centre could be made sufficiently flexible to accommodate this variety of offenders. The council thought it impractical to suggest that special detention centres should be established for the medically unfit and mentally subnormal. Meanwhile it reported that the Prison Commissioners were considering how to cater for these special needs. However, as we have already seen, the wardens had pleaded not to be sent unsuitable boys ever since the centres opened and they clearly believed it was extremely difficult to accommodate such offenders within a 'brisk and exacting'[172] system.

The Advisory Council's proposals concerning the length of a detention centre sentence accorded more closely with the wardens' views. In order to allow 'a period of progressive treatment to be given'[173] the council recognized that there would have to be some uniformity of sentence. They therefore proposed standard three-month and six-month sentences. A six-month sentence was necessary, it argued, because something was needed to fill the gap between a three-month sentence and the indeterminate six- to twenty-four-month borstal sentences. Those offenders needing a more severe punishment would be sentenced to a minimum of three years' imprisonment.

The council expected that its proposals would be criticized on two grounds. Some would feel the proposed alternatives to prison were 'too soft'. This, it felt, was not true because the detention centre regime was 'more exacting' than that of prison, and anyway 'the fundamental principle of penal treatment was that the treatment of young offenders should be primarily remedial'.[174] Others would argue that there was need for more research. Certainly the Home Secretary thought that research was necessary. Only a few months after the publication of the Advisory Council's report he argued that it was needed 'to ensure that the enlarged resources of the penal system are used to the best advantage and to throw the light of reason on the basic problems of penal treatment which have so often in the past been battlefields of emotion and prejudice'.[175] The council, while admitting that its proposals were not based on research, felt this was no reason for not making the proposed changes because *'they are based on principles which would not be affected by the results of further research into the effects of different methods of treatment ...* At some future date the results of any research that

[171] *Ibid.*, p. 11.
[172] *Ibid.*, p. 7.
[173] *Ibid.*, p. 7.
[174] *Ibid.*, p. 7.
[175] Butler, R. A., *Penal Reform and Research*, Eleanor Rathbone Memorial Lecture, 1960, Liverpool University Press, 1960, p. 3.

is carried out may, of course, suggest some modification of the present proposals'[176] (our italics). Detention centre policy was clearly being determined as much by emotion and conviction as by the 'light of reason' and this became increasingly apparent in the following months as pressure on detention centre places increased and demands for the reintroduction of corporal punishment gathered strength. In July 1959 disorders at the Carlton Approved School served to remind the public that the approved school system was dealing with difficult boys, many of whom it was believed needed firmer discipline. This incident added strength to the staff lobby within the Home Office who wanted such offenders to be dealt with firmly.[177]

The Magistrates' Association Council approved the Advisory Council's proposals and at its annual general meeting in the autumn of 1959 passed a resolution urging the Home Secretary to provide sufficient detention centres for all courts in England and Wales as soon as possible. It emphasized again the need for the provision of compulsory after-care and recommended that one detention centre should be provided for girls. Lord Chief Justice Parker, addressing this meeting, declared that he wanted corporal punishment restored and short terms of imprisonment used as deterrents for young offenders.

By the autumn of 1959 a substantial increase in the number of detention centre places available to courts all over England and Wales had become a certainty. At least the Home Secretary had acquired sufficient resources from the Treasury to double the number of places in the near future and proposals for making a detention centre order the standard short-term custodial sentence had gained widespread approval from the Advisory Council on the Treatment of Offenders, the Magistrates' Association and many others concerned with young offenders.[178] Some of those who had studied detention centres closely were, however, rather less optimistic about their effectiveness in stemming the rising tide of crime amongst the young.[179]

In the Queen's Speech at the beginning of the Parliamentary Session in 1959 it was announced that: 'Further advance will be made in penal reform. A Bill will be introduced to provide more effective means of

[176] *The Treatment of Young Offenders, op. cit.*, p. 8.
[177] *Disturbances at Carlton Approved School: Report of Inquiry*, Cmnd. 937, 1959. Note the similar effect to that of the Standon Farm Approved School shooting of a staff member earlier.
[178] See for example, *Justice of the Peace and Local Government Review*, vol. 123, 31 Oct., 1959.
[179] For example, see Grünhut, M., 'After-Effects of Punitive Detention', *op. cit.*, p. 191. Also Rose, G., 'Training Young Offenders', in *Penal Practice in a Changing Society: A Critical Examination of the White Paper Policy*, Institute for the Study and Treatment of Delinquency, 1960.

dealing with young offenders and to extend compulsory after-care for prisoners who, by supervision on discharge, may be prevented from reverting to crime.'[180] In November 1960 the promised Criminal Justice Bill was introduced in the House of Commons with the aims of making 'wider provision for the use of borstal training and of detention centres in dealing with young offenders, to discontinue short sentences of imprisonment as more detention centres became available and to extend the provision of compulsory after care'.[181] The proposals contained in the Bill closely resembled those first put forward by the Prison Commissioners and, as we have seen, endorsed by the government in its white paper and by the Advisory Council on the Treatment of Young Offenders. As well as replacing short terms of imprisonment with sentences of detention, after-care was to be compulsory although a detention centre inmate could only be recalled once. There was no outright opposition to the clauses relating to the treatment of young offenders. As in 1948 the proposals relating to detention centres were extremely hard to oppose. The reasons were much the same.

First, the debate took place against a background of concern about the rising number of young offenders. As Butler said when introducing the Second Reading of the Bill, 'one third of persons convicted of indictable offences were between fourteen and twenty-one'.[182] As we have already seen, tough measures were being demanded from many quarters and proposals to reintroduce corporal punishment were being widely discussed in the press.[183] The pressure was such that in January 1960 the Home Secretary had asked the Advisory Council on the Treatment of Offenders to consider whether there were any grounds for reintroducing corporal punishment as a judicial penalty. The council reported in November, on the same day that the Criminal Justice Bill was introduced into the House of Commons. After considering all the evidence the council unanimously came down against such a proposal although at the outset some members had thought it might be desirable. It offered the extension of detention centre provision as one of the more appropriate methods of dealing with young offenders. Therefore, once again detention centres were being offered as an alternative to corporal punishment, and failure to provide sufficient numbers of them would certainly 'cause an increased demand

---

[180] *H. C. Deb.*, vol. 612, col. 51.

[181] *H. C. Deb.*, vol. 629, col. 183.

[182] *H. C. Deb.*, vol. 630, col. 562.

[183] See *News Chronicle*, 21 Mar., 1960, and also Report of the Advisory Council on the Treatment of Offenders, *Corporal Punishment*, Cmnd. 1213, 1960, p. 7.

for the reintroduction of corporal punishment. That is a fact to be recognized by its opponents'.[184]

The second reason why the extension of detention centres was hard to oppose was because it met the need for an alternative to short terms of imprisonment which could be available to all the courts. The urgency of this need had been demonstrated time and again in recent years as more young people experienced a spell in prison. Altogether 3,099 persons under twenty-one went to prison under sentence in 1960, very nearly double the number sent to prison only three years earlier. As many again experienced short spells in prison whilst awaiting trial or before conviction, including some young people under seventeen. Between January and November 1960, 585 boys and twenty-three girls were remanded in an adult prison. Several such instances were widely reported and deplored in the press and in Parliament.[185] Although severe measures against young offenders were demanded there was also widespread agreement that prison was not the place for them. Meanwhile the courts were filling existing detention centres beyond their capacity because some magistrates were committing offenders to them without first establishing that there was a vacancy.[186] It was argued that it was harder to get a delinquent boy into a detention centre than a normal boy into public school.[187] It was impossible to deny, therefore, that an alternative to short terms of imprisonment had to be found.

Although there was, therefore, little outright opposition, the government's proposals concerning the expansion of detention centres were criticized mainly because of the implications they would have for the selection of offenders considered suitable for punitive detention, and thus on the future development of the regimes in detention centres. James MacColl, for example, was concerned about detention centres becoming 'an all-purpose institution' dealing with a very wide variety of offenders. The evidence from Dr Grünhut's studies of detention centres showed that careful selection was important and James MacColl introduced an amendment requiring that courts 'obtain such information as to the conduct, home surroundings and medical history of the person as may enable it to decide whether he is suitable for and likely to profit from training in a detention centre'.[188] The amending clause was defeated.

As in 1948, the objectives of detention centres were queried and

---

[184] *Justice of the Peace and Local Government Review*, Vol. 124, Notes of the Week, 9 July, 1960, p. 452.

[185] For example, see *H. C. Deb.*, vol. 627, Adjournment Debate on Juvenile Offenders (Accommodation), col. 2082.

[186] *Report of the Prison Commissioners for the Year 1960*, Cmnd. 1467, 1961.

[187] *H. C. Deb.*, vol. 630, col. 1299.

[188] *H. C. Standing Committee of the Criminal Justice Bill*, vol. 1, 1960, col. 123.

there was again some discussion about how to achieve a balance between punishment and remedial treatment. Many, like the Lord Chief Justice Parker, were 'alarmed at the element of reform creeping into detention centres';[189] rather fewer saw the centres as consisting of a lot of sterile 'square-bashing'[190] and were at a loss to see the benefit of detention centre training which was described by such adjectives as 'brisk', 'bracing', 'energetic', and 'disciplined'.[191] Government spokesmen were at pains to assure Parliament that they had no intention of making detention centres any less rigorous. 'There have been rumours that the regime in detention centres has weakened ... there is no intention whatever of not having the strictest regime for young people at detention centres.'[192] How this was to be done remained rather vague. A clearer definition of the way in which detention centre regimes might develop in the future would, of course, have sharpened the differences between these opposing views. It was no longer possible to obscure the character of detention centres behind the label 'experimental' as had been done in the early days, but the government remained guarded about the precise nature of future changes in the routines at the centres. One intended departure from previous policy was, however, revealed during the debates in the House of Lords when it became clear that the government was planning a detention centre for girls. While the Magistrates' Association had recommended this, the Advisory Council on the Treatment of Offenders, the Ingleby Committee (which had by now reported)[193] and a body of opinion within the Home Office were opposed to the idea. Attempts in the House of Lords to prohibit this development were defeated. Apart from that, government statements about the future pattern of the regimes in the detention centres were characterized by 'coy elusiveness'.[194]

[189] Quoted in the *Daily Telegraph*, 13 Jan., 1961.

[190] *H. C. Deb.*, vol. 630, col. 626 (Christopher Mayhew).

[191] *H. C. Deb.*, vol. 230, col. 1154 (Baroness Wootton).

[192] *H. C. Deb.*, vol. 638, col. 92 (R. A. Butler).

[193] The Ingleby Committee reported in October 1960. See *Report of the Committee on Children and Young Persons*, Cmnd. 1191, 1960. Its report contained very little about detention centres but, briefly, it endorsed the proposals to increase the numbers of centres so that one would be available to every court. It was opposed to sentences of more than three months and was in favour of compulsory after-care.

[194] James MacColl, *H. C. Deb.*, vol. 638, col. 440.

IV THE END OF THE EXPERIMENT: MORE DETENTION CENTRES

The clauses in the Bill relating to the custodial treatment of young offenders were passed largely unaltered by both Houses in the summer of 1961. And so the rapid expansion of detention centre places, sufficient to replace short terms of imprisonment for the young offender, became approved Home Office policy. Four more senior detention centres were opened during 1961 and a further three, including Moor Court for girls, the following year. By the end of 1964 there were fourteen senior detention centres. In that year nearly six thousand young offenders experienced a period in a detention centre, over four times as many as in 1960.

In August 1963 prison sentences of medium length were abolished for offenders under twenty-one years and subsequently the proportion of offenders in this age group sentenced to custodial treatment who were sent to detention centres, doubled. The proportion sent to prison or borstal fell.[195] Detention centres continued to receive boys who, on the whole, were a good deal less criminal than those sent to borstal or to prison except that after 1963 the centres received many more who were convicted of breaking and entering.[196] The Criminal Justice Act, 1961, had also provided for compulsory supervision on leaving a detention centre and this was implemented in January 1964.

The regimes in the centres continued to undergo modifications with further emphasis, it is said, 'not only on proper discipline and fair discipline, but also on the establishment of relationships between individual members of staff and boys'.[197] In order to assist this process. in 1962 the appointment of a social worker to each detention centre was given official encouragement. There has also been more emphasis on education, especially remedial education,[198] and to some they appear to be becoming more like short-term borstals.

Yet the inherent contradictions in the regime remain: it still attempts to be both deterrent and reformative. Detention centres continue to be controversial. They have been the subject of much review and enquiry since 1961 and as late as 1967 they were still con-

[195] Field, E., 'Research Into Detention Centres', *British Journal of Criminology*, vol. 9, no. 1, 1969, p. 70.

[196] *Ibid.*, p. 70.

[197] *The Sentence of the Court*, A Handbook for Courts on the Treatment of Offenders, HMSO, 1969, p. 29.

[198] Remedial education was provided for one in seven boys at detention centres by 1960. The Advisory Council on the Treatment of Offenders recommended this be increased, for it estimated that one in four detainees at a detention centre had a reading age of ten or below. See Advisory Council on the Treatment of Offenders, *Detention Centres*, 1970, p. 20.

sidered by some to be experimental.[199] It could be argued that the greater the emphasis placed on *treatment* in a detention centre, the greater the contradictions. The 'sharp' aspects of detention centres may have been blunted over the years but since 1968 when the maximum remission which could be earned increased to four weeks, mainly in order to increase the capacity of existing detention centre provision which was once more under pressure, the sentence has become shorter. And yet it was precisely the brevity of the sentence which in the early days both advocates and critics alike believed made any serious attempt at constructive training impossible. As a further illustration of the conflicting pressures in the development of detention centre regimes, we may note two events which occurred in 1962. First, the appointment of social workers to the centres was encouraged, and second, the staff changed from wearing civilian clothes to uniform.[200]

The type of offender sent to detention centres continued to be very varied. Although, as we have seen, it was widely held that the selection of offenders was important, the courts continued to send boys regarded by the centres as 'unsuitable'. One study of boys sent to senior detention centres between 1960 and 1962 concluded that twenty-eight per cent were unsuitable.[201] First offenders, with whom detention centres appear to have the most success, continued to form a small minority of their intake. Former approved school boys, nearly three-quarters of whom are likely to be reconvicted within three years of leaving detention centres, are still sentenced to these centres.[202] Making detention centres the *standard* short-term custodial treatment was unlikely to make the courts more selective although, as a result of the Streatfield Committee's report,[203] they are now given more informa-

[199] *Justice of the Peace and Local Government Review*, vol. 131, 25 Mar., 1967, p. 177.

[200] It is difficult to be sure of the reasons for this change, for only a year earlier Mr Butler saw no reason to do so when questioned in Parliament. With the expansion of detention centres, it was no longer possible to staff them entirely by volunteers from the prison service. Therefore, there may have been an influx of staff who felt happier in uniform, especially as in 1962 there were allegations of attacks on them by boys. Alternatively we have been told that the staff prefer uniform because it is provided free by the Prison Department.

[201] Banks, C., 'Boys in Detention Centres', in Stephanos, A. (ed.), *Studies in Psychology*, University of London Press, 1965, quoted by Field, E., *op. cit.*, p. 67. Banks found twenty-six per cent were not suitable for detention: half of them having severe psychological handicaps; nearly a quarter were too physically handicapped and ten boys were innocent of the offence for which they were convicted.

[202] See *The Sentence of the Court, op. cit.*, Annex.

[203] *The Report of the Interdepartmental Committee on the Business of the Criminal Courts*, 1961, Cmnd. 1289, studied ways in which the courts could be better informed about every kind of sentence, what it involved, what it achieved and so on. They recommended the publication of a handbook. This was done in 1964.

tion about the nature and the likely success of the sentences available to them. Moreover, as long as detention centres are regarded as punitive then the sentence is likely to fit the crime rather than the offender. For instance, as the Lord Chief Justice recommended with reference to attacks on the police: 'Some form of detention whether it be a detention centre, borstal or imprisonment, must be meted out in all cases, regardless of whether they have a good character or not.'[204]

As an experiment in a method of custodial treatment which deters the young offender who is subjected to it, detention centres could not, in 1961, be judged a great success. Statistics published by the Prison Commissioners showed that by the end of 1960, 45·2 per cent of those released from senior detention centres in the previous four years had been reconvicted and that of those released in 1959, 36·8 per cent had offended again before the end of 1960.[205] As a commentator in the *Justice of the Peace and Local Government Review* wrote: 'This success cannot be regarded as other than disappointing, even allowing for the fact that the figures refer to boys and young men for whom no other method of treatment had been thought appropriate.'[206] More recent evidence suggests that detention centres are marginally less successful than borstals in deterring the young offender.[207]

The rapid expansion of detention centre provision in the early 1960s and the change in emphasis from a form of custodial treatment suitable only for a minority of offenders to a standard short-term custodial sentence was not, therefore, soundly based on the *successful* outcome of an experiment. Rather it was a response to pressure from the courts, Parliament, and public opinion as reflected in the press, to take tough measures to combat the rising number of young offenders. The Prison Commissioners wanted more detention centres because of the pressure on existing places and the problems created for their staff by the inappropriateness of other forms of custodial treatment. Moreover, a detention centre place could be used on average five times a year which compared very favourably with prisons and borstals where the majority of sentences are longer and hence the turnover rate lower. Therefore, to a prison system beginning to feel overwhelmed by numbers, an increase in detention centre places was a cheap and comparatively speedy method of coping with some of the extra pressure. At the same time an increase in the number of

[204] *Guardian*, 18 June, 1966.
[205] *Report of the Prison Commissioners for the Year 1960, op cit.*, p. 50.
[206] Magisterial Punishment – I: 'The Detention Centre', *Justice of the Peace and Local Government Review*, vol. 126, 8 Sept., 1962, p. 558.
[207] *The Handbook of the Court, op. cit.*, Annex.

detention centre places was the only policy the government could offer which would be widely regarded as punitive enough (and therefore believed to be a deterrent), given that the majority view in the Home Office and in the Prison Commission was that corporal punishment should not be reintroduced, and given that there were widespread criticisms of the practice of sending young offenders to prison. The *introduction* of detention centres was the price paid for the abolition of corporal punishment at a time when there was much concern about crime rates among the young. Their *expansion*, when the criminal activities of the young were again causing alarm and the prison system as a whole was under great pressure, was the 'civilized alternative'[208] to its reintroduction.

V CONCLUSION

There are aspects in this case study which we consider may prove of more general importance in explaining social policy change.

1. Penal policies not only have a variety of objectives attached to them but these objectives conflict. Very broadly, on the one hand a penal policy is seen to be a means of punishment and retribution and on the other a means of education and training. The former is concerned with deterrence, the latter with reform, although both aim to reduce the extent of wrongdoing in society. Detention centre policy is an illustration of the way in which the development of a penal policy is determined to a large extent by the outcome of the contradiction between these two views.

2. Because the conflict between these two views is fundamental and continuing, progress in one direction must be seen to be counterbalanced by moves in the other. Thus a move to take young offenders out of prison and abolish an entirely punitive method of dealing with them, namely corporal punishment, had to be seen to be replaced by a 'tough' new measure also embodying a large element of punishment. When public concern about the extent of criminal activity is high, that is when crime rates appear to be rising, it is harder to move in the direction of education and reform without making substantial concessions to those wanting to see punitive penal policies. Therefore, it is very probable that at the end of the 1930s corporal punishment could have been replaced by Howard houses which were intended to be far less punitive than detention centres, but not ten years later when anxiety about rising crime rates among the young had increased.

---

[208] *H. C. Deb.*, vol. 630, col. 635 (William Deedes).

3. The controversial detention centre policy gained acceptance by being labelled 'experimental', because it is very difficult to oppose an experiment. Such a tactic allowed its proponents to remain vague about the actual methods to be employed in implementing the policy on the grounds that it would restrict the experiment too much.

4. The extent of discretion the ill-defined detention centre policy left in the hands of those who had to implement it was considerably reduced by lack of resources. The nature of the early detention centres in particular was determined partly by the availability of staff and buildings. The Prison Commissioners could not get the specially trained staff and purpose-built premises that they needed, because they could not command extra resources. Old attitudes and ideas will inevitably be carried over into the new institutions in this situation.

5. Butler, a strong, able Minister with clear views about the kind of policies he wished to see implemented, arrived at the Home Office with a definite interest in penal reform. The Prison Commissioners therefore gained a powerful ally in their efforts to get additional resources. Nevertheless, even a strong Minister in a favourable economic climate could not ignore trends such as a rising crime rate and Butler's policies were undoubtedly tempered by these trends. We wonder what the Criminal Justice Act, 1961, would have looked like if the crime rates had remained at the level they were when Butler became Home Secretary. Would it have then been possible to declare that detention centres were an experiment that had failed? Certainly there would have been no need to promise a large increase in detention centre provision to counterbalance moves towards bringing back corporal punishment.

6. The judiciary, like the medical profession, has a large degree of autonomy and it needed a strong Home Secretary even to consider giving it advice and information about the impact of its sentencing policies on the staff and offenders in penal institutions. The Home Office and Prison Commissioners could not ensure that detention centres were used selectively from the outset, although, without a variety of forms of treatment, together with remand centres, the courts justifiably did not feel that they had much opportunity to be selective.

7. Pressures for change were generated both inside and outside the Home Office and Prison Commission. Inside the Home Office it is difficult to ascertain the roles played by the senior civil servants during this period and particularly to know how much importance to attach to Butler's appointment of Peterson as vice-chairman and then chairman of the Prison Commission. We can be sure that some favoured penal policies with an emphasis on education and training, others on more deterrent methods, for the establishment of a girls' detention centre, for example, was hotly contested within the Home

Office. How the balance between these views changed over the period we do not know. In addition there are powerful lobbies within the Home Office representing the staff of penal institutions.

8. Unlike the internal interest groups, a promotional pressure group like the Howard League for Penal Reform can only persuade, not threaten. Its role in the development of detention centre policy was to modify the punitive elements and encourage variety in the kind of regimes practised in the centres, and develop alternative forms of short custodial training, rather than to press for the total abandonment of detention centres. After 1957 the latter would have been an unrealistic proposal until the mid-sixties when such a proposition gained serious support in several quarters. The Howard League gained much of its strength in the 1950s from being well informed at a time when the Home Office and Prison Commission were undertaking very little in the way of research and evaluation. Butler's establishment of an internal research unit, thus giving the government control over more information relating to penal policy, has weakened the League's position in this respect.

9. The development of detention centres depended little on whether they were judged to be a 'success' or a 'failure'. The evaluation of their effect on young offenders was interpreted in the most optimistic light by the Prison Commissioners because, at the end of the fifties, they needed a relatively cheap and quick method of expanding custodial training to meet the increasing demands that the rising crime rate was making on their penal institutions; magistrates were determined to use them whatever the research findings said and ten weeks in a detention centre was considered preferable to corporal punishment or a short spell in prison. In this sense detention centres were an experiment which could not be allowed to fail.

CHAPTER THIRTEEN

The Struggle for Clean Air

This is a study of the events and the circumstances which preceded the Clean Air Act of 1956. That Act is of great importance to us all, for it won the first substantial foothold in the quest for an unpolluted atmosphere. We deal mainly with the period from 1952 to 1956. On the face of it the prospects for new, firm and effective legislation were as good as they had ever been. Yet, during those years, the campaign for clean air was a struggle; not so much against open opposition as against the reluctance, apprehension and tardiness of government in according the issue the priority it warranted.

I THE BACKGROUND

Legislation to prevent or reduce air pollution was fragmentary and largely ineffective before 1956. The Public Health Act of 1936 defined the emission of smoke[1] in any trade or manufacturing process or from other than domestic chimneys as a 'nuisance'. Local authorities could serve a notice requiring the abatement of the nuisance, but although the person or organization responsible could be taken to court for not complying with the order, the maximum penalty was only £50. There were also many loopholes. It was a defence in any proceeding to show that the 'best practical means' for preventing the nuisance had been used. Domestic premises were completely exempt, as were certain industrial processes and, in any case, local authorities often found it difficult to identify the precise source of a smoke nuisance.[2]

There was no general provision for the declaration of smokeless zones and when special powers were obtained by local Acts the regulation of smoke had to be achieved through a succession of separate

[1] Smoke was defined to include 'soot, ash, grit or gritty particles'.

[2] Smoke from railway engines was an offence under the 1868 Regulation of Railways Act, but no particular body was responsible for enforcement.

orders.[3] As far as smoke was concerned, the greatest shortcoming of the pre-1956 legislation was the omission of domestic premises. This deficiency was important because, as the Beaver Committee on Air Pollution reported in 1954, 'nearly half of all the smoke in the air comes from domestic chimneys'.[4]

Other forms of air pollution were also poorly controlled. Dust could constitute a statutory nuisance under the 1936 Public Health Act, but there were similar problems of enforcement to those connected with smoke. Legislation to control the pollution from motor vehicles only covered 'smoke or visible vapour' and action against offenders had to be taken by the police under the Road Traffic Acts. Certain industries producing 'noxious gases' and other pollutants were subject to the Alkali Acts and required to be registered as 'scheduled processes'. This meant that they were under the supervision of the alkali inspectors of central government who only permitted registration if the 'best possible means' had been adopted to avoid pollution.

Regulatory legislation was, therefore, clearly deficient in these and other respects. The shortcomings had been noted by several committees of enquiry and, on various occasions, periods of high atmospheric pollution had led to significant increases in morbidity and mortality. Yet such evidence of the need for improved and co-ordinated clean air legislation was, to all intents and purposes, ignored by successive governments.

In 1946 there was, for example, the report of the Simon Committee on Domestic Fuel Policy.[5] Its terms of reference were 'to consider and advise on the use of fuels and the provision of heat services in domestic ... premises', and to do so 'with special regard to the efficient use of fuel resources and *the prevention of atmospheric pollution*' (our italics). The committee's position was unequivocal. 'We cannot', they said, 'afford to maintain our low standard of heating; we cannot afford to depress and destroy the life of our cities by smoke pollution; we cannot afford to waste our limited national coal resources.'[6] It recommended that housing subsidies should be conditional upon the installation of multi-fuel appliances and also pressed that

---

[3] By 1953 only two authorities – Manchester and Coventry – had put the 'smokeless zone' provisions of their local Acts into operation.

[4] *Report of the Committee on Air Pollution* (Beaver), Cmd. 9332, 1954, para. 68, p. 21.

[5] *Domestic Fuel Policy: Report of the Fuel and Power Advisory Council*, Cmd. 6762, 1946. Lord Simon was a past president of the National Smoke Abatement Society and a notable figure in the smoke abatement campaign. He was joint author of *The Smokeless City* with Marion Fitzgerald (Longmans, Green, 1922). In it he wrote, 'Parliament has appointed committee after committee to enquire into it [smoke pollution], and has with great consistency paid no attention to their reports, except to pigeon-hole them' (p. 2).

[6] *Ibid.*, p. 3.

'the necessary legislation be passed to enable smokeless zones to be established'.[7] Professor MacIntosh's appendix to the report struck an even more forceful note. 'Smoke abatement', he wrote, 'like any other measure of public health, must come, not from the free choice of individuals, but from concerted action by the State through the agency of local authorities'.[8] However, it was the view of Viscount Ridley,[9] set out in his Memorandum of Reservation, which appears to have prevailed. He argued that 'legislation should be delayed until there is more widespread knowledge of modern methods of burning fuel, until public opinion has been further educated on the subject, and until there are adequate supplies of smokeless fuel and suitable appliances.'[10] The main clean air recommendations of the Simon Committee were duly placed on one side, as indeed had most of those of an earlier committee in 1921.[11]

There are several possible reasons why this happened. In 1946 the housing shortage loomed as a dominating problem of vast proportions. There were shortages of building materials and labour and no substantial start had been made towards the government's house building targets. In these circumstances it is not surprising to find, for example, that the replacement of old-fashioned grates secured little priority. Moreover, Simon was a Fuel and Power committee; it was not the child of the Ministry of Health. In addition, of course, Ridley's doubts about the adequate supply of smokeless fuel, indeed of coal itself, were amply justified by the events of the succeeding years.

Five years later, in 1951, Ridley himself chaired another committee to consider national policy for the use of fuel and power resources. Although his terms of reference made no mention of the air pollution issue the problem was discussed and limited proposals put forward in the report.[12] The committee sought to encourage the installation of solid fuel appliances by, for example, using concessions under schedule A taxation and by making subsidies and building licences dependent upon 'approved designs'. It did not, however, suggest that new general legislation was required.

Despite the passage of some six years the much less ambitious clean air proposals of the Ridley report received little support from the newly elected Conservative government. As the report itself pointed out, fuel and power remained in short supply (coal rationing con-

---

[7] *Ibid.*, p. 30.

[8] *Ibid.*, p. 45.

[9] During the war he had been closely involved in the Ministry of Supply with similar issues. His view therefore carried weight.

[10] *Ibid.*, p. 36.

[11] Ministry of Health, *Departmental Committee on Smoke and Noxious Vapours Abatement* (Newton), Interim Report, Cmd. 755, 1920.

[12] Ministry of Fuel and Power, *Report of the Committee on National Policy for the Use of Fuel and Power Resources*, Cmd. 8647, 1952.

tinued and the load shedding of electricity was a frequent necessity in winter months). There was, additionally, a new target of 300,000 dwellings a year to be achieved which might well be delayed by introducing all Ridley's recommendations about domestic heating.[13]

What little public discussion there was about air pollution continued to focus upon smoke. This, in its turn, served to emphasize coal burning as the key causative factor and this directed attention to domestic premises. Characteristically, the most tangible smoke problems were the winter 'fogs' which enveloped our industrial towns. Of course, there had been dense fogs in this country, especially in London, since the eighteenth century and certainly their occurrence in disaster proportions was being recorded in the second half of the nineteenth century: December 1873, January 1880, February 1882, December 1891 and 1892.[14] There were notable fogs in Glasgow in 1909 and in Manchester in 1930. On the continent too and in the United States similar events occurred. In December 1930 there was a killer fog in the Meuse valley which, because conditions were similar to those in the Thames valley, should have acted as a warning signal to Britain. Indeed, a Professor Firket estimated that the public services in London could be faced with the responsibility of 3,200 sudden deaths if a similar fog occurred there.[15] Later, in 1948, there was the Donora fog in Pennsylvania which was fully investigated in a subsequent report of the US public Health Service.[16]

Only a month after Donora came a dense London fog that 'established a record, not for density but for duration'. It lasted from 26 November until 1 December 1948. Despite the fact that the number of deaths registered during the fog was some twenty to thirty per cent higher than in the previous four weeks, little attention appears to have been paid to its significance. In the first week of January 1949 the *Lancet* carried a short note by Logan, who was assistant medical statistician at the General Register Office.[17] The press seemed to be more concerned about the fog's effect upon the 'travelling public'. This was remarkable when the cost in life was estimated at between 700 and 800:[18] a catastrophe many times greater than either that in the Meuse

[13] It is noteworthy that this housing target appears to be a relevant factor in the initial retardation of health centres and detention centre policy as well.

[14] See for example, Prindle, R. A., 'The Disaster Potential of Community Air Pollution', in Farber, S. M. (ed.), *The Air We Breathe*, Thomas, 1961.

[15] Firket, J. (University of Liege), 'Fog Along the Meuse Valley', in *Transactions of the Faraday Society*, April, 1936.

[16] *Air Pollution in Donora*, Public Health Bulletin No. 306, Federal Security Agency, US Public Health Services, 1949.

[17] See Logan, W. P. D., 'Fog and Mortality'. *Lancet*, 8 Jan., 1949, p. 73.

[18] See Martin, A. E., 'Epidemiological Studies of Air Pollution', *Monthly Bulletin of the Ministry of Health and Public Health Laboratory Service*, 20, 42, 1961.

or at Donora, both of which led to major enquiries.

Despite such historical, comparative and contemporary evidence that periods of acute and killing smoke pollution were a recurrent risk, no British government had shown any marked concern for the air pollution problem. Two questions, therefore, arise. First why should this issue have secured so little priority and second, why, during the mid-1950s was there a change which led to firmer and more effective regulation? The years 1952–6 saw developments which furnish some answers and these can be broadly and conveniently discussed in terms of the events, the participants, and the context.

II THE EVENTS

From 5–9 December 1952 London was again subjected to a dense fog of catastrophic proportions, which was responsible for at least four thousand deaths. As Logan wrote in the *Lancet* early in 1953, 'for a few days, death rates attained a level that has been exceeded only rarely during the past hundred years – for example, at the height of the cholera epidemic of 1854 and of the influenza epidemic of 1918–19'.[19] Deaths from bronchitis in the County of London increased ninefold in the week ending 13 December and from pneumonia by four times. These additional deaths were concentrated in the older age groups and, to a lesser extent, amongst infants. There was great pressure on the hospitals: 'Applications to the Emergency Bed Service for the admission of general acute cases far exceeded all previous records.'[20] Furthermore, deaths from respiratory illnesses in London remained abnormally high for some two months after the December smog.

Measured against the effects of other dense fogs, epidemics or the east coast floods this was a public health catastrophe of alarming magnitude. It was probably the worst and most devastating fog that the country had ever faced. The events have been vividly described by Wise, whose account underlines the remarkable public complacency and official unpreparedness.[21] There was no plan for a public alert

[19] Logan, W. P. D., 'Mortality in the London Fog Incident, 1952', *Lancet*, 14 Feb., 1953, p. 336.
[20] Abercrombie, G. F., 'December Fog in London and the Emergency Bed Service', *Lancet*, 31 Jan., 1953, p. 234. *The Interim Report of the Committee on Air Pollution*, Cmd. 9011, 1953, noted that whereas on 1 Jan., 1951, at the height of the influenza epidemic, 293 applications for hospital beds were received, on 9 Dec., 1952, at the height of the fog period, there were 492 applications.
[21] Wise, W., *Killer Smog*, Rand McNally, 1968.

system and the radio news on the 8th, which initially contained a modest warning of the dangers, was eventually broadcast without it.[22] Indeed, as Wise clearly demonstrates, 'for more than twenty-four hours, the great city of London had been experiencing a growing air pollution disaster, yet the astonishing fact was that hardly a soul in the city realized it or even suspected that there was the slightest danger'.[23]

The press certainly did not appear to appreciate what was happening. As Sanderson has shown, an examination of the newspapers during the smog reveals that the public health aspects received little or no attention at the time. He points out that 'the aspect of the whole business which first attracted the headlines was undoubtedly the death or enforced destruction of several prize animals at the Smithfield Agricultural Show'.[24] Not until a week after the onset of the fog did any newspaper turn to the impact upon the health of the *people* of London. On 6 December, the second day, *The Times* devoted some space and two back page pictures to the fog. On Monday the 8th it carried a substantial report under the heading 'Transport Dislocated by Three Days of Fog'. Traffic hold-ups received most attention; then the cancellation of sporting events over the weekend; then the increase in crime, particularly street attacks which the fog was said to encourage and, also, there were the cattle affected at the Smithfield Show. Not a word from *The Times* about sickness and death until the 20th, some two weeks after the fog started. Even then there was only a three-inch note of the National Smoke Abatement Society's demand for an enquiry and a sentence reporting that 'it was announced in the House of Commons on Thursday [the 18th] that deaths from all causes in Greater London during the week ended December 13, totalled 4,703 compared with 1,852 in the corresponding week of 1951'. There was also some correspondence about the costs of the fog but not a single letter mentioned the major health issue. Incredibly, during the fog itself, *The Times* carried a fourth leader that waxed euphoric about British fogs which, 'taking advantage of a northern island, rich in rivers and diversity of soils, roam about on their little cat feet as freely as they did before anyone had heard of smoke abatement'.[25]

Reaction to the catastrophe was very slow to develop and certainly the government did not respond with any sense of urgency. There were several reasons for this apparent apathy. One, of course, as Logan pointed out, was that 'some weeks had to elapse before the mortality returns could be analysed and the total number of deaths due to the

[22] *Ibid.*, p. 152.
[23] *Ibid.*, p. 116.
[24] Sanderson, J. B., 'The National Smoke Abatement Society and the Clean Air Act, 1956', *Political Studies*, vol. ix, no. 3, 1961.
[25] 'Fog in the Fields', *The Times*, 9 Dec., 1952, p. 9.

fog estimated'.[26] The most obvious evidence and most quickly available calculation of the scale of the havoc wrought could be seen in the traffic disruptions, not in the increased number of deaths. It was not at first realized that the lethal effects of the fog were some five or six times greater than those of 1948.

The task of analysing the mortality returns was undertaken by the London County Council health department and by Logan, who was now chief medical statistician at the General Register Office. The LCC's Medical Officer of Health reported in detail to his committee some six weeks after the peak period. Although the abnormally large number of people dying from causes connected with difficulty in breathing was stressed, the report did not contain the estimate of four thousand extra deaths which later commanded such wide currency. Indeed, reading the report, the figure of 445 'excess deaths over normal' for the week ending 13 December 1952 is the one which catches the attention.[27] The aftermath of the fog had yet to be studied. Logan's report which more fully plotted the emerging dimensions of the catastrophe, was not published until ten weeks after the disaster[28] and even his estimate of four thousand deaths was later considered by some to be much too conservative.[29] Neither of these reports appeared in a popular form. One was 'for members' information only' (with an amended version appearing in the *Medical Officer*) and the other was available to readers of the *Lancet*. References to the LCC analysis did, however, appear in the press.

There was another important reason why, at the time, so little concern was expressed. Fog exacted its major toll from amongst those already suffering from chest troubles of one kind or another. Typically, though not exclusively, these were the elderly with chronic bronchitis. To varying degrees they succumbed each winter to the cold, the damp and the fogs. A particularly dense or lengthy fog could be regarded as doing no more than advancing slightly the death of those who were, in any case, ailing. Like the polluted atmosphere, bronchitis had become an unremarkable part of the lives of many people; especially the industrial working classes. In medical terms the fog had a 'nonspecific effect on persons already having serious respiratory or cardiac lesions'.[30] Paradoxically, the much higher rates of morbidity and mor-

[26] Logan. W. P. D., 'Mortality from Fog in London, January, 1956', *British Medical Journal*, 31 Mar.. 1956, p. 722.

[27] LCC Health Committee. *Fog and Frost in December, 1952, and Subsequent Deaths in London*, Report by the Medical Officer of Health (J. A. Scott), 19 Jan., 1953. See also the *Medical Officer*, 7 Feb., 1953, p. 64.

[28] *Op. cit., Lancet*, 14 Feb., 1953.

[29] See Wilkins, E. T., 'Air Pollution and the London Fog of December, 1952', *Proceedings of the Royal Sanitary Institute*, 11 Nov., 1953.

[30] See Martin, A. E., 'Mortality and Morbidity Statistics and Air Pollution', *Proceedings of the Royal Society of Medicine*, vol. 57, no. 10, Oct. 1964.

tality in this than in previous fogs was attributed by some to the war-time discoveries of new forms of treatment and the inception of a National Health Service. Both, it was argued, resulted in more old people being kept alive, thereby increasing the number of them endangered by dense fog.

Thus, before the severity of the fog could be established the *specificity* of its effects as well as its dimensions had to be proved. This was difficult because, as the National Smoke Abatement Society pointed out, the smoke-fog 'induces an attitude of apathetic acceptance. If, as with other plagues, it was followed by its own distinctive disease it would be very different, but when John Smith dies of bronchitis three days after the fog ... well, he might have died of bronchitis anyway'.[31]

Nevertheless, the seeming unconcern of the government about this devastating fog remains difficult to explain, certainly when contrasted with its reaction earlier in the year to the Lynmouth flood disaster or to the slaughter on the road of a marching column of Chatham cadets in the previous summer. There were questions in Parliament from Labour Members about a week after the fog.[32] Information was sought about the number of casualties and on December 16 Macleod, the Minister of Health, replied that there were some five hundred extra deaths in London during the week ending December 6.[33] Two days later the figure rose to over a thousand as the Minister's next answer updated the returns to the end of the following week.[34] An interdepartmental committee to look into the causes and cure of the fog was demanded but refused.[35] No information could be given about the connection between high levels of atmospheric pollution and the incidence of pulmonary TB or cancer of the lungs and bronchiae.[36] Even by the middle of February 1953 the questions were still being parried. In a written reply to Lipton, the parliamentary secretary to the Ministry of Works said that no further action was being taken by the Department of Scientific and Industrial Research Atmospheric Pollution Committee with respect to the heavy mortality caused by the London fog.[37] The question did elicit, however, the information that the committee had met twice in 1952, that £33,000 had been spent on its work during the year and that there was no medically qualified member.

By February 1953 there was still no sign that the government intended taking any steps, either to inquire into or to reduce the risks of severe air pollution, notwithstanding the fact that by then the LCC

[31] *Smokeless Air*, vol. XXIII, no. 85, Spring, 1953, pp. 97–8.
[32] See p. 393 for a fuller discussion.
[33] *H. C. Deb.*, vol. 509, col. 188.
[34] *H. C. Deb.*, vol. 509, col. 237.
[35] *H. C. Deb.*, vol. 509, col. 265.
[36] *H. C. Deb.*, vol. 509, cols 289–90.
[37] *H. C. Deb.*, vol. 510, col. 382.

and GRO data were available. The LCC had been pressing for an inquiry. So too had the National Smoke Abatement Society, which played a major role in awakening concern about the implications of the fog. For some of the reasons which have already been discussed there appeared to be a growing probability that, left unattended, the London disaster would fade into the background despite its magnitude. 'The Society immediately urged upon the Government a full inquiry and later [their secretary] ... had an informal meeting with the medical advisers of the Ministry of Health and was assured that a full investigation was contemplated.'[38] The society, however, was not satisfied, believing that such an investigation would be a protracted task. Speedily, it undertook its own survey, the purpose of which was 'to present the facts in a readily comprehensible and striking manner before memory of the event had faded'.[39] The report was published in the Spring 1953 issue of its journal[40] and copies were widely distributed to MPs, the press and notable individuals.

This document was followed by two articles in *The Times* (20 and 21 April, 1953) written by Dr Lessing, a leading member of the NSAS.[41] The two parts were sub-titled the 'Lessons of the London Fog' and 'Remedies and their Costs' The tone was subdued but critical. A 'thorough and impartial investigation' was called for and the absence of reasonable doubt about the existence of a formidable problem of air pollution emphasized. However, there was no editorial comment and only a desultory and short correspondence.

In May 1953, Macmillan, the Minister of Housing and Local Government, at last announced that he intended to appoint a committee of inquiry, after having steadfastly refused to do so for six months since the December disaster. The first perplexing question is why should he have refused earlier? The second equally puzzling question is why, eventually, he gave way?

Although the full extent of the catastrophe took time to determine, certainly by February 1953 the facts were reasonably well known and indeed it has been contended that the Minister of Health's 'statement in the Commons on 18th December giving the numbers of deaths during the week ended 13th December, produced an immediate impression and it was apparent that the problem of preventing further disasters of this nature was urgent'.[42] Admittedly the formation of a committee or the introduction of a Bill take time but a statement of intent could have been made.

[38] Sanderson, J. B., *op. cit.*, p. 244.
[39] Sanderson, J. B., *ibid.*
[40] 'The London Fog: A First Survey', *Smokeless Air*, Spring, 1953.
[41] 'Polluted Air Over Towns', *The Times*, 20 and 21 April, 1953.
[42] Ministry of Health. *Mortality and Morbidity During the London Fog of December, 1952*, 1954.

One explanation for the delay and the resistance may be found in the divided ministerial responsibility for air pollution. Until January 1951 this had unequivocally resided with Health. After this the former responsibilities of the ministry were divided: local government, housing and environmental regulation passed to what was first called the Ministry of Local Government and Planning and later Housing and Local Government.[43] Most of the pollution research was carried out under the aegis of Fuel and Power. When the crisis broke, air pollution was only a part of the responsibilities of one civil servant in the Ministry of Housing and Local Government. There were, of course, the Alkali Inspectors but they were also few in number and were rarely concerned in local government matters. What relevant civil service experience and concern existed remained in the Ministry of Health.[44] Indeed, early in 1953 the Minister of Health (MacLeod) set up an internal committee of 'officers and expert advisers to marshall and examine the facts' about the London smog.[45] At the completion of its work in 1954 the committee acknowledged the main sources of the help it had received: the London medical officers of health; general practitioners; coroners and coroners' pathologists; the Meteorological Office; the Fuel Research Station; together with the Ministries of Agriculture and Fisheries and Pensions and National Insurance. All placed information from their departments at the committee's disposal. There was nothing, apparently, from the Ministry of Housing and Local Government.[46]

Yet if action was to be taken, Macmillan, as Minister of Housing and Local Government, had to initiate it.[47] His attention and commitment were, however, elsewhere. The Conservatives had won the 1951 General Election pledged to a target of 300,000 new houses a year. The task fell to Macmillan and he accepted it as the primary responsibility before him. He makes clear in his autobiography that

[43] *The Medical Officer*, journal of the public health doctors, frequently criticized this division of responsibility, lack of co-ordination and leadership. 'Is this why, in the fight against atmospheric pollution, there is no leadership from the centre?' ('Fog over London', vol. LXXXIX; 14 Feb., 1953, p. 73.) 'Was there ever a greater fog over Whitehall than on this problem of Air Pollution?' (Barnett, J. S. G., 'Smoke-Laden Fog', 10 Jan., 1953, p. 10.)

[44] After the smog catastrophe, however, one particularly knowledgeable and well-informed officer from the Ministry of Health acted in an advisory capacity at the Ministry of Housing and Local Government as well.

[45] See the preparatory note to the Ministry of Health report, *Mortality and Morbidity During the London Fog of December, 1952, op. cit.*

[46] Lipton summed up this problem in an exchange at question time: 'A London fog concerns a number of departments between whom there is a lack of co-ordination and a lack of initiative.' *H. C. Deb.*, vol. 510, col. 992.

[47] It may be significant, as in the health centre study, that after the division of Health and Housing in 1951 the Minister of Health did not become a member of the Cabinet again until 1962.

during this period housing and related issues absorbed the major part of his time and energy as well as that of his senior civil servants.[48] Nonetheless, the east coast floods of February 1953 did engage his personal attention, and a committee of inquiry was set up under Lord Waverley. Perhaps the longer-term implications of action to curb air pollution were more complex and open-ended.

This too was a period when the austerities of wartime regulation were just beginning to be lifted. The government, moreover, wished to move as quickly as possible to lessen public control; to a reduction in the size of the civil service and to checking the growth of public expenditure.[49] Indeed, its election manifesto of 1951 proclaimed that 'multiplying orders and rules should be reduced'.[50] In that general climate the prospect of introducing a *further* major sphere of governmental regulation and developing new responsibilities and expertise at the ministry was hardly likely to be viewed sympathetically. At that time too, as Wise has pointed out, 'there were no votes to be gained from scouring the atmosphere'.[51] To the extent that effective legislation would have to restrict the use of open domestic fires the probability of popular opposition must have been judged high; certainly in mining areas where concessionary coal was available.

None of these factors convincingly explains Macmillan's tardy response to the London smog. Probably the high priority attached to housing production and the related matters of development charges, rents and subsidies placed the issue in an acutely competitive position. There was no existing commitment or experience within the ministry; thus no *group* of senior civil servants to advance the cause of clean air.

Why then, by May 1953, was Macmillan prepared to appoint a committee of inquiry? Typically, 'mounting public concern' is held to be responsible and certainly *The Times*' articles, the continuing parliamentary questioning and the work of the NSAS provide some corroboration for this view. There was, however, also the *persistence* of the issue. It was kept well to the fore over a comparatively long period. The NSAS were influential in this as were certain public health doctors. The government could hardly welcome the prospect of the issue being sustained *into* the following winter, with its attendant risks of another smog disaster. Certainly it was the theme of public alarm at the likelihood of further smog the following winter to which Dodds returned time and again in the adjournment debate

[48] Macmillan, H., *Tides of Fortune, 1945–55* (ch. XIII), Macmillan, 1969.
[49] It is interesting to note the importance attached to this general commitment in both the health centre and detention centres studies.
[50] Craig, F. W. S., *British General Election Manifestos, 1918–1966*, Pol. Ref. Pubs, 1970, p. 146.
[51] Wise, W., *op. cit.*, p. 165.

on air pollution in May 1953, at the end of which Marples (for Macmillan) announced that a committee of inquiry would be appointed.[52]

A further factor influencing the government in its decision may, however, need to be sought in the debate about fuel policy which was renewed during the first half of 1953. For the first time since the war the annual productivity of the coal mining industry had declined in the previous year. There had been poor labour relations and an increase in strike action. Amongst the Conservative backbenchers a campaign was developing for an inquiry to be made into the operation of the National Coal Board and for a more coordinated national fuel policy. By April 1953 these demands were supported in the Conservative's Parliamentary Fuel and Power committee and by a substantial section of the 1922 Committee. More efficiency in coal burning (i.e. less smoke) was needed as well as the more economical use of its by-products which were obtained in the coking process. To the extent that the nation reduced its dependence upon coal it might, so some thought, break the stranglehold which the mineworkers were supposed to maintain upon important sections of the nation's economy. Whether or not Conservative backbench pressure for a fuel policy which would achieve these various ends had reached sufficient strength by April 1953 to weigh in the Government's deliberations about atmospheric pollution is hard to judge; but certainly the one issue merged into the other.

No single explanation seems to account satisfactorily for the government's ostensible change of heart; a change formally denoted by the announcement of the membership and terms of reference of an interdepartmental committee of inquiry towards the end of July 1953.[53] Sir Hugh Beaver, managing director of Guinness, was to be chairman. The other eleven members were drawn from industry, local government and from people outside these two spheres who possessed special knowledge of the problem. Three of the members were also leading figures in the NSAS.[54] As well as the members, 'assessors' from the Ministries of Health; Fuel and Power; Housing and Local Government and from the Department of Scientific and In-

---

[52] To support his contention Dodds informed the House that, as an MP, he had never had more correspondence on any subject and he quoted an editorial from the *Star* of 16 April, 1953 which stated that: 'A Government Committee to inquire into the more technical aspects of smoke abatement must get down to practical business and yield results before the next fog season. December's killer fog, like the flood disaster, caught many experts unawares. This must not happen again.'

[53] Established by the Ministers of Housing and Local Government, Fuel and Power and the Secretary of State for Scotland.

[54] See Sanderson, J. B., *op. cit.*, p. 247.

dustrial Research were appointed to assist in the committee's work.[55] The combined team of members and assessors looked impressive, comprising as it did leading administrators and scientists. There was every indication, therefore, that the air pollution issue was at last to be taken seriously. The committee's task was 'to examine the nature, causes and effects of air pollution and the efficacy of present preventive measures; to consider what further preventive measures are practicable; and to make recommendations'.

Having launched this inquiry the government was not absolved from further pointed questions in Parliament about its progress. For example, in October Macmillan had to deal with questions from Nabarro. In the course of answering them he promised that the committee would provide a speedy interim report. Indeed, this was actually completed by November 18 1953 and published in December.[56] It seems likely that Beaver had earlier decided to produce such a document, and that by October it was already in the process of preparation.

One part of the interim report contained a short technical survey of the problem whilst the other proposed some modest measures which could be introduced at once. These included a public alert system and the use of a 'closely-fitting simple gauze mask, or woollen scarf wrapped round the mouth and nose'.[57] In fact 'smog masks' were to become available through the National Health Service soon afterwards. But the winter of 1953–4 passed without any substantial period of smog.[58]

By the standards of other committees of inquiry Beaver worked fast. There are several reasons why the final report, which was published in November 1954, only sixteen months after the committee's appointment, was finished so quickly. Certainly the drive, conviction and experience of the chairman were of the utmost importance. He considered that speed was essential if the whole issue of air pollution was not to lose the momentum it had so far achieved. Wise contends that 'Sir Hugh believed ... the Government hoped the public furore would subside in the meantime', and that the demand for the control of air pollution would lessen. He goes on to suggest that 'the Chairman remained sceptical of Whitehall's real

[55] They included the chief alkali inspectors of England and Wales and Scotland; the DSIR director of fuel research; the Chief Scientist at the Ministry of Fuel and Power; a principal medical officer and an assistant secretary from the Ministry of Housing and Local Government. The Director of the Meteorological Office of the Air Ministry was a member, not an assessor.

[56] *Committee on Air Pollution: Interim Report*, Cmd. 9011, 1953.

[57] *Ibid.*, p. 9.

[58] For a good summary of the position soon after Beaver's interim report see 'The Menace of Air Pollution', PEP, *Planning*, vol. XX, no. 369, August, 1954.

intentions. He could not easily forget that the Minister of Housing and Local Government, who represented the department most concerned with the air pollution problem, had failed to consult him on even a single occasion during the first eight months of the committee's existence.'[59]

The committee also worked in a way that allowed it to progress quickly. It 'took little formal evidence: rather taking the view that all interests were in agreement as to the objective and that therefore it was a matter for joint discussion to find the means'.[60] This approach was made possible by the prior existence of much technical knowledge and information about the problem, albeit scattered and needing to be drawn together. The technical expertise of the members and the assessors certainly helped in doing this, as did a variety of informal discussions with individuals and groups with special knowledge. There was also relevant American experience, some post-war local experiments in smokeless zones as in Manchester[61] and the work being done at the same time by the Minister of Health's own 'officers and experts' committee concerned with an analysis of the London fog. Thus there were facts to be drawn on and, with evidence like that of the NSAS or the LCC, firm recommendations to hand.[62]

In a comparatively short time, then, the final report appeared in November 1954. Its most important recommendations were that 'local authorities should have power under general legislation, by means of Orders requiring confirmation by the appropriate Ministers, to establish (i) smokeless zones in which the emission of smoke from chimneys would be entirely prohibited, and (ii) smoke control areas in which the use of bituminous coal for domestic purposes would be restricted'. In addition 'financial assistance should be provided by local authorities and by the Exchequer towards the costs incurred by house owners in converting appliances in smokeless zones and smoke control areas'.[63] Many other proposals were made but the main thrust of the recommendations was aimed at domestic smoke. As the report pointed out, 'no cure can be found for the heavy smoke pollution of

[59] Wise, W., *op. cit.*, p. 169.

[60] Wise, W., *op. cit.*, p. 168.

[61] The town clerk of Manchester later wrote: 'the Beaver committee were not disposed to regard smokeless zones as a feasible answer to their terms of reference ... it was only when they had visited some smokeless zones that they accepted the principle. When they visited Manchester and were taken on to the roof of a building in the middle of the central area it happened to be a clear day with little wind and the evidence of the value of a smokeless zone was irrefutable.' Dingle, P., 'What Manchester Thinks Today ...', in the *Municipal Review*, vol. 36, Dec. 1965, p. 721.

[62] See *Smokeless Air*, Summer 1954, which reproduces the NSAS evidence to Beaver.

[63] *Committee on Air Pollution*, *op. cit.*, para. 121, p. 34.

our cities and towns unless the domestic chimney is dealt with'.[64] Nonetheless, certain proposals to curb industrial smoke were included although other industrial pollutants received comparatively little attention. The most immediate and pressing problem was seen as smoke and especially domestic smoke.

The report was unanimous, outspoken in its condemnation of air pollution and authoritative. It put forward practical and comparatively modest proposals for new legislation. The final report received a full and sympathetic press. Given these favourable aspects and the sequence of events so far, the prospects for legislative reform looked good. A month before the publication of the Beaver report Macmillan left Housing and Local Government to become Minister of Defence, and was replaced by Duncan Sandys who was considered by some to be more concerned with the air pollution issue. The target of 300,000 houses was about to be achieved and clean air was, in any case, becoming increasingly feasible on technical grounds as time passed.

The government gave no indication that it accepted the broad principles of the report until the end of January 1955 when Duncan Sandys did so in answer to a parliamentary question from Nabarro.[65] The Minister contended that no time had been lost. During the Recess, he said, the government had necessarily to study the report's implications. In the meantime, however, Nabarro had won first place in the ballot for Private Members' Bills and had chosen to introduce a clean air measure incorporating most of the Beaver recommendations.[66] The Bill was duly framed, with the technical and financial assistance of the NSAS, and obtained its first reading in December 1954 supported by a distinguished group of Members from both parties.[67]

An unequivocal assurance that the government would introduce comprehensive clean air legislation 'within the session' was finally given by the Minister during the second reading debate of Nabarro's measure early in February 1955. His Bill was accordingly withdrawn; taken over, in effect by the government.[68] The puzzling question is whether, without the additional pressure and embarrass-

---

[64] *Committee on Air Pollution, op. cit.*, para. 68, p. 21.

[65] *H. C. Deb.*, vol. 536, cols 38–42.

[66] See Nabarro, G., *Nab 1: Portrait of a Politician*, Maxwell, 1969, pp. 290–3.

[67] The maximum number of eleven supporters included: Alf Robens, Col Lancaster (chairman of the Conservative Parliamentary Fuel and Power Committee); Philip Noel-Baker; Enoch Powell; Angus Maude (director of the Conservative Political Centre); Hilary Marquand (former Labour Minister of Health); Anthony Greenwood; Dr Horace King; Leslie Lever (former Labour mayor of Manchester); Sir Walter Darling, and Sir John Barlow (a leading Conservative industrialist).

[68] *H. C. Deb.*, vol. 536, cols 1422–1510.

ment of a Private Members' Bill, this would have happened. The fact that just before the Beaver report was published some dozen experienced MPs (who subsequently lent support to the Nabarro Bill), representing both sides of the House agreed that they would present a Clean Air Bill should they be fortunate in the ballot, suggests that there were real fears for the report's fate. Since, moreover, the NSAS was also ready to spend its time and money helping Nabarro prepare his Bill it can be assumed that they too were dubious about the government's intentions. Sir Hugh Beaver also appeared unconvinced that his committee's labours would necessarily bear fruit.[69] The *Municipal Review*, mouthpiece of the Association of Municipal Corporations, speculated that there was a 'nice, clean, empty pigeonhole the same shape and size as the Beaver report ... after all the report suggests interference with one of the most sacred of our national habits and one can't be too careful'.[70]

Duncan Sandys explained that the government's delayed response was due solely to the need for consultations with interested parties. Certainly these had been started with the local authority associations and with the Federation of British Industry (now the Confederation), both of whom, the Minister reported, were willing to collaborate in the implementation of new clean air legislation. Despite such apparently favourable soundings there remains more than a hint of government hesitation to proceed with Beaver's proposals: why?

His report was almost certainly considered in the Cabinet Home Affairs Committee before or soon after its publication. The political and financial costs and benefits of action must have been considered. What factors were likely to have entered into such calculation? There was little evidence that industry generally would respond adversely to the broad sweep of proposals, although the detail might be contested. But intervention to ensure a cleaner atmosphere would also have to change longstanding habits of open fire *domestic* heating. There was substantial room for doubt about how the public might react. A general election was looming fast on the horizon (May 1955 in the event). Eden was about to succeed Churchill as leader of the Conservative Party and it was unclear how this might affect the outcome. The Conservatives were far from confident that they would be returned. As Macmillan wrote: 'no one can tell how this election will turn out'.[71] Given these kinds of uncertainties the government might have judged it prudent to introduce clean air controls *after* the General Election. In practical terms too this would have seemed

[69] Report in the *Manchester Guardian*, 7 Jan., 1955; quoted in the debate (*Ibid.*, col. 1449).

[70] 'Wholly Smoke' (Anon.), *Municipal Review*, vol. 26, Jan. 1955, p. 33.

[71] *The Tides of Fortune, op. cit.*, Diary entry 6 May, 1955, p. 583.

a sensible postponement, given the pressure on parliamentary time towards the end of an administration.

The availability of the resources needed to embark upon a comprehensive clean air policy is also likely to have been considered by the Cabinet Home Affairs Committee. The Beaver report had pointed out the difficulties connected with the supply of solid smokeless fuels but had concluded that the situation was sufficiently promising to make a start. The notion that even without government intervention the smoke problem would resolve itself in God's good time must, by 1955, have seemed plausible. Ahead there was a clear prospect of the end of steam locomotion; the growth of domestic central heating and the development of nuclear power.[72] If the problem would gradually solve itself why introduce supposedly unpopular legislation which might soon be redundant anyway? It seems likely therefore that the Nabarro Bill did tip the balance when probably the only member of the Cabinet advocating positive action was Duncan Sandys.[73] Whether the Bill worked as an ·accelerator or a precipitator is difficult to determine.

The Government's own Clean Air Bill received its first reading just before the summer Recess of 1955. The second reading debate eventually took place in November that year.[74] The committee stage did not start until the following February. The major criticism of the Bill at both points came from those who wished to see it made stricter and more extensive in its application, particularly in the case of industry. Few modifications were made, however, and the final Act of 1956 closely resembled the original Bill.

III THE PARTICIPANTS

In describing and analysing the events of the period 1952–6 various participant groups and individuals have already been noted. We turn now to a more specific and detailed examination of the part played by the most important of them.

The National Smoke Abatement Society (now the Clean Air Society) was the only group with a well established and special commitment to clean air reform. It originated in the Coal Smoke Abatement Society which was formed in 1899, primarily to press for the enforcement of the smoke nuisance provisions of the 1875 Public Health Act: 'It was the neglect of these powers that finally

[72] See p. 399.
[73] 'Let me say straightaway that if my hon. friend [Nabarro] has been pushing us along a little, nobody resents it less than I do.' Duncan Sandys (in the second reading debate on Nabarro's Bill). *H. C. Deb.*, vol. 536, col. 1484.
[74] *H. C. Deb.*, vol. 545, cols 1221–1333.

brought together the people who ... decided to set up a Society.'[75] In its early years the society, through the work of an inspector, submitted complaints to the local authorities about industrial smoke; undertook investigations such as the testing of domestic grates; and held conferences. At its 1912 International Smoke Abatement Conference and Exhibition held in London, resolutions were adopted 'calling for support for a Smoke Abatement Bill ... and for a Royal Commission to investigate the problem. From these resolutions came the activities that led to the setting up of the Newton Committee on Smoke and Noxious Vapours Abatement, and eventually – after the serious setback caused by the 1914–18 war and its aftermath – the Public Health (Smoke Abatement) Act of 1926.'[76] Both the Coal Smoke Abatement Society and the Manchester-based Smoke Abatement League submitted important evidence to the 1921 Newton Committee and between the publication of its report and the 1926 legislation pressed, with little success, for as strong a Bill as possible 'in the face of much opposition from industry'.[77]

In 1929 the society and the league amalgamated to form the NSAS which adopted the league's previous policy of extending the range of membership and welcoming the association of any vested interests. As well as local authorities and individuals, commercial and public undertakings (such as the National Coal Board) subsequently joined, creating a mixed and, at times, contentious support base.[78]

During the 1930s the cause of clean air was extremely hard to advance because of the depression and 'a surplus of coal and unemployment in the mines and ... national preoccupation with the threat of war'.[79] The society's membership nevertheless increased; it published a quarterly journal; held conferences; generated ideas such as the conception of 'smokeless zones' and assembled relevant information from this and other countries. But, as the society's own account of its history admits, 'many opportunities were lost', mainly through the lack of resources. When the 1952 smog struck, these opportunities increased relatively faster than the society's capacity to grasp them.[80]

[75] 'The Society's Story', in *Sixty Years for Clean Air*, report of the Diamond Jubilee Conference and Exhibition, 1959, p. 12.

[76] *Sixty Years for Clean Air, op. cit.*, p. 15.

[77] *Ibid.*, p. 16.

[78] As Sanderson notes, 'this diversity of membership, though a source of strength in some respects, can lead to internal dissension. In 1952, for instance, the NCB attempted (unsuccessfully) to prevent the Society from issuing a report criticising the use of "nutty slack" which had been recommended by the Minister of Fuel and Power.' *Op. cit.*, p. 237.

[79] *Sixty Years for Clean Air, op. cit.*, p. 17.

[80] 'The event severely stretched the Society's small organisation by reason of the many inquiries we received, and especially the many visits and telephone

Even so, the London smog provided the society with *the* opportunity for exerting effective influence. It was the only body adequately prepared with ideas and information. Despite its limited resources it acted quickly; for instance in undertaking and distributing the results of its own survey of the smog and in formulating evidence to Beaver. Later, it was able to brief Nabarro and provide him with a parliamentary adviser and, further, to assist other MPs during the passage of the eventual government Bill.

In 1952 there was no other single group in such a *generally* authoritative position as the NSAS on the clean air issue. It was to it that the press first turned for information when the magnitude of the smog catastrophe became apparent. It was the society which was able to submit the kind of general evidence *and* recommendations for feasible action which the Beaver committee could incorporate into its report. It also spanned and, to some extent, co-ordinated a research field which was fragmented into a variety of specialist and technical contributions. The views of the society could not be dismissed as uninformed or impractical, and it had an impressive and respectable membership list behind it. Had it possessed more organizational resources its impact might have been greater than it was. Even in 1951 the society's annual expenditure was only £4,800, half of which was devoted to salaries and nearly another £1,000 to printing and publishing its journal and other material. There was little, if any, elbow room and few reserves which could be thrown into an intensified campaign. Perhaps the most important part played by the NSAS during the years immediately after 1952 was to *sustain* atmospheric pollution as a public issue once, partly because of its influence, it had gained that position after the London smog.

Although we have argued that there were no other bodies with a comparable general grasp of the clean air question in the early 1950s there were groups concerned with, and knowledgeable about, specific aspects. Within the Ministry of Housing and Local Government the Alkali Inspectorate might have been expected to have played a more significant part in the events of those years. Admittedly both the chief inspectors for England and Wales and for Scotland sat as assessors on the Beaver committee but the Inspectorate as such offered no formal evidence. Their role appears to have been largely consultative rather innovative. The history of this branch of government may help to explain their seemingly passive part in this particular episode in the struggle for clean air.

The Alkali Inspectorate was established in 1863 for the purpose

discussions with eager but not always technically minded representatives of the press, *at the very time we should have liked to have been making our own more specific inquiries and investigations*' (our italics). Report of general secretary to NSAS in *Proceedings of the Annual Conference*, 1953, p. 33.

of regulating the release of 'noxious gases' by the fast growing chemical industry, and although the Acts were subsequently extended to other industries the work remained directed to selected industrial processes. The Inspectorate was, and is, recruited from scientists with relevant (often industrial) experience. It has worked in an essentially collaborative style directly with industry, persuading and advising rather than enforcing. The Inspectorate has comprised a small group working, as McLeod puts it, 'just within the "safety zone" of public ignorance and national apathy'.[81] Indeed, its relatively untroubled existence for a hundred years and its ability to exercise influence in the application of scientific knowledge to industrial processes in the interests of greater public welfare is partly the result of avoiding the limelight of debate which, from time to time, erupted in its area of concern. The Alkali Inspectorate was, therefore, not only small, separate, technical and specialized but also lacked the kind of tradition which would have made it likely to play a significant part in the more general issue of clean air which emerged in the 1950s.

Another branch of government which had also been concerned with aspects of air pollution over many years was the Department of Scientific and Industrial Research. The department first undertook studies in atmospheric pollution in 1927. In 1952 this work was centred in the Fuel Research Station at Greenwich under the general direction of an Atmospheric Pollution Research Committee,[82] a committee of the Fuel Research Board of the DSIR. Amongst other things the work involved maintaining a Standing Conference of Co-operating Bodies in the systematic and regular measurement of atmospheric pollution throughout the country. The 'co-operating bodies' were given advice in approved methods of measurement and, if necessary, provided with apparatus. The monthly results were published in the *Atmospheric Pollution Bulletin*. In addition, various investigations of a technical nature were conducted; for example, on 'the recovery of sulphur compounds from flue gases' and on 'the combustion problems of industrial boilers and domestic heating and cooking appliances'. There were technical papers on the composition and measurement of smoke and detailed surveys in certain localities.[83]

[81] McLeod, R. M., 'The Alkali Acts Administration, 1863–84: the Emergence of the Civil Scientist', *Victorian Studies*, Dec. 1965, p. 112.

[82] The committee's terms of reference were: 'To carry out the supervision, co-ordination, and collation of the local records of atmospheric pollution, and to advise on research into the amount, nature and prevention of pollution'.

[83] See for example, the *27th Report of the work of the DSIR* 1955; Wilkins, E. T., 'Review of the Fuel Research Station's Investigations of Atmospheric Pollution', in NSAS, *Proceedings of the Annual Conference*, 1952, pp. 29–32; and DSIR Atmospheric Pollution Research Committee, Technical Paper, no. 1, *Atmospheric Pollution in Leicester: A Scientific Survey*, 1945.

The fact that the Fuel Research Station was primarily concerned with the problems of measuring atmospheric pollution, and with technological innovation and improvement may partly explain its apparent lack of *policy* initiative in the clean air issue. Although it supplied important technical evidence to the Beaver Committee, and three members of its Atmospheric Pollution Research Committee served on it, there was a singular lack of any public contribution. The report of the Director of Fuel Research on the 'Investigation of Atmospheric Pollution for the Ten Years ending 1954' devoted only nine lines to the London smog, concluding: 'since that time arrangements have been made for more detailed and extensive surveys during any future occurrences of this kind'.[84]

The lack of any policy component in the role of the Fuel Research Station is paralleled in many respects by other research stations, for example Building Research and, to a lesser extent, the Road Research Laboratory. It has been suggested that the DSIR's cherished independence of its related central government departments was only won at the price of 'no public interference' in the policy spheres of these departments. The stations were not to be promotional but provide information to bodies *seeking* assistance. How far any of this took the form of specific instructions or agreements is hard to judge but the similar pattern of work of a number of these stations suggests some general DSIR policy.[85] Whatever the explanation, the DSIR, which had been concerned with atmospheric pollution at least as long as the NSAS played a considerably lesser part in the events which we have described.[86]

Those involved in medical research on the effects of atmospheric pollution might also have been expected to figure prominently in the debate between 1952–6. But the Medical Research Council's unit on Atmospheric Pollution was not established at St Bartholomew's Hospital until 1955. Its contribution to the more rigorous investigation of the relationship between polluted air and, for example, lung cancer

[84] *27th Report of the Work of the DSIR*, 1955, p. 22. It should be noted, however, that in the less acute London smog of January 1956 the DSIR did issue a press release providing certain facts (9 Feb., 1956).

[85] Indeed such a policy is implied by the comments of a former secretary to the DSIR. He wrote: '... but whenever scientific facts are relevant to a practical problem this should be sought out independently of existing and preconceived practical policy, and be made available in scientific accuracy, to be brought by those *administratively responsible* into correlation with the relevant consideration, economic, financial, social and so on' (our italics). Melville, H., *The Department of Scientific and Industrial Research*, Allen & Unwin, 1962, p. 27.

[86] In this section we are indebted to D. L. Simms of Nuffield College for valuable suggestions and ideas.

or bronchitis, was still to be made.[87] Some work had been undertaken on the relationship between lung cancer and polluted air and had been published at various times in the *British Journal of Cancer*;[88] and there were Logan's statistical analyses of the effects of fog to which we have already referred.[89]

In the early 1950s there was no cohesive and well-developed medical interest group concerned primarily with the consequences of atmospheric pollution. It was, of course, widely agreed that polluted air and the absence of sunlight were deleterious to health but precise and hard evidence was not readily available. The single most committed and vigorous medical voice came from the local authority medical officers of health and certainly leading clean air campaigners were to be found amongst their number.[90] But they had other community health problems to consider as well, and outside the industrial and metropolitan areas atmospheric pollution was not regarded as so pressing. The fact that the smog catastrophe was, in effect, a local London issue perhaps made it difficult to generalize the urgency outside the group of London medical officers of health and to create *new* commitments over and above those already held by a number of notable doctors in local authorities elsewhere.

Despite the absence of any general lead from the medical profession the importance of quantified data about the effect of the London smog must be re-emphasized. It was upon those measurements, supplied from medical sources, that much subsequently turned. Epedemiological investigations by the GRO, at the Ministry of Health, and by local medical officers of health were of the utmost importance. That this was not matched by a forceful policy involvement may in part be attributed to the divided responsibility at central government level in a situation where the major responsibility for action lay with the Ministry of Housing and Local Government and not Health. This may have affected adversely the ability of public health doctors outside the ministry to influence central government. Until 1951 their main contacts in these matters would have been with their professional colleagues and civil servants at the Ministry of Health. They were less familiar with the comparatively new set-up at Housing and Local Government; and in any case, as we have noted already, with respect to air pollution there was little enough to become familiar with, apart from the Alkali Inspectorate.

[87] *Report of the Medical Research Council for 1955–6*, Cmnd. 180, p. 114.
[88] For example, work by Goulden, F.; Kennaway, E. L. and Urquhart M. E.; by Waller, R. G. and by Stocks, P.
[89] See p. 377.
[90] 'It [the public health service] has hammered at this problem for years ... the apathy and disinterest has been at the centre.' J. S. G. Barnett, *Medical Officer, op. cit.*, p. 20.

Industries, particularly the chemical and coal industries, were obviously interested parties in the clean air issue. It is difficult, however, to determine what part such industrial interests played in the development with which we are concerned. The achievement of a cleaner atmosphere is very difficult to oppose openly and it is likely that those in industry or elsewhere who wished to do so had to manoeuvre obliquely and not in public view. The fact that the clean air issue became focused upon domestic smoke, although certainly justified at the time, meant that the problem of industrially caused pollution was less prominent. Indeed, the 1956 Clean Air Act was sharply criticized for lacking the necessary teeth to deal with industrial pollution. Whether or not this reflected 'the influence of industry', as Nabarro contended, is difficult to test, but it seems likely that some of the 'escape clauses' which the Act contained did represent concessions won by industrial interests.

The close relationship between efficient combustion and clean air, however, meant that industrial smoke pollution was the hallmark of wasteful (and hence expensive) fuel consumption. Firms could be encouraged to support smoke control measures, at least in the installation of new or replacement equipment, by the favourable loans which were administered by the Ministry of Fuel and Power for projects saving fuel. The capital costs, moreover, could be charged against revenue for tax purposes. It is reasonable, therefore, to conclude that industry (for instance, the Federation of British Industry as it then was) did not collectively and actively oppose in principle the kind of clean air reforms being proposed. Whilst the problem continued to be seen mainly as one of smoke, industry could play its part and reap certain advantages from lower fuel costs.

The role of Parliament, and especially certain backbenchers of both parties, must not be underestimated in the clean air campaign. Their prominence in our story is a reflection of the almost complete lack of interest and involvement of either of the political parties. Until 1955 neither had included anything about cleaning the atmosphere in their election manifestos.[91] In pressing for government action, and thereby helping to keep alive the issue of atmospheric pollution, two features of backbench intervention are noteworthy. They are parliamentary questioning and Nabarro's Private Members' Bill. We have already discussed the second of these; now we turn to the first.

Prior to the 1952 London smog there were parliamentary questions about air pollution, but from one question in the session 1951–2 the number jumped to thirty-five in the next. The acceleration began soon after the December smog, which, it will be recalled, dispersed on the 9th. On the 16th Driberg asked the Minister of Health 'how

[91] Craig, F. W. S., *op. cit.*

many persons died of bronchial or other ailments in the Greater London area as a result of the recent severe fog?'[92] On the following day he asked whether an inquiry into the whole matter would be set afoot. Questions addressed to various Ministers followed on the 18th and 19th,[93] upon which day the House adjourned for the Christmas Recess. The main thrust of these initial questions was twofold. First, they sought to obtain a 'public' estimate of the dimensions of the catastrophe and second, they pressed for an immediate inquiry. The first objective met with some success but the second encountered firm blocking. When the Commons reassembled on January 20 1953, questioning was resumed at once. There was Greenwood on the 20th; Dodds on the 21st; Lipton, Keeling, Noel-Baker and Hastings on the 22nd; Dodds, Janner, Noel-Baker, Gibson, Blenkinsop and Lipton on the 27th and Mallalieu on the 29th. Questions continued throughout February and into March until the Easter adjournment. Most of them were asked by Labour Members, but not all. The questions which were dealt with orally often gave the opportunity for telling exchanges. For example, Macmillan himself dealt with the oral questions on January 27, which covered 'requests' for the setting up of an inter-departmental committee of inquiry; for making the powers of local authorities more effective; for the implementation of the Ridley committee's recommendations; for information about the connection between atmospheric pollution and lung cancer and for an account of what the Chief Alkali Inspector was doing about the London smog. Macmillan argued, amongst other things, that it was a big undertaking to alter the whole fuel system of the country and also said that he 'did not feel further general legislation was required at that time'. This particular flurry of questions and answers ended with Dodds stating that because of 'the amazing display of apathy' he would raise the matter on adjournment.[94]

A second phase of questioning followed the announcement, made in the last minutes of Dodds' promised adjournment debate on May 8, that a committee of inquiry would be set up.[95] Questions now mainly

[92] *H. C. Deb.*, vol. 509, col. 188.

[93] *H. C. Deb.*, vol. 509, cols 22, 237, 265 and 289.

[94] *H. C. Deb.*, vol. 510, col. 828. Members may use the motion for the adjournment of the House to obtain a debate on particular issues. Normally time is allotted to such discussion the day before recess or for thirty minutes at the end of public business. 'A member wishing to raise a matter during the half-hour adjournment period must give notice to the Speaker in writing; a ballot is held once a fortnight, and eight members obtain the right to speak during the following two weeks.' Central Office of Information, *The British Parliament*, 6th edn, HMSO, 1968, p. 31.

[95] *H. C. Deb.*, vol. 515, col. 850. Marples (Parliamentary Secretary to the Ministry of Housing and Local Government) said, 'the Government have decided to appoint a committee, under an independent chairman, to undertake

concerned its intended membership, terms of reference and date of commencement. These continued until July 21 1953 when, in response to a series of questions from Dodds, Medlicott, Hastings and Blenkinsop, the Parliamentary Secretary to the Ministry of Housing and Local Government (Marples) provided details about the committee's composition and brief.[96] Again, however, the manner of the announcement hardly suggested vigorous enthusiasm on the part of the Ministers concerned.

The House adjourned at the end of July and reassembled in the middle of October, whereupon a third stage in questioning immediately began. Questions were now of two kinds. First, there were those about the progress of the Beaver committee since its inception in the summer and second, there were questions demanding to know what 'emergency plans' the Minister had prepared for the forthcoming winter, with its risk of a recurrence of the London smog of the previous year. The initial answers gave little encouragement that any preparations whatsoever were being made. 'Is the Minister not aware', asked Lipton, 'that his activity or in-activity in the matter is regarded with considerable misgiving?'[97] Perhaps what served to dramatize the impending smog risk more vividly than anything else was the whole idea of the need for 'smog masks'. On November 13 Gough asked the Minister of Health whether he would make a statement about the provision of such masks under the National Health Service. McLeod replied that, by regulation, from November 17 1953 onwards doctors would be able to provide smog masks for patients likely to be at risk.[98] Some commentators noted similarities between smog masks and the wartime gas masks.

By the end of November 1953 Beaver's interim report had appeared and Macmillan then made a short statement about the government's emergency proposals for the winter. These included the smog masks, a Meteorological Office alert system and an increase of half a ton in the domestic allocation of coke.[99] The *need* for emergency plans, was, of course, emphasized in the interim report but the questioning in Parliament also served to expose the absence of any preparations for reducing the risk of another London smog episode, or dealing with it if it occurred.

After the uneventful passage of the winter months of 1953–4 questions were fewer but regular, mainly querying the progress and

---

a comprehensive review of the causes and effects of air pollution, and to consider what further preventive measures are practicable'. The announcement was made to a chamber containing less than a dozen members.

[96] *H. C. Deb.*, vol. 518, cols 201–3.
[97] *H. C. Deb.*, vol. 518, cols 1791–3.
[98] *H. C. Deb.*, vol. 520, cols 104–6.
[99] *H. C. Deb.*, vol. 521, cols 1161–2.

expected date of publication of Beaver's final report. A fourth phase
in the questioning effectively began once the report had appeared
in November 1954. 'Will the Minister make a statement?' asked
Dodds, Marquand and Blenkinsop in the second week of December.
Duncan Sandys 'hoped to clear the air about the Government's intentions as soon as possible'.[100] However, when Nabarro, during the
'Business of the House' on 9 December asked the Lord Privy Seal 'for
early facilities for a debate on Beaver' he was refused.[101] On January
25 1955, the first day after the Christmas Recess, both Nabarro and
Dodds had questions on the order paper asking what action the
government intended to take following its consideration of the *Report
on Air Pollution*. Duncan Sandys chose to answer Nabarro's question
orally, although it had not been reached at Question Time. He informed the House that preliminary discussions had been instigated
with various interest groups and that, in principle, the government
accepted the policy recommendations contained in the report.[102]

This review of the part played by parliamentary questions in the
progress towards Clean Air legislation suggests that a group of members acted in some unison, though not organized by the Opposition. Most were Labour members representing constituencies suffering
from high levels of atmospheric pollution (e.g. Stross, Dodds, Lipton,
Ellis Smith, and Hastings), but Conservative backbenchers also played
a part, especially Nabarro. Although questions are a regular and
unexceptional feature of our parliamentary system they appear to
have played an important role in sustaining the issue of air pollution
by keeping up a steady and critical pressure upon the various
Ministers, but especially upon Macmillan and McLeod. In his adjournment debate Dodds quoted the *Evening Standard* of January 24
1953 in which it was reported that 'Mr Iain McLeod, the Minister
of Health, was another of the speakers at The Fan Makers' Dinner.
He said he seemed to get nothing except questions about the fog
and its effect upon people's health.'[103] Clearly, the Minister was not
referring to parliamentary questions alone, but their special contribution is important to recognize. In this case they required facts and
figures which were not always available; they revealed the central
departments' lack of involvement in research and their unpreparedness in several directions. Chester and Bowring suggest that whilst
'a matter remains only in the press or in private discussion he
[the Minister] is not compelled to make a public statement about it.
If, however, it becomes the subject of a Question, he is brought in
personally, he has to give an answer, an answer which may receive

[100] *H. C. Deb.*, vol. 535, col. 771.
[101] *H. C. Deb.*, vol. 536, cols 38–42.
[102] *H. C. Deb.*, vol. 536, cols 38–42.
[103] *H. C. Deb.*, vol. 515, col. 842.

a fair amount of publicity ...'[104] This, gradually, is what happened.

The effect of the parliamentary questions about air pollution, though somewhat diluted by having to be addressed to several Ministers, must also have caused a diversion of civil service resources to the issue and, from time to time, they provided newsworthy items for the press. But essentially, like the NSAS involvement, the parliamentary questioning first helped to stress the crisis proportions of the London smog and second, served to keep the issue going beyond that particular event. A harassing barrage over nearly two years was maintained partly, one suspects, precisely because many of the answers conveyed a stolid reluctance on the part of the Ministers concerned (except perhaps Sandys when he replaced Macmillan) to respond to the problem with any apparent sense of urgency or commitment.

In this section we have not attempted to explore the roles fulfilled by all the identifiable participants, but have looked at some in more detail than was possible in discussing the events of 1952–4. We have also endeavoured to explain why some groups that might have been expected to have made a substantial contribution did not do so. We move now to a fuller discussion of what might be regarded as the environment in which the developments with which we are concerned took place. Like all environments this offered opportunities but it also imposed limitations and constraints upon what could be accomplished.

IV THE CONTEXT

There are various features of the 'environment' in which the events of the period 1952–6 occurred which help in understanding what did or did not happen. Certain developments in the campaign for clean air harmonized with prevailing trends and were encouraged thereby. Others ran counter to them and were impeded. In the discussion which follows we look in particular at technical, economic and political aspects of this environment.

Technically, the control of smoke presented no problem. The control of other pollutants, both gases and dust, was less easy. Speakers in the second reading debate on the Clean Air Bill returned repeatedly to the absence of any mention of the control of the unseen oxides of sulphur. 'One of the most deleterious products of the combustion of fuels is sulphur, present in the form of its oxide', explained the Beaver committee, continuing: 'Sulphur dioxide is discharged

[104] Chester, D. N. and Bowring, N., *Questions in Parliament*, Clarendon Press, 1962, p. 255.

into the atmosphere with the chimney gases wherever fuel in the form of coal, coke, fuel oil or unpurified gases is burnt. *The degree of efficiency of combustion does not affect the quantity of sulphur dioxide evolved'* (our italics).[105] Some reduction of this sulphur dioxide could be achieved by cleaning coal at the pits. As far as the large power stations were concerned sulphur dioxide could be washed from the flue gases.[106] But unless this is highly efficient the beneficial effect is largely offset by the reduced buoyancy of the moisture-laden gases which results in less dispersion and then a quicker descent to ground level. 'In general industry', Beaver explained, 'the scale of operations is so much less than in the electricity industry that no system of gas washing likely to operate at a reasonable cost is yet in sight. No known methods exist whereby the greater part of the sulphur from industrial and domestic chimneys can be prevented from being poured into the atmosphere in the form of corrosive gases ... there is thus no present prospect of substantially reducing the emission of sulphur oxide.'[107] Hence, with the exception of the power stations, the technical problems of controlling sulphur pollution were considered to be insurmountable, pending more knowledge or the replacement of coal, coke and fuel oil by electricity or town gas. This line of argument was developed by the Minister in defending the omission of sulphur oxides from the 1956 Bill. His view was corroborated by the technical committee of the NSAS which said, in a report on sulphur dioxide, that 'apart from a provision to prevent its discharge through higher chimneys it was not possible to include in the Clean Air Act, 1956, any measures for its control, because none for general application existed'.[108]

There were, likewise, technical constraints on the control of certain dusts, especially the cement dust in the Northfleet area of north-west Kent. Since 1935 new kilns had had to be fitted with electrical precipitators to mitigate the problem but, as Beaver concluded, 'even with precipitators working at full efficiency it is problematical whether dust emission from cement manufacture can be kept below a rate equivalent of 0·5 per cent of the cement made'.[109] Thus the problem of fine cement dust found no nice technical solution and in any case further costly screening was likely to affect adversely the costs of building and, by implication, the housing programme.

[105] *Committee on Air Pollution, op. cit.,* para. 48, p. 16.

[106] For an account of clean air policies and problems in the electricity industry see *Central Electricity Generating Board, First Report and Accounts, 1958–9,* H. C. 313, 1959, pp. 20–1.

[107] *Ibid.,* p. 18, para. 56.

[108] NSAS, *Sulphur Dioxide: An Examination of Sulphur Dioxide as an Air Pollutant* (undated), p. 5.

[109] *Committee on Air Pollution, op. cit.,* p. 16, para. 46.

Unlike smoke, therefore, certain other sources of air pollution were often technically difficult to prevent given the continuation of the processes responsible. Additionally there were, in these cases, few instances of a coincidence between clean air and potential economy. Technically some things were easier to do than others. Some were, as yet, not feasible at all.

By the mid-1950s other technological changes were becoming evident which would contribute to a more favourable outlook for clean air. The British Transport Commission's Railway Modernisation Plan was substantially worked out and broadly accepted by 1955 and, as the commission contended, this represented 'a landmark in the history of British Railways, *if only* [our italics] because it envisages the final abandonment of steam traction in favour of diesel and electric motive power'.[110] Since the steam engine was a substantial source of pollution in many urban and industrial areas these developments were indeed important. The number of steam locomotives had reached a peak during the war years but fell steadily from 20,000 in 1950 to 13,000 in 1960; that is a reduction of thirty-five per cent. By 1965 only 3,000 still remained.[111] The last ran in 1968. The consumption of locomotive coal is perhaps a better indicator of the consequences of replacing steam by diesel and electric locomotion. In the decade 1950–60 this fell by approximately fifty per cent – from fourteen million tons each year to seven million tons.[112] It is necessary to remember, however, that these changes did not really begin to have noticeable effects until the second half of the 1950s: between 1952 and 1954 they were still largely in the future, although clearly discernible. Commenting on the new electrification of the Sheffield to Manchester line in September 1954 the *Manchester Guardian* considered that, together with other similar schemes, it would probably be 'the biggest single contribution ever made to the anti-smoke campaign'.

In other industries too the replacement of coal could also be foreseen. In the Potteries, for example, gas and electric fired kilns began to be installed. In power stations and in the blast furnaces of the iron and steel industry greater efficiency in combustion was gradually achieved. In 1955 the government announced a provisional programme of nuclear power station construction. In the same year the Central Electricity Generating Board could claim that rapid progress was already being made towards nuclear power.[113] On the domestic

---

[110] British Transport Commission, *Seventh Annual Report and Accounts, 1954*. Vol. 1 'Report': H. C. 20–1, p. 31.

[111] Calculated from various tables in BTC (after 1962 British Railways Board), *Annual Reports and Accounts*, 1952–65.

[112] *Ibid.*

[113] Central Electricity Generating Board, *First Report and Accounts, op. cit.*

front, space heating, the next step after solid smokeless fuel, might just be perceived, although it only really gathered momentum after the 1961 report of the Parker–Morris committee on housing standards.[114]

In contrast to these obviously favourable trends was, of course, the growth of motor transport. In 1952 there were only some five million licensed motor vehicles in the United Kingdom; by 1960 the number had risen to ten million and by 1970 to fifteen million. Between 1952 and 1970 the average annual increase was about 500,000, although in the years 1961–4 nearly two million additional vehicles appeared on our roads.[115] In 1955, however, Beaver was able to say that 'the contribution of exhaust gases to the total volume of air pollution is still relatively small'.[116]

Throughout the debate concerning smoke pollution the question of the adequate supply of fuel and appliances was frequently raised. In its interim report the Beaver committee explained the problem quite simply: 'the replacement of bituminous coal by smokeless solid fuel presents two difficulties: the supply of the latter is insufficient, and coke – which forms the greater part of smokeless fuel supplies – cannot be burnt satisfactorily by itself in most old-fashioned open grates still in use in most houses'.[117] In reviewing the alternative sources of fuel to replace the nineteen million tons a year of bituminous coal then used for domestic purposes, its final report concluded that 'for as long as we can foresee the main substitute for house coal must be solid smokeless fuel'.[118] Would the supplies of these fuels be sufficient to support a substantial clean air policy chiefly aimed at the domestic grate? The Beaver committee thought there would be enough to keep pace with the rate at which smoke control areas would be established over the first five years.

The possibility of shortages could not be discounted however, and certainly at any point much earlier than the mid-1950s they were often acute. The production of smokeless fuels depended upon the carbonization of coal, which primarily resulted from the manufacture of gas. Hence, the future depended upon 'the requisite coal supplies being available to the gas undertakings; on the extent to which the gas industry is able ... to widen the range of coals carbonized; on the enterprise they display in widening their markets for gas; and on the extent to which oil or non-coking coal releases coke now used by other

[114] Ministry of Housing and Local Government, *Homes for Today and Tomorrow*, 1961.

[115] See Department of the Environment, *Highway Statistics*, 1970, table 1, p. 12.

[116] *Committee on Air Pollution: Interim Report*, op. cit., para. 64, p. 20.

[117] *Ibid.*, para. 59, p. 23.

[118] *Committee on Air Pollution* (final report), op. cit., para. 72, p. 22.

than domestic consumers'.[119] Clean air was placed, even more clearly than before, in the context of fuel policy and, despite Beaver's show of confidence, the outlook was uncertain. The supply of the grates which were needed to replace the estimated twelve million not suitable for burning solid smokeless fuels looked unpromising. Although 'approved appliances' had been installed in all new council houses since 1948 their output fell far short of what would be required to support a clean air programme. Until the old grates were replaced the question of appropriate fuel supplies remained academic.

We have already considered the extent to which the government might have been uneasy about the reaction of the general public to the effect of a clean air policy upon the open fire. Yet it was not only the somewhat Dickensian affection for the 'good coal fire' which was involved, real though this was. The obligatory installation of new appliances at some cost might well be opposed unless it was generously subsidized; coke was more difficult to store because of its bulk and low density, and coke fires had to be kept fairly high and more frequently made up. In addition, in most parts of the country coke cost more per ton than coal and the differences widened after 1954.[120] Price per ton was the crude measure familiar to the public, albeit the Prices and Tariffs sub-committee of Beaver was able to conclude that 'for every type of appliance using solid fuel, coke costs less per *useful therm* than any other solid fuel'[121] (our italics). Notwithstanding this more technical and accurate conclusion individual householders would not be easily persuaded that a change to solid smokeless fuels, with all that that involved, was an especially attractive proposition.

We have endeavoured to examine some of the salient background features which affected, in a more general way, the clean air struggle in the years 1952–6. Some of these were technological and helped form prevailing assumptions about what was and was not feasible and what soon might be possible. There were relevant economic issues which arose from the shortages of the early post war years, but which were expected to become less pressing in the future. Another important aspect of the economic and political context of the clean air struggle concerned the likely public reaction to the costs and inconvenience to them personally of a shift to solid smokeless fuels.

[119] *Committee on Air Pollution*, Appendix XI, Foxwell, G. C., 'The Provision of Smokeless Fuels', para. 40, p. 4.
[120] For example, in Birmingham the difference was 11s 1d; in Glasgow 4s 5d; in Leeds 10s 7d and in Liverpool 2s 7d (table 2, Appendix X, *Committee on Air Pollution*).
[121] *Committee on Air Pollution*, Appendix X, p. 63.

V THE OUTCOME

The introduction of legislation was forestalled by the General Election in May 1955[122] but the Clean Air Bill was given its first reading before the summer recess of the new Parliament. The Bill obtained its second reading in November and its third in April 1956. The main clauses of the Act may be briefly summarized.

It was to be an offence to allow the emission of dark smoke from any chimney.[123] But there were important escape clauses which the critics, during the debates, attributed largely to the government's lack of firmness in confronting the pressures from industry.[124] For example, it was to be a defence that the contravention was solely due to the use of unsuitable fuel, although even poor fuel can be burnt without dark smoke if combustion is efficient. It was also to be a defence, for seven years, to prove that the offence was due to the nature of the building or its equipment and was not the result of a failure to maintain them. Additionally there was a defence if the occupier could show that it had not been practicable to alter or re-equip the building to avoid contravening the Act. Despite the criticism of these so called escape clauses about dark smoke no changes were made at the committee stage. It is interesting to note the stricter terms of Nabarro's Private Member's Bill in which the period of 'escape' was three rather than seven years.[125] He explained in the debate that he believed 'the FBI hand is writ large between the lines of this Bill ... because it was members of the FBI representing industrialists, who have been responsible for persuading the Minister to put three years up to seven'.[126]

Other clauses concerned the control of new industrial furnaces. They were to be, 'so far as practicable', smokeless and fitted with plant to arrest grit and dust. The height of new chimneys for carrying away smoke, grit, dust or gases was to be subject to the prior approval of local authorities.

Provisions were more widesweeping with regard to domestic smoke. Local authorities could, by order, declare all or parts of their

---

[122] The Conservative Manifesto said: 'we wholeheartedly accept the need for a national "clean air" policy ... and comprehensive legislation on smoke abatement will be introduced'. Craig, F. W. S., *op. cit.*, p. 172.

[123] Railway engines and vessels were also broadly included in the coverage of this section.

[124] For example, Ellis Smith asserted that they 'have not framed this Bill in the interest of the people but ... as a result of the desires of the organised employers'. *H. C. Deb.*, vol. 545, col. 1311.

[125] Several of the local Acts, such as the Manchester one in 1948, were also stricter in a number of respects.

[126] *H. C. Deb.*, vol. 545, col. 1249.

district a 'smoke control area'. Once such an order was confirmed by the Minister any smoke in that area would be an offence. But there were provisos here too; for example, it was a defence to prove that smoke was caused despite the use of an authorized fuel; the local authority could, in its order, exempt certain buildings or classes of buildings and the Minister retained the power to suspend or relax the operation of an order.

If the owners of dwellings in a smoke control area incurred expenditure in adapting appliances to meet the requirements of the order then the local authority would pay seventy per cent of the cost and any part of the remainder at their discretion. An Exchequer contribution would be made towards these local authority expenses amounting to twenty per cent in the case of council houses and approximately sixty per cent for other dwellings.

The Minister of Housing and Local Government was to appoint a consultative Clean Air Council in order to review progress in 'abating the pollution of the air' and to secure advice. In addition, provisions were made for local authorities to undertake or contribute towards the cost of research and general publicity.

Such, then, were the principal aspects of the 1956 Clean Air Act some three and a half years after the London smog disaster. It was much criticized at the time for not being sufficiently bold and for leaving too many loopholes; for not tackling the problem of industrial air pollution and for only dealing with smoke. There were, as we have explained, both technical and political reasons for these deficiencies. The subsequent early difficulties in attaining even these modest objectives are perhaps some vindication of a fairly cautious approach.

The difficulties were mainly twofold. First there was the problem of householders obtaining enough solid smokeless fuel to support the smoke control area programmes. In April 1959 the Minister of Power appointed a small committee (Peech) on Solid Smokeless Fuels with the task of looking into 'the availability and suitability of smokeless fuels and plans for their future production' and into 'the adequacy of present arrangements and future plans for their distribution'.[127] Its terms of reference were set in the context of the expected effect of the Clean Air Act. In general the committee did not find that there were overall shortages in production but warned that imbalances might be expected between the different varieties of solid smokeless fuel, particularly a shortage of reactive fuels suitable for unimproved open grates. What the committee also emphasized, however, was that it had received evidence 'that many complaints about the availability of solid smokeless fuels arise from distribution

---

[127] Ministry of Power, *Report of the Committee on Solid Smokeless Fuels*, (Peech), Cmnd. 999, 1960.

difficulties and not from inadequate production or producers' stocks'.[128] The extra bulk of these fuels compared with coal created difficulties of storage for retailers; the necessity for more frequent deliveries and less opportunity for householders to lay in stocks. These distributional problems were overshadowed in the earlier debates by concern with output: in the event they proved to be the first hurdle. Retailers complained about insufficient notice of smoke control area orders which left them uncertain about how and when to modify their stocking and delivery practices.

Although the Gas Council had assured the Peech committee that the industry could meet certain of the threatened deficiencies, rapid technological changes in gas production had, by 1963, created a new situation. The production of gas by coal carbonization was clearly in decline. Oil gasification reduced the gas industry's dependence on coal, reduced its labour requirements and was easier to site. Already by 1961 the Minister of Power had approved the Gas Council's decision to import the equivalent of ten per cent of the industry's output as liquified natural gas from the Algerian fields. Natural gas had also been discovered in Holland and exploration was beginning in the North Sea.[129]

'Whereas hitherto it had been possible to rely on open-fire gas coke for domestic grates as the basic replacement for raw coal in smoke control areas, a major increase in the production of gas coke could no longer be expected.' So read the preamble to the government's white paper on *Domestic Fuel Supplies and the Clean Air Policy* published at the end of 1963.[130] The white paper concluded that supplies of solid smokeless fuel, although sufficient to support the existing smoke control areas, would fall increasingly short of requirements as more areas were declared. It advocated the greater use of closed appliances in which various fuels could be used, as well as urging a shift to gas, oil and electricity for domestic heating in smoke control areas.

Despite the shift in this direction shortages of solid smokeless fuel, often regional or local in character, continued to impede the smoke control areas programme from time to time. As recently as 1970 indeed 'there was a severe shortage of solid smokeless fuels ... which caused the suspension of more than 550 smoke control orders'.[131] By 1971 the situation had again eased and a circular in July stated that 'the Secretary of State hoped that authorities who

[128] *Op. cit.*, para. 87, p. 21.

[129] See PEP, *A Fuel Policy for Britain*, ch. IV, 1965. The first commercially worthwhile North Sea natural gas was discovered in 1965.

[130] Ministry of Power, *Domestic Fuel Supplies and the Clean Air Policy*, Cmnd. 2231, 1963.

[131] National Society for Clean Air, *Clean Air Year Book*, 1973, p. 5.

during the past two or three years have reduced or discontinued their smoke control programmes will now resume them energetically'.[132] It is clear that the advance towards clean air was sharply affected by solid smokeless fuel supply and distribution problems and that, partly because of this, progress was slower than had been contemplated in the Beaver report and in later debates.

The second major reason for this slow movement is to be found in the local authorities.[133] They, it will be recalled, retained the responsibility for initiating smoke control orders. In the so called 'black areas' some responded sluggishly and others not at all for several years. A series of circulars and letters exhorting local authorities to take action were dispatched by the Minister from 1959 onwards. In the 1959 circular black area authorities were asked to draw up comprehensive plans for establishing smoke control areas and set targets.[134] The replies were published in 1960.[135] Of the 324 authorities involved eighty-five did not respond to the invitation, thirty of them indicating that they were concerned about the effect of a clean air programme upon people receiving concessionary coal. By the end of 1960 only modest progress had been made: there were some 250 orders in England and Wales covering about a quarter of a million dwellings.

The great majority of English authorities in the 'black areas' had orders in operation by mid-1972 and about one in ten had reached their final target. In Scotland thirty-two authorities had smoke control areas in operation. By contrast only one of the authorities in the thirty 'black areas' in Wales had obtained an order.

Obviously progress has been made but there are marked regional variations. Some authorities have been notable for their enthusiasm, others for their lack of achievement. An explanation of the latter must be offered. There are two general factors to be taken into account.

First, there is the issue of concessionary coal and local interest in the future of the coal mining industry. Local authorities in mining areas have faced a considerable dilemma which was somewhat mitigated after 1962 when, by agreement, miners could receive either smokeless fuel or a cash payment in lieu of their coal allowance.[136] This was not a complete answer and the concern of mining com-

[132] Department of the Environment, circular 53/71.

[133] For a further discussion of the differential response of local authorities and certain other matters covered in this section see Scarrow, H. A., 'The Impact of British Domestic Air Pollution Legislation', *British Journal of Political Science*, vol. 2, part 2, 1972.

[134] Ministry of Housing and Local Government, circular 5/59.

[135] Ministry of Housing and Local Government, *Smoke Control (England and Wales)*, Cmnd. 1113, 1960.

[136] See the Ministry of Housing and Local Government, circular 4/62, *Smoke Control in the Black Areas*.

munities about the effects of a clean air policy upon their livelihood remained. Second, there is the question of the availability of appropriate resources to embark upon systematic smoke control programmes. Of the 250 local authorities in England and Wales which were designated 'black' in 1972, two thirds were second tier authorities, municipal boroughs, urban and rural districts. The resources needed for an energetic programme were not always readily available. One such resource was smoke control officers. As Beaver and others[137] had pointed out, these men were not immediately available and in most areas had to be recruited or transferred from other public health inspector duties. Some of the smaller authorities did not find this easy.[138]

Despite all the difficulties, however, the air over Britain is much less polluted by smoke now that it was twenty years ago.[139] In some areas the reduction has been quite dramatic. Several developments have contributed to this; for example, the disappearance of the steam locomotive and the growth of domestic central heating. But there is little doubt that the Clean Air Act has also played a substantial part, although it is impossible to gauge its contribution precisely.

Two million tons of smoke were discharged into the atmosphere of the United Kingdom in 1954; by 1971 this had fallen to 700,000 tons, a reduction of sixty-five per cent. These overall figures conceal the fact that, relatively, industrial smoke has been reduced more than domestic smoke. They also obscure the considerable variations between local areas. Greater London, where we began our account, has, for example, made substantial progress. The capital experienced other severe winter smogs after 1952: in January 1956, December 1957, and December 1962. In 1956 the estimated number of additional deaths was a thousand; in 1957 seven to eight hundred and in 1962 seven hundred.[140] There have been no smogs since then. By 1962 a quarter of all domestic premises in London were under a control order and firmer regulations had been secured over industrially caused air pollution. Reviewing the position in 1970, Plank wrote: 'the work of the London boroughs under the Clean Air Acts has been notably successful. With an outlay of only three shillings per head per annum the boroughs

---

[137] See, for example, Ministry of Health, *Report of the Working Party on the Recruitment, Training and Qualification of Sanitary Inspectors*, 1953.

[138] See, for example, Ministry of Housing and Local Government *Clean Air Act, 1956: Memorandum on Smoke Control Areas*, 1956, which indicates the extent of detailed work involved in creating a smoke control area.

[139] For a summary of the progress to date see pp. 11–13 in the *Royal Commission on Environmental Pollution*, First Report, Cmnd. 4585, 1971.

[140] See Logan, W. P. D., 'Mortality from Fog in London, January 1956', in *British Medical Journal*, 31 Mar., 1956, p. 722. Also LCC, *Fog in London: 3–7 December, 1962*, Report by the MOH to the Health Committee (4 Feb., 1963).

and central government have changed London's environment to the benefit of Londoners' health and amenity'.[141] Not only has smoke emission in London declined but so too, though less dramatically, has sulphur dioxide. Plank points out that in central London the winter average of smoke fell eighty per cent between 1958 and 1969 and that sulphur dioxide fell by forty per cent. Perhaps even more telling are his figures for sunshine. From these he concludes that 'the reduction of air pollution in central London appears to have increased the duration of sunshine since 1958 by about fifty per cent during the months November to January'.[142]

The story is less encouraging in certain other parts of the country and it can be argued that the situation in London has been sufficiently different to make it an easier task to secure a smoke-free atmosphere. This may be so. As we have emphasized throughout there is a complicated network of related factors involved. Nevertheless, the impact of the Clean Air legislation has played a crucial part in the battle against atmospheric pollution. The Acts[143] are by no means the complete answer, but where they have been vigorously implemented they do provide an example of what can be done to keep the air fit for breathing.

VI CONCLUSION

There are certain aspects of this case study which may prove useful pointers in the explanation of social policy change. We note below those which we consider most important.

1. The *event* (the London smog) appears crucial. It caused a shift in public awareness of and tolerance for a particular social risk. A phenomenon which had been regarded as an inevitable feature of the winter months began to be seen as an unnatural and unacceptable hazard which could at least be reduced if not wholly removed. The emergence of the term 'smog' instead of 'fog' reflects this change. Nevertheless, the event needed exploitation lest its impact was lost as memories faded. The existence of a ready and authoritative pressure group was vital.

2. The pressures for change appear to have been generated outside the traditional bureaucracies. The ministries did not provide any

---

[141] Plank, D., 'The Progress and Effects of Smoke Control in London', in the *Quarterly Bulletin of the Research and Intelligence Unit of the GLC*, no. 10, Mar. 1970, p. 54.

[142] *Ibid.*, p. 52.

[143] There was a further Act in 1968 (Private Members') which tidied up certain parts of the earlier legislation and removed certain anomalies.

leadership, perhaps because they lacked experience and because no *one* had clear responsibility. The medical profession as a whole showed little sense of outrage, with the notable exception of certain local authority medical officers of health. The scope for effective unilateral action by local authorities was limited simply because of the problem; smoke drifts across boundaries. Others directly involved in dealing with or studying the problem (the Alkali Inspectorate and the Fuel Research Station, for instance) were few in number and in any case did not regard it as their business to influence policy.

4. The existence of hard information seems, throughout this story, to be of considerable importance. Until it became available the dimensions of the smog catastrophe remained unclear and the feasibility of action remained in question. The work of the Beaver committee provided a collection point for much of the relevant but diverse data although a lot of material had already been brought together by the NSAS. Not only was the existence of information important but also its organization, and the speed at which it became available.

5. The major problem in achieving change was not one of overcoming outright opposition but of dispelling the apparent apathy of the government, for without its concern and intervention little progress could be made. Priority had to be won against the competition of other issues. The eventual capture of government interest owes much to the way in which the issue was sustained after 1952; by backbench parliamentary questions; by the NSAS; by Nabarro's Private Members' Bill and, to a lesser extent, by the press. Because of the seasonal nature of the smog risk this was, of course, easier than it might otherwise have been: the spectre of 'next winter' was never far away.

6. The costs of the reform were comparatively light as well as being widely borne. Its benefits, moreover, were also widespread and fairly obvious in industry. The virtues of clean air tended to coincide with good business. In these senses the 'climate' for change was by no means unfavourable.

7. Similarly, certain technological and economic changes were becoming apparent which indicated the greater feasibility of clean air legislation. At the very least controlling legislation would be going with rather than against the tide.

8. Many of the considerations listed above suggest that the campaign for clean air had much in its favour after 1952. The key problem, therefore, is to account for the tardy response of government. We have suggested that there was a combination of reasons. There, were for instance, other pressing and competing priorities (particularly the commitment to build 300,000 houses) and the Minister most concerned showed no special enthusiasm for the air pollution issue. Neither was there a well-established civil service interest which

might have exercised its influence internally. Doubts existed about the adequate supply of solid smokeless fuel. There was probably a fear of losing support from the general class of open fire, coal burning householders as well as some industrial interests. Anxiety about householders' reaction is understandable when one considers the numbers involved and therefore the near universality of the issue. Finally, there was an ideological reluctance to embark upon more controls. Indeed, the in-coming Conservative government in 1951 was committed to *removing* controls, many of which had been imposed during war-time.

CHAPTER FOURTEEN

The Abolition of National Assistance: Policy Changes in the Administration of Assistance Benefits

In 1966 a Bill was introduced to Parliament which proposed the abolition, by merger with the Ministry of Pensions and National Insurance, of the National Assistance Board. When this measure came into force later in the same year it marked the abandonment of a system of administering assistance benefits through an independent board which had been in existence for just over thirty years. The administration of assistance benefits for the unemployed had been centralized in 1934 when an entirely new central government agency, the Unemployment Assistance Board, was created.[1] As a result of the needs of wartime this agency acquired new functions and a new title, the Public Assistance Board, in 1940. It subsequently became the National Assistance Board in 1948 with responsibility for making means-tested assistance payments to all categories of people, except the gainfully employed, whose financial needs were not met by the national insurance schemes and family allowances. It was a residual service within the basically universal social security system.

When the National Assistance Board (NAB) ceased to exist in 1966 it was replaced by the Supplementary Benefits Commission (SBC), which became responsible for the provision of a similar range of services. The most immediate difference was that the commission

---

[1] For a detailed study of this policy development see Millet, J. D., *The Unemployment Assistance Board*, Allen & Unwin, 1940. For a new and important interpretation of this development see Briggs, E. and Deacon A., 'The Creation of the Unemployment Assistance Board', *Policy and Politics*, vol. 2, no. 1, Sept. 1973.

operated *within* the new Ministry of Social Security. For the first time a single ministry was directly responsible for the full range of social security schemes – contributory and means-tested alike. Other substantial changes in benefits, in the criteria of eligibility, in nomenclature and in administrative procedures were made at the same time. Whether or not these were important and whether they resolved the problems they were designed to meet will be mentioned briefly; but this is not the main purpose of the case study. The object is to try to explain why the Labour government considered it necessary to create a new administrative structure and a new image for the assistance system.

The 1966 changes were but one episode in the long history of central government involvement in the administration of assistance benefits which certainly goes back to 1934 and, for some purposes, much earlier. Although these antecedents must be borne in mind we shall confine ourselves to a more limited question: namely, what was the relationship between the Labour Party's social security plans evolved during its years in Opposition (1951–64) and the way in which, as a government, it reformed national assistance in 1966.[2] As an opposition party it had developed a strategy which, on the face of it, should have led to the abolition of national assistance – but in a rather different way from what actually happened. We shall endeavour to explain why the 1966 policy differed in important respects from what was proposed in Labour's election manifesto of 1964 and from what was verbally promised during the election campaign. This raises at least two general issues of considerable importance: first, the quality of planning achieved within an opposition party and, second, the nature of the constraints which determine how, and how far, election pledges are converted into effective policies once a party gains power.

I NATIONAL ASSISTANCE AND THE LABOUR OPPOSITION: 1951–54

It is hardly surprising to find the Labour Party, which had created the national assistance system in 1948, claiming in its 1951 election manifesto that it had 'a national insurance system covering the whole population with greatly improved pensions and a humane National Assistance scheme'.[3] However, by 1955 its manifesto contended that

[2] This case is part of a larger study which will be published separately and at a later date.

[3] Labour Party Election Manifesto, 1951, in Craig, F. W. S., *British General Election Manifestos, 1918–1966*, Political Reference Publication, 1970, p. 147.

'social security must be carried one stage further. In order to remove the last taint of "public assistance", a Ministry of Social Welfare will be established to take over the work not only of the Ministry of Pensions and National Insurance, but also of the NAB'.[4]

In just four years the note had changed from one of self congratulation to one of concern with the image of national assistance. This partly reflects the party's change of role from that of outgoing government defending its record (in 1951) to that of a critical opposition; but it also reflects the beginning of a gradual increase in the degree and specificity of the disenchantment with which members of the Labour Party viewed national assistance. The reference to national assistance in the 1955 manifesto was an isolated commitment to change. By 1959 the nature of the problem was explained more fully. 'The living standards of more than half our old-age pensioners are a national disgrace. About a million are driven by poverty to seek National Assistance and *another 500,000 would be entitled to receive it*' (our italics). Two rather different criticisms were contained in this statement. First, there was concern that national assistance was needed far too frequently by pensioners as a means of avoiding poverty and, second, that even this source of help was unavailable to many of them because of their unwillingness to ask for it. Although the two different *types* of problem being identified are quite distinguishable, the Labour Party responded to them as a single issue for policy purposes. The primary need was seen to be an improvement in pensions. This response was an understandable one for several reasons: the Labour Party did not favour a means-tested solution to pensioner poverty; the national assistance system was a ready means of monitoring the weaknesses of national insurance benefit whereas there were no comparable administrative statistics on the failure of national assistance; and pensioners were by far the largest group of people depending on assistance. The national assistance problem was first and foremost a pensioner problem, especially during the fifties, and this was firmly reflected in Labour planning. Let us therefore, briefly trace the development of Labour's response to the pension issue in order to place its plans for national assistance in perspective.

The flat-rate national insurance system introduced in 1946 was under considerable stress throughout the fifties. On the one hand the current and projected costs of social security benefits – especially pensions – and their distribution between employee, employer and the Exchequer were issues of controversy. On the other hand despite their apparent costliness, insurance benefits had visibly failed to achieve the goal of removing the retired, the sick, the unemployed and

---

[4] *Forward with Labour*, 1955, in Craig, F. W. S., *op. cit.*, p. 179.

the widowed from poverty.[5] Unless they had income from other sources, or very low rents, people drawing these benefits were almost certainly living below the 'official' poverty line defined by national assistance scale rates. National insurance benefits were judged inadequate, particularly within the Labour Party, on three main counts: the flat rate benefits were low relative to the concept of poverty embodied in national assistance; they were almost continuously eroded by inflation but only periodically revised; and they bore no close relationship either to the individual standards of living experienced by people before they became recipients or to any measure of the national average standard of living. The system of financing the scheme left little room for removing these defects. Unless costs were shifted towards the Exchequer substantial improvements in benefits could only be financed by greatly increasing the burden of the regressive flat-rate contributions on lower paid workers.

The position of the elderly was obviously central to the discussion of national insurance and assistance not only because they were the largest group of beneficiaries but also because they were permanently obliged to live on a very low income. Until the results of the poverty research conducted by Abel-Smith and Townsend became available in the mid-1960s it was almost exclusively the poverty of old age that attracted attention.[6] As Crossman said during the 1957 Labour Party Conference – 'just as unemployment was the great social disgrace of the 1930s, poverty in old age is the great social disgrace and the great challenge of the 1950s'.[7] He might have added that a stigmatized means-tested service was, in the last resort, the only way great hardship was avoided in both these decades and that in many cases it was the same generation of people who faced these threats to their self esteem. The inadequacies of national insurance were underlined by the fact that some, but by no means all, employees received occupational benefits which were additional to their entitlement under the state scheme. The core issue, as perceived by the Labour Party, was summarized in another speech at the 1957 conference: 'the system we have at the present time is creating wider inequalities in old age than exist in working life. We are developing two classes in our society; a class dependent on the national pension and more and

[5] See Titmuss, R. M., 'pensions systems and population change', in *Essays on the Welfare State*, Allen & Unwin, 1958. Also see Abel-Smith, B., 'Social Security', in Ginsberg, M. (ed.), *Law and Opinion in England in the Twentieth Century*, Stevens, 1959; Bull, D. (ed.), *Family Poverty*, Duckworth, (2nd edn), 1972; George, V., *Social Security: Beveridge and After*, Routledge & Kegan Paul, 1968; and Atkinson, A. B., *Poverty in Britain and the Reform of Social Security*, Cambridge University Press, 1969, on the strengths and weaknesses of the flat-rate insurance system.

[6] Abel-Smith, B. and Townsend, P., *The Poor and the Poorest*, Bell, 1965.

[7] *Report of the 56th Annual Conference of the Labour Party*, 1957, p. 124.

more National Assistance, and another class gaining from private superannuation schemes.'[8]

National Superannuation: the foundation of Labour's plan

In May 1957 the Labour Party published *National Superannuation* which was, in the words of its subtitle, *Labour's Policy for Security in Old Age*. It was placed before the party for discussion and approval during the 1957 Conference. Despite the fact that its central proposal – the introduction of a comprehensive earnings-related state pension scheme – was not introduced by the 1964–70 Labour government, it remains an historic document. It marked a complete break with the Beveridge flat rate scheme, some of the defects of which were outlined above. It served as the cornerstone of Labour's social security policy from 1957 until it formed a government in 1964, going through several revisions during this period. At the very least it implied a great reduction in the number of old people dependent on national assistance; but it gradually became apparent that this was not the only change in national assistance that would be involved in moving away from the flat-rate insurance system.

The Labour Party planners clearly believed that a long-term solution to the shortcomings of flat-rate pensions rested with a State earnings-related scheme, but that in the short run flat-rate pensions were too low and that the Conservative government, along with demographic pessimism, were ensuring that they remained that way.[9] The national superannuation scheme was published during a by-election at East Ham fought by Reg Prentice. As he told the 1957 conference the scheme 'aroused a lot of interest, but the most important issue in that by-election was the plight of the old-age pensioners. That was the number one issue, it has overshadowed even the impending Rent Act. What people kept on saying was: What is Labour going to do for the old people who are already on pensions?'[10] A short as well as a long-term strategy was needed. Part of the short-term strategy existed in 1957. In *National Superannuation* a commitment was made to raise the basic rate of pension to three pounds a week. This was, the pamphlet explained, 'a special concession to present pensioners, who through no fault of their own, will not be able to share the full benefits of National Super-

[8] *Ibid.*, Mackenzie, N., p. 107. The expression 'two nations in old age', which made the same point, was used in the Labour Party policy document, *National Superannuation*, 1957.

[9] Although the very pessimistic demographic assumptions of the forties were modified in the early fifties, the 'burden' of the elderly continued to preoccupy government. See Titmuss, R. M., 'Pensions systems and population change', *op. cit.*, for an early and valuable discussion of this problem.

[10] 1957 Party Conference, *op. cit.*, p. 118.

annuation'.[11] Other features of a short-term solution were developed later, as we shall see.

Both the long-term plan and this promise to existing pensioners had implications for national assistance, but the problem was somewhat more complex than has been implied so far. Apart from future generations of old people who would reap the full benefit of the newly proposed system of pensions and the existing pensioners who were to get higher flat-rate pensions, there were also the older workers (not yet retired) who would draw only limited benefits from the gradual build-up of earnings-related pension rights. The tentative proposal was to 'blanket them in to some extent', but further thought was promised on this issue. Prentice also raised a further problem for the short-term; that was the period of time that might elapse between a Labour government securing power and introducing its pension scheme. He felt that a short Bill raising pensions to the suggested three pounds immediately a Labour government came into power would be appropriate.[12] Could the short-term issues be resolved quite that simply? The three pounds pension would raise many pensioners above national assistance, but not all of them. Indeed, as Atkinson has shown, the national superannuation scheme itself would not have completely removed the need to supplement pensions.[13] One delegate to the 1957 Conference made the issue quite specific and asked the National Executive Committee 'to consider whether it is not possible to create some kind of national minimum income during the transitional period – in other words to revise the present conditions and standards of the National Assistance scheme'.[14]

The 1957 Conference accepted the 'National Superannuation' policies in general outline, but no one doubted that a lot of work remained to be done if comprehensive and viable proposals were to be framed in readiness for a future Labour government. The new role of national assistance within the social security system was just one of the areas that needed close examination. Had Labour won the 1959 election it would have come to power without any very explicit policies in this area, but its defeat did at least give the party time to look beyond the bare bones of its national superannuation proposals. Indeed, few other areas of social policy can have benefited from such a long period of planning in opposition. The powerful internal conflicts which were absorbing so much energy within the party during the years in opposition were not conducive to detailed policy planning. Yet in the case of social security, as we have seen, the foundations of a policy were apparent by 1957 and this allowed

---

[11] *Ibid.,* p. 36.
[12] *Ibid.,* p. 119.
[13] Atkinson, A. B., *op. cit.,* pp. 111–19.
[14] Labour Party Conference, 1957, *op. cit.,* Mackenzie, N., p. 107.

detailed planning to extend over a further period of seven years before Labour eventually came to power. This work was carried out in a study group on 'Security in Old Age' under the aegis of the Home Policy Sub-Committee of the party's research department. The group was chaired by Richard Crossman and consisted of members of the National Executive Committee, co-opted MPs, members of the permanent staff of the research department, a group of academics and, in the later years, several TUC observers.[15] How did they use their time?

It was only after the 1959 election defeat that Labour's social security planning moved beyond the basic proposals for a wage-related pension. The 1960 Conference signalled the changes. The expenditure of energy on pensions planning was a good investment for Labour. Demographic trends and the limitations of national insurance had made this clear from the mid-1950s, but it was the position of *existing pensioners*, rather than the long-term pension plan, that came sharply into focus in the 1960 Conference debate on social security. The plight of these pensioners emphasized that national assistance was an unacceptably stigmatized, but by now fundamental, part of the social security system.

Some of the references to national assistance were strongly worded. 'Let us be frank about National Assistance', one speaker urged, 'we despise and loath it. We despise the Poor Law and hate the Means Test. These are relics of the past and have no place in a real affluent society.'[16] There were specific criticisms going beyond the rhetoric. Another delegate argued:

> It is entirely wrong that old-age pensioners should have to beg an existence ... I think it is damning, in this age of prosperity, that even when you send an old-age pensioner along to the National Assistance office, the Assistance officer will send that person to the WVS to receive second-hand clothing. *That was not our intention of National Assistance.*[17] (Our italics.)

Reference was also made to the 'thousands who are too proud to accept relief however needy they may be, and who also detest the Means Test'.[18] Such expressions of horror about a stigmatized service were familiar enough in the 1920s and 1930s, but they had not

---

[15] The academic members of the study group were Richard Titmuss, Brian Abel-Smith and Peter Townsend in the first instance. Tony Lynes was added to their number at a later date. Throughout the period to 1964 the NEC members included Harold Wilson, Richard Crossman and Miss Herbison (who became Minister of Pensions and National Insurance in 1964).

[16] Labour Party Conference, 1960, *op. cit.*, p. 98.

[17] *Ibid.*, pp. 98–9 (Our italics).

[18] *Ibid.*, p. 100.

been publicly expressed to any great extent in Labour Conferences for many years.

Whilst flat rate national insurance remained the unrivalled basis of social security in the early and mid-1950s, policy debates concentrated on the levels of benefit. There were no clear differences in the underlying policy of the parties. As we have seen, however, a distinct divergence began to appear in the late fifties with the Labour initiative on earnings-related benefits. By the beginning of the sixties the divergence was marked and the Labour Party was then accusing the Conservatives of gradually abandoning the existing national insurance system. While both parties were devising new policies, Labour spokesmen certainly felt that they were moving in opposite directions. The differences of approach centred on the role of the State system. Labour was aiming at State earnings-related benefits with occupational schemes in the background. The Conservative government was seen by Labour to be restricting the State scheme to a limited service for the supplementation of occupational schemes. This pattern has now been made explicit.[19] At that time Labour criticism focused on the increasing number of pensioners who were, and would in the future continue to be, dependent on national assistance as a result of this approach. Occupational pensions provided only very limited cover for low income workers and for women. National assistance supplementation of pensions would, therefore, be necessary on a considerable scale for the foreseeable future under Conservative policies. The national assistance system had acquired an apparently permanent role that had certainly not been envisaged in 1948 when the Labour government created it. This was at the heart of the discussions in the 1960 Labour Conference. The Labour response was to try to move away from national assistance altogether.

Months of inconclusive Opposition pressure on the government to raise pensions, the bitterness of electoral defeat, and the vulnerability of the Conservative record on pensions at this point combined to introduce a new edge of hostility and determination into the debate.[20] As the service of last resort for pensioners, national assistance had been brought into prominence. Crossman summarized the issue in his concluding speech. He reiterated that the situation which the conference deplored was 'part of Tory policy: they are quite deliberately

[19] See *Strategy for Pensions,* Cmnd. 4755, 1971.

[20] The Conservative record on pensions was a major theme of the 1960 Conference debate. The last increase in pensions had been in January 1958. Between that time and the 1960 Conference 'the Parliamentary Labour Party [had] pressed continuously for further increases. Between November 1958 and July 1959 there were nine debates, and on every occasion the Tories voted against an increase. The Tories have further refused in five debates between November 1959 and July 1960 in this new Parliament, to grant an increase.' Labour Party Conference, 1960, *op. cit.,* p. 98.

keeping the rate of benefit at a point where you are compelled to go to National Assistance in order to live. I have only to quote to you the figures: 82,000 more pensioners have had to go to national assistance this year than last.'[21] The figures for people drawing sickness, unemployment and widows' benefits and also having recourse to national assistance had risen similarly. Consequently the arguments were not about reforming national assistance; they were about abolishing it. Tom Brown, MP, did 'ask delegates who [had] passed a very strong condemnation upon the National Assistance Board: what would you put in its place?'[22] He concurred with his colleagues when providing the answer: higher pensions.

Yet this was *not* a complete answer. Although replacing national assistance by higher pensions was the one thought in all minds, it concealed the need to reform national assistance as well. Until pensions could be raised very substantially by national super-annuation, pension supplementation would be necessary on a large scale. The short-term problems of the transition had not been resolved and neither had the problem of the non-pensioner clientele of the NAB. The discussion had been dominated by a concern for pensioners and had neglected substantial minority groups who would continue to depend heavily upon the services of the NAB. Crossman focused attention upon this. As he noted:

> When we look at the Agenda there is not a single resolution on sickness benefit or unemployment benefit. This is my blame as much as anybody else's because three years ago at Brighton [the 1957 Conference] we decided to pick out the problem of the old people and produce a concrete solution for it to put before the people in time for the last election ... if we concentrate solely on the old age pension we are neglecting a large part of the problem of poverty.[23]

He assured the delegates that the members of the study group on social security were going to broaden their solution to encompass these other problem areas. The influence of the academic members of the group is partly reflected in this new departure. Abel-Smith and Townsend were about to realign the whole of post-war thinking on poverty by quantifying the number of the non-elderly, as well as the elderly, poor. Another dimension of poverty, and therefore of national assistance and its future role, was being brought into focus. Only if the existing solution – earnings-related benefits – could be extended to the unemployed and sick could the Labour Party begin to abolish national assistance by making it largely redundant. Crossman also

[21] *Ibid.,* p. 103.
[22] *Idem.*
[23] *Ibid.,* p. 104.

indicated a further task for the coming years: the schemes must be costed and the public must be told how the money was to be raised. 'In the last election', he asserted, 'we made tremendous inroads on the old people who never voted Labour before – and I am quite sure we did it by candidly saying how to pay the bill.'[24] The policy-making programme on social security was clearly mapped out for the years leading up to the next election. If it was completed sucessfully the long-term impact would be to remove not only pensioners but many other insurance beneficiaries from the ambit of national assistance. However, its short-term future remained obscure. The social security study group was reformed and its terms of reference extended to include a review of the operation of national assistance.[25]

The Income Guarantee: a short-term strategy
In the course of a supply day debate on social security in 1962 a new Labour commitment was made public: to replace 'the system of national assistance very largely by a new system of supplements to income'.[26] It was the first indication that the social security study group had found a means of removing people from national assistance in the short-run. The commitment emerged more clearly in the 1963 policy pamphlet *New Frontiers for Social Security* and in a supply debate of the same year, as a guaranteed minimum income for pensioners.[27] This new proposal was not a *major* feature of *New Frontiers*. The pamphlet rehearsed the arguments for earnings related pensions, but went on to explain how this principle would be applied to sickness, unemployment and widows' benefits. It also promised that family allowances would be reorganized (with benefits graduated according to the age of the child). Crossman's undertaking to look beyond the elderly poor was being honoured, the plan was now a far more comprehensive policy for social security. The income guarantee was a relatively small part of this policy. It filled a gap in short-term strategy. It catered for existing pensioners and the period of transition from flat-rate to earnings-related pensions by offering a presumably less stigmatized method of supplementing pensions than national assistance.

The transitional period was to last seven years and the central purpose of the income guarantee was to remove an increasing proportion of old people from national assistance during this time.[28] The elderly and widows would have their incomes supplemented up to the

[24] *Ibid.*, p. 105.
[25] *Ibid.*, p. 43.
[26] *H. C. Deb.*, vol. 668, col. 51.
[27] *New Frontiers for Social Security*, Labour Party, 1963.
[28] *New Frontiers* introduced this rapid rate of transition by means of generous 'blanketing-in'.

level of the guaranteed income without recourse to a detailed and individualized means-test. The guaranteed income would be high enough in the first year to remove, say, half of the elderly from national assistance and would rise at a faster rate than national assistance over the seven years. By the end of the transitional period it would be high enough to relieve the great majority of pensioners of the need to seek supplementation from the NAB. This level 7 would then be 'dynamised'; that is, increased annually so as to retain a constant relationship with wage rates. Although some people would continue to depend on the income guarantee for many years, new pensioners would gain earnings-related pensions above this level as national superannuation began to make a real impact. This was the key advantage of the guarantee. It would be quite expensive during the early years but would decline as the new pension system expanded. The alternative approach would have been much more expensive. A very large flat-rate pension increase would have been needed at the beginning of the transition period if it was to remove most existing pensioners from national assistance.[29] Such an increase would have been unselective and therefore wasteful in the short-run. In the long-run it would have posed problems for the earnings-related pension scheme since this was to consist of the flat-rate pension with an earnings-related element added to it.

This is the picture of the income guarantee that was presented in *New Frontiers*; it gave little away. The details of the new proposals, which would determine its scope, timing, effectiveness and administrative machinery, were conspicuous by their absence. In succeeding months Labour spokesmen showed every sign of not wanting to be too specific. The questions to be asked, therefore, are first whether agreement had been reached on a detailed policy or whether the reticence indicated a failure to reach agreement. Second, if firm decisions had been made, did they amount to an attractive and feasible policy to which a future Labour government would want to be committed? Third, what was planned for the national assistance system and its remaining clientele?

An indication of the level of income to be guaranteed and the cost of the scheme was not only absent in *New Frontiers*, it was also lacking at the press conference which took place the day before its publication. The scheme could not have progressed this far without some estimates being made of the possible benefits, rate of take-up and cost. It must be presumed that the NEC had decided not to publicize any of these estimates. *The Times* reported Crossman as explaining at the press conference that the details of *National Super-*

---

[29] See Atkinson, A. B., *op. cit.*, for a discussion of the relationship between national insurance and national assistance.

annuation had been 'shot to pieces' before and during the 1959 election and that this would not happen again.[30] Crossman insisted that he had been misquoted, but the incident highlighted Labour's reticence to publish details of its new proposals. Whether, in the case of the income guarantee, this reflected a failure to take decisions on its most important features was not clear at the time. But amid the substantial coverage of *New Frontiers*, press criticism concentrated on the absence of figures on cost. Despite Crossman's earlier conference pledge to tell the people how the money would be found, estimates of the likely cost of the income guarantee were never published.

One point on which *New Frontiers* was explicit was that national assistance would be abolished by a future Labour government. A Ministry of Social Security would be set up, incorporating both the NAB and the MPNI. The pamphlet made the study group's thinking clear on this issue:

> This proposal – first made in the Beveridge Report – has been strongly pressed since 1951 by those who wish to mitigate the stigma of accepting means-tested relief by changing the name of National Assistance. A change of name which leaves the essential evil unchanged makes little appeal to us. But it would be appropriate to signalize the abolition of poverty by creating a new Ministry to administer our new system of social security.[31]

National Assistance was to be abolished as a logical outcome of the total package of proposals. The relatively small number of people who would continue to be dependent on some form of means-tested benefit could be given 'more generous treatment and greater care and attention' in the new ministry.[32] But had any clear decisions been made about the income guarantee that was to make this possible?

The main work on the income guarantee had taken place in the social security study group during 1962. The initial proposal was drafted by Tony Lynes as a guaranteed pension for those who qualified for national insurance pensions. The idea was modified considerably before it was included in *New Frontiers*. By then it had become a guaranteed *income* covering the old people who did not qualify for retirement pensions as well as those who did. It also implied some means of gathering data on individual's incomes to ensure that a person's total income, not just his pension, was raised to a guaranteed level. The details changed quite quickly during this first year of discussion. But, details apart, it was the concept which attracted early and enthusiastic support from some MPs and from staff members of the Labour Research Department. The great merit of the guarantee was

[30] *The Times*, 2 April, 1963.
[31] *New Frontiers, op. cit.*, p. 19.
[32] *Ibid.*, p. 19.

the immediacy of the help it could bring pensioners. The great disadvantage was that it was innovative. Titmuss had suggested in 1960 that many people had 'put too much faith in the 1940s in the concept of universality as applied to social security'.[33] The income guarantee was an attempt to provide selective benefits without recourse to a detailed and stigmatizing means test. It was also the first firm proposal in the post-war period to advocate a liaison between the social security and tax systems.[34] The price to be paid for innovative change (even of this relatively modest kind) can be high, as we shall see.

There have been sharp ideological disputes over selectivity, but this was not the key issue in the case of the income guarantee. It was designed to replace existing selective benefits (NA) as part of a plan greatly to extend universal pension benefits. The central problems were the political and administrative feasibility and relevance of the scheme. Despite its obvious merits the guarantee involved yet another change in social security, with all the attendant uncertainties. It could easily have deflected an unreasonable amount of energy and resources from the implementation of the core of the programme – national superannuation. If this was to be avoided, decisions had to be made during the period of opposition planning so as to provide a clear basis for implementation once Labour came to power.

The study group's key decision to guarantee a given level of *income* to old people implied the need for an income return to be obtained. This would not necessarily have to be made to the tax authorities; but since it would have to be compulsory if the guarantee were to apply to all old people, there were obvious advantages to be gained from tying it to the taxation system. Not the least of these was that direct taxation involved the one almost universal 'means test'. To the extent that means-testing was itself a source of stigma, an income guarantee tied to the taxation system would stand a good chance of being acceptable to the people it was designed to help. Whether or not to try to effect this kind of link between the social security and taxation systems was a strategic decision that had to be resolved by the study group. Many of the detailed features of the scheme would be influenced by this decision. What of these details, what kinds of questions did they raise?

What kind of Income Guarantee – and at what cost?
The cost of any such proposal is determined by the level of the guaranteed income, by the scope of the scheme, and by whether some items of

[33] Titmuss, R. M., *The Irresponsible Society*, Fabian Tract 323, 1960, p. 10.
[34] The income guarantee must be seen against this background of a reanalysis of universal social services. This was taking place, for different reasons, within both the major British political parties.

income are disregarded in calculating eligibility or some additional payments are included to cover special needs. A few comments are necessary on each of these factors. As we have seen, the scope of the guarantee was largely decided by making it a guaranteed income for all of the elderly, not just retired pensioners. The stress on income also implied that capital was not to be considered as such; but this immediately raises the problem of 'disregards'. Under national assistance rules, the first thirty shillings (and half of the next twenty) of weekly income were disregarded at the time. Under national insurance provisions the 'earnings rule' allowed pensioners to earn £4 5s a week before their pensions were reduced. Whether the income guarantee included a disregard at the national assistance or the national insurance level, or none at all, would affect the cost of the scheme and its relation to existing benefits. Similarly, it was important to decide if 'notional income' (as from owner occupation) should be calculated, and whether disregards should apply only to earnings or to unearned and pension income as well (e.g. occupational pensions). If the income guarantee was to be seen as a partial substitute for 'across the board' pension increases then there was a strong argument for some kind of disregard. Similarly, without a disregard the guarantee would have been a major disincentive to pensioners who worked part-time after retirement.

A rent allowance, like a disregard, was also persuasively argued for within the study group and must have been a cause of disagreement. Rent is the most important variable item of expenditure for old people. In 1964, when the national assistance scale rates were £3 3s 6d for a single person and £5 4s 6d for a couple, average payments in respect of rent varied from £1 17s 1d in London to £1 2s 10d in Wales (discretionary payments on the other hand were received by sixty-five per cent of pensioners on national assistance but averaged under 9s a week).[35] If a *standard* rent allowance had been built into the guarantee it would have been 'over generous' to many if high, and inadequate for most if low. A *variable* rent allowance on top of the guarantee would have raised old people above national assistance in far greater numbers and a smaller *basic* income could have been guaranteed. Indeed, a generous rent allowance as of right would have raised a substantial proportion of the elderly above national assistance even without

[35] These are the average rent payments for all types of beneficiary in the region in question. The payments show an even greater variation if one breaks them down by type of beneficiary: from £2 16s 5d in the case of assistance paid in supplementation of unemployment benefit in London, to 16s 9d where the assistance was in supplementation of old-age pensions in Wales. The average rent payment in Great Britain was £1 7s 2d. *Report of the National Assistance Board* (1964), Cmnd. 2674, 1965. Appendix XII, p. 73. See appendices XIII to XVII on the levels of rent paid by recipients.

the income guarantee. Such was its attraction; the disadvantages are obvious. The scheme would begin to look like national assistance and require a similar range of information.

Although essentially policy decisions, these are precisely the kind of problems which also demand good data. One of the disadvantages of policy planning in opposition is the scarcity of administrative data. Data on the rent paid by independent pensioners (those not applying for national assistance) were not available to the NAB, but the Opposition had even less information than the NAB and MPNI could have amassed on these questions of rent and disregards. Having outlined the kinds of problems that had to be resolved, let us now turn to the public discussion of the scheme in search of clues about what decisions, if any, were made on these questions during Labour's period in opposition.

The Labour Conference debate on *New Frontiers* in October 1963 was the first for some time in which Crossman had not been the main speaker on the party's social security plans. Miss Herbison introduced the pamphlet and was alluded to by several speakers as possibly the next Minister of Pensions. Her warmth of personality and great concern for poor pensioners and widows were extolled. She in her turn, however, gave little away about Labour's proposals. Richard Marsh specifically argued that it was 'about time the Executive told us some of the figures in the new scheme ... there is no reason at all why this Conference cannot be told what the guaranteed minimum income is. We are entitled to know this ... whether it is three pounds or six pounds a week is important.'[36] Margaret Herbison only referred in fact to the cost of the whole social security scheme, and then in the very broadest terms.

Can this country afford this ambitious scheme? ... Well, employees with an average pay – that is sixteen pounds today – will pay exactly the same as at present. Those above average pay will pay more than they do now ... under our scheme employers will have to pay more; but again [they] ... will not be paying as much under our scheme as many of their competitors in Western Europe are doing today.[37]

'This document', she added, 'is based on the most detailed and rigorous technical, financial and actuarial advice.'[38] It was a theme which re-emerged in 1964 both during and after the election.

In a parliamentary debate initiated by the Opposition in December 1963, Crossman came under considerable Conservative pressure to elaborate on the 'certain level' at which the income guarantee would

[36] *Labour Party Conference Report*, 1963, p. 233.
[37] *Ibid.*, p. 227.
[38] *Idem.*

operate. Some of the features of the scheme became a little clearer. He indicated that it would be closely related to the prevailing (at the time of implementation) level of national assistance with something extra for rent (a figure of twenty to twenty-five shillings a week was suggested) plus an addition of a further fifteen per cent or so.[39] The concept of income to be employed in the income return was broadly that subject to tax and would involve some disregards similar to those allowed in assessing eligibility for national assistance. In the course of the debate it certainly became clear that the scheme was to be closely geared to the income tax system.

The guaranteed income was apparently to be provided through the joint efforts of two organizations outside the MPNI: the Post Office and the Board of Inland Revenue. The former would be used to distribute benefits, but the latter would have the crucial responsibility of collecting the data (via simplified tax returns) about old people's incomes on which eligibility would be determined. This was the cricital administrative innovation from which the proposal drew its strength; thus would the sting of the means test be drawn.

The decision to build the guarantee scheme around the tax system must have been strongly influenced by one member of the Labour study group – Douglas Houghton. In his 1964 election address he described himself as Labour's expert on taxation and finance. He had been secretary to the Inland Revenue Staff Federation from 1922 to 1960 and was certainly better placed than most of the Labour planners to assess the likely administrative consequences of linking the income guarantee to the taxation system. In the circumstances of opposition planning the opinion of one person with relevant experience can be crucial, for there is no army of civil servants to explore the administrative consequences of a proposal. The form that the income guarantee would take must have rested to a considerable extent on Houghton's judgement of the feasibility of 'putting the tax system into reverse'. Having decided upon this course many of the details of the scheme fell into place. The most convenient approach was to approximate Inland Revenue procedures as closely as possible. For example, data on earnings, as for PAYE, would be based on the current tax year, and for unearned income on the previous tax year. The study group co-opted Mr Callaghan, the future Labour Chancellor of the Exchequer, at the end of 1962 after these fundamental issues of the income guarantee had been raised.

The level at which the income guarantee would operate was not entirely clear, but as we have noted Crossman had indicated in the Commons that it would be based on the scale rates for national

[39] The details of the scheme were outlined in speeches by Mitchison and Crossman. *H. C. Deb.*, vol. 686, cols 231–300.

assistance plus an additional element in recognition of rents and other such variables.[40] To make it worthwhile it had to be, say, a full pound more than the prevailing level of national insurance pensions and it would be progressively increased during the seven years of transition to the new earnings-related system of social security. The first likely date for the introduction of the scheme was 1966. Extrapolating from 1962 to the likely 1966 rates of national insurance and national assistance benefits the study group would have begun working (in 1962) with an income guarantee in the region of £4 5s for a single person and £6 10s for a couple. An article published in 1964 by Geoffrey Gibson, who was the secretary of the study group, confirms these levels (he suggested £4 7s 6d and £6 19s a week rising to £5 19s and £7 19s after seven years).[41] The important point is that at this level the guarantee would not have been impossibly expensive, but it would progressively have raised a substantial proportion of the elderly poor above national assistance.

The actual cost of the guarantee would depend on the rate of take-up and therefore on such factors as the level of disregards and personal savings. In 1962 the Labour Party could have expected to launch a scheme at a cost of something like £200 million in the first year and, allowing for savings on national assistance, it would have been reasonable to estimate the *net* cost at near £150 million. This was a substantial amount of money. The figure would be higher if national assistance and national insurance rates were more generous when the scheme was introduced than was anticipated in 1962 and higher still if generous disregards or a variable rent allowance was added. Nevertheless, it was a relatively small sum compared with the cost of national superannuation and it was less than the long-run cost of raising flat-rate pensions by anything like an equivalent amount (a comparable across the board increase for pensioners would have cost something like £300 million in the first year).

This does raise a complication. Labour had promised a three pounds basic pension in 1957 and had continually criticized the Conservative government for not increasing the pension substantially. The Labour leadership was under pressure from constituency delegates in annual conferences and from the trade union movement to introduce a generous increase in flat-rate benefits immediately on gaining office. A specific figure was carefully resisted during the 1960 conference debate, but both the pressure and the 1957 commitment were real. If the 1957 promise of three pounds was to be updated when Labour gained power to take account of changes in the standard or cost of living, the increase would be a substantial one and an income

[40] *H. C. Deb.*, vol. 686, cols 231–300.

[41] Gibson, G., 'The Income Guarantee', *New Society*, vol. 4, no. 113, 26 Nov., 1964.

guarantee which improved upon this would therefore be more expensive to implement. But having invented the guarantee the study group had an *alternative* to a large flat-rate increase.

This alternative strategy – a *combination* of a smaller flate-rate increase and an income guarantee – was obviously foreshadowed in *New Frontiers.* The relative weight attached to each would determine the total cost. The speed of implementation of the income guarantee would in turn influence this relationship. If the guarantee was introduced very quickly after Labour gained power this would reduce the pressure for immediate and substantial increases in national insurance and national assistance benefits. Alternatively, if these benefits were raised immediately the guarantee could be phased in with less haste, but at a higher rate. As the scheme was apparently to be tied to the tax system, the time of year that Labour came to power would be important. It would determine which tax year the scheme could be based on. An optimistic timetable would see it operative twelve to fifteen months after the party came into power. Given the commitment to improving the pensioners' lot, a longer time scale would probably entail immediate and substantial flat-rate increases as an interim compensatory measure. Yet a mere fifteen months' delay in implementing an entirely novel scheme is very little.

Despite the attempts to produce a blueprint which could be acted on quickly, the Opposition's plans for an income guarantee were obviously fraught with uncertainties as it approached the 1964 election. The level and cost of the scheme depended on decisions that would have to be taken once it was in power: that is, upon decisions about the level of flat-rate benefits and a viable timetable for implementing the various proposals; about rent allowances and disregards; and about the details of administration and the precise responsibilities of the different government departments involved. This last question, like many others, just could not be answered in opposition. The Labour planners knew roughly what they wanted and the likely order of maximum and minimum cost. They did not know what future ministers would be able to secure in practice. It is also almost certain that they did not agree among themselves about some of the fundamental features of their scheme. Two dominant ideas, each with its own merits, seem to underlie the proposed income guarantee: a relatively high flat-rate guarantee without a variable rent allowance; or a lower guaranteed level plus a rent allowance. Some rapid decisions would have to be made, not least on disregards and administration, if either one of these models was to be implemented within the first eighteen months of a Labour government.

The Income Guarantee and National Assistance
One final point must be made about the income guarantee and the years of Labour planning in opposition. The scheme arose, as we have seen, in response to the transitional problems connected with the introduction of National Superannuation. It would raise pensioners and widows above national assistance and *inter alia* justify a complete refurbishing of the remaining national assistance system. As such it would be a subsidiary, relatively minor and temporary programme. Yet the role outlined for it did not tie it exclusively to the introduction of the new Labour pension system. Not all proposals which serve party interests also relate to existing problems faced by civil servants and the government, but the income guarantee clearly was relevant in this wider context. Its fate was not necessarily dependent on that of the national superannuation scheme.

The supplementation of pensions through national assistance was an important issue in its own right and the administrative dilemma had become more apparent over time. Low insurance benefits forced many pensioners to seek augmentation from the NAB. This was a relatively inexpensive way to raise their standard of living, but it had real disadvantages. It was a source of some discomfort for the Conservative administration because it contravened the original policy of subsistence pensions. Although the report of the Philips Committee in 1954 could be cited as justification for departing from this policy, pensioner poverty was a potential electoral embarrassment.[42] In particular, attention was being focused on this issue throughout the early sixties because of accumulating evidence about the numbers of old people in financial need who were failing to use national assistance.

We have already mentioned this last phenomenon in passing; it was referred to in speeches by Labour spokesmen in parliamentary and conference debates. Nevertheless, it is important to note that this was in essence a different and parallel criticism of national assistance to that mounted within the Labour Party and reflected in its planning. Labour policy was founded on a determination to get people, especially the elderly, off national assistance. On the other hand, the fact that even *some* needy old people did not go to the NAB for help raised questions about the suitability of a service of this kind as a means of preventing poverty. The implication was that assistance was under-utilized because it was felt to cast a stigma, or possibly for a mixture of other reasons such as ignorance of the benefits available.

[42] *Report of the Committee on the Economic and Financial Problems of the Provision for Old Age*, Cmd. 9333, 1954.

As early as 1954 Peter Townsend had found evidence of old people who had a *prima facie* entitlement to national assistance but who were not claiming it it.[43] Although his book, *The Family Life of Old People*, was not published until 1957 it is important to remember that a substantial proportion of the elderly poor were probably failing to apply for national assistance from the earliest years of its existence. His findings tended to confirm the unsystematic evidence of the stigma attaching to assistance which MPs detected in their constituencies, and which was alluded to in Labour's 1955 manifesto. Surprisingly, then, there was no real public debate on this issue until research conducted by Cole and Utting was published in 1962.[44] In their book they suggested that at least 500,000 (and probably as many as 700,000) old people who would be eligible for national assistance were not applying for it. Perhaps the most important thing revealed by these findings and their discussion in Parliament, was the degree of ignorance which existed about the effectiveness or the defects of the national assistance system and the way in which potential clients perceived such a service. The Conservative government eventually responded to the mini-political storm caused by the Cole and Utting findings. In the summer of 1964 it accepted a proposal to conduct, within the MPNI and NAB, a research based enquiry into the extent and causes of the under-utilization of national assistance by retirement pensioners.[45]

The apparent size of the problem should have had an impact on *both* the major political parties. It made the Conservatives' reliance on national assistance as a means of supplementing pensioners doubly embarrassing. Supplementation by the NAB could be said to be undesirable in principle and also ineffective in practice. The income guarantee, which was a potential solution to this dilemma, should have begun to find friends within the Conservative Party and within the departments, especially the MPNI and the NAB, which had to absorb much of the criticism aimed at the government. The Labour Party seemed to be in a much happier position since it had developed a solution to this immediate political issue as a by-product of its more elaborate long-term plans; but the problem of under-utilization was a warning to them as well. The income guarantee would still leave a residual role for a service similar to national assistance and its exact form therefore deserved attention. Moreover, the income guarantee's potential importance had grown during the early sixties as the dis-

[43] Townsend, P., *The Family Life of Old People*, Routledge & Kegan Paul, 1957.

[44] Cole, D. with Utting, J., *The Economic Circumstances of Old People*, Codicote, 1962.

[45] With academic advice (from Professors Marsh and Ilersic) the MPNI and NAB conducted the research themselves. The results were published as a report, *Financial and Other Circumstances of Retirement Pensioners*, 1966.

satisfaction with national assistance increased. Added to which, because it had planned to dispense with assistance not reform it, Labour did not have an alternative solution to the issue of national assistance if the income guarantee failed it.

The Conservative government did not take up the idea of the income guarantee, although *The Times* had suggested that it might do so when *New Frontiers* was first published.[46] That it did not do so is hardly surprising. The Labour scheme was published only fifteen months before the 1964 election, which left little time for the government to transform the germ of an idea into a programme. There had been indications of what the Labour plan might be in 1962, but the government faced other more pressing problems between 1962 and 1964. It had to make difficult decisions in the economic field and was shaken by the Profumo and other crises, including a change of leadership. Even if the idea had proved attractive, the government simply lacked the drive and confidence to capitalize on it. Hence the Conservatives' rather tame manifesto promise in 1964 of a complete review of social security policy.[47]

In the case of the Labour Party, the income guarantee had apparently begun to gain a certain autonomy as a policy. It is difficult to be dogmatic on such an issue, but the 1963 Commons debate if read now leaves the impression that the proposal was given more prominence than when it first appeared in *New Frontiers*. It had obvious political merit as a short-term programme with appeal for existing pensioners. They were a large group of the electorate and one that Labour had courted in the 1959 election. The promise of pension increases was important, but predictable, and it could be neutralized by the government introducing actual pension increases during the run-up to the election. National assistance rates were raised before the 1959 election and both assistance and insurance benefits were again raised substantially in May 1963. By way of contrast, the income guarantee was novel and immune from this kind of pre-emption. The government would have had to take over the idea *in toto* or come up with an equally attractive alternative in order to counteract it. This it had failed to do.

For Labour the income guarantee presented a classic policy dilemma; accentuated by the uncertainties of being in opposition. It could prove to be electorally popular, but it could also embroil a future Minister in delay, considerable expenditure of staff and financial resources as well as the expenditure of influence in winning co-operation between different government departments. How much priority and emphasis

---

[46] *The Times*, 2 Apr., 1963.

[47] Conservative policy-making in the social security field and its relationship with that in the Labour Party cannot be examined in the compass of this case study but will be included in a future publication.

should be given to this one item of the social security plan? It is not unusual for a party to place one set of emphases on its proposals in its own blueprints and stress another when appealing to the electorate or to constituency workers. In the event the Labour Party certainly accepted that the income guarantee *could* be introduced ahead of the other proposals. The 1964 manifesto specifically committed a future Labour government to its introduction and during the election campaign Harold Wilson strengthened the pledge. This question, of what priority was given to the idea, will be explored more fully at the beginning of the next section.

For the first time since the inception of the NAB, however, there was the semblance of a plan for reforming the income maintenance safety net on which so many low-income households depended. National assistance was to be reduced to a 'national scheme to assist people in peculiar and special circumstances',[48] operating within a new Ministry of Social Security. Through the aegis of the income guarantee, widows and the elderly were being offered the chance to escape from national assistance entirely. Precisely who would benefit, to what extent, and under what conditions, was still unclear. These details, though basic to the scheme, were hostages to fortune. The decisions would have to be made by a future Labour government.

II THE LABOUR GOVERNMENT: 1964–66

By its victory in the 1964 election, the Labour Party won the opportunity to bring its social security plans to fruition. Let us be clear about the relationship between its plans and national assistance. The proposed earnings-related benefits, backed by an income guarantee, promised rapidly to reduce national assistance to a small-scale service for non-pensioners. The residual assistance functions were to be absorbed into a new Ministry of Social Security, thus ending the structural separation of the insurance-based and means-tested services. This part of the reform was not spelled out in any detail. What we have tried to show is that the novel idea of an income guarantee was a solution to more than one problem. It had been designed as a primarily short-term complement to earnings-related benefits. But it could possibly be seen as an electorally attractive idea in its own right given the severe criticism of national assistance as a means of supplementing pensions.

[48] The words were those used by Aneurin Bevan on 24 November, 1947, when introducing the National Assistance Bill. They were quoted in the 1963 debate, *H. C. Deb.*, vol. 686, col. 232.

Curiously enough these two parts of the story did not really come together at the time. The Cole and Utting data on the under-utilization of national assistance by pensioners produced demands for its reform, or at least for an enquiry. Yet the data were hardly used to underline the merits of the income guarantee. Perhaps this was due to a disagreement within the Labour Party about the form the income guarantee should take, its feasibility, or even its desirability. However, whatever the cause, it remained an adjunct to national superannuation throughout the period of Labour *planning*. The priorities of a long-term plan and the needs of an election campaign are obviously likely to differ. Labour's social security planners had not neglected the short-term needs of pensioners but both the income guarantee and the future of the residual assistance system were subordinate to the long-term pension plans. It was during the 1964 election that the income guarantee really acquired a different status (and the fate of national assistance came into prominence later still). Let us see how this change in emphasis occurred.

Provision for the elderly was one of the key features of Labour's social policies during the 1964 election. Mark Abrams had shown in 1962 that only thirty-nine per cent of 'target voters' felt that Labour would do most for the elderly. By February 1964 this figure was fifty-one per cent and it was rising.[49] Labour's social security plans were gaining credibility among the crucial 'floating' voters. Butler and King argue that Abrams' findings on this and other similar issues did not affect Labour's policy priorities but were reflected in the way policy proposals were *publicized*. What this argument neglects is the subsequent effect of this publicity; the effect on the party once it was in power. The income guarantee is a case in point.

The Labour manifesto noted that, '*with the exception of the early introduction of the Income Guarantee* the key factor in determining the speed at which new and better levels of benefit can be introduced, will be the rate at which the British economy can advance'.[50] The Labour Party's extensive programme of social policy developments was specifically founded on the hope of attaining a faster rate of economic growth. Care had been taken to avoid the tag: 'socialism means higher taxation'. Yet the income guarantee, and the immediate benefits it would bring to the elderly poor, were clearly not to be contingent on the economic situation. It was promised unconditionally. An increase in flat-rate benefits was also given a high, though less categorical, priority. Harold Wilson personally gave prominence to the short-term needs of the elderly in a television broadcast during the election and thereby stored up problems for his party. Pensions

[49] Quoted in Butler, D. and King A., *The British General Election of 1964*, Macmillan, 1965, pp. 67–71.
[50] 1964 Labour Manifesto in Craig, F. W. S., *op. cit.*, p. 240 (our italics).

and security of tenure for private tenants, were at the top of his list of social policy priorities. The income guarantee was promised 'without delay'.[51] In practice the prologue was a poor guide to the main drama. The income guarantee was far from being the success story that Labour would have wished. Instead of being implemented quickly it was delayed and apparently given low priority. The consequences of the saga were important for the reform of national assistance.

Government and Opposition: the Income Guarantee
Even if a party does not feel bound by all its election pledges once it gains power, they do give the Opposition something to work on. One of the Conservatives' first parliamentary responses to finding themselves out of office in 1964 was to harry the new Labour government on its pension pledges. In the very first weeks of Opposition the Conservatives took up the income guarantee as a Labour weak spot. Other social security issues were not ignored. The delay in implementing earnings-related pensions was criticized throughout the Labour government. But the Opposition took its lead from the election propaganda and concentrated on the short-term needs of the elderly. The debate on the Queen's speech was not an auspicious start for the Government in the field of social security. Despite the planning in opposition the Speech noted that:

They [the Government] believe that radical changes in the national schemes of social security are essential to bring them in line with modern needs. They will therefore embark at once upon a major review of these schemes. Meanwhile, they will immediately introduce legislation to increase existing rates of National Insurance and associated benefits.[52]

As the leader of the Opposition (Sir Alec Douglas-Home) observed, the Labour 'manifesto said that the Socialist Party was poised to swing its plan for social security into instant operation,' but he could find 'no mention in the Gracious Speech either of a minimum income guarantee, or half-pay on retirement'.[53] Nor were details available on the size and cost of the increases that were to be made in pensions and other existing benefits. He felt this was odd since 'the Right Hon. Lady [Miss Herbison, the new Minister of Pensions and National Insurance] told us last year that all this had been costed and was

---

[51] See the Labour Party Conference, 1965, and *H. C. Deb.*, vol. 702, cols 1391–2, for a summary by Sir Keith Joseph of the priority given to this proposal.
[52] *H. C. Deb.*, vol. 701 cols 39–40.
[53] *Ibid.*, col. 56.

ready'.[54] The omission of the more innovative social security proposals from the Queen's Speech, which meant they would not be introduced for at least a year, suggested that Labour planning in Opposition had been less than perfect. The costing of its proposals, in particular, had been a strong point in the Labour campaign and was one that the Conservatives consistently attacked during the first period of Labour government. The Opposition clearly felt that something had gone wrong with Labour's proposed income guarantee and it probed its costing as one of the most likely areas in which the pre-election planning had proved unsatisfactory.

Crossman has argued that for a few months after losing office ex-ministers can fairly easily reconstruct what is happening within their old departments and that this gives them considerable edge in criticising the new government.[55] The Conservatives had the additional advantage in 1964 of Labour's vulnerability. The party came to power with a list of pledges which would keep any government busy and involve substantial extra public expenditure. The economy was a critical problem not only because of a very heavy balance of payments deficit and an inflationary trend, but also due to the fact that the government's economic management skill was 'on trial'.[56] Social policy expenditure largely depended on getting the economy right. Unfortunately for Labour not all of it could be deferred that long; yet new commitments could be denounced as economically 'irresponsible' by the Conservatives and by domestic and international economic elites. In addition to these difficulties another emerged in the white paper on the economic situation which was released at the end of October 1964. In the words of the white paper:

> The large public expenditure programme which the Government found on taking office would, if left unchanged, fully absorb for the years ahead the future growth of revenue at present rates of taxation, even on the assumption of a regular 4% per year rate of growth of gross national product.[57]

The Opposition was on a good wicket. Economic growth was below the four per cent target and hard choices therefore faced the government. It felt that it had to prune existing public expenditure whilst giving priority to some of its own proposals and deferring the rest

[54] *Ibid.*, cols 55–6.
[55] Crossman, R. H. S., *Inside View*, Cape, p. 15.
[56] For discussion of Labour's problems in the economic field and their impact on social policy see Brittan, S., *Steering the Economy*, Secker & Warburg, 1969, chs 7 and 8; Cohen, C. D., *British Economic Policy, 1960–69*, Butterworth, 1971; Beckerman, W. (ed.), *The Labour Government's Economic Record: 1964–1970*, Duckworth, 1972; and Townsend, P. and Bosanquet N., *Labour and Inequality*, Fabian Society, 1972.
[57] Paragraph 9 of the white paper, quoted in *H. C. Deb.*, vol. 701, col. 57.

until the economic situation had improved. In this situation broken election pledges, especially in the field of social expenditure, were a weakness that the Opposition was bound to exploit. The parliamentary battles over social security took place in this context. Let us first look at the short-term decisions made by the government and then examine the parliamentary exchanges that ensued.

Labour's priorities in social security

Douglas Houghton, Chancellor of the Duchy of Lancaster and 'social service overlord with small "o"', outlined the programme that the government had decided upon. Apart from the immediate increases in national insurance benefits, there were to be 'improved social benefits along traditional lines, which means that National Assistance will be retained for the present but with improved scales to tide over until we can bring in the income guarantee'.[58] Priority was also to be given to the development of earnings-related sickness and unemployment benefits, which the previous administration had already begun to discuss with the TUC, and to the abolition of prescription charges. Though not mentioned in Houghton's list of priorities, the government also acted quite quickly on a scheme of redundancy payments. Together these amounted to a substantial set of short-term improvements, but the other items of the original plan were relegated to a major review of social security policies.

On the face of it the review of social security policy can only be explained as a mantle to throw over the deferment of promised reforms. A review hardly seemed justifiable on policy grounds in view of the effort devoted to the social security plans from the mid-fifties onwards. Neverthless, the detailed negotiations needed to pave the way for national superannuation would take time and Labour's planning, when in Opposition, had only just begun to catch up with the problem of *family* poverty. Whether the decision to review social security policy meant that gaps and defects had already been noticed in the pre-election planning was not made clear. What did emerge was that the review would be conducted not by Miss Herbison, but by Douglas Houghton – the 'overlord'.

Quite why the Cabinet decided upon the review and created the machinery of government that it did is difficult to answer conclusively; but the Opposition had its theories and criticisms. It welcomed the fact of a review as a conversion to its own approach as outlined in its 1964 manifesto. Labour's initial reluctance to conduct one had arisen, Sir Keith Joseph argued, 'because they were wedded and dedicated to panaceas which they thought would stand up to examination – now they are in power they have discarded some of those schemes, some

[58] *H. C. Deb.*, vol. 701, col. 870.

temporarily, and some perhaps permanently'.[59] He readily conceded that major changes (national superannuation) would take time despite the quality of the planning Labour claimed they had done in Opposition; but he could see no reason for delay in the introduction of the income guarantee. He detected some doubt in the government's mind about the policies that had been designed while in Opposition. These remarks on the reasons for the review were clearly party-political, but some of the Opposition's criticisms of the administrative machinery were more neutral and practical.

Douglas Houghton's role consisted of overall co-ordination of the social services. As such he had responsibility for the social security review among other things. He described his own role thus:

> My own part will be that of an overseer, guide and if you will, philosopher as well. The hard work will be done by my right hon. friends the Minister of Pensions and National Insurance, the Minister of Health and other Ministers who will have responsibility for some sections of the social services. I see that *The Times* newspaper said that I have got my work cut out. Of course I have.[60]

The Conservatives were more explicit than *The Times*. They noted that he had only a handful of civil servants and no departmental backing.[61] Although he was a member of the Cabinet, and the Ministers for Pensions and Health were not, it was a curious position from which to effect co-ordination, change, or a review of policy options. The rhetoric was impressive. Harold Wilson, for example, saw the co-ordination role as a means 'to ensure that no longer do we have the scandal of poverty in the midst of great potential abundance'.[62] Houghton in turn promised to look at such questions as the role of redistribution in securing economic growth and 'how much of the redistribution should be in money and how much should be in free or subsidized services'.[63] But a Minister without executive responsibility can be administratively isolated. If he is not very careful, and lucky, his contribution may not amount to much more than fine words.

The Opposition also argued consistently in debates and at question time, notably through Lord Balniel and Sir John Eden, that the social security review should not be a private ministerial affair. It demanded a public enquiry or, at the least, a systematic gathering of evidence from 'outside bodies' including 'those who run private occupational schemes'.[64] Since the reform of social security had been delayed there

[59] *H. C. Deb.*, vol. 702, cols 1389–90.
[60] *H. C. Deb.*, vol. 701, col. 868.
[61] *H. C. Deb.*, vol. 702, cols 1248–9.
[62] *H. C. Deb.*, vol. 701, col. 65.
[63] *Ibid.*, col. 871.
[64] *H. C. Deb.*, vol. 705, cols 699 and 1049–50.

may have been merit in a wide-ranging review of poverty and income maintenance; although it would have reduced Ministers' opportunities to introduce solutions in an *ad hoc* way as they became economically and administratively feasible. But the Opposition's argument against the 'hole-in-the-corner' review undertaken by prejudiced Ministers' had clear party overtones.[65] A public review would have publicized opposition to the idea of State earnings-related pensions as such and to their early introduction given the state of the economy. Sir Cyril Osborne underlined the point by asking Douglas Houghton 'to bear in mind the very serious warning of the Governor of the Bank of England on Monday, when he said that the only salvation for the country economically was a severe cut in Government expenditure, when conducting the social security review'.[66] The review remained a 'closed' ministerial planning process.

The fate of the Income Guarantee
From the debate on the 1964 Queen's Speech onward, Miss Herbison was kept under pressure over the income guarantee. The pressure largely came from MPs' questions; most, but by no means all of them, from Conservatives. They were all addressed to three broad issues: the date when the income guarantee would be announced; the cost and level of benefit it would provide; and its administrative features. No details were ever given in reply. The standard response from the beginning was that work was progressing on the scheme but that none of its features, such as cost, could be given until its precise form had been decided upon. The only real impact of all this activity, though perhaps an important one, was to make the Ministry constantly aware of the cost, in parliamentary terms, of failing to introduce the guarantee. If election pledges are indeed a force for change it is this continuing pressure, not least from the Opposition, which makes them so. Although Ministers on several occasions discussed the scheme with backbench Labour MPs interested in social security, there was no concerted pressure from the backbenches to introduce the income guarantee quickly. Labour had a hair-line majority and the income guarantee was far from being its only worry.

The extent of the difficulties facing the government are well illustrated by the Chancellor of the Exchequer's budget statement in November 1964 and by the problems of raising national insurance benefits. The budget statement outlined the action that had been taken to reduce the balance of payments crisis and to prune the Conservative legacy of public expenditure commitments. The Chancellor then turned to 'a very important priority in public expenditure. I

[65] *H. C. Deb.*, vol. 705, col. 1049.
[66] *Ibid.*, col. 1050.

believe that all of us found during the course of the recent election that there is widespread public concern ... about the condition of the elderly, the sick and the needy in this country'.[67]

He announced increases in national insurance benefits (from £3 7s 6d to £4 for single persons and from £5 9s to £6 10s for a couple), war pensions and industrial injuries benefits as well as the abolition of the earnings rule for widows' benefit. Comparable increases were announced in national assistance rates. He felt it was 'in accordance with the feeling of the country that we should not delay bringing about these improvements for the old, the sick and the widows while we are working on our longer-term plans'.[68]

In fact the benefits were not to be paid until the end of March 1965, a delay of nearly six months. The Opposition harried the government on this question for some time. The official explanation offered for the delay was that the MPNI was administratively unprepared for a rise in pensions when Labour came into power. As a measure of compensation for these administrative shortcomings an additional lump-sum grant of four pounds was paid to the elderly who were on national assistance in December 1964. It cost the Exchequer £6m – rather less than the cost of introducing the increased benefits several months earlier.[69] The nature of the economic constraints within which the government was operating is illustrated by Sir Keith Joseph's suggestion that it was the Treasury that would not let the government introduce any of the increases before March.[70] A short while after this George Brown specifically offered the economic situation as the reason for the delay. When taxed with the divergence between this explanation and her own, Miss Herbison agreed that the economic situation had *subsequently* been seen as a problem, although administrative problems were the initial reason.[71] The important point is that the pressure on public expenditure arising from the economic situation was certainly sufficient in the winter of 1964 for it to have been one factor in the tardy payment of higher benefits. The delay had occurred despite, according to Sir Keith Joseph, 'a major row' between Miss Herbison and some of her colleagues and considerable pressure from Labour backbenchers.[72]

The income guarantee clearly could not have been introduced early in 1965 in view of the tremendous pressure on public expenditure. This pressure had grown considerably during the first months of the Labour government. During the second reading debate on the national

[67] *H. C. Deb.*, vol. 707, cols 1031–2.
[68] *Ibid.*, col. 1032.
[69] *H. C. Deb.*, vol. 702, cols 17–20.
[70] *H. C. Deb.*, vol. 702, col. 1395.
[71] *H. C. Deb.*, vol. 705, cols 706–7.
[72] *H. C. Deb.*, vol. 702, col. 1394.

insurance increases, Douglas Houghton felt 'bound to say that if we had not made the announcement [to increase benefits] when we did, it would have been very difficult to make it now, having regard to the worsened economic situation'.[73] The government had in effect mortgaged its future to a substantial extent (with regard to social security policy) when it introduced these increases. As Houghton said, 'what we are doing is undoubtedly anticipating a growth rate that we have not yet seen and that represents an act of economic faith as well as an act of social justice'.[74] The previous government had estimated that with a four per cent growth rate it could spend another '£360 million at constant prices in real terms between now [1964] and 1967–8'; the national insurance increases had taken up £285 million of this and the four per cent growth rate was nowhere in sight.[75]

During the same debate Douglas Houghton explained, not surprisingly, that the income guarantee had been delayed by the economic situation. The introduction of the guarantee would probably have added half as much again (i.e. £150 million) on to the cost of the benefit increases, and they had caused great anxiety as it was. Indeed, the cost of the scheme could have been more than this by 1965 (the figure of £150 million derived from Labour planning before the 1964 election), although nowhere near the £700 million suggested by one Conservative MP.[76] It is also important to note that the income guarantee would have been a direct charge on the Exchequer; it could not have been defrayed by contributions (unless it could have been introduced as part of the earnings-related pension system). Although the estimated total cost of the benefit changes and the abolition of prescription charges was nearly £300 million in 1965–6, *only £130 million fell as a direct charge on the Exchequer.*[77] The net cost of the income guarantee could, therefore, have more than doubled the charge on the Exchequer.

More unexpectedly, Houghton also blamed the delay of the income guarantee on the late election. He soundly berated the Conservatives for having clung to office until the bitter end. He argued that this unfortunate decision on their part had made it impossible to phase the new scheme into the income tax system in time for the 1965 tax year. The failure to harmonize the introduction of the guarantee with the benefit increases had left Labour, he admitted, in an 'exposed position'. Nevertheless, he gave the assurance that the guarantee was a 'must' in the legislative programme and that room

---

[73] *H. C. Deb.*, vol. 702, col. 1404.
[74] *Ibid.*, col. 1403.
[75] *Ibid.*, col. 1403.
[76] *H. C. Deb.*, vol. 721, col. 4.
[77] *H. C. Deb.*, vol. 701, cols 1033–4.

would be found for it.[78] The point he was acknowledging, of course, was that although they were not over-generous compared with earlier suggestions,[79] the national insurance benefit increases could possibly have been lower if 'harmonized' with the introduction of the income guarantee. They had now been introduced at a time and at a level which restricted Labour's future room for manoeuvre. The important question at this point was not whether the income guarantee would be introduced without further delay, but whether it could be introduced even when the economic situation improved. Ministerial replies to questions mentioned that progress was being made, but no further information was given. The guarantee had become an embarrassing non-starter, for the time being at least.

On July 27 1965, the Chancellor of the Exchequer made a Commons statement on the balance of payments position. The essence of the message was simple: earlier measures were having effect and the deficit was being reduced, but this trend needed to be reinforced. Cuts were announced in the 'swollen programmes of public expenditure left behind' by the previous government, a further tightening on capital expenditure was imposed, and some of the government's 'desirable social reforms' were deferred.[80] In the social security field it had been decided that priority must go to 'wage-related unemployment and sickness benefits'. The income guarantee had now been officially postponed.[81]

Two days later the Opposition initiated a major debate devoted to the proposition that the government had failed to fulfil its election pledges. This reviewed the whole saga of achievements, crises, and failures of the first nine months of Labour rule. The Conservative case was not only that the government had failed to honour individual pledges, such as the income guarantee, but that it had substantially increased taxation despite a promise to finance higher public expenditure from economic growth and that the economic crises were largely the product of the government's own mishandling of affairs.

The Prime Minister presented his view of Labour's record on social security. He argued, at this time a very familiar theme, that the economic situation left by the Conservatives was much worse than

---

[78] *Ibid.*, cols 1397–8.

[79] The actual increases in 1965 were no higher than those urged on the Conservatives by Labour in 1963, when the former had last raised benefits. Both the cost of living and average wage rates had risen in the meantime. See *H. C. Deb.*, vol. 702, col. 1403.

[80] *H. C. Deb.*, vol 717, cols 228–32. For discussion of the economic context of Labour's decisions on public expenditure see Brittan, S., *Steering the Economy, op. cit.*; Cohen, C. D., *British Economic Policy, 1960–1969, op. cit.*; Beckerman, W. (ed.), *The Labour Government's Economic Record: 1964–1970, op. cit.*

[81] *Ibid.*

had been expected. He also noted that an incoming government is not armed with a sheaf of drafted Bills that it can introduce quickly and that, in the case of the Ministry of Pensions, there was not even a pension increase Bill 'on the stocks'. Despite these problems the parliamentary session had resulted in sixty-five Bills, 'a pretty good record'.[82] He then suggested that even in the face of these pressures the priorities set during the election had been honoured. The emphasis that had been given to pensions was reflected in the first Bill produced by the government (to restore bus fare concessions for retirement pensioners) and by the Pensions (Increases) Bill which was first read 'fifteen days after Parliament met'.[83] This case ignored the unqualified pledge to introduce the income guarantee. Mr Barber reminded the Prime Minister that this scheme had not been dependent on the progress of the economy.

The Prime Minister's explanation of why the scheme was deferred contained three elements. The first was the need for further action on the balance of payments; not least to 'reassure the world trading community and the holders of sterling balances, of our utter determination to make Britain strong and sterling strong'.[84] The second, which followed from this, was summed up in the phrase 'viability means sacrifices'. Action on mortgages and the income guarantee were two of the 'cherished and important political programmes' deferred until 1967.[85] The third point brought the Prime Minister back to problems of administration and the effect they had on priority decisions:

> We had hoped on coming in [to office] that it would be possible, dependent on the administrative machinery we found, to introduce the income guarantee very quickly indeed ... this would be a way of increasing pensions without the full cost of a general pension increase ... *The administrative machinery was nothing like sufficient* to do this. What we did ... was to carry through immediately as our first priority the biggest pensions increase for twenty years.[86]

What were the chances of the income guarantee being re-introduced in 1967, the date mentioned by the Prime Minister? One clear ground for pessimism was that he had implied in his speech that the pension increases honoured the pre-election pledge. However, in reply to the continued flow of questions on the subject Margaret Herbison said that the scheme was deferred, not abandoned, and that preparations

[82] *H. C. Deb.*, vol. 717, col. 731.
[83] *Ibid.*, col. 748.
[84] *Ibid.*, cols 8, 746-7.
[85] *Ibid,*, col. 748.
[86] *Ibid.*, col. 748 (our italics).

for its introduction were continuing.[87] National Superannuation had not yet emerged as a firm policy and it was still possible, therefore, for the income guarantee to be introduced alongside a new pension system as was originally intended, or for it to be launched ahead of the pension changes if the economic situation permitted. During the debate on the Queen's Speech at the beginning (November) of the 1965-6 session, Douglas Houghton also affirmed that nothing had been abandoned. Both as one of the earliest (and arguably the strongest) supporters of the income guarantee, and as social service overlord, Houghton could be expected to watch over its progress with particular interest. He was also given every reason to do so by the weight of parliamentary criticism. The income guarantee was very much at the forefront of the institutionalized conflict between government and Opposition over the government's record. But social security priorities had been further clarified: wage-related unemployment and sickness benefits were to be introduced ahead of any other proposals that might eventually emerge from the social security review.

On the one hand this was a real achievement and one which gave rise to an amusing exchange when Houghton fulsomely praised Miss Herbison:

> Douglas Houghton: 'She is so full of good works that hardly a week passes but that something upon which we can congratulate her is done. This session she is going to have quite a bundle of good things.'
> Sir D. Glover: 'Mother Christmas.'[88]

On the other hand, yet more resources were now committed to social security changes even before the social security review resulted in proposals for graduated pensions (which would affect the long-term role of national assistance), or the income guarantee. Houghton acknowledged this dilemma in explaining that only 'the most pressing economic reasons persuaded us to bring forward a scheme for earnings-related short-term benefits ... in advance of the general review'.[89] Graduated unemployment benefits would, along with the redundancy payments, soften the blow of 'redeployment' at the price of a shift in the priorities enunciated during the election.

Let us illustrate the problem. The overall cost of the improvements to *existing* social security benefits mentioned above was £325 million in the first full year (1965-6) and it was estimated that the new short-

---

[87] See for example her answer to a question from Mr William Hamilton on 22 Nov., 1965; *H. C. Deb.*, vol. 721, col. 4.
[88] *H. C. Deb.*, vol. 720, col. 179.
[89] *Ibid.*, col. 178.

term graduated benefits would cost a further £60 million in their first year.[90] If the economy permitted, the next major set of improvements might have been expected to come into operation by, say, 1969. The *National Plan* allowed for an additional social security expenditure of £387 million in 1969–70.[91] What room for manoeuvre did this projected sum allow? There were several possible demands in the queue: a further increase in existing flat-rate benefits; increases in the cost of the new graduated short-term benefits; the introduction of the income guarantee; and the introduction of graduated pensions. The cost of each would depend not only on the level of benefit decided upon, but also upon the composition of the total package as well as the level of unemployment. Introducing graduated pensions and the income guarantee together would avoid the cost of a large increase in existing flat-rate benefits. If existing benefits alone were raised the increase would have to be considerable; coupled with an income guarantee it could be lower, but the total cost could still be very substantial. The tightness of the projected limits can be seen from the fact that (at 1964 prices) the 1964–5 improvements had cost nearly the total increment budgeted for in 1969–70. By 1969 a ten per cent real increase in *existing* benefits would probably have cost an extra £436 million[92] This kind of improvement would have barely left room for the introduction of an income guarantee, even at the original rates tentatively proposed and costed back in 1962.

The problem is clear enough. Social security involves such large expenditures that in a period of economic restraint one can use up all available resources in just meeting (or failing to meet) the expectations of *existing* beneficiaries. There is little room for innovation and virtually none for untried and uncertain experimental schemes which are difficult to cost. The income guarantee, and the changes in the role of national assistance that were promised, seemed a financial albatross during the economic troubles of 1965.

Yet there was pressure to honour the income guarantee pledge by doing something about national assistance. The Conservatives produced the fruits of their own thinking on social security in the autumn of 1965, in time for the debate on the Queen's Speech. They promised to transform the role of the NAB and to merge it into a new Department of Health and Social Security. The transformation consisted of more generous arrangements, including higher disregards, and the imposition of a positive duty on officials to seek out those in need

[90] *Ibid.*, cols 170–1 and 178.

[91] The plan allowed for a total increase in expenditure of £541 million, of which £154 million was to meet increases in expenditure that would be likely to arise even if benefits remained unchanged after 1966; leaving a balance of £387 million. *The National Plan*, Cmnd. 2764, 1965, pp. 203–4.

[92] *H. C. Deb.*, vol. 721, col. 223.

from all age groups.[93] In addition to the pressure this placed on the government, the ministry's survey of pensioners had been completed and was ready for publication. It confirmed the original Cole and Utting contention that three-quarters of a million pensioners who seemed to be eligible for national assistance were not in fact applying for it.[94] The Ministry now had hard evidence of the failure of national assistance in this respect at least. Since Labour members had been very critical of the Conservative government for not resolving the problem when it was highlighted by research in the early sixties, the Labour government would now have to act or lose face with the Opposition and many of its own supporters.

On March 7 1966, Miss Herbison announced in the Commons that national assistance was to be reformed. The NAB was to be merged with the MPNI and the benefits system was to be improved and renamed.[95] These changes are discussed below. The clear intention was that the elderly in particular should not be deterred from obtaining these new benefits, for they were the potential losers now that the income guarantee was finally being jettisoned as a short-term strategy. In one sense the policy was an attempt to salvage something from the income guarantee and it looked very much like the newly announced Conservative proposal, although in another sense it was an extension of the more general reform of national assistance that had been implicit throughout Labour's plans for social security. The major difference between the Labour Party's plans and performance was that pensioners were to remain *within* the means-tested supplementary benefits system. This was an important difference, but although the income guarantee had 'failed' this does not mean that the new proposals were necessarily second best. This is a point to which we shall return. Let us first look at the 'failure' side of the equation and specify some of its possible causes and implications.

III THE FAILURE OF THE INCOME GUARANTEE PROPOSAL: POSSIBLE EXPLANATIONS

A number of possible explanations for the demise of the income guarantee are worth examining.

(1) The state of the economy and the high level of existing public expenditure constrained new initiatives
On the face of it this is the most likely explanation. Of course it

[93] *Ibid.*, col. 192.
[94] *Financial and other Circumstances of Retirement Pensioners, op. cit.*
[95] *H. C. Deb.*, vol. 725, col. 178.

does imply a re-shaping of social service priorities, since the income guarantee had been given very high priority during the election. The economic problems faced by the government did not prevent some increases in public expenditure, including such new initiatives as earnings-related short-term benefits and redundancy payments. This shift in priorities would, therefore, need to be explained.

(2) The government was preparing for a quick election
A second election was obviously likely when Labour came to power with a bare majority of six in 1964. Only one direct reference was made in Parliament to the possibility that the improvements in existing insurance benefits introduced during 1964–5 were in preparation for a snap election. Nevertheless, it is possible that such considerations shaped Labour strategy and pre-empted the resources (financial and administrative) necessary for more fundamental reforms.

(3) The commitments entered into immediately on gaining power left the government little room for manoeuvre later when the economy did not improve
The government clearly did not expect it to take virtually its whole six years in office to attain its basic economic objectives. Its short-term strategy may, therefore, have been a much greater constraint on its long-term policies than it imagined back in 1964–5 when the decisions were taken.

(4) The income guarantee was a novel proposal with high costs
Apart from its financial cost, the income guarantee would have required a large amount of inter-departmental co-operation and a complete re-structuring of the residual national assistance scheme. These may have proved to be insurmountable obstacles.

(5) The social service review and the social service 'overlordship' complicated and delayed planning
The administrative machinery created, and indeed the individual Ministers appointed by Harold Wilson to run it, may have been important variables, but it is difficult to estimate their impact.

(6) Labour planning in Opposition was inadequate
As we have noted, the Conservatives made this suggestion in November 1964, and it is certainly possible that mistakes had been made about the cost and administrative feasibility of the income guarantee. It is also possible that too few decisions were made before coming into power about the details of this scheme and that it subsequently became embroiled in the process of civil service con-

sultations. Although decisions made in Opposition relate mainly to what is *desired*, they can serve as a basis from which to negotiate what is feasible. If too many loose ends are left unconnected an incoming government may find that what is *desired* becomes hopelessly confused with the question of *feasibility*. Unless the Minister gives priority to a scheme and says 'this is what I and the party want', ideas hatched in Opposition can easily run into trouble if they are only partly formulated *and* propose quite new policies. This raises the question of the conditions in which manifesto commitments, Crossman's 'battering-ram of change', can be effective in forcing the pace of governmental policy-making.

These factors almost certainly provide the central elements of the explanation. What is important is the weight to be attached to each and their consequences for the subsequent reform of national assistance. A definite answer cannot be provided, but the following argument seems the most likely.

The obvious explanation – the economic crisis and pressure on public expenditure – is the essential background to, and a large element in, the story. But it is not conclusive. Other programmes were introduced; money was found for social policy initiatives. Set against this is the fact that the Treasury had good reason to oppose the income guarantee since it was a new scheme and its exact cost was unpredictable (because the rate of applications and the numbers eligible were both unknown). Depending on the decisions arrived at about disregards and rent allowances, it could have cost far more than Labour had estimated. Perhaps, crucially, it would logically be a direct charge on the Exchequer rather than being paid for by higher insurance contributions. It seems unlikely that the income guarantee would have gained Treasury support in Cabinet during the early years of the government; Treasury Ministers had too many problems to be sympathetic to this proposal. By comparison, the social security proposals that were given priority had a direct relevance to the economic situation. Graduated unemployment benefits and redundancy benefits were an important gloss on the unemployment caused by deflation and the 'shake-out' of labour.[96]

Yet the same arguments did not apply in the long run. Douglas Houghton was in a position as overlord to fight for the guarantee. The scheme could have been kept in readiness for a more opportune moment. Work had certainly proceeded on it. Some of the thought given to simplifying procedures, for example, was incorporated into the later reform of national assistance. What is clear is that the restructuring of social security priorities and the early increases in flat-

---

[96] The *National Plan* was bluntly frank about this: as it noted the income guarantee, unlike the redundancy and earnings-related unemployment benefits, would not contribute to faster growth, *op. cit.*, pp. 203–4.

rate benefits represented a major commitment of available resources. If it had been kept in reserve, the income guarantee would have become viable only much later in the period of Labour government than was suggested during the 1964 election.

It is unlikely that any changes in social security priorities arising from the necessity of an early election were the crucial factor. Although the increases in flat-rate benefits announced in 1964 would have proved an advantage if a second election had occurred within a matter of months, the continued delay of the income guarantee became a troublesome 'broken pledge' as time wore on. This really leaves only one possibility. As the Prime Minister implied, the initial decision to delay the income guarantee must in fact have arisen from *administrative* considerations, in addition to the economic ones. But which administrative considerations? Was it the social security review and the complication of an overlord that caused difficulties?

This was certainly an area of some tension and possibly a source of delay for the long-term plans. A non-departmental Minister co-ordinating and planning policies across two other departments is a recipe for problems in British government. Douglas Houghton had a very small staff and was in the position of having to request information and papers from the civil servants in the departments he was supposedly co-ordinating. The traditions and procedures of the civil service and of ministerial government inevitably produce strains in this kind of situation. Although Houghton held the Cabinet seat and chaired the relevant Cabinet sub-committee he lacked the immediate access to ideas, opinions and data which departmental Ministers have. For example, Miss Herbison (the Minister for Pensions) had daily briefings with her departmental civil servants, but Houghton did not. The officials working on the social security review formed Houghton's own small office and were not attached to the Ministry of Pensions. The overlord arrangement could easily have resulted in the Ministers vetoing each other's proposals, rather than giving them greater weight in Cabinet and in negotiations with the Treasury.

It is hard to imagine a modern prime minister being unaware of the potential dangers of appointing an overlord who has no real departmental backing. War-time experiments of a related kind should have warned Harold Wilson of the possible consequences of his decision. However the problem, seen from his position, was difficult to resolve. He would not have wanted all the social service Ministers in his Cabinet as this would have made it impossibly large. The ideal solution may have been to rationalize ministries into fewer large departments in 1964, as has subsequently happened, but after thirteen years in Opposition Wilson had a team of colleagues who were something of an unknown quantity on the one hand and who had to be given office on the other. After a long stretch out of power a party has to reward many of its most faithful workers with a taste of office. This combination of circumstances made a rationalization of departments difficult and may account for the curious overlord role created and retained in the social service field for several years.

Nevertheless, given Houghton's enthusiasm for the income guarantee, these administrative problems need not have delayed the proposal, providing it had been planned sufficiently carefully for *both* the Ministers concerned to agree what the scheme entailed and to push it along firmly. Had this happened it would have been difficult for the officials in the Ministry of Pensions to have quietly buried the scheme even if they had opposed it from the start. Providing the Ministers were in agreement they would have been in a much stronger position to overcome difficulties brought to light by their officials than would a non-Cabinet Minister of Pensions who had no real voice in the higher echelons of government decision-making.

In practice the problems which seem to have led to the lack of action on this proposal in 1964–5 were intrinsic to the scheme itself and to the governmental process. The Opposition planning had not resulted in firm decisions on many of the working arrangements – regarding fluctuations in incomes and needs (especially rents), disregards, the retirement rule and wives' earnings – to be incorporated in such a scheme. Once in government, the civil service would have brought many differing viewpoints to bear on these issues. The same is true of the numerous other technical questions that arise when introducing a new element into a system of benefits with a long history of administrative procedures and rules reflecting both pragmatic decisions and powerful social attitudes and prejudices. For example, the related issues of not deterring the elderly from working and not penalizing the thrifty would alone have raised complex questions of existing precedents and underlying social values when devising rules. A party which came into power with its own detailed proposals would still face unforeseen facets of these issues raised within the department and in inter-departmental consultations. The Labour Party had an outline scheme, *not* a detailed blueprint. The income guarantee could not have been introduced without considerable work being done on these details. These problems were outlined by Conservative Ministers of Pensions while Labour was still in Opposition.[97]

The final nail in the coffin of the income guarantee was the inter-departmental arrangements which the scheme entailed. The NAB, the MPNI, the Board of Inland Revenue and the Post Office were all affected by the original concept. This fact in itself represents a for-

[97] For example, see the comments made by Boyd-Carpenter in 1963, *H. C. Deb.*, vol. 686, cols 340–41.

midable programme of inter-departmental planning; but the real stumbling block was the Board of Inland Revenue. The longstanding separation between the social service and taxation systems has been partially bridged since 1964–5. The academic and governmental re-examination of the relationship between these systems has developed slowly; the income guarantee was in the van as a positive proposal demanding such a reappraisal. But in 1965 the Board of Inland Revenue had good reason to resist being entangled in the income guarantee. The 1965 Finance Act brought an almost overwhelmingly heavy increase in its work-load. The Commissioners were in a more powerful position than almost any permanent secretary to insist that their Minister (the Chancellor of the Exchequer) should avoid additional burdens.[98]

It could be argued that strong and determined Ministers could have pushed the scheme through reasonably quickly with the support of a sympathetic Chancellor of the Exchequer, but this misses the point. The Labour Party's optimism in Opposition seems to have been misplaced. The income guarantee raised far too many questions for it to be introduced 'without delay'. The civil servants had taken a first look at these before Labour came to power.[99] The new Minister of Pensions would have been briefed on the difficulties the scheme raised as soon as she took up office and this certainly would have necessitated an initial delay. As we have seen, once the guarantee had been delayed other commitments were entered into; consequently, if the administrative issues were to be resolved and the money earmarked, the scheme would have had to be delayed for several years.

Labour planning whilst in Opposition

The system of two-party democratic government hinges on the proposition that the Opposition provides a real choice, an alternative government. Consequently, an Opposition party must be able to make its mark on national policies within a reasonable time after gaining office. Whether it can do this depends on two sets of circumstances; there are those which determine the quality of its planning while in Opposition and there are those which limit its freedom to implement its policies once in power. In Chapter 5 it was argued than an incoming government's ability to determine events may be declining in both respects. In this case study attention has been concentrated on the problem of planning in Opposition,

---

[98] The Commissioners are being appointed by letters-patent and dismissable only on the agreement of both Houses.

[99] Crossman mentions the civil service practice of making preliminary preparations, during an election, for whichever party gains office. Crossman, R. H. S., *op. cit.*, p. 13.

although this is obviously not unrelated to what can be achieved once a party is in power. The whole issue is most critical to a party like Labour which has traditionally held a programmatic or reforming image of its role and destiny.

In the case of the income guarantee there were four major areas of weakness in the Labour Party's plans, despite the expertise harnessed to social security issue during the years of opposition.

(1) The main principles of the scheme were not spelled out at all clearly. It was not decided, for example, whether the guarantee would include a variable individual allowance for rents even though these are the largest and most fundamental component of need.

(2) The administrative dependence on the Inland Revenue (if the guarantee was not to be means-tested through the NAB) seems not to have been taken very seriously by the scheme's proponents. The problem of having to effect this administrative linkage may in itself have wrecked the scheme. In view of the extra work planned for the Inland Revenue the outcome seems to have been inevitable. There was apparently no pre-election attempt to look at the interaction of different policy proposals one with another, or if there was it did not lead to caution over the way in which the income guarantee was presented to the electorate.

(3) The guarantee was devised to take pensioners off national assistance, but the consequences of this for the rump of the system that would remain were not seriously discussed. The Labour Party did not have a policy for national assistance; only a policy for reducing its importance. Many questions that would have to be resolved before enacting the guarantee were therefore left to the civil service, including the most fundamental issue of whether a quite different solution might not be more appropriate if one looked at national assistance as a whole and not just at those pensioners living at or below its 'poverty line'.

(4) The timing of the guarantee was originally fixed by its relation to the National Superannuation proposals for graduated pensions. The Labour Party planning group apparently did not consider the possibility that the income guarantee could be introduced in its own right as a measure of short-term help for pensioners until the pre-election months of 1963–4. This might have seemed an obvious and attractive idea both because of the great political capital to be gained and because of the complexity and probable length of the negotiations which would have preceded the introduction of a new pension system. Nevertheless, the guarantee had remained a relatively minor proposal as far as the Labour social security planners were concerned; much of the available energy was devoted to the wage-related benefits.

It may reasonably be argued that the failure of the income guarantee arose from factors which no amount of planning in Opposition could have avoided. In addition to those already mentioned it can be seen that two others laid the foundations for a debacle. First, the Labour social security group was obviously not unanimous about the scheme's merits and one enthusiast (Houghton) may have carried the day against the better judgement of others, or simply because they were preoccupied with the wage-related benefit schemes. Second, Harold Wilson seems to have taken a problem, pensioners' grievances, plus a ready-made but embryonic Labour solution, the income guarantee, and projected them into prominence during the heat of the election. It was this prominence which made the failure notable. Arguably no one can prevent party leaders pursuing their political instinct simply by the quality of their planning.

Nevertheless, Labour planning was weak at this point and its inadequacies contributed to the events of 1964–5. The full-time input of research staff was negligible compared with the size of the problem. However enthusiastic and expert they may be, a group of academics and politicians doubling as part-time policy planners and a handful of staff servicing the whole range of policy committees, cannot be expected to devise workable proposals; but they are expected to do so. The fact that they sometimes succeed is not an answer to the problem. The administrative pitfalls of a proposal cannot always be seen by individuals, few of whom have had experience in the civil service or a recent taste of ministerial office. When problems are detected, as they undoubtedly were in the case of the income guarantee, they may not be pursued vigorously enough. A way through the problem may remain unperceived. Alternatively, a tentative and largely unexplored proposal may be allowed to pass for a well re-searched and costed scheme, as seems to have happened in this case. It is just possible that a reasonably large Labour research staff would have found time to look more closely at the divergences of opinion within the social security group and either strengthened the income guarantee scheme or have shown it to be unworkable. Equally, they may have been able to warn Harold Wilson not to enter into firm commitments; or, alternatively, to have focused attention on the scheme once he had done so and thereby rapidly to have improved it.

As it was, the social security planning group had effectively ceased to exist during the election just as the leader of the party was up-grading perhaps their weakest proposal into a scheme that would be implemented 'without delay'. Most importantly, however, a wider opportunity was wasted. The failure of the guarantee was important not for what was lost but for what might have been achieved. Had the whole issue been opened up beyond the question of pensioners it might have led to a more fundamental reappraisal of social security and taxation policies.[100] The Labour planning group included Richard Titmuss, who was a very early critic of the insularity which typified these areas of policy. What seems to have been lacking were the resources to pick up the germs of ideas and broaden them into a wider debate about basic policy proposals while adding detailed advice on administrative feasibility. Given the limited planning resources, not least the scarcity of data on many key variables, the planning group concentrated heavily on one major theme – new schemes of earnings-related benefits.

The final questions that must be asked, therefore, are why the income guarantee was abandoned in 1966 and not simply delayed further, and why national assistance was reformed in the way it was. The answer to the first question points to the administrative complexities of the income guarantee. If the economic position had been the only consideration the scheme could have been deferred. But if the scheme could not be based on the Inland Revenue system this was good reason to look for an alternative. If income returns were made to a body like the NAB, and not to the Board of Inland Revenue, the major advantage of the guarantee would be lost. In these circumstances a reform of national assistance was the obvious approach and one that had anyway been promised in general terms as part of the social security package. There were good arguments for responding in this way. The Conservative Opposition was making great play of Labour's broken pledges as we have seen and the government could not survive on a tiny majority for long.

It is probable that Miss Herbison would have sought the opportunity to reform national assistance and regain the initiative even without the threat of an election. But the election was surely a factor in the timing of change; to salvage something from the original manifesto promise would clearly be an advantage. This point did not escape the Conservatives and they were quick to accuse Miss Herbison in March 1966 of announcing her new policies for national assistance purely because of the pending election.[101] The 1966 campaign was about to begin. The 1964 manifesto pledges, combined with the likelihood of a further election, provided a reason for speedy reform. This situation introduced urgency into the MPNI and probably the Cabinet as well; it may also have had an impact on the Treasury Ministers.

---

[100] The Conservatives have approached this issue in their own way: *Proposals for a Tax-Credit System*, Cmnd. 5116, 1972. However, as Townsend points out, the Labour government could have channelled help to poor pensioners more effectively than it did in 1966 by adding to the existing universal services. Townsend, P. and Bosanquet, N., *op. cit.*, p. 283.

[101] *H. C. Deb.*, vol. 725, cols 1732–3.

IV THE REFORM OF NATIONAL ASSISTANCE: THE POLICY CHANGES OF 1966

The preceding argument presents the reform of national assistance as a negative outcome of the failure of the income guarantee. This is one perspective. The Labour social security plans had meant, *inter alia*, a change in national assistance and it was in this wider context that the party had committed itself to such a course. The reform of national assistance had not arisen as an independent, self-contained proposal.[102] The driving force had come from the attempt to produce a comprehensive plan. But there is another perspective. There were good reasons for looking at national assistance as a whole and not simply as a residual system to be dealt with once pensioners had been removed from its responsibilities.

One of the major disadvantages of having approached the problems of national assistance via the needs of the elderly was the effect this could have on the service provided to the non-elderly. A residual service for these clients would have offered a potentially more individualized approach, as the 1964 Labour manifesto claimed, but it could also have resulted in a far more stigmatized service. The elderly were the largest and the only socially approved group of national assistance applicants. Without them the service would have changed in unpredictable ways. This was certainly one of the arguments the Minister had to consider once she was in office.

Although the loss of the income guarantee left the Minister with one option less, it also opened up the possibility of a different kind of approach. A comprehensive reform of national assistance was an alternative to introducing the income guarantee – an alternative which could only gain momentum as a proposal when the latter had been abandoned. This approach had been developed within the MPNI and the NAB under Margaret Herbison, whereas Douglas Houghton had argued strongly for the income guarantee to be retained as a proposal even after the initial reverses had made it look less economically and administratively feasible. While Crossman had promised in Opposition not to reform national assistance before its role had been greatly reduced, the fact of a pending election now favoured this course of action. Miss Herbison personally saw it as a worthwhile policy in itself and not merely as an attempt to rescue something

---

[102] That bastion of reformative zeal, the Fabian Society, had not totally ignored the defects of national assistance. The nearest approach to a blueprint for change was published as Glennerster, H., *National Assistance: Service or Charity?* Fabian Society, Young Fabian Pamphlet no. 4, 1962. However, it *also* assumed that an income guarantee would provide for pensioners, leaving the remaining functions of the NAB to be absorbed within the MPNI.

from the original proposals. The Minister and the social services overlord (and their respective officials) had been working in somewhat different ways since Labour had first come into office. Although the income guarantee had been considered, and preparations for it had been made, it was just one and not the only possibility that was being studied within Miss Herbison's ministry. She seems justified in her claim that, despite the timing of the announcement before the 1966 election, the reform of national assistance was something 'on which my Department has been working for a considerable time'.[103] In fact a 'considerable time' could be interpreted to mean as much as five or six years. Though the income guarantee has overshadowed what was happening to national assistance in this account, and did so at the time to some extent, national assistance was not simply an administrative island unwashed by the seas of social and political change. Things had been happening; change was beginning to take place spurred on by the intellectual energy and later by the pressure group activity that followed on the 'rediscovery of poverty'.

Pressures for the reform of national assistance in the years immediately preceding 1966
Changes had begun to occur in national assistance during the early 1960s. In particular the amount of publicity given to benefits had been increased even before 1964. The problem of eligible pensioners who did not apply had also focused attention on the nature of stigma – the impact of domiciliary visiting, discretion and uncertainty – and on the service's image. The results of the ministry's survey of pensioners had concentrated further attention on stigma and related issues in 1965. A piecemeal reappraisal was gathering momentum within the NAB throughout the early sixties. Similarly, while the fate of the income guarantee had been the main focal point, there had also been a steady flow of parliamentary questions about national assistance during the 1964–6 period. These covered several topics which are discussed below, and amounted to a considerable pressure for change.

(1) The appropriateness of existing national assistance regulations
Two main aspects of the existing scheme were questioned. They were disregards and the wage stop.[104] The former arose on only a few

---

[103] *H. C. Deb.*, vol. 725, col. 1732.
[104] 'Disregards' concerned that income not taken into account in calculating the amount of benefit or indeed eligibility itself. The 'wage stop' was the provision whereby a recipient's benefit was restricted to what he might normally expect to earn when in full-time work.

occasions, most notably at the end of 1964 when Mrs Thatcher urged that the level of disregards should be raised immediately. The only increase since national assistance first began had been in 1959. She felt that too much attention had been given to people who would not apply, to the detriment of those who just failed to qualify.[105] By comparison, the wage stop was frequently challenged during these years, both in general and in relation to particular problems (such as regional variations in its incidence and delays in revising its application to families as wage rates increased). A small number of MPs – most of them Labour – kept this issue before the Minister, using such evidence as the estimates of low income families produced by the Allen Committee on Rating to reinforce their case.[106]

The only real *discussion* of the wage stop also occurred at the end of 1964 during the debate on increases in national assistance scale rates. On this occasion Mr Curran (Conservative) urged the Minister 'to review the wages stop so as not to penalise the man with a large family and to recognise that, as we are doing it now, we are clamping down on the loafer at the expense of his children'. He felt it was possible to 'put up with a certain amount of cheating and fiddling rather than penalise the man with a large family'.[107] Unfortunately, throughout the period there were virtually no ideas brought forward about how to deal with the wage stop, apart from some Labour pleas to abolish it altogether. The front bench spokeswomen, Miss Herbison and Mrs Thatcher, seemed in agreement that the wage stop was 'far easier to debate than to solve as a problem'.[108] Miss Herbison, as Mrs Thatcher noted, had defended the principle of the wage stop as an Opposition speaker when Mrs Thatcher had been under fire from the Labour front bench. As Minister, Miss Herbison now argued that 'the crux of the problem was family allowances' and that 'scandalously low wages' were a matter for the TUC with whom she had communicated on the wage stop issue during her backbench days in opposition. She admitted that the issue was one to which she had 'not found an acceptable solution in the short time I have been Minister'.[109] At this time a review of the wage stop was promised in order to ensure that it was being applied appropriately in individual cases. At a later date, in reply to further questions on this topic, it was also announced that an inter-departmental committee

[105] *H. C. Deb.*, vol. 704, cols 334–5.
[106] *Report of the Inquiry into the Impact of Rates on Households* (Allen), Cmnd. 2582, 1965. Wage stop questions were too numerous in this period to list. The most interesting are to be found in *H. C. Deb.*, vol. 704, cols 330–42; vol. 709, cols 17–18; vol. 707, col. 13 (written answer); vol. 708, col. 5 (written answer), vol. 709, col. 537; and vol. 713, cols 1–8.
[107] *H. C. Deb.*, vol. 704, cols 331–2.
[108] *Ibid.*, col. 336.
[109] *Ibid.*, cols 340–2.

was examining the whole problem of low-wage families.[110]

The importance of this area of concern is that it marks a change in the type of criticism levelled at the national assistance system. The way in which the NAB dealt with *family* poverty was being questioned. It was the first political fruit of the turn-around in attitudes about poverty. Throughout the fifties the NAB had been almost exclusively criticized for its handling of pensioner poverty. A wider perspective was beginning to emerge and the interests of non-pensioner claimants were being expressed with some force.

(2) The name and independent status of the NAB

Although wage stop questions were the largest single category, the name and separate identity of the NAB were also challenged on a number of occasions.[111] The 'independence' of the board was questioned because its separateness from the MPNI was felt to be a source of stigma for clients. The main demand, therefore, was for a merger with the MPNI, although one Labour MP asked in March 1966 for a larger reorganization to include the Ministry of Health.[112] By 1966 this idea had emerged as an element of Conservative policy. A merger of the NAB and the MPNI had also been promised by Labour, but only as a minor tidying-up operation within the context of the social security plan.

(3) A new role for national assistance

The most interesting speculation on the future role of national assistance came in a speech by Douglas Houghton in which he looked forward to the time when Labour had implemented its social security plans. His vision implied not only the removal of any remaining stigma, but the creation of an entirely new welfare role for the NAB.

> Whether the Board remains separate or is merged with the Ministry [MPNI] is largely a matter of administration and presentation. A good deal of work of the NAB will continue though on a greatly diminished scale. But the NAB has built up a staff with a spirit of service in the care of people which must not be lost It is the only national welfare service we have ... is there here a foundation of an agency to which any citizen could turn in time of trouble or difficulty, of sickness, bereavement, incapacity or personal plight, a service which could call upon and co-ordinate other services to meet the needs of the particular situation – in two words, the citizen's friend?[113]

[110] *H. C. Deb.*, vol. 713, cols 1–8.
[111] See *H. C. Deb.*, vol. 702, col. 72 (written answer); vol. 704, cols 332 and 342; vol. 709, cols 13–14 and 102; and vol. 713, cols 12–13.
[112] *H. C. Deb.*, vol. 725, cols 1484–5.
[113] *H. C. Deb.*, vol. 707, cols 872–3.

During this same period, November 1964, Houghton also argued that there are 'three institutions in Britain about which no hard word can be said in this House – the Crown, the Church, and the National Assistance Board'.[114] Both these references to national assistance were proved wrong in the first eighteen months of Labour government. The scale of work of the NAB was *not* greatly diminished, due to the failure to implement the policies which would remove the elderly from its ambit. Consequently its role remained basically unchanged. At the same time (and partly for this reason) the NAB, or at least the scheme it operated, came under steady criticism. The stigma of assistance in relation to the elderly was one, by now traditional, source of criticism. The principle and administration of the wage stop was the other prominent source. The elderly poor still attracted the most public sympathy, but the needs of other recipients were being publicized more fully than they had been in the late fifties and early sixties when Labour first developed its social security proposals. What effect did this have on the objectives, philosophy and content of the Social Security Act of 1966?

1966: the Social Security Bill and the abolition of national assistance
Miss Herbison summarized the main changes that were being introduced when she opened the Second Reading debate on the Social Security Bill: a new Ministry of Social Security incorporating both insurance and assistance schemes; supplementary benefits and pensions in place of national assistance payments; simplified rules governing resources; a more flexible system of application; less routine visiting of recipients and other changes in the administration of supplementary benefits; and a lay commission within the ministry to ensure 'responsiveness to human need'. The Minister claimed that these arrangements would provide a 'form of guaranteed income ... for the old and others with long-term need such as the chronic sick'.[115] Emphasis was placed on the new status of benefits. Eligible applicants would have a *right* to them; there would be an attempt to reduce stigma; and publicity would be given to the new scheme. In essence the proposals were designed to make the old assistance system more readily understandable and predictable, less conspicuously different from national insurance and, in some respects, more generous.

The Times expressed one reaction to the scheme in a leading article entitled 'Change for Change's Sake'.[116] The proposals were seen as an unnecessary fulfilment of Labour's 1955 pledge to abolish the NAB and, at the same time, unadventurous. The theme of this leading article was unduly negative. The Act changed more than just a name.

[114] *H. C. Deb.*, vol. 702, col. 1400.
[115] *H. C. Deb.*, vol. 725, col. 178.
[116] *The Times*, 17 May, 1966.

Admittedly, some developments such as the increase in the level of benefits, the improvement and rationalization of disregards and the replacement of some discretionary grants by a standard (nine shillings a week) payment to long-term recipients could have been introduced within the existing framework of national assistance. These changes were important for recipients, but they were precisely the kind of incremental improvements which can be expected in any longstanding programme. Apart from increases in benefits and some improvement in publicity, the fact is that such developments had been sorely lacking in the eighteen years of national assistance. A number of these kinds of changes filled out the package and made it a useful reform, but as *The Times* implied, they hardly amounted to a radical departure from the national assistance system.

Nevertheless, changing the name to supplementary benefits, which was at the heart of what was new in this policy, was of more fundamental importance than *The Times* suggested. It is difficult to express a change of attitude in legislation and even more difficult to ensure that it has practical effects, but this was what the reform was about. It was a belated attempt, still based on only limited knowledge of the phenomenon, to reduce the stigma that attached to assistance benefits. Apart from the changes in terminology and the promised merger of offices at field level, pensioners were also going to receive supplementary pensions through the same order book as their pension, the amount of discretion was to be reduced, and above all the language, if not the legal substance, of a right to benefit was officially recognized as appropriate to assistance. Several, not just one, of the facets of stigma were being acted on. Although the improvements were mainly aimed at the elderly, other long-term recipients stood to gain something if there was an across the board improvement in the image of the new service.

The financial cost of the scheme was quite modest by comparison with the income guarantee. The basic increase in public expenditure was only £51 million in the first full year. In addition to this the changes ought, if they were at all successful, to attract more claimants and therefore to involve subsequent and unpredictable increases. The size of these would depend on the success of the publicity given to the new benefits, on the extent to which potential clients felt that the stigma and uncertainties of making an application had been reduced, and on how many people had become newly eligible for benefit due to changes in the treatment of resources. Miss Herbison estimated, for example, that an extra 250,000 successful claimants would add £13 million to the total cost. In the event, the final cost to the Exchequer was higher than this. A net increase of 356,000 weekly payments to persons over pensionable age was recorded between October and December 1966. Nevertheless, the total cost must have been half, or less, of that which the income guarantee would have entailed. This reform of national assistance was within the expenditure limits to which the Minister was working.

The policy accorded with needs and interests in both political parties; the Bill received a smooth passage to Royal Assent. The Opposition welcomed the retention, by a Labour Government, of means-testing; it accorded with its emphasis on providing 'selective' social services. Some Conservatives evidently saw the Bill as the final chapter in Labour's opposition to means-testing. It was suggested that Miss Herbison (and other Labour Members too) had 'finally been able to exorcise the [means test] demon from her subconscious'.[117] The Opposition's response to the Bill underlined the nature of the reform. It was hailed as 'one of the most important measures which we have had or will have in this Parliament'; but there were also criticisms of the limited nature of the changes that were being made. Two wider reforms were urged on the Minister by the Conservatives in debate and in committee. The first was to extend the administrative reorganization to include the Ministry of Health. This was resisted by Miss Herbison on grounds of efficiency and size. She did not see sufficient advantages in such a change to offset the problems that would arise in a very large department.

The second proposal was more germane to the issue of assistance. The Minister was urged to place a positive duty on local officials of the new Ministry to seek out those in need of financial assistance. It echoed a demand expressed by some MPs in 1947 (during the second reading debate on the National Assistance Bill) that the NAB should be directly and legally responsible for meeting all financial need falling within the scope of its regulations. If accepted, this proposal would have had unforeseeable long-term consequences for the administration of the scheme, but in the short-run it could have strengthened the emphasis placed upon the potential client's entitlement to benefit. The possible role of a reformed national assistance system that Douglas Houghton had outlined in 1964 bore some similarities to the Conservative proposal, although the circumstances were not what Houghton had envisaged. The elderly had not been removed from national assistance and it therefore remained a large-scale service for the supplementation of insurance benefits. Because of this, and because of the comparative haste with which the policy was developed, the Bill did not introduce any immediate changes in the duties and functions of the field staff (except that it foreshadowed a substantial reduction in the amount of domiciliary visiting).

Other Conservative suggestions – notably those to establish a 'welfare inspectorate' to co-ordinate health and welfare policy and to

[117] *H. C. Deb.*, vol. 729, col. 356.

reconsider the financial needs of the disabled as a whole – were also rejected. This is not surprising for they were general rather than specific and clearly thought-out proposals. They could not have been taken seriously at this stage of the policy process. Careful consideration would have been needed before they could be presented in a form that could be implemented. The point that these proposals highlighted, however, was that the reform of national assistance had not arisen from, or produced, a wider public debate of the several issues upon which it touched. The whole range of problems confronting the elderly, the chronically sick and disabled, poor families, one-parent families and the long-term unemployed were relevant to the task of reforming national assistance. Many of these need groups would have benefited from closer study at the time. With the possible exception of family allowances, which were increased during the succeeding two years, there was little fear of delaying action on these fronts by opening them up to wider debate because there were few policy proposals in the pipeline. The unique feature of national assistance, arising from its residual function, was the number of need groups (most of them greatly neglected in research and policies) which it served. In addition its work touched on the equally unexplored problems of the co-ordination of services for these groups of people; the relationship between cash and in-kind services; patterns of referral within the social services; and the whole question not simply of stigma but the relationships between client groups, the general public and the social services.

Not all these topics could have been studied in preparation for, or in response to, the reform of national assistance. Most of them remain areas in which only limited progress has been made. But there were few signs that even the purpose, role and administration of supplementary cash benefits had been closely questioned prior to the reform. They had certainly not been publicly discussed. This raises a number of questions about the relationship between the policies incorporated in the 1966 Act and the policy process that preceded them.

V POLICIES AND PROCESSES

The history of the administration of assistance schemes by the central government illustrates a complex inter-relationship of innovative and reformative policies which can be roughly divided into two broad sequences. The first centres on a slow movement from conflict towards consensus about the administration of a centralized assistance scheme. One can, rather arbitrarily, select the creation of the Unemployment

Assistance Board in 1934 as the crucial part of this phase.[118] The sequence extended into the 1950s, but its apogee was the passing of the National Assistance Act in 1948. The second sequence reveals the gradual splintering of this consensus. The scope, role and future of national assistance were questioned and new policies were devised. By the beginning of the 1960s opposition to the contemporary operation of national assistance was quietly vehement, particularly in some quarters of the Labour Party. Although there was not the bitterness that existed in the thirties and the elderly had replaced the unemployed as the key client group, many of the old questions were being re-opened. Above all the extent and role of means-tested benefits in the social security system was being challenged and the persistence of stigma was being rediscovered.

This case study has outlined the way in which the Labour Party contributed and responded to this concern with the operation and role of national assistance. The two questions that must be asked of the party's short-term policies, which were based on the proposed income guarantee, are closely related and concentrate attention on the same features of the policy process. The first is why it was that its proposed income guarantee was a failure, and the second is whether the problem to be solved was appropriately diagnosed and defined.

A two-part answer has been provided to the first of these questions. The income guarantee was abandoned because of difficulties which arose once Labour was in power and which forced the responsible Minister to restructure the plans developed in Opposition. But the quality of that planning was also a contributory factor. The economic and administrative constraints which prevented the income guarantee being adopted have been examined in detail. The Labour Party could perhaps have been expected to have some contingency plans in the event of an economic crisis; it certainly could have been expected to anticipate the administrative problems of uniting parts of the social security and tax systems. In practice it had developed neither during its years in Opposition and had not made decisions on some of the key features of its proposed income guarantee. The consequence, as we have seen, is that national assistance was reformed on the basis of only a limited amount of data, conceptual analysis, or exploration of policy alternatives. The reform that had become necessary in 1966 had never been intended and was not a product of the detailed, long-term planning that had preceded the 1964 election.

Does this mean that the Labour Party had been concentrating upon the wrong issue during its years in Opposition? In one sense the answer must be no. The Labour planners had been anxious to get people off national assistance, not simply to change the system. This is the

---

[118] See Millett, J. D., *op. cit.*, and Briggs, E. and Deacon, A., *op. cit.*

larger issue. Their emphasis was appropriate given the weaknesses and the unpopularity of national assistance. However, in another sense, they had defined the problem incorrectly, both in terms of what eventually happened and in terms of their own stated objectives. They had for too long concentrated on the needs of the elderly to the exclusion of the rest of the poor and they had neglected the problems of the residual means-tested service that would have to continue to operate on national assistance lines. The 'rediscovery' of family poverty was spearheaded by academics working on Labour's social security plans. It was reflected in the emphasis placed during the early sixties on short-term earnings-related benefits and increases in family allowances. Again the emphasis was on the broader issue, but the neglect of national assistance as a service meant that the nature of stigma and the hazards of means-testing were not studied. There was not an adequate conceptual or empirical basis on which to devise policies to *minimize* these problems when the attempt to circumvent them was forestalled in the first years of government. The scarcity of resources in the days of Opposition planning seemed to have led to an inadequately prepared proposal for an income guarantee and a neglect of the second-order, but crucial, issues thrown up by the failings of national assistance as an income maintenance programme. How did this influence the policy-making that took place once the party was in power?

It could be argued that the reform of 1966 reflected a broader conception of the problem than that on which the party's manifesto pledges were based. The consequences for the non-pensioner clientele of separating them from the higher status group of pensioners was one consideration that influenced the 1966 policies. Similarly, the language of 'rights' and the attempt to create a more easily understood, somewhat less discretionary, system of benefits offered hope of improvement for groups other than just the elderly. Nevertheless, the Act was at best based upon hunch and good intentions. One does not have to minimize the merits of the Act or the sincerity of the desire to create a less stigmatized service to argue that the context in which the policy was developed was less than perfect. Despite the official survey of pensioners,[119] little was known about why people failed to use national assistance.

Quite apart from the priorities the Labour Party had set itself in its planning, national assistance had been a neglected service for other reasons. Parliamentary scrutiny had not been very effective, MPs' questions had highlighted a few problems but not produced a deeper understanding of the operational problems. No pressure groups had concentrated their attention upon national assistance despite the fact

---

[119] *Financial and other Circumstances of Retirement Pensioners, op. cit.*

that it had been in existence for eighteen years. The Child Poverty Action Group initially did more than any other group to broaden the poverty issue and take it beyond that of pensioners; it was later followed by claimants groups. But these developments came too late to influence the reform of national assistance. Could the planning process have operated more effectively than it did? An obvious possibility is that a longer and more public period of policy discussion may have led to the proposal and testing of a wider range of policy options and the elaboration of a much fuller understanding of key factors like stigma.

In the introduction to their book of case studies Schaffer and Corbett raise a familiar theme in public administration, the incremental nature of much decision-making.[120] Their point is that bureaucracies mainly settle for incremental change and carefully avoid the type of policy-making which involves substantial commitments. They therefore see this form of inertia, and the impetus needed to overcome it, as a key feature of the policy-making process. The reform of national assistance was certainly of an incremental kind. Was this because there had been no public debate to provide the impetus for a wider review of policy? The question is important but difficult to answer. The term 'incremental' is elusive and imprecise. It is used to refer both to decision-making *processes* and *outcomes*; in both situations it is far from value free. Although Braybrooke and Lindblom have defended the incremental approach it can easily be equated with mere conservatism.[121]

Nevertheless, the reform of national assistance could be reasonably described as an incremental policy in terms of both process and outcome. It is certainly possible that a more 'open' policy process would have produced a fundamental reappraisal of policy; a rigorous search for alternative solutions and a more radical reform. It is possible but by no means certain. The policy process which gave rise to the original Labour social security plan was equally closed, but in that instance the resulting proposals did involve major changes. The real point about 'open' phases in a policy process is that they can communicate levels of dissatisfaction with existing policies and suggest solutions to policy-makers who would otherwise remain ignorant of, or immune from, such forces. But the net effect may be to inhibit policy-makers rather than encourage them to consider radical change. Only when there is a consensus of respected or powerful opinions in

[120] Schaffer, B. B. and Corbett, D. C., *Decisions: Case Studies in Australian Administration*, Cheshire, 1966.
[121] Braybrooke and Lindblom are chiefly concerned to defend an incremental decision-making *process*. Schaffer and Corbett apply the term to decision *outcomes*. Braybrooke, D. and Lindblom, C. E., *A Strategy of Decision, op. cit.*, ch. 5.

favour of a fundamental reform which authorities are trying to resist will 'open politics' be a necessarily radical force.

By the time national assistance was reformed a body of informed and vocal opinion *was* questioning its effectiveness in dealing with the whole range of poverty that fell within its ambit. If the failure of the income guarantee and the need to do something about national assistance had led to the appointment of a committee publicly to examine the poverty problem, would this have been a more satisfactory basis for policy-making? There is little point in such speculation, except to illustrate the way in which the issues may have been differently defined and the consequences this might have had in terms of policy proposals.

The surprising feature of the policy sequence that led up to the 1966 Act is that it was contained within narrow boundaries. The elderly poor were at the centre of the stage rather than poverty itself. Means-testing in national assistance was questioned, but not the problems of means-testing throughout the social services. The assumed stigma of national assistance did not lead on to a wider debate about how clients perceive the social services. The fact that these issues were not generalized to other situations and need groups *during* the policy-making process is reflected in the resulting policies. Despite the criticisms of national assistance that found a voice during the decade before 1966, a new consensus emerged on the basis of only limited changes. The immediate break with the past was hardly dramatic and the reform was a fairly isolated policy rather than one item in a comprehensive programme of measures to deal with poverty and inequality.[122]

This outline of a case for a more open and wide-ranging discussion of policies throws the nature of the actual policy process into relief. Why did it take the form it did and did it in turn have merits? The elements of an explanation have been indicated earlier. A public discussion of poverty would have brought hostile attacks on the earnings-related pension scheme which was the cornerstone of Labour's strategy. Miss Herbison and her officials had presumably been aware of the disadvantages as well as the strengths of the income guarantee from the beginning. A solution which utilized some of the thinking that had been fed into the income guarantee, while avoiding a split between the pensioner and non-pensioner poor, certainly did not lack advocates in the ministry. Moreover, the pressure to fulfil an election pledge was considerable, both because of the priority Harold Wilson had given to it and because of the necessity of a further election (which took place in 1966). The Opposition's pursuit of the Labour Party over its broken election pledges made it virtually

---

[122] For further discussion of this feature of the story and a broader discussion of the Labour governments' record on poverty see Townsend, P. and Bosanquet, N., *op. cit.*, especially chs 2, 8, 9, 12, 13, 14 and 16.

impossible for the government publicly to re-examine its policies. Finally, the government had every opportunity to avoid the policy debate becoming a public one. Quite apart from the weakness of the client and promotional groups, there was no body of independent professionals involved in administering national assistance and the necessity of developing an alternative policy was not officially accepted until the new strategy was announced. The government could control the policy-process.

As we have seen there were many questions, obscured by the 'closed' policy process, which would have benefited from fuller study. If the pressure to act on national assistance had not been so great it should have been possible, for example, more effectively to concentrate the available resources on *the most needy old people* by a measure such as a disability allowance.[123] In this sense it does seem as if an opportunity was lost. But one can by no means assert that a wider *debate* would have produced better *policies* in the prevailing circumstances. It is certainly unlikely that it would have resulted in a greatly improved short-term strategy; time and financial resources were both in short supply in 1965-6. This, of course, is the final and perhaps crucial consideration that must be borne in mind. A different type of policy process may have considerably delayed the reform of national assistance whereas the 'closed' process harnessed administrative experience to the fundamental desire to improve the lot of poor pensioners and produced an answer quite speedily. A lot of people benefited who might not have done so, at least not for a number of years, if a more open style of government had been adopted. This has to be weighed against the fact that the Act was a product of its antecedents, it had primarily arisen because of the plight of pensioners. It could have little impact in itself on the problems faced by single-parent families, the unemployed, or other groups of low-income families whose poverty and experiences of means-tested services were even more difficult to resolve than those of the elderly.

Stigma and the 1966 Act

The concluding comment must be on the 1966 Act and its consequences for national assistance clients. Stigma is an administrative as well as a value problem and it was at the heart of the administrative reform of 1966. Has the problem diminished as a result of the reform? In terms of most dimensions of stigma the answer must be no. The stigma of declaring oneself poor remains however the administrative process of doing so is changed and however confidential the declaration. It is inherent in a means-tested service for the poorest minority which operates within a value system that strongly

---

[123] Townsend, P. and Bosanquet N., *op. cit.*, p. 283.

approves materialism, economically productive roles, and economically 'independent' families. These values have in fact been reinforced since 1966. Equally, other forms of deviance which correlate, or are *believed* to correlate, with poverty (such as unemployment, social inadequacy and even criminal intent) continue to stigmatize the service and its clientele just as they did before 1966. The concern with abuse of the system, and attempts to prevent such abuse, have noticeably grown during the past few years. This has certainly made it more likely that particular groups of clients will feel stigmatized by using the service. In 1966 a considerable effort was made to improve the detailed administration of the service and this clearly increased confidentiality for some clients. On the other hand such factors as inadequate office design are only slowly overcome, but they can make application a painfully public and embarrassing experience for many clients. Like public attitudes and the public prejudices intentionally or unwittingly reflected by officials, premises cannot be improved by a single reformative Act.[124]

The two changes which might have been expected to have had an immediate, direct and beneficial impact on stigma for all clients, were the departmental amalgamation and the new terminology of a right to benefit. The merger did end the clear distinction between contributory and supplementary social security. For the elderly in particular this was almost certainly a gain. But a firm conclusion is impossible on both these points. We possess so little information (especially relating to the years before 1966) on how far and why the Supplementary Benefits Commission's clients feel stigmatized that an opinion must be largely personal. The only firm but tangential evidence we have relates to changes in the numbers of claimants. A net increase of 356,000 weekly payments to people over pensionable age was reported between October and December 1966. The Ministry of Social Security noted that, of these, 300,000 were 'new' beneficiaries in the sense that there was no record of their having received national assistance in recent years.[125] This suggests that the elderly did feel more able to apply; the figures seem to justify the reform. Unfortunately, they reflect the effects of changes in levels of benefit, disregards and greater publicity, as well as any reduction in unwillingness to apply. Atkinson's analysis of the upward trend in applications leaves much less room for optimism. He argues that 'between a half and two-thirds of the increase between December 1965 and November 1968 ... can be attributed to the more generous assistance scale' and that 'a substantial increase would have taken place in any case if

[124] Report of the Committee on Abuse of Social Service Benefits (Fisher), Cmnd. 5228, 1973.
[125] Ministry of Social Security, *Annual Report (1966)*, Cmnd. 3338, 1967.

National Assistance had remained in force'.[126] The image of the service was not radically transformed as far as one can tell from his evidence. There are still substantial numbers of old people with an *a priori* entitlement to benefit who do not apply.

This does not mean that the changes were irrelevant; they were not. In one sense it rather points to the intractable nature of stigma and the almost equally persistent problem of ignorance (of levels of benefit, conditions of entitlement, etc.) in a low status, means-tested service. The most interesting speculation on which to end is whether the subsequent growth of client organization was stimulated by the publicity, stated intentions, and entitlement terminology of 1966. The administrative changes may have been irrelevant to this trend, but it is at least arguable that they were a contributory factor. If the policies of 1966 did encourage client militancy this was an important, though unintended, consequence. It has certainly ended the quiet obscurity into which the administration of national assistance had sunk in the mid-fifties. Though to a limited extent, clients' expectations and responses must now be considered in this as in other social services. This, rather than party policy-making or research, may be the primary force for future reform in the supplementary benefit system.

VI CONCLUSION

Four features of the policy process examined in this case study are selected and commented upon below. They are: the way in which the 'problem' was delineated and its relationship to the 'solution' that was enacted in 1966; the nature of problems of planning in Opposition: the effect of the 1964 election on policy-making; and, finally, the constraints within which the Labour government had to act between 1964 and 1966.

(1) The reform of national assistance in 1966 was a solution to a problem; but neither the problem in question, nor the solution, was what one might have expected given the long period of Labour planning for a complete restructuring of the social security system. By 1966 the Labour government was under considerable pressure to do *something* about the obvious defects of national assistance and, as has been argued, its merger of the insurance and assistance system had real merits. Nevertheless, this approach was not the product of a sustained pressure group campaign and it had been specifically denounced by

---

[126] He concludes his analysis by suggesting that the *proportion* of those eligible for benefit who claim it may have fallen since 1966. Atkinson, A. B., *op. cit.*, pp. 75–6.

Crossman while in Opposition. In fact the *reform* of national assistance was always a minor and rarely even a noteworthy feature of the Labour Party's policy during the years of Opposition. The main issue was seen to be that of reducing the *role* of the assistance system rather than changing the way it worked and was perceived by its clients and potential clients. The Labour Party was least prepared for the course of action that actually emerged in 1966 – a change in national assistance unaccompanied by a major reduction in the types and numbers of people dependent on it. Moreover, although the problem of national assistance touched on many little understood issues of social administration and despite this lack of preparation, the changes of 1966 were not preceded by public debate or much detailed research.

The case study has offered explanations for both the way in which the perception of the problem crystallized and then changed over time, and for the 'closed' nature of the policy process. One factor common to both was the absence, until the mid-sixties, of pressure groups concerned with how national assistance actually worked. During the period from 1948 (when the National Assistance Board was established) to 1966 there were demands from MPs of both parties for specific changes in regulations and procedures, but very few people felt a need to reform national assistance comprehensively. The most vociferous demand was for better pensions and the problem of national assistance was seen as an index of this need rather than as a separate issue. It was primarily within the Labour Party that the search for a new approach to social security was concentrated and although evidence on the defects of national assistance did accumulate, the origins of the 1966 policies have been traced to the Labour Party's plans, not to specific criticisms of the National Assistance Board and its work.

The dominance of pensioner poverty in the early post-war history of national assistance and the promise of earnings related benefits as a means of lifting many of the elderly, sick or unemployed out of poverty further explains why there was little discussion of national assistance problems. However, even after the Labour Party had come to power and its hopes of quickly resolving social security issues had been dashed, the policy process continued to be a 'closed' one. It is at this point that there could perhaps have been a useful 'open' phase. It was not allowed to develop because, given the failure to meet election pledges based on detailed planning in Opposition, Labour's competence and credibility were on trial. In addition a public enquiry or study of the poverty issue would have made a flexible and *ad hoc* introduction of policies impossible, while exposing the earnings-related pension scheme to hostile criticism. The Labour government succeeded in controlling the policy process (and limiting the discussion of national assistance) by denying that its original proposal of an income guarantee had fallen by the wayside until the very moment the new programme of reforms was announced. Obligingly no one forcibly argued that even the income guarantee and earnings-related pensions would leave many people dependent on assistance. There were always rather larger issues to be debated during the tumultuous period from 1964 to 1966.

(2) Labour's planning in Opposition has been criticized in this case study primarily because of the inconclusive and perhaps unsystematic exploration of the proposed income guarantee. Firm decisions were not reached on key points and the administrative complications were apparently not taken seriously enough by some members of the study group. On the other hand the study group was surely right to concentrate its resources on reshaping the national insurance system. The questions that arise are fundamental to the party system. How far do we expect the parties to plan the details of their programmes? How far do they feel that detailed planning is essential if changes in policy are to be effected speedily and with minimal deviation from their intentions? The electoral cycle provides only a limited time in which to legislate and introduce major changes in policy. A party with substantial changes in mind must therefore plan carefully or face disappointment. Does it really have a chance of doing so?

The limited capacity for planning in Opposition is partly a product of insufficient knowledge and experience of the day-to-day problems within government departments and the way which they are handled; the Opposition party is deprived of data relevant to the formulation of its own plans. This problem is particularly acute when a party has spent many years in Opposition. It can be argued that a full awareness of the administrative problems to be encountered would constrain party policy-making, but even when general principles have been agreed it can be difficult for an Opposition party to plan realistically. Additional planning resources within the parties might help them overcome some of these problems. However, it must be said that Labour's indecision on aspects of the income guarantee may have reflected fundamental differences of opinion, which more planning staff would not have resolved, as well as a lack of time to devote to the more peripheral features of the social security plan.

(3) The Open University case study raises the question of the effect of election strategy on policy-making. This case study illustrates one way in which they can be related. This relationship has three main features – the election led to an increase in the commitment to the proposed income guarantee; it revealed a divergence between the priorities of Labour's planning group and those of their leader during the heat of the election; and the promises made during the election provided a basis for Opposition criticism and thereby acted as constraints on the Labour government. It was hardly sur-

prising that Harold Wilson should highlight the short-term gains pensioners would enjoy under Labour, but in doing so he substantially increased the commitment to the income guarantee. Unfortunately for Labour it had not received the attention that its new status would have warranted, but the position had become irreversible – the Opposition did not let the commitment to the income guarantee pass from view.

(4) Although it was important, this election promise was not the only constraint on Labour's actions once it came to power in 1964. The most obvious one was the economic situation combined with the high level of public expenditure commitments into which the Conservative government had entered. This is not the appropriate place to assess the relative contributions of Conservative and Labour mismanagement of the economy to the successive crises experienced from 1964 to the end of Labour's period in office. What is clear is that these crises and the lack of economic growth together undermined Labour's programme of changes in social policy. If the previous Conservative government had been abstemious with public funds Labour's problem might have been a little easier. It would have had more room to move in reshuffling its own proposals. As it was it had to defer programmes especially in the major sectors, such as social security, where the expenditures needed to maintain *existing* services leave little room for innovation at the best of times.

However, the failure to introduce the income guarantee has not simply been explained in terms of these economic problems. A weighting of factors has been implied. It is impossible to say (at least until the official records become available) whether the income guarantee would have been considered to be financially feasible in 1964, but it has been argued that such a course *was not an administrative possibility*. Labour planning in Opposition had been sketchy and over-optimistic about the changes needed in the machinery of government if the income guarantee was to be keyed into the taxation system. Because the scheme was delayed the government produced short-term remedies which narrowed the scope of its options in the long-term. Substantial increases in flat-rate benefit in 1965 absorbed much of the extra resources available for social security.[127] The administrative costs of an innovative proposal had been the first barrier to introducing the guarantee. Its financial cost became a further reason for delay once existing benefits had been raised.

At this point the many factors in the story began to converge and point to one outcome. Because the commitment to help existing pen-

---

[127] In fact Labour did not achieve such a substantial improvement in benefits during its remaining five years in office, Atkinson, A. B., 'Inequality and Social Security' in Townsend, P. and Bosanquet, N., *op. cit.*, p. 16.

sioners escape from national assistance was high and additional evidence on the defects of national assistance was becoming available, something had to be done; if possible before the imminent election. Reforming national assistance was the obvious course and one that was anyway favoured for a number of reasons by the Minister and some of her officials. By declensions the policy process had moved from one definition of a problem which bore tangentially on the national assistance problem (fundamentally reshaping the national insurance system) to a solution which few had specifically argued for in the intervening years – a modification of the assistance system which did not immediately fit into a wider strategy for change in social security. The timetable within which the Minister worked may have resulted in a more *ad hoc* and piecemeal approach to the poverty issue than might have emerged if Labour had had a more secure parliamentary majority. But this was only one item in a series of decisions and policy situations outlined in this case study. The 1966 policies reflected the nature and context of Labour's planning in Opposition as well as the constraints and misfortunes it experienced once in power. Although not based on a momentous development in social policy this case study therefore illustrates features of the several policy arenas and processes within which British political parties operate.

PART IV

Discussion

In this section we draw together the evidence of our case studies in the form of general propositions about the circumstances in which issues attain priority.

CHAPTER FIFTEEN

Emerging Propositions

The case studies enable us to advance certain propositions about what determines the priority that an issue attains.[1] These propositions relate to two things. First, they concern the general criteria against which the claims of an issue are assessed. There are, in our view, three main ones: legitimacy, feasibility and support. Hypothetically, any issue can be scored against each of these items and its likely progress then estimated. Issues with high levels of legitimacy, feasibility and support will usually do best and vice versa. These three criteria are, of course, concepts which help to simplify, organize and understand our evidence. We do not contend that authorities consciously apply them as a necessary calculus. Nor do we wish to imply that the way they are interpreted is fixed. It is what authorities believe to be legitimate, feasible and well-supported that is important. Different governments will make different interpretations and, in this sense, the meaning of the criteria is affected by ideology.

The second things to which our propositions refer are the particular attributes of the issues themselves which determine the outcome of applying the general criteria. What is it about an issue which, for example, increases its feasibility in the eyes of authorities or is felt to erode support? How must issues be presented in order to improve their perceived legitimacy? These are the kinds of questions that we shall consider after having first discussed the notion of general criteria.

I THE GENERAL CRITERIA

Legitimacy

To determine legitimacy we must ask: is this an issue with which government considers it should be concerned? At the most general

---

[1] No word is entirely satisfactory in describing the variety of claims, bids, proposals, demands, suggestions or exhortations that 'something must be done'. We have chosen the term 'issue' to refer to all these things. It covers demands that particular problems be attended to as well as demands that particular solutions or remedies be applied.

level, how this question is answered will reflect assumptions about the proper role and sphere of government action. More specifically it is likely to vary with the ideology of the party in power and with its suppositions about what 'public opinion' or important interest groups consider the limits of State action to be. The precise nature of these limitations is rarely clear cut but it is possible and useful to think in terms of prevailing *levels* of legitimacy. At the one extreme there are those issues to which government must traditionally respond if it is to retain credibility; for example, disorder on the streets. At the other end of the scale there are those which do not even get into the hypothetical queue competing for its attention; for instance, the selection of marriage partners.

As our case studies are concerned with identifiable changes in social policy all the issues attained or were ascribed a measure of legitimacy. However, in some of them, such as family allowances and clean air, there was a comparatively low level of legitimacy early on which was only later improved by other changes. War in particular alters widespread assumptions about the legitimate spheres of government. But part of the tactical skill in strengthening the position of an issue may be in persuading government that it is indeed a legitimate (or more legitimate) candidate for attention. Conversely, of course, those wishing to play down an issue may aim to show that it is not a proper concern of government and hence, in effect, not an issue at all. For many issues the legitimacy of government intervention has already been established by precedent; for instance, in the Open University the involvement of the State in providing adult education was at no time questioned although the particular kind of provision was disputed.

The importance of so-called 'temporary' measures in times of exceptional circumstances, the initiation of experiments, or the introduction of State intervention in 'special cases' can all contribute important precedents in this matter of legitimacy. The control of private rents, first implemented in 1915 to deal with problems assumed to be of limited duration, is a good example of the way in which the temporary redefinition of the acceptable sphere of intervention created new patterns of public expectation and changed the situation in such a way that it was extremely difficult for government to revert to non-intervention.

It may also prove difficult to limit State intervention to 'special' areas or cases when circumstances change in ways which challenge the grounds for distinguishing between the special and the general or which serve to make this distinction an issue in itself. For instance, it is hard to sustain the case for the special payment of dependants' allowances or the provision of comprehensive medical care to servicemen when, through the effects of total war, that case is widely seen to apply to the population as a whole.

What is or is not considered to be a legitimate concern of government is not immutable and not everything which is legitimate gains priority. Consequently it is sometimes difficult to be sure when this factor significantly contributes to an explanation of the priority which an issue obtains. It can probably best be recognized when the opposition is conducted as a dispute about the proper limits of government. Although clean air was, and is, a difficult issue to oppose, and although in the industrial field government had exercised various pollution controls since the second half of the nineteenth century, the control of domestic smoke was openly resisted. Certainly, until 1952, and indeed for some time afterwards, this opposition argued that it was improper for government to interfere with the private citizens' preference for coal as a source of domestic heating. It was not until the predominance of domestic smoke as a cause of the London smog became widely recognized that the question of the legitimacy of government control in this sector substantially disappeared. Even so, a Conservative government pledged to reduce controls of all kinds was probably susceptible to the residual arguments about legitimacy which continued sporadically throughout the period 1952–6.

In the earlier history of the family allowances campaign the concept of legitimacy helps, in part, to explain the lack of much progress. Family allowances are a means by which the State shares with parents the financial responsibility for the maintenance of children – it is a way in which families with fathers in full-time work can be assisted financially outside the wages system. Whether or not this was a legitimate function of government remained a vexed question until the Second World War. The change can be accounted for in several ways, but essentially it occurred because, as a solution, family allowances were seen to impinge upon other issues as well, such as the management of the economy, which were indisputably the concern of the government. As a programme it became linked with 'legitimate' problems and was made more legitimate in the process.

In contrast to these two examples it is valuable to note the detention centre case study where the question of legitimacy not only does not arise but where there is an almost imperative general expectation that government should respond to the problem of rising rates of delinquency. Public order issues rarely raise disputes about whether they are the proper concern of governments, although what they actually do or should do may be fiercely contested.

Our discussion of the concept of legitimacy should not lead to the conclusion that where it is useful in explaining the progress or retardation of an issue other considerations do not underlie it. All we wish to suggest is that issues with low levels of legitimacy can be more readily opposed or resisted (for whatever reason) and that those where legitimacy is not in question do not have to overcome this particular hurdle. They are, therefore, more firmly placed in our hypothetical queue: indeed, without a modicum of legitimacy they do not enter it. These may be pertinent considerations in certain circumstances. We now discuss what these are.

Earlier we classified the changes with which our case studies were concerned as *initiation* (policies which are new departures); *development* (policies for changing the scale of an activity which already exists); and *reform* (the recasting of policies in existing spheres of involvement). We suggest that questions of legitimacy will be important when the recognition of an issue is likely to require government action in quite new areas or in radically different ways; that is, where the changes fall into our first category above. Furthermore, we suggest that this will be especially the case when the origins of the issue are extra-governmental or when the basis of opposition to it mainly rests upon questions of legitimacy. Usually, when the issue is about administrative reform or the development of existing government responsibilities this factor plays no substantial part as, for instance, in the case of the abolition of the National Assistance Board and in expanding the provision of detention centres.

However, we must note that these propositions may also be applicable to issues involving termination rather than initiation. It is possible that if the present functions of the 'welfare state' are increasingly challenged, the question of legitimacy will emerge again in spheres where it has not seriously been contested for several decades. Our case studies do not provide any instances of such situations but there are several contemporary examples which illustrate the point. Changes in policy have occurred which appear to reflect an influential view that the control of certain behaviour and relationships is no longer the legitimate concern of government: the regulation of homosexual behaviour is one. The Wootton committee struggled with another: the smoking of cannabis. It may be, therefore, that levels of legitimacy are a particularly relevant consideration in understanding the introduction or termination of policies which are concerned directly with altering existing patterns of individual freedom or responsibility. This formulation accepts that an issue may gain priority by the *reduction* of its assumed legitimacy, in which case the solution or change will involve the termination of policies rather than their initiation.

Legitimacy is a central and longstanding subject of political philosophy and it arises in all realms of government activity. However, historical accounts of the growth of the 'welfare state' are much occupied with the relationship between these developments and the establishment and enlargement of the legitimate role of government. Good reasons for this may be found in the fact that social policies are concerned with more than the regulation of social relationships.

The supply of goods and services is also involved, and on an increasingly large scale. Although regulation can only be achieved in most instances through the collective action of the State, welfare goods and services may be (and are) supplied by other systems. There are alternatives – principally the family, the market, employers, and voluntary or philanthropic bodies. It is by no means immediately apparent what, in any particular area of supply, the balance between these systems should be. Unlike matters of defence or foreign policy, in the sphere of the social services the legitimacy of State intervention has had to be established, as it were, against the claims of these other systems.

Feasibility

The concept of feasibility can be elusive. It is, nevertheless, important because the possibility (or the assumed possibility) of taking steps to deal with a problem may well determine its chances of gaining attention. Considerations of feasibility are also likely to influence the choice between several alternative solutions; and hence it can probably help us answer the question of why one remedy is introduced rather than another. There are several different elements in the notion of a 'feasible policy' which must be identified.

First, feasibility is, in its broadest sense, determined by the prevailing structure and distribution of theoretical and technical knowledge. Developments in these fields may alter quite radically the possibility of dealing with a problem which was previously considered to be an inevitable or unresolvable state of affairs. But it is important to note that neither the theory nor its application necessarily has to be correct; merely that they are generally believed to be so. There are also areas in which theoretical knowledge outstrips the ability to apply it to practical problems or where it waits upon adequate and convincing validation. As well as these aspects, new theory or growing knowledge may serve to redefine a problem in such a way that certain solutions take on a fresh relevance.

However, the general state of knowledge, understanding or technology only set the boundaries to the concept of feasibility. Our second point is more specific: it is that feasibility is not entirely independent of who does the judging. Particular ideologies, interests, prejudices and information will affect the kinds of conclusions which are drawn about the feasibility of different alternatives. In particular, actors in the policy-making process are likely to assess feasibility differently to the extent that they are aware of and are influenced by different sets of constraints. Thus there may well be several competing views about feasibility; and the progress of a proposal can be affected by how this competition is resolved.

The third noteworthy feature about feasibility is that it is rarely immediately apparent. As we pointed out earlier, much of the work undertaken by the civil service is concerned with assessing the feasibility of various courses of action or inaction. Consequences will be estimated and modifications made. We argued that this was a key phase in the progress of an issue, where considerable regulation was likely to occur. The personal accounts of both Ministers and senior civil servants bear witness to the importance of this 'testing for feasibility'.[2] Certain aspects tend to reappear in the calculations. Three in particular must be noted. They are: concern about resources, collaboration and administrative capacity.

The feasibility of a particular change in policy (or of continuing a policy unchanged) will be assessed against the resources available and those required (or released) by the change. There are various kinds of resources – money, manpower, parliamentary time, or capital equipment. Let us take the first two as examples. Money is always scarce and different items of public expenditure compete with each other. Therefore, solutions involving less rather than more expenditure will usually commend themselves and those which distribute additional costs in ways which do not concentrate them on the Exchequer will be preferred. In testing financial feasibility, however, the calculation is usually more complicated than this suggests. It is not only a matter of more or less but especially of just how much is involved now and in the future. For example, some solutions are very difficult to cost, whether in terms of the economies they achieve or the extra costs they impose. They may be open-ended either because no accurate figure can be put on the financial implications or because the emerging expenditures are not controllable by central government. To take some specific examples, we may note that the introduction of family allowances could be accurately costed and estimates of the costs in subsequent years could be made with some confidence – at least in the short-term. In any case the control of costs was firmly in the hands of central government from year to year. In contrast, the Open University could not be costed accurately. Once in operation, however, costs were broadly controllable; similarly with health centres. No government is likely to sign what amounts to a blank cheque.

The distribution of the financial costs and benefits is also likely to be pertinent when the feasibility of a scheme is being tested. For example, in the clean air study the cost of introducing control could be, and was, arranged in such a way that it was borne by the local authorities, householders, and industry as well as by the Exchequer. In the case of the health centre developments costs were, to some extent, also spread. But the health centre programme was related to

[2] See, for example, Lord Bridges, 'The Treasury as the most Political of Departments', in Friedrich, C. J. and Harris, S. E. (eds), *Public Policy*, vol. XII, 1963, Harvard.

the encouragement of community care and to a shift away from the increasingly expensive hospitals. On balance, therefore, additional expenditure on health centres could be offset against the assumed savings to be made by reducing institutional care.

What financial feasibility actually amounts to is difficult to say. It varies over time, between governments and probably between departments; but the key questions will be about amount, distribution, and longer-term implications. The importance of each of these questions is sharpened by the fact that the radical reallocation of public spending on a massive scale is, at least in the short run, itself unlikely to be judged feasible. Changes in the level and in the pattern of expenditure will occur most often at the margin.

Manpower resources are another aspect of feasibility which is likely to be assessed. Raising the school leaving age, extending the social work services, improving the take-up of supplementary benefits by seeking out potential claimants or opening more detention centres, all require more staff or their transfer from one sector to another. Just as there are limitations upon relocating the fixed capital equipment of the social services, so too there are certain restrictions upon the movement of staff. Questions about the feasibility of recruitment and training are, therefore, likely to be involved and will be especially relevant if government has undertaken, as an election promise for instance, to reduce the number of civil servants. Where, as in the case of the Open University, it may be argued that change will achieve a more economical use of scarce manpower its progress could be eased.

The clean air study provides another interesting example. If radical changes in the control of atmospheric pollution were to be achieved at least two kinds of staff had to be considered. On the industrial side efficient combustion not only depended upon good boilers but also upon the existence of stokers with sufficent skill to fire them well. The Beaver committee spent a considerable amount of time examining the problems created by the widespread lack of training for stokers and how this could be rectified quickly enough for the proposed reforms to be feasible. On the domestic side the local work involved in the implementation of new controls and in public education would have to be undertaken by smoke control officers, probably public health inspectors. But such men were in short supply and certainly the possibility of introducing key parts of the clean air programme of 1956 depended upon the practicability of increasing their number.

Certain changes in social policy not only require extra resources but also new patterns of collaboration and new levels of commitment on the part of those individuals and organizations upon whom successful implementation depends. The likelihood of obtaining the right kind and amount of collaboration will form part of the calculation of feasibility. Commonly it is the local authorities that government relies upon for putting new policies into practice. They in their turn may respond to central government proposals on the basis of their own estimations of local feasibility. The health centre study shows the extent to which both central and local government assessed feasibility against the expected and known attitudes of doctors towards working in the centres. Little progress could be made where few general practitioners were willing to participate. In the case of the Open University an essential collaborator was the BBC and, clearly, had its facilities not been forthcoming the whole project would have foundered. The processes of 'sounding out' and of 'informal approaches' are part of the exploration which is often needed in order to determine the reactions of vital collaborators in the operation of a new policy.

Tests of administrative feasibility will also be applied to proposals. Can particular schemes be implemented? Does adequate administrative capacity exist, or can it be created? In the NAB case study considerable doubt arose on these counts concerning the minimum income guarantee. Objections were, at least in part, that it could not be made to work. More recently proposals for a system of negative income tax have been confronted with similar criticisms. Two kinds of question appear to be involved in estimations of administrative feasibility. First, there are issues about authority. Certain policies may be judged not feasible because they are unenforceable. With hindsight, prohibition in the United States might so have been judged. Second, there are questions about the availability of administrative means. Does a suitable administrative organization exist? Can one be adapted? Will it become overloaded? Is the necessary up-dating, recording, selecting or identifying possible? Part of the growing opposition to selective secondary education, for example, derived not from whether selection was right or wrong in principle but from conclusions that it could not be done within a tolerable margin of error and was therefore wasteful. A similar consideration can be detected in the debates about the future of the public schools; how, in administrative terms, do you incorporate these schools in the maintained sector? Or, to take another example, how administratively, could the municipalization of privately rented accommodation actually be organized?

We do not suggest that considerations such as these about resources, collaboration, or administrative practicalities are the overriding determinants of whether it is judged feasible to embark upon new or changed social policies. Although some things are not possible before the advent of certain technical developments (for instance, the Open University and national television coverage), one suspects that issues rarely emerge until there is at least the *prospect* of practical action. The process of testing for feasibility is more often a testing for the costs of converting those prospects into reality. For example, the prevention of air pollution by cement dust is not possible without an adverse effect upon the output and price of cement, and thus upon the housing programme and the balance of payments. Authorities assess feasibility as they see it and usually within a restricted time span. In the long-run almost anything could become possible (and indeed legitimate) but, typically, feasibility is being considered as between now and, say, the election after next. Or it is bounded by the planning periods to which authorities become accustomed: in universities it would probably be the quinquennium after next.

Support

In Chapter 3 we introduced the concept of 'support' and considered how and why authorities strove to secure its regulation. We argued, following Easton, that 'diffuse support' enabled governments to act in ways which were, in any one case, damaging to the interests of some individuals, groups or classes. As Gamson explains, in discussing the similar notion of 'political trust', when 'the supply in the reservoir is high, the authorities are able to make new commitments on the basis of it and, if successful, increase such support even more. When it is low and declining, authorities may find it difficult to meet existing commitments and govern effectively'.[3] The concept of diffuse support concerns what, in everyday language, are referred to as the 'stock' or the 'credit' of a government. It locates the prevailing boundary of tolerable discontent.

None of these concepts can be applied in a precise fashion or set out in a tidy equation but authorities do make assessments of this kind. Questions about the expected acquisition or erosion of support are posed and the answers or uncertainties taken into account in drawing conclusions about political feasibility. Because policy change alters, or is thought to alter, some features of an existing distribution of power, influence, benefits, status or values, inevitably it will create some satisfaction and some discontent. The notion of the political feasibility of an issue is closely connected with its implications for this balance. Two considerations determine how it is estimated by authorities. The first is *whose* discontents and *whose* satisfactions are involved and the second is the general state of the reservoir of support.

The question of whose reactions are involved is answered in both general and specific terms, and we shall discuss each in turn. Measures which attract extensive approval will, obviously, improve a government's stock of general support. Conversely, widely unpopular policies will reduce it. However, the amount of active support or opposition

[3] *Op. cit.*, pp. 45–6.

rarely indicates their full extent. Gamson, especially, has pointed out that potential partisans (those who are affected by a policy decision) greatly outnumber the actual partisans who deliberately seek to affect its outcome. The extent of the support enjoyed, or likely to be enjoyed, by different policies cannot readily be assessed except occasionally by such means as opinion polls or referenda, and these are crude and subject to error. The degree of support that alternative governments attract is only practically tested in the elections. Despite all these difficulties estimations are made of the state, or likely reaction, of public opinion to different issues and endeavours are made to modify it. Although what 'public' feeling actually is about an issue can rarely be determined empirically, what it is *thought* to be by authorities is more important in the short-term.

In spite of the elusiveness of the notion of public opinion it does serve as a means of applying one test of support. Since all governments must pay some attention to the likely effect of their actions upon general levels of support or acquiescence some such concept is needed. This is not to say that all issues are examined against this yardstick or that only those which are thought not to jeopardize general support gain prominence. But, hypothetically, some kind of ledger has to be kept by government in order that the overall or cumulative effect of many different decisions can be estimated. In the clean air case study, for example, the delay in government action and the obvious reluctance to respond to the situation created by the London smog must be viewed against a general belief on the part of the government that support was to be won by reducing the extent and variety of statutory controls. In the NAB study the Labour government's policy was affected by the belief that a reduced dependence on means tests would be widely welcomed. Assumptions about the pervasiveness of certain public values and beliefs are moulded by the values and beliefs of those who do the judging, as well as by the sources from which they obtain their information. Furthermore, the attitudes of their significant constituencies are likely to be generalized to the population as a whole.

So far, we have looked at the question of whose satisfactions and discontents enter into the calculus of support only in connection with a broadly conceived public opinion or response. But the sensitivity of an electoral group's support for a project may depend not so much on whether it likes it, or the government, as on the marginality of the issue and the group. Will they change sides at the election – and on this issue? Indeed, the language of electoral analysis includes frequent reference to marginal voters and marginal constituencies.

Electoral support is, of course, rarely the only consideration. Particular sets of interests and interest groups are involed in specific policy proposals or changes. They may include other departments, backbenchers, industrial organizations, the trade unions, local authorities, promotional groups and so on. How much a group's support is assumed to matter will vary with the issue as well as with the general level of support accorded by that group to the relevant authority. How seriously these consequences are regarded will depend upon the extent to which the future or continuing collaboration of the body in question is felt to be necessary in general or for the operation of particular policies. The generalized discontent of groups which control certain key resources will be avoided where possible. The level of a government's standing with such bodies will affect how far it is prepared to antagonize them on any one issue and whether, in turn, they mobilize and exercise their potential influence in Opposition.

Since the case studies are all concerned with actual changes in social policies, they satisfied, as it were, the criterion of support. Nonetheless, as we have already suggested, in some of them an initial absence of progress can be related to assumptions about the implications of action (or inaction) for support. Considerations of general support also appear to influence the kind of solution adopted in response to a particular problem. In the detention centre study, for example, it was suggested that the public were seen to be unsympathetic and sceptical towards the abandonment of corporal punishment. Certainly this was the picture portrayed by the mass media. More crimes of violence as well as a general rise in crime rates did nothing to alleviate such misgivings. In these circumstances it was difficult to remove a supposedly deterrent form of penal 'treatment' without putting in its place something which could at least be presented as a tough deterrent alternative. A shift in the attitude of important partisan groups towards certain issues may alter the support implication of related policy decisions. Evidence about such changes is likely to be influential. In the health centres case the commitment of central government to the development followed the local demonstrations that there were general practitioners willing to collaborate.

At the beginning of this section we maintained that two considerations affected a government's evaluation of the support implications of any courses of action. We have, so far, discussed only one of these; namely, the question of whose discontents and whose satisfactions are involved. The other consideration concerns the assumed general state of a government's support or credit. This will vary over time. It will ebb and flow, be consumed and be replenished. Its particular level and trend will create somewhat different constraints and opportunities. Broadly, issues which authorities feel will affect support adversely are better placed at times when this support is high or rising and weakly placed when it is low or falling. These considerations will apply with especial force when general elections are impending, since only then is this level actually tested. As the NAB study suggests, there was more pressure upon the Conservative government to respond to new evidence about the extent of poverty amongst the old prior to the 1964 election than there would have been at an earlier period in its administration; and Labour felt obliged to find an alternative to the minimum income guarantee before it went to the polls in 1966.

Our contention that the criterion of support is, explicitly or implicitly, applied to all issues in the process of determining their priority should not obscure the fact that issues do advance despite scoring low, or even negatively, on this scale. Capital punishment was abolished; homosexual law reformed and health service charges introduced. In almost all circumstances government finds itself in a position in which its actions have mixed consequences for support. There are some potential gains and some losses: trade-offs are assessed and the effects of cancelling out taken into account. Perhaps we should refer to the net implications for support of a government promoting or ignoring an issue. We should also consider the comparatively short time perspective within which such calculations seem to be made. But in whichever way reference to the support criterion is qualified we contend that it constitutes a permanent and initial hurdle for all issues.

II ISSUE CHARACTERISTICS

So far, we have argued that there are aspects of our political system which, in general terms, help to explain the formation and progress of issues. In particular we have utilized the concepts of legitimacy, feasibility and support and regarded them as criteria against which issues are broadly assessed. In theory any issue can be located at a point upon each of these continua. However, drawing upon the evidence of our case studies, there appear to be factors affecting the overall 'image' of an issue which more specifically influence its fortunes within the context of the general considerations which we have discussed.[4] It is to these more particular characteristics which we now turn.

Association and scope

Few issues remain unrelated to others. One problem is linked with another and one solution overlaps another. In particular, problems and solutions are continually being matched and associated. Any one issue tends, therefore, to form part of a pattern of issues. The manipulation of these relationships is an important political tactic,

[4] For an interesting discussion of the notion of images in politics see Boulding, K. E., *The Image*, University of Michigan Press, 1966, especially ch. VII.

but whether deliberately arranged or not, the design of this pattern will exert a considerable influence upon the individual priorities of the issues within it.[5] Successful pressure group activity, for instance, is often the result of an ability or an opportunity to present a particular issue together with or separate from certain other issues. The way issues are related is, moreover, likely to reflect alliances. An interest group may try to fuse certain issues in an attempt to win allies, or it may strive to keep them apart to avoid unwanted ones.

Whether or not an association or convergence of issues advances or retards them individually or collectively is not a question which can be answered without examining the particular circumstances of the case. Sometimes an issue may achieve and retain priority because it remains in isolation. Alternatively, issues may rely upon their relationship with others to carry them forward. Our cases provide examples of the development of social policies where both the association of issues and their separation appear to have been substantial features of the political process. The first situation is illustrated in the family allowances study and the second in the creation of the Open University.

The problems to which family allowances were related before the last war varied, but were largely 'weak' issues as far as government was concerned. The early members of the Family Endowment Society saw family allowances as concerned with problems about the status of women; as a means of removing certain obstacles to equal pay by meeting various family responsibilities outside the wage system; and as a way of combatting family poverty. During the 1920s their earlier concern with the issue of a declining birth rate (particularly amongst the middle classes) was tempered by the emerging fear of over-population. By the latter part of the 1930s fears of a declining population had reversed this position. There were, for instance, a million fewer children in 1940 than in 1930, a situation considered serious by those concerned with our trading and military potential. In particular, Germany was introducing pro-natalist policies. Thus, by the end of the 1930s family allowances were positively associated with at least one 'strong' issue; namely the decline in population. They were also advocated as a means of ameliorating the considerable

---

[5] This assumption formed an important theme in some of the more perceptive general studies of British social policy. Take for example this passage about the reforms of 1906–14 in Ford, P., *Social Theory and Social Practice* (Irish University Press, 1968). They 'were thus brought about by an unusual conjunction of forces by no means always found working together – a wide variety of opinion at once critical and constructive, an insistence on new ethical standards in social matters, the increase of knowledge and theoretical advance, the creation of a bureaucracy at once sympathetic and dynamic, able to devise new institutions and practices needed for their operation; and the resolution of the deadlock in one of the great political parties' (p. 131).

poverty and malnutrition, primarily amongst children, revealed by the inter-war surveys; but poverty, as an issue, was confused by the effects of widespread unemployment.

During the war years, partly through the work and special position of Beveridge, Keynes and Henderson, family allowances became connected with other issues as well. In particular they were seen by government as relevant to the problems of less eligibility in the proposed new system of social security and, most important of all, to the management of the economy, especially the control of inflation and demands for wage increases. Indeed, the close relationship of family allowances to wages policy largely explains their tardy acceptance by the TUC.

After their introduction family allowances were mainly associated with concern for reducing poverty and maintaining the birth rate. But by the late 1950s it was recognized that the population trend had again changed and the spectre of over-population reappeared. Poverty was widely considered to have been abolished among the employed and their families. Women's increased participation in the labour force, particularly married women, supplemented many family incomes and secured an increasing number of women an economic status of their own. Family allowances became completely separated from considerations of equal pay.

Thus during the war years, family allowances became relevant to an increasing number of issues. Government attached high priority to some of these, economic problems in particular. Had these convergences not occurred it is possible that family allowances would not have received priority in the government's programme. After the war the set of issues to which family allowances had been related weakened. Significantly, they attracted less and less attention. There were only two modest increases in the allowances in almost twenty years, although their real value was severely eroded and other social security benefits were increased at fairly regular intervals.

The case of the Open University provides an example of an opposite situation in which the isolation of an issue partly accounted for its successful inauguration against apparently considerable odds. The proposal was entirely pertinent to the general problems arising in higher education during the early sixties. It might have been expected that it would be considered and treated together with these. In fact this did not happen. Jenny Lee assumed special responsibility for its development and it was kept as separate as possible for as long as possible. Had this degree of insulation not been achieved then the Open University would probably have failed to survive in the highly competitive situation in which it would otherwise have been located. Of course, there were also convergences in this case, particularly where a solution (a TV university) became technically feasible at roughly the same time that the pressure built up for the expansion of higher education Moreover, Harold Wilson deployed a number of overlapping arguments to support his ideas; namely that there would be technological, economic, egalitarian and political advantages to be gained from establishing an Open University. However, although important in explaining the inception of the idea these were secondary factors in explaining its survival.

The case studies led us to consider *why* the association or disassociation of issues may be relevant in explaining the development of social policies. One reason can be found in their relationship to the scope of the conflict which surrounds an issue. We found the work of Schattschneider of value in developing this line of thought. He advances two main propositions early in his study entitled *The Semi-Sovereign People*. He writes that 'at the nub of politics are, first, the way in which the public participates in the spread of the conflict and, second, the processes by which the unstable relation of the public to the conflict is controlled'. In consequence, he argues that 'the most important strategy of politics is concerned with the *scope* of conflict. So great is the change in the nature of any conflict likely to be as a consequence of the widening involvement of people in it that the original participants are apt to lose control ...'[6]

How issues are separated or brought together has a profound bearing upon the control and determination of the scope of the conflict about them. Different individuals and groups will judge differently the advantages or disadvantages of either limiting or extending this. Sometimes events alter the capacity of participants to exercise control over the scope of an issue (the London smog and clean air, for instance). Yet, despite this, the ability to influence the scope or determine the arenas in which an issue is debated and assessed, is a component of political power. It is, for instance, this potential capacity and the manner of its utilization which constitute an important feature of the power of the mass media.

In general we suggest that a strategy of *limitation* will be preferred by those who advance controversial issues from existing positions of strength, usually within or close to government. In contrast, groups or individuals who are, or feel themselves to be, pursuing popular issues from initial positions of weakness may find their influence enhanced by strategies of *extension*. Where an issue is unwelcome and embarrassing to government the threat of extension may be enough to gain it priority.

Another reason why the association of issues is relevant to the pattern of policy development may be found in the concept of demand reduction by 'collection and combination' which Easton has sug-

[6] Schattscheneider, E. E., *The Semi-Sovereign People*, Holt, Reinhart & Winston, 1960, p. 3 (our italics).

gested.[7] Amongst other things the various gatekeepers of a political system are engaged in tasks of 'economizing' since, whatever the will, few issues can pass through the net. Sometimes their jobs are defined quite clearly in these terms, in other cases they are not. But it is likely that of any two issues seeking attention, that which eases the process of 'economizing' will be preferred to that which disrupts it. Hence, a solution or policy proposal which appears to solve more than one pressing problem will be in a stronger position than one which has only a narrow application. Likewise problems which lend themselves to treatment in existing programmes, or by existing administrative machinery and technologies are likely to make better progress than those which require the creation of quite new agencies or ways of working. It may be illuminating to conceive government response to issues as based upon an economy of remedies; that is, upon the convergence of general issues to which a single solution may be applied.[8]

This would suggest that there is a complicated relationship between problems and solutions which is in itself one of the important explanations of why certain policies emerge. Logically, the identification and analysis of a problem precedes proposals for a remedy, but in reality the sequence is less tidy. Solutions may become detached from the problems which originally prompted them; one problem may elicit several solutions and one solution, as we have pointed out, may bear upon more than one problem. The very fact that remedies are attractive and available may advance the priority of certain problems to which they can be applied. On the other hand, new and pressing problems may rekindle interest in solutions previously rejected or placed in cold storage. Although we have used the term 'issues' for demands that steps be taken to deal with problems (such as homelessness or the rising cost of living) as well as for demands that particular solutions be adopted (for instance, abortion law reform, nuclear disarmament or metrication) the question of association cannot be fully explored unless we bear in mind this difference. It was when health centres, as a solution, became relevant to new kinds of problems arising in the organization of general practice that they began to develop. The possibility of amalgamating the MPNI and the NAB was rejected on grounds of administrative tidiness alone but accepted later when it formed part of the solution to other problems faced by the Labour government. Thus, our propositions about the association of issues must be understood also to apply to the interrelationships between problems and solutions.

We have suggested that the combination or convergence of issues

[7] See p. 25.
[8] See Parker, R. A., 'Social Ills and Public Remedies', in *Man and the Social Sciences*, ed. Robson, W. A., LSE – Allen & Unwin, 1972, pp. 122–3.

can, under certain circumstances, enhance the chances of each receiving attention. There is, however, probably a limit to this possibility which is approached when, by amalgamation and juxtaposing, several issues move from the realm of the specific to that of the general. Sets of issues which are brought together to form a broad radical programme will be open-ended and hence not easily regulated. Of course, the question of why the prospects of comprehensive social policy changes should be poor in our political system can be answered in several other ways as well. For example, it may be explained from the standpoint of a pluralist interpretation which emphasizes the diversification of power and commitment, or in terms of such related theories as 'disjointed incrementalism' developed by analysts like Braybrooke and Lindblom. The latter stress that 'only policies are considered whose known or expected consequences differ incrementally from the status quo'.[9] Alternatively, if one prefers the class model of contemporary politics and assumes a concentration of economic power inimical to radical social policies, this too may explain the poor chances of comprehensive issues or programmes gaining priority.[10] Whichever approach is adopted, however, the implications seen similar: beyond a certain point an individual issue's chances will probably be reduced by amalgamation.

In summary then, the case studies suggest that the relationship between issues is of considerable importance in understanding changes in social policies. Since, in reality, such associations often transcend the conventional administrative or political boundaries which are used to classify issues, the study of social policy formation cannot be restricted to the social services alone. For example, it may be precisely because social policy issues are considered together with (or as if they were) economic policy issues that accounts for the attention they receive and for their subsequent progress.

We suggest that the association or separation of issues is important for at least three reasons.
  (i) It can modify the legitimacy of one issue by linking it with or divorcing it from issues with different levels of legitimacy.
 (ii) It is closely related to the process of demand regulation; that is, to the process of seeking an economy of remedies. In this it affects the calculus of feasibility.
(iii) It provides a means of influencing the scope of disputation about an issue: this is likely to bear upon levels of political support and discontent and to affect the alignment of interests.

[9] Braybrooke, D. and Lindblom, C. E., *A Strategy of Decision*, Free Press, 1963, p. 85.
[10] See Miliband, R., *op. cit.*

Crises

Students of social policy have been inclined to accord a special place to crises in their analyses and explanations. Myrdal, for example, writing more generally about the extension of state interventions, claims that 'all the time new measures were introduced *ad hoc*, to serve limited and temporary purposes, to safeguard special interests, and often to meet an immediate emergency of one sort or another'. He continues that 'new intervention was usually not only motivated by special circumstances – a particular need, an emergency or a pending crisis – but also designed accordingly, as limited and often temporary measures'.[11] These propelling crises and emergencies he sets upon an international scene, placing special emphasis on the 'unending upheavals in international relations, beginning with the First World War' and the effects upon all nations of 'successive and cumulative waves of violent economic crises'.[12]

Certainly, both war and cold war, as dramatic examples of international crises, have affected the development of social policy. Titmuss has documented and discussed some of the effects and consequences of the Second World War.[13] The impact of the 1914–18 war on social policy remains to be studied in as much detail. The influence of Korea, the cold war or Vietnam also lack systematic study, although their importance is probably considerable. For example, to understand the introduction of health service charges by the Labour government in 1951 it must be placed in the context of massive defence expenditures connected with the Korean war and their repercussions upon other spheres of public spending.

Likewise, as we have previously argued, the repeated economic crises faced by this country have left an indelible imprint upon social provision and policy, the most massive probably being the years of depression between the wars. Perhaps of even greater significance has been the assumption, since the last war, that the management of the economy was a feasible and overriding responsibility of government, and that the modification of expenditures on public social services was one of the tools of management. This assumption has, in effect, forged a close link between social policy and even the smaller domestic economic crises. But economic crises and war are mainly examples on a large scale. Our case studies provide less global instances of the effect of crises on social policy development.

The concept of crisis is useful in accounting for the relatively sudden and prominent attention paid by government to certain issues. Crises are urgent situations which demand a response from government and sometimes to government; issues, that is, which cannot

---

[11] Myrdal, G., *Beyond the Welfare State*, Duckworth, 1960, p. 13.
[12] *Op. cit.*, p. 15.
[13] Titmuss, R. M., *Problems of Social Policy*, HMSO, 1950.

be ignored or deferred without jeopardizing a government's credibility or even, in extreme situations, its chances of survival. As Coral Bell writes with regard to international relations, 'the essence of true crisis in any given relationship is that the conflicts within it rise to a level which threatens to transform the nature of the relationship. In adversary crisis it is from peace to war; in intramural crisis it is from alliance to rupture.'[14]

Different governments, and in particular the two parties, will have somewhat different structures of credibility to maintain and different alliances endangered by rupture. Hence, what is a crisis for one may not be a crisis for the other. Similarly, what is a crisis for the BMA is not usually a crisis for the NUT.

Typically, crises arise from episodes or events, like specific disasters or public scandals, which require an unqualified and immediate commitment to *some* kind of action.[15] But they may also be generated by the redefinition or discovery of existing situations, such as the Cole and Utting research in the NAB study, or by the identification of an emerging trend as with delinquency in the case of detention centres. Histories of social policy usually provide a number of examples of crises. In the post-war period there is the death of Dennis O'Neill in a foster home and, more recently, the incidents at several mental sub-normality hospitals. Sir Keith Joseph probably had these in mind when, speaking at a conference of the National Association for Mental Health, he said: 'I must tell you that one day ... somebody will write a book ... about the part that scandal has to play in procuring reform.'[16]

Whether or not an issue assumes the character of a crisis will depend upon many factors apart from what actually happened or is happening. It is, for instance, noteworthy that a child died in a foster home in 1936 in circumstances similar to those of the O'Neill case eight years later. The earlier tragedy made little if any impact upon the development or reform of child care policy. Neither did deaths which occurred later. Similarly, although our study of clean air demonstrates the central importance of the London smog crisis of 1952, it must be remembered that it was by no means the first such incident. There had been killer London smogs before and these had not led to any noticeable progress in the control of atmospheric pollution. Thus, it is important to try to identify those general factors which help to make a potential crisis into an actuality.

[14] Bell, C., *The Conventions of Crisis: A Study in Diplomatic Management*, Oxford University Press, 1971, p. 9.
[15] See Paige, *Korean Crisis, op. cit.* He stresses the threat to values and the lack of time to respond as characteristically related to the idea of crisis.
[16] *Minds Matter*, Annual Conference Report, National Association for Mental Health, 1971, p. 39.

Timing is one element. An event may provoke a crisis a month before a general election but not if it occurs soon afterwards. It may demand a political response if it follows close in the wake of similar events but not if it happens in apparent isolation. Prevailing patterns of public concern also vary over time and whether, for instance, a catastrophe occurs in a climate of general indifference or one of existing keen interest and concern will influence how it is treated.

Another factor which seems of the utmost importance in translating a potential into an actual crisis is the availability and distribution of information about it. For a situation to become a crisis it has to be known about. A hushed up situation remains a potential crisis, even though it may have far reaching consequences. The mass media obviously contribute to the process of publicity but, equally the activity of pressure groups in advertising and providing facts is one of the ways in which potential crises can be exploited. Indeed, such activities may be essential if the matter is to be dealt with forcefully in the press or television. It should not be concluded, however, that the partisans have a monopoly in the political exploitation of situations of scandal or catastrophe. A Minister may, for instance, utilize the opportunity presented by such events to take action in response to the crisis which has developed. Opposition from within the Cabinet or from strong interest groups may thereby be counteracted and reduced. One suspects, for example, that something rather like this occurred in the case of the Court Lees Approved School; the Home Secretary making this a reason for the initiation of certain difficult reforms in the Approved School system. Sir Keith Joseph also said at the NAMH conference already mentioned that '*the sudden revelation of conditions*, well known to the experts, of which the public is unaware gives Ministers a chance to galvanize their colleagues and get the resources to improve things'.[17]

Yet another factor in determining whether a particular event or situation becomes a crisis is likely to be the generally assumed feasibility of the government actually taking any kind of relevant action. This will depend upon precedent, popular expectation, or technology – in short, upon the ability of the government to alter, prevent or learn about what has happened. In this respect a scandal or catastrophe in areas where there is an existing and well established public responsibility for providing services or exercising control is likely to lead to a more immediate and unqualified response than those in spheres where there is no such responsibility. In these latter situations questions of legitimacy, the creation of relevant administrative machinery or the acquisition of expertise and knowledge may all have to be resolved before action is realistically possible.

[17] *Op. cit.*, p. 39 (our italics).

Given these kinds of determining factors there are broadly two ways in which political crises may arise. They may be spontaneous like the London smog, or they may be engineered. The Child Poverty Action Group's campaign for higher family allowances after the publication of Townsend and Abel-Smith's *The Poor and the Poorest* is the kind of engineered crisis by which pressure groups sometimes endeavour to force their issue into greater prominence. This is not to assume, however, that an engineered crisis abandons an empirical basis although, as in the case of the film *Cathy Come Home*, a dramatic presentation may contribute to a sense of crisis; in that instance about homelessness.

The actions arising from the perception of a crisis situation may not lead directly to changes in social policy. An enquiry may be promised or set afoot; heads may roll or ranks be closed. But *prima facie* the existence of a crisis will often accelerate or initiate policy changes. Whether it does so or not is likely to depend upon the general attitude of government (or the Minister) towards the issues involved. More particularly, whether it falls into an existing area of public responsibility will be crucial and so will be the ability of partisans to exploit the opportunities such situations present.

Some of our case studies illustrate the propositions about crises that we have put forward, the clean air developments in particular. The role played by the catastrophic London smog of 1952 in achiev-ing the first effective clean air legislation is undoubtedly considerable. It was not unique and it could be expected to happen again with no less severity. There was a well-informed pressure group (NSAS) of long standing, broadly based in its membership and independent. They, together with the press once it had realized what had actually hap-pened, kept the issue alive, as did regular questions in Parliament. It was a catastrophe which was gradually understood as man-made and not a natural phenomenon. It was not a situation, however, which would respond to private actions; the dangers could only be reduced by a more widespread public intervention. This hardly existed at the time.

Thus the smog was a warning of crisis dimensions which, it would be imagined, no government could ignore. However, the newly elected Conservative government was anxious to reduce the areas of govern-ment regulation after years of austerity and the widespread public control of many aspects of life. There was, furthermore, no one estab-lished department or section of government with experience in these problems. What responsibility there was divided between the newly-separated Ministry of Health and Ministry of Housing and Local Government at the national level and many councils at the local level. Nor was it immediately apparent that a ready solution was to hand – coal was in short supply but so too were oil, electricity, solid smokeless fuels and, to some extent, gas. The patterns of political interest and the various strengths and weaknesses of the groups involved were largely untested. For these, and possibly other reasons, the government was reluctant to act, and for several months after the event adopted a defensive attitude and only tardily set up the Beaver Committee.

The important reason why the smog catastrophe was influential was not that it happened, but that in circumstances in which speedy and effective government action was by no means assured, the issue was kept alive. It was sustained by the work of the well-prepared NSAS; later by the Beaver Committee itself (note the importance and effect of the quick interim report), and to some extent by the press. But it was also an eminently sustainable issue because of the clear threat of repetition and escalation and because it became plain, with the help of the evidence assembled by the Beaver Committee, that it could be prevented or at least mitigated. Also it might affect almost anyone in contrast to, say, the O'Neill tragedy, which was of a sort that few could envisage happening to them or their children.

In summary the generalizations which may help us to understand the effect of crises upon policy development are these. First, given the relative nature of crisis situations at different times and for different governments, they represent an opportunity for change and the re-ordering of priorities. It is their assumed urgency which is important, for this short-circuits many of the processes of issue regulation which we have previously discussed. Second, the extent to which these opportunities are realized will depend upon the ability of partisans or the willingness of authorities to exploit the situations created. Third, there will be important differences in a government's response depending upon their existing involvement in the area concerned and upon the level of legitimacy. In a crisis a quick response is required. This becomes more possible the greater the existing responsibility and preparedness. A careful assessment and search for potential solutions takes time, more or less depending upon the extent to which the research and intelligence functions within government or elsewhere are already organized around the issue in question.

Crises certainly appear to have played a particular role in the initiation, development and reform of social policies, possibly more so than in many other fields. If this is the case, and it is difficult to prove, there may be two kinds of explanation. One is to be found in the nature of many of the social services. They are frequently concerned with the individualization of treatment, control or benefit; that is, with the provision of services to identifiable individuals and families in ways which involve the exercise of administrative and professional discretion at the point of supply. There is a risk therefore that some bad decisions will be made and some bad practices develop.

Moreover, many of the situations contain a high level of what might be termed 'social risk'; for example, the placement of deprived children in foster homes or for adoption; gathering together numerous mentally sub-normal adults in residential premises; or treating offenders in the open community or, for that matter, keeping them together in closed prisons.

Thus there are real and particular risks in this field. Equally important, however, is the fact that it is possible for an individual MP, interest group or others to pursue 'scandalous cases', especially where the young, old or sick are involved. A high degree of technical or legal knowledge is not usually required and 'sensations' are, moreover, eminently newsworthy. In these fields the authorities are vulnerable to the discovery of case scandals. It is interesting to note the extent to which, in the background discussion to the NAB study, governments at various times endeavoured to protect the Ministers from having to assume direct responsibility for questions about individual cases by the creation of semi-independent boards or commissions.

The second possible explanation for any special influence that crises exert on social policy is simply one of scale. About half of all public expenditure is devoted to the social services. Almost every member of society is in contact with them at some time and they account for a major proportion of all employees of the State. The likelihood of crisis will be greater the larger the scale of collective social provision.

The origins of changes in social policies may involve crises more often than other areas of public policy for reasons like these. We would, however, repeat our earlier contention that it is in existing areas of government commitment that crises (as we have defined them) are more likely to occur and lead to social policy change. Outside these spheres the scale, intensity, or public impact of events or situations will have to be greater in order to effect change, since it will often require new departures in collective social action and call for the reappraisal of ideas about legitimacy.

Trend expectation and prevention
There are obviously some issues which, if not attended to, will become more acute and more urgent; they are expected to be cumulative and progressive. There are others which do not have this characteristic. When a situation is likely to degenerate, action may be taken not because it is yet a crisis but as an insurance, as it were, against this happening.

It is for this reason that the identification of trends and the formulation of convincing predictions is a relevant aspect of the process of social policy development. We suggest that issues which can be shown to be growing more pressing can gain priority *before* a crisis is reached, as a form of prevention. Certainly they will obtain more attention than problems which are thought to be static or considered susceptible to spontaneous remission.

Our case studies provide several examples of the influence of trend expectations. In the development of detention centres it was not only the fact that the criminal statistics showed a rise in delinquency amongst the young but that this trend was assumed to reveal a prospect of a future deterioration. Moreover, more young offenders were believed to mean more adult offenders. These expectations posed two questions. One was what steps could or should be taken to check the trend and, preferably, reverse it; the other was how the additional offenders were to be dealt with should this prove impracticable. The development of detention centres was seen to be relevant to both these problems and provides another example of the convergencies which we discussed earlier.

Population forecasts played an important part in the family allowances case study, with trends at one time indicating that decline was likely to reach 'crisis proportions' and, at other times, that growth loomed as an ominous threat. Unlike trends in public order (or disorder), government is likely to view a shift of the birth rate in *either* direction as potentially critical. In the case of the Open University as well, demographic changes led to assumptions about a rising demand for higher and further education.

There are numerous other examples in which forecasts about future trends appear to have prompted action to prevent or prepare for what was thought to be in store. Titmuss has shown, for example, how expectations about the scale of the civilian casualties which would be caused by air raids was one of the crucial factors in the establishment of the Emergency Medical Service at the beginning of the last war. The fact that the number of casualties was, in the event, considerably overestimated shows the importance of what was *believed*. The forecasts which authorities accept will partly be determined by the assumed reliability of the source. Where expert predictions are at variance action is less likely. One of the means whereby the effect of forecasts can be counteracted is for partisans or authorities to demonstrate the credibility of alternative conclusions. The longer term the forecasts the more possible this becomes.

In the same way that authoritative forecasts about aspects of population, health or public order are likely to influence their present priority, so too predictions about the pattern of development of existing policies will influence whether or not their reform is thought necessary. In particular, estimates of rising costs may be regarded as issues in themselves. The health centre developments were influenced by the expected further increases in the costs of hospital care. The first scheme for graduated social security contributions and pensions was introduced in 1959 primarily to forestall the steeply rising costs to the Exchequer forecast by the government actuary on the basis of emerging changes in the age structure of the population.

So far we have suggested that it is forecasts and expectations of deteriorating situations, especially in spheres where government is already involved, which are likely to bring certain issues into prominence. But, as the earlier history of detention centres illustrates, an 'improving' trend may enable different kinds of solutions to a problem to be adopted. When, in the 1920s, crime rates amongst the young were falling, less deterrent alternatives to short-term imprisonment could be considered more readily than when, subsequently, rates were following an upward course. It may be that contentious policies will be more readily introduced when, in a specific area, improvement is assumed to be occurring and continuing.

Thus, we would argue that the presumed location of an issue in relation to a relevant trend is a factor which helps to explain its priority. On the one hand, when matters are considered to be getting worse, and threaten a crisis, policies which can be viewed as precautionary or preventive will gain ground. This will apply with special force when the deterioration occurs in a sphere of existing government responsibility; when the forecasts are authoritative and not in dispute; and when the time span is short rather than long. On the other hand, when the relevant trend is improving this may give government the opportunity to introduce changes which, when the situation was reversed, it considered impossible without endangering support. This will mainly arise in connection with government issues; that is, issues emanating from the party in power or from the departments. If government has no enthusiasm for an issue an apparently improving situation will hardly be conducive to securing change. Support is not in jeopardy.

Origin

Issues do not arise spontaneously. They are formulated by particular groups or individuals. This is true of both 'problems' and 'solutions'. Hence, it is important to know whose issue it is or is seen to be.

There is a difference between the progress of those issues which government (and we include here the civil service) formulate and raise themselves and those originating outside the government system. This is demonstrated quite clearly in comparing the Open University and the clean air case studies. Pressure groups (although they existed) were of little importance in the former case since interest in the idea was generated mainly within the government party. Throughout its development the Open University also received crucial support from the Prime Minister. The case for clean air made slow progress despite otherwise favourable circumstances partly because, at that time, it was neither a politician's nor an administrator's issue.

The notion of 'opposition issues' also seems appropriate in helping to explain the events in some of the case studies. One of the reasons why health centres obtained little encouragement from successive Conservative governments was probably because proposals for such centres had a longstanding association with socialist ideas about the organization of medical services. When issues are closely identified with one of the political parties this obviously assists them when that party is in power but obstructs them when it is in Opposition. Even though a particular social problem may be accorded similar priority by both parties there will almost certainly be disagreement about the appropriate solution. In many instances this springs from different assumptions about its cause and nature as well as ideological commitment to certain kinds of remedies.

Where an issue constitutes a challenge to a government's competence *and* is advanced from 'outside', its recognition is likely to be resisted or ignored. In these circumstances other factors (irrefutable evidence or crises) will have to be particularly favourable if the issue is to make progress. Where issues arise out of the administration of existing policies or programmes whether it is an administrator's issue or a critic's issue will affect the outcome. Indeed, when a critic's issue threatens to become inescapable there seems to be a tendency for it to be annexed by the administration. In the NAB study the government's decision to undertake its *own* study of the financial circumstances of old people following upon the publication of the Cole and Utting findings is a case in point.

We do not contend that only issues originating in or close to government gain priority, for this is patently not so. Issues of keen interest and concern to a Minister can be blocked or diverted by his Cabinet colleagues and pressure groups do win victories. But *prima facie* the closer to government the point of origin the better the prospects. There are several reasons why this should be.

First, in broad terms any government has a programme which represents its preferred priorities. Certain issues are preselected and the likelihood of their receiving attention will, therefore, be considerable. Second, no such programme, however detailed, will remain unaltered. Modifications will have to be made in light of new circumstances or unforeseen difficulties. Nevertheless, a government will strive to retain as much control over the reordering of priorities as possible. Only in this way can the main features of a programme be protected from the constant competition from other issues. But issues originating outside government are likely to introduce a degree of diversity and disorder which threatens the survival of anything resembling a programme. Third, the number of regulative hurdles to be surmounted is likely to decrease the 'closer' to government an issue is initiated.

These propositions tend to simplify the problems of actually identifying the origin of an issue. There is rarely a single source and, in any case, ideas about both problems and solutions may be in circulation well before they crystallize into a demand for action. It is, therefore, useful to think in terms of the sponsorship of issues as well as their origin. For example, although the origins of family allowances are to be found mainly outside the government system, sponsorship moved 'into' government during the war in the persons of Keynes and Henderson. It was their special position and advisory roles which made their sponsorship of crucial importance. In contrast the sponsorship of the clean air issue remained substantially outside government, despite the work of the Beaver Committee and the later intervention of Nabarro. The health centre developments were accelerated by the *extension* of sponsorship to numerous local authorities instead of the few.

Not only may the progress of an issue depend upon the proximity of its origin or sponsorship to government but also upon the network of support or opposition which it is expected to create. The prestige, expertise or power of the sponsors will influence the fate of an issue. The nature of likely opposition is related to the pattern of support. These are considerations which pressure groups, for example, are taking into account when they canvass patrons or members whose association is felt to enhance the standing of their cause. A particular government will view some origins or sponsorships as more reputable than others. The first move in gaining a foothold for an issue may, therefore, involve getting it accepted by just such a body or individual. It may mean a successful resolution at the party conference; obtaining the backing of a professional body or persuading key civil servants or Ministers that *this* is an issue which warrants their especial attention. Certainly we would argue that the image of an issue is much affected by whose issue it is seen to be.

Information

Although issues are advanced and supported on the basis of beliefs and theories about them, the extent to which their existence or urgency can be substantiated by accepted facts has, we maintain, a particular impact upon their progress. With an increasingly 'quantitative approach to the problems of life'[18] the facts are frequently, but not always, numerical. There are facts about issues as social problems and facts about different solutions. We shall consider each in turn and draw out certain propositions from our case studies.

[18] See Abrams, M., *Social Surveys and Social Action*, Heinemann, 1951.

There are innumerable references to the importance of social facts in the development of social policy. Reconstruction, says Ford, 'implies planning and inventing, but before one can undertake either, *the facts must be known*'.[19] In a similar vein, Simey, writing of Charles Booth's influence upon social policy, maintains that 'after his work had become generally known, no amendment of social policy was possible without a carefully tested appeal to experience and the evaluation of proposals in light of relevant evidence'.[20] More recently Joyce Warham has claimed that 'unless poverty can be defined, its extent cannot be measured; and until its extent is known it cannot take shape as a problem demanding collective action'.[21]

There is a widespread conviction amongst students of social policy that new facts have mattered. In particular, that they have enabled issues to be formulated in ways which demanded a response from government. The empirical demonstration that certain problems actually exist is regarded as an essential step in securing State action to deal with them. However, it is plain that the exposition of the facts about an issue in no way guarantees it attention and that issues are accorded priority on only the flimsiest factual basis. In what situations then, is the emergence of 'new facts' likely to have a bearing upon the progress of an issue? The case studies suggest some possible answers.

In the NAB development the publication of the Cole and Utting research concerning the non-take up of assistance benefits by old people appears to have applied the kind of pressure upon government which is frequently noted in historical studies of the development of social policy. But that part of the story has certain noteworthy features. First, the findings related to an existing area of governmental responsibility and indicated a substantial gap between policy and practice. Second, it concerned a sphere in which there is a high level of legitimacy, namely the elderly poor. Third, contrary or alternative data did not exist and the facts, moreover, were verifiable. Indeed, the subsequent government inquiry set out to do just that. Had it arrived at different conclusions disputation about the gravity of the problem could well have blunted the impact. Fourth, the data did not readily allow alternative interpretations. They dealt simply with a basically simple problem. Fifth, the facts were deployed and used politically. Facts are potiential influence which may be exerted in acts of rational persuasion or coercively; but for this they have to be used and not allowed to rest where they fall. Lastly, the Cole study reinforced certain doubts and misgivings in the Labour Party about means-testing and

[19] Ford, P., *Social Theory and Social Practice*, Irish University Press, 1968, p. 10 (our italics).
[20] Simey, T. S. and Simey, M. B., *Charles Booth*, Oxford, 1960, pp. 265–6.
[21] Warham, J., *Social Policy in Context*, Batsford, 1970, p. 62.

probably encouraged a greater sense of urgency in its deliberations, as an Opposition, about relevant aspects of its social security programme.

In the clean air study the fact of a London smog was indisputable but it was not until later that its proportions could be charted accurately from the morbidity and mortality statistics. These showed that the ill-effects were more far-reaching than had at first been assumed *and* that they were worse than on previous occasions. The data came from official sources and were universally accepted as valid. The facts, therefore, did not serve to verify the event or the existence of a new problem. Essentially, they revealed a change in its scale. It seems likely, though impossible to prove, that had these figures indicated less mortality and morbidity than in the previous smogs it would have been harder to press the urgency of the general problem. As with the Cole study, these data were used politically, first by the NSAS and later by the Beaver Committee itself.

New facts have other effects as well. In the case of health centres we argued that the high costs and limited achievements of the early post-war centres contributed to their subsequent fall from favour. The experimental evidence was not encouraging and until this was superseded by new evidence from the much later round of experiments the prospects could hardly be assessed optimistically. Where a commitment in a particular area or programme is regarded as experimental, information about adverse performance may lead to abandonment rather than rectification. The experimental label makes the responsible authorities less vulnerable to criticisms arising from unfavourable facts.

We have already discussed the impact of the criminal statistics upon the development of detention centres but there was also Max Grünhut's commissioned evaluative study. Detention centres were claimed to be experimental. The relatively low level of success which the study revealed might, therefore, have been expected to lead to a backtracking on the policy. It is difficult to be sure why the full results of Grünhut's work were, apparently, interpreted favourably but two explanations seem plausible. First, that detention centres were not in practice intended to be experimental. They were labelled 'experimental' in their early stages to justify their introduction on a very modest scale when the Prison Commissioners were unable to get additional resources. Second, they were an indispensable part of the resources for dealing with a particular problem (rising crime rates) in a particular political climate (the desire to avoid the even harsher alternatives being demanded from certain quarters). In any case the findings were capable of various interpretations because of the inherent difficulties in defining success and failure; and they did show that after being at a detention centre certain types of offender were unlikely to be convicted again.

There are several general conclusions which we feel can be drawn from such examples in our case studies. First, there is the question of the authority of the facts. The more authoritative they are seen to be the more potentially influential. But authority derives from several sources. Official facts collected and disseminated by government departments have *prima facie* an advantage in that they are widely assumed to be correct. Facts supplied by bodies with reputations for impartiality and special authority in their field will, likewise, be difficult to challenge; for instance, the Institute of Municipal Treasurers and Accountants or the Royal Colleges. As well as their source the authority of facts derives from their verifiability. This is most relevant for partisans whose facts may be considered unreliable. The verification of facts becomes important to the extent that they are likely to be disputed; the onus being more often upon partisans to verify *their* facts rather than upon the authorities. 'Arguments which can be *shown* to have no factual foundation can be disposed of easily by opponents',[22] says Becker, but where verification is difficult the advantage will tend to go to the official interpretation or view.

Second, unless facts reinforce or confirm the priorities or choices of authorities their effect will depend upon the extent to which they are politicized (i.e. put to use as instruments of influence). This may take various forms. It may involve popular publication through the mass media; informal discussions; the drafting of memoranda or questions in Parliament. The mere existence of facts about an issue may have little impact unless, literally, they are discovered and used. This implies individuals or bodies ready and capable of undertaking these tasks. Of course, in certain circumstances there may be a deliberate decision not to use some facts. Indeed, the *control* of information is crucial because of its great tactical value.

Third, facts which show an indisputable failure of an existing programme or policy in attaining publicly stated (or legally codified) objectives or standards are more capable of being politically effective than those which demonstrate shortcomings when measured against other criteria. Government (and other authorities) is especially vulnerable to verified facts which show failure in its own terms. It is less vulnerable to the disclosure of failures defined in other, essentially private, terms; or when the policy concerned is assumed to be of an experimental nature.

Fourth, even when the facts which identify certain problems cannot be disputed their impact will generally be slight unless remedial action is possible. If it is widely believed that there is an absence of the

---

[22] Becker, H. S. (ed.), *Social Problems*, Wiley, 1966, p. 6 (our italics).

knowledge or skill necessary for action to be taken the issue can be more easily shelved. There may be exceptions when authorities wish to tackle such problems or when the facts reveal situations to which government must make *some* response in order to acquire the appropriate skill, understanding or theory which is lacking. Ford, in particular, has stressed the importance of theory in determining ideas about what is possible. Writing of the spate of enquiries towards the end of the last century he pointed out that 'what is of interest ... is not the evils they described, vivid as the accounts of them sometimes were, but the way those dealing with national policy tried to think their way out from accepted views to new principles suitable for grappling with them'.[23]

So far we have said little about the relevance of their factual basis for the adoption of solutions. This is partly because the most influential facts appear to be simple descriptions of unsolved *problems*. The factual case for a proposed remedy tends to be more complicated and much less conclusive. As Donnison reminds us, 'research workers [cannot] present authoritative findings for others to apply; neither [can] others commission them to find the "correct" solution'.[24] It is more difficult to show convincingly that one solution is markedly superior to another than it is to shame governments into taking *some* action by the revelation of intolerable conditions. Yet, as we have argued earlier, remedies must at least appear to be feasible. What new facts may do is to undermine, and in some cases overthrow, existing assumptions about the nature, effect or wisdom of a proposed course of action. Indeed, they may more often relegate rather than promote a solution. Better information about the likely consequences or implications of policy proposals may immobilize rather than activate government on certain issues.

Nothing we have said should be taken to imply that *all* facts which are authoritative and used politically will exert a major influence. They can be overriden by other factors such as ideological commitment. However, the circumstances in which facts are likely to be of most importance are, we suggest, the following:

(i) When government cannot ignore them without risking a substantial loss of support; for instance, when gross inadequacies in social welfare services with a high level of legitimacy are shown to exist. The actual magnitude of issues indicated by the facts is also likely to affect their impact.

(ii) When the question of the legitimacy of an issue is in dispute *and* the dispute is essentially about matters which are susceptible to

---

[23] Ford, P., *op. cit.*, p. 49.
[24] Donnison, D. V., 'Research for Policy', *Minerva*, vol. X, no. 4, Oct. 1972, p. 527.

factual determination. There are situations in which, for example, whether government should intervene in new fields or use new kinds of solutions is widely accepted to rest upon questions of severity, urgency, size or trend.

(iii) When issues are advanced from positions of weakness the deployment of factual evidence will be more important in affecting their progress than when they are advanced from positions of strength. Somewhat similarly the onus of proof is normally upon those who wish to change what exists rather than upon those who wish to retain it.

Ideology

We have already noted that the criteria of legitimacy, feasibility and support are interpreted in ways which reflect ideological convictions. We have also discussed the concept of opposition issues. There is, however, a more general sense in which issues can be viewed as carrying different ideological loadings. Some, like the clean air or detention centre issues, are not seen as party political, in contrast to others like the Open University. What difference does this make to the progress of an issue?

Clearly for an issue to accord with the prevailing ideology of the party in power improves its likelihood of gaining priority. Indeed, it may serve as one of the marker flags by means of which the parties publicly distinguish their positions. The decontrol of rents in 1957 was one such example; circular 10/65 on the general introduction of comprehensive secondary education was another. There are many other issues which, although they do not serve this dramatic purpose, broadly correspond with the ideology of the party in power. Others do not offend against it or can at least be presented in ways which do not. At the other end of the scale, ranged in a similar order, are issues which are more or less associated with the Opposition. In the middle area stand numerous supposedly non-ideological issues. There are yet other issues which, although they may blend with the ideological commitments of some members of the party in power, make poor progress because they are precisely the kinds of issues which threaten the uneasy coalitions upon which the parties are built.

Whilst a party remains in power an issue will gain advantage from possessing the appropriate ideological flavour. When political power changes hands, however, these same characteristics are likely to prove a handicap. This poses difficult tactical problems for some pressure groups, particularly those concerned with long-term or permanent issues. Take, for example, the National Smoke Abatement Society which was and is (as the National Society for Clean Air), involved in this way and which carefully avoided associating the clean air issue with any one party. The Howard League for Penal Reform has acted in a similar fashion. In contrast, for partisans within parties (and in some cases within the civil service) the ability to show a close correspondence between 'their' issue and general party ideology will be an advantage to be sought. Harold Wilson almost certainly argued for an Open University on these kinds of grounds with his Cabinet colleagues. On the other hand when, within a party, issues are canvassed which appear to be out of ideological step it will be necessary to play down the divergence; possibly by presenting the issue mainly as an administrative or technical matter. To some extent this occurred within the Labour Party with respect to both the creation and the later reform of the NAB.

We suggest that the following conclusions might be drawn concerning the effect of ideological loadings in the priority of issues:

(i) For short-term issues or those which can be dealt with within the span of one party's power it will be advantageous for them to be compatible with that party's broad ideology.

(ii) For long-term issues, that is those which will require sustained priority, more advantage may accrue from their being seen as non-ideological, given that their legitimacy is established.

(iii) Issues which are ideologically distinctive will tend to make poor progress when they risk exposing differences within the parties; when they invite extensive opposition which, within Parliament for example, consumes scarce resources of time; and when their pursuit is likely to generate discontents which can be generalized to other fields of government activity; that is, when they seem to endanger the level of diffuse support.

III SUMMARY

If we regard an issue as having a natural history[25] then, at any particular time, certain levels of legitimacy, feasibility and support will be ascribed to it by authorities having the power to settle its priority. However, this will rarely be enough to explain its progress to or from that point. In order to account for such movements at least one of three further considerations must be added.

(i) Since many issues with broadly similar claims compete for priority, even when they are well to the fore in our hypothetical queue, progress depends upon *comparative* strengths. A clear example of what we have in mind is the way in which certain

[25] See Becker, S., *Social Problems, op. cit.*, pp. 11–23.

issues are set aside at the outbreak of war in preference to others which, in the changed circumstances, take on a special urgency.[26]

(ii) The characteristics of an issue may change, or be believed to have changed, in ways which enhance or lessen its legitimacy, feasibility or support. It may, for instance, become associated with a new set of other issues. It may reach 'crisis proportions' or threaten to do so. It may accord with a refashioned party programme or it may, perhaps, capture the interest of a Minister or a senior civil servant.

(iii) The criteria of legitimacy, feasibility or support are not fixed. Changes in their interpretation will bring changes in the pattern of issue priorities. An ideological shift on the part of the authorities may well alter conceptions of legitimacy. In a similar fashion a change of party in power will alter the relevance of certain kinds of support.

Change in an issue's priority is, therefore, either the outcome of alterations in its comparative strength, in its characteristics, or in the basic criteria against which it is judged. Sometimes it involves a combination of all these things. The aim of partisans is usually to modify the image of the issue in which they have an interest so that it satisfies the three main criteria more or less well. What they actually do depends upon whether they wish to advance or retard its progress. Either way this, and any counter moves by authorities, constitute the tactics of social policy politics. The strategy, on the other hand, seeks to secure shifts (or a firmer consolidation) in what are considered to be the legitimate spheres of government, in how feasibility is assessed and in the broad structure of support.

Our case studies cover certain periods in the natural histories of the issues with which they deal. The stories could begin earlier and could continue beyond the point at which we bring them to a close. Each period does, however, contain a recognizable policy change which needs to be explained. In order to do so it may be helpful to think in terms of the issue obtaining a score on the scales of legitimacy, feasibility and support at the 'beginning' and then to ask how this was subsequently improved by the 'end'. More specifically, it is helpful to consider which of the three component scores was raised in particular and as a result of which changes. Were the criteria redefined? Was the image of the issue recast by changes in its characteristics and, if so, in which ones and how did this happen?

None of our cases involve fundamental redefinitions of the general criteria. The changes they recount are primarily the result of altera-

[26] The pre-war Criminal Justice Bill is a good example. Having been introduced in 1939, war halted further progress. It was not until 1948 that it was reintroduced (see the detention centre case study).

tions over time in the characteristics of specific issues. It would be hard to say which of the six characteristics that we discussed in the last section was most important. All, in our view, were noteworthy because, once they were seen to change, they began to modify the orientation of influential groups, not least governmer: itself, towards the issues concerned.

Select Bibliography

We have not included all the references in the book in this bibliography. Instead we have selected the more important and the more general references in each chapter. For Chapters 1 and 2 we have provided an extended list of key books and articles for the student of social policy development.

Part I

Chapters 1 and 2

Beales, H. L., *The Making of Social Policy*, Hobhouse Memorial lecture, no. 15, 1950.

Briggs, A., 'The Welfare State in Historical Perspective', *Archiv. Europ. Sociol.* II, 1961.

Boulding, K. E., 'The Boundaries of Social Policy', *Social Work* (US), vol. 12, no. 1. Jan., 1967.

Bruce, M., *The Coming of the Welfare State*, Batsford, 1961.

Donnison, D. V., 'Ideologies and Politics', *Journal of Social Policy*, vol. 1, part 2, Apr., 1972.

Donnison, D. V. *et al.*, *Social Policy and Administration*, Allen & Unwin, 1965.

Ford, P., *Social Theory and Social Practice*, Irish University Press, 1968.

Gilbert, B. B., *British Social Policy, 1914–39*, Batsford, 1970.

Ginsberg, M., 'Social Change', in *Essays in Sociology and Social Philosophy, vol. 3, Evolution and Progress*, Heinemann, 1961.

Goldthorpe, J. H., 'The Development of Social Policy in England 1800–1914: notes on a Sociological Approach to a Problem in Historical Explanation', in *Transactions of the Fifth World Congress of Sociology*, vol. iv, 1962.

Marsh, D. C. (ed.), *An Introduction to Social Administration*, Routledge & Kegan Paul, 1965.

Marshall, T. H., *Social Policy*, Hutchinson, 1965 (3rd edn, 1970).

Marshall, T. H., *Sociology at the Crossroads*, Heinemann, 1963.

Myrdal, G., *Beyond the Welfare State*, Duckworth, 1960.

Pinker, R., *Social Theory and Social Policy*, Heinemann, 1971.
Parker, R. A., 'Social Ills and Public Remedies', in *Man and the Social Sciences*, Robson, W. A. (ed.), Allen & Unwin, 1972.
Rein, M., *Social Policy: Issues of Choice and Change*, Random House, 1970.
Robson, W. A. and Crick, B. (eds), *The Future of the Social Services*, Penguin, 1970.
Saville, J., 'The Welfare State: an Historical Approach', *The New Reasoner*, Winter, 1957–8.
Slack, K. M., *Social Administration and the Citizen*, Joseph, 1966.
Titmuss, R. M., *Essays on the Welfare State*, Allen & Unwin, 1958.
Titmuss, R. M., *Commitment to Welfare*, Allen & Unwin, 1968.
Titmuss, R. M., *Problems of Social Policy*, HMSO, 1950.
Warham, J., *Social Policy in Context*, Batsford, 1970.
Wedderburn, D., 'Facts and Theories of the Welfare State', *The Socialist Register*, 1965.

Part II

The selected bibliography for Chapters 3–8 contains references that have been chosen for one or more of three reasons: because they provide good coverage to a particular topic; because they are collections of useful readings; or because a strand of the argument presented in these chapters hinges upon them.

Chapter 3

Easton, D., *A Systems Analysis of Political Life*, Wiley, 1964.
Easton, D., *Varieties of Political Theory*, Prentice-Hall, 1966.
Vickers, G., *Value Systems and Social Processes*, Tavistock, 1968.

Chapter 4

Benewicke, R. and Dowse, R. E. *Readings on British Politics and Government*, London University Press, 1968.
Birch, A. H., *Representative and Responsible Government*, Allen & Unwin, 1964.
Crossman, R. H. S., *Inside View*, Cape, 1972.
Gamson, W. A., *Power and Discontent*, Dorsey, 1968.
Hanson, A. H. and Crick, B. (eds), *The Commons in Transition*, Fontana, 1970.
MacKenzie, R. T., *British, Political Parties*, Heinemann, 1955.

Mackintosh, J. P., *The British Cabinet*, Methuen, 1968.

Chapter 5

Barnett, M. J., *The Politics of Legislation*, Weidenfeld & Nicolson, 1969.
Boyle, E., Crosland, C. A. R. and Kogan, M. (ed.), *The Politics of Education*, Penguin, 1971.
Braybrooke, D. and Lindblom, C. E., *A Strategy of Decision*, Free Press, 1963.
Brittan, S., *Steering the Economy*, Secker & Warburg, 1969.
Chapman, R. A., *The Role of Commissions in Policy Making*, Allen & Unwin, 1973.
Dror, Y., *Public Policy-Making Re-examined*, Chandler, 1968.
Faludi, A., *A Reader in Planning Theory*, Pergamon, 1973.
Griffith, J. A., *Central Departments and Local Authorities*, Allen & Unwin, 1966.
Hill, M. J., *The Sociology of Public Administration*, Weidenfeld & Nicolson, 1972.
Keeling, D., *Management in Government*, Allen & Unwin, 1972.
Rose, R., *Policy-Making in Britain*, Macmillan, 1969.
Self, P., *Administrative Theories and Politics*, Allen & Unwin, 1972.

Chapter 6

Beer, S., *Modern British Politics*, Faber, 1965.
Finer, S. E., *Anonymous Empire*, Pall Mall Press, 1958.
Guttsman, W. L., *The British Political Elite*, MacGibbon & Kee, 1965.
Moodie, G. C. and Studdert-Kennedy, G., *Opinions, Publics and Pressure Groups*, Allen & Unwin, 1970.
Wootton, G., *Interest Groups*, Prentice-Hall, 1970.

Chapter 7

Brown, R. G. S., *The Administrative Process in Great Britain*, Methuen, 1970.
Butt, R., *The Power of Parliament*, Constable, 1967.
Hill, A. and Whichelow, A., *What's Wrong with Parliament?* Penguin, 1964.
Richards, P. G., *Parliament and Conscience*, Allen & Unwin, 1970.
Stankiewicz, W. J., *Crisis in British Government*, Collier-Macmillan, 1967.

Chapter 8

D'Antonio, W. V. and Erhlich, H. J. (eds), *Power and Democracy in America*, University of Notre Dame Press, 1961.

Bachrach, P. and Baratz, M. S., *Power and Poverty: Theory and Practice*, Oxford University Press, 1970.

Dahl, R. A., *Modern Political Analysis*, Prentice-Hall, 1963.

Dahl, R. A., *Pluralist Democracy in the United States: Conflict and Consent*, Rand McNally, 1967.

Guttsman, W. L. (ed.), *The English Ruling Class*, Weidenfeld & Nicolson, 1969.

McKenzie, R. T., and Silver, A., *Angels in Marble*, Heinemann, 1968.

Miliband, R., *The State in Capitalist Society*, Weidenfeld & Nicolson, 1969.

Schattschneider, E. E., *The Semi-Sovereign People*, Holt, Reinhart & Winston, 1960.

Urry, J. and Wakeford, J. (eds), *Power in Britain*, Heinemann, 1973.

Part III

These references all deal with the particular case studies.

Chapter 9

Beveridge, J., *Beveridge and His Plan*, Hodder & Stoughton, 1954.

Bullock, A., *The Life and Times of Ernest Bevin, vol. II*, 'Ministry of Labour, 1940–45', Heinemann, 1967.

Keynes, J. M., *How to Pay for the War*, Macmillan, 1940.

Macmillan, H., *The Middle Way*, Macmillan (Revised edn.), 1958.

Rathbone, E., *Family Allowances*, Allen & Unwin (2nd edn.), 1949.

Sayers, R. S., *Financial Policy, 1939–45*, HMSO, 1956.

Stocks, M., *Eleanor Rathbone*, Gollancz, 1949.

Social Insurance and Allied Services, A Report by William Beveridge, Cmd. 6404, 1942.

White Paper on Family Allowances, Memorandum by the Chancellor of the Exchequer, Cmnd. 6354, 1942.

Report of the Royal Commission on the Population, Cmd. 7695, 1949.

H. C. Deb., vol. 380 (Debate on Family Allowances).

Chapter 10

Jackson, B., *The Times*, 25 Nov., 1969.

Wilson, H., *Speech to the First Congregation of the Open University at the Royal Society*, London, 23 July, 1969.

Young, M., 'Is Your Child in the Unlucky Generation?' *Where*, no. 10. Autumn, 1962.

New Ventures in Broadcasting: a Study in Adult Education, BBC & the British Institute of Adult Education, 1928.

The Post Office, *Report of the Committee on Broadcasting, 1960*, Cmnd. 1753, 1961–2.

Memorandum on the Report of the Committee on Broadcasting, 1960, Cmnd. 1770, 1962.

'Labour and the Scientific Revolution', *Report of the 62nd Annual Conference of the Labour Party*, 1963.

A University of the Air, Cmnd. 2922, 1966.

The Open University, Report of the Planning Committee to the Secretary of State for Education and Science, 1969.

Conservative Central Office (press release), *Statement by Rt Hon. Sir Edward Boyle*, 27 Jan., 1969.

Chapter 11

Curwen, M. and Brookes, B., 'Health Centres: Facts and Figures', *Lancet*, ii, 1969.

Eckstein, H., *The English Health Services*, Harvard University Press, 1958.

Ryan, M., 'Health Centre Policy in England and Wales', *British Journal of Sociology*, Mar., 1968.

Interim Report of the Committee on the Future of the Medical and Allied Services (Dawson), Cmd. 693, 1920.

A National Health Service, Cmd. 6502, 1944.

Medical Practitioners' Union, *Design for Family Doctoring*, 1966–7.

Ministry of Health, *Circular, 7/67*.

Chapter 12

Choppen, V., 'The Origins of the Philosophy of Detention Centres', *British Journal of Criminology*, vol. 10, no. 2, 1970.

Fox, L., *The English Prison and Borstal System*, Routledge & Kegan Paul, 1952.

Grünhut, M., 'Juvenile Delinquents under Punitive Detention', *British Journal of Delinquency*, vol. 5, no. 3, 1955.

Grünhut, M., 'After-Effects of Punitive Detention', *British Journal of Criminology*, vol. 1, no. 1, 1960.

Rose, G., *The Struggle for Penal Reform*, Stevens, 1961.

Watson, J., *The Child and the Magistrate*, Cape, 1942.

Annual Reports of the Prison Commissioners for the years 1951–60.

Detention in Remand Homes: A Report of the Cambridge Department of Criminal Science on the Use of Section 54 of the Children and Young Persons Act, 1933, Macmillan, 1952.

Advisory Council on the Treatment of Offenders, *Penal Practice in a Changing Society*, Cmnd. 645, 1959.

Institute for the Study and Treatment of Offenders, *Penal Practice in a Changing Society: A Critical Examination of the White Paper Policy*, 1960.

Advisory Council on the Treatment of Offenders, *Corporal Punishment*, Cmnd. 1213, 1960.

Advisory Council on the Treatment of Offenders, *Detention Centres*, 1970.

Chapter 13

Logan, W. P. D., 'Mortality in the London Fog Incident, 1952', *Lancet*, 14 Feb., 1953.

Plank, D., 'The Progress and Effects of Smoke Control in London', *Quarterly Bulletin of the Research and Intelligence Unit of the GLC*, no. 10, Mar., 1970.

Sanderson, J. B., 'The National Smoke Abatement Society and the Clean Air Act, 1956', *Political Studies*, vol. ix, no. 3, 1961.

Scarrow, H. A., 'The Impact of British Domestic Air Pollution Legislation', *British Journal of Political Science*, vol. 2, part 2, 1972.

Wise, W., *Killer Smog*, Rand McNally, 1968.

'Fog and Frost in December 1952 and Subsequent Deaths in London', Report by the MOH of the LCC in *Medical Officer*, 7 Feb., 1953.

'The London Fog: A First Survey', *Smokeless Air*, Spring, 1963.

'Polluted Air over Towns', *The Times*, 20 and 21 Apr., 1953.

Interim Report of the Committee on Air Pollution (Beaver), Cmnd. 9332, 1954.

Report of the Committee on Air Pollution (Beaver), Cmnd. 9332, 1954.

Ministry of Health, *Mortality and Morbidity During the London Fog of December 1952*, 1954.

Political and Economic Planning, 'The Menace of Air Pollution', *Planning*, vol. xx, no. 369, 1954.

'NSAS Evidence to the Beaver Committee', *Smokeless Air*, Summer, 1954.

National Society for Smoke Abatement, *Sixty Years for Clean Air*, 1959.

See also NSAS *Clean Air Year Books* for data and commentaries.

Chapter 14

Abel-Smith, B., 'Social Security', in Ginsberg, M. (ed.), *Law and Opinion in England in the Twentieth Century*, Stevens, 1959.

Abel-Smith, B. and Townsend, P., *The Poor and the Poorest*, Bell, 1965.

Atkinson, A. B., *Poverty in Britain and the Reform of Social Security*, Cambridge University Press, 1969.

Beckerman, W. (ed.), *The Labour Government's Economic Record: 1964-70*, Duckworth, 1972.

Briggs, E. and Deacon, A., 'The Creation of the Unemployment Assistance Board', *Policy and Politics*, vol. 2, no. 1, 1973.

Bull, D. (ed.), *Family Poverty*, Duckworth, (2nd edn), 1972.

Butler, D. and King, A., *The British General Election of 1964*, Macmillan, 1965.

Cohen, C. D., *British Economic Policy, 1960-69*, Butterworth, 1971.

Cole, D. and Utting, J., *The Economic Circumstances of Old People*, Codicote Press, 1962.

Graig, F. W. S. *British Election Manifestos, 1918-66*, Political Reference Publications, 1970.

George V., *Social Security: Beveridge and After*, Routledge & Kegan Paul, 1968.

Glennerster, H., *National Assistance: Service or Charity?* Fabian Society, Young Fabian Pamphlet, no. 4, 1962.

Schaffer, B. B. and Corbett, D. C., *Decisions: Case Studies in Australian Administration*, Cheshire, 1966.

Titmuss, R. M., 'Pensions Systems and Population Change', in *Essays on the Welfare State*, Allen & Unwin, 1958.

Townsend, P. and Bosanquet, N., *Labour and Inequality*, Fabian Society, 1972.

Part IV

Chapter 15

Most of the references relevant to this last section have already been noted but the following should also be consulted.

Becker, H. S. (ed.), *Social Problems*, Wiley, 1966.
Boulding, K. E., *The Image*, University of Michigan Press, 1966.
Donnison, D. V., 'Research for Policy', *Minerva*, vol. x, no. 4, Oct., 1972.

Index

Index compiled by Sheila Payne

NOTES

NOTES

NOTES

NOTES

NOTES